International Financial Issues in the Pacific Rim

NBER–East Asia Seminar on Economics
Volume 17

International Financial Issues in the Pacific Rim
Global Imbalances, Financial Liberalization, and Exchange Rate Policy

Edited by **Takatoshi Ito and Andrew K. Rose**

The University of Chicago Press

Chicago and London

TAKATOSHI ITO is professor of economics at the University of Tokyo and a research associate of the National Bureau of Economic Research and the Tokyo Center for Economic Research. ANDREW K. ROSE is the Bernard T. Rocca Jr. Professor of International Trade, director of the Clausen Center for International Business and Policy at the Haas School of Business, University of California, Berkeley, and a research associate of the National Bureau of Economic Research.

The University of Chicago Press, Chicago 60637
The University of Chicago Press, Ltd., London
© 2008 by the National Bureau of Economic Research
All rights reserved. Published 2008
Printed in the United States of America

17 16 15 14 13 12 11 10 09 08   1 2 3 4 5
ISBN-13: 978-0-226-38682-9 (cloth)
ISBN-10: 0-226-38682-1 (cloth)

Library of Congress Cataloging-in-Publication Data

East Asian Seminar in Economics (2006 : Kapaau, Hawaii)
    International financial issues in the Pacific Rim : global
imbalances, financial liberalization, and exchange rate policy / edited
by Takatoshi Ito and Andrew K. Rose.
        p. cm.—(NBER-East Asia seminar on economics; v. 17)
    Includes index.
    ISBN-13: 978-0-226-38682-9 (cloth : alk. paper)
    ISBN-10: 0-226-38682-1 (cloth : alk. paper)
        1. Foreign exchange rates—East Asia—Congresses. 2. Capital
movements—East Asia—Congresses. 3. Finance—East Asia—
Congresses. 4. Foreign exchange rates—Congresses. 5. Capital
movements—Congresses. 6. Finance—Congresses. I. Ito, Takatoshi,
1950— II. Rose, Andrew, 1959– III. Title.
HG3976.5.E23 2006
332'.042095—dc22

                                                        2007035486

Relation of the Directors to the
Work and Publications of the
National Bureau of Economic Research

1. The object of the NBER is to ascertain and present to the economics profession, and to the public more generally, important economic facts and their interpretation in a scientific manner without policy recommendations. The Board of Directors is charged with the responsibility of ensuring that the work of the NBER is carried on in strict conformity with this object.

2. The President shall establish an internal review process to ensure that book manuscripts proposed for publication DO NOT contain policy recommendations. This shall apply both to the proceedings of conferences and to manuscripts by a single author or by one or more coauthors but shall not apply to authors of comments at NBER conferences who are not NBER affiliates.

3. No book manuscript reporting research shall be published by the NBER until the President has sent to each member of the Board a notice that a manuscript is recommended for publication and that in the President's opinion it is suitable for publication in accordance with the above principles of the NBER. Such notification will include a table of contents and an abstract or summary of the manuscript's content, a list of contributors if applicable, and a response form for use by Directors who desire a copy of the manuscript for review. Each manuscript shall contain a summary drawing attention to the nature and treatment of the problem studied and the main conclusions reached.

4. No volume shall be published until forty-five days have elapsed from the above notification of intention to publish it. During this period a copy shall be sent to any Director requesting it, and if any Director objects to publication on the grounds that the manuscript contains policy recommendations, the objection will be presented to the author(s) or editor(s). In case of dispute, all members of the Board shall be notified, and the President shall appoint an ad hoc committee of the Board to decide the matter; thirty days additional shall be granted for this purpose.

5. The President shall present annually to the Board a report describing the internal manuscript review process, any objections made by Directors before publication or by anyone after publication, any disputes about such matters, and how they were handled.

6. Publications of the NBER issued for informational purposes concerning the work of the Bureau, or issued to inform the public of the activities at the Bureau, including but not limited to the NBER Digest and Reporter, shall be consistent with the object stated in paragraph 1. They shall contain a specific disclaimer noting that they have not passed through the review procedures required in this resolution. The Executive Committee of the Board is charged with the review of all such publications from time to time.

7. NBER working papers and manuscripts distributed on the Bureau's web site are not deemed to be publications for the purpose of this resolution, but they shall be consistent with the object stated in paragraph 1. Working papers shall contain a specific disclaimer noting that they have not passed through the review procedures required in this resolution. The NBER's web site shall contain a similar disclaimer. The President shall establish an internal review process to ensure that the working papers and the web site do not contain policy recommendations, and shall report annually to the Board on this process and any concerns raised in connection with it.

8. Unless otherwise determined by the Board or exempted by the terms of paragraphs 6 and 7, a copy of this resolution shall be printed in each NBER publication as described in paragraph 2 above.

Contents

Acknowledgments   xi

Introduction   1
Takatoshi Ito and Andrew K. Rose

I. GLOBAL IMBALANCES

**1. Life on the Tri-Polar Sphere: How Should
Interest and Exchange Rates Realign Next?**   13
Michael P. Dooley, David Folkerts-Landau,
and Peter Garber
Comment: John Simon

**2. Liquidity Risk Aversion, Debt Maturity,
and Current Account Surpluses:
A Theory and Evidence from East Asia**   39
Shin-ichi Fukuda and Yoshifumi Kon
Comment: Linda S. Goldberg
Comment: Andrew K. Rose

**3. Are Currency Appreciations Contractionary
in China?**   71
Jianhuai Shi
Comment: Ashvin Ahuja
Comment: Dante B. Canlas

II. MONETARY POLICY AND EXCHANGE RATES

4. **The Relationship between Openness and Inflation in NIEs and the G7**   109
Chung-Shu Wu and Jin-Lung Lin
Comment: Peter Blair Henry
Comment: John Simon

5. **Pass-Through of Exchange Rates to Consumption Prices: What Has Changed and Why?**   139
José Manuel Campa and Linda S. Goldberg
Comment: M. Chatib Basri
Comment: Kiyotaka Sato

6. **Price Impacts of Deals and Predictability of the Exchange Rate Movements**   177
Takatoshi Ito and Yuko Hashimoto
Comment: Eli Remolona

7. **Adopting a Common Currency Basket Arrangement into the ASEAN Plus Three**   219
Eiji Ogawa and Kentaro Kawasaki
Comment: Michael P. Dooley
Comment: Kiyotaka Sato

III. LIBERALIZATION, MARKET ACCESS, AND THE COST OF CAPITAL

8. **Growth and Returns in Emerging Markets**   241
Peter Blair Henry and Prakash Kannan
Comment: Takatoshi Ito
Comment: Etsuro Shioji

9. **Bond Markets as Conduits for Capital Flows: How Does Asia Compare?**   267
Barry Eichengreen and
Pipat Luengnaruemitchai
Comment: Eiji Ogawa

10. **Financial Liberalization under the WTO and Its Relationship with the Macro Economy**   315
Lee-Rong Wang, Chung-Hua Shen, and
Ching-Yang Liang
Comment: Shin-ichi Fukuda
Comment: Roberto S. Mariano

11. **Cross-Border Acquisitions and Target Firms' Performance: Evidence from Japanese Firm-Level Data**   347
Kyoji Fukao, Keiko Ito, Hyeog Ug Kwon, and Miho Takizawa
Comment: M. Chatib Basri
Comment: Roberto S. Mariano

12. **Stock Market Opening and the Cost of Capital: The Case of Korea**   391
Inseok Shin and Chang-Gyun Park
Comment: Yuko Hashimoto
Comment: Chulsoo Kim

Contributors   415
Author Index   419
Subject Index   425

Acknowledgments

This volume is a collection of papers that were presented at the 17th annual East Asia Seminar on Economics (EASE). EASE is co-organized by the National Bureau of Economic Research (NBER) in Cambridge, Massachusetts; the Productivity Commission of Australia; the Hong Kong University of Science and Technology; the Korea Development Institute in Seoul; Singapore Management University; the Chung-Hua Institution for Economic Research in Taipei; the Tokyo Center for Economic Research; and the Chinese Center for Economic Research in Beijing. EASE 17 was held at the Kohala Coast, Hawaii, June 22–24, 2006; the NBER was the local organizer.

We thank all our sponsors—the NBER, All Nippon Airways, the University of Tokyo's Center for Advanced Research in Finance, and especially the Center for Global Partnership—for making EASE 17 possible. The conference department of the NBER led by Carl Beck, and the publication department led by Helena Fitz-Patrick, as usual, made the organization and publication process run smoothly. Brett Maranjian deserves special praise for making the conference run flawlessly.

Introduction

Takatoshi Ito and Andrew K. Rose

This volume is a collection of papers that were presented at the 17th East Asian Seminar in Economics (EASE) on June 22–24, 2006. The conference was organized around three inter-related research interests: global imbalances, monetary and exchange rate policy, and the liberalization of capital accounts.

Global Imbalances

The first three chapters deal with the global imbalances, which has been one of the important and puzzling policy issues in the international policy arena since 2003. The global imbalance consists of a number of related and remarkable developments primarily in the United States and East Asia (although oil-producing nations are also involved): large American current account deficits (reaching over 6% of American GDP in 2005 and 2006), large Chinese current account surpluses, a large accumulation of foreign reserves among the Asian countries, low global real interest rates, and large current account surpluses of oil-producing nations (thanks mostly to high oil prices). Many of these developments are unprecedented, especially in size. Such imbalances might be expected to point to substantial dollar

Takatoshi Ito is a professor at the Graduate School of Economics, Tokyo University, and a research associate of the National Bureau of Economic Research. Andrew K. Rose is the Bernard T. Rocca Jr. Professor of International Business in the Economic Analysis and Policy Group, Haas School of Business at the University of California, Berkeley and a research associate of the National Bureau of Economic Research.

During the revision process of the volume, we received very helpful and thoughtful comments from two anonymous reviewers of the original manuscript. Both the editors and the authors have greatly benefited from their detailed comments on each chapter. We are extremely grateful to the reviewers from both the NBER and the University of Chicago press.

depreciation and a Chinese currency appreciation. Yet the dollar, as measured by the real effective exchange rate, has not depreciated much in recent years, while the Chinese yuan has been a currency de facto (if no longer *de jure*) pegged to the U.S. dollar. The Chinese currency has been highly managed and its stability is maintained with heavy intervention by the Chinese central bank (the People's Bank of China). Many economists have predicted (or wished for) a fall of the dollar, but all have been disappointed—at least so far.

Clearly a number of different actors are present in the global imbalance phenomenon, and it is difficult to pinpoint a single cause that is most important. Nevertheless, each of the first three chapters sheds light on the issue from a different angle; the collection as a whole is a contribution to the resolution of the puzzle. Dooley, Folkerts-Landau, and Garber (chapter 1 in this volume) review one view of an important minority about the origin and sustainability of global imbalances. They argue that the current situation of large U.S. current account deficits and large East Asian surpluses can be expected to continue for some time, since it is in the interest of all the relevant parties. Fukuda and Kon (chapter 2 in this volume) are also concerned with the origins of global imbalances; it argues that a preference for dollar assets exhibited by East Asian countries can help explain flows of Asian capital to the United States. Shi (chapter 3 in this volume) argues, consistent with Dooley, Folkerts-Landau, and Garber, that any real appreciation of the Chinese currency can be expected to contribute to the decline in Chinese output. This in turn explains the hesitation of the Chinese government to alter its exchange rate policy.

The Dooley, Folkerts-Landau, and Garber chapter states that the global imbalance situation not only has lasted for a substantial period of time, but can be expected to last considerably longer. The low medium- and long-term American interest rates are used as a key point to suggest that the financial markets do not show signs that any substantial changes are imminent. The same authors have already argued in an influential series of papers that no country has an incentive to deviate from the current situation. The view of the authors is that the world has emerged into a new international financial system that has been dubbed the "Revived Bretton Woods" or "Bretton Woods II" system. In this system, developing countries maintain de facto fixed exchange rates vis-à-vis the U.S. dollar. The East Asian countries have deliberately adopted this mercantilist stance, undervaluing their currencies in order to induce rapid economic development via export-lead growth. In the current chapter, Dooley, Landau-Folkerts, and Garber offer a dynamic element to their world view. They show that the patterns of imbalances and the low real interest rates, observed over the past few years in the United States and elsewhere, are empirical evidence that support the Revived Bretton Woods hypothesis. They argue that a sudden change in an increase in capital outflows (exports of saving) from Asia to well-developed capital markets in the United States and Europe produces an immediate rise in the U.S. dollar and Euro, followed by gradual depreciation. They argue that sterilized intervention does not work and those countries that wished to peg their currencies to the dollar, in particular China, can and will do so when the dollar pegs accord with their economic policy objectives. Thus, in their view, the global imbalances are neither problematic nor unsustainable, and are likely to unwind only slowly.

A complimentary approach is taken in the next chapter. Instead of relying on public policy preferences, Fukuda and Kon attempt to explain the U.S. current account deficits through a shift in preference towards American assets by the rest of the world, most notably East Asian countries. In this view it is reminiscent of recent influential work by Blanchard and Giavazzi, among others. The authors examine the impact of aversion towards liquidity and note that different results occur in response to increases in risk aversion among private agents and the government. The shock causes large current account surpluses and substantial depreciation of the real exchange rate against the international currency. Thus, they argue that the U.S. current account deficits can be caused by reasons that originate from outside the United States, most conventional explanations rely on a decline in American savings, especially from the public sector. Though their chapter points to this possibility, it does not, of course, prove that it is the only or most important reason. The authors do persuasively argue that the decrease in short-term debt immediately after the East Asian crises is consistent with an increase in risk aversion among private agents, while the subsequent increase in reserves is consistent with an increase in aversion on the part of the government.

One important part of the global imbalance problem is the inflexibility of the Chinese currency, which many regard as undervalued. Shi examines the macroeconomic effects of the changes in the value of RMB (the Chinese currency) on output, using a vector autoregression (VAR) approach. The variables analyzed in the model include the real exchange rate, foreign gross domestic product (GDP), the inflation rate and domestic GDP. Using a data set that spans the relevant period—from 1991 through 2005—Shi finds that fluctuations in the real effective exchange rate have a strong and sensible impact on domestic output. In particular, a real RMB appreciation has indeed caused output to decline historically. This is certainly consistent with the Bretton Woods II idea, and helps explain the reluctance in China to revalue the RMB. However, it is important to point out a key cautionary finding in the paper. When Shi adds in the international finance linkage of the Chinese economy by adding the U.S. interest rate into the system, the contractionary effect of RMB real exchange appreciation is diminished.

Monetary Policy and Exchange Rates

It is widely agreed that any resolution of the global imbalances problem (discussed in the first three chapters), will almost surely require some sort of exchange rate adjustment. Thus, understanding the link between the exchange rate and domestic economic activity is a key goal of international and macro economists. Accordingly, studying the causal relationship between the exchange rate and macroeconomic phenomena is a valuable undertaking that has been widely pursued in the literature. (It might be said that the most important aspects of the entire field of international finance concern the determination of the exchange rate and its linkage to the domestic economy.) The next four chapters examine various aspects of monetary policy and the foreign exchanges in East Asia. These chapters are directly relevant to a number of issues and puzzles of the global financial system, including the topic of global imbalances discussed in the first set of chapters of this volume.

The first examines the relationship between openness and national inflation performance. In a highly open economy the cost of policy mistakes is higher, in part because of the presence of foreign capital works as a competitive force. This is a positive aspect of openness, which helps restrain inflation. However, more open economies experience larger external shocks, and the transmission of these shocks into the economy may be faster, reducing the stability of the domestic economy. Thus, openness has its costs as well as benefits, and monetary policy will tend to be more prudent in an open economy. Using this framework, Wu and Lin (chapter 4 in this volume) critically examine the relationship between economic openness (measured by ratios of imports and exports) and inflation, searching for signs of a tradeoff. The conventional wisdom established by David Romer is that greater openness leads to lower inflation, because the cost of loose monetary policy and the resulting inflation are higher if the economy is more open. The negative relationship between openness and inflation is predicted by time consistency in the context of a monopolistically competitive production sector. Wu and Lin conduct their empirical analysis using a panel data set of thirteen countries (the Group of Seven countries plus four newly industrialized economies, the Philippines, and Mexico). However, among these thirteen countries, Wu and Lin find no clear evidence of the relationship between openness and low inflation.

One of the most important and substantial channels between the exchange rate and the domestic economy is the effect that exchange rate changes have on inflation. Measuring the speed and size of this *pass-through* effect is accordingly viewed as one of the major tasks for policymakers in international finance. A large and fast pass-through effect means that the central bank must pay close attention to the exchange rate when setting its policies. The issue is especially topical since in the literature, it has been argued that the degree of pass-through has declined in recent years. Campa and Goldberg (chapter 5 in this volume) examine pass-through effects using cross-country, time-series pooled data for OECD countries. They focus on sector-specific import price sensitivities to the exchange rate. To simulate the impact of a change in import prices on the overall consumer price index, Campa and Goldberg use a model of pricing behavior that incorporates a distribution sector. This is potentially important, since before they affect the overall price level, exchange rate changes are commonly thought to show up first in import prices; further pass-through to retail prices can then be expected to be influenced by sectoral distribution patterns and import input use. The degree of pass-through may also be influenced by various other factors, including market structures, pricing policies (since the distribution margin can also be adjusted), product substitutability, slow adjustment of nontradable prices and wages, exchange rate policies, and so forth. One of the major findings of Campa and Goldberg is that the degree of pass-through into import prices is more closely defined by industry than by country; the only exception is the United States. Pass-through into import prices is noisiest and least precisely measured with respect to energy imports. This may be due to regulatory changes in the energy sector in many countries. It is also interesting to note that pass-through effects are very precisely estimated among manufactured goods and food in many countries. Campa and Goldberg argue that growth in imported input use, especially in distribution services, has increased the predicted sensitivity of retail prices of imported goods to exchange rates. In the second part of the paper, the authors calibrate the effects of import prices on consumer prices using observed distribution expenditures and import usage.

Campa and Goldberg analyze the effects of exchange rate on the macroeconomy. The next chapter, by Ito and Hashimoto (chapter 6 in this volume), is completely different. The authors are interested in understanding the determination of exchange rates (not their effects), from a high-frequency microeconomics perspective (instead of taking a macroeconomic view). Their focus is quite narrow; they examine patterns of exchange rate volatility within a single day. Since the influential work of Meese and Rogoff in the early 1980s, many academic economists have come to believe that the exchange rate follows a random walk and is thus nonpredictable. On the other hand, the financial industry spends millions of dollars in purchasing hardware and hiring physics PhDs to develop software programs and trading strategies, all based on the idea of predictability. This shows the serious gap between the academic literature and the real world, a difference that is clearest in the realm of high-frequency exchange rate dynamics. Ito and Hashimoto exploit a new data set of extremely high-frequency that contains actual ready-to-transact quotes and actual transaction prices and volumes, all of which can be combined to construct *order flows.* Using standard techniques, Ito and Hashimoto establish that a shock to buying order flow results in prices that rise within one to five minutes. However, these effects disappear completely within even as short a period of time as thirty minutes. It is also interesting that the persistence of some key price impacts has declined over time. This paper is one of the first papers to exploit the rich data set made available by EBS, an actual trading platform widely used in the real world. The authors observe a variety of trading patterns as intra daily *seasonality,* and show that order flows proxied by the number of deals are important in predicting the price movements. This controversial finding needs to be established in the out-of-sample exercises in the future work before it is firmly established. Nevertheless, the paper may well encourage the private sector to analyze the exchange rate dynamics further, something that has been the province of academic work to date.

One of the most damaging effects that an exchange rate can have on the economy is when it crashes. There have been many failures of fixed exchange rate regimes, and the East Asian failure in 1997–98 is one of the most important. The fixed exchange rate policy played an important role in both developing financial vulnerabilities in East Asian economies before the crisis, and exacerbating them after it. The dollar peg regime had encouraged easy money to flow into East Asia, resulting in currency overvaluation and double mismatches (of both maturity and currency) in balance sheets. It is thus no surprise that studying East Asian exchange rate policy has been a popular topic in recent policy discussions. The last chapter of this section is by Ogawa and Kawasaki (chapter 7 in this volume); it examines feasible exchange rate regimes in East Asia. In the regional tradition of East Asia, the goal is to find a way to stabilize intraregional exchange rates, since this both reflects and may also encourage a high degree of intraregional trade. More precisely, the authors search for co-integrating vectors for groups of real bilateral exchange rates. They interpret the existence of co-integrated real exchange rates as evidence that supports an optimal currency area among involved countries. Ogawa and Kawasaki examine monthly data from 1987 to 2005 for the East Asian, U.S., and Euro area currencies. They find that before the Asian crisis of July 1997, the yen was not in the East Asian group of countries that showed co-integration. However, after the crisis the yen needs to be included in order to detect co-integration. Although the Japanese yen is sometimes viewed as a currency outside the region, they find that it has indeed been inside the group recently.

Liberalization, Market Access, and the Cost of Capital

Capital flows have been identified as important elements in a host of economic phenomena, and are potentially critical in issues ranging from economic development through currency crises. The benefits for increased capital inflows to developing countries seem obvious: they provide valuable capital inputs, enhance the efficacy with which capital is deployed, and may also allow risks to be diversified. However unlike trade liberalization, not all economists are enthusiastic toward general capital account liberalization in developing countries. It is appropriate then to reconsider the costs and benefits of capital liberalization.

The last five chapters deal with various issues related to the liberalization of capital accounts, market access, and the cost of capital; they are mainly concerned with examining the hypotheses that capital inflows bring benefits. Liberalization will, in principle, provide much-needed capital to developing countries and thus contribute to development. Opening up previously closed markets should lower the cost of capital and thus enhance economic growth. Henry and Kannan (chapter 8 in this volume) study the relationship between stock market returns and growth rates among emerging market countries. Shin and Park also examine this theme in chapter 12, focusing on Korea. Foreign direct investment especially helps companies in developing countries acquire good governance, managerial improvement, and technological edge. Fukao and colleagues examine FDI data (chapter 11 in this volume), and show that foreign acquisitions improved the productivity and profitability of target firms quicker and to a significantly greater degree than acquisitions by domestic firms. Eichengreen and Luengnaruemitchai (chapter 9 in this volume) examine regional bond holdings in order to measure the degree of financial integration. Finally, the chapter by Wang, Shen, and Liang (chapter 10 in this volume) exploits data on financial service commitments at WTO negotiations, and examines the correlation between financial liberalization and economic growth.

The Henry and Kannan chapter examines the relationship between the stock market returns of emerging markets and their aggregate growth rates. They use the standard aggregate indices—the S&P Emerging Markets Data Base (EMDB) and a data set that spans 1976 through 2005. It would be reasonable to guess that emerging markets that grow faster would also have higher stock market returns. However, the authors find that this conjecture is not in fact confirmed by the data. First, among emerging market countries there seems to be no correlation between growth rates and stock market returns over the last 30 years. Second, emerging market countries have grown faster than the United States, but stock returns of these very different countries have been about the same. Third, Asian emerging markets grew faster than Latin American emerging markets, but experienced lower stock returns than those of Latin America! After establishing this set of interesting puzzles, the authors then set out to explain them. Several hypotheses are considered by Henry and Kannan. First, it turns out that a simple Solow growth model does not predict the results. However, two new ideas prove to be more fruitful. For instance, expected returns may be higher in Asia but the actual returns became higher in Latin America. That is, unexpected favorable growth surprises may explain the returns. Alternatively, stock prices may already have incorporated expected future economic growth at the beginning of the sample, so that the levels of Asian stock prices were rationally high at the outset. The stylized fact obtained in this paper is new and will become standard reference in the future. The incorporation of estimates of direct rates of return from the EMDB database is particularly convincing evidence.

One of the lessons that Asia learned from the crisis of 1997–98 was the importance of avoiding "double mismatches"—namely, currency and maturity mismatches—in the balance sheets of financial institutions and corporations. In order to mitigate the double mismatch problem, regional central banks and ministries of finance have tried to push the initiative of promoting bonds issued in the local currencies. Progress, however, has been slow. The chapter focuses on financial integration by examining the match between the countries that issue and those that actually hold bonds. They do this using the popular *gravity* model, augmented with other institutional, policy, and economic variables. The data are drawn from the IMF's increasingly important Coordinated Portfolio Investment Survey (CPIS) database. If residents in the region tend to hold more bonds from the same region, the region is said to be more financially integrated. Eichengreen and Luengnaruemitchai explain the variation in bilateral holdings of long term bonds for a large number of country-pairs over the 2001–03 period. The confidence in their basic results is high since the model works well; other factors such as capital controls, exchange rate volatility and stock market and financial sector size are all significant with the expected signs. To provide a natural comparison, they ask how Asia compares with Europe and Latin America. Europe is clearly ahead of others in terms of financial integration, but Asia has made considerable progress compared to Latin America. This may occur because of institutional advantages that are conducive to intraregional cross-holding of Asian bonds. The authors' findings are highly relevant for the current policy discussion in the region.

The last three chapters all examine the opening or liberalization of domestic markets and the associated effects on market performance. Wang, Shen, and Liang examine financial liberalization as measured by General Agreement on Trade in Services (GATS) commitments. Fukao and colleagues examine performance of firms acquired by foreign firms and compares them with those acquired by domestic firms. Shin and Park examine foreign participation in the Korean stock market and the effect on the cost of capital.

The Wang, Shen, and Liang chapter examines the contribution of liberalization of trade in services to economic growth. A unique feature of this paper is the measurement of financial liberalization through the degree of commitments in the GATS. Indeed, one of the most valuable and original contributions of this paper lies in the coding, analysis, and inclusion in the growth equation of these GATS commitments. The de jure liberalization measures pertain to the 1994–00 and 01–04 periods. Wang finds that mode 1 (cross-border supply of services), mode 2 (consumption abroad), and mode 3 (commercial presence) are all positively correlated with the income level, but mode 4 (movement of natural persons) is not. The paper also finds a positive link between indicators of financial sector competition and financial sector liberalization; it also finds a positive correlation between economic growth and financial sector competition. A scenario is presented that opening financial markets will increase procompetitive pressure and ultimately lead to large differences in growth rates.

The Fukao, Ito, Kwon, and Takizawa chapter analyzes foreign direct investment (FDI) into Japan. In particular they examine whether a firm is chosen as an acquisition target based on its productivity level, profitability, and other characteristics. They also check whether the performance of Japanese firms acquired by foreign firms improves after acquisition. Their firm-level data set extends from 1994 to 2002. In earlier work, Fukao and colleagues have found that acquisitions by foreigners brought a large and quick improvement in total factor productivity (TFP) and profit rates. However, firms being acquired by foreign firms performed better simply because foreign investors acquired more promising Japanese firms than Japanese investors did. In order to solve this selection bias problem in this paper, the authors combine a difference-in-differences approach with a propensity score matching technique. Thus they first identify comparable firms as defined as firms sharing similar characteristics. They then compare acquired firms and nonacquired firms. Both results from unmatched samples and those from matched samples show that foreign acquisitions improved target firms' productivity and profitability significantly more and quicker than acquisitions by domestic firms. The technology of propensity matching is not new in this literature, but this chapter is probably the first paper to apply the technique to the Japanese M&A case.

Shin and Park study changes in the cost of capital after the opening of the Korean stock markets to foreigners, as proxied by the dividend yield. They employ a firm-level panel regression approach, focusing on the relationship between foreign participation rates and the dividend yield. The latter variable is a standard proxy for the cost of capital. Shin and Park find that the larger the foreign participation rate is, the lower is the dividend yield. But, the relationship is only significant in the post-crisis period when the Korean stock market was fully opened and foreign participation rate became higher. These results are different from those of existing studies based on cross-country data that tend to find the effects of market opening are realized in the early stage of opening. Although the exact mechanism for this finding is left for future research, the finding itself is provocative.

We are extremely happy to have these papers collected into this book. We believe that this volume will contribute to the growing literature on financial markets, regional integration, and economic growth in East Asia.

I

Global Imbalances

Life on the Tri-Polar Sphere
How Should Interest and
Exchange Rates Realign Next?

Michael P. Dooley, David Folkerts-Landau, and
Peter Garber

1.1 Introduction

A useful model of the international monetary system today must recognize
two important facts. First, an economically important periphery of poor
countries has emerged in recent years and these countries are now large
enough to have a material effect on the rest of the world. Second, the standard assumptions about domestic financial markets and capital mobility
that fit the rest of the world are not useful in understanding the behavior of
these countries or their interaction with the rest of the world. Our description of a framework that does recognize these facts has come to be known
as Bretton Woods II.[1]

In our model Asian financial markets are not integrated with international markets. One important implication is that for these countries sterilized intervention "works" in the sense that real exchange rates are influenced for extended time periods by governments' portfolio choices. We
also offer an argument for why such countries will find it in their interest to
keep their real exchange rates undervalued for an extended time period as
a part of a coherent development strategy.

Our conjecture is that export of domestic savings to the well-integrated
capital markets in the industrial world by governments following this development strategy is driving unusual behavior of macro variables in the

Michael P. Dooley is a professor of economics at the University of California, Santa Cruz
and a research associate of the National Bureau of Economic Research. David Folkerts-
Landau is Global Head of Research at Deutsche Bank. Peter Garber is a global strategist at
Deutsche Bank and a research associate of the National Bureau of Economic Research.

1. For the sequence of articles we have written on Bretton Woods II, see Dooley, Folkerts-
Landau, and Garber (2003a, b; 2004a, b, c, d; 2005a, b).

industrial world. In particular, low interest rates in the United States and Euroland are attributed not to the behavior of savings or investment in poor countries, but to the unusual decisions of these governments to place a large share of domestic savings into the well-integrated capital markets of industrial countries. This generates historically low interest rates not just in the United States, but in all markets that are integrated with U.S. financial markets.

In this paper we also take seriously the overwhelming evidence that financial markets in the United States and Euroland are very highly integrated. To make analysis with a three region model manageable we go to the extreme assumption that assets generated in the industrial world are perfect substitutes. The important implication is that sterilized intervention in these markets does not work. A less familiar implication is that the choice of dollar or euro assets by governments in the periphery makes no difference for interest rates in Euroland and the United States and has no effect on the dollar–euro exchange rate. It follows that the dreaded diversification of reserves that is often cited as a threat to the stability of the Bretton Woods II system is not a threat at all.

Finally, our approach offers interesting predictions for the dynamic paths for interest rates, exchange rates, and current account balances. We expect the United States to absorb a disproportionate share of the savings exported by periphery governments for an extended, but finite, time period. The U.S. current account deficit will shrink as the supply of savings from the periphery is reduced and interest rates in the integrated international financial markets rise. The supply of savings from the periphery will shrink as their successful development policy results in an improvement in their domestic financial markets. We expect the dollar-euro exchange rate to follow the usual cyclical patterns but with no long-run trend. Both the dollar and the euro will slowly depreciate in real terms against the managed periphery currencies.

That our forecasts have been on target for the last three years may be a matter of good analysis or good fortune. But it has, in the nature of things, led to a more general acceptance of the view in the financial markets, to the extent that market participants now want to hear the risk scenarios around this central view. This is much less true of the academic and official sector discourse, where, even after several years, debate is dominated by the view that the system will collapse very soon, all the more so for not having collapsed already.[2]

Whatever the judgment that hindsight will deliver on these disputes, it is clear that the global monetary system that we have described has some legs to it. So rather than fight old battles over the probability of collapse, we

---

2. See Eichengreen 2004, Obstfeld and Rogoff 2004, Obstfeld 2005, and Roubini and Setser 2005.

think it is time to analyze the dynamics and evolution of the system given that its basic parameters will last for some time.

1.2 A Differing Base of Premises

In this paper we set out in greater detail how we think about the dynamic forces emanating from the emergence of China and Asia as major players in world capital and foreign exchange markets. Conventional analyses have been based for several years on the assertion that the Bretton Woods II system cannot hold together for much longer. This may or may not turn out to be correct, but it does not offer any guidance if the system does survive for an extended time period, as we believe it will. The framework developed below also provides a guide to the dynamics of the system following a variety of changes in the economic environment.

For simplicity, our framework has divided the world into three regions: emerging Asia, the United States, and Euroland.[3] Euroland includes all countries outside the United States with open capital markets and market-determined exchange rates. We will use the euro to stand for the currencies of these countries since it is the dominant currency among them. Asia includes all countries with relatively closed capital markets and managed exchange rates and we use the renminbi to stand in for their currencies.

Some observers have questioned the usefulness of aggregating the managed rate countries into a single zone because of the differing incentives and constraints facing these countries. We agree, for example, that current account surpluses and reserve growth for China, oil-exporting countries, and Japan are products of quite different developments and incentives and are likely to have different degrees of persistence over time.[4] Our forecast is that individual countries will join and exit the bloc of countries that manage their dollar exchange rates, and their management will find different degrees of success, but the bloc will nevertheless remain a lasting and economically important feature of the international monetary system.[5]

The analysis will lean on four assumptions. We believe these assumptions are realistic, and they dramatically simplify the dynamics of a three-region analysis:

---

3. Because there is no necessity of geographic contiguity, we have referred to these regions in other essays from the functional viewpoint as the trade account region, the center country, and the capital account region.

4. See Dooley and Garber (2005, p. 158–160).

5. We have consistently argued that the system, *not its current manifestation in the orientation of particular countries to these three blocs,* would last for the foreseeable future. "Fixed exchange rates and controlled financial markets work for twenty years and countries that follow this development strategy become an important periphery. These development policies are then overtaken by open financial markets and this, in turn, requires floating exchange rates. The Bretton Woods system does not evolve, it just occasionally reloads a periphery." (Dooley, Folkerts-Landau, and Garber, 2003b, p. 3).

1. Asian financial markets are poorly integrated with the other two regions because of capital controls and the threat of sovereign interference with capital flows. This allows Asia to manage the dollar-renminbi exchange rate so that the renminbi appreciates in real terms slowly over an adjustment period of many years.

2. The United States and Euroland financial markets, in contrast, are very well integrated and their respective assets are very close substitutes, an assumption consistent with a great deal of empirical work, especially on the inefficacy of sterilized intervention. The United States and Euroland do not manage the euro-dollar exchange rate.

3. The dominant change in the economic environment that is driving the main features of the world economy is the rapid growth of savings rates and the level of savings in Asia *and* their exportation to the rest of the world.

4. The United States and Euroland differ in their capacities to utilize Asian savings, with the United States having a much greater absorptive capacity.

Some of the significant departures of our analysis from the conventional approach include the following:

1a. Conventional analysis considers Asian financial markets sufficiently integrated with international markets so that Asian governments will not be able to manage real exchange rates at reasonable costs. In particular, they will be unable to fend off hot money inflows. Moreover, they will not want to distort real exchange rates for much longer to encourage export-led growth.

2a. Conventional analysis assumes that United States and Euroland financial markets are not well integrated. Diversification of Asian reserves is thought to have an important effect on the dollar-euro exchange rate. This assumption seems to us inconsistent with substantial evidence that intervention and reserve management by U.S. and Euroland authorities have not had a large or lasting effect on industrial country exchange rates.

3a. The conventional analysis usually identifies a fall in the U.S. household savings rate or a rise in the government fiscal deficit rate as the driving force behind the U.S. current account deficit.

4a. Interest rate movements have not been consistent with this assumption—falling instead of rising. To circumvent this contradiction, it is conventionally asserted that interest rates and asset prices are driven by incorrect expectations, a misunderstanding of the dangerous nature of the system, or bubbles.

To summarize results in the rest of the paper, following a sudden shift to a global system with a long-term rise in exports of Asian savings and an understanding that this system will persist include:

- There is a substantial *immediate* appreciation of the euro against the dollar. As one of the only key prices allowed to move freely, this is a painful overshooting.
- Real interest rates in the United States and Euroland remain low relative to historical cyclical experience but converge slowly toward normal rates as Asian markets become integrated with international markets.
- The dollar and the euro gradually depreciate relative to the renminbi but, after the initial euro appreciation versus the dollar, *remain constant relative to each other in the absence of further disturbances.*
- A shift to a more rapid expected growth in Europe would *depreciate* the euro relative to the dollar and renminbi and raise interest rates in the United States and Europe.
- More rapid expected growth in the United States would tend to *depreciate* the dollar relative to the euro and renminbi. Because the dollar–renminbi is managed, the dollar would not fall immediately but would begin to depreciate more rapidly. The euro would appreciate immediately and then match the dollar's more rapid rate of depreciation against the renminbi.
- Shifts in currency composition of Asian reserves from dollars to euros would have *little or no lasting effect* on dollar-euro exchange rates.
- Effective protection in the United States and Euroland or a fall in the savings rate in Asia would generate a stronger dollar in the long run. The immediate effect would be less rapid dollar depreciation against the renminbi. The euro could go either way against the dollar.
- In real terms, the dollar will eventually have to depreciate relative to the renminbi, but most of the adjustment in the U.S. trade account will come as U.S. absorption responds to increases in real interest rates. Slow adjustment in the composition of U.S. output toward traded goods over an extended time period will not require unprecedented dollar depreciation.
- High oil prices and high consumption by oil exporters would generate a slower rate of dollar depreciation against the renminbi and higher interest rates in the United States and Euroland. The dollar-euro rate could go either way.

1.3   Analysis

In our framework, the fundamental shock to the system is a change in the supply of savings from Asia and a suspension of the usual home bias in allocating these savings across world markets. It may not seem all that important to decide whether it was because U.S. savings fell or Asian savings increased to drive the pattern of current accounts we now see. But it is, in fact, crucial for understanding the system and the direction it will take.

Asian real exchange rates are not market-determined prices, but are heavily and successfully managed by Asian governments. As noted above, the conventional analysis assumes this troublesome fact will soon go away. We argue that this policy behavior will *eventually* go away but is a central feature of Asian development policies and will not dissipate for a long time. It follows that if the rest of the world is to adjust now to a savings shock emanating from Asia the primary adjustment mechanism will not be changes in Asian real exchange rates.

To manage real exchange rates, Asian governments must intervene in foreign exchange markets. That part of the intervention that is sterilized is, in fact, intervention in credit markets. Asian finance ministries or central banks sell domestic securities, reducing the supply of loanable funds to domestic borrowers, and buy foreign securities, thereby increasing the supply of loanable funds in the U.S. and Euroland. The resulting shift in interest differential is possible because of effective capital controls. That is, Asian governments can manage exchange rates and interest rates because their domestic assets are made imperfect substitutes for foreign assets in private portfolios by policy, if not by private preference.

Figures 1.1 and 1.2 summarize the current state of the global system. Long term U.S. real rates fell to half their previous cyclical peak for two years during the rapid growth phase of this business cycle. They have recently begun to rise, but they are still substantially below their cyclical peak. This is reflective of low real interest rates throughout the industrial world. Simultaneously, the current account deficit has grown steadily as a ratio to U.S. GDP. Whatever one might think about low savings in the United States this is clear evidence that the supply of savings pushing into the United States, regardless of price, has dominated a demand pull of savings into the United States for half a decade.

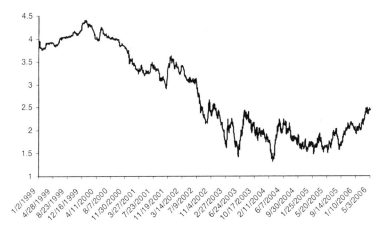

Fig. 1.1   Ten year TIPS yield

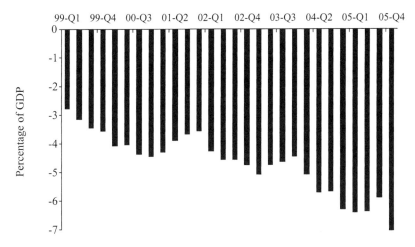

Fig. 1.2   U.S. current account balance

Because Asian exchange rates are managed, adjustment must proceed through current account balances and real interest rates. To understand current accounts we have to understand savings and investment. The question is: how are savings and investment changed in the United States, Euroland, and elsewhere as Asian savings are offered to the rest of the world? In particular, can we understand why real interest rates might fall in both the United States and Euroland while current account balances adjust by very different amounts? In our view, this is a very easy case to understand.

We can illustrate our approach first with a set of figures focusing on interest rates and current accounts for Asia, the United States, and Euroland, and then with another set focusing on net foreign debt positions and exchange rates.

Figure 1.3 shows real interest rates for the United States, Euroland, and Asia on the vertical axes. The horizontal axes represent the domestic savings, investment, and current accounts for these three regions. The upward sloping curves labeled S are national savings. The curves labeled S' are national savings augmented by imports or exports of savings through horizontal shifts. The downward sloping curves labeled I are investment. For convenience, we start with balanced current accounts at a common interest rate, but any starting point for the separate economies will do as long as real rates are the same in the United States and Euroland.

A policy to divert Asian savings to the United States and Euroland reduces the supply of savings available in Asia and shifts the Asian supply curve to the left. A current account surplus is generated and interest rates in Asia rise. In this exercise, we assume that savers in Asia are paid the initial interest rate r_0, investors are charged r_1, and the resultant excess of savings is dumped on the global financial market for whatever rate of return it may bring. The financial markets allocate these new savings to the

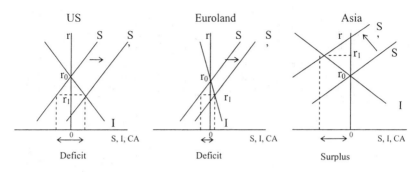

Fig. 1.3   Current account and interest rates

United States and Euroland to re-equate the real rates of interest in the two zones.

In the United States and Euroland, the augmented savings supply curves shift to the right as Asian savings push in. The real interest rate in the United States and Euroland falls as we move down the investment demand curves and the financial markets distribute the added savings across the two zones. The demand curves are downward sloping because investment increases relative to domestic savings as interest rates fall. Moreover, consumption rises with a fall in interest rates, so domestic savings fall as well. The rise in consumption and investment is matched by an inflow of foreign savings and by definition the current account deficit, initially marked at zero, increases. The increase in Asia's current account surplus is matched by the sum of the increases in the current account deficits of the United States and Euroland.

In the United States, the increase in savings demanded is large because investment and savings are quite sensitive to the rate of interest.[6] Euroland sees the same qualitative changes. But investment and the current account deficit increase only slightly because there are few profitable investment opportunities and consumption is not very responsive. The fundamental factor driving the different responses of the United States and Euroland current account deficits is the different opportunities to efficiently utilize foreign savings as the interest rate falls in both regions.

An important aspect of the adjustment process is the equalization of real rates of return on capital invested in the United States and Euroland through private arbitrage. When we turn to exchange rate determination in the following, we will use the result that real interest rates are equalized by flows of savings. It is clear, however, that expected rates of return on capital in the United States and Euroland could be equalized by expected real exchange rate changes in addition to real interest rates.

---

6. This means that there are many viable projects or confident consumers ready to go with a small improvement in financing costs relative to Euroland.

This apparent indeterminacy between real interest rates and expected changes in real exchange rates during the adjustment period is resolved at the end of the period. When the new equilibrium is established there is no reason to predict that the real exchange rate between the euro and the dollar will continue to change over time. Since the capital stocks must have the same expected rate of return looking forward at the end of the adjustment period, it follows that real interest rates must be the same at that time. Arbitrage across time will ensure that any capital put in place in the United States and Euroland during the adjustment period that will remain in place in a new steady state must have the same rate of return.

The preferred policy over time for Asian governments is to allow gradual real exchange rate appreciation. Over time, this reduces their intervention in credit markets and their exports of savings. By the end of the adjustment period real interest rates will have equalized across the three regions.

We now turn to the foreign exchange markets. There are three keys to understanding the three cross exchange rates.

First, for some years, Asian governments can and will manage the real dollar value of their currencies. They can do so because capital controls make Asian domestic assets imperfect substitutes for United States and Euroland assets in private portfolios. Their ability to manage their real exchange rate will erode over time as capital controls become less effective and their domestic asset markets are integrated with international capital markets. Their desire to maintain the system will also erode as their surplus labor is absorbed. But they will manage rates as long as they can because undervaluation is an important part of their development strategy.

Second, in the long run, say ten years more or less, the real value of the three currencies will have to adjust to changes in the international investment positions of the three regions generated during the adjustment period. Asia's net asset position will improve while the U.S. and Euroland positions will deteriorate by relatively large and small amounts, respectively.

The relationship between the long run exchange rate and the net foreign debt position of each region is not controversial and is the centerpiece of most analyses about the ultimate depreciation of the dollar. As net foreign debt increases, larger trade balance surpluses are needed to service net debt (balance the current account). So a fall in net foreign assets is associated with a depreciation of the real exchange rate. The implication is that the dollar and the euro must depreciate against the renminbi, but the dollar must depreciate by more. Therefore, the dollar must depreciate against the euro.[7]

---

7. In our view, the amount of the eventual dollar depreciation is often overestimated. Recall that the primary factor driving the increase in the U.S. trade and current account deficit is the relatively strong response of U.S. investment and consumption to a decline in interest rates. Over the adjustment period interest rates will rise, thereby causing an equally strong reverse effect, and this will help reduce the U.S. deficit. The exchange rate adjustment therefore must be consistent with a slow shift in U.S. output toward traded goods.

Third, exchange rates today would normally reflect these long run expectations to some degree. But intervention by Asian governments is sufficient to strictly manage the dollar-renminbi exchange rate. Intervention will not keep the renminbi undervalued forever, but it can extend the adjustment period. As we have argued elsewhere, the preferred path (from China's perspective) for Asian real exchange rates is a gradual appreciation toward their new long run values.

In contrast, the euro cross-rates both today and along the adjustment path are determined by private investors. The relevant context for these portfolio choices is that dollar and euro assets are close substitutes.[8] The key implication is that once the system comes to be understood the euro and the dollar must depreciate at the same rate over time relative to the renminbi. Recall that real interest rates on capital invested in the United States and Euroland are equalized by net savings flows. It follows that investors must expect the euro-dollar exchange rate to remain unchanged. Put another way, both currencies must depreciate, and be expected to depreciate, at the same rate against the renminbi.

The result of a shift in Asian savings exports is then an immediate euro appreciation against the dollar and the renminbi, followed by a constant dollar/euro rate. This means that there will be immediate, maximal political pressure for relief in a Euroland unable to absorb the shock easily, and continuous, though declining, pressure thereafter.

These results are illustrated in figure 1.4. Starting from an initial value of the renminbi-dollar rate in the top panel and a renminbi-euro rate in the bottom panel, we can follow the effects of an increase in Asian savings exports and intervention. These increases raise interest rates faced by domestic investors in Asia and lower interest rates in the United States and Euroland. Asia generates a current account surplus matched by deficits in the United States and Euroland. This continues until Asian savings exports and intervention return to normal levels. In figure 1.2, this interval is from 0–T. The eventual fall in the dollar against the renminbi from A to B is required to close the trade deficit and even to generate the trade surplus needed to service the higher level of U.S. debt at time T and after.

Without intervention, we would expect an immediate depreciation of the dollar; but this can and will be delayed by intervention.[9] Along the adjustment path AB, the dollar is supported by a flow of intervention. Private investors know the dollar will depreciate but nevertheless are willing to

8. See Henderson and Leahy (2005) for a three country analysis of intervention where imperfect asset substitution is assumed for all three regions.

9. We could replace time with net debt on the horizontal axis and have a diagram similar to that presented in Blanchard, Giavazzi, and Sa (2005). The case we present here is similar to their discussion of intervention following a shift in preferences away from U.S. goods. The interested reader is encouraged to work through their analysis of an imperfect substitutes model. Their analysis assumes that interest rates are unchanged and changes in absorption are assumed to be related to fiscal policies.

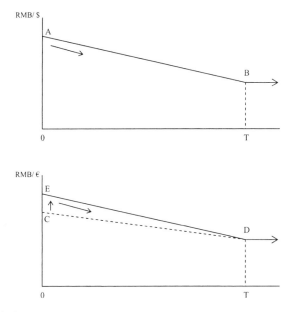

Fig. 1.4   Exchange rates

hold the stock of dollars, reduced by Asian purchases of U.S. assets.[10] U.S. debt to foreigners is growing more rapidly than it would have if the fall in interest rates had been partially offset by a market-determined depreciation of the dollar.

The renminbi-euro rate starts at C and must eventually move to D, a much smaller depreciation. Like the United States, Euroland will accumulate debt (or reduce net assets below their previous path) during the adjustment period. But in this case Asian governments are not intervening to manage the exchange rate either at point C or along the adjustment path. The question is then: where will the market set euro exchange rates?

We can make our analysis more realistic and much more transparent by assuming that U.S. and Euroland assets are close substitutes in private portfolios. This is an important departure from the usual portfolio balance model because it implies that the currency composition of Asian intervention is of secondary importance. If euro and dollar assets are close substitutes in private portfolios, Asian governments could intervene in either dollars or euros to stabilize the dollar value of their currencies. Moreover, diversification of Asian reserves would have little or no lasting effect on the dollar-euro exchange rates, contrary to a key conclusion of the conven-

10. The portfolio balance equilibrium is based on the idea that residents of all countries prefer home assets, but can be moved away from their preferred portfolio by differences in expected yields; that is, by interest differentials adjusted for expected changes in exchange rates.

tional view.[11] The irrelevance of Asian reserve diversification is consistent with a very large body of empirical evidence that sterilized intervention has had no lasting effect on exchange rates among industrial countries.[12]

The practical importance of this assumption is that the two adjustment paths in figure 1.2 must have the same slope. If they did not, more rapid dollar depreciation against the renminbi, relative to euro depreciation against the renminbi, implies expected depreciation of the dollar against the euro. Since interest rates in the United States and Euroland are the same, arbitrage would be profitable. Private investors would immediately bid for euros against dollars and would do so until the euro jumps to E. From this initial appreciation the euro now depreciates against the renminbi at the same rate as the dollar. Note that along this adjustment path the euro, as the key and only freely determined price in the global system, overshoots and remains overvalued relative to the dollar and the renminbi throughout the adjustment interval, although the degree of overvaluation shrinks over time.

Therefore, for senior European financial officials to claim that a small Euroland current account position means that the EU is part of neither the problem nor the solution is a divorce from reality. In particular, successfully arguing that China should not speed up the appreciation of the renminbi places maximal pressure on the euro to appreciate against the dollar, exactly the opposite of the intent.

We can now iterate through the current account analysis. The euro has appreciated against the renminbi and the dollar, so Euroland's current account deficit, already increased by the fall in interest rates, tends to widen. The dollar is unchanged against the renminbi and has depreciated against the euro, so the already increased U.S. current account deficit is reduced. These second round effects on the current account positions of the three regions would not alter our basic story assuming the reactions of absorption to interest rates is very different in the United States and Euroland.

1.4 Interest and Exchange Rates with Disturbances Along the Adjustment Path

Of course, changes in many conditions will shift the dollar-euro exchange rates along the adjustment path set out in the previous section. The

---

11. See Eichengreen (2005).

12. We have also explored the effects of diversification under the assumption of imperfect substitution between dollar and euro assets. Our conclusion is that it is not the interests of Asian governments to diversify, and recent data from the IMF shows that they have not done so through the end of last year. See Dooley, Folkerts-Landau, and Garber (2004a). The argument presented here suggests that Asian governments can diversify if they choose to do so, but that this would have no lasting effect on dollar exchange rates.

framework developed above is useful to evaluate changes in the economic environment during the adjustment process, and the peculiar nature of the global system produces some remarkable and unanticipated results.

1.4.1   A Stronger Euroland Outlook

Suppose, for example, that at time t_1 an improved outlook for profits in Euroland generates a positive shift in the demand for investment in Euroland. Figure 1.5 suggests that Asian savings will be shifted from the United States to Euroland for the balance of the adjustment period and that interest rates in both regions will rise.

The effects on exchange rates are illustrated in figure 1.3. With more Asian savings going to Euroland and less to the United States, at the end of the adjustment period, at T, the euro will be weaker and the dollar stronger than would have been the case. If Asian intervention at t_1 keeps the dollar from jumping from its initial value at F in figure 1.3, the euro depreciates sharply at t_1 for two reasons. First, it must now reach level J at T and it must now depreciate more slowly to match the dollar's reduced rate of depreciation.

1.4.2   A Weaker Euroland Outlook

A weaker outlook for Euroland investment would have symmetric effects. In this case there would be deterioration in the final expected debt position of the United States and an improvement in the final debt position of Euroland. This would require a more rapid rate of dollar depreciation against the renminbi and another move up for the euro. Interest rates in both regions would fall).

1.4.3   A Stronger U.S. Outlook

Changes in U.S. growth and investment would have similar effects. As U.S. growth increases, so does the expected stock of U.S. debt. The greater long run depreciation would not affect the current level of the renminbi-dollar but would require a more rapid appreciation of the renminbi against the dollar for the balance of the adjustment period.

The euro would appreciate against the renminbi and the dollar for two reasons. First, its long run level would jump up as Euroland would have a higher net asset position than before, and it would have to appreciate immediately in order to match the dollar's higher expected depreciation rate against the renminbi.

This is illustrated in Figure 1.6. The expected renminbi-dollar exchange rate at T shifts down from B to G and the expected renminbi-euro rate moves up from D to K. The euro immediately jumps from H to I as again the change in the euro is amplified by arbitrage between dollar and euro assets. Interest rates in both regions would rise.

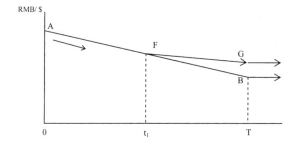

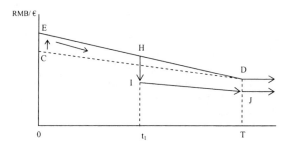

Fig. 1.5 Exchange rates, increase in Euroland growth

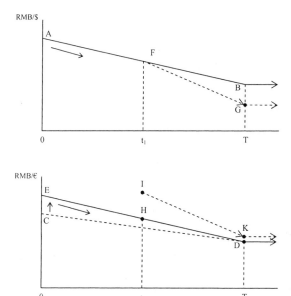

Fig. 1.6 Exchange rates, increase in U.S. growth

1.4.4   More War or Katrina

A larger fiscal deficit and demand for capital following destruction of U.S. capital or expanded expenditure for war increases U.S. demand for foreign savings and will lead to an increased U.S. indebtedness at T. Therefore, scenario 3 analysis applies. The euro appreciates against the dollar. Global interest rates rise.

1.4.5   Protectionism Surges; Oil Exporters Start Consuming Asia's Surplus Savings

It turns out that all of these have the same impacts on interest and exchange rates. For example, effective protection against Asian exports in both the United States and Euroland would forcibly reduce net savings transfers to the United States and Euroland from Asia by forcing a reduction in Asia's net trade surplus. Similarly, a decline in net Asian savings exported to the United States and Euroland would occur if a larger share of U.S., Euroland, and Asian income is transferred to oil exporters via terms of trade shifts. As the oil exporters start to consume a high fraction of this transfer, fewer excess savings are available to accumulate U.S. and Euroland debt. Each of these developments can be analyzed as illustrated in Figure 1.7.

In these events expected U.S. net debt at T is reduced, which raises the terminal exchange rate from B to G. Euroland net debt also falls, which raises the renminbi-euro rate from D to K. We assume that on its new path the renminbi-dollar rate does not jump up at t_1, but the rate of dollar depreciation is reduced so that the new path for the renminbi-dollar rate is FG. The renminbi-euro rate must reach K at T and the path from t_1 must have the same slope as FG; that is, the renminbi-euro rate must have the same expected rate of depreciation as the renminbi-dollar rate. The conclusion is that the euro can either depreciate or appreciate immediately against the dollar depending on the relative change in debt stocks in response to the new environment. There is no necessary direction of effect for this key exchange rate. Interest rates will rise both in the United States and Euroland because of the reduction in available savings.

A useful rule of thumb is that events that change expected U.S. and Euroland debt stocks and real exchange rates in opposite directions generate large and immediate changes in the dollar-euro rate when expectations change. The market rate changes in the same direction as the change in the expected future rates. Events that move both expected debt stocks in the same direction have ambiguous effects on the exchange rate at the point where expectations change.

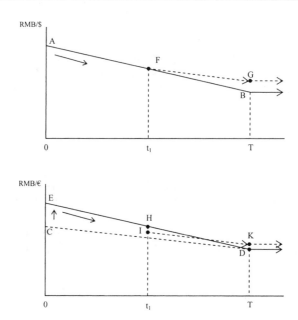

Fig. 1.7   Exchange rates

1.5   Further Thoughts on Asset Markets

The apparent failure of dollar exchange rates to respond to unprecedented recent and projected U.S. current account deficits is an important challenge for economic analysis. It is generally agreed that a substantial increase in projected debt levels should be associated with expectations that the real exchange rate will eventually depreciate. If private investors regard financial assets denominated in different currencies and issued by residents of different countries as perfect or very close substitutes, then the current exchange rate should be tied to the expected future exchange rate through the interest parity condition. Taken together, these ideas suggest that the dollar should have declined several years ago against the floating currencies when expectations about future U.S. debt levels were revised.

Suppose, for example, that some event generates a forecast that U.S. debt will increase from zero to sixty percent of U.S. GDP and then stabilize at that level at some arbitrary future date, T. Most analysts would agree that a real depreciation of the dollar by time T will be a part of the adjustment required to service this higher level of debt.[13] If the dollar is expected to be lower at T, if interest parity holds, and if real interest rate differentials are not affected by the shock that generated the increase in expected debt, then

---

13. See Lane and Milesi-Ferretti (2004, 2005) for discussion and evidence.

the real exchange rate must depreciate immediately and by the same amount as the long run expected value when expectations change.

Research on exchange rates since the early 1970s has been dominated by attempts to reconcile the data to this elementary notion. In the early years of floating rates the question was why exchange rates were much more variable than reasonable estimates of long run expected values. The current debate asks why market rates now are so stable in the face of strong presumption that the long run expectation has changed by a large amount.

To be sure, the market could have gotten it wrong then and could be getting it wrong now. If so, a crisis with sharply rising interest rates and sharply falling dollar exchange rates could be imminent, as conventional analysts predict. But it seems prudent to carefully consider alternative possibilities that are *currently* consistent with the salient evidence.

1.6   An Attempt to Reconcile Current Exchange Rates and Expectations

Market exchange rates need not move in lock step with expected exchange rates if interest rates change or if interest rate parity does not hold. An approach that was popular in the early 1980s to explain excess volatility of market exchange rates explored the assumption that interest parity may not hold if assets denominated in different currencies or issued in different countries are not close substitutes.[14] That is, if residents of a country for some reason prefer domestic assets, they would have to be compensated with higher expected yields to move away from their preferred portfolio. If rates of change toward a stable long-run equilibrium varied, it follows that current exchange rates could be much more variable than long run expected exchange rates. Moreover, sterilized intervention alters relative supplies of securities and could have some influence on expected rates of change and the levels of exchange rates.

In the current context, the implications of this portfolio balance approach are straightforward. If foreign residents prefer home securities and those preferences are unchanged, U.S. residents must pay a premium to finance a current account deficit. If we assume domestic interest rates are not affected by the shock that increases U.S. foreign debt, foreign investors must be induced to hold the growing stock of dollar-denominated claims on the United States by an extra expected return in the form of expected appreciation of the dollar. Since at T the dollar has to be below its current level because of increased U.S. indebtedness to foreigners, and since it must be expected to appreciate from now to T, the dollar must depreciate by even more now.

At first glance, this does not seem to help much in understanding the current situation where, it is argued, the dollar has not depreciated enough.

---

14. See Branson and Henderson (1985) for a survey.

But this can be rationalized by assuming the initial shock was a spontaneous increase in preferences for dollar assets (Blanchard et al. 2005). If foreigners want dollar assets, they can obtain them through current account surpluses and in the interim will accept a lower expected yield on the dollar assets they do hold. It follows that even though the dollar is expected to be lower at T, it may not fall much initially because an expected depreciation is consistent with an otherwise unsatisfied demand for dollars during the adjustment period.

1.7   Is Intervention a Plausible Driver of the System?

Identifying plausible reasons for a shift in preferences toward dollars remains a serious problem.[15] As one explanation, if changes in governments' balance sheets are not systematically offset by private investors the shift in currency preferences could be associated with government policies. In particular, sterilized intervention could account for expected increases in U.S. net international debt but only gradual adjustment in dollar exchange rates.

But there are a number of reasons that the portfolio balance approach was placed on a back burner of the profession's research agenda. First, a very large empirical literature was unable to find any lasting effect of intervention on interest rates or exchange rates. Second, imperfect substitution is usually modeled as aversion to exchange rate volatility. But sensible estimates of the degree of risk aversion needed to match exchange rate data seemed implausible. Third, imperfect substitution could be related to default risk or capital controls, but this has generally been assumed to be irrelevant for industrial countries.

Finally, Dornbusch (1976) showed that monetary policy and associated changes in real interest rate differentials could account for exchange rate volatility with perfect substitution and stable long run expected values for real exchange rates. In an era when monetary policies were quite variable, this solved the theoretical puzzle of the day and moved portfolio balance models to the history of thought reading list.

Nevertheless, it is clear that home bias in goods, equities, and other financial assets remains a central fact and puzzle for international economics.[16] Obstfeld (2004) presents a thoughtful review of these issues and offers a guess that a new theoretical basis for the portfolio balance approach will emerge from his work with Ken Rogoff on the implications of imperfect goods market integration. This would be welcome, but in the interim we re-

---

15. Cooper (2001, 2004) offers a compelling argument for a change in private preferences for U.S. assets. We agree that this is part of the story, but focus here on governments' portfolio choices.
    16. See Obstfeld and Rogoff (2000).

main largely in the dark about the source of home bias for assets and the implications for models of portfolio behavior.

Our own home bias in these matters is that capital controls and the threat of sovereign interference with foreign investment is the most compelling argument behind a portfolio balance framework.[17] It follows that the portfolio balance approach is more likely to be useful in understanding the behavior of countries or groups of countries whose governments dominate private portfolio decisions through controls and intervention and manage their exchange rates.

In our framework, the shift in preferences toward dollars is not just *qualitative,* but is *measured* by increases in international reserves of governments managing their exchange rates. Moreover, sterilized intervention is effective in altering interest differentials and exchange rates *between* managed economies and an integrated international capital market. But shifts in the composition of reserves do not change exchange rates *within* the larger integrated market.

While we use China/Asia and the renminbi as shorthand for the managed fixed rate region and its currency, we do not argue that China alone is large enough to dominate international interest and exchange rates. However, we estimate that countries that actively manage their exchange rates comprise about one third of world GDP and savings. The shock to the global system that we model is a substantial increase in savings rates and levels among this group. These are coupled with a decision of governments in the region to put a large share of the increase, about half, into foreign assets.

We could extend the portfolio balance model as well to economic relationships within the international capital market, that is, to the relations between the United States and Euroland, but we do not do so for two reasons. First, the reasons for rejecting this model in the past are still very powerful. Second, a three-zone portfolio balance model is very difficult to work with, particularly when we are interested in studying the endogenous responses of exchange rates and real interest rates to various shocks. Since such models have a low insight to equation ratio, we stick with the perfect substitutes model for the United States and Euroland. Our guess is that introducing a little bit of home bias in these portfolios will do little violence to our results.

References

Blanchard, O., F. Giavazzi, and F. Sa. 2005. The U.S. current account deficit and the dollar. NBER Working Paper no. w11137. February.

17. See Dooley and Isard (1980).

Branson, W., and D. Henderson. 1985. The specification and influence of asset markets. In *Handbook of International Economics,* vol. 2, eds. R. W. Jones and P. B. Kenen. New York: North Holland.

Cooper, R. N. 2001. Is the U.S. current account sustainable? Will it be sustained? *BPEA,* 1:217–26.

———. 2004. U.S. deficit: It is not only sustainable, it is logical. *Financial Times* (October 31).

Dooley, M., D. Folkerts-Landau, and P. Garber. 2003a. Dollars and deficits: Where do we go from here? Deutsche Bank Global Markets Research (June 18).

———. 2003b. An essay on the revived Bretton Woods system. NBER Working Paper no. 9971. September.

———. 2004a. The Revived Bretton Woods system: The effects of periphery intervention and reserve management on interest rates and exchange rates in center countries. NBER Working Paper no. 103332. Cambridge, MA: National Bureau of Economic Research, March.

———. 2004b. Direct investment, rising real wages and the absorption of excess labor in the periphery. NBER Working Paper no. 10626. Cambridge, MA: National Bureau of Economic Research, July.

———. 2004c. The U.S. current account deficit and economic development: Collateral for a total return swap. NBER Working Paper no. 10727. Cambridge, MA: National Bureau of Economic Research, September.

———. 2004d. The revived Bretton Woods: Alive and well. Deutsche Bank Global Markets Research. Frankfurt: Deutsche Bank AG. December.

———. 2005a. Savings gluts and interest rates: The missing link to Europe. NBER Working Paper no. 11520. Cambridge, MA: National Bureau of Economic Research, July.

———. 2005b. Interest rates, exchange rates and international adjustment. NBER Working Paper no. 11771. Cambridge, MA: National Bureau of Economic Research, November.

Dooley, M., and P. Garber. 2005. Is it 1958 or 1968? Three notes on the longevity of the revived Bretton Woods system. *Brookings Papers on Economic Activity* 1:147–187.

Dooley, M., and P. Isard. 1980. Capital controls, political risk, and deviations from interest parity. *Journal of Political Economy* 88:370–84.

Dornbusch, R. 1976. Expectations and exchange rate dynamics. *Journal of Political Economy* 84:1161–76.

Eichengreen, B. 2004. Global imbalances and the lessons of Bretton Woods. NBER Working Paper no. 10497. Cambridge, MA: National Bureau of Economic Research, May.

Eichengreen, B. 2005. Sterling's past, dollar's future: Historical perspectives on reserve currency competition. NBER Working Paper no. 11336. Cambridge, MA: National Bureau of Economic Research.

Gourinchas, P. O., and H. Rey. 2005. From world banker to world venture capitalist: U.S. external adjustment and the exorbitant privilege. NBER Working Paper no. w11563. Cambridge, MA: National Bureau of Economic Research, August.

Henderson, D., and M. Leahy. 2005. A note on alternative exchange rate policies with three currencies. New York: Board of Governors of the Federal Reserve System.

Lane, P. R., and G. M. Milesi-Ferretti. 2004. The transfer problem revisited: Net foreign assets and real exchange rates. *Review of Economics and Statistics* 86:841–57.

———. 2005. Financial globalization and exchange rates. IMF Working Paper no. 05/03. Washington, DC: International Monetary Fund, January.

Obstfeld, M. 2004. External adjustment. *Review of World Economics,* vol. 140:541–68.

———. 2005. Sustainability and the U.S. account: Dark musings. Available at http://www.frbsf.org/economics/conferences/0502/Obstfeld.ppt. Retrieved February, 2005.

Obstfeld, M., and K. Rogoff. 2000. The six major puzzles in international macroeconomics: Is there a common cause? In *NBER Macroeconomics Annual 2000,* eds. B. S. Bernanke and K. Rogoff. Cambridge, MA: MIT Press.

———. 2004. The unsustainable U.S. current account position revisited. Available at http://www.frbsf.org/economics/conferences/0502/Obstfeld.pdf. Retrieved October, 2004.

Roubini, N., and B. Setser. 2005. Will the Bretton Woods 2 Regime Unravel Soon? The Risk of a Hard Landing in 2005–2006. Available at http://www.frbsf.org/economics/conferences/0502/index.html. Retrieved February 4, 2005.

Comments   John Simon

This chapter by Dooley, Folkerts-Landau, and Garber deals with their contentious model of the international monetary system and their explanation, based on the saving and intervention behavior of Asian countries, for the current pattern of interest and exchange rates around the world. At the beginning of the paper the authors state, "rather than fight old battles over the probability of collapse, we think it is time to analyze the dynamics and evolution of the system given that its basic parameters will last for some time." The paper then provides a diagram in figure 1.1 and discusses some of the implications of moving around the lines representing their model for future interest and exchange rate movements.

Assuming that everything is as the authors have said would lead to a rather short discussion from me. The framework the authors provide in the paper is short and uncomplicated. Indeed, it is little more than their set of assumptions. And, if all the authors' assumptions are true, you get the results they do. So hopefully the authors will forgive me if I, in an effort to stimulate some interesting discussion, do not agree with everything they say.

The authors set out four assumptions: Asian financial markets are poorly integrated and, so, can manage their exchange rate; the United States and Euroland are well integrated, so sterilized intervention here is ineffective; the dominant driver of the world economy is the pattern of Asian savings; and the United States has a greater absorptive capacity for Asian savings than the Euro area. I am happy, for the purposes of this discussion, to take these as given. I will focus, however, on part of their first assumption where they state, "This allows Asia to manage the dollar-renminbi exchange rate

John Simon is Chief Manager in the Payments Policy Department of the Reserve Bank of Australia.

so that the renminbi appreciates in real terms slowly over an adjustment period of many years." China *can* do this. But will it want to?

Much of the discussion in the paper is focused on the international environment and treats the individual countries as somewhat of a black box. It is tempting to assume that, just because China has been managing its exchange rate for a while, it will continue to do so regardless of future developments. But in addressing the question of whether China will want to continue its current arrangements for the indefinite future, it is worth looking inside the black box. At this stage it is also worth commenting that a similar observation could be made about the United States and Euroland. They have many more policy tools at their disposal than sterilized intervention in the foreign exchange market. Thus, even assuming, as this paper does, that sterilized intervention doesn't work, that doesn't mean they are completely powerless to influence interest and exchange rates. Consider, for example, the likely effects of trade policy or, indeed, the effect that the color of Greenspan's tie could have on interest and exchange rates in days gone past.[1]

The basic story is fairly well known. China has been intervening heavily to maintain the level of its exchange rate, which has lead to large accumulations of foreign reserves and significant bond issues to sterilize the intervention. Figure 1C.1 shows the growth in China's foreign exchange reserves.

As can be seen, reserves have been growing at around 35 to 50 percent per year since 2003. This alone has been cause for some to question the sustainability of the fixed exchange rate arrangements. The internal consequences of this can be seen in the growth in the People's Bank of China's bond liabilities (figure 1C.2).

China has had to issue significant quantities of bonds to sterilize its foreign exchange intervention. Despite this, the economy is still awash with liquidity. Figure 1C.3 shows the growth rate of money and credit in China. Much of this strength can be traced to the increased export earnings that are a direct consequence of China's currently preferred exchange rate.

This strong monetary growth, despite the best attempts of the government to constrain it, is the most obvious sign of the internal stresses that the economy is dealing with. One consequence of this liquidity is the high rate of investment in China. As can be seen in figure 1C.4, it is over 40 percent of GDP and growing. This is a sign of an economy that is facing significant imbalances. While other Asian countries have occasionally experienced this level of investment before, it has invariably been followed by a sharp contraction.

In addition to the monetary stresses, there are a number of other stresses

---

1. See, for example, the opening statement of Senator Dodd during Greenspan's testimony before the Senate Committee on Banking, Housing, and Urban Affairs on July 18, 1996.

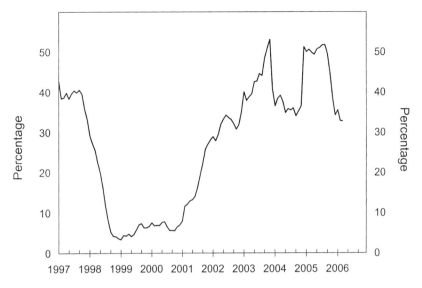

Fig. 1C.1   China—Forex reserves, year-ended percentage change

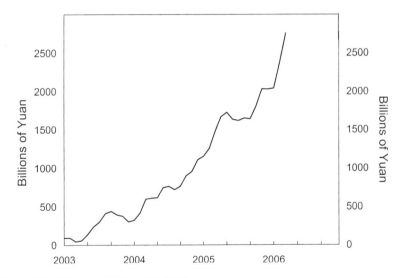

Fig. 1C.2   China—PBC bond liabilities

evident in the Chinese economy. A consequence of the export oriented policies of the government is that labor markets are undergoing significant structural change. The strength of export oriented industries has led to significant labor demand from these industries—which are predominantly located in the coastal areas of China. The wages in these areas have increased

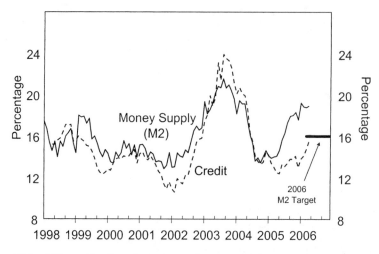

Fig. 1C.3   China—Credit and money supply, year-ended percentage change

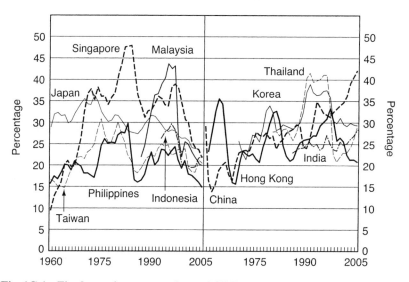

Fig. 1C.4   Fixed asset investment, share of GDP
Sources: CEIC; RBA

rapidly and induced significant internal relocation of workers. Consequent to this relocation have been significant stresses on urban infrastructure and housing prices that have increased rapidly.

In response, the government of China has implemented a number of policies to try to contain these pressures. It has increased lending rates to limit borrowing, it has raised reserve ratios on banks to restrict lending, it has enforced capital gains taxes on housing and implemented other restrictions to limit house price appreciation, and it has provided support for rural wages to limit the flow of labor. Indeed, a number of these policies have been implemented in quick succession quite recently. These are not the signs of a stable economy.

In predicting the outcome of these circumstances, the experience of industrialized countries under monetary targeting may be instructive. Such targeting was invariably associated with quite detailed controls on the actions of banks. These controls, however, had limited effectiveness because economic activity tended to move to the less regulated areas of the financial system rather than being completely suppressed. It is somewhat like squeezing on a balloon. You can restrict one area of the economy, but the fundamental pressures still bubble out in other areas. Thus, in China's case, there are fundamental pressures in its economy that need to be addressed. And the current policies deal not so much with the causes as with the symptoms.

Given this environment, it seems that an obvious question is how long China will be willing to maintain its current policies. As I indicated above, even if we assume that China can maintain a gradually appreciating exchange rate, it is still an open question as to whether it will want to. As such, my fundamental comment on the paper by Dooley, Folkerts-Landau, and Garber is that they treat the various economic blocs too much like black boxes. It may well be that Bretton Woods II survives for many years, but even if it does, an appreciation of the risks around that forecast is important for understanding its evolution.

So, to conclude on a rhetorical note, perhaps it is worth asking how good a label is Bretton Woods II for the current situation? Bretton Woods II invokes the spirit of an agreement that sought to bind countries into a fixed exchange rate regime. While countries are not renowned for their selfless spirits when making international agreements, unless one makes the assumption that Bretton Woods had no effect on its signatories it seems misleading to put the current situation in the same category. No countries have agreed to do anything, and the current arrangements have no more permanence than China gives them. As such, a prediction of the likely future path of interest and exchange rates that doesn't consider the motivations behind China's current policy, and the chance these may lead to different policies, would significantly understate the inherent risk of the forecast— if not change the forecasts themselves.

References

Barro, R. J., and D. B. Gordon. 1983. A positive theory of monetary policy in a natural rate model. *Journal of Political Economy* 91(4): 589–610.

Romer, D. 1993. Openness and inflation: Theory and evidence. *Quarterly Journal of Economics* 108:869–903.

Terra, M. C. T. 1998. Openness and inflation: A new assessment. *Quarterly Journal of Economics* 113:641–48.

Liquidity Risk Aversion, Debt Maturity, and Current Account Surpluses
A Theory and Evidence from East Asia

Shin-ichi Fukuda and Yoshifumi Kon

2.1 Introduction

In recent literature, it has been widely discussed why the U.S. current account has deteriorated dramatically during the past decade (see, among others, Obstfeld and Rogoff, 2004; Roubini and Setser, 2004; Blanchard, Giavazzi, and Sa, 2005). Although the U.S. current account had been in deficit for most of the 1980s and 1990s, its deficits were almost balanced by Japan's current account surpluses until the mid-1990s. However, the U.S. current account started to show a dramatic deterioration after 1997 and is now far from balanced by surpluses of the other industrialized countries (see figure 2.1). The first strand of studies proposed that the recent deterioration in the U.S. current account primarily reflects a decline of the U.S. domestic saving and an increase in the U.S. demand for foreign goods. The second strand of studies, in contrast, pointed out that an increase in the global supply of saving, especially an increase in Asian and Middle Eastern savings, would help to explain the increase in the U.S. current account deficit. In particular, these studies stress a remarkable reversal in global capital flows that has transformed emerging-market economies from borrowers to large net lenders in international capital markets (see, for ex-

Shin-ichi Fukuda is a professor of economics at the University of Tokyo. Yoshifumi Kon is a Ph.D. student of economics at the University of Tokyo.

This is a substantially revised version of the paper "International Currency and the US Current Account Deficits" that was prepared for the 17th Annual East Asian Seminar on Economics, held at Kohala Coast, Hawaii, June 2006. We would like to thank A. Rose, L. Goldberg, M. Dooley, two anonymous referees, and the other participants of the conference for their constructive suggestions.

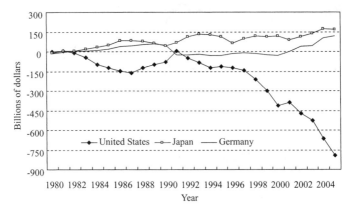

Fig. 2.1   Current account balances of the U.S., Japan, and Germany
Source: International Financial Statistics, IMF

ample, Bernanke, 2005; Dooley, Folkerts-Landau, and Garber 2005; and Caballero, Farhi, and Gourinchas, 2006).

When looking at the recent remarkable reversal in global capital flows, East Asian economies have been one of the major net lenders after the currency crisis in 1997. Table 2.1 reports total trade balances of eight East Asian economies from 1990 to 2004. It also reports their trade balances against the United States and the other trade partners. It shows that except for Hong Kong and the Philippines, the East Asian economies had trade balance surpluses in total after the crisis. In particular, except for the Philippines, they have had big trade balance surpluses against the United States since the crisis and the surpluses have widened in the 2000s. The trade balance surpluses have been one of the main sources of the U.S. current account deficits since the late 1990s, especially since the early 2000s.

In this paper, we explore some theoretical and empirical implications of the changed international capital flows in East Asian economies after the currency crisis. During the crisis, East Asian economies with smaller liquid foreign assets had a hard time preventing panics in financial markets and sudden reversals in capital flows (see, for example, Corsetti, Pesenti, and Roubini 1999 and Sachs and Radelet 1998). Many developing countries thus came to recognize that increased liquidity is an important self-protection against crises. Among the strategies for the self-protection, replacing liquid short-term debt by illiquid long-term debt was initially one popular advice that many economists suggested. However, what most Asian economies took more seriously was raising foreign reserves (see, for example, Aizenman and Lee 2005 and Rodrik 2005). Foreign exchange reserves held by developing nations, especially East Asian economies, are now record-breaking and stand at levels that are a multiple of those held by advanced countries. The purpose of this paper is to show that

Table 2.1   Trade balances of East Asian economies

	China			Korea			Singapore			Hong Kong			Thailand			Indonesia			Malaysia			Philippines		
	Total	U.S.	Non-U.S.	Total	U.S.	Non-U.S.	Total	U.S.	Non-U.S.	Total	U.S.	Non-U.S.	Total	U.S.	Non-U.S.	Total	U.S.	Non-U.S.	Total	U.S.	Non-U.S.	Total	U.S.	Non-U.S.
1995	16.8	8.6	8.2	-9.8	-6.2	-3.6	-6.2	2.9	-9.1	-19.2	23.0	-42.2	-16.5	1.6	-18.1	3.8	1.9	1.9	-3.9	2.7	-6.5	-10.9	1.0	-11.9
1996	12.1	10.6	1.6	-19.8	-11.5	-8.3	-6.6	1.5	-8.1	-18.0	22.7	-40.7	-17.6	0.8	-18.4	7.0	1.7	5.2	-0.2	2.1	-2.3	-11.2	0.7	-11.9
1997	40.8	16.5	24.3	-8.4	-8.4	0.0	-7.2	0.7	-8.0	-20.8	24.7	-45.5	-5.4	2.5	-7.8	9.2	2.0	7.1	-1.5	1.3	-2.9	-19.9	1.6	-21.6
1998	43.4	21.0	22.4	39.3	2.7	36.7	8.3	3.1	5.2	-10.9	26.9	-37.8	11.4	6.1	5.3	21.5	3.5	18.0	15.2	4.4	10.7	0.0	3.6	-3.6
1999	29.2	22.5	6.7	23.9	4.7	19.3	3.7	3.0	0.6	-5.9	28.8	-34.6	8.1	6.2	1.9	24.7	4.1	20.6	19.1	7.1	11.9	4.7	4.1	0.6
2000	24.0	29.8	-5.8	11.3	8.5	2.8	3.3	3.6	-0.3	-11.3	32.6	-43.9	7.0	7.4	-0.4	28.6	5.1	23.5	16.0	6.5	9.5	3.7	5.0	-1.3
2001	23.1	28.2	-5.0	8.7	8.9	-0.2	5.7	-0.4	6.1	-11.6	28.9	-40.6	3.1	6.0	-3.0	25.3	4.6	20.8	14.8	6.0	8.9	-0.9	2.6	-3.5
2002	30.3	42.8	-12.5	9.4	9.8	-0.5	8.6	2.5	6.1	-7.8	31.1	-38.8	4.1	7.3	-3.2	25.9	4.9	20.9	13.9	5.7	8.2	-0.2	1.4	-1.6
2003	25.4	58.7	-33.3	13.9	9.4	4.5	16.1	2.6	13.6	-8.7	29.0	-37.7	4.5	6.5	-2.0	28.5	4.7	23.8	22.2	7.7	14.6	-1.3	-0.1	-1.1
2004	31.8	80.4	-48.6	28.7	14.1	14.6	16.5	2.5	14.0	-12.1	29.5	-41.6	2.1	8.2	-6.2	25.0	5.6	19.5	22.2	8.5	13.7	-4.4	-1.1	-3.3

Source: IMF, *Direction of Trade Statistics Yearbook,* various issues.

Note: Units in billions of U.S. dollars.

macroeconomic impacts will be very different depending on which strategy developing countries take for self-protection.

In the first part of this paper, we investigate what impacts an increased aversion to liquidity risk can have on current account and the other macroeconomic variables in a simple open economy model. In the model, each representative agent maximizes the utility function over time. Since Obstfeld and Rogoff (1997), usefulness of utility-based models has been widely recognized. A key feature in our model is that relative size of net foreign liquid debt to foreign reserve reduces the utility. This is one of the simplest forms that capture costs from holding liquid foreign debts. At period τ, there is an unanticipated shock that increases aversion to liquidity risk. When the government keeps the amount of foreign reserves constant, the increased aversion among private individuals reduces liquid debt and increases illiquid debt. However, because the sum of liquid and illiquid debts does not change much, the macroeconomic impacts are not large, causing only small current account surpluses. In contrast, when both private individuals and the government respond to an unanticipated increase of liquidity risk aversion, the increased aversion increases foreign reserves and may lead to a rise of liquid debt. In particular, under some reasonable parameter set, it causes large macroeconomic impacts, including current account surpluses accompanied by depreciation of the real exchange rate.

In the second part of the paper, we provide some empirical evidence in East Asia that supports to the theoretical implications. In particular, we focus on the changes of foreign debt maturity structures and their implications in East Asian economies. We find that many East Asian economies temporarily reduced short-term borrowings soon after the crisis, but increased short-term borrowings in the early 2000s. Since short-term debt is liquid debt, the former change after the crisis is consistent with the case where only private agents respond to the increased aversion to liquidity risk. However, the latter change is consistent with the case where the government also started to respond and accumulated substantial foreign exchange reserves.

Since macroeconomic impacts of the increased liquidity risk aversion depend on which strategy the East Asian economies take, our results have several important implications. In particular, by accumulating foreign exchange reserves, the U.S. dollar is the dominant reserve currency in the currency compositions. This suggests that substantial rises in foreign exchange reserves will increase capital inflows into the United States. We point out that trade account surpluses have been widening against the United States, but not against non-U.S. countries in several Asian economies in the 2000s. Finally, we find that there were substantial depreciations of East Asian real exchange rates against the U.S. dollar even after the economies recovered from the crisis. We point out that the result is also consistent with the model.

There are several previous studies that address determinants of debt maturity structure. For example, Rodrik and Velasco (1999) argue that international investors with informational disadvantages may choose to lend short-term to better monitor and discipline borrowers (see also Fukuda 2001 and Jeanne, 2004). Broner, Lorenzoni, and Schmukler (2004) argue that emerging economies borrow short term due to the high risk premium charged by international capital markets on long-term debt (see also Schmukler and Vesperoni, 2006). However, unlike ours, none of them discussed interactions between debt maturity and foreign reserves that prevailed in emerging markets in the late 1990s and the early 2000s.

The paper proceeds as follows. Section 2.2 sets up our small open economy model and section 2.3 discusses its implications under constant foreign reserves. Section 2.4 discusses macroeconomic consequences when the government chooses foreign reserves so as to minimize its loss function, and section 2.5 presents the simulation results. Section 2.6 shows some supporting evidence in East Asia, and section 2.7 considers an implication for the U.S. current account deficits. Section 2.8 discusses implications for real exchange rates. Section 2.9 summarizes our main results and refers to their implications.

2.2   A Small Open Economy Model

The main purpose of our theoretical model is to investigate macroeconomic consequences when the economy suddenly increased its aversion to liquidity risk. We consider a small open economy that produces two composite goods, tradables and nontradables. For analytical simplicity, we assume that outputs of tradables and nontradables, y^T and y^N respectively, are fixed and constant over time. Each representative agent in the economy maximizes the following utility function:

$$(1) \qquad \sum_{j=0}^{\infty} \beta^j \left[U(c_{t+j}^T, c_{t+j}^N) - C(\lambda b_{t+j}^A, R_{t+j}) \right], \quad 0 < \lambda,$$

where c_t^T = consumption of tradable good, c_t^N = consumption of nontradable good, b_t^A = net liquid debt, b_t^B = net illiquid debt, and R_t = foreign reserve. The parameter β is a discount factor such that $0 < \beta < 1$. Subscript t denotes time period. The utility function $U(c_{t+j}^T, c_{t+j}^N)$ is increasing and strictly concave in c_{t+j}^T and c_{t+j}^N, while the disutility function $C(\lambda b_{t+j}^A, R_{t+j})$ is strictly increasing and strictly convex in b_{t+j}^A.

The budget constraint of the representative agent is:

$$(2) \ b_{t+1}^A + b_{t+1}^B = (1 + r_A)b_t^A + (1 + r_B)b_t^B - y^T - p_t^N y^N + c_t^T + p_t^N c_t^N + T_t$$

where T_t is lump-sum tax, p_t^N is the price of nontradable goods, r_A is real interest rate of liquid debt, and r_B is real interest rate of illiquid debt. For simplicity, we assume that $r_A < r_B = (1/\beta) - 1$. The assumption that $r_A < r_B$ reflects a liquidity premium that makes real interest rate of liquid debt lower than that of illiquid debt. Since the numeraire is the traded good, the real interest rates and the price of nontradable goods are defined in terms of tradables.

A key feature in equation (1) is that net liquid debt and foreign reserve are in the utility function. In our model, net supply of domestic debt is always zero, so that b_t^A denotes net liquid foreign debt. We assume that the relative size of net liquid foreign debt to foreign reserve reduces the utility. This is one of the simplest forms that capture potential costs from holding liquid foreign debts. Panics in financial markets and sudden reversals in capital flows are more likely to happen when the country has higher (net) levels of liquid foreign debts, but are less likely when it has higher levels of foreign reserves. To the extent that $\partial C(\lambda b_{t+j}^A, R_{t+j})/\partial(\lambda b_{t+j}^A) > 0$ and $\partial C(\lambda b_{t+j}^A, R_{t+j})/\partial R_{t+j} < 0$, the function $C(\lambda b_{t+j}^A, R_{t+j})$ is a reduced form that captures the disutility from such potential costs.

One may interpret the function $C(\lambda b_{t+j}^A, R_{t+j})$ as a shopping time model where either a decline of b_t^A or a rise of R_t saves labor time for reducing liquidity risk. In a closed economy, fiat money provides such liquidity services in the money-in-the-utility function model. In a small open economy that has a potential liquidity risk, either a decrease of liquid foreign debt or an increase of foreign reserve provides a similar service. In the following analysis, we assume that $\partial^2 C(\lambda b_{t+j}^A, R_{t+j})/\partial(\lambda b_{t+j}^A)\partial R_{t+j} < 0$. The assumption reflects the fact that a foreign reserve accumulation relieves the marginal disutility from increased liquid foreign debt. The parameter λ represents the degree of risk aversion to potential liquidity shocks. An increased aversion to liquidity risk generally increases the marginal disutility from the increased liquid foreign debt.

The first-order conditions are derived by maximizing the following Lagrangian:

(3) $$L = \sum_{j=0}^{\infty} \beta^j [U(c_{t+j}^T, c_{t+j}^N) - C(\lambda b_{t+j}^A, R_{t+j})]$$
$$+ \sum_{j=0}^{\infty} \beta^j \mu_{t+j} [b_{t+1+j}^A + b_{t+1+j}^B - (1 + r_A) b_{t+j}^A - (1 + r_B) b_{t+j}^B$$
$$+ y^T + p_{t+j}^N y^N - c_{t+j}^T - p_{t+j}^N c_{t+j}^N - T_{t+j}].$$

It holds that $c_t^N = y^N$ in equilibrium. Assuming interior solutions, the first-order conditions thus lead to:

(4a) $$\partial U(c_t^T, y^N)/\partial y^N = \mu_t p_t^N,$$

(4b) $$\partial U(c_t^T, y^N)/\partial c_t^T = \mu_t,$$

(4c) $$\lambda \partial C(\lambda b_{t+1}^A, R_{t+1})/\partial(\lambda b_{t+1}^A) = (r_B - r_A)\mu_{t+1}.$$

Since the numeraire is the traded good, the price of nontradable good p_t^N denotes the real exchange rate of this small open economy at time t, where a decline of p_t^N means depreciation of the real exchange rate. Equation (4a) thus implies that the real exchange rate depreciates when y^N increases. Equation (4b) determines the amount of consumption of tradable good. Equation (4c) implies that the amount of liquid foreign debt b_t^A is inversely related with the amount of foreign reserves R_t. This is because foreign reserves, which reduce liquidity risk, allow the representative agent to hold more liquid foreign debt.

Under the assumption that $r_B = (1/\beta) - 1$ where the real interest rate of illiquid debt is equal to the rate of time preference, Lagrangian multiplier μ_t is constant over time and equals to $\mu > 0$. This implies that all of the macro variables c_t^T, p_t^N, b_t^A, and $b_t^A + b_t^B$ are constant over time without unanticipated external shocks.[1] However, an unanticipated change of the parameter λ affects the equilibrium values of these variables. In particular, the parameter λ affects the choice between liquid and illiquid foreign debts because of potential costs from holding liquid foreign debt, and may affect the current account of the economy.

2.3   The Macroeconomic Impacts under Constant Foreign Reserves

The main purpose of the following analysis is to explore the impacts when the economy suddenly increased its aversion to liquidity risk. To achieve this goal, we explore what impacts an unanticipated change of λ has on various macroeconomic variables. This section first considers the case where the amounts of foreign reserves R_t and lump-sum tax T_t are exogenously given and remain constant over time. Under the balanced budget, the government issues no bond to finance its activity. This corresponds to the case where only private individuals respond to an unanticipated increase of disutility from liquidity risk.

Suppose that there was an unanticipated increase of λ at period τ. Then, both c_t^T and p_t^N instantaneously jump to the new steady state at period τ, while both b_t^A and $b_t^A + b_t^B$ move to the new steady state at period $\tau + 1$. Since $c_t^N = y^N$, the budget constraint thus leads to:

(5a) $$0 = r_B(b_0^A + b_0^B) - (r_B - r_A)b_0^A - y^T + c_0^T + T,$$

(5b) $$b_1^A + b_1^B = (1 + r_B)(b_0^A + b_0^B) - (r_B - r_A)b_0^A - y^T + c_1^T + T,$$

(5c) $$0 = r_B(b_1^A + b_1^B) - (r_B - r_A)b_1^A - y^T + c_1^T + T,$$

where the variables with subscript 0 are those in the old steady state and the variables with subscript 1 are those in the new steady state. Denoting the change of the variable x's steady state value by Δx, it therefore holds that:

---

1. When $r_B \neq (1/\beta) - 1$, Lagrangian multiplier μ_t changes over time and consequently some macrovariables such as c_t^T have a time trend. However, even when $r_B \neq (1/\beta) - 1$, a basic message in the following analysis is essentially the same.

(6)
$$\Delta(b^A + b^B) = \frac{(r_B - r_A)}{(1 + r_B)} \Delta b^A = \Delta c^T.$$

Since equations (4b) and (4c) respectively imply that:

(7a)
$$\Delta\mu = \frac{\partial^2 U(c^T, y^N)}{\partial c^{T2}} \Delta c^T,$$

(7b)
$$\lambda^2 \frac{\partial^2 C}{\partial(\lambda b_{t+1}^A)^2} \Delta b^A + \left[\frac{\partial C}{\partial(\lambda b_{t+1}^A)} + \lambda b^A \frac{\partial^2 C}{\partial(\lambda b_{t+1}^A)^2} \right] \Delta\lambda = (r_B - r_A)\Delta\mu,$$

we also obtain:

(8a)
$$\frac{\Delta b^A}{\Delta\lambda} = -\frac{1}{\Omega} \left[\frac{\partial C}{\partial(\lambda b^A)} + \lambda b^A \frac{\partial^2 C}{\partial(\lambda b^A)^2} \right] < 0,$$

(8b)
$$\frac{\Delta(b^A + b^B)}{\Delta\lambda} = \frac{\Delta c^T}{\Delta\lambda} = \frac{r_B - r_A}{1 + r_B} \frac{\Delta b^A}{\Delta\lambda} < 0,$$

(8c)
$$\frac{\Delta\mu}{\Delta\lambda} = \frac{\partial^2 U(c^T, y^N)}{\partial c^{T2}} \frac{\Delta c^T}{\Delta\lambda} > 0,$$

where $\Omega \equiv \lambda^2[\partial^2 C/\partial(\lambda b_{t+1}^A)^2] - [(r_B - r_A)^2/(1 + r_B)][\partial^2 U(c^T, y^N)/\partial c^{T2}] > 0$.

Since there is no net supply of domestic debt, b_t^A and b_t^B denote net liquid foreign debt and net illiquid foreign debt respectively. Equations (8a) and (8b) thus imply that the unanticipated decline of λ decreases not only the amount of net foreign liquidity debt, but also the sum of net foreign liquidity and illiquidity debts. Since the economy's current account balance over period t is defined by:

(9)
$$CA_t \equiv [(b_t^A + b_t^B) - (b_{t+1}^A + b_{t+1}^B)] + (R_{t+1} - R_t),$$

they also indicate that an unanticipated decline of λ improves the current account at period t because R_t is constant over time. However, since $\Delta(b^A + b^B) = [(r_B - r_A)/(1 + r_B)] \Delta b^A$, the change of $b^A + b^B$ is much smaller than the change of b^A because $(r_B - r_A)/(1 + r_B)$ is small. This implies that the increased aversion may have a limited impact on the sum of net foreign debts, although it changes the component of net foreign debts substantially through decreasing liquid foreign debt and increasing illiquid debt when private individuals increase disutility from liquidity risk.

The inequality (8c) implies that $\Delta c^T/\Delta\lambda < 0$. Therefore, equations (4a) and (4b) lead that $\Delta p^N/\Delta\lambda < 0$. These inequalities imply that an unanticipated increase in the aversion decreases consumption of tradable good and leads to the depreciation of the real exchange rate. Since $r_B > r_A$, the shift from liquidity debt to illiquid debt increases the burden of total interest payments. Given consumption of nontradable goods, this decreases both

c^T and p^N. However, to the extent that the sum of liquid and illiquid debts does not change much, the macroeconomic impacts are not large, causing only small current account surpluses.

2.4   The Government Loss Minimization Problem

In the last section, we assumed that the amount of foreign reserves is exogenously given. This exercise is useful to see macroeconomic consequences when only private individuals respond to an unanticipated increase in the aversion to liquidity risk. It is, however, natural that the government also chooses the amount of foreign reserves so as to minimize the social costs. The purpose of this section is to explore what impacts an unanticipated change of liquidity risk aversion has on various macroeconomic variables, especially the current account balance, when both private individuals and the government respond to an unanticipated increase in the disutility from liquidity risk. In the analysis, we assume that the government minimizes the following loss function:

$$(10) \qquad \text{Loss}_t = \sum_{j=0}^{\infty} \beta^j C^G(\lambda^G b_{t+j}^A, R_{t+j}).$$

In equation (10), the government losses arise solely from disutility from liquidity risk. The government's loss function, $C^G(\lambda^G b_{t+j}^A, R_{t+j})$, is strictly decreasing and strictly convex in R_{t+j}. This reflects the fact that foreign reserves relieve the country's liquidity risk. The parameter λ^G represents the degree of the government's aversion to the potential liquidity risk, where $\partial C^G(\lambda^G b_{t+j}^A, R_{t+j})/\partial(\lambda^G b_{t+j}^A) > 0$. An increased aversion to the risk generally increases the marginal loss from decreased foreign reserves because $\partial^2 C^G(\lambda^G b_{t+j}^A, R_{t+j})/\partial(\lambda^G b_{t+j}^A)\partial R_{t+j} < 0$. We allow that the government's disutility function $C^G(\lambda^G b_{t+j}^A, R_{t+j})$ is generally different from that of the representative private agent $C(\lambda b_{t+j}^A, R_{t+j})$.

When increasing the amount of foreign reserves, the government has alternative methods to finance it. However, because of the Ricardian equivalence, the government method of finance does not affect resource allocation. We thus focus on the case where the increases of the foreign reserves are solely financed by lump-sum tax increases. In this case, the government budget constraint at period t is written as:

$$(11) \qquad T_t = G^* + R_{t+1} - (1 + r) R_t,$$

where G^* is exogenous government expenditure and r is real interest rate of the foreign reserves. We assume that the rate of returns from foreign reserves is very low in international capital market, so that $r < r_A < r_B$.

Assuming interior solution, the government's first-order conditions that minimize (10) lead to:

(12)
$$\frac{\partial C^G(\lambda^G b_{t+1}^A, R_{t+1})}{\partial R_{t+1}} = 0.$$

Equation (12) means that the government changes the amount of foreign reserves up to the satiation point. Equations (11) and (12), together with equations (4a)–(4c) and (5a)–(5c), determine the equilibrium allocation when the government chooses the amount of foreign reserves so as to minimize the loss function.

Since there is no net supply of domestic debt, both b_t^A and b_t^B are net foreign debts, the sum of which is still constant without external shocks even when the government chooses the amount of foreign reserves endogenously. However, unanticipated changes of λ and λ^G affect the equilibrium allocation. Suppose that there were unanticipated increases of λ and λ^G at period τ. Then, both c_t^T and p_t^N instantaneously jump to the new steady state at period τ, while three stock variables b_t^A, $b_t^A + b_t^B$, and R_t move to the new steady state at period $\tau + 1$. Since $c_t^N = y^N$, the budget constraints in periods $\tau - 1, \tau$, and $\tau + 1$ respectively lead to:

(13a) $0 = r_B(b_0^A + b_0^B) - (r_B - r_A) b_0^A - y^T + c_0^T + G^* - rR_0,$

(13b) $b_1^A + b_1^B = (1 + r_B)(b_0^A + b_0^B) - (r_B - r_A) b_0^A$
$\qquad\qquad - y^T + c_1^T + G^* + R_1 - (1 + r)R_0,$

(13c) $0 = r_B(b_1^A + b_1^B) - (r_B - r_A) b_1^A - y^T + c_1^T + G^* - rR_1,$

where the variables with subscript 0 are those in the old steady state, and the variables with subscript 1 are those in the new steady state. It therefore holds that:

(14) $\Delta(b^A + b^B) - \Delta R = \Delta c^T = \left[\dfrac{(r_B - r_A)}{(1 + r_B)}\right]\Delta b^A - \left[\dfrac{(r_B - r)}{(1 + r_B)}\right]\Delta R.$

The condition (14) degenerates into the condition (6) when $\Delta R = 0$. However, since $\Delta R \neq 0$ when the government optimally chooses R, the following results become very different from those in the last section.

When the government chooses the amount of foreign reserves endogenously, equation (4c) implies:

(15) $\lambda^2 \left[\dfrac{\partial^2 C}{\partial(\lambda b^A)^2}\right]\Delta b^A + \left[\dfrac{\partial C}{\partial(\lambda b^A)} + \lambda b^A\dfrac{\partial^2 C}{\partial(\lambda b^A)^2}\right]\Delta\lambda + \lambda\left[\dfrac{\partial^2 C}{\partial(\lambda b^A)\partial R}\right]\Delta R$

$$= (r_B - r_A)\Delta\mu,$$

while equation (4b) still leads to (7a). Since equation (12) leads to:

(16) $\lambda^G\left[\dfrac{\partial^2 C^G}{\partial(\lambda^G b^A)\partial R}\right]\Delta b^A + b^A\left[\dfrac{\partial^2 C^G}{\partial(\lambda^G b^A)\partial R}\right]\Delta\lambda^G + \left(\dfrac{\partial^2 C^G}{\partial R^2}\right)\Delta R = 0,$

we therefore obtain that:

(17a) $\dfrac{\Delta R}{\Delta \lambda} = \dfrac{-\dfrac{\partial^2 C^G}{\partial(\lambda^G b^A)\partial R}\left\{b^A\Omega\left(\dfrac{\Delta\lambda^G}{\Delta\lambda}\right) - \lambda^G\left[\dfrac{\partial C}{\partial(\lambda b^A)} + \lambda b^A\dfrac{\partial^2 C}{\partial(\lambda b^A)^2}\right]\right\}}{\dfrac{\partial^2 C^G}{\partial R^2}\Omega - \lambda\lambda^G\dfrac{\partial^2 C}{\partial(\lambda b^A)\partial R}\dfrac{\partial^2 C^G}{\partial(\lambda^G b^A)\partial R}}$,

(17b) $\dfrac{\Delta b^A}{\Delta\lambda} = -\dfrac{1}{\Omega}\left[\dfrac{\partial C}{\partial(\lambda b^A)} + \lambda b^A\dfrac{\partial^2 C}{\partial(\lambda b^A)^2} + \lambda\dfrac{\partial^2 C}{\partial(\lambda b^A)\partial R}\dfrac{\Delta R}{\Delta\lambda}\right]$,

(17c) $\dfrac{\Delta(b^A + b^B - R)}{\Delta\lambda} = \dfrac{\Delta c^T}{\Delta\lambda} = \dfrac{r_B - r_A}{1 + r_B}\dfrac{\Delta b^A}{\Delta\lambda} - \dfrac{r_B - r}{1 + r_B}\dfrac{\Delta R}{\Delta\lambda}$,

(17d) $\dfrac{\Delta\mu}{\Delta\lambda} = \dfrac{\partial^2 U(c^T, y^N)}{\partial c^{T2}}\dfrac{\Delta c^T}{\Delta\lambda}$

where Ω, which is positive, was defined following equations (8a)–(8c).

As you see in (17a), $\Delta R/\Delta\lambda$ depends on various derivatives and parameters. Therefore, we cannot conclude that $\Delta R/\Delta\lambda$ is positive in general. However, to the extent that the government chooses the amount of foreign reserves to minimize the liquidity risk, it is natural to suppose that the government increases R when aversion to liquidity risk increases. We thus focus on the case where $\Delta R/\Delta\lambda > 0$ in the following analysis. When $\Delta R/\Delta\lambda > 0$, equation (17b) implies that $\Delta b^A/\Delta\lambda$ depends on two opposite effects. One is $(-1/\Omega)[\partial C/\partial(\lambda b^A) + \lambda b^A\partial^2 C/\partial(\lambda b^A)^2]$ that is negative, reflecting the private agent's responses to the increased aversion to liquidity risk. The other is $(-\lambda/\Omega)[\partial^2 C^G/\partial(\lambda b^A)\partial R](\Delta R/\Delta\lambda)$ that is positive, reflecting the government's responses to the increased aversion to liquidity risk. The sign of $\Delta b^A/\Delta\lambda$ generally depends on which effect is bigger.

Given $\Delta b^A/\Delta\lambda$ and $\Delta R/\Delta\lambda$, equations (17c) and (17d) determine $\Delta(b^A + b^B - R)/\Delta\lambda$, $\Delta c^T/\Delta\lambda$, and $\Delta\mu/\Delta\lambda$. The signs of $\Delta(b^A + b^B - R)/\Delta\lambda$, $\Delta c^T/\Delta\lambda$, and $\Delta\mu/\Delta\lambda$ in general depend on whether $(r_B - r)\Delta R$ is bigger than $(r_B - r_A)\Delta b^A$ or not. Since the current account balance over period t is still defined by (9), this indicates that the effect on the current account is not clear. However, when $\Delta b^A/\Delta\lambda < 0$, we can pin down the signs of $\Delta(b^A + b^B - R)/\Delta\lambda$, $\Delta c^T/\Delta\lambda$, and $\Delta\mu/\Delta\lambda$. In this case, the macroeconomic impacts of an unanticipated change of λ work in the same directions as those in the last section, even if both the government and private individuals increase disutility from liquidity risk.

Moreover, to the extent that $(r_B - r)\Delta R > (r_B - r_A)\Delta b^A$, the conditions (17c) and (17d) imply that an unanticipated increase of λ leads to a temporal improvement of the current account when the economy moves from the old steady state to the new steady state, and that the increase of λ reduces the amount of tradable consumption and leads to the depreciation of the real exchange rate. When the government increases foreign reserves substantially, the representative private agent may not need to increase costly illiquid foreign debt. However, since the rate of returns from foreign reserves is very low, the private agent's disposal income declines through increasing lump-sum tax. Given consumption of nontradable goods, this may decrease both c^T and p^N and derive a temporal improvement of the current account.

It is noteworthy that in terms of the magnitude, an unanticipated change of λ generally has different macroeconomic impacts when both the government and private individuals increase liquidity risk aversion as opposed to when only private individuals do. For example, suppose that two types of economies initially have a common value of Ω. This happens when two types of economies initially have common values of b^A_t, R, and c^T. In this case, it is easy to see that the absolute value of $\Delta b^A / \Delta \lambda$ is larger when only private individuals increase liquidity risk aversion. However, even in this case, $\Delta(b^A + b^B - R)/\Delta\lambda$ and $\Delta c^T/\Delta\lambda$ can be larger when both the government and private individuals increase liquidity risk aversion because of the effect of $\Delta R/\Delta\lambda$. In other words, an increased aversion to liquidity risk may lead to larger current account surplus in the short-run, and may lower social welfare when the government minimizes the costs from liquidity risk and increases the amount of foreign reserves. The next section will investigate this possibility by specifying the functional forms in the model.

2.5   Some Numerical Examples

In the last section, we explored what impacts an increased aversion to liquidity risk have on current account and other macro variables when the government minimizes the costs from liquidity risk. However, the magnitude is not necessarily clear without using specific functional forms. The purpose of this section is to explore the quantitative impacts by specifying the functional forms in the model.

In the experiment, we use the following functional forms:

(18a) $U(c^T_t, c^N_t) \equiv \gamma \ln[(c^T_t)^\alpha (c^N_t)^{1-\alpha}]$

(18b) $C(b^A_t, R_t) \equiv \dfrac{1}{2R_t}(\lambda \dfrac{b^A_t}{R_t} - D)^2$, when $\dfrac{b^A_t}{R_t} \geq \dfrac{D}{\lambda}$,

$\equiv 0$,   otherwise,

(18c) $C^G(b^A_t, R_t) \equiv \dfrac{1}{2R_t}(\lambda^G \dfrac{b^A_t}{R_t} - D^G)^2$, when $\dfrac{b^A_t}{R_t} \geq \dfrac{D^G}{\lambda^G}$,

$\equiv 0$,   otherwise,

In (18a), the utility from consumption represents the case where an elasticity of substitution in consumption between the tradable good and the nontradable good equals to one. The disutility functions (18b) and (18c) imply that the satiation ratio of b^A_t/R_t is D/λ for the private agent and D^G/λ^G for the government.

To explore the impacts of unanticipated changes of λ and λ^G, we set the structural parameters as $\alpha = 0.7$, $\beta = 0.9$, $\gamma = 10$, $r_B - r_A = 0.05$, $r = 0.01$, $G^* = 1.5$, $D = 1.05$, and $D^G = 1$ and domestic outputs as $y^T = y^N = 10$. We also set that $R = 15$ when the government does not choose R endogenously. These parameters and variables remain constant throughout the period. However, at period τ, there was an unanticipated preference shock in holding liquid foreign debt, and the value of λ and λ^G increased from 1 to 1.1 permanently. Then, when $b_t^A + b_t^B = c_t^T$ before period τ, the equilibrium values of macro variables are summarized in tables 2.2–2.4.

Table 2.2 reports the case where the government does not respond to the shock, while table 2.3 reports the case where the government responds to the shock. The change of λ has very small impacts on c_t^T, p_t^N, and $b_t^A + b_t^B$ in table 2.2. In contrast, in table 2.3, the changes of λ and λ^G increase R_t substantially and cause large declines of c_t^T, p_t^N, and $b_t^A + b_t^B - R_t$. As we discussed in the last section, it is not clear in general what impacts the changes of λ and λ^G have when both private individuals and the government respond to the shock. However, table 2.3 indicates that under the parameter set and exogenous variables specified above, rises of λ and λ^G increase R_t, b_t^A, b_t^B, and $b_t^A + b_t^B$ at period $\tau + 1$, decrease c_t^T and p_t^N at period τ, and lead to a temporal current account surplus at period τ. We can also see that the changes of these macrovariables are substantial in table 2.3. For example, tradable good consumption declines at period τ only by less than 1 percent in table 2.2 but nearly 10 percent in table 2.3. A large decline of $b_t^A + b_t^B - R_t$ in table 2.3 implies that the economy runs larger substantial current account surplus when the government also responds to the shock than when only the private individuals respond.

However, each of b_t^A and b_t^B shows a dramatic change even when only private individuals respond to the shock. That is, b_t^A declined by about 10

Table 2.2   The impacts of an increase in λ: Numerical examples when R is always constant.

	R	b^A	b^B	$b^A + b^B$	CA	c^T	p^N $(x10)$
period $\tau - 1$	15.00	16.38	7.01	23.39	0.00	8.39	1.80
period τ	15.00	16.38	7.01	23.39	0.07	8.32	1.78
period $\tau + 1$	15.00	14.84	8.48	23.32	0.00	8.32	1.78

Table 2.3   The impacts of an increase in λ: Numerical examples when R is always endogenously chosen.

	R	b^A	b^B	$b^A + b^B$	CA	c^T	p^N $(x10)$
period $\tau - 1$	14.86	15.60	6.26	21.86	0.00	7.00	9.85
period τ	14.86	15.60	6.26	21.86	0.64	6.36	9.55
period $\tau + 1$	26.77	15.56	7.58	33.14	0.00	6.36	9.55

percent and b_t^B increased by about 20 percent in table 2.2. This reflects the fact that the increased aversion to liquidity risk causes a shift from liquid debt to illiquid debt when private individuals try to reduce the risk. When the government responds to the shock, b_t^A and b_t^B also show significant changes in the table. However, both b_t^A and b_t^B increase in table 2.3. It is not clear in general whether the increased liquidity aversion increases b_t^A or not when both private individuals and the government respond to the shock. But if the government increased R_t and reduced the liquidity risk, the private individuals would have less incentive to shift their debts from liquid ones to illiquid ones. Table 2.3 shows that this effect can dominate the other under some reasonable parameter set.

The different responses of b_t^A and b_t^B may have interesting implications when the private individuals respond to the shock first and then the government follows it. In this case, the increased liquidity aversion would have very different impacts before or after the government responds. Table 2.4 summarizes the changes of macro variables under the circumstance. In table 2.4, we still assume the parameter set and exogenous variables specified above. But we suppose that before period 1, the economy was in the steady state where only private individuals maximized. At period 1, there was an unanticipated shock and the value of λ increased from 1 to 1.1 permanently. At period 1, only private individuals respond to the shock, while the government keeps foreign reserves constant. The changes of the variables from period 0 to period 1 are thus exactly the same as those in table 2.2. However, after period 2, λ^G increased from 1 to 1.1 permanently and the government also starts to respond to the shock so as to minimize the loss function. The steady state values are thus adjusted to those in table 2.3.

It is noteworthy that the introduction of the government's minimization reduces the amount of tradable good consumption from 8.32 to 6.36 in table 2.4. This implies that the welfare of the representative agent is not necessarily enhanced by the government's optimization. In fact, when $\lambda = \lambda^G = 1$ permanently, we can confirm that the introduction of the government's optimization reduces the lifetime utility of the representative agent from 10.4 to 9.9. This is partly because the government's loss function is different from that of the private agent. However, low real interest of for-

Table 2.4		The impacts of an increase in λ: Numerical examples when the government responds only after period 2.					
	R	b^A	b^B	$b^A + b^B$	CA	c^T	p^N (x10)
period 0	15.00	16.38	7.01	23.39	0.00	8.39	1.80
period 1	15.00	16.38	7.01	23.39	0.07	8.32	1.78
period 2	15.00	14.84	8.48	23.32	1.95	6.36	9.55
period 3	26.77	25.56	7.58	33.14	0.00	6.36	9.55

eign reserves is another crucial factor that reduces the welfare of the representative agent. The accumulation of foreign reserves is useful in reducing the liquidity risk for the representative agent. However, since the accumulation of foreign reserves reduces available resources, it may deteriorate the welfare of the representative agent through reducing consumption of tradable goods.

2.6   Some Evidence in East Asia

After the Asian crisis, most Asian economies came to recognize that economic growth that relies on liquid external borrowings is not desirable, given their vulnerability to a sudden reversal of capital flows. Soon after the crisis, they thus started to increase liquidity as an important self-protection against crises. Our theoretical model, however, implies that they had alternative strategies for the self-protection depending on whether the government cares about liquidity risk or not.

Based on the data in *BIS Quarterly Review,* figure 2.2 reports the changes of short-term, medium-term, and long-term borrowings in seven East Asian economies before and after the crisis. Reflecting dramatic capital inflows into East Asia before the crisis, we can observe large increases of all types of debts in 1995 and 1996. We can also observe that there were substantial declines of short-term borrowings not only during the crisis, but for some periods after the crisis. The declines of short-term borrowings during the crisis clearly happened because of capital flight under the panicking crisis. It is, however, noteworthy that the declines of short-term borrowings continued even in 1998, when East Asian economies started their economic recovery. At the same time, there were dramatic increases of medium-term borrowings and some increases of long-term borrowings in several East Asian economies after the crisis.

These results indicate that many East Asian economies shifted their borrowings from liquid short-term debt to illiquid long-term debts soon after the crisis. However, the shift from liquid debt to illiquid debt did not persist. Instead, liquid short-term debt increased again in the early 2000s. Korea was the only East Asian country that had significant increases of short-term borrowings since the late 1990s. But several East Asian economies also experienced increases of their short-term borrowings in the early 2000s. In contrast, in the East Asian economies, medium-term debt and long-term debt slowed in growth and sometimes declined during the same period. This indicates that many East Asian economies may have reversed their maturity structures, shifting their borrowings from illiquid long-term debt to liquid short-term debt.

An essentially similar result can be obtained from the alternative data set in *Global Development Finance* issued by the World Bank. Table 2.5 summarizes average maturity of private credits to six East Asian countries

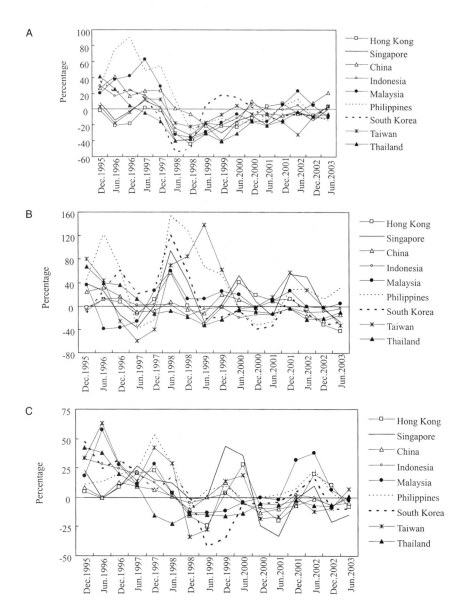

Fig. 2.2   Annual loan growth rates: *A*, Short-term; *B*, Medium-term; *C*, Long-term

Source: Table 9A in *BIS Quarterly Review* (June 12, 2006).

Notes: The data are percent changes of international claims from a year earlier in average amounts outstanding. Short-term is up to and including one year, medium-term is 1 up to 2 years, and long-term is over 2 years.

Table 2.5   **Average maturity of new commitments in private credit to East Asia**

	China	Indonesia	Korea	Malaysia	Philippines	Thailand
1995	7.3	11.0	5.8	16.9	10.9	8.9
1996	7.0	11.5	12.3	18.1	13.9	7.9
1997	6.4	16.1	6.6	12.7	14.4	10.9
1998	11.1	n.a.	6.4	13.7	6.3	6.8
1999	10.9	14.3	5.1	10.3	13.5	8.8
2000	10.5	6.9	4.6	7.6	11.4	7.3
2001	10.2	8.0	4.1	11.6	4.7	5.9
2002	10.1	9.4		10.2	9.4	4.3
2003	8.7	7.9		6.1	8.3	4.7
2004	9.0	8.2		8.3	8.5	5.0

Source: Global Development Finance, The World Bank.
Note: Units in years.

from 1995 to 2004. In the East Asian countries, the average maturity increased during the crisis and remained high until late 1999. This indicates significant shifts from liquid short-term debt to illiquid long-term debt soon after the crisis. However, as in figure 2.2, Korea reduced average maturity in the late 1990s. The other East Asian countries also gradually reduced maturity in the early 2000s. This alternative data set also supports the view that many East Asian economies may have reversed their maturity structures in the early 2000s.

Since short-term borrowing is liquid debt and medium-term and long-term borrowings are illiquid debts, shifting their debt from short-term to long-term is consistent with the case in our theoretical model where only private agents responded to the increased aversion to liquidity risk. In contrast, increasing their short-term borrowings and decreasing long-term borrowings are consistent with the case in the model where the government also responded. The above evidence suggests that in East Asia, the former case prevailed soon after the crisis but the latter became dominant in the early 2000s.

Among the strategies for self-protection, replacing liquid short-term debt by illiquid long-term debt was one of the most popular pieces of advice that many economists suggested for developing countries. However, what step most Asian economies eventually took was to raise foreign reserves. Table 2.6 reports the ratios of foreign exchange reserves to GDP for ten East Asian economies (Japan, China, Hong Kong, Indonesia, Korea, Malaysia, the Philippines, Singapore, Thailand, and Taiwan) from 1990 to 2004. It shows that the ratios went up substantially after the crisis and showed further increases in the early 2000s, except for Indonesia. The ratios are now over 10 percent in all East Asian economies and over 20 percent except for Japan, Indonesia, and the Philippines. It is highly possible

Table 2.6   The ratios of foreign exchange reserves to GDP in East Asia

	Japan	China	Hong Kong	Indonesia	Korea	Malaysia	Philippines	Singapore	Thailand	Taiwan
1990	2.7	9.7	32.8	7.0	5.8	22.8	2.1	76.0	15.6	45.2
1991	2.2	12.6	33.5	8.0	4.7	23.1	7.2	80.7	17.8	45.9
1992	2.0	5.6	35.0	8.3	5.6	29.9	8.3	82.2	18.3	38.8
1993	2.3	5.5	36.4	7.1	5.6	40.7	8.6	82.9	19.6	37.3
1994	2.6	9.8	37.0	6.9	6.1	34.1	9.4	82.4	20.3	37.8
1995	3.5	10.8	39.1	6.8	6.3	26.8	8.6	81.8	21.4	34.1
1996	4.6	13.0	40.8	8.0	6.1	26.8	12.1	83.4	20.7	31.5
1997	5.1	15.8	53.4	7.7	3.9	20.8	8.9	74.7	17.3	28.8
1998	5.5	15.6	54.2	23.8	15.0	35.4	14.2	91.3	25.8	33.8
1999	6.4	15.8	59.9	18.9	16.6	38.6	17.4	93.1	27.8	36.9
2000	7.5	15.6	65.1	17.3	18.8	32.7	17.2	86.6	26.1	34.4
2001	9.5	18.1	68.3	16.6	21.3	34.6	18.9	87.8	28.0	43.7
2002	11.6	22.3	69.9	15.5	22.2	36.0	17.7	92.7	30.0	57.4
2003	15.4	27.8	76.3	14.7	25.5	42.9	17.6	103.7	28.7	72.2
2004	17.9	37.3	75.8	13.6	29.3	56.4	15.5	105.1	29.8	79.2

Sources: Except for Taiwan, *International Financial Statistics*, IMF. For Taiwan, Key Indicators, ADB.

that the accumulated foreign reserves discouraged the private agents to replace liquid short-term debt by illiquid long-term debt in these economies.

One may argue that the rapid rise in reserves in recent years has little to do with the self-insurance motive, but is instead related to policymakers' desire to prevent the appreciation of their currencies and maintain the competitiveness of their tradable sectors. The aggressive intervention could maintain the competitiveness of their tradable sectors and manifest itself in the massive accumulation of foreign reserves by Asian central banks. This argument may be relevant in explaining China's reserve accumulation, where de facto dollar peg has been maintained for a long time. To some extent, it may also explain recent reserve accumulation in the other East Asian economies. However, it may not explain why the dramatic rise in foreign reserves started to happen after the crisis, because the policymakers had an incentive to maintain the trade competitiveness even before the crisis.

2.7   An Implication for the U.S. Current Account Deficits

In previous sections, we provided some theoretical and empirical analyses on the changes in international capital flows in East Asian economies after the currency crisis in 1997. The analyses were motivated by what happened in East Asia after the crisis. However, the changes of capital flows in East Asia will have a special implication for the U.S. current account when the government accumulates foreign reserves. This is because the U.S. dollar is the dominant reserve currency in international capital market, so that it became indispensable for developing countries to accumulate the U.S. government bonds that would make crises less likely.

Unfortunately, each government keeps the currency composition of the foreign exchange reserves a well-guarded secret. But IMF annual report provides average currency composition for industrialized countries and developing countries every year. In addition, Tavlas and Ozeki (1991) reported average currency composition for selected Asian countries in the 1980s.[2] Table 2.7 summarizes the reported currency compositions. The shares of the U.S. dollar have been high in both industrialized and developing countries. In particular, the shares of the U.S. dollar in developing countries were close to 70 percent from 1991 to 2001. Although updated data is not available for the selected Asian countries, more than half of these reserves are likely to have been invested in the United States, typically U.S. treasuries or other safe U.S. assets.

Some comparable data sets are also available from the U.S. side. The U.S. Treasury does have estimates of major foreign holders of treasury securi-

2. Tavlas and Ozeki (1991) did not clarify which countries they included in their selected Asian countries. China is likely to be excluded in their estimates.

Table 2.7   Official holdings of foreign exchange (in percent)

	1980	1984	1989	1994	1999	2004
U.S. dollar						
Industrial countries	54.3	57.0	48.4	51.2	75.3	71.5
Developing countries	58.1	57.0	60.5	61.8	68.2	59.9
Selected Asian countries	48.6	58.2	56.4	n.a.	n.a.	n.a.
Japanese yen						
Industrial countries	2.1	5.3	7.5	8.3	6.7	3.6
Developing countries	4.9	4.1	6.9	8.2	6.0	4.3
Selected Asian countries	13.9	16.3	17.5	n.a.	n.a.	n.a.
Pound sterling						
Industrial countries	0.5	1.4	1.2	2.3	2.2	1.9
Developing countries	5.3	4.1	5.8	4.9	3.7	4.8
Selected Asian countries	3.0	3.5	6.4	n.a.	n.a.	n.a.
Deutsche mark						
Industrial countries	9.4	12.9	20.6	16.4	—	—
Developing countries	15.4	8.8	11.7	11.8	—	—
Selected Asian countries	20.6	14.6	15.2	n.a.	—	—
ECUs or Euro						
Industrial countries	29.0	20.6	15.0	14.1	16.1	20.9
Developing countries	0.0	0.0	0.0	0.0	19.9	29.2
Selected Asian countries	0.0	0.0	0.0	n.a.	n.a.	n.a.
Swiss franc						
Industrial countries	1.1	1.2	1.1	0.2	0.1	0.1
Developing countries	4.8	2.6	2.2	2.0	0.4	0.2
Selected Asian countries	10.6	4.9	3.0	n.a.	n.a.	n.a.
French franc						
Industrial countries	0.0	0.4	1.1	2.1	—	—
Developing countries	2.6	1.7	2.1	2.1	—	—
Selected Asian countries	0.6	0.6	0.5	n.a.	—	—
Netherlands guilder						
Industrial countries	0.4	0.6	1.1	0.2	—	—
Developing countries	1.3	0.9	1.0	0.9	—	—
Selected Asian countries	2.8	1.9	0.9	n.a.	—	—
Other currencies						
Industrial countries	3.2	0.7	4.0	5.3	1.4	2.0
Developing countries	7.6	20.8	9.9	8.3	1.7	1.6
Selected Asian countries	0.0	0.0	0.0	n.a.	n.a.	n.a.

Sources: Except for selected Asian countries, *IMF Annual Report*. For selected Asian countries, Tavlas and Ozeki (1991).

ties holdings from 2000 to 2005. Table 2.8 summarizes the estimates for Japan, China, Korea, Taiwan, Hong Kong, Singapore, and Thailand. The changes of treasury securities holdings were modest in Hong Kong, Singapore, and Thailand. However, there were dramatic increases of treasury securities holdings in China and Japan. In Korea and Taiwan, the amount of treasury securities holdings was more than doubled from 2000 to 2005. Although the data includes both official and private holdings, it is more likely

Table 2.8   **Major foreign holders of U.S. treasury securities**

	2000	2001	2002	2003	2004	2005
Japan	317.7	317.9	378.1	550.8	689.9	671
China	60.3	78.6	118.4	159	222.9	310.9
Korea	29.6	32.8	38	63.1	55	68.9
Taiwan	33.4	35.3	37.4	50.9	67.9	68.1
Hong Kong	38.6	47.7	47.5	50	45.1	40.3
Singapore	27.9	20	17.8	21.2	30.4	33
Thailand	13.8	15.7	17.2	11.7	12.5	16.1

Source: http://www.ustreas.gov/tic/mfhhis01.txt.
Note: All data are those in the end of December. Units in billions of U.S. dollars.

that recent increases in central bank reserves account for a large share of those assets.[3] The reserves, which are typically held in the form of U.S. Treasury bills and agency bonds, pay a low rate of return. It is less likely that private investors accumulated such low interest assets.

The evidence supports the view that substantial rises in foreign exchange reserves increase capital inflows into the United States. It is, however, noteworthy that similar capital inflows from East Asia would not happen outside the United States when the East Asian economies adopt the strategy of replacing liquid short-term debt by illiquid long-term debt for self-protection. In fact, several East Asian economies came to run frequent trade balance *deficits* against other countries in the early 2000s. For example, Korea's trade balance against non-U.S. countries was in deficit in 2001 and 2002. China and Thailand have run deficit against non-U.S. countries since 2000. The change of the strategies from the late 1990s to the early 2000s may explain why the East Asian economies widened their trade account surpluses only against the United States in the 2000s.

Needless to say, our results do not necessarily deny alternative views in explaining recent increases in the U.S. current account deficits. One may argue that the recent deterioration in the U.S. current account primarily reflects economic policies and other economic developments within the United States itself. One popular argument for the "made in the U.S.A." explanation of the rising current account deficit focuses on the burgeoning U.S. federal budget deficit. That inadequate U.S. national saving is the source of declining national saving and the current account deficit must be true at some level. However, the so-called twin-deficits hypothesis, that government budget deficits cause current account deficits, does not account for the fact that the U.S. external deficit expanded by about $300 billion between 1996 and 2000, a period during which the federal budget was

---

3. When Treasuries are resold, it is difficult to identify who holds what U.S. Treasury securities. Private custodial transactions on behalf of governments also cloud matters.

in surplus and projected to remain so. It seems unlikely, therefore, that changes in the U.S. government budget position can entirely explain the behavior of the U.S. current account over the past decade (see also Erceg, Guerrieri, and Gust 2005). The U.S. national saving is currently very low and falls considerably short of domestic capital investment. Of necessity, this shortfall is made up by net foreign borrowing. The increased capital flows from the East Asian economies to the U.S. economy may provide one of the promising answers to the question of why the United States has been borrowing so heavily in international capital markets.

2.8   Implications for Real Exchange Rates

One of the byproducts of our theoretical analysis is the impacts of increased liquidity risk aversion on the real exchange rate. If recent current account surpluses in East Asia primarily reflect either an increase in the U.S. demand for East Asian products or increased productivity of East Asian exports, they would naturally lead to currency appreciation of East Asian currencies in a world of floating exchange rates. However, when the economy increases its liquidity risk aversion, large current account surpluses could persist for long years accompanied by the real exchange rate depreciation. This is particularly true for current account surplus against the United States, the currency of which has been widely held as an international reserve currency. The purpose of this section is to investigate these implications empirically. Figure 2.3 reports real exchange rates of eight East Asian economies from 1990 to 2004. In the figure, lower values mean depreciation. It shows that except for China, the real exchange rates depreciated substantially against the U.S. dollar after the crisis and remained low even after the economies recovered from the crisis. The rate of depreciation from 1996 to 2004 is more than 20 percent in Korea, Thailand, Malaysia, and the Philippines.

The basic result still remains true even when we use absolute PPP data to evaluate the real exchange rates after the crisis. By using the balanced panel data of the Penn World Table (PWT 6.2) from 1990 to 2003, we estimated the simple following logarithmic equation over the 2000 observations:

$$(19) \qquad \log P_j/P_{U.S.} = \text{constant} + a \cdot \log Y_j/Y_{U.S.},$$

where $P_j/P_{U.S.}$ is the price level of country j relative to the United States, and $Y_j/Y_{U.S.}$ is country j's income level relative to the United States. We included $\log Y_j/Y_{U.S.}$ in the regression because Rogoff (1996) found that the Balassa-Samuelson effect leads to a clear positive association between relative price levels and real incomes.

To examine the real exchange rate depreciation in East Asia after the crisis, we include the post-crisis dummy and the post-crisis East Asian dummy. The post-crisis dummy is a time dummy that takes one from 1998 to 2003 and zero otherwise. The post-crisis East Asian dummy is an East Asian re-

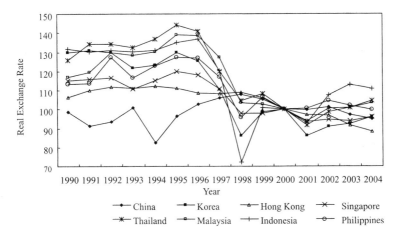

Fig. 2.3   Real exchange rates in East Asia

Sources: International Financial Statistics, IMF.

Notes: All real exchange rates are normalized to be 100 in 2000. "Real Exchange Rate" of country c in year y = $[p_{c,y} \times (e_y/e_{2000}) \times 100]/p_{USA,y}$ where e = nominal exchange rate (dollar per national currency), p = except for China, Producer Price Index (for China, Consumer Price Index). Lower values mean depreciation.

gional dummy times a post-crisis dummy that takes one from 1999 to 2003 only for eleven Asian economies (China, Hong Kong, Indonesia, Korea, Macao, Malaysia, the Philippines, Singapore, Taiwan, Thailand, and Vietnam) and zero otherwise. We started the post-crisis East Asian dummy from 1999 because the East Asian economies may have had a different strategy for the self-protection in 1998. Because China, former centrally planned countries, and post-crisis Indonesia can be outliers, we also include the China dummy, the East Europe dummy, and the post-crisis Indonesia dummy in some regressions. The China dummy or the East Europe dummy takes one from 1990 to 2003 for China or two East Europe countries (Romania and Russia) and zero otherwise. The post-crisis Indonesia dummy takes one from 1998 to 2003 for Indonesia and zero otherwise.

Table 2.9 reports the results of our regressions with and without the three extra dummies. Like Rogoff's result, the coefficient of the relative income level always takes significantly positive, showing a clear positive association between relative price levels and real incomes. However, the coefficients of the two time dummy variables are significantly negative. The negative coefficient of the post-crisis dummy implies that there was worldwide undervaluation of real exchange rates against the U.S. dollar after the crisis. The negative coefficient of the post-crisis East Asian dummy implies that the degree of the undervaluation of the real exchange rates was more conspicuous among the East Asian economies after the Asian crisis.

It is noteworthy that the negative coefficient of the post-crisis East Asian dummy is much larger than that of the post-crisis dummy in the absolute

Table 2.9   The Balassa-Samuelson Regression

	dependent variable $\log P_j/P_{U.S.}$		
constant	−0.0996	−0.0881	−0.0889
	(−5.66)	(−5.07)	(−5.13)
$\log Y_j/Y_{U.S.}$	0.3420	0.3428	0.3423
	(46.69)	(47.49)	(47.50)
post-crisis dummy	−0.0991	−0.1007	−0.0976
	(−5.60)	(−5.78)	(−5.60)
post-crisis East Asian dummy	−0.3112	−0.2827	−0.2268
	(−5.37)	(−4.88)	(−4.06)
China dummy		−0.4125	−0.4179
		(−3.70)	(−3.74)
East Europe dummy		−0.6340	−0.6352
		(−8.14)	(−8.18)
post-crisis Indonesia dummy			−0.6101
			(−3.48)
adj.R-squared	0.4898	0.5066	0.5102

Source: The Penn World Table (PWT 6.2), where Y_j = nominal GDP per capita in country j, and P_j = price level of Y_j. The data was downloaded from http://pwt.econ.upenn.edu/.
Notes: Number of observations is 2,338 (14 periods for 168 countries) for each regression. Data period is from 1990 to 2003 (balanced panel). Eleven Asian countries are: China, Hong Kong, Indonesia, Korea, Macao, Malaysia, Philippines, Singapore, Taiwan, Thailand, and Vietnam. t-statistics are in parentheses.

value. The result is consistent with our theoretical model, where the East Asian economies that increased the liquidity risk aversion had current account surpluses accompanied by the real exchange rate depreciation. The result does not change even if we include the China dummy, the East Europe dummy, and the post-crisis Indonesia dummy. All of the three dummies had significantly negative coefficients.[4] However, both the post-crisis dummy and the post-crisis East Asian dummy kept having negative impacts, implying undervaluation outside the United States and larger undervaluation in East Asia after the crisis.

2.9   Concluding Remarks

During the last decade, financial globalization has been accompanied by frequent and painful financial crises. Some of the well-known crises include Mexico in 1995, East Asia in 1997, Russia in 1998, Brazil in 1999, and Argentina in 2002. During the crises, countries with smaller liquid foreign assets had a hard time preventing panics in financial markets and sudden

4. The negative coefficient of the China dummy implies that the Chinese Yuan had been undervalued throughout the 1990s. It reconfirms the conclusion of Frankel (2005) that China's prices have been well below the level that one would predict from the Balassa-Samuelson equation.

reversals in capital flows. Many developing countries thus came to recognize that increased liquidity is an important self-protection against crises. However, developing countries have alternative strategies for the self-protection. Replacing liquid short-term debt by illiquid long-term debt and raising foreign reserves are two popular strategies that many economists advised. The first strategy would be taken when private individuals respond to the shock, because an increased aversion to liquidity risk among private individuals reduces liquid debt and increases illiquid debt. We found that the East Asian economies may have taken this course soon after the crisis. However, we also found that what most Asian economies have taken seriously in the 2000s is the second strategy. Under a reasonable parameter set, it may lead to larger liquid debt, smaller illiquid debt, and larger current account surpluses, accompanied by depreciation of the real exchange rate when the government responds to an unanticipated increase in the liquidity risk aversion. Macroeconomic impacts of the increased liquidity risk aversion can be very different depending on which strategy developing countries will take.

When looking at remarkable recent reversals in global capital flows, East Asian economies have been one of the major net lenders after the currency crisis in 1997. Foreign exchange reserves held by East Asian economies are now record-breaking, and stand at levels that are a multiple of those held by advanced countries. In particular, because of the role of the U.S. dollar as an international currency, it became indispensable for developing countries to accumulate the U.S. government bonds that would make crises less likely. Consequently, after the crisis, the increased preference for international liquidity allowed a large proportion of the U.S. current account deficit to be financed by developing countries, especially East Asian economies. It is important to reconsider what impacts the increased liquidity risk aversion in East Asia had on international capital flows, including the U.S. current account deficit.

Needless to say, our model is too simple to describe a variety of macroeconomic phenomena in East Asia after the crisis. For example, our model neglected the role of capital stock investment, which showed dramatic fluctuations before and after the crisis. It also did not take into account risk premium for long-term debt that prevailed in emerging markets. Incorporating these factors is left for our future research.

References

Aizenman, J., and J. Lee. 2005. International reserves: Precautionary versus mercantilist views, theory and evidence. NBER Working Paper no. 11366. Cambridge, MA: National Bureau of Economic Research.

Bernanke, B. S. 2005. The global saving glut and the U.S. current account deficit. The Sandridge Lecture. Richmond, VA: Virginia Association of Economics.

Blanchard, O., F. Giavazzi, and F. Sa. 2005. The U.S. current account and the dollar. NBER Working Paper no. 11137. Cambridge, MA: National Bureau of Economic Research.

Broner, F., G. Lorenzoni, and S. Schmukler. 2004. Why do emerging economies borrow short term? Policy Research Working Paper Series no. 3389. The World Bank.

Caballero, R., E. Farhi, and P.-O. Gourinchas. 2006. An equilibrium model of "Global Imbalances" and low interest rates. NBER Working Paper no. 11996. Cambridge, MA: National Bureau of Economic Research.

Corsetti, G., P. Pesenti, and N. Roubini. 1999. What caused the Asian currency and financial crisis? *Japan and the World Economy* 11:305–73.

Dooley, M. P., D. Folkerts-Landau, and P. M. Garber. 2005. Savings gluts and interest rates: The missing link to Europe. NBER Working Paper no. 11520. Cambridge, MA: National Bureau of Economic Research.

Erceg, C., L. Guerrieri, and C. Gust. 2005. Expansionary fiscal shocks and the trade deficit. International Finance Discussion Paper 2005–825. Washington, DC: Board of Governors of the Federal Reserve System.

Frankel, J. 2005. On the Renminbi: The choice between adjustment under a fixed exchange rate and adjustment under a flexible rate. NBER Working Paper no. 11274. Cambridge, MA: National Bureau of Economic Research.

Fukuda, S. 2001. The impacts of bank loans on economic development: An implication for East Asia from an equilibrium contract theory. In *Regional and global capital flows: Macroeconomic causes and consequences,* eds. T. Ito and A. O. Krueger, 117–145. Chicago: University of Chicago Press.

Jeanne, O. 2004. Debt maturity and the international financial architecture. IMF Working Paper no. 04/137. Washington, DC: International Monetary Fund.

Obstfeld, M., and K. Rogoff. 1997. *Foundations of International Macroeconomics.* Cambridge, MA: MIT Press.

Obstfeld, M., and K. Rogoff. 2004. The unsustainable U.S. current account position revisited. NBER Working Paper no. 10869. Cambridge, MA: National Bureau of Economic Research.

Rodrik, D. 2005. The social cost of foreign exchange reserves. *International Economic Journal* 20 (3). Forthcoming.

Rodrik, D., and A. Velasco. 1999. Short-term capital flows. NBER Working Paper no. 7364. Cambridge, MA: National Bureau of Economic Research.

Rogoff, K. 1996. The purchasing power parity puzzle. *Journal of Economic Literature* 34 (2): 647–68.

Roubini, N., and B. Setser. 2004. The United States as a net debtor: The sustainability of the U.S. external imbalances. Unpublished draft.

Sachs, J., and S. Radelet. 1998. The East Asian financial crisis: Diagnosis, remedies, prospects. *Brookings Papers on Economic Activity* Issue no. 1. Washington, DC: Brookings Institute.

Schmukler, S., and E. Vesperoni. 2006. Financial globalization and debt maturity in emerging economies. *Journal of Development Economics* 79:183–207.

Tavlas, G. S., and Y. Ozeki. 1991. The Japanese yen as an international currency. IMF Working Paper no. WP/91/2. Washington, DC: International Monetary Fund.

Comment   Linda S. Goldberg

The main goal of this chapter is to explore the consequences of heightened demand for liquidity by Asian economies in the period following crises of 1997. The authors argue that this heightened demand led to appreciation of the key international currency of liquidity, the U.S. dollar. To make this point, the authors develop a model wherein a liquidity demand shock generates a period of persistent strength for the high liquidity asset and currency. The chapter is well-written and draws logical conclusions from its modelling exercise.

My main comments on the chapter will focus on the specific application of the chapter to the data since 1997. I then offer some suggestions for expanding the modeling to make this application conform more closely to recent experience. I will make suggestions pertaining to the following themes: (a) How can the authors supplement the model to provide richer dynamics? (b) Is liquidity demand for dollars really the key issue in the last decade, beyond perhaps the initial period of reserve accumulation in East Asia? (c) If liquidity demand is so important, can the authors motivate why there appears to have been such a bias towards dollars over, for example, euros?

Supplementing the Model to Provide Richer Dynamics

Within the model of the chapter, utility from consumption of goods is a substitute for utility from having liquid investments. Shocks to demand for liquidity therefore lead to persistent consumption collapse. Savings rise, consumption falls. The authors may consider providing more motivation for their specific way of introducing a useful concept. One alternative approach is to have more separability in utility from consumption and liquidity, with the relevant margin of substitution instead to be between liquid and illiquid investments.

Another aspect of the model that can be extended is the treatment of investment and production. Within the model, fixed endowments are assumed without any investment dynamics. It would be interesting to see a richer approach to investment choices. This richer approach is especially relevant since, with events in East Asia motivating the paper, we also observe a dynamics of real investment and output that have been an integral part of recent events.

Linda S. Goldberg is a Vice President of International Research at the Federal Reserve Bank of New York and a Research Associate of the National Bureau of Economic Research.

The views in this discussion are those of the author and do not necessarily reflect the position of the Federal Reserve Bank of New York or the Federal Reserve System.

Two recent papers present a nice treatment of investment and can suggest useful ways to have more fully dynamic modelling of investment and exchange rates. Within a dynamic stochastic general equilibrium approach (DSGE), the paper by Erceg, Guerrieri, and Gust (2006) is useful. If you want a model with rudimentary portfolio choice and exogenous risk premiums, which like the Fukuda and Kon chapter doesn't capture reasons for a sudden change in appetite for risk, the work by Faruqee, Laxton, Muir and Pesenti (2005) is carefully specified.

Interpreting the Empirics

Within the Fukuda and Kon chapter, increased liquidity demand shows up in growth of foreign exchange reserves relative to GDP across East Asia. This growth in foreign exchange reserves probably played a substantial role during the first year or two after the crisis. Yet, how do the authors explain the continued accumulation of reserves by the same countries? The liquidity argument has a substantially different emphasis than arguments focused on the "global savings glut."

The authors present some regression analysis. This section could be expanded, with more discussion of both the testing methodology and interpretation of the results. One point that could be addressed is why and if the authors view the demand for liquidity exclusively as a post-Asia crisis phenomenon? Why would this demand not arise for larger groups of countries and across other crises?

Overall, in thinking about the emphasis of the paper, it is important to determine the importance of *liquidity demand* in recent imbalances and the duration of its effects. According to the International Monetary Fund's WEO Report for 2005, a key feature of the East Asia events instead involves a focus on *investment rates.*

> Investment rates have fallen across virtually all industrial country regions, although this has been most noticeable in Japan and the euro area countries, where they reached historic lows in 2002. . . . In volume terms, the fall in average investment rates in industrial countries has been more modest.

> Investment rates differ substantially across emerging market economies . . . With the exception of China and a handful of other countries, however, investment rates have fallen in emerging market economies since the Asian financial crisis. Indeed, investment rates in East Asia have declined by more than 10 percentage points of GDP since their peak in the mid-1990s and have not rebounded. WEO 2005, Ch. 2.

These observations support the suggestion made earlier in these comments that the authors should provide a richer modeling of investment in the paper. For example, when we examine data for the United States in figure 2C.1, the growth in the current account deficit, defined as the difference between national savings and investment, is dominated by low national savings since 2000.

Figure 2C.2 shows the savings and investment by Asia, outside of China since 1990. Observe the interesting dynamics of savings and investment in this region in the period from 1997 to 2006. The model of the paper predicts substitution between consumption and liquidity, while investment is stable. Yet in the data we observe a reduction in savings and an even larger collapse in investment spending.

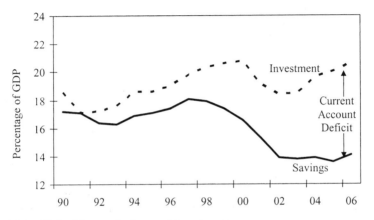

Fig. 2C.1   United States: Savings and Investment
Source: IMF April 2006 *World Economic Outlook,* OECD, authors' calculations. 2006 values are based on IMF *WEO* and OECD forecasts.

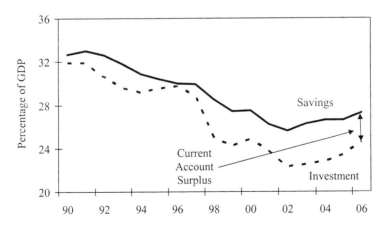

Fig. 2C.2   Asia outside China: Savings and investment
Source: IMF April 2006 *World Economic Outlook,* OECD, authors' calculations. 2006 values are based on IMF *WEO* and OECD forecasts.

Table 2C.1   **Global current account balances**

	2002	2005	Change
Surpluses			
Oil Exporters[a]	88	398	310
Emerging Asia	128	241	113
Japan	113	164	51
Western Europe[b]	52	23	−29
Others + Errors	95	−20	−116
Deficit			
United States	−475	−805	−330

Sources: IMF September 2005 *World Economic Outlook,* national sources.
Note: Figures in billions of U.S. dollars.
[a]IMF WEO fuel exporters plus Norway.
[b]EMU plus Denmark, the United Kingdom, Sweden, and Switzerland.

If the dollar strength post-1997 is a focal point of the modeling exercise, and liquidity demand from Asia is emphasized, it is useful to provide context on the extent to which global current account balances are dominated by particular regions. As shown in table 2C.1 in the early 2000s (for example 2002) the surpluses of Emerging Asia and Japan accounted for more than half of the current account deficit of the United States. This situation changed by the mid-2000s, when the surpluses of oil exporters basically matched those of emerging Asia and Japan. Could it still be that the strength of dollar was attributable to liquidity demand at this time? The authors of the paper could elaborate more on the timing and strength of the liquidity motive behind a demand for dollars in the period well after 1997.

Why is liquidity demand biased towards dollars over, for example, euros?

The arguments of the paper lead Asian economies to purchase dollars, and generate an associated dollar appreciation in the wake of strong liquidity demands. It would be useful to have more exposition of why this liquidity demand is so strongly biased toward dollars, instead of euros, for example. Evidence on bid-ask spreads in foreign exchange markets may be informative, as would information on the depth of dollar versus euro bond markets.

Is it because of the low transaction costs of operating in dollar markets, and the prevalence of the dollar in trade invoicing? Goldberg and Tille (2006) argue that the special role of the dollar in international markets makes for asymmetric effects of exchange rates across the U.S. and its trading partners. Models need to recognize such asymmetry, when consequences for dollars, rather than alternative currencies, are postdated.

Conclusions

This well-written and thought-provoking paper focuses our attention on the special position of and effects on countries with highly liquid assets. The demand for liquidity appears to have been especially important in the immediate aftermath of the Asian crises of 1997. The challenge for the authors is to make the paper both more specific and more general at the same time. More specific to this event means that we could have richer modelling of investment decisions—the liquidity versus consumption trade-offs. It could be more general in the sense that we would like to see whether this liquidity demand phenomenon was present in other crises and observe how it was manifested. If not, the model and empirical application may be able to tell us why.

References

Erceg, Christopher, L. Guerrieri, and C. Gust. 2006. Trade Adjustment and the Composition of Trade. *International Finance Discussion Papers,* no. 859.

Faruqee, Hamid, D. Laxton, D. Muir, and P. Pesenti. 2005. Smooth Landing or Crash? Model-Based Scenarios of Global Current Account Rebalancing. NBER Working Paper no. 11583. Cambridge, MA: National Bureau of Economic Research.

Goldberg, Linda, and C. Tille. 2006. The International Role of the Dollar and Trade Balance Adjustment. NBER Working Paper no. 12495. Cambridge, MA: National Bureau of Economic Research.

International Monetary Fund. 2005. *World Economic Outlook,* September. Washington, DC: International Monetary Fund.

International Monetary Fund. 2006. *World Economic Outlook,* April. Washington, DC: International Monetary Fund.

Comment   Andrew K. Rose

This is an interesting paper on an important set of related issues that has been much discussed in the literature of late. The authors are interested in whether the American current account deficit is fundamentally sustainable. Linked to this is the question of how special the United States is since it happens to be the country that issues the world's favored reserve currency (at least the current favorite). Alternatively expressed, are the fundamental causes of "global imbalances" mostly American or foreign? Mostly permanent or transitory? I congratulate the authors for a stimulating piece of work on such a relevant and topical set of issues.

Andrew K. Rose is the Bernard T. Rocca Jr. Professor of International Business in the Economic Analysis and Policy Group, Haas School of Business at the University of California, Berkeley and a research associate of the National Bureau of Economic Research.

While praise is appropriate, the role of the discussant is intrinsically critical. I want to begin by pointing out three strategic choices the authors made that I would have made differently.

The first place where I diverge from the authors is in the approach they take to modeling the exogenous parameter shock that starts the ball rolling. Why exactly does the taste for foreign liquidity suddenly rise? Why is the taste limited to Asian countries? And why does it take place when it does? To me, if the fundamental source of the shock was the Asian crisis (as seems perfectly reasonable), then this should be modeled more directly. As it is, assuming that there is a shock to preferences for net foreign assets of a specific currency seems perilously close to assuming the solution to the problem of interest. It is also restrictive, since it doesn't allow one to really address the question of what's special about the United States other than by assumption.

A separate issue is the implicit linkage in the paper between bilateral and multilateral balances—or, more precisely, between trade and financial imbalances. In the paper, a country that develops a taste for the assets of, for example, the United States runs a current account surplus vis-à-vis the United States. That seems natural—but only at first. Usually we model bilateral trade flows independently of the aggregate trade balance; a country may have a deficit vis-à-vis a particular country and still run an aggregate surplus. More importantly, we also usually model trade in goods (and services) independently of trade in assets. I can obtain euros by running a surplus vis-à-vis Japan and then trading the yen for euros. So the setup here is restrictive and at odds with the literature. That's not necessarily bad, of course, it's simply worth pointing out (and defending).

The final and most important issue, at least to me, is whether we really believe that agents get utility from holding net foreign assets. I am not wholly convinced that this is intrinsically plausible. It seems hard for me to believe that net foreign assets (NFA) deliver welfare in a way similar to the satisfaction I get from consuming goods and services. Do I really benefit from NFA per se, that is assets that *aren't* converted into goods and services? Even if I do, isn't there satiation in NFA? Do the net foreign assets of different countries really yield substantially different utility? Do Asians have different tastes for NFA than say Europeans, and does this really vary a lot over time? Could the size of this effect be comparable to that from goods? After all, ρ and λ are big in the paper (as recognized by the authors). Finally, if NFA holdings are inherently valuable, why do so few countries seek to increase them by reducing liabilities (as opposed to increasing reserves)? All this strikes me as a set of issues worthy of discussion in future work.

Are Currency Appreciations Contractionary in China?

Jianhuai Shi

3.1 Introduction

In recent years, the renminbi (RMB) exchange rate and China's exchange rate policy have received the extensive concern of the international community. Has RMB been undervalued? If so, by how much it is undervalued? Should RMB be revaluated or appreciated? These questions have all caused a hot debate at home and abroad. Though there is no unanimous conclusion on how much RMB is undervalued, it is the more unanimous view of researchers that RMB *is* undervalued. For example, Goldstein (2004) estimates that RMB has been undervalued by 15–30 percent in 2003 according to a simple fundamental equilibrium exchange rate (FEER) model. Frankel (2004) uses a modified purchasing power parity method to estimate that RMB was undervalued by 35 percent in 2000, and judges that it is undervalued at least that much at present. Shi and Yu (2005) use a behavior equilibrium exchange rate (BEER) model to draw that RMB was undervalued by about 12 percent on average during 2002–2004, and Coudert and Couharde (2005) use a FEER model to estimate that the RMB exchange rate was undervalued by 23 percent in 2003.

No matter if currency is being undervalued or overvalued, exchange rate

Jianhuai Shi is a professor at the China Center for Economic Research (CCER) at Peking University.

This is a revision of a paper presented at the 17th Annual East Asian Seminar on Economics on International Financial Issues around the Pacific-Rim, Hawaii, June 22–24, 2006, organized by the National Bureau of Economic Research. I thank Ashvin Ahuja, Dante Canlas, Michael Dooley, Peter Garber, Takatoshi Ito, and Andrew Rose for insightful comments, and Guoqing Song for help in obtaining data used in this research. The views expressed herein are those of the author and do not necessarily reflect the views of the National Bureau of Economic Research.

misalignment certainly results in a distortion of the economy that exerts a negative impact on economic structure and macroeconomic performance of the economy. For example, in recent years, the Chinese economy has been in a state of obvious external and internal imbalance,[1] which certainly has something to do with the undervaluation of RMB. According to the Swan Diagram, a classic framework for analyzing the macroeconomic policy of an open economy, allowing RMB to appreciate is a direct and effective method to resolve the imbalances of the Chinese economy (Shi 2006), but the Chinese government seems hesitant to allow RMB to appreciate[2] and would rather adopt other measures such as adjusting export tax rebates, relaxing the controls on capital outflow, and adjusting the interest rate or deposit reserve ratio to deal with external and internal imbalances of the economy.

Why then, considering that there is obviously an undervaluation of RMB and that the Chinese economy suffers from external and internal imbalances, does the Chinese government still resist RMB appreciation? According to a traditional macroeconomics textbook model, currency appreciations are contractionary; at least in the short run, appreciations will raise the price of domestic goods relative to the price of foreign goods (namely the real exchange rate appreciation), cause exports to drop and consumers to substitute home produced goods with imported goods, and thus reduce the aggregate demand.[3] So, the hesitation of the Chinese government is consistent with the view of traditional macroeconomic theory. Though the Chinese government has announced that China does not pursue too big a trade surplus, indicating that the Chinese policymakers would like to reduce the surplus through various means, the Chinese government certainly worries that RMB appreciations are contractionary, as traditional macroeconomic theory states, and thus would have a negative impact on China's economic growth and employment—even causing the Chinese economy to fall into a long time recession, as happened in Japan during the 1990s (as is often, but maybe not correctly, cited by those who argue against the RMB appreciation). This is the main reason the Chinese government is unwilling to allow RMB to appreciate. Considering that there is a high rate of unemployment caused by economic reform and economy transition into the market economy, maintaining the high rate of economic growth and sustaining employment are obviously the higher priorities of the Chinese government.

1. Specifically, external imbalance is evidenced by the large current account surplus and a large growth in foreign exchange reserves; the internal imbalance manifests itself in the overheating of the economy and the pressure of inflation.

2. Under China's new exchange rate regime, if the monetary authority reduces the intensity of exchange market intervention, or widens the band of RMB exchange rate floating, the market will promote RMB to appreciate progressively because of the steady expectation of RMB appreciation. In this paper, we do not distinguish appreciation from revaluation.

3. This is the expenditure-switching effect of exchange rate change.

Must appreciations be contractionary and depreciations expansionary? For a long time, at least since Hirschman (1949), economists have realized that appreciations are not necessarily contractionary, nor are depreciations necessarily expansionary. Marked by Krugman and Taylor (1978), there appears a so-called *contractionary devaluations* literature.[4] On the demand side, the literature emphasizes the expenditure-changing effects of exchange rate change ignored by the traditional macroeconomic theory and provides a series of mechanisms and channels through which devaluation can cause outputs to drop. On the supply side, the literature demonstrates the *contractionary devaluations* effect mainly through the influence of devaluation on the cost of imported intermediate goods, the cost of wages and, firm's working capital.[5] After the 1994 Mexico currency crisis and 1997–98 East Asian financial crisis, the contractionary devaluations literature obtained renewed attention of economists (Kamin and Rogers 2000), and has received new development. The new development emphasizes the importance of the balance sheet effects in explaining the economic recession caused by the devaluation in the financial crisis (Frankel 2005).

According to the contractionary devaluations literature, currency revaluations are likely to have an expansionary rather than a contractionary impact on the economy in developing countries. For instance, currency revaluation has real cash balance effect and real wealth effect: It lowers the domestic price level, therefore leading to real cash balance and real wealth increase, which tends to expand personal spending (Bruno 1979, Gylfason and Radetzki 1991). Currency revaluation also has an income reallocation effect (Diaz-Alejandro 1963, Cooper 1971, Krugman and Taylor 1978): it tends to transfer real income from groups with high marginal propensity to saving toward groups with low marginal propensity to saving, causing total domestic expenditure to expand. This is because revaluation raises the real wage through reducing the price level, causing the real income to shift from entrepreneur to the laborer, and the laborer has higher marginal propensity to consume than that of entrepreneur. This income reallocation effect may be remarkable in developing countries, because the laborers in developing countries usually have limited wealth and are subject to strong liquidity constraint, so their marginal propensities to consume are nearly equal to 1. Moreover, in developing countries, new equipment investment usually includes a large amount of imported capital goods, and currency

4. This literature is mainly about the exchange rate policy of developing countries. Devaluations are usually included in stabilization programs of developing countries and the balance of payment problems in developing countries generally are devaluation pressure. Therefore, the contractionary devaluations literature mainly investigates the issue of devaluation. However, many channels of the contractionary devaluations are equally suitable to the issue of revaluation.

5. See Lizondo and Montiel (1989) for a survey of contractionary devaluations literature. Caves, Frankel, and Jones (2002) provide a simple introduction of ten kinds of contractionary devaluations effects.

revaluation will lower domestic prices of those goods, which will help to expand investment expenditure and, therefore, total expenditure (Branson 1986, van Wijnbergen 1986).[6] Finally, currency revaluation will lower the domestic prices of imported intermediate goods and raw materials (such as petroleum and minerals) which, in turn, will lower the production costs of all final goods (including nontradable goods) and the lowering of marginal costs relative to the prices of final goods will lead to increased output and employment (Bruno 1979, van Wijnbergen 1986). Therefore, even if the net effect of revaluation on aggregate demand is contractionary (the expenditure-switching effect is large enough to dominate the expenditure-changing effect), the existing supply side effect may still make the revaluation expansionary.

Regarding the empirical literature, the majority of research on the relationship between the real exchange rate and output in developing countries has demonstrated that real devaluations are contractionary while real appreciations were expansionary, suggesting that the channels the contractionary devaluations literature revealed are important in developing countries. For example, in an influential early research Edwards (1986) used a reduced form equation model to study a panel data set of 12 developing countries, and found that devaluations were contractionary in the short-term, but turned out to be expansionary after one year, and were neutral in the long-term. Gylfason and Radetzki (1991) used a macroeconomic simulation method to find that for the 12 developing countries studied, devaluations were all contractionary in the short-term as well as in the mid-term. Kamin and Rogers (2000) used a vector autoregression model (VAR model) to study the relation between real exchange rate and output in Mexico, and found that real devaluations were contractionary while real appreciations were expansionary. Other recent researches, such as Hoffmaister and Vegh (1996) on Uruguay, Moreno (1999) on six East Asian countries, Akinlo and Odusola (2003) on Nicaragua, and Berument and Pasaogullari (2003) on Turkey, all support the contractionary devaluations hypothesis.

What is the relationship between RMB real exchange rate and China's output then? Are RMB appreciations contractionary as the textbook says, or expansionary as the contractionary devaluations hypothesis suggests? The purpose of this paper is to study the effects of RMB real exchange rate on China's output by using VAR models with a sample of 1991q1–2005q3. The rest of the paper is organized as follows: section 2 gives a brief historical review of China's exchange rate regime, the evaluations of the RMB real exchange rate, and China's output during the past decade, in order to provide a background for the issues to be discussed; section 3 describes the models to be employed and the data to be used, and discusses the time se-

6. Those are the expenditure-changing effects of exchange rate change.

ries characteristics of the variables; section 4 takes an econometric analysis of the VAR models through impulse-response function graphs and variance decompositions of forecast errors; and finally, section 5 summarizes the conclusions drawn from this research.

3.2   A Brief History of RMB Exchange Rate Evaluation and China's Output Fluctuation: 1991–2005

In the early part of the 1990s, China implemented a double exchange rate system; an official fixed exchange rate coexisted with a market exchange rate formed in the swap foreign exchange market. By 1992, up to 80 percent of the foreign exchange transactions were conducted at the swap foreign exchange market and the market exchange rate essentially reflected the demand for and the supply of the foreign exchange. Because the swap market exchange rate was higher than official exchange rate, implying a subsidy to exporters, the double exchange rate system caused unfair competition and resource distortion, and was unfavorable for attracting foreign direct investments.[7] Against these negative effects, the official exchange rate of RMB was increasing (devaluating) constantly, from 4.7 yuan per U.S. dollar in 1990, devalued to 5.4 yuan per dollar in 1992, until it reached 5.8 yuan per dollar by the end of 1993. On January 1, 1994, China reformed its double exchange rate system by unifying the two exchange rates and established a single and managed floating exchange rate system based on market supply and demand. Afterward, the nominal rate of RMB had gone through disconnected, small bouts of appreciation, and this course went on until 1997 and the financial crisis of East Asia.

When the external demand dropped and the currencies of China's principal trade partners devalued against the U.S. dollar by a wide margin (except Hong Kong), the market participators generally anticipated that RMB would follow those currencies and devaluate. In order to stabilize the regional exchange rates and prevent the currencies from competitive devaluation, the Chinese government announced against the market expectation that RMB would not be devalued. From then on, the RMB exchange rate was fixed at 8.28 yuan per U.S. dollar, and the so-called managed float became a de facto dollar peg. This system lasted until July of 2005. On July 21, 2005, China instituted a reform of its exchange rate regime by revaluating the RMB by 2.1 percent and terminating its peg to the U.S. dollar in favor of a managed float based on a basket of currencies. Under the new exchange rate regime, the daily fluctuation of RMB exchange rate is restricted within 0.3 percent on both sides, and the RMB exchange rate has

7. Under this kind of system, the foreign investment must be converted into RMB according to the official exchange rate first. When the foreign investors need foreign exchanges, however, they can only obtain them through the foreign exchange swap market, at the market exchange rate.

not moved very much because of the market intervention conducted by the People's Bank of China (PBOC). Figure 3.1 portrays the track of RMB nominal exchange rate against the U.S. dollar during the past sixteen years.

In contrast with the relative stableness of the bilateral nominal rate of RMB, the real effective exchange rate (hereafter referred to as the real exchange rate) of RMB presented a large fluctuation in the past periods of more than ten years. As can be seen from figure 3.2, the real exchange rate of RMB had gone through six different stages. (a) 1991q1–1993q2—the real exchange rate of RMB experienced a large amount of depreciation, mainly because the nominal rate of RMB had presented a large devaluation; (b) 1993q3–1998q1—the real exchange rate of RMB experienced a large amount of appreciation, mainly because of higher inflation in China during the period and a small appreciation of RMB nominal rate. After the financial crisis of East Asia, the appreciation of RMB real exchange rate was due to the sharp devaluations of the currencies of some China's trade partners. (c) 1998q2–1999q4—the real exchange rate of RMB experienced a certain degree of depreciation, mainly because there appeared to be a deflation in China; (d) 2000q1–2002q1—a certain degree of appreciation of RMB real exchange rate appeared in this period, mainly the reflection of mild inflation in China and a deflation in the trade partners in this period. The real exchange rate of RMB of 2002q1 rebounded to the level of 1997q4. (e) 2002q2–2005q1—the real exchange rate of RMB turned to the course of large depreciation, mainly influenced by the fact that the U.S. dollar depreciated largely against Euro, Japanese yen, and other key currencies, so RMB also depreciated largely against those currencies; (f) 2005q2 and q3—subject to the influence of appreciation of the U.S. dollar

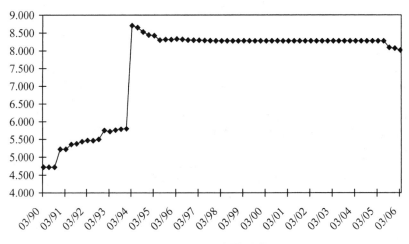

Fig. 3.1   RMB nominal exchange rate (yuan/U.S. dollar)

Source: IMF, International Financial Statistics

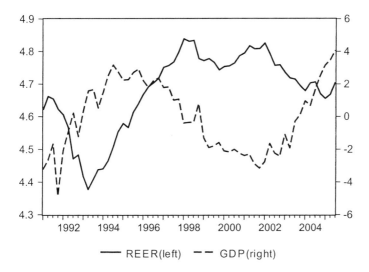

Fig. 3.2   RMB real exchange rate and real GDP

Note: REER stands for RMB real exchange rate index with a rise indicating an appreciation. GDP stands for detrended real gross domestic product. See section 3 for the definition and explanation of the variables.

against the Euro and Japanese yen, the RMB real exchange rate turned to an appreciation state again.

By investigating the detrended real output data of China, we can find that China's real output also experienced a large fluctuation over the past ten plus years. Concerning the correlation of the two variables, as figure 3.2 shows, during the whole sample period (1991q1–2005q3) the relationship between the RMB real exchange rate and China's cyclical output is not very clear, but since 2000q1 the two have presented an obvious negative correlation; namely, appreciations of the real exchange rate have been associated with falls of the cyclical outputs, while real depreciations have been followed by expansions of the cyclical output. The relation between RMB real exchange rate and China's output accords with the forecast of the traditional open economy macroeconomics—RMB appreciations are contractionary, while RMB depreciations are expansionary.

However, for the shown correlation between the RMB real rate and China's output in figure 3.2, two issues are still needed to be clarified: First, may the tight correlation between the RMB real rate and China's output be spurious? That is, is it just reflecting the response of both variables to the third external variable, and do the two variables have nothing to do with each other? For example, a change in government spending will influence the real exchange rate while influencing aggregate demand. Models in the Mundell-Fleming tradition predict that an increase in government spending raises the real interest rate and leads to an appreciation of the real exchange rate.[8] Second, if real exchange rate and output are really relevant, what then is the causality between them? In other words, does the change of the real exchange rate of RMB cause the change of output, or, conversely, does the change of the output cause the change of the real exchange rate of RMB? In order to draw the answers to the above-mentioned questions, we employ a preliminarily pairwise Granger causality test to examine the Granger causality between the RMB real rate and China's output. The Granger causality tests will indicate whether a set of lagged variables has explanatory power on the other variables. If the computed F-statistics are significant, we can claim in Granger's sense that one variable does cause the other variable.

Table 3.1 reports the results of the Granger causality test. The result of the test on the whole sample (1991q1–2005q3) shows that, with a 95 percent level of confidence, the sample data reject the null hypothesis, indicating that China's output Granger causes the RMB real rate, and the RMB real rate Granger causes the output as well. Because there seems a difference on the relationship between RMB real rate and China's output before and after 2000q1, we divide the whole sample into two subsamples (1991q1–1999q4 and 2000q1–2005q3) and conduct a Granger causality test on the two subsamples separately. The results turn out to be surprise. For the first subsample, the data reject the null hypothesis with a 99 percent level of confidence, suggesting the output Granger causes the real exchange rate, and the real exchange rate Granger causes the outputs as well. For the second subsample, upon which there seems to be a strong correlation between the output and real exchange rate, the date instead cannot reject the null hypothesis, showing the strange result that the output does not Granger cause the real exchange rate and the real exchange rate does not Granger cause the outputs either. That means no variable is helpful in explaining the movement of the other. One explanation to this strange-looking result may be that the number of observations in the second subsample is too small, resulting in a small F-Statistic. Another explanation may be that there are other variables influencing both RMB real rate and China's output at the same time that has limited the usefulness for the pairwise Granger causality test.

So, in order to investigate the relationship between the RMB real exchange rate and China's output more precisely, we employ VAR models to control the influence of variables that may have impacts on both RMB real exchange rate and China's output, in order to answer the above-mentioned questions. The estimated VAR models also let us study other interesting issues.

---

8. The sticky-price intertemporal models of the New Open Economy Macroeconomics predict a fall in the real interest rate in response to an increase in government spending (Obstfeld and Rogoff 1995), hence a depreciation of the real exchange rate.

Table 3.1   **Pairwise Granger causality tests**

Null Hypothesis	Obs.	F-Statistic	Probability
Sample: 1991Q1–2005Q3			
GDP does not Granger Cause REER	55	2.65	0.04
REER does not Granger Cause GDP		2.85	0.03
Subsample: 1991Q1–1999Q4			
GDP does not Granger Cause REER	32	3.69	0.02
REER does not Granger Cause GDP		9.38	0.00
Subsample: 2000Q1–2005Q3			
GDP does not Granger Cause REER	23	0.86	0.51
REER does not Granger Cause GDP		0.52	0.72

3.3   Model and Data

3.3.1   The Models

We use the VAR model to study the relationship between the real exchange rate of RMB and China's output in order to find out whether the correlation indicated by figure 3.2 is spurious or not, and the direction of causality between the real exchange rate and output in China. Owing to the relatively small sample size, we can't include all interested variables within one VAR model,[9] so we adopt the modeling strategy of Kamin and Rogers (2000) as follows: we estimate a basic model at first, and then expand the basic model by entering another external variable to the basic model each time. Following Kamin and Rogers (2000), the basic model includes China's gross domestic product (GDP), RMB real effective exchange rate (REER), China's inflation rate (INFL) and foreign gross domestic product (GDPF). Following the tradition of business cycle literature, we detrend the data of gross domestic product so as to focus upon the growth cycle. Therefore, GDP and GDPF represent the cyclical components of gross domestic product (or GDP gap) of China and foreign countries respectively. The reasons for selecting these four variables are as follows: GDPF is taken as a proxy of external shocks. This variable lets us examine the effect on Chinese economy of external shocks. GDP and REER are the variables we want to study. INFL is the *intermediate* variable in between the real exchange rate and output, proxying all possible channels link the real exchange rate to output. Being different from Kamin and Rogers (2000), we choose GDPF instead of the U.S. interest rate as the proxy of external factors. This is based on the following consideration: China still implements

9. Because a VAR model involves quite a lot of parameters to be estimated, introducing too many endogenous variables will cause serious loss in the degrees of freedom, thus affecting the statistic dependability of the results.

the capital controls, therefore, the relation between the U.S. interest rate and China's interest rate should not be very close. On the other hand, after fulfilling the RMB convertible for current account transactions and formally joining the World Trade Organization, the openness of China's real economy is increasing constantly, and the ratio of foreign trade to GDP in China has reached a level of 70 percent at present. In this situation, the business cycles of trading partners have important influence on China through the channels of import and export.

The basic model is too parsimonious to allow us to investigate more comprehensive influences of the variables that influence both the real exchange rate and the output; it may not be very efficient to study the problem of spurious correlation. For example, it provides us with little sense of which channels link the real exchange rate to output. Therefore, we enter one endogenous variable into the basic model each time, and estimate other VAR models in addition. That lets us see whether our final results are robust or not, and at the same time lets us control the size of the VAR model within the appropriate level according to the sample. We enter government spending (GOV) and money supply (M2) into the basic model respectively to examine fiscal and monetary channels in the relationship between real exchange rate and output. In addition, we enter the U.S. interest rate (RUS) so as to investigate the international financial linkage of Chinese economy and examine the efficiency of capital controls in China. Therefore, besides the basic model that is indicated as model 1, we further estimate three more VAR models. The models can be expressed in the form of an unrestricted VAR model as follows:

$$Y_t^l = \sum_{i=1}^{k_l} A_t^l Y_{t-i}^l + \varepsilon_t^l, \quad \varepsilon_t^l \sim IID[o^l, \Omega^l], \quad l = \overline{1, 4}$$

where,

$Y_t^1 = (GDPF_t, INFL_t, REER_t, GDP_t)'$,

$Y_t^2 = (GDPF_t, INFL_t, GOV_t, REER_t, GDP_t)'$,

$Y_t^3 = (GDPF_t, M2_t, INFL_t, REER_t, GDP_t)'$,

$Y_t^4 = (RUS_t, GDPF_t, INFL_t, REER_t, GDP_t)'$.

k_l indicates the lags of l-th VAR model. A_t^l is parameter matrix of l-th VAR model for $i = 1, 2, \ldots, k_l$, ε_t^l is a random residual vector of l-th VAR model, o^l is the zero mean vector of ε_t^l, and Ω^l is a covariance matrix of ε_t^l. Accordingly to AIC criterion and SC criterion, the different numbers of lags are tried for each VAR model, and the optimum lags turn out to be 4 for all four models.

We take the familiar two-stage approach to estimate the VAR models. At the first stage, the variables are regressed on lags of all the variables in the system, and at the second stage, the Cholesky decomposition technique used by Sims (1980) is employed to orthogonalize the residuals so as to identify the primitive structural system. The Cholesky decomposition imposes a recursive contemporaneous causal structure on the VAR models. The model variables are ordered in a particular sequence, and variables higher in the ordering are assumed to cause contemporaneous changes in variables lower in the ordering. Variables lower in the ordering are assumed to affect variables higher in the ordering only with a lag. Because of this, determining a reasonable order for endogenous variables is an important issue in employing a VAR model. We select the variable orders of our four models as above, and the rationale for the orderings are as follows.

GDPF is ordered first because GDPF captures the external shocks that may have significant contemporaneous effects on Chinese economic variables like INFL, REER, and GDP due to the openness of Chinese economy. On the other hand, the outputs of China's trade partners as a whole are unlikely affected contemporaneously by any Chinese economic variables. For REER, INFL, and GDP, we adopt an ordering a little bit different from that of Kamin and Rogers (2000);[10] we order INFL prior to REER and GDP by assuming that inflation shocks have a contemporaneous effect on RMB real exchange rate (since RMB nominal exchange rate is stable due to high official intervention) and on aggregate demand. In contrast, we assume that price is sticky in the short run, so it responds to real exchange rate and aggregate demand shocks only with lags. REER is ordered prior to GDP, as we assume that real exchange rate shocks have a contemporaneous effect on aggregate demand through traditional channel or those indicated by the contractionary devaluations literature, while aggregate demand shocks do not affect contemporaneously the real exchange rate. In model 2, GOV is ordered after INFL by assuming that government spending shocks affect inflation only with a lag. In model 3, M2 is ordered prior to INFL under the assumption that as the monetary policy instrument in China, money supply reacts not to realized inflation but to expected inflation. In model 4, RUS is ordered prior to GDPF because U.S. interest rate shocks affect contemporaneously the world aggregate demand, but due to the relative closeness of U.S. economy, the U.S. interest rate is unlikely affected contemporaneously by world aggregate demand and any Chinese economic variables.

3.3.2   The Data

The data are quarterly; the sample interval is 1991q1–2005q3. 1991q1 is the earliest time for which the quarterly gross domestic product data are available in China. The gross domestic product data of 2005q4 is collected according to a new statistical method and without comparability with the

---

10. Kamin and Rogers (2000) adopt following ordering: REER → INFL → GDP.

data in the past, and therefore we exclude it from our sample. Except for inflation rate, variables are the real ones. U.S. real interest rate is obtained by subtracting the U.S. inflation rate from the nominal interest rate, and other real variables are drawn from the nominal ones divided by consumer price index. The base period is 1992.

The foreign gross domestic product index, GDPF, is calculated according to the trade-weighted average of the gross domestic product indices of 14 principal trade partners of China. GDP and GDPF are detrended gross domestic products. In business cycle literature, the Hodrick-Prescott (H-P) filter is widely used to generate the cyclical components. It is well known, however, that the H-P filter has an end-of-sample problem, that is, at the end of the sample the estimates are particular unreliable. In addition, the filter depends on the choice of the "smoothness parameter" which makes the resulting cyclical component and its statistical properties highly sensitive to this choice. Those problems become serious when sample size is small. Because of the relatively small sample we have, we do not use the H-P filter in this study. Instead, we use quadratic detrending to construct GDP and GDPF data, which is implemented by regressing the logarithm of quarterly real gross domestic product on a trend and its quadrate. The regression with a quadratic time trend has higher degree of fit than one with a linear time trend in our case.

REER (RMB real effective exchange rate index) is taken from the International Financial Statistics database of the International Monetary Fund (IMF), a rise in REER indicating an appreciation. China's inflation rate, INFL, is obtained by differencing the logarithm of consumer price index. GOV expresses the Chinese government spending. M2 is China's broad money supply. RUS indicates the U.S. real interest rate of three-month treasury bills. Except for INFL and RUS, variables are in the logarithm. GDP, GOV, INFL, and GDPF have been seasonally adjusted. Data of other countries or regions come from the International Financial Statistics database of IMF. The data of China's variables, except REER, come from the State Statistics Bureau, the People's Bank of China, China's Ministry of Finance, and General Customs of China. Taiwan GDP annual data come from the IMF World Economic Outlook Database 2006, which have been translated into quarterly data.

3.3.3   The Time Series Characteristics of the Data

Because many macroeconomic variables are not stationary, to avoid spurious regressions we need to test if the time series of relevant variables in our models are stationary or not. If the variables turn out to be nonstationary, we further need to know whether there exist long run steady relations among those endogenous variables or not. We take the unit root tests and cointegration tests for those purposes below.

Table 3.2   **Unit root tests**

	Level		First Difference	
	ADF Test	Phillips-Perron Test	ADF Test	Phillips-Perron Test
GDP	–1.53*	–1.45*	–1.88*	–9.26**
REER	–1.27*	–1.37*	–5.56**	–5.69**
INFL	–1.24*	–1.89*	–12.00**	–11.38**
GDPF	–2.26*	–2.64***	–7.00**	–7.02**
GOV	1.12*	1.21*	–6.10**	–10.10**
M2	0.20*	–0.44*	–3.91**	–6.01**
RUS	–1.61*	–1.87*	–6.42**	–6.44**

* denotes that the hypothesis that the variable contain unit root cannot be rejected at the 10 per cent level of significance.

** denotes the rejection of the hypothesis that the variable contain unit root at the 1 per cent level of significance.

*** denotes that the hypothesis that the variable contain unit root cannot be rejected at the 5 per cent level of significance.

Unit Root Tests

We use both the augmented Dickey-Fuller (ADF) test and the Phillips-Perron test for unit root tests. Table 3.2 reports the results of the unit root tests of all relevant variables in our models. For the level variables, both tests reveal that we cannot reject the presence of a unit root, which shows these variables are all nonstationary. On the other hand, the Phillips-Perron test rejects the null hypothesis of the presence of a unit root at the 1 percent level of significance for the first difference of all variables, while the ADF test rejects the null hypothesis at the 1 percent level of significance for the first difference of all variables except GDP. The ADF test cannot reject the presence of a unit root for the first difference time series of GDP. Here, we adopt the result of the Phillips-Perron test for GDP, and therefore assert that all variables in our models are the first order integrated variables, namely variables of I (1).

Cointegration Tests

Because all variables in our models are variables of I (1), we need to further test if there are cointegration vectors for each model. We implement VAR-based cointegration tests using the methodology developed in Johansen (1995). Table 3.3 reports the results of Johansen cointegration tests, which indicate that there is at least one cointegration vector for each VAR model. Therefore nonstationary data needs less concern in this study. In fact, as elaborated in Sims, Stock, and Watson (1990), when variables are cointegrated using a VAR in levels model is not misspecified, and the estimates are consistent. Some economists suggest that when one really doesn't know whether there is cointegration or what the cointegration vec-

Table 3.3   Cointegration tests for alternative specifications

Hypothesized No. of CE(s)	Eigenvalue	λ-Trace Statistics	λ-Max Statistics
Model 1: Series: GDPF INFL REER GDP			
None	0.68	94.67*	62.30*
At most 1	0.26	32.38*	16.73
At most 2	0.19	15.65*	11.54
At most 3	0.07	4.11*	4.11*
Model 2: Series: GDPF INFL GOV REER GDP			
None	0.70	149.45*	65.79*
At most 1	0.56	83.66*	45.72*
At most 2	0.35	37.95*	23.93*
At most 3	0.17	14.01	10.02
At most 4	0.07	4.00*	4.00*
Model 3: Series: GDPF M2 INFL REER GDP			
None	0.69	137.91*	63.97*
At most 1	0.62	73.94*	52.53*
At most 2	0.25	21.42	15.68
At most 3	0.10	5.73	5.70
At most 4	0.00	0.03	0.03
Model 4: Series: RUS GDPF INFL REER GDP			
None	0.70	154.51*	66.46*
At most 1	0.67	88.04*	60.79*
At most 2	0.27	27.25	17.00
At most 3	0.15	10.25	8.79
At most 4	0.03	1.47	1.47

Note: Lags interval (in first difference): 1 to 3.
* denotes rejection of the hypothesis at the 0.05 level of significance.

tor is, the VAR in levels approach is probably better than the approach that tests for cointegration, estimates cointegrating relations, and then estimates a vector error correction (VEC) model (Cochrane 2005). We follow the suggestion and conduct our study on the relationship between RMB real exchange rate and China's output by using VAR in levels model in the next section.

3.4   Empirical Results

This section comprises two subsections. The first subsection presents the empirical results derived from our VAR in levels models. The estimation results of the VAR models are given in the form of impulse response functions and variance decompositions, and based on those, the empirical analysis of the relationship between RMB real exchange rate and China's output is then conducted. In the second subsection, the robustness of the results obtained in the first subsection is investigated by adopting different ordering of variables, using VEC model specification, and substituting

RUS for GDPF in the first three models as a proxy of external shock. We want to know whether the results change significantly or not when we make those changes.

3.4.1 Results from the VAR in Levels Model

In a VAR analysis, the dynamic interactions between the variables are usually investigated by impulse response functions or forecast error variance decompositions. In this subsection, we obtain our empirical results concerning the relationship between RMB real exchange rate and China's output by using these two instruments.

Impulse Response Functions

The impulse response functions (IRFs) display the responses of a particular variable to a one-time shock in each of the variables in the system. Figure 3.3 and figure 3.4 plot the IRFs of GDP and REER respectively calculated from four VAR models. By investigating those IRFs graphs, the following results can be drawn:

First, when one standard deviation positive (appreciation) shock to REER takes place, there is an obvious decline of GDP, indicating that RMB real rate shocks have a negative impact on China's output. From the 8th quarter, the contractionary effect is weakened to some extent but obviously still exists. After 18 quarters, the impact of RMB real rate shock on output turns to be positive. This effect of RMB real appreciation occurs in all models estimated, suggesting the robustness of the result. This result is in contrast with that of, say, Edwards (1986) and Kamin and Rogers (2000). In Edwards (1986), for 12 countries studied, devaluations (revaluations) were contractionary (expansionary) in the short-term, but after one year devaluations turned out to be expansionary. In Kamin and Rogers (2000) devaluations (revaluations) were contractionary (expansionary) in short-term as well as in medium-term in Mexico.

Second, in model 4, which includes RUS, the contractionary effect of positive shocks to REER on GDP is significantly less than that in other three models that do not include RUS. The former is only about half of the latter. On the other hand, shocks to RUS have a remarkable contractionary effect on GDP; the magnitude of the effect is even larger than that of REER shocks. These two findings seem to indicate that on one hand the capital control in China is less efficient than we thought. On the other, capital flows have a significant impact on the Chinese economy, which is even larger than the impact of trade (the impact of REER) on the economy.[11] In other words, after accounting for the effect of international finance

---

11. The impact of a rise in RUS on the Chinese economy may function through the following channel: a rise in RUS results in a decline in U.S. demands, which in turn causes the demand for China's export to decline. But because we have entered GDPF into model 4, the influence of this channel has already been controlled.

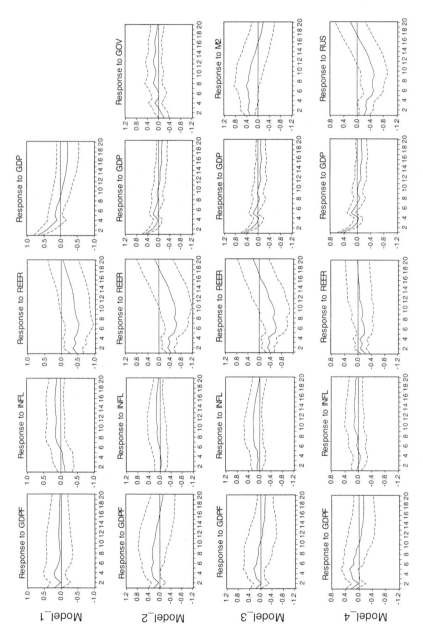

Fig. 3.3 Impulse responses of GDP to Cholesky one S.D. shocks ± 2 S.E.

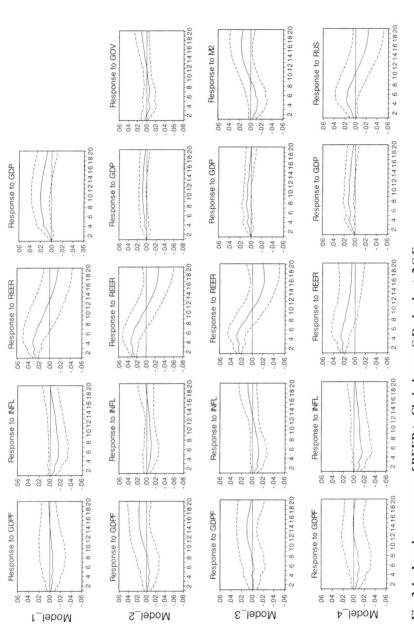

Fig. 3.4 Impulse responses of REER to Cholesky one S.D. shocks ± 2 S.E.

linkage, the effect of RMB real appreciation on China's real economy may be smaller than what we have expected.

Third, one standard deviation shock to GDP has no obvious impact on REER. After the 3rd quarter, the shock causes REER raise for some extent. This effect of output shock occurs in all models estimated, suggesting the robustness of the result. Because the measure of the IRFs graphs of REER is only about one tenth relative to the measure of those of GDP, we think that the magnitude of impact of output shocks on RMB real rate is much less than that of the impact of RMB real rate shocks on output.

Fourth, the impact of shocks to other variables virtually accords with the economic intuition. For example, an increase in money supply has an obvious expansionary effect and causes the real exchange rate depreciation in short-term. GDPF shocks have expansionary effect too; an increases in government spending results in RMB real appreciation in first 2 quarters, and inflation shocks cause a decline of GDP in short-term. An important exception is the effect of INFL shocks on REER. An increase in inflation causes real exchange rate depreciation. We should expect that an increase in inflation causes the RMB real exchange rate to appreciate, because the nominal rate of RMB has been very steady since 1997. In addition, an increase in government spending causes GDP to drop in the first two quarters. One possible explanation of this may be that in the short run government spending has a strong crowding-out effect in China.

In summary, the analyses based on IRFs suggest that the RMB real appreciation shock has contractionary effect on China's output. After controlling the influence of other variables, the RMB real appreciation shock still causes GDP to decline, which excludes the spurious correlation between RMB real exchange rate and China's output. The empirical results also seem to support the guess that the direction of the causality between the RMB real rate and China's output runs from the former to the latter. Finally, the external shocks have remarkable effects on China's output. In particular, U.S. interest rate shocks have a significant impact on China's cyclical output. When the effect of RUS is included in VAR model, the effect of REER turns out to be weaker for certain degree.

Variance Decompositions

The IRFs provide a useful tool to assess the direction as well as the magnitude of response of a variable to various kinds of shocks. However, the variance decompositions give the fraction of the forecast error variance for each variable that is attributable to its own shocks and to shocks in the other variables in the system, so allow us to appraise the relative importance of the contribution of different shocks to the variance of a particular variable. Table 3.4 provides the variance decompositions of GDP and RMB real exchange rate from four VAR models. The following results emerge from table 3.4.

Table 3.4 **Variance decompositions of GDP and REER from VAR models**

Model 1

T	S.E.		GDPF		INFL		REER		GDP	
1	0.9	0.6	4.6	0.8	2.4	1.4	30.7	97.8	62.3	0.0
2	1.2	0.7	3.3	1.0	2.9	5.1	33.0	93.4	60.8	0.5
3	1.5	0.7	4.9	1.8	2.6	6.1	40.3	89.9	52.2	2.2
4	1.6	0.7	7.1	1.5	2.5	8.6	44.5	83.1	45.9	6.8
8	1.8	1.3	5.0	2.0	3.0	14.8	63.4	65.8	28.5	17.4
12	1.8	1.6	4.4	2.0	4.9	16.5	68.1	53.8	22.6	27.7
20	1.9	1.8	3.9	1.7	8.2	15.2	63.2	49.4	24.8	33.8

Model 2

T	S.E.		GDPF		INFL		REER		GDP		GOV	
1	1.0	0.6	8.4	0.8	0.0	0.2	36.7	96.0	47.5	0.0	7.3	3.1
2	1.3	0.6	6.7	1.0	0.2	1.3	43.2	96.3	43.1	0.0	6.9	1.4
3	1.5	0.7	11.0	2.0	0.3	2.0	50.6	94.3	32.9	0.0	5.1	1.8
4	1.7	0.8	16.0	2.0	0.3	3.2	51.4	91.7	26.7	0.9	5.7	2.4
8	1.8	1.2	16.0	2.1	0.7	6.6	68.0	85.9	12.3	2.6	3.5	2.7
12	1.9	1.4	14.0	4.0	1.7	8.4	72.4	78.8	8.1	6.2	3.9	2.6
20	2.1	1.8	13.0	15.6	3.5	5.2	70.2	68.6	8.4	6.0	5.3	4.7

Model 3

T	S.E.		GDPF		INFL		REER		GDP		M2	
1	1.0	0.0	5.8	0.5	1.6	1.4	29.4	96.3	48.2	0.0	15.0	1.8
2	1.3	0.0	3.9	0.3	2.1	6.8	30.7	88.0	37.3	0.3	25.9	4.5
3	1.5	0.0	5.3	0.4	1.8	7.9	36.4	82.3	27.6	0.7	28.9	8.8
4	1.7	0.0	7.3	0.3	1.9	8.7	37.9	78.6	22.5	2.1	30.4	10.2
8	1.8	0.0	6.1	0.5	4.8	12.0	51.5	72.5	9.9	4.3	27.7	10.7
12	1.9	0.1	4.6	3.1	7.5	12.1	54.8	66.8	7.3	6.4	25.8	11.6
20	2.1	0.1	6.5	5.5	9.0	8.9	52.3	59.9	7.8	4.0	24.4	21.6

Model 4

T	S.E.		GDPF		INFL		REER		GDP		RUS	
1	0.5	1.0	13.2	2.6	0.7	8.2	12.4	85.3	61.9	0.0	11.8	3.9
2	0.8	1.2	10.5	3.4	0.5	13.3	10.7	77.1	53.5	1.5	24.7	4.7
3	0.9	1.5	14.8	5.5	0.8	12.2	11.2	70.7	42.8	3.7	30.4	7.9
4	1.0	1.7	18.5	4.7	1.1	13.1	9.5	63.9	35.1	6.3	35.8	12.0
8	1.2	1.8	14.8	6.3	0.6	15.1	9.3	54.6	16.3	8.6	58.9	15.4
12	1.4	1.9	10.2	5.6	2.2	16.5	7.8	52.6	11.3	12.1	68.5	13.1
20	1.7	2.0	12.0	4.1	4.1	13.5	6.6	40.4	12.8	11.6	64.6	30.4

Notes: The two columns below a variable give the fraction of the forecast error variance for GDP and REER that is attributable to shocks to the variable at the given forecast horizon, with the bold column in left indicating the fraction for GDP. The columns below "S.E." contain the forecast error of GDP and REER at the given forecast horizon.

First, concerning the source of variation in GDP forecast error, for those models that do not include RUS, "own shocks" is the first most important source at the horizons of the first and second quarters, while RMB real exchange rate shock is the second most important source. Beginning from the third quarter, however, the RMB real exchange rate shocks become the first most important source of variation in GDP, and accounts for 36–70 percent of the GDP forecast error variance in models 2 and 3. In the medium and long-term horizon, "own shocks" is the second most important source in model 1, which accounts for about 24 percent of the GDP error variance, while the contributions of "own shocks" in model 2 and 3 decrease greatly, and only account for about 8 percent of the GDP error variance. In contrast, shocks to GDPF and M2 turn out to be the second most important source of the GDP error variance in model 2 and 3 respectively, in the medium and long-term horizon, and account for about 14 percent and 26 percent of the GDP error variance respectively.

Second, in model 4, which includes RUS, "own shocks" to GDP is the first most important source of the GDP error variance only at the horizons of the first, second, and third quarters. Beginning from the 4th quarter, however, the RUS shocks become the first most important and predominant source of variation in GDP, accounting for 36–69 percent of the GDP error variance, while in the long-term horizon "own shocks" and GDPF shocks turn to be second and the third most important source of the GDP error variance, accounting for about 13 percent and 11 percent respectively. In contrast, REER shocks become the fourth important source of variation in GDP, only accounting for 7 percent of variation in the long-term horizon. When RUS is included in VAR model, the power of REER shocks in explaining the error variance of GDP has significantly declined. This result is consistent with what we obtained in IRFs analysis.

Third, in the source of variation in RMB real exchange rate forecast error, "own shocks" is the first most important and predominant source, accounting for 63–98 percent of the forecast error variance at the horizons of the first to fourth quarters, and 40–70 percent after eight quarters. On the other hand, the contribution of GDP shocks to the error variance of REER is negligible at the horizons of the first to fourth quarters. In the medium- and long-term horizon, the contribution of GDP shocks to the error variance of REER is about 30 percent in model 1, but drops by a large margin to under 7 percent in model 2 and model 3 and about 12 percent in model 4. On the contrary, shocks to M2, GDPF, and RUS in the other three models all have relatively large contribution to the error variance of REER. What merits attention is that GOV has very little contribution to the error variance of REER.

In summary, the analyses based on the variance decompositions suggest that (a) the shocks to the RMB real exchange rate have a large contribution to the variation in China's output in models that do not include the U.S. interest rate, and some contribution to the variation in China's output in the model that includes the U.S. interest rate, suggesting the possibility that the spurious correlation between the RMB real exchange rate and China's output can be excluded; (b) except for the basic model (Model 1), the shocks to GDP have small contribution to the variation in RMB real exchange rate, and the contribution is negligible at the horizons of the first to fourth quarters, suggesting the possibility of reverse causation running from the GDP to the RMB real exchange rate can be excluded; and (c) when the U.S. interest rate is included in VAR model, the power of REER shocks in explaining the error variance of GDP significantly declines.

3.4.2   Robustness Analysis

The results obtained in the previous subsection may be specific to the selected ordering of endogenous variables. Therefore, it is interesting to estimate our VAR models with different and plausible ordering. In addition, because all variables in our models are variables of I (1) and there are cointegration vectors for each model, it is worth trying to check the results obtained from the VAR in level models with those obtained from the cointegration restricted VAR models, that is, the VEC models.[12] Furthermore, the results of previous subsection suggest that the magnitude of the effect of the RMB exchange rate shocks on China's output is diminished remarkably by including the U.S. interest rate in the VAR model, therefore it is also interesting to substitute RUS for GDPF as a proxy of external shock in our first three VAR models. In this subsection we therefore investigate the robustness of the results as regards these three points.

Different Ordering

Kamin and Rogers (2000) adopt orderings a little bit different from ours in their VAR models. Except for GDPF, variables in our four VAR models are ordered as in Kamin and Rogers (2000) as follows: model 1: REER$\rightarrow$ INFL$\rightarrow$GDP; model 2: GOV$\rightarrow$REER$\rightarrow$INFL$\rightarrow$GDP; model 3: REER $\rightarrow$ M2$\rightarrow$INFL$\rightarrow$GDP; and model 4: RUS$\rightarrow$REER$\rightarrow$INFL$\rightarrow$GDP. If we relax the assumption of price stickiness in the short run, the above orderings seem plausible. For example, in model 1, an appreciation of real exchange rate shifts demand away from nontraded goods and decreases the price of nontraded goods and the general price level for a given level of nominal exchange rate. The adjustment of the price level then causes the change of output.

We reestimate our four VAR models by adopting the above orderings and find that the results are quite similar to those of previous subsection. Owing to the space limitation, we only present the impulse response func-

---

12. Some economists argue that it is appropriate to estimate VEC model when variables are I (1) and there are cointegrating relations between them (Engle and Granger 1987).

tions of GDP from the four VAR models using orderings adopted by Kamin and Rogers (2000) (figure 3.5).

Results from VEC Model

The VEC models to be estimated have following forms:

$$\Delta Y_t^l = \alpha^l ECM_{t-1}^l + \sum_{i=1}^{k_l-1} \Gamma_i^l \Delta Y_{t-i}^l + \varepsilon_t^l, \ \varepsilon_t^l \sim IID[o^l, \Omega^l], \ l = \overline{1, 4}$$

where $ECM_{t-l}^l = \beta^{l\prime} Y_{t-1}^l$ is the error correction terms, reflecting the long-run equilibrium relationship between the variables. $\beta^{l\prime}$ is the matrix of cointegration vectors. The coefficient vector α^l reflects how fast the deviation from the long-run equilibrium is corrected through a series of partial short-run adjustments. Γ_i^l is parameter matrix of variables in differences, the elements of these matrices reflect the short-term effect of the variables on a dependent variable.

We estimate four VEC models adopting the same orderings of the previous subsection. By investigating the estimation results of four VEC models, we find that the IRFs of VEC models are very similar with those of VAR models in direction and dynamic path of the responses. The results of variance decompositions are basically similar too. But one difference is: the effect of various shocks in VEC models case seems more lasting than that in VAR models. Taking the response of GDP to the REER shocks as an example the contractionary effect of an appreciation of REER sustains longer before the expansionary effect appears. Because restricted by space, we only provide the results of variance decompositions of GDP and REER and impulse response functions of GDP from the VEC models (table 3.5 and figure 3.6).

Substitution RUS for GDPF in VAR Model

When we substitute RUS for GDPF in VAR Models and reestimate the first three VAR models of the previous subsection we find that comparing the original models using GDPF as proxy variable for external shocks: (a) the IRFs of three new VAR models are similar with those of model 4 of the previous subsection—the magnitude of the effect of RMB exchange rate shocks on China's output is diminished, especially in medium and long-term; (b) the expansionary effect of REER shocks appears earlier; (c) concerning the source of variation in GDP forecast error, in all three new VAR models the RUS shocks become the most important and predominant source of variation in GDP error variance respectively. The contributions of "own shocks" and M2 to variation in GDP have exceeded the contribution of REER in the second and third new models; (d) the effects of other shocks on GDP are similar between new models and original ones. Figure 3.7 and table 3.6 provide IRFs and variance decompositions of GDP from

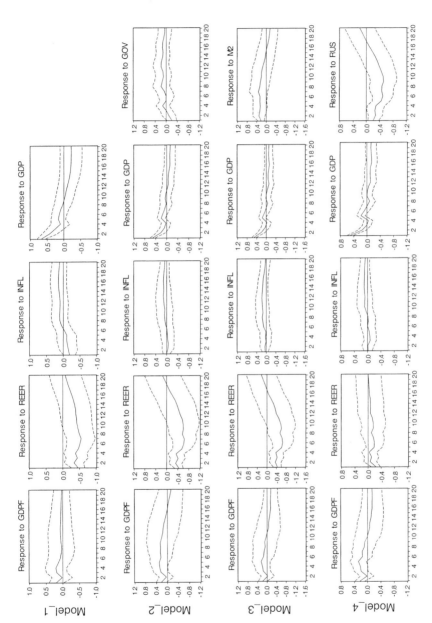

Fig. 3.5 Impulse responses of GDP from VARs with different ordering

Table 3.5 Variance decompositions of GDP and REER from VEC models

T	S.E.		GDPF		INFL		REER		GDP	
					Model 1					
1	1.0	0.6	2.7	0.2	3.1	2.8	30.4	97.1	63.8	0.0
2	1.5	0.7	1.7	0.1	4.2	8.4	29.9	91.0	64.2	0.6
3	2.0	0.7	2.0	0.2	4.0	11.1	35.2	86.6	58.8	2.2
4	2.5	0.8	2.8	0.1	4.5	14.6	39.0	79.4	53.8	5.9
8	3.3	1.9	1.6	0.0	3.7	22.7	59.9	67.6	34.8	9.7
12	4.0	2.8	1.1	0.1	3.3	24.9	70.1	63.8	25.4	11.2
20	5.1	4.2	0.8	0.1	2.8	26.2	78.6	61.5	17.8	12.1

T	S.E.		GDPF		INFL		REER		GDP		GOV	
						Model 2						
1	1.0	0.6	8.3	0.5	0.1	0.4	37.8	95.3	45.9	0.0	7.8	3.8
2	1.4	0.6	6.7	0.8	0.2	1.7	45.6	95.7	40.6	0.0	6.9	1.8
3	1.8	0.7	11.9	2.0	0.3	2.3	53.2	94.2	29.7	0.0	5.0	1.5
4	2.0	0.7	18.4	2.1	0.3	3.0	53.6	92.7	22.6	0.4	5.1	1.8
8	2.4	1.3	23.0	6.0	0.1	3.1	67.0	88.8	7.6	0.6	2.2	1.5
12	2.7	1.5	27.2	10.0	0.1	2.6	67.3	84.9	3.5	1.0	2.0	1.6
20	3.8	1.6	33.0	11.3	0.1	2.4	63.2	82.9	1.6	1.2	2.2	2.1

T	S.E.		GDPF		INFL		REER		GDP		M2	
						Model 3						
1	1.0	0.0	4.4	0.7	2.3	1.8	29.9	94.8	46.4	0.0	17.0	2.7
2	1.5	0.0	3.0	0.4	2.9	7.0	32.1	86.2	33.9	0.2	28.1	6.3
3	2.0	0.0	3.3	0.4	2.9	8.2	39.1	79.6	23.2	0.3	31.5	11.5
4	2.5	0.0	4.5	0.3	3.1	8.9	42.0	76.3	17.4	1.0	32.9	13.5
8	3.3	0.0	5.0	0.3	4.1	9.8	55.8	70.5	5.6	0.7	29.5	18.8
12	4.1	0.1	5.2	0.3	4.6	10.3	58.6	68.1	2.6	0.6	29.0	20.7
20	5.5	0.1	5.6	0.9	4.8	10.6	58.6	66.8	1.3	0.7	29.6	21.0

T	S.E.		GDPF		INFL		REER		GDP		RUS	
						Model 4						
1	*0.5*	*1.0*	*13.6*	*1.5*	*1.0*	*10.4*	*12.0*	*81.5*	*58.9*	*0.0*	*14.6*	*6.6*
2	0.7	1.5	10.4	1.4	0.7	17.1	10.3	71.1	47.8	1.4	30.8	9.0
3	1.1	2.0	14.9	2.0	0.6	17.0	11.3	63.6	34.1	2.9	39.2	14.5
4	1.3	2.5	19.4	1.3	0.6	18.4	9.7	55.8	24.7	4.1	45.7	20.4
8	2.0	3.5	17.1	0.5	0.3	22.6	12.4	43.5	7.1	2.9	63.2	30.5
12	2.4	4.4	12.3	0.9	1.2	26.3	13.9	39.6	2.9	2.4	69.7	30.8
20	2.9	5.6	8.1	2.2	2.7	31.3	14.3	37.9	1.2	2.0	73.7	26.6

Notes: The two columns below a variable give the fraction of the forecast error variance for GDP and REER that is attributable to shocks to the variable at the given forecast horizon, with the black column in left indicating the fraction for GDP. The columns below "S.E." contain the forecast error of GDP and REER at the given forecast horizon.

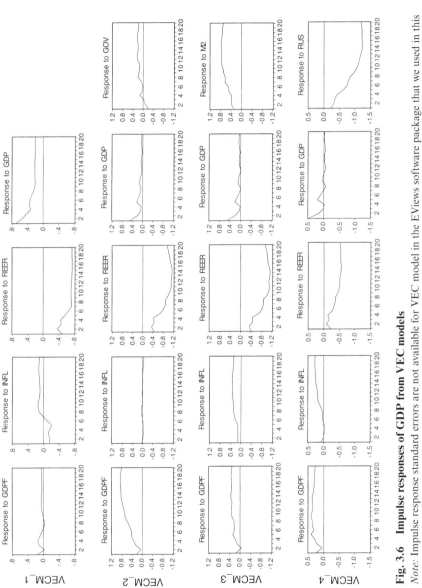

Fig. 3.6 Impulse responses of GDP from VEC models

Note: Impulse response standard errors are not available for VEC model in the EViews software package that we used in this study.

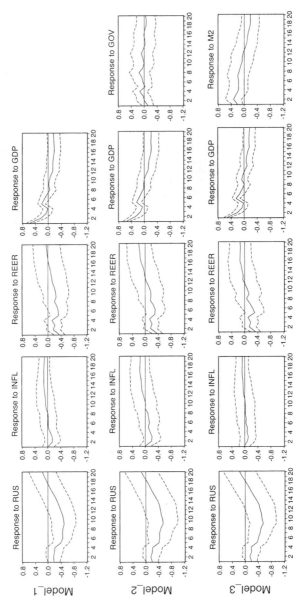

Fig. 3.7 Impulse responses of GDP from VARs with RUS substituting for GDPF

Table 3.6   Variance decomposition of GDP from VAR models with RUS

T	S.E.	RUS	INFL	REER	GDP	
			Model 1			
1	0.5	6.8	0.1	24.4	68.8	
2	0.8	10.1	3.7	23.4	62.8	
3	0.9	13.7	6.0	26.2	54.18	
4	1.0	18.2	6.4	25.8	49.6	
8	1.2	46.9	2.7	26.9	23.6	
12	1.4	58.0	2.3	23.4	16.2	
20	1.7	55.7	4.7	20.1	19.6	

T	S.E.	RUS	INFL	REER	GDP	GOV
			Model 2			
1	0.6	8.0	0.0	26.6	63.1	2.3
2	0.8	9.8	5.9	23.9	58.7	1.7
3	0.9	13.0	10.3	25.2	49.9	1.5
4	1.0	16.5	11.4	24.3	44.4	3.4
8	1.2	42.8	7.0	23.4	23.7	3.1
12	1.3	59.1	4.7	17.6	16.2	2.4
20	1.6	54.9	7.6	16.5	19.0	2.1

T	S.E.	RUS	INFL	REER	GDP	M2
			Model 3			
1	0.5	7.8	0.1	22.3	59.6	10.2
2	0.8	8.6	0.8	18.3	48.4	23.9
3	0.9	11.7	2.2	18.9	39.9	27.3
4	1.0	14.5	2.5	18.3	36.3	28.4
8	1.1	42.9	1.6	16.7	20.1	18.7
12	1.3	60.6	1.1	11.7	13.6	13.0
20	1.6	57.9	1.9	12.1	14.3	13.9

Notes: The column below a variable gives the fraction of the forecast error variance for GDP that is attributable to shocks to the variable at the given forecast horizon. The column below "S.E." contains the forecast error of GDP at the given forecast horizon.

the three new VAR models, with RUS replacing GDPF as a proxy variable of external shocks.

In summary, the robustness analysis confirms that our basic result, namely that the shocks to RMB real exchange rate have a contractionary effect on China's output, essentially does not change even if we adopt the orderings of Kamin and Rogers (2000) or use VEC model in our model specification. But after including the international finance linkage of the Chinese economy, the effect of REER shock on China's output and the power of REER shocks in explaining the changes of China's output turn to be relatively small, while the U.S. interest rate shock has relatively large effect on China's output, the magnitude of its effect exceeding that of RMB exchange rate shocks.

3.5 Conclusion

This paper has investigated the relationship between the RMB real exchange rate and China's output by using the VAR model technique. The empirical analysis reveals several interesting findings. First, even after source of spurious correlation is controlled for, RMB real appreciation has led to a decline in China's output, suggesting that currency appreciations have been contractionary in China, as traditional open economy macroeconomics forecasts. Second, when the international finance linkage of Chinese economy is accounted for, the effect of RMB real exchange rate shocks on China's output and the power of the shocks in explaining the change of China's output are relatively small, while the effect of U.S. interest rate shocks on China's output is relatively large. The intuition behind this finding may be that the effectiveness of China's capital controls has eroded over time and the scales of capital inflows and outflows have become large enough that external shocks through international finance channels have significant influence on the Chinese economy, exceeding the influence of external shocks through international trade channels. Third, besides shocks to RMB real exchange rate and the U.S. interest rate, shocks to domestic money supply and foreign demand all have important effects on China's output. However, government spending shocks have less power in explaining the change of China's output.

The conclusion that currency appreciations have been contractionary in China is remarkably different from those made by similar empirical works on developing countries. The possible explanations of this difference are as follows. First, in the existing research on contractionary devaluations effect in developing countries, devaluations usually take place under an abnormal environment of currency or financial crisis, and thus have been associated with economic recession, but RMB devaluations did not happen in case of currency or financial crisis until now. Second, the urban economic reform begun in the early 1990s has made many people lose their jobs and traditional benefits of medicare, pensions, education, and so on, which has strengthened the motive of precautionary saving of households in urban and township areas. Under that situation, the income reallocation effect as well as the real cash balance and the real wealth effects of currency appreciation may not play a very great role.

Third, China has absorbed a large amount of foreign direct investment for many years. As a result, the technological progress and production capacity of China's manufacturing industry have been promoted rapidly, the substitutability of home produced capital goods (included those produced by foreign investment enterprises) to imported goods has been strengthened, and therefore, the effect of RMB exchange rate on domestic invest-ment spending is not clear. Fourth, one condition that devaluation can lead to a reduction in national output is that imports initially exceed exports (Krugman and Taylor 1978). China's trade balance has been in the favorable surplus for more than ten years except for 1993, and therefore does not satisfy that condition.

Finally, because of the characteristics of processing trade in China's manufacturing industry and administrative controls on prices (especially on those of service sector), the supply side effect of the RMB exchange rate on output is also uncertain. In a word, it seems that the expenditure-changing effect and supply side effect of the RMB exchange rate change are not remarkable in practice until now. Therefore, the effect of RMB exchange rate shock on China's output is mainly embodied through the expenditure-switching effect, as traditional macroeconomic theory emphasized. In that situation, the appreciations of RMB are likely contractionary.

It is worth pointing out, however, that the conclusion that appreciations have been contractionary in China does not necessarily mean that China should continue maintaining the undervalued RMB exchange rate, since the undervalued RMB has already caused the Chinese economy to run into internal and external imbalances in the past several years. Figure 3.2 tells us that China's real GDP has been running above its long-term trend since 2003, and this kind of deviation is expanding. Indeed, the overheating of the Chinese economy is obvious. There is no doubt that continuing the undervaluation of RMB exchange rate will further aggravate the imbalances of the Chinese economy. In fact, the conclusion that appreciations have been contractionary in China implies that relative to other effects of exchange rate change, the expenditure-switching effect has been predominant in China until now. Therefore, it is effectual to use the orthodox Swan Diagram to analyze macroeconomic policy issues in China.[13] According to the Swan Diagram of Shi (2006), allowing RMB to appreciate is helpful for the Chinese economy to realize internal and external balances.

In addition, China's capital account surplus has increased rapidly along with the rapid increases in the current account surplus in recent years. The rapid increase in the "double surplus" causes China's foreign exchange reserve to expand in a wild manner and causes the money supply and the domestic credit to expand passively, which have aggravated the overheating of the Chinese economy and the difficulty in the government's attempt at macromanagement. In particular, as China's capital account liberalizes gradually and the effectiveness of capital controls erodes over time, the hot money will flow into China in great amounts, becoming one of the impor-

13. If appreciations (depreciations) are expansionary (contractionary), the Swan Diagram is less insightful about the combination of policy instruments to simultaneously fulfill both internal and external balances, because it it difficult in this case to decide where and how the internal and external balance schedules intercross. See, for example, Frankel (2005).

tant reasons the foreign exchange reserve increase so fast. Our empirical work indicates that the effect of shocks on China's output through international finance channel (as represented by U.S. interest rate shocks) exceed that through international trade channels (as represented by RMB real exchange rate shocks), suggesting it is important for the Chinese authorities to handle the capital inflows problem correctly. The inflow of hot money in recent years is mainly a response to the expectations of RMB appreciation, and one of the important reasons for the persisting existence of the expectations is the undervaluation of RMB. Therefore, allowing RMB to appreciate at faster speed, so as to restore the equilibrium level of RMB exchange rate, will lessen the expectations of RMB appreciation, thus relaxing the pressure of the rapid increase in foreign exchange reserve on the Chinese authorities.

References

Akinlo, A. E., and Odusola, A. F. 2003. Assessing the impact of Nigeria's naira depreciation on output and inflation. *Applied Economics* 36:691–703.

Berument, H., and M. Pasaogullari. 2003. Effects of the real exchange rate on output and inflation: Evidence from Turkey. *The Developing Economies,* XLI-4:401–35.

Branson, W. H. 1986. Stabilization, stagflation, and investment incentives: The case of Kenya, 1979–1980. In *Economic adjustment and exchange rates in developing countries,* eds. S. Edwards and L. Ahamed, 267–93. Chicago: University of Chicago Press.

Bruno, M. 1979. Stabilization and stagflation in a semi-industrialized economy. In *International economic policy: Theory and evidence,* eds. R. Dornbusch and J. A. Frenkel, 270–89. Baltimore, MD: Johns Hopkins University Press.

Caves, R. E., J. A. Frankel, and R. W. Jones. 2002. *World trade and payments: An introduction.* Reading, MA: Addison-Wesley.

Cochrane, J. H. 2005. *Time Series for Macroeconomics and Finance.* University of Chicago. Unpublished Manuscript.

Cooper, R. N. 1971. Currency devaluation in developing countries. In *Government and economic development,* ed. G. Ranis. New Haven, CT: Yale University Press.

Coudert, V., and C. Couharde. 2005. Real equilibrium exchange rate in China. CEPII Working Paper no. 2005-01. Paris: Center for International Prospective Studies.

Diaz-Alejandro, C.F. 1963. A note on the impact of devaluation and the redistributive effects. *Journal of Political Economy* 71:577–80.

Edwards, S. 1986. Are devaluations contractionary? *The Review of Economics and Statistics* 68:501–508.

Engle, R. R., and C. W. J. Granger. 1987. Co-integration and error correction representation, estimation, and testing. *Econometrica* 55:251–76.

Goldstein, M. 2004. Adjusting China's exchange rate policies. Revised version of the paper presented at the International Monetary Fund's seminar on China's Foreign Exchange System. May 26–27. Dalian, China.

Gylfason, T., and M. Radetzki. 1991. Does devaluation make sense in the least developed countries? *Economic Development and Cultural Change* 40 (1): 1–25.

Frankel, J. A. 2004. On the Yuan: The choice between adjustment under a fixed exchange rate and adjustment under a flexible rate. Paper presented at an International Monetary Fund seminar on China's foreign exchange system. May 26–27. Dalian, China.

Frankel, J. A. 2005. Mundell-Fleming lecture: Contractionary currency crashes in developing countries. *IMF Staff Papers,* vol. 52, No. 2, pp. 149–92.

Hirschman, A. O. 1949. Devaluation and the trade balance: A note. *The Review of Economics and Statistics* 31:50–53.

Hoffmaister, A. W., and C. Vegh. 1996. Disinflation and the recession-now-versus-recession-later hypothesis: Evidence from Uruguay. *IMF Staff Papers* 43:355–94.

Johansen, S. 1995. *Likelihood-Based Inference in Cointegrated Vector Autoregressive Models.* Oxford, England: Oxford University Press.

Kamin, S. B., and J. H. Rogers. 2000. Output and the real exchange rate in developing countries: An application to Mexico. *Journal of Development Economics* 61 (1): 85–109.

Krugman, P., and L. Taylor. 1978. Contractionary effects of devaluation. *Journal of International Economics* 8:445–56.

Lizondo, S., and Montiel, P. J. 1989. Contractionary devaluation in developing countries: An analytical overview. *IMF Staff Papers* 36:182–227.

Moreno, R. 1999. Depreciations and recessions in East Asia. *Federal Reserve Bank of San Francisco Economic Review,* 3, 27–40.

Obstfeld, M., and K. Rogoff. 1995. Exchange rate dynamics redux. *The Journal of Political Economy* 103 (3): 624–60.

Shi, J. 2006. Adjustment of global imbalances and its impact on China's economy. *China and World Economy* 14 (3): 71–85.

Shi, J., and H. Yu. 2005. Renminbi equilibrium exchange rate and China's exchange rate misalignment: 1991–2004. *Economic Research Journal (Jingji Yanjiu),* 40 (4): 34–45.

Sims, C. 1980. Macroeconomics and reality. *Econometrica* 48:1–48.

Sims, C., J. Stock, and M. Watson. 1990. Inference in linear time series models with some unit roots. *Econometrica* 58 (1): 113–44.

Van Wijnbergen, S. V. 1986. Exchange rate management and stabilization policies in developing countries. *Journal of Development Economics* 23:227–47.

Comment   Ashvin Ahuja

Shi's main contribution is in his measurement of the extent to which the RMB-USD exchange rate movement can affect important macroeconomic aggregates in China. In this regard, his handling of the data is careful and the result useful to Chinese policymakers.

The results he obtains also gives observers an idea why China's policy-

Alvin Ahuja is a senior economist at the Bank of Thailand.
Comment read at the 17th East Asian Seminar on Economics on "International Financial Issues Around the Pacific Rim," held on June 22–24, 2006 at Kona, Hawaii.

makers are so reluctant to let the RMB float more in the short run. Shi's approach is as solid as can be expected from the classical econometric method of enquiry, given the time series limitation. Since the chapter has a nice summary of the history of the exchange rate regimes of China and of the main results, I will focus on policy implication and the robustness of the results with suggestion for further research.

How much should China revalue or let the RMB appreciate is the central issue in Asia and the world today. China and its currency are part and parcel of the global imbalances issue, and the relevance to Asian central banks is beyond question. When a relatively large trading nation such as China pegs, other central banks are forced to intervene in the foreign exchange market quite extensively as well, regardless of their appetite for such activity. This is evident in the pace at which Asian central banks accumulated international reserves, starting from 2002.

The chapter does not offer an extensive policy prescription for the Chinese policymakers on what they should do with the RMB exchange rate going forward. Having the economy grow briskly with price stability has helped lift millions out of poverty and raise the welfare of most ordinary Chinese citizens. Essentially, there is a strong case for China to be cautious about letting the nominal peg go. It needs to carry the public with it on the road of market reform. An economic slowdown that lasts longer than necessary can put those reforms at risk. Shi makes this important point. On a more palpable level, as a dollar peg is one way to anchor inflation expectations in China, a legitimate question is: what is the implication of leaving the peg or revaluation on inflation? Would it imply deflation? From Shi's conclusion, price stability would not be compromised.

There are policy implications for Asian regional economies as well. In Asia, one concern is the slowdown in the People's Republic of China (PRC) if the revaluation takes place, but there is also another in the excessive accumulation of U.S. dollars (USD), which can make regional economies more vulnerable when large USD correction comes. Also, Chinese and other Asian central banks' dollar reserves buildup has become increasingly harder to sterilize fully: the sterilization costs have mounted alongside shrinking central bank profits when measured in dollar terms; a politically important issue in some countries.

At issue may be not only whether RMB revaluation is contractionary to China, but also how much of an impact it makes on the regional economies in the short run. The answer may depend on the timing: if it takes place soon, when confidence is strong, capital is still flowing in, short-term foreign debt is small and reserves are large, the fallout could be more limited, for example. So, the timing matters a great deal. Taking these standard variables into account, the model used seems unable to give insight to the appropriate timing issue.

The approach Shi takes is quite standard and expected from the first serious attempt to answer his well-posed question. But as a reader, I am left with doubt when it comes to a methodology that does not recognize the importance of the difference between structural relationships between economic variables and reduced-form variables. I am also uncomfortable with a model that suggests that currency appreciation is usually contractionary or associates depreciation with expansionary phases, regardless of the underlying shocks or economic and financial structure. We have plenty of examples whereby such associations only exist under specific contexts, as acknowledged in the paper itself.

I would also like to see subsequent work asking the same question, but using an alternative approach, by now standard, which is founded on microeconomic behavior of economic agents and uses the language of general equilibrium. It would allow us to probe the question in a deeper way and be more certain that the Chinese do not make systematic errors in reacting to (or anticipating) different policies over time. We could study the underlying forces or disturbances that may affect the Chinese GDP and the RMB in different ways from both the supply and demand sides. These underlying shocks may also be faced with other regional economies within the same timeframe. The policy implications may be drastically different from Shi's under this new approach, as different shocks are modeled and their effects on macroaggregates are studied.

The alternative approach can also afford us an opportunity to explore different policy alternatives under different setups. For instance, under a tightly managed floating system used in China, what is the implication on economic resiliency (how costly it is to the economy before it gets to a new equilibrium) when domestic prices and nominal wages are flexible or not so flexible? Theory predicts that a recession should be quick and less painful when prices are flexible. In the context of this unknown (not measured or documented in the paper, at least) flexibility of nominal wage-price contracts in China, how efficient or how long will it take Chinese farms and firms to adjust to an exchange rate shock? This, to me, seems central to the analysis and a policymaker's decision.

I'd also expect to see different policy responses if the government targets some sector's prosperity in particular. For instance, commodity (e.g., farm product) prices may be set differently in China from manufacturing tradables, for example. Shi's approach has its limit. However, policymakers' decision to allow appreciation at a faster pace may depend on pleasing different constituencies at different times. Moreover, we need to have the analysis under different policy alternatives in the United States, European Union, or Japan, which affect what China may do in response.

Overall, I think the chapter is solid, and it accomplishes what it sets out to do. Policymakers should take heed that Shi's model implies costly economic adjustment from RMB appreciation only for a short period of time. With domestic wage-price flexibility, adjustment may also be less painful than Shi's model implies.

Comment   Dante B. Canlas

The chapter of Mr. Jianhuai Shi empirically assesses the output effects of currency revaluation in China using vector autoregression (VAR). To be forthright, Mr. Shi's answer to his question, which is the title of his chapter, is a "Yes."

The chapter departs from two observed imbalances in China's economy. One is external, the other, internal. China is posting a huge trade surplus in relation to the United States and other major trading partners. At the same time, China is experiencing some serious inflation pressure. In view of these twin imbalances, the exchange value of the renminbi (RMB) has been placed squarely in the policy hot seat.

The United States, in particular, is pressuring China to revalue the renminbi in an effort to scale up China's imports. At this stage, however, China's policymakers in charge of monetary policy are hesitating to do so for fear of inducing an output contraction. Instead, China is offering to tax its exports, ease capital controls, and adjust interest rates.

In aid of resolving the policy debate, Shi opens up a VAR-based investigation of the output effects of the RMB's revaluation using time series data for the period 1991Q1–2005Q3. Mr. Shi conducts the requisite tests—unit root and co-integration—and proceeds to estimate impulse-response functions. One of the results worth highlighting is the GDP decline from a contemporaneous shock to RMB's real exchange value. This result, according to Shi's results, wanes after 12 quarters. Granger causality tests confirm that the effects run from the RMB shock to GDP.

One question that arises as a matter of course from the VAR results is this: How much of the knowledge generated from the VAR tests translates into knowledge about the proper conduct of exchange-rate based stabilization? In other words, do VAR tests have the power to discriminate among alternative exchange-rate adjustment rules that would allow people in charge of monetary policy to determine the most effective rule for stabilization?

This is doubtful even if after doing a decomposition-of-variance analysis, the researcher is able to rank-order the contribution of various shocks to the variance of a particular variable, say, GDP. If VAR tests have the power to discriminate, then Mr. Shi should have been more definite about his policy recommendations. For example, would he have concluded the

Dante B. Canlas is a professor of economics at the University of the Philippines.

following: "First of all, the conclusion that revaluations are contractionary in China does not mean that China would continue maintaining RMB exchange rate undervalued"? But who is the policymaker in China who is sufficiently brave to engineer a revaluation after being appraised by the best technical minds that such an action would be contractionary?

What I'm trying to do here is counsel caution in extracting policy recommendation from the results of the VAR tests. If one is bent on deriving appropriate exchange-rate adjustment measures in China, additional analytical work is indicated on other real factors that are causing the twin imbalances. Labor-market factors, for instance, deserve to be looked into. It is clear that political debates are being fueled by claims of a massive export of jobs to China, an issue that ultimately finds its way into the RMB exchange-rate debate. Neglect of aggregate labor-market variables like the real and money wage results in specification errors that ought to be rectified theoretically and empirically.

II

Monetary Policy and Exchange Rates

4

The Relationship between Openness and Inflation in NIEs and the G7

Chung-Shu Wu and Jin-Lung Lin

4.1 Introduction

Investigating a sample of 114 countries, Romer (1993) found a significant negative relationship between openness and inflation. For a cross-section data set that covers so many countries, it is difficult for a researcher to understand the economic situation of every country in the sample set. If the set includes some countries that have a special economic structure, the empirical results might be significantly distorted. In this paper, we investigate the relatively familiar economies, such as Newly Industrialized Economies (NIEs) and the G7, to verify the robustness of Romer's findings. Our empirical results show that openness and inflation do not have a regular relationship as stated by Romer (1993).

Romer (1993) interpreted his findings by using the time consistency theory of inflation, which states that in the more open economies the inflation caused by a surprising monetary expansion will be higher. Therefore, the monetary authorities in these countries tend to follow a more conservative policy than those of less open economies. Since this argument has important implications not only on the validity of time consistency policy, but also on economic cooperation and integration, many researchers have followed his footsteps and continue discussing the relationship between openness and inflation. Among them, Lane (1997) built a small open economy model which has a monopolistic distortion and nominal price rigidity in

Chung-Shu Wu is a professor of finance at National Dong Hwa University, and a professor of economics at National Chengchi University and at National Taiwan University. Jin-Lung Lin is a professor of finance at National Dong Hwa University.

The authors thank Peter B. Hendry, Andrew K. Rose, John Simon and the other conference participants for their valuable comments and suggestions. Chih-Ping Fan provided excellent research assistance.

the nontraded sector to illustrate that the gains at a surprising monetary expansion are lower in a more open economy. In his empirical results, Lane also found a significant inverse relationship between openness and inflation. However, by dividing Romer's sample into four groups of countries according to the indebtedness level, Terra (1998) found a significant negative relationship between openness and inflation only in the severely indebted countries. Moreover, using a variety of measures of the trade-off between output and inflation (the slope of the Phillips curve), Temple (2002) could not find a stable correlation between the trade-off and openness, which cast doubts about the argument raised by Romer (1993).

Although the literature does not reflect a consensus about the relationship between openness and inflation, most derived their results based on a period averaged cross-section data. It is clear that a country's openness or inflation may vary dramatically during a certain period. To represent a country's characteristics by period averaged indexes may not reflect the actual phenomenon. Moreover, traditionally, researchers use the share of imports in GDP or GNP as a proxy for openness. It is quite possible that some countries have a very high imports share because of geographical or other reasons, and have low inflation due to other factors (which may or may not be explained by the time consistency theory). If we include these data into a sample that does not have a regular relationship between openness and inflation, it is very likely for us to find a spurious "significant relationship" result. However, it is not because the theory is right, but because we have not taken into account the problem of extreme value. To compare the empirical results between Romer (1993) and Temple (2002), it can be noted that the difference may result from excluding some countries with special property.[1] In this paper, we use a panel data set that includes some NIE countries (Hong Kong, Korea, Mexico, Philippines, Singapore, and Taiwan) and the G7 (Canada, France, Germany, Italy, Japan, U.K. and the United States)[2] to reinvestigate the relationship between openness and inflation. Since the number of countries under investigation is only thirteen, it is relatively easy for us to go through the patterns of openness and inflation of each country. Therefore, we can check the robustness of our empirical results with regard to the extreme value problem. In addition, using the panel data, we can verify the time consistency theory by examining the corollary of the theory that the effect of a monetary expansion on output is smaller in a more open economy.

The rest of the paper is organized as follows. Section 4.2 describes the historical patterns of openness and inflation of NIEs and the G7. Section 4.3 investigates the relationship between openness and inflation using an-

1. Countries with high openness and low inflation, such as Singapore and Lesotho, are not included in the sample set of Temple (2002).
2. Since we run the time series regression in the latter part of this paper, we select the countries that have a complete quarterly data before 1990.

nual panel data. The empirical results of a time series approach to the relationship for each individual country are presented in section 4.4. In section 4.5 we adopt a VAR analysis to examine the impacts of money supply on output in order to check the corollary of Romer's model (1993). Section 4.6 offers some conclusions.

4.2   Historical Patterns of Openness and Inflation of NIEs and the G7

The historical patterns of imports (imports/GDP), shares, and the annual growth rate of the GDP deflator of thirteen countries are plotted in figure 4.1 and figure 4.2. From figure 4.1 it can be noticed that some countries such as Canada, Hong Kong, Italy, Korea, the Philippines, Taiwan, and the United States have a significant upward trend for imports shares. However, some countries like Japan, Singapore, and United Kingdom the imports shares do not show an obvious trend.[3] Nevertheless, to our knowledge, Japan and Singapore have been steadily opening their capital market and restructuring their tariff system. The import shares seemingly cannot appropriately reflect the actual openness conditions for those countries. Moreover, it can be seen from table 4.1 that compared to the G7 countries, the NIEs have a relatively high imports share. Especially for Hong Kong and Singapore, their periods of averaged import shares are as high as 89.6 percent and 152.2 percent respectively. Since Hong Kong is an international harbor and Singapore is a city country, it is not strange for them to have such high imports shares.

If we compare the openness and inflation in the NIEs, it is easily noticed that Singapore, who has the highest openness but enjoys the lowest inflation, is the standard model that fulfills the argument of time consistency theory. However, there exist some cases that are not satisfied by the theory. Hong Kong has a much higher openness than Taiwan, yet its inflation is higher than Taiwan. If we examine the relationship among the G7 countries, we can find the same phenomena. For some comparisons, they accord with Romer's findings, such as Germany vs. Italy, and Canada vs. France. In contrast, some comparisons do not fit the theory, for example, the United Kingdom vs. the United States, and France vs. Japan. If we compare the two different regions' countries, it is easy to find some Asian countries like Hong Kong and Korea whose openness is higher than most the G7 countries, but also have higher inflation, contradicting the time consistency theory.

There are many reasons to account for the contradiction. For example, it can be seen from table 4.1 that Taiwan has a lower inflation than Hong

---

3. Different definitions of openness such as exports/GDP share or (exports + imports)/GDP share have a similar pattern. In addition, the empirical results of this paper are robust with regard to the opening definition.

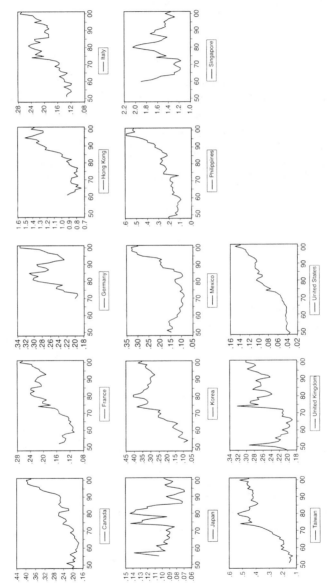

Fig. 4.1   Historical patterns of imports/GDP shares of thirteen countries

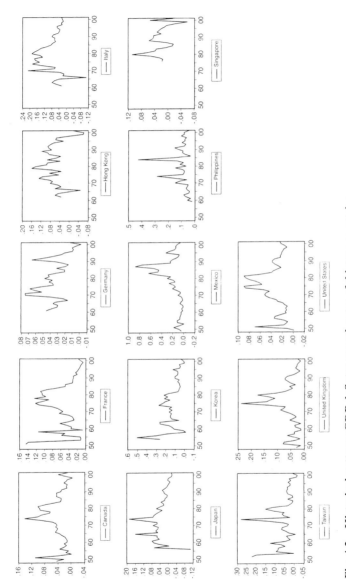

Fig. 4.2   Historical patterns GDP deflator growth rates of thirteen countries

Table 4.1   Related indexes of openness and inflation of thirteen countries (%)

	RIM	REX	DPGDP	DCPI
Singapore	152.23	119.86	3.16	3.19
Hong Kong	89.60	98.34	6.99	7.23
Taiwan	31.41	32.14	6.61	5.84
Korea	24.62	18.71	15.31	10.88
Philippines	19.32	17.70	9.98	7.95
Mexico	12.25	12.49	18.64	18.20
Germany	25.54	27.02	3.88	2.76
United Kingdom	23.67	23.10	6.58	6.36
Canada	21.50	22.09	4.85	4.51
Italy	17.30	16.29	9.55	6.96
France	16.72	16.72	6.52	6.28
Japan	10.54	11.51	4.94	5.35
United States	7.16	6.78	3.82	4.02

Source: International Financial Statistics, August 2005, IMF.

Note: In order to compare with the empirical results of Romer (1993), the period of average annual growth rate is from the beginning of each country's variable for which the data is available to 1990.

Kong and Korea. One of the factors that can be attributed to the low inflation is that in the late 1940s Taiwan experienced a hyperinflation period during which the whole country suffered.[4] Since then, the Taiwanese government has paid close attention to inflation when conducting monetary or fiscal policy. As for Singapore, from figure 4.2 we can see that in the mid-1980s Singapore's economy experienced a three to four year economic recession, which caused a serious deflation. Therefore, if we use the period's averaged inflation rate to represent the inflation condition, a country that experienced deflation naturally would have a lower inflation. However, deflation is not a desire of the Singapore central bank (Monetary Authority of Singapore). A similar situation also existed in the mid 1980s in the Hong Kong economy.

From the above discussion, it can be noted that the extent of one country's openness is determined by geographic condition, traditional culture, and economic development policy, among other factors. The difference of inflation among countries also is determined by many factors that may or may not be related to time consistence theory. If we investigate the relationship between openness and inflation without taking into account these factors, we may obtain a misleading result. By using a period of averaged data that includes a period containing an abnormal event, we may have a wrong description about country's monetary policy, which may seriously distort the interpretation of empirical results.

4. In early 1920s Germany also experienced a hyperinflation episode.

4.3   Empirical Analysis of Panel Data

From figure 4.1 it can be seen that the openness (imports/GDP) of some countries have an obvious increasing trend. If an inverse relationship exists between openness and inflation, the empirical result will be enhanced by using panel data. In this section we analyze the panel data of thirteen countries to verify the relationship.[5] In order to compare, we adopt the empirical model suggested by Romer (1993) which is of the form:

$$\pi_{it} = a_0 + a_1 OPEN_{i,t} + a_2 y_{i,t} + \varepsilon_{i,t}, \quad i = 1, 2, \ldots, 11 \quad t = 1, 2, \ldots, n,$$

where π_{it} is country i's inflation at period t; $OPEN_{i,t}$ is country i's openness at period t, which is measured by imports/GDP share; and $y_{i,t}$ is country i's real per capita Gross Domestic Product at period t.

Table 4.2 shows the empirical results of panel data regression of thirteen countries. Since we argue that each country has its own characteristics concerning inflation, we include different constant terms for different countries. Column (1) is the model proposed by Romer (1993). It can be seen that in most cases there exist a positive instead of negative sign for openness, though the per capita real output and real growth rate have the right signs.[6] In addition, this result is robust to different openness, inflation definitions and estimating periods.[7] If we compare our empirical model with Romer (1993), the only difference is that we take into account different constant terms. In order to check whether it is appropriate to restrict those constant terms to be the same, we do a Wald test for the restriction. The result shows, for all cases, a significant rejection of the null hypothesis that those constants are the same. However, for verifying that imposing the constant constraint will result in different coefficient estimates for openness, we re-estimate our model and show the empirical results in table 4.3. It is surprising to find from the table that if we constrain the constant terms to be the same, the sign on openness is consistent with Romer's argument, that is, openness and inflation have an inverse relationship.

By dividing the sample into developing and developed countries, Romer (1993) found that the inverse relation between openness and inflation is significant in developing countries, but insignificant in developed countries.

5. The data of NIEs and The G7 have different properties. Quarterly data from NIEs are seasonally unadjusted, whereas data from The G7 is seasonally adjusted. In order to avoid the seasonality problem, we use the annual data to engage in panel estimation.

6. Romer (1993) chose real per capita income to serve as a general measure of development. However, this variable has a different order from other variables such as inflation or imports share. Therefore, we use the change of real GDP as an alternative.

7. In the Romer (1993) paper, he adopted the imports/GDP share to represent a country's openness. In order to check the robustness of empirical results, we have tried various measures of openness, such as exports/GDP share, and (imports + exports)/GDP share, and the empirical results are similar. Though Hsu & Wu (1993) pointed out that the dynamic structure of the wholesale price index is different from the consumer price index, in this paper we have estimated the case of the wholesale price index and achieved similar results.

Table 4.2   Panel regression of NIEs and G7 (without constant restriction)

| | Period (1973~1999) | | | | Period (1973~2001) | | | |
| | DPGDP | | DCPI | | DPGDP | | DCPI | |
Variable	(1)	(2)	(3)	(4)	(5)	(6)	(7)	(8)
C_CA	0.6364	0.0070	0.6353	−0.0026	0.1445	0.0321	0.1453	0.0357
C_FRA	0.6468	0.0271	0.6444	0.0162	0.1448	0.0428	0.1432	0.0435
C_GER	0.5770	−0.0214	0.5718	−0.0349	0.1238	0.0193	0.1193	0.0174
C_HK	0.5638	−0.1147	0.5040	−0.1830	0.2396	0.0463	0.2398	0.0559
C_ITA	0.7071	0.0718	0.6962	0.0522	0.1825	0.0791	0.1747	0.0737
C_JAP	0.5945	−0.0008	0.6029	0.0001	0.1054	0.0076	0.1109	0.0150
C_SING	0.4047	−0.2768	0.3307	−0.3628	0.2407	0.0103	0.2322	0.0129
C_SKOR	0.6214	0.0172	0.5874	−0.0242	0.1963	0.0550	0.1749	0.0377
C_ME	1.1181	0.0246	1.1215	0.0216	0.3782	0.0269	0.3767	0.0358
C_PH	0.5899	0.0634	0.5883	0.0547	0.1967	0.0938	0.1948	0.0949
C_TW	0.5134	−0.0659	0.5036	−0.0829	0.1501	0.0020	0.1522	0.0088
C_UK	0.6574	0.0399	0.6531	0.0270	0.1661	0.0611	0.1642	0.0617
C_US	0.6410	0.0168	0.6529	0.0205	0.1214	0.0204	0.1281	0.0290
RIM	0.0964**	0.1489***	0.1416***	0.1974***	−0.0980**	−0.0288	−0.0936*	−0.0295
	(2.5315)	(3.4162)	(2.9468)	(2.8503)	(−2.4318)	(−0.8696)	(−1.8599)	(−0.7664)
ARGDP	−0.0592**		−0.0600		−0.0068		−0.0067	
	(−2.5478)		(−2.4439)**		(−0.7469)		(−0.7064)	
DGDP		0.7941***		0.7826***		0.8189***		0.7909***
		(6.6540)		(6.1663)		(9.2430)		(7.9405)
$\bar{R}^2$	0.6085	0.6943	0.5724	0.6421	0.4207	0.6656	0.3963	0.6179

Notes: T-statistics based on robust standard errors are in parenthesis; C_X represents the constant term in X country; RIM is the imports/GDP share; ARGDP is the real per capita GDP; DGDP is the annual average.

*Significant at the 10 percent level.

**Significant at the 5 percent level.

***Significant at the 1 percent level.

Table 4.3   **Panel regression of NIEs and the G7 (with constant restriction)**

| | Period (1973~1990) | | | | Period (1973~2001) | | | |
| | DPGDP | | DCPI | | DPGDP | | DCPI | |
Variable	(1)	(2)	(3)	(4)	(5)	(6)	(7)	(8)
C	-0.1317**	0.0634***	-0.1281*	-0.0636***	-0.0399	0.0451***	-0.0470	0.0454***
	(-2.0083)	(8.3244)	(-1.8071)	(8.1081)	(-0.6855)	(8.0426)	(-0.7747)	(7.8809)
RIM	-0.0300***	-0.0429***	-0.0357***	-0.0470***	-0.0339***	-0.0387***	-0.0346***	-0.0385***
	(-3.1066)	(-6.2503)	(-3.8907)	(-6.4646)	(-4.2782)	(-6.7348)	(-4.8026)	(-6.5716)
ARGDP	0.0253***		0.0249***		0.0135**		0.0142**	
	(3.6730)		(3.3384)		(2.1964)		(2.2075)	
DGDP		0.7588***		0.7512***		0.7764***		0.7616***
		(12.1504)		(10.6919)		(13.8723)		(11.7866)
$\bar{R}^2$	0.1051	0.6238	0.1053	0.5883	0.0476	0.6048	0.0507	0.5720

*Significant at the 10 percent level.
**Significant at the 5 percent level.
***Significant at the 1 percent level.

In tables 4.4 and 4.5 we restrict the constant and estimate two different groups, which are NIEs and the G7. From the tables we can see that openness has a significant negative relationship with inflation for NIEs, but have mixed results for the G7. For the period between 1973 and 1990, which is the same sample period used as Romer, the sign on imports/GDP share is positive rather than negative in the case of the G7, and this result is consistent with Romer. However, when we extend our sample period to 2001, the sign on imports share of the G7 become insignificantly different from zeros. To check the robustness of the empirical results with regard to constant restriction, we re-estimate the models and summarize the results in table 4.6 and table 4.7. It can be seen from the tables that the signs on imports share for NIEs are no longer significantly negative. On the contrary, for some cases they have a significant positive sign. As for the G7 countries, the empirical results for those without restriction on constants are similar to the cases with restriction. It can be noted that in the case of included constant terms the coefficients on imports share of the G7 are significantly negative in the extended period. This result may be because a country, like Germany, has a relatively high openness but experiences a sharp declining of inflation due to a weakening economy.

It can be noted from table 4.1 that Singapore is the country with the highest period averaged openness and the lowest period averaged inflation among the Asian 4. If we regard it as an outlier and take it out of the sample, in tables 4.8 and 4.9 it can be shown that even with a constant constraint, in most cases the openness has an insignificant sign.[8]

From the above discussion, it is quite clear that the empirical result of the relationship between openness and inflation is sensitive to the model selection and sample set. Under the more flexible models without constant constraint, or by eliminating the country with special characteristics, Romer's argument is not supported.

4.4 Time Series Approach

It can be seen from figure 4.1 that some countries such as Hong Kong, Korea, Taiwan, Canada, France, Italy, and the United States have an upward trend of imports share. Theoretically, they are good examples for verifying the relationship between openness and inflation by using the time series.[9]

From table 4.10 we show the empirical results of time series regression for the inflation model of each individual country. It can be seen that only few cases—France, United Kingdom, and Mexico—show a significant

8. Romer (1993) in footnote 8 pointed out that "re-estimating the regression with Singapore and Lesotho excluded, however, lowers the t-statistic on openness only modestly." Nevertheless, our empirical results show a different aspect.

9. We include seasonal dummies into the model whose data is seasonally unadjusted, and only dummies significantly different from zeroes are reported in tables.

Table 4.4   **Panel regression of NIEs (with constant restriction)**

	Period (1973~1990)				Period (1973~2001)			
	DPGDP		DCPI		DPGDP		DCPI	
Variable	(1)	(2)	(3)	(4)	(5)	(6)	(7)	(8)
C	-0.0379	0.0739***	-0.0437	0.0679***	-0.0459	0.0594***	-0.0564	0.0537***
	(-0.5452)	(3.3118)	(-0.5796)	(2.8139)	(-0.8522)	(3.6660)	(-0.9584)	(3.1332)
RIM	-0.1015***	-0.0539***	-0.1003***	-0.0536***	-0.1038***	-0.0510***	-0.0988***	-0.0464***
	(-5.0950)	(-3.8102)	(-5.1805)	(-3.6955)	(-6.4325)	(-4.6771)	(-6.2728)	(-4.1690)
ARGDP	0.0248***		0.0250***		0.0234***		0.0240***	
	(3.2535)		(3.0032)		(3.6404)		(3.4073)	
DGDP		0.7613***		0.7684***		0.7661***		0.7691***
		(9.3190)		(8.6769)		(10.5168)		(9.7068)
$\bar{R}^2$	0.2494	0.6985	0.2317	0.6544	0.2478	0.6889	0.2300	0.6528

*Significant at the 10 percent level.
**Significant at the 5 percent level.
***Significant at the 1 percent level.

Table 4.5 **Panel regression of the G7 (with constant restriction)**

| | Period (1973–1990) | | | | Period (1973–2001) | | | |
| | DPGDP | | DCPI | | DPGDP | | DCPI | |
Variable	(1)	(2)	(3)	(4)	(5)	(6)	(7)	(8)
C	−0.2873*	0.0659***	−0.1904	0.0782***	0.2061*	0.0468***	0.2606**	0.0597***
	(−1.8198)	(5.0160)	(−1.1688)	(5.4828)	(1.8324)	(4.7452)	(2.2700)	(5.8653)
RIM	0.1382**	0.1092**	0.1133**	0.0727	0.0433	0.0483	0.0159	0.0201
	(2.5183)	(2.0620)	(1.9872)	(1.3010)	(1.1519)	(1.2726)	(0.4298)	(0.5431)
ARGDP	0.0337**		0.0245		−0.0163		−0.0210*	
	(2.1526)		(1.5165)		(−1.4622)		(−1.8661)	
DGDP		−0.5089**		−0.6578***		−0.1466		−0.3748**
		(−2.2406)		(−3.0805)		(−0.7973)		(−2.0074)
$\bar{R}^2$	0.0905	0.0801	0.0482	0.1018	0.0102	0.0015	0.0145	0.0213

*Significant at the 10 percent level.
**Significant at the 5 percent level.
***Significant at the 1 percent level.

Table 4.6   Panel regression of NIEs (without constant restriction)

| Variable | Period (1973~1990) | | | | Period (1973~2001) | | | |
| | DPGDP | | DCPI | | DPGDP | | DCPI | |
	(1)	(2)	(3)	(4)	(5)	(6)	(7)	(8)
C_HK	0.6047	-0.1092	0.5505	-0.1547	0.1893	0.0201	0.1759	0.0268
C_SING	0.4469	-0.2622	0.3847	-0.3162	0.1839	-0.0259	0.1631	-0.0250
C_SKOR	0.6564	0.0147	0.6198	-0.0211	0.1613	0.0438	0.1328	0.0252
C_ME	1.1677	-0.0080	1.1632	-0.0141	0.3376	0.0026	0.3280	0.0063
C_PH	0.6220	0.0635	0.6174	0.0593	0.1656	0.0849	0.1573	0.0853
C_TW	0.5469	-0.0672	0.5362	-0.0765	0.1140	-0.0116	0.1088	-0.0061
RIM	0.0914**	0.1364***	0.1256**	0.1652**	-0.0814*	-0.0087	-0.0729	-0.0090
	(2.2842)	(2.9550)	(2.4744)	(2.2842)	(-1.9205)	(-0.2485)	(-1.3454)	(-0.2186)
ARGDP	-0.0630**		-0.0631**		-0.0035		-0.0028	
	(-2.4641)		(-2.3326)		(-0.3532)		(-0.2685)	
DGDP		0.8798***		0.8821***		0.8838***		0.8720***
		(8.5288)		(7.7941)		(11.3144)		(9.9555)
$\bar{R}^2$	0.6031	0.7379	0.5667	0.6863	0.3972	0.7303	0.3795	0.6883

*Significant at the 10 percent level.
**Significant at the 5 percent level.
***Significant at the 1 percent level.

Table 4.7   Panel regression of the G7 (without constant restriction)

| | Period (1973~1990) | | | | Period (1973~2001) | | | |
| | DPGDP | | DCPI | | DPGDP | | DCPI | |
Variable	(1)	(2)	(3)	(4)	(5)	(6)	(7)	(8)
C_CA	0.1799	0.0480	0.2247	0.0122	0.5379	0.1151	0.5645	0.1030
C_FRA	0.1955	0.0600	0.2424	0.0260	0.5267	0.1067	0.5546	0.0950
C_GER	0.1365	0.0077	0.1709	−0.0360	0.5076	0.0936	0.5290	0.0755
C_ITA	0.2461	0.1087	0.2862	0.0663	0.5674	0.1436	0.5897	0.1261
C_JAP	0.1750	0.0503	0.2422	0.0422	0.4590	0.0535	0.5000	0.0598
C_UK	0.2021	0.0676	0.2396	0.0239	0.5563	0.1355	0.5806	0.1192
C_US	0.1960	0.0562	0.2736	0.0519	0.4880	0.0678	0.5314	0.0750
RIM	0.1941	0.1536	0.3690**	0.3257**	−0.2816***	−0.2293***	−0.2193***	−0.1483*
	(1.2938)	(1.0439)	(2.2399)	(2.0121)	(−3.9141)	(−2.8578)	(−3.1322)	(−1.8755)
ARGDP	−0.0159		−0.0244		−0.0410***		−0.0451***	
	(−1.0274)		(−1.5335)		(−4.3543)		(−4.6446)	
DGDP		−0.5098***		−0.6449***		−0.0466		−0.3142*
		(−2.6928)		(−3.5350)		(−0.2652)		(−1.8222)
$\bar{R}^2$	0.3562	0.4007	0.3063	0.3742	0.2732	0.2018	0.2344	0.1647

*Significant at the 10 percent level.
**Significant at the 5 percent level.
***Significant at the 1 percent level.

Table 4.8   Panel regression of twelve countries with constant restriction (excludes Singapore)

Variable	Period (1973~1990)				Period (1973~2001)			
	DPGDP		DCPI		DPGDP		DCPI	
	(1)	(2)	(3)	(4)	(5)	(6)	(7)	(8)
C	-0.1410**	0.0572***	-0.1368**	0.0562***	-0.0497	0.0405	-0.0560	0.0395***
	(-2.1772)	(6.8069)	(-1.9769)	(6.3620)	(-0.8501)	(6.5016)***	(-0.9217)	(6.2217)
RIM	-0.0117	-0.0190	-0.0193	-0.0178	-0.0256*	-0.0215	-0.0261*	-0.0172
	(-0.6067)	(-1.2245)	(-0.8664)	(-0.8414)	(-1.8275)	(-1.9254)*	(-1.9136)	(-1.4431)
ARGDP	0.0258***		0.0254***		0.0144**		0.0149**	
	(3.7817)		(3.4627)		(2.3226)		(2.3119)	
DGDP		0.7624***		0.7578***		0.7814***		0.7708***
		(12.1270)		(10.8043)		(13.9304)		(12.0216)
$\bar{R}^2$	0.0847	0.6193	0.0804	0.5827	0.0316	0.6037	0.0327	0.5715

*Significant at the 10 percent level.
**Significant at the 5 percent level.
***Significant at the 1 percent level.

Table 4.9 Panel regression of NIEs with constant restriction (excludes Singapore)

	Period (1973–1990)				Period (1973–2001)			
	DPGDP		DCPI		DPGDP		DCPI	
Variable	(1)	(2)	(3)	(4)	(5)	(6)	(7)	(8)
C	0.0916	0.1324***	0.2836	0.1866***	0.3712***	0.0811***	0.4494***	0.0979***
	(0.5206)	(4.2789)	(1.3338)	(5.0487)	(2.8717)	(3.9495)	(3.4202)	(4.3981)
RIM	−0.0197	−0.0228	0.0298	−0.0349	0.0090	−0.0259	0.0385	−0.0183
	(−0.4426)	(−0.6896)	(0.5509)	(−0.9015)	(0.3539)	(−1.3099)	(1.5067)	(−0.8746)
ARGDP	0.0015		−0.0245		−0.0333**		−0.0447***	
	(0.0709)		(−0.9397)		(−2.1948)		(−2.8963)	
DGDP		−0.3236		−1.1095***		0.0997		−0.3352
		(−1.2613)		(−3.4587)		(0.5368)		(−1.5845)
$\bar{R}^2$	−0.0336	−0.0025	−0.0260	0.1847	0.0550	0.0042	0.0793	0.0095

*Significant at the 10 percent level.
**Significant at the 5 percent level.
***Significant at the 1 percent level.

Table 4.10   Time series regression for each individual country

Dependent variable: DPGDP; period: 1968:Q1–1990:Q4

Variable	Hong Kong	Korea	Mexico	Philippines	Singapore	Taiwan	Canada	France	Germany	Italy	Japan	United Kingdom	United States
C	-0.0746 (-0.1242)	0.5127** (2.0948)	6.4206*** (3.8672)	-0.7722 (-0.7069)	-0.4522 (-1.5407)	0.4895*** (2.9592)	0.1550 (0.3904)	3.0077** (2.5920)	0.8438*** (3.4831)	0.5590*** (3.5515)	-0.5941*** (-3.0361)	0.3053 (0.4526)	-0.1404 (-0.4996)
RIM	-0.06341 (-1.0304)	-0.1243 (-1.5757)	-1.3701*** (-3.3842)	-0.0313 (-0.1756)	0.1205*** (5.0950)	0.2187*** (3.4860)	0.1588* (1.7417)	-0.2082* (-1.7626)	-0.1237 (-1.3726)	-0.3337 (-1.0405)	0.8307*** (3.5647)	-0.2376* (-1.7528)	0.2436** (2.4662)
RGDP	0.0229 (0.3862)	-0.0246 (-1.4861)	-0.5696*** (-3.6737)	0.0880 (0.7503)	0.0216 (0.9902)	-0.0511*** (-3.0262)	-0.0136 (-0.3404)	-0.2802** (-2.4821)	-0.0864*** (-3.0801)	-0.0253*** (-6.3254)	0.0370*** (2.8647)	-0.0218 (-0.2520)	0.0167 (0.5906)
DUM11	0.0517** (2.7929)												
DUM21		0.1063*** (3.3553)											
DUM41						0.0841*** (5.0614)							
DUM42				0.4976*** (3.0106)		0.0493*** (2.9974)							
S1						0.0073** (2.2113)							
AR(1)		0.5765*** (6.2744)	0.7359*** (6.2101)		0.5436*** (4.4767)	0.9291*** (15.9983)	1.1155*** (25.3718)	1.0720*** (13.3607)	0.7795*** (10.5156)	1.1982*** (13.0128)	0.9377*** (32.9554)	1.1059*** (24.3318)	1.4985*** (19.6544)
AR(2)		0.5232*** (5.5402)											-0.5286*** (-6.9224)
AR(3)		-0.2735*** (-2.9903)						-0.1437* (-1.9449)					
AR(4)						-0.2006 (-3.5642)	-0.1691*** (-3.8555)					-0.1743*** (-3.7736)	
$\bar{R}^2$	0.244	0.721	0.662	0.156	0.753	0.892	0.948	0.936	0.865	0.876	0.819	0.912	0.977
Q_p	0.258	0.703	0.613	0.945	0.278	0.201	0.288	0.474	0.202	0.597	0.394	0.185	0.102

Notes: DUM11 is a dummy variable which sets 1989:Q2 to be one, the other periods to be zeroes; DUM21 is a dummy variable which sets 1963:Q4 to be one, the other periods to be zeroes; DUM41 is a dummy variable which sets 1973:Q4 to 1974:Q3 to be ones, and the other periods to be zeroes; DUM42 is a dummy variable which sets 1980:Q4 to be one, and the other periods to be zeroes; S2 is a seasonal dummy; AR(i) is the ith order serial correlation correction of residual; Q_p represents the significance level of Liung-Box Q statistics.

*Significant at the 10 percent level.

**Significant at the 5 percent level.

***Significant at the 1 percent level.

negative sign on imports share. The cases that have a significant positive sign on imports share outnumber those that have a negative sign. Even countries like Canada, Taiwan, and the United States, who have an upward trend of imports share, also have a significant positive sign on imports share.[10]

Although the empirical cross-section model proposed by Romer (1993) may not be an appropriate empirical model for time series approach, it provides an alternative to verify the relationship between inflation and openness.[11] There is room for improving the time series empirical model, and we believe that different models may have different results. However, under our current framework, we cannot find a strong support for the time consistency theory.

4.5 Money Supply and Real Output

Romer (1993) is based on a partial rigidity price model to derive a reverse relationship between openness and inflation. From that model we can also derive a corollary that the effect that a monetary expansion on output is smaller in a more open economy. Since we have quarterly time series, it is convenient for us to verify this hypothesis. In this section, we adopt the VAR model to do the impulse response analysis to examine the impacts of money supply on real output.[12]

It is well-known that the impulse response analysis may be significantly affected by variable ordering. Pesaran and Shin (1988) proposed a procedure to solve the ordering problem. In this section, we follow the approach of Pesaran and Shin (1988) and Lin (2003) to perform the impulse response analysis. Since variables in our VAR model are stationary (first difference of logarithm money supply and logarithm real GDP), it is appropriate for us to ignore the co-integration issues raised by Phillips (1998).

In figure 4.3 we show the impulse response of money growth on real GDP growth according to the order of degree of openness. From the figure it is difficult to find regularity between openness and the impacts of money supply. Singapore has the highest openness, and its money supply also has the most significant impact on real output among the NIEs. Germany has

---

10. To save space in this paper, we only report the empirical results based on Romer's model in Table 10, and the results are robust to different openness, inflation definitions, and sample periods.

11. Exchange rate is one of the factors that are important determinants of inflation rates. When we incorporate it into the model, the properties of empirical results do not change.

12. Alternatively, we may use transfer function analysis to discuss the dynamic structure between money supply and output. However, in that analysis we have to assume there is no feedback effect between variables, which is inappropriate to our model. See Liu (1987), Liu and Hudak (1985). The VAR impulse response analysis is widely used by researchers to investigate the relationship between malpractice and economy, e.g., Juselius (1998), Oxley (2000), Wu and Hu (2000), Morsink and Bayoumi (2001), and Fung (2002).

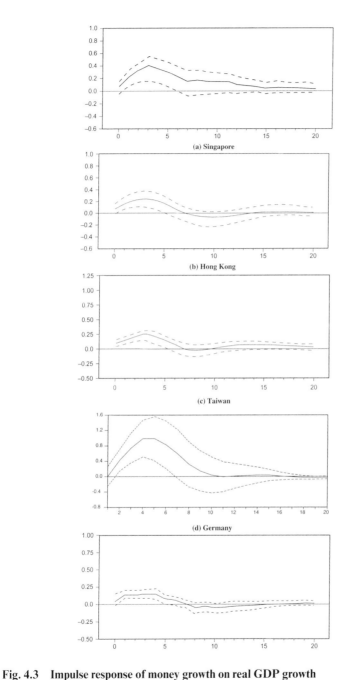

Fig. 4.3   Impulse response of money growth on real GDP growth

Note: (a) Singapore; (b) Hong Kong; (c) Taiwan; (d) Germany; (e) Korea; (f) United Kingdom; (g) Canada; (h) Philippines; (i) Italy; (j) France; (k) Mexico; (l) Japan; (m) United States

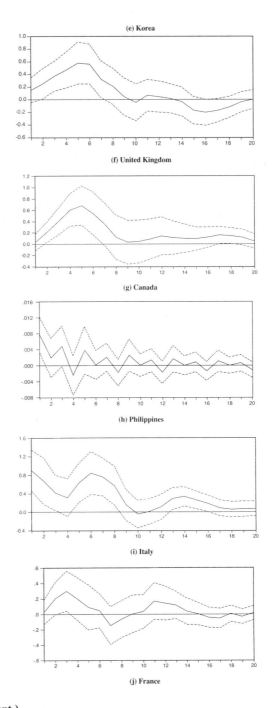

Fig. 4.3 (cont.)

Note: (a) Singapore; (b) Hong Kong; (c) Taiwan; (d) Germany; (e) Korea; (f) United Kingdom; (g) Canada; (h) Philippines; (i) Italy; (j) France; (k) Mexico; (l) Japan; (m) United States

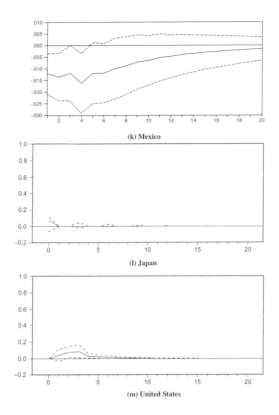

Fig. 4.3   (cont.)

Note: (a) Singapore; (b) Hong Kong; (c) Taiwan; (d) Germany; (e) Korea; (f) United Kingdom; (g) Canada; (h) Philippines; (i) Italy; (j) France; (k) Mexico; (l) Japan; (m) United States

a similar situation as Singapore, which has the highest openness among the G7. However, Germany also has a relatively significant impact of money supply on real output. Interestingly, France, Japan, and the United States, who have a relatively low openness among eleven countries, have a relatively insignificant impact of money supply on real output, which contradicts the corollary derived from Romer (1993).

4.6   Conclusion

Romer (1993, 1998) argued that the more open economies are, the higher cost for them to adopt a stimulative monetary policy, hence they will choose a more conservative policy than less open economies. Therefore, there exists a reverse relationship between openness and inflation. Since one country's openness is determined by geographic condition, historical experience, and economic development policy, among other variables, inflation can be attributed to factors that may or may not be related to time consistency theory. If we investigate the relationship between openness and inflation without taking those factors into account, we may have an inappropriate interpretation of the empirical results. In this paper, we reexamine the relationship by discussing more familiar economies, NIEs and the G7, which can provide us more information about empirical findings.

Our empirical results show that for a panel data set of thirteen countries, models with or without constant constraint give different relationships between openness and inflation. If we restrict the constant terms to be the same, the empirical results are similar to Romer (1993). However, if we relax the restrictions, which are supported by empirical testing, the empirical results do not show a certain relationship between openness and inflation. In addition, leaving out some countries with special structures, the empirical results also change significantly. When we use the time series approach to analyze the relationship between openness and inflation in each individual country, for most cases the negative relationship cannot be supported even in those countries that have an obvious upward trend of imports share. Moreover, we employ a VAR model to check the corollary of Romer (1993) that the affects of money on real output are smaller in a more open economy. From the results of impulse response analyses, we cannot find a regular relationship between openness and the impacts of money supply.

Each country has its own characteristics, including geographic, cultural, and historical background, and through time many factors drive the changing patterns of openness and inflation of each country. It is difficult for a period averaged data to reveal that information, and show a stable regularity between openness and inflation. Though our empirical results are not in accordance with the findings of Romer (1993, 1998), they do not mitigate the importance of the time consistency theory. The primary purpose of this paper is to point out that perhaps researchers should pay more attention to the reasons why openness and inflation have different relationships among different countries, rather than searching for a uniform relationship.

References

Fung, B. S. C. 2002. A VAR analysis of the effects of monetary policy in East Asia. BIS Working Paper no. 119.

Hsu, J. D., and C. S. Wu. 1993. Current prices and policy (in Chinese). Research Report of Research, Development and Evaluation Commission. Taipei, Taiwan: Executive Yuan, pp. 1–151.

Juselius, K. 1998. Changing monetary transmission mechanisms within the EU. *Empirical Economics* 23 (1): 455–81.

Lane, P. R. 1997. Inflation in open economies. *Journal of International Economics* 42:327–47.

Lin, J. L. 2003. An empirical investigating of interest rate policy transmission mechanism and its impacts on macroeconomic and financial system (in Chinese). *Quarterly Journal of Central Bank* 25 (1): 5–47.

Liu, L. M. 1987. Sales forecasting using multi-equation transfer function models. *Journal of Forecasting* 6:223–38.

Liu, L. M., and G. B. Hudak. 1985. Unified econometric model building using simulations transfer function equations. In *Time series analysis: Theory and practice*, vol. 7, ed. O. D. Anderson, 277–88. Amsterdam: Elsevier Science Publishing.

Morsink, J., and Tamim Bayoumi. 2001. A peek inside the black box: The monetary transmission mechanism in Japan. *IMF Staff Papers* 48 (1): 22–57.

Oxley, L. 2000. Identifying an interest rate transmission mechanism for New Zealand. Australasian Econometric Society Meeting, Auckland, July.

Pesaran, H. H., and Y. Sin. 1988. Generalized impulse response analysis in linear multivariate model. *Economic Letters* 58:17–29.

Phillips, P. C. B. 1998. Impulse response and forecast error variance asymptotics in nonstationary VARS. *Journal of Econometrics* 83:21–56.

Romer, D. 1993. Openness and inflation: Theory and evidence. *Quarterly Journal of Economics* 108:869–903.

Romer, D. 1998. A new assessment of openness and inflation: Reply. *Quarterly Journal of Economics* 113:649–52.

Temple, J. 2002. Openness, inflation, and the Phillips curve: A puzzle. *Journal of Money, Credit and Banking* 34 (2): 450–68.

Terra, M. C. T. 1998. Openness and inflation: A new assessment. *Quarterly Journal of Economics* 113:641–48.

Wu, C. S., and S. C. Hu. 2000. Interest rates, credit rationing and banking deregulation in Taiwan. *Deregulation and Interdependence in the Asia-Pacific Region*, ed. T. Ito and A. O. Krueger, 255–76. Chicago: University of Chicago Press.

Comment   Peter Blair Henry

Professors Wu and Lin have provided us with a useful study of openness and inflation. Previous work documents that openness and inflation are negatively correlated across countries (Romer 1993). Wu and Lin take exception with this result and demonstrate that the relationship uncovered by Romer is not robust. In the context of the Newly Industrialized Economies (NIEs) and the Group of Seven (G7), there is no systematic relationship between openness and inflation. More generally, Wu and Lin argue that there are many pitfalls associated with using purely cross-sectional data to study the relationship between openness and inflation, and implicitly warn us not to do so in future work.

The authors begin very sensibly by taking us through the raw data. This is instructive, because it immediately raises questions about Romer's find-

Peter Blair Henry is professor of economics and Gunn Faculty Scholar at Stanford University, Graduate School of Business, a faculty research associate of the National Bureau of Economic Research, and a Nonresident Senior Fellow of the Brookings Institution.

ings, at least within this particular subsample. There are four observations in table 4.1 that do not accord with the view that greater openness is associated with lower inflation: (a) Hong Kong is more open than Taiwan but has had higher inflation than Taiwan; (b) The United Kingdom is more open than the United States but has had higher inflation than the United States; (c) France is more open than Japan but has also had higher inflation than Japan; and (d) Both Hong Kong and South Korea are more open than most G7 countries but have had higher inflation.

Moving beyond the raw data, formal panel regressions also do not show a systematic negative relationship between openness and inflation. Panel data allows the authors to include country-specific dummies to account for sundry differences across countries (culture, geography, etc.) that Romer was not able to account for in his strictly cross-sectional set up. With and without country dummies, Wu and Lin find little evidence to suggest that openness and inflation are negatively correlated. While the authors succeed in their modest aim of demonstrating the fragility of the relationship between openness and inflations in this sample, I have a few quibbles with what they have done.

First, although I am sympathetic to the general point of the paper, I think that it is a little unfair of the authors to make a direct comparison of their study of 13 countries with the Romer study, which has 114. With the 13 countries in the Wu and Lin sample, empirical power is a nontrivial issue, and the question then becomes: is the relationship between openness and inflation really not in the data, or is there simply too much noise to reliably detect its presence?

Second, is this a paper about the time consistency theory of inflation or is it a comparative study of inflation in the NIEs and the G7? If it is the former, then the comments about small sample size in the previous paragraph hold with greater force. If it is a comparative analysis then I would like to know more about the inflation histories of these countries than is conveyed in figure 4.2. For example, is the story behind the fall in inflation in the NIEs similar to that of the great 1980s disinflation that took place in the G7 countries? This kind of institutional focus would add a lot to the paper. The authors convincingly argue that strictly cross-sectional analyses miss important insights conveyed by the heterogeneity of country-specific experiences through time. Indeed, there is much to be learned by reducing sample size and focusing on country experiences. I only wish that the paper would have delivered a bit more in this regard.

Third, I would have liked the paper to be a bit more ambitious. The authors focus exclusively on the time-inconsistency theory of monetary policy that motivated the Romer study. This approach focuses on the insight that in an open economy, policies that stimulate aggregate demand have two offsetting effects. The first effect is that stronger aggregate demand stimulates production and raises national income. The second is that stronger aggregate demand also increases imports, which reduces national income. Because the second effect is not present in a closed economy, expansionary monetary policy has a smaller impact on real output in an open economy than it does in a closed one. Therefore, the incentive for the monetary authority to surprise the public with a monetary expansion is lower in an open economy.

This is a perfectly good theory to test, but it seems to me that there are other important mechanisms through which openness may help to maintain low inflation. In particular, an increasingly popular view is that increased integration of goods and labor markets helps to hold down the worldwide level of inflation, because the threat of global competition reduces the pricing power of firms and the bargaining power of workers (Rogoff 2003). Because the countries in this sample are all active participants in the ongoing process of global economic integration, it would seem natural to test whether any of these other channels have any empirical relevance. For instance, instead of just looking at the correlation between consumer-price-and-deflator-based measures of inflation, why not bring wages into the story? Is it the case that wage growth is slower in more open economies, controlling for things like changes in productivity?

References

Rogoff, K. 2003. Globalization and global disinflation. *Federal Reserve Bank of Kansas City Economic Review* 88 (4): 45–81.
Romer, D. 1993. Openness and inflation: Theory and evidence. *Quarterly Journal of Economics* 108 (4): 869–903.

Comment   John Simon

This paper reinvestigates the results of Romer (1993) and suggests that the negative correlation between openness and inflation found by Romer may not be robust. In my comments I would like to focus on a particular difference between the approach of Romer and Wu and Lin—the use of time series data rather than cross sectional data—and its implications for these findings.

To provide a reference point for my comments I consider the data for Australia shown in figure 4C.1. Openness, measured as the ratio of imports to GDP, is strongly trending and rises from a little under 10 percent in the 1960s to over 20 percent today. Inflation, captured here by the GDP defla-

John Simon is chief manager of the Payments Policy Department of the Reserve Bank of Australia.

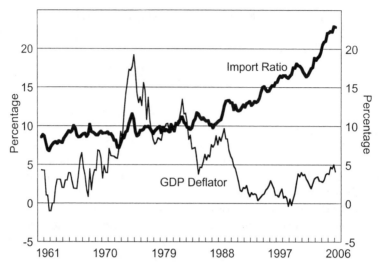

Fig. 4C.1   Inflation and Openness
Source: ABS

tor, was below 5 percent in the 60s, and rose significantly in the 70s before returning below 5 percent in the early 90s. This pattern, if not the specific numbers, is common to many countries. (See figure 4C.1).

The first observation is that time series regressions on this data will have to deal with the integration of the series. Openness is clearly I(1). But there is a question about whether to treat inflation as I(1) or I(0) with breaks. Since the return of low inflation in the early 90s it is I(0). However, when using the full sample its properties are ambiguous, and it can be classified as either I(1) or I(0) depending upon the particular test used. Similarly, tests of cointegration between inflation and openness are ambiguous. Although, once again, it is pretty clear that inflation and openness are not cointegrated over the recent low inflation period (primarily because inflation is not integrated). Given this, interpretation of time series regression results on these variables will be problematic.

A further complication to the interpretation of this relationship is the addition of output per capita to the model. This variable is included in both Romer and Wu and Lin as a control for openness on the argument that richer countries trade more. But from an econometric point of view, the relevant point is that it is a strongly trending series. A long run relationship between inflation and openness could be obtained if openness and output per capita were cointegrated and inflation was I(0), or a more complicated cointegrating relationship between all three variables may exist. Regardless, I think the paper would benefit from careful attention to these issues.

Related to the use of output per capita is the question of whether it is the best control for openness. There is a large literature on the expected amount of trade between various countries. And while output per capita is an important variable, it is not the only one used. For example, geographic location has an effect on trade. The appropriate variables to use will be affected by the panel estimation technique chosen; static variables cannot be used in a fixed effects regression. For example, while a country's location does not change, the group of countries it trades with and, thus, its weighted average distance from those countries does. Therefore, as the Asian region has expanded, the center of gravity for many country's trade has also changed.

The second observation is that Australia, along with many other countries, has experienced a fair number of exchange rate and monetary policy regimes over the sample period. Prior to 1973, Australia was in the Bretton Woods arrangement. In Romer's original paper he excluded data from before 1973 to avoid problems created by this arrangement. Wu and Lin also follow this approach for their panel regressions, but not for the individual country regressions in section 4 of the chapter. Following Bretton Woods, Australia used a variety of managed exchange rate regimes before floating the dollar in 1983. Finally, an inflation targeting regime was adopted in the early 1990s. Each of these regimes has implications for the basic Romer hypothesis that, when there is an inability to commit to low inflation outcomes, greater openness ought to be associated with lower inflation. The most significant conceptual problem is with inflation targeting regimes, which have now been adopted by a significant range of countries. An inflation targeting regime presumably involves a credible commitment by the monetary authority to a particular inflation rate. Under such a regime, the relationship posited by Romer should be inoperative. It would be an interesting extension for the paper to investigate this further.

Finally, and most importantly, a question that arises in my mind is whether one would expect to see the Romer relationship between inflation and openness in a country time series in the first place? The basic Barro and Gordon (1983) model used by Romer posits that a central bank has an incentive to generate surprise inflation in the pursuit of higher output growth. Romer extends this by suggesting that the incentive becomes weaker in more open economies and, thus, that lower inflation results. Imagine then, that imports rise in a given country. Is a central bank really going to respond to this arise by producing slightly less surprise inflation that very year? What if the higher imports are a consequence of lower tariffs? Would a central bank really work to offset the inflationary consequences of lower tariffs by generating surprise inflation, albeit less than it usually does?

The first hypothetical question points to the possibility that any relationship will, at best, be present over the longer run and not observable in year-to-year movements in inflation and openness. A related point is that the model emphasized by Romer is static. A consideration of the dynamics involved is likely to involve significant complication compared with the cross-sectional model estimated by Romer. The latter questions raise the possibility that inflation and openness may be negatively related for reasons unrelated to the model proposed by Romer—trade has generally been increasing in recent years as trade barriers have gradually been lowered throughout the world. That is, even if the Romer effect were present in the time series data, there is no reason to expect that a time series regression of the two would be able to identify its existence, given the confounding factors likely present in the data.

More conceptually, it seems to me that the Romer model is one that is much more likely to be relevant in explaining the differences between countries than within countries. In part it is because the fundamental model is static, but it also reflects the fact that each country is likely to make its own evaluation of its preferred trade-off between output and inflation (and the plethora of other macroeconomic variables); any variation in those variables is likely to be much more muted than the differences observed across countries. For example, the difference in labor market outcomes between Sweden and the United States is much larger than the changes one would expect to observe over time in either country. In particular, the kind of tradeoffs one would identify within the countries would be very different from those that would emerge in cross country comparisons.

In light of these general considerations, I have a more specific observation about the paper by Wu and Lin. They emphasize the fixed effects results, but also conduct random effects regressions. An important feature of a fixed effects regression is that it removes any cross country variation and focuses on the time series dimension. Thus, if the Romer result is one that only applies across countries, the lack of results in a fixed effects regression would be expected. In this respect it is particularly interesting that Wu and Lin find that the Romer result is observed in the random effects panel regression—that is, without country specific dummy variables. This is suggestive of the idea that the Romer effect is a cross-country effect rather than a within country effect.

My final comment is on section 4.5, which introduces a VAR model as an alternative test of the Romer hypothesis. As a central banker, I have had intimate acquaintance with the raw data that is used to generate monetary aggregates. As such, I place very little faith in any empirical work that relies on them. There are sufficient breaks in the series caused by changing categorizations of financial institutions, that any given monetary aggregate can give a misleading impression about actual monetary growth. Furthermore, given the time periods covered by this study encompassed monetary targeting in a number of countries, I think the Lucas critique is very apposite. At a very practical level, one of the consequences of monetary targeting is that money moves to the financial institutions that are not subject to controls. Thus, when banks are subject to lending controls, nonbank financial institutions are very popular. As a result, the targeted variable, say M2, becomes misleading and a broader aggregate needs to be considered. As such, I think the lack of results in section 4.5 cannot be considered particularly conclusive—it could just be that the data are flawed.

To summarize my comments and make some suggestions for further extension of the work in this paper, let me suggest a hypothesis that Wu and Lin would be well placed to answer. Is the Romer result a reflection of cross sectional institutional differences and country regimes, or is it one that truly applies within countries over time? A further question is whether the result is a reflection of a third factor rather than being a reflection of a direct relationship between inflation and openness? I think the paper already has some intriguing results that point in a particular direction. I would suggest that putting the lack of time series results into the context of the cross sectional results that do work may help to identify what institutional features are relevant for countries that experience higher openness and lower inflation. For example, the work of Terra (1998) identifying high debt countries as the ones that exhibit a relationship between inflation and openness suggests that all three variables may be indicators of a country's institutional inheritance. With this sort of extension, I believe this paper could provide a valuable complement to the existing literature and a deeper understanding of the inflationary process across countries.

References

Barro, R. J., and D. B. Gordon. 1983. A positive theory of monetary policy in a natural rate model. *Journal of Political Economy* 9 (4): 589–610.

Romer, D. 1993. Openness and inflation: Theory and evidence. *Quarterly Journal of Economics* 108:869–903.

Terra, M. C. T. 1998. Openness and inflation: A new assessment. *Quarterly Journal of Economics* 113:641–48.

Pass-Through of Exchange Rates to Consumption Prices
What Has Changed and Why?

José Manuel Campa and Linda S. Goldberg

5.1 Introduction

Both traded and nontraded goods prices can be sensitive to exchange rate movements. There are a number of forces that contribute to less than complete pass-through of exchange rates into the final consumption prices of imported goods. First, pass-through into prices at the border is incomplete, and varies considerably across goods and across countries. Second, distribution services, like local storage, transportation, and retail costs, provide some insulation of consumption prices of traded goods, both by diluting the import content of the final consumption good and because distributors may actively adjust profit margins to absorb currency fluctuations. For home produced tradable goods, production costs are expected to become more sensitive to exchange rates and import prices as production increasingly relies on imported components. Indeed, a producer of tradable goods achieves such production cost sensitivity both through his own reliance on imported components, and through the reliance of his domestic suppliers and distributors on imported inputs. Imported goods play a role, directly introducing sensitivity to exchange rates in the domestic economy through costs, as in Campa and Goldberg (2006), or alternatively, by keeping pass-through into import prices low in a model of foreign exporting firms selling intermediate goods to domestic producers who

José Manuel Campa is the Grupo Santander Professor of Finance and Director of Research at IESE Business School, University of Navarre, and a research fellow of the Centre for Economic Policy Research. Linda S. Goldberg is a Vice President of International Research at the Federal Reserve Bank of New York and a Research Associate of the National Bureau of Economic Research.

compete with nontraded goods producers, as argued by Bacchetta and van Wincoop (2003).[1]

In this paper, we consider the evolution over the past decade in the predicted sensitivity of consumption prices of imported and domestically-produced goods with respect to exchange rates. For this work, we focus on changes in distribution margins and imported inputs use, as well as on pass-through into import prices at the border for five broad categories of goods: manufactured, nonmanufactured, food, energy, and raw materials. Thus, we build on Campa and Goldberg (2006), where we explored the role of the distribution sector and imported inputs in levels of consumer price index (CPI) sensitivity to exchange rates across twenty-one Organization for Economic Cooperation and Development countries. That study documented that distribution expenditures associated with goods consumed by households are between 30 and 50 percent of the purchasers' prices. These distribution expenditures are dominated by wholesale and retail sector costs, with transportation and storage costs relatively low except in the case of various raw materials and mining industries. In tradable goods production, imported inputs are shown to account for between 10 and 48 percent of the final price. Nontradable goods are produced with lower shares of imported inputs, ranging from 3 percent in the United States to 22 percent in Hungary. Using this evidence across countries within a calibrated model, we found that predicted and actual CPI sensitivity to exchange rate movements are low, often below 10 percent of any exchange rate change.

Yet that study did not address changes over time in the effects of exchange rates on the consumption prices of different types of goods. With distribution expenditures partially insulating final consumption prices from import price changes at the border, consumption price sensitivity to exchange rates can rise if the structure of the retail and distribution sector leads to lower distribution costs. In particular, we ask whether there has been something like a "Wal-Mart effect" influencing exchange rate pass-through, whereby expenditure on such services declines as large-box retailers and distributors are increasingly present in local markets.

One issue is the potential for changing pass-through into the prices of imports at the border. Some studies present evidence that pass-through into the import prices of industrialized countries has declined in the past decade, particularly on finished goods (Marazzi, Sheets, and Vigfusson 2005; Otani, Shiratsuka, and Shirota 2005; Frankel, Parsley, and Wei 2005), while other studies dispute the magnitude and significance of such changes (Campa and Goldberg 2005; Campa, Goldberg, and González-Minguez 2007; Ihrig, Marazzi, and Rothenberg 2006; Daly, Hellerstein, and Marsh 2006; Thomas and Marquez 2006).

---

1. Corsetti and Dedola (2005) make related arguments in a different production chain and pricing setup.

Another relevant issue is the growth of globalization of production over the recent decade. If more imported components are used in production, and these components are priced as other imports at the border, then there is more opportunity for local costs to be sensitive to exchange rates. This growth in imported inputs could raise the sensitivity of final consumption prices to exchange rates.

In this paper, we pull together evidence on these three sources of changing pass-through into consumption prices of types of goods using data drawn from eighteen countries. We compare the roles of expenditures on distribution services, use of imported inputs and components in production, and of changes in the rate of exchange rate pass-through into border prices of goods across countries, across sectors, and for pre- and post-1995 time periods. The analysis yields the following observations. Pass-through into the prices of imports, at the border, is defined more by industry than by country. The notable exception is the United States, where pass-through into import prices is unusually low. Pass-through into import prices is noisiest and least precisely measured for energy imports. Pass-through into import prices of manufactured goods and, less so, food prices, are the only categories measured with precision across countries. Evidence of declining pass-through into the border prices of imports is concentrated within some manufactured goods categories (Marazzi and Sheets 2006; Campa, Goldberg, and González-Minguez 2007), but only for some countries.

Across countries and industries, distribution expenditures have a large industry-specific component but are not trending in a consistent direction across these industries. Imported input use likewise has industry characteristics, but—unlike distribution expenditures—trend changes have been significant and widespread. Imported input use has tended to grow over time, both across countries and across industries. These findings together will suggest that changes in distribution margins have not been the key contributor to changing pass-through into consumption prices of goods over the past decade. By contrast, the significant expansion of imported input use, including its use in distribution services, has increased the predicted sensitivity of retail prices of imported goods and other tradable goods to exchange rates.

It is important to point out that our exercise is one of generating changes in prices imputed to be associated with exchange rate movements. This exercise is one of "all else equal." The exercise shows pressures on prices that are generated by exchange rates. However, these price pressures may not be observable in realized consumption price data. As Gagnon and Ihrig (2005) compellingly argue, and Gust and Sheets (2006) build into general equilibrium models, the inflationary impetus from a home currency depreciation may be met with monetary tightening. In this case, some of the inflationary pressures from depreciation are offset by policy.

Section 5.2 begins our exposition by presenting evidence on industry-specific exchange rate pass-through into import prices and the (more sparse) evidence available on pass-through into consumption prices at the level of particular industries. In section 5.3 we delve into the industry-specific features of distribution margins and imported input use, and focus specifically on decomposing patterns into ones associated with specific countries, industries, and points in time. Section 5.4 pulls together this information and evidence on exchange rate pass-through into import prices to generate predicted values for the consumption price sensitivity to exchange rates of different types of goods across countries. Section 5.5 concludes by summarizing key findings and discussing implications for trade balance adjustment to exchange rates.

5.2   Import Price Elasticities with Respect to Exchange Rates

There is a large literature that has looked at the extent to which exchange rate changes affect import prices of goods. Most of these studies generally have found that pass-through is incomplete, implying that import prices are less volatile than exchange rates. Goldberg and Knetter (1997) present a review of the literature in this area and concluded that pass-through into U.S. import prices was on the order of 50 percent. Large variations around this estimate occur by industry. Antzoulatos and Yang (1996), Yang (1997), and Olivei (2002) all perform estimation of pass-through rates into import prices at the industry level and conclude that pass-through varies across industries. The existing evidence has been obtained by either focusing on a subset of narrowly defined industries, using data at the firm or product level (microstudies) or, more broadly, by looking at a cross-section of relatively aggregated industry statistics (industry studies).

Micro-oriented studies generally focus on pass-through from one country's firms into another's and concentrate on a particular product or industry. For example, Feenstra (1989) and Gron and Swenson (1996) examined the pass-through of movements of the yen into U.S. import prices for Japanese shipments of cars, trucks, and motorcycles. Gil-Pareja (2003) and Goldberg and Verboven (2001) also focus on the degree of pass-through in the automobile industry by looking at detailed product imports from different countries. In other industries, Bernhofen and Xu (2000) examined the exchange rate pass-through into U.S. petrochemical imports from Germany and Japan, and Blonigen and Haynes (2002) looks at Canadian exports of iron and steel into the United States.

The cross-industry studies focus on import prices for more than one industry at a time, often with more aggregated data than found in the micro-oriented studies. Feinberg (1989), Yang (1997), and Pollard and Coughlin (2005) provide estimates of pass-through at broader industry classifications for imports in the manufacturing sector in the United States. Similar evidence for five industry categories is presented for OECD countries in Campa and Goldberg (2005, 2006), Marazzi, Sheets, and Vigfusson (2005), Gagnon and Ihrig (2006) and, for European Union countries, in Campa, Goldberg, and González-Mínguez (2007). Across the OECD countries, industry considerations, and particularly the sectoral composition of a country's imports, have been more important than macroeconomic volatility in explaining changes in exchange rate pass-through into aggregated import prices.

Table 5.1 reports estimated pass-through rates into import prices for all imports and for five broad industry categories across 16 countries. The reported coefficients are the estimated pass-through rates from a regression of changes in import prices on changes in nominal exchange rates and foreign prices using quarterly data for the period 1976:1 to 2004:1.[2] The reported estimates of pass through of exchange rate changes are the contemporaneous effect and the cumulative one-year impact from an exchange rate shock. These estimates come from a partial-adjustment model of the form:

$$\Delta p_t^j = \alpha + \sum_{i=0}^{4} a_i^j \Delta e_{t-i}^j + \sum_{i=0}^{4} b_i^j \Delta w_{t-i}^j + c^j \Delta gdp_t^j + \vartheta_t^j,$$

where p_t^j are local currency import prices or the local consumer price index, e_t^j is the exchange rate, w_t^j is the foreign production costs, gdp_t^j is real GDP, and the final term is the regression residual. The short-run relationship between exchange rates and the respective price series of country j is given by the estimated coefficient a_0^j. The long run elasticity is given by the sum of the coefficients on the contemporaneous exchange rate and four lags of exchange rate terms $\Sigma_{i=0}^{4} a_{it}^j$. While the theoretical antecedents of this equation suggest a log-levels relationship among variables, for estimation the variables in these equations are first differences in logarithms to control for the possibility of unit roots (Campa and Goldberg 2006; Osbat 2006).

Across the eighteen countries for which pass-through rates are presented in table 5.1, the (unweighted) average pass-through elasticity of import prices is 0.59. Consistent with the findings of prior studies, most industries exhibit a striking degree of partial pass-through. In the "all imports" category the hypothesis of zero exchange rate pass-through is rejected for more than half of the countries. Across industries, pass-through rates equal to 1, or complete pass-through, are strongly rejected for manufacturing and for food.

Pass-through is smaller in manufacturing than in commodities such as energy and raw materials. The precision of the estimates also is tightest for

---

2. The sample period begins later for the Netherlands (1977:2), Norway (1978:2), Portugal, and Sweden (1980:2), Australia and Belgium (1981:2), Italy (1982:2), Denmark and New Zealand (1987:3), and Hungary (1995:2) and ends earlier for Netherlands (1997:4), Portugal (1998:4), Austria (1999:4), Denmark and New Zealand (2002:4). France is missing data from 1987:1 to 1996:1.

Table 5.1   Pass-through-rates into industry import price indices

	All Imports	Food	Energy	Raw Materials	Manufacturing	Nonmanufacturing
Australia	0.67*+	0.35*+	−0.69+	0.43*+	0.93*	0.66+
Austria	0.10	0.06	2.24	1.74	−0.32+	1.50
Belgium	0.68	0.55	−0.70	1.72*	0.43	0.51
Denmark	0.82*	0.99*	3.50	1.14*	0.57*+	1.61*
Finland	0.77	0.83	1.46	0.28	0.74	1.08
France	0.90*	1.41*	1.89	—	0.99*	1.27
Germany	0.80*	0.48*+	2.72*	1.12*	0.42*+	1.54*
Hungary	0.78*	0.63*	0.89	−0.00	0.79*+	0.67
Ireland	−0.06	1.23*	1.78*	2.06*	1.19*	1.70*
Italy	0.35+	0.81*	−.80	0.76	0.56*+	0.07
Netherlands	0.84*	0.54*+	2.19	1.72*	0.32*+	1.44*
New Zealand	0.22+	0.23+	0.27	−0.04+	0.24+	0.18
Norway	0.63*	0.15+	−0.69	0.69	0.61*	0.07
Portugal	1.08*	1.07*	0.79	1.41*	1.02*	0.85
Spain	0.70*	1.01	−0.01	1.23*	1.06+	0.61
Sweden	0.38*+	0.85*	−1.64+	0.11+	0.66*+	−0.66+
United Kingdom	0.46*+	0.52*+	0.39	0.47*+	0.46*+	0.39+
United States	0.42*+	0.21+	0.20	0.44*+	0.44*+	0.33
Average	0.59	0.66	0.77	0.90	0.62	0.77
Standard Deviation	0.30	0.39	1.42	0.67	0.36	0.68

Sources: Nominal exchange rate and consumer prices come from the IFS; import price comes from the OECD. Specific start and end dates by country are detailed in the data appendix. Long-run elasticities (four quarters) shown.

Note: *Significantly different from zero (5%), + Significantly different from one (5%). Most data are quarterly, spanning 1975 through the end of 2004.

manufacturing and for food, with dispersion of estimated rates of pass-through across countries lowest for these categories. Our 2005 study reached similar conclusions for both short-run and long-run pass-through rates in the OECD countries. These differences across industries also occur at more disaggregated levels within manufacturing, as Yang (1997) and Pollard and Coughlin (2005) show for manufacturing industries in the United States, and Campa, Goldberg, and González-Minguez (2007) show for the euro-area countries. Pass-through into the import prices of non-manufactured goods, energy, and raw materials appears to be poorly measured by the basic estimating equation.[3]

Recent studies have debated whether pass-through of exchange rates

3. There are many reasons why the pass-through estimation equation can generate poor results. One of these reasons is that the proxies for production costs may be poor. Another reason could be codetermination of exchange rates and the prices of some goods. In recent years, the dollar and petroleum prices have exhibited stronger comovement than in the preceding decade.

into import prices may have declined since 1997, particularly for the United States (Marazzi, Sheets, and Vigfusson 2005; Ihrig, Marazzi, and Rothenberg 2006). Campa, Goldberg, and González-Minguez (2007) argue that the evidence is mixed across European countries. We replicate these tests for fifteen of the eighteen countries[4] in table 5.1 and find that it is difficult to make a case that pass-through into import prices has systematically declined. Typically, the relationship between exchange rates and the local currency import prices of energy, raw materials, and nonmanufactured goods are found to be noisy and unstable. It is difficult to make definitive statements about whether pass-through rates have altered meaningfully for these sectors. By contrast, for manufactured goods estimates of exchange rate pass-through are more informative. We observe some instances of increasing pass-through of exchange rate movements into import prices and other instances of declining pass-through as we look across the sample of countries. Importantly, we stress here that the presumption that pass-through rates have systematically declined across countries, and across a wide spectrum of goods, is not supported. It is not yet appropriate to conclude that persistent change has occurred in the distribution of pass-through into import prices of manufactured goods.

5.3   Mapping Imported Inputs and Distribution Margins into Consumption Prices of Goods

One goal of the analysis is to understand the feedback between exchange rate changes and stimuli to consumption prices or goods across countries.[5] In order to move from exchange rate sensitivity in the border prices of goods to sensitivity in retail prices, analyses need to account for the role of the distribution sector and imported inputs used in production. For this purpose, we use a basic approach of a two country model with wage stickiness and monopolistically competitive producers. Our specific formulation closely follows our 2006 study, and the prior studies discussed therein.

5.3.1   The Mapping

This approach follows a utility-based framework that explicitly tracks the degree of substitutability of imported and domestic products, and presents the explicit cost functions faced by producers. C.E.S. utility functions

4. We are able to compare a pre-1995 period with the period from 1995 to the present for all countries except France and the Netherlands, for which the import price data ends in 1997, and Hungary, for which the available data begins in 1993.
5. Another goal of the analysis of pass-through and consumption prices of categories of goods is to understand the signal sent to consumers to induce expenditure switching between imported and home produced goods. This signal is a critical link in trade balance sensitivity to exchange rate fluctuations. See Goldberg and Tille (2006).

are assumed over nontraded (n) and traded goods (t) consumption, with both sectors producing a continuum of varieties with similar elasticities of substitution, θ. Prices for any good i are a markup over costs $c_t(i)$, with the markup rate as $\theta/(1 - \theta)$. Consumption of tradable and nontradable products are also governed by a constant elasticity of substitution ϕ. Home (h) and foreign (f) tradable goods are imperfect substitutes in consumption, with an elasticity of substitution of $\phi_T > 1$. Bringing one unit of good i where $i \in (h, f, n)$ to consumers requires units of a basket of differentiated nontraded goods for distribution services.[6] We denote these distribution costs per unit of output by $m_t(i : e_t)$, where this basket of differentiated nontraded goods includes expenditures on wholesale and retail sector services, as well as expenditures on transportation and storage. These distribution expenditures are permitted to be sensitive to the exchange rate e_t, which is defined as the domestic cost per unit of foreign exchange. Per unit production requires domestic labor and imported inputs. Labor inputs required per unit of output are inversely related to sectoral productivity parameters Z_i. W_t refers to the wage per unit of labor at home, and W_t^* refers to foreign wages. Productivity parameters as well as domestic and foreign wages are assumed sticky over the relevant pricing horizon. Imported input shares per unit of output are denoted by $\mu_t(i : e_t)$ for home tradable goods and home nontradable goods. These imported cost shares also are sensitive to exchange rates. Foreign currency variables are indicated by superscript "$*$." The pricing equations $P_t(i)$ for home nontradable goods n, home tradable goods h, and imported consumption goods f are given by:

$$(1) \quad P_t(n) = \frac{\theta}{\theta - 1}c_t(n) = \frac{\theta}{\theta - 1}\left[\frac{W_t}{Z_N} + \mu_t(n : e_t)\frac{e_t W_t^*}{Z_F}\right]$$

$$(2) \quad P_t(h) = \frac{\theta}{\theta - 1}c_t(h) = \frac{\theta}{\theta - 1}\left[\frac{W_t}{Z_H} + m_t(h : e_t) \cdot P_t(n) + \mu_t(h : e_t)\frac{e_t W_t^*}{Z_F}\right]$$

$$(3) \quad P_t(f) = \frac{\theta}{\theta - 1}e_t c_t^*(f) = \frac{\theta}{\theta - 1}\left[\frac{e_t W_t^*}{Z_F} + m_t(f : e_t) \cdot P_t(n)\right]$$

Differentiating equations (1) through (3), we derive expressions for exchange-rate pass-through elasticities into home tradable, home nontradable, and imported goods prices. The respective pass-through rates into the consumption prices of these goods are shown in equations (4) through (6). Notationally, $\eta^{a,b}$ terms denote elasticities of a with respect to changes in b.

---

6. Burstein, Neves, and Rebelo (2003) highlight the role that distribution margins can play in lowering exchange-rate pass-through into consumption prices.

$$(4) \quad \eta^{P(n),e} = \frac{\dfrac{\partial P(n)}{\partial e}}{\dfrac{P(n)}{e}} = (1 + \eta^{u_t(n:e),e}) \left[\frac{\mu_t(n:e)\dfrac{ew^*}{Z_F}}{c_t(n)} \right] =$$

$$\frac{\theta}{\theta - 1} (1 + \eta^{u_t(n:e),e}) \left[\frac{\mu_t(n:e)\dfrac{eW^*}{Z_F}}{P_t(n)} \right]$$

$$(5) \quad \eta^{P(h),e} = \frac{\dfrac{\partial P(h)}{\partial e}}{\dfrac{P(h)}{e}} = \frac{\theta}{\theta - 1} \left[(\eta^{P(n),e} + \eta^{m(h),e}) \frac{m(H:e)P(n)}{P_t(h)} + \right.$$

$$\left. (1 + \eta^{u_t(h:e),e_t}) \frac{u(h:e)\dfrac{eW^*}{Z_F}}{P_t(h)} \right]$$

$$(6) \quad \eta^{P(f),e} = \frac{\partial P(f)/\partial e}{P(f)/e} = 1 - \frac{\theta}{\theta - 1} \frac{[m(f:e)P_t(n)]}{P(f)} \left[1 - (\eta^{m(f),e} + \eta^{P(n),e}) \right]$$

Equation (4) shows that pass-through into the consumption price of nontradables occurs only when this sector has cost sensitivity to exchange rates through its use of imported inputs. Some of the exchange rate pass-through in nontradables can be mitigated to the extent that nontradable producers can substitute away from these imported inputs as they become more expensive, $\eta^{\mu_t(n:e),e} < 0$.

Equation (5) shows exchange rate pass-through into the consumption prices of tradables produced in the home market. This pass-through occurs both because home tradables use imported inputs and also because sectoral expenditures on nontraded distribution services can be sensitive to exchange rates. Such sensitivity can be passive, because nontradables prices can respond to exchange rates through imported inputs (as in 4). More active sensitivity arises if distributors strategically adjust the markups they take on home tradables that compete with imported brands. This phenomenon, called double marginalization, is explored in our 2006 study, and Hellerstein (2004).

Pass-through into the consumption prices of imports, equation (6), differs from border price sensitivity of imports. For the derivations of equations (4) through (6), exchange-rate pass-through at the border is assumed to be complete, that is, equal to one. If pass-through at the border is different than one, the actual border pass-through rate simply multiplies equations (4) through (6). Whatever the border price sensitivity, local expenditures on distribution dilute the import content of this consumption good (the first term), even more so if distributors also actively reduce the margins changed during home currency depreciations to limit changes in market shares of the products being distributed. One force magnifying the pass through of exchange rates, and therefore working in the opposite direction, is that from equation (4), whereby distribution costs rise if these services rely on imported inputs into production and have costs that are sensitive to exchange rates.

Equations (4) to (6) also show the impact that increases in the distribution margins have on the expected pass-through rates of a given change in imported prices of final goods, or intermediate inputs in final consumer prices. In general, increases in the share of the distribution sector in the final price of a good decrease the impact on the final consumption price of the good. For nontraded goods, this effect occurs mainly through imported inputs used in production. For domestically-produced traded goods, the impact in equation (5) occurs through a decrease in the foreign value added part of the product. Moreover, as the share of imported inputs in the production of the good increases, changes in border prices of imported products have a higher percentage impact in the production cost of domestically produced goods. This results in higher pass-through into consumer prices.

The existing evidence on pass-through into import prices at the aggregate level suggests that the pass-through may have declined in the last decade, at least in developed countries (see Pollard and Coughlin 2005; Marazzi et al. 2006; and Olivei 2002). We have argued that such evidence is not definitive and requires further monitoring. Yet, despite this possible change in pass-through at the border, the outcome of the debate does not impinge on the key roles that imported inputs and distribution costs have in the final impact of import prices on consumer prices. Increases in imported inputs and in vertical trade that have occurred in the last decade would suggest a rise in import price pass-through. Increases in vertical trade also raise the likelihood that imported products have value added that originates in the home market. For example, U.S. imports of cars from Canada could contain engines that were first produced in the United States, exported to Canada, and ultimately re-exported to the United States. The result is a smaller share of Canadian value-added in U.S. imports, and less Canadian content to be acted upon by exchange rate movements. In this context, we could expect declining sensitivity to exchange rate changes of auto import prices from Canada as Canadian content falls. At the same time, increases in the imported input component of domestically produced goods imply a higher exposure of domestically produced products to exchange rate changes, and a higher pass-through from import prices into final consumer prices.[7] To quantify the relative size of each of

---

7. Feenstra (1998) and Rauch (1999) show the increasing role that the vertical integration of production across borders has on international prices and trade. This discussion has not

these effects and the insulating role of the distribution sector, in the next section we examine the evolution of imported input shares and distribution margins over the last decade.

5.3.2   Patterns in Imported Input Use and Distribution Expenditures

We measure the share of imported inputs and distribution expenditures for industries by using country-specific input-output tables.[8] Our full sample of imported input data spans 16 countries, 59 homogeneous manufacturing, primary-industry, and service industry groupings, and 1 to 2 years per country-industry observation.[9] The data on distribution margins span all but one of the same countries, but with narrower availability in terms of industries. The reduced availability occurs because, in some cases, service industry inputs into industry production are unavailable. Details on data construction and availability are provided in appendix table 2.

Our analysis extends information reported in our 2006 study, which looked at the disaggregated data across countries. That study observed that industries with the highest imported input share are Coke, refined petroleum products, and nuclear fuel manufacturing. Within the manufacturing sector, the next highest imported input shares are in computers and communication equipment, at around 50 percent. More generally, industries involved in services, agriculture, and commodity production have much lower shares of imported inputs than industries in manufacturing. For instance, real estate services, and forestry, logging and related services have average imported input shares between 6 percent and 14 percent of total costs, respectively. By contrast, almost all manufacturing industries have imported input shares above 20 percent. The industry within manufacturing with the lowest imported input share is food and beverage manufacturing.

The dispersion of imported input shares in production differs significantly by country. In general, larger countries have lower shares of imported inputs while smaller countries have higher shares. The United States has by far the lowest ratio of imported inputs into production of all countries in our sample. Ireland, with 51 percent, has by far the largest reliance on imported inputs with other smaller countries like Belgium, Hungary and the Netherlands also heavily reliant on imported parts and components.

More formally, we consider the extent to which industries versus countries versus time explain the prevalence of import input use. We run re-

---

dealt with the issue of transfer pricing, which pertains to intra-firm pricing policies. For instance, a multinational may differentially price sales of goods to subsidiaries versus to unrelated parties.

8. Details on construction methods are in Campa and Goldberg (2006).

9. Compared with table 5.1, we drop Australia and Greece from the analysis due to lack of input-output information to allow us to compute the data on imported inputs.

Table 5.2   Imported input variance decomposition

	Adjusted R^2 for regression excluding each set of dummies	Adjusted R^2 for regression with only each set of dummies	Percent of full regression specification adjusted R^2 explained by each set of dummies
Industry dummies	0.19	0.48	68.3
Country dummies	0.60	0.19	26.7
Year dummies	0.69	0.10	14.2

Note: We define the percent of the full regression adj. R^2 explained by the industry dummies as (adjusted R^2 from the regression including only the industry dummies)/(adj. R^2 of the full specification). The alternative, (adj. R^2 from the regression including everything but the industry dummies)/(adj. R^2 of the full specification), would yield slightly higher percents. Adjusted R^2 for the full regression specification with all dummy variables = 0. 70.

gressions using 1,394 imported share observations, covering 59 industries and 16 countries. Variance decompositions are used to identify the portions of the observational variance within this data base that are attributable to industry fixed effects, country fixed effects, or time dummies. With the exception of France, Ireland, Norway, Portugal, Spain, and the United Kingdom, each country included in the sample has two years (typically five years apart) of imported input data.

The full regression specification accounts for 70 percent of the variation in imported input use (table 5.2). In order of importance, imported input use is determined first by industry identity, then country, then by time. Having already discussed industry and country highlights, it is interesting to focus attention on time trends in imported input use across countries. Of the 57 industries with enough observations to run a regression, 16 industries had time trends that were statistically significant at a 10 percent level. All of these trends were positive.[10] On average, the industries with significant trends had imported input use increase by 0.9 percentage points per year. The manufacturing industries Coke, refined petroleum products, and nuclear fuel had the largest (statistically significant) increase in imported input share, rising 3.4 percentage points per year, on average. Real estate activities had the smallest significant increase, averaging 0.2 percentage points per year.

While this regression analysis has used disaggregated industry data, it also is useful to consider broader aggregates. The results of this aggregation are provided in table 5.3. Across the broadly aggregated sections it is clear that energy and manufactured goods have by far the highest imported input shares at, on average, 43 percent and 38 percent of total inputs respectively. Nonmanufactured goods, food, raw materials, and the

10. The industries with significant time trends include food, energy extraction and refining, manufacture and servicing of computers and other machinery, and some service industries.

Table 5.3   Imported input share

	Year	All Industries	Manufactured Goods	Nonmanufacturing	Energy	Food	Raw Materials	Distribution Sector
Austria	2000	0.29	0.48	0.18	0.46	0.18	0.15	0.17
Belgium	2000	0.35	0.53	0.23	0.61	0.34	0.32	0.28
Denmark	2000	0.23	0.39	0.16	0.30	0.20	0.19	0.17
Finland	2000	0.25	0.35	0.16	0.58	0.15	0.11	0.17
France	2000	0.14	0.22	0.09	0.47	0.11	0.17	0.07
Germany	2001	0.19	0.31	0.12	0.44	0.16	0.19	0.17
Hungary	2000	0.44	0.63	0.21	0.71	0.20	0.16	0.21
Ireland	1998	0.52	0.68	0.42	0.48	0.30	0.48	0.46
Italy	2000	0.20	0.30	0.13	0.54	0.16	0.18	0.17
Netherlands	2000	0.30	0.46	0.22	0.45	0.35	0.44	0.28
Norway	2001	0.21	0.30	0.17	0.13	0.14	0.17	0.22
Portugal	1999	0.24	0.40	0.13	0.36	0.25	0.06	0.15
Spain	1995	0.18	0.27	0.11	0.40	0.12	0.08	0.08
Sweden	2000	0.25	0.37	0.18	0.57	0.20	0.20	0.20
United Kingdom	1995	0.18	0.29	0.12	0.12	0.16	0.15	0.13
United States	2002	0.06	0.09	0.03	0.28	0.04	0.07	0.03
Average		0.25	0.38	0.17	0.43	0.19	0.20	0.19
Standard Deviation		0.11	0.15	0.08	0.16	0.08	0.12	0.10

distribution sector all have average imported input shares at or just under 20 percent. Across countries we confirm the observation that Ireland, at 52 percent, and the United States, at 6 percent, span the spectrum of intensities for the group of sixteen countries.

Comparable data analysis of expenditures on distribution services also generates interesting observations. First, we conduct a variance decomposition exercise across the most disaggregated industry level data (59 industries, 16 countries). As shown in table 5.4, this decomposition explains substantially less of the sample variation than was the case when we examined patterns of imported input use. Industry fixed effects had the strongest explanatory power. There are common patterns across countries in the incidence of high and low distribution margin expenditures for industries. Distribution expenses are consistently high in apparel (18 percent), leather (19), furniture manufacturing (36), and fishing and related services (5). Distribution expenses appear to be lowest on some commodity-type products and industries, such as petroleum and natural gas extraction (11 percent); uranium, thorium, and metal ore mining (12 and 13), and nonautomobile transportation equipment manufactures (35).

Time fixed effects explain little of the variation observed in distribution expenditures. Each country in the sample typically had two years of distribution margins data included in the analysis. Of 30 industries with enough observations to examine trends, only 7 had statistically significant time trends. Among these industries, 4 had positive time trends (agriculture, mining, manufacturing of food products, and pulp, paper, and paper products) and 3 had negative time trends (manufacturing of radio and television, motor vehicles, and medical and precision equipment). Thus, the number of industries with strong distribution expenditure trends was low, and the pattern of changes in distribution expenditures was not persistent for all industries in either a positive or negative direction. Hungary and Finland have the lowest overall level for distribution expenditures. On the other extreme, the United States had the largest distribution expenditures in the sample (0.29 in 2002). This observation contrasts sharply with what was observed for imported input use, where increasing globalization of production was readily apparent across many industries. Over the past decade, imported input use and globalization of production has grown substantially, while changes in distribution expenditures have been more diffuse and bidirectional.

One short-coming of this distribution margin data, as explained in our 2006 study, is that there is a trade-off in getting information expenditure margins at the industry-level and getting information relevant for the consumption of households. The total distribution margins with industry-level detail encompass margins on total final consumption. This total includes distribution margins for household consumption, investment, public sector, and export markets. In our modelling of CPI sensitivity to exchange

Table 5.4   **Distribution expense variance decomposition**

	Adjusted R^2 for regression excluding each set of dummies	Adjusted R^2 for regression with only each set of dummies	Percent of full regression specification adjusted R^2 explained by each set of dummies
Industry dummies	0. 13	0. 34	69. 1
Country dummies	0. 44	0. 13	26. 9
Year dummies	0. 49	0. 09	18. 3

Note: Adjusted R^2 for the full regression specification with all dummy variables = 0. 49.

rates and import prices we use the distribution expenditure specifically for the household sector, eschewing the more extensive industry-specific information used in the variance decomposition. In part, the country-fixed effects in the variance decomposition just discussed reflect the components of final demand in each country. Distribution margins in fixed capital formation and exports are substantially lower than those on household consumption.

5.4   Calibrating Pass Through of Exchange Rates into Consumption Prices

Pass-through of exchange rates into consumer price indices has two main components. First, we require information on how exchange rates pass through into import prices. This information was presented in section 5.2 and in table 5.1. Second, we require a model of import price transmission into consumer prices. This model was provided in section 5.3.1 and is based on Campa and Goldberg (2006). In this section of the paper, we focus on calibrating the model using our information on changes in key parameters, including sectoral distribution expenditure and imported input use. Our goal is to track, quantitatively and qualitatively, the sources of change in predicted pass-through of exchange rates into consumption prices. We begin by assuming relevant parameters for calibrating equations (4) to (6).

Assumptions are made for the values of demand elasticity (θ), the elasticities of substitution among groups of products, and elasticities of response to exchange rates of distribution margins and imported inputs.[11] Our assumed estimate of the demand elasticity, θ, is consistent with evidence on the steady state price over cost markups, defined by markup = $\theta/(\theta - 1)$. Basu and Fernald (1997) find markups for U.S. industries in the range of 11 percent. Oliveira Martins, Scarpetta, and Pilat (1996) find

11. The calibrations basically shut down the role of initial conditions and substitution between tradables and nontradables goods by setting the relative price terms to equal one in the calculations. Accordingly, values of ϕ do not matter for these calibrations.

markups ranging between 10 and 35 percent, in data spanning 14 OECD countries and 36 manufacturing industries. These markup values imply a range for θ between 10 and 4. For our calibration we assume θ = 7. Using higher demand elasticities would yield lower values of pass-through into home tradables and now tradeable goods prices.

The simple model of equations (4) through (6) is able to explore many alternative specifications on substitution elasticities, changes to industry competitive structures, and state-contingent markups. Likewise, a range of assumptions could be made about the ability of producers to substitute between home-produced inputs and imported inputs when exchange rates alter the relative prices of inputs from different sources, or about proactive adjustment of profit margins of distributors of goods. These important themes, explored at length in our 2006 paper, are not emphasized here.

Our specific goal is to explore the changes in pass-through into consumer prices that are specifically attributable to changes in pass-through at the border, changes in imported input use, and changes in distribution sector expenditures. With this objective in mind, we shut down some of the other forces that would influence the exchange-rate transmission into the final consumption prices of goods. Specifically, the initial relative prices of imported and home tradables, and of home tradables and nontradables, are assumed to be the same. Imported input shares are assumed inelastic with respect to exchange rates and are assumed to be identical across the production of nontradables and home tradables. Finally, distribution expenditures are assumed inelastic with respect to exchange rates, so that $\eta^{m(f:e),e}$ and $\eta^{m(h:e),e} = 0$.

We focus on data for all industries, manufacturing, nonmanufacturing, energy, food, and raw materials, which are the industry groupings for which we also have information on import prices and exchange rate pass-through at the border. While there are eighteen countries for which we have been able to estimate exchange rate pass-through into import prices at this level of index disaggregation, changes in both imported input use and distribution expenditures are available only for ten of these countries.

5.4.1   Calibrated Pass-through

Table 5.5 reports the calibrated pass-through elasticities into final prices of imports and domestically produced traded goods according to equations (5) and (6). These pass-through coefficients imply the transmission into final prices of a given percentage change in the import price at the border. The estimates use the imported input shares and distribution ratios calculated as described in the previous section for the years indicated in the second column of the table.

The pass-through transmission to final prices of imported products is relatively high and fluctuates for the aggregate of all industries between

Table 5.5   Pass-through of a change in import prices at the border into the consumption prices of imported and domestically-produced traded products

	Year	All Industries	Manufactured	Nonmanufactured	Energy	Food	Raw Materials
For imported products							
Austria	1995	0.851	0.858	0.809	0.842	0.831	0.875
Belgium	1995	0.886	0.887	0.874	0.877	0.853	0.911
Denmark	1995	0.825	0.819	0.851	0.884	0.821	0.760
Finland	1995	0.887	0.881	0.918	0.900	0.762	0.976
Germany	1995	0.844	0.852	0.784	0.863	0.757	0.764
Hungary	1998	0.902	0.905	0.892	0.857	0.848	1.000
Ireland	1998	0.939	0.930	0.987	1.000	0.939	0.974
Italy	1995	0.847	0.857	0.754	0.864	0.744	0.932
Netherlands	1995	0.878	0.873	0.899	0.928	0.849	0.876
Portugal	1999	0.859	0.859	0.858	0.828	0.814	0.904
Spain	1995	0.866	0.875	0.822	0.922	0.807	0.732
Sweden	1995	0.903	0.891	0.948	0.901	0.858	0.966
United Kingdom	1955	0.846	0.833	0.925	0.967	0.750	0.914
United States	1997	0.684	0.696	0.518	0.497	0.620	0.876
For domestically produced products							
Austria	1995	0.354	0.496	0.276	0.372	0.211	0.291
Belgium	1995	0.389	0.607	0.245	0.528	0.429	0.431
Denmark	1995	0.259	0.463	0.144	0.401	0.201	0.194
Finland	1995	0.259	0.376	0.149	0.517	0.192	0.151
Germany	1995	0.195	0.295	0.137	0.307	0.218	0.142
Hungary*	1998	0.443	0.661	0.273	0.668	0.273	0.169
Ireland	1998	0.648	0.837	0.502	0.560	0.391	0.581
Italy	1995	0.243	0.228	0.181	0.612	0.223	0.147
Netherlands	1995	0.376	0.563	0.257	0.392	0.442	0.423
Portugal	1999	0.306	0.489	0.184	0.454	0.329	0.087
Spain	1995	0.227	0.329	0.151	0.475	0.163	0.128
Sweden	1995	0.326	0.365	0.295	0.372	0.054	0.331
United Kingdom	1995	0.230	0.361	0.150	0.146	0.231	0.184
United States	1997	0.068	0.101	0.042	0.262	0.058	0.069

Note: The numbers reported here are the estimated values of equations (5) and (6). The computation further assumes an elasticity of demand of 7, and zero elasticities of exchange rate changes to distribution margins in home products, and to the share of imported inputs used in production.

0.68 for the United States and 0.9 for Hungary and Sweden. This means that, given a change in imported goods prices at a country's border, nearly 70 percent of this price signal will be transmitted to the final consumption prices of the imported goods in the United States, and nearly 90 percent in Hungary and Sweden. The two key determinants of variations in this rate of pass-through are the share of imported inputs in the production of non-traded services that enter the distribution sector, and the share of the distribution sector into final prices of the product. For a given share of imported inputs into the production of nontraded goods in the country, the higher the share of distribution costs the lower the rate of transmission into final prices. However, as the share of imported inputs into nontraded goods increases, so does the sensitivity of distribution costs to changes in import prices.

Differences in calibrated pass-through across industries for a given country are relatively small. Such differences arise due to differences in the share of distribution costs in different sectors, and these tend to be relatively small. Larger differences arise across countries. For instance, the United States has the highest share of distribution costs in the sample (see table 5.5) and a low share of imported inputs in production in distribution services (see table 5.3) leading to the result that the predicted transmission into final prices of imported goods is the lowest. On the other extreme, Hungary has the lowest share of distribution margins (0.07 in table 5.5) and the second highest, after Ireland, ratio of imported inputs into production (0.44 in table 5.3). Its rate of pass-through into final prices of imported products is 0.90, the highest in the sample.

Pass-through into final prices of domestically produced traded goods is reported in the lower panel of table 5.5. Transmission rates are significantly lower than the transmission rates for imported products. The transmission rates for all industries (column 3) fluctuate between 0.65 for Ireland and 0.07 for the United States. Looking at equation (5), two key differences explain the lower transmission rates. First, and most important, is the ratio of imported inputs into the production of domestic goods (the last term in the square brackets of equation [5]). The lower this ratio, the less sensitive are input costs to changes in prices of imported products and the weaker are cost pressures arising from exchange rates into the prices of domestically produced goods. The second factor is the importance of the distribution sector and the sensitivity of this sector to changes in import prices (the first term in the square brackets of equation [5]). The lower the sensitivity of the distribution sector to import prices, the lower the pass-through into final prices of domestically produced goods.

The United States shows the lowest sensitivity of domestically produced goods prices. This is due mainly to two factors: its low sensitivity of final prices of imports reported above and its lower share of imported inputs into production of domestic goods. In contrast, Hungary again shows the highest predicted sensitivity of the prices of domestically-produced goods to changes in the border prices of imported goods.

Differences across industries are much larger for the case of domestically produced goods. Transmission rates are substantially larger for energy and manufacturing than for the other three industries in almost all countries in the sample. This is mainly due to the higher ratio of imported inputs into the production of manufacturing and energy products relative to the other industries (see table 5.3).

5.4.2   Changes Over Time in Calibrated Pass-through

To evaluate the evolution of changes in these transmission rates over time we compute the same transmission rates as those reported in table 5.5 using the latest available information on distribution margins and imported input shares for each country.[12] Table 5.6 reports the difference between the estimated values for equations (5) and (6) using data from these later years and the estimated transmission rates using 1995 data and reported in table 5.5.

Increases in the pass-through for imported products can be due, following equation (6), to decreases in the share of distribution costs in the final price of imported products. Increases in the prices of nontraded goods due to increases in the imported inputs used in the production of nontraded goods can result in an increase in pass-through of exchange rates into final prices of imported products.

The results in the top-panel of table 5.6 indicate that there has been an increase in the calibrated pass-through of movements in border prices of imports into the final prices of imported and domestically-produced goods for most countries. For aggregated imported goods, this increased transmission of border prices to final consumption prices has happened in all countries shown, with the exception of the United States, Italy, and, to a very small degree, Belgium and Sweden. The countries with an increase in the rate of transmission have this result mainly because imported inputs are more extensively used in the production of nontraded goods that factor into the costs of distribution services.

For the United States and Italy, the decline in border price transmission into the final prices of imported goods is a feature of manufacturing, food, and raw materials. For the United States, pass through into nonmanufactured imports and energy imports rose, while it declined for these sectors in Italy. The share of imported inputs into production on nontradables in these countries has also increased, although relatively less than for other countries, in the last decade. Therefore, this lower calibrated sensitivity of the final consumption prices of imported goods has been mainly due to in-

---

12. The year used for each country to calculate the measure of imported inputs is reported in table 5.3, and the corresponding date for the share of distribution costs is reported in table 5.5.

Table 5.6   **Changes in implied pass-through into the consumption prices of imported and domestically produced traded products**

	All Industries	Manufactured	Nonmanufactured	Energy	Food	Raw Materials
		For imported products				
Austria	0.016	0.009	0.063	-0.013	-0.029	0.121
Belgium	-0.003	-0.002	-0.011	0.033	0.007	0.044
Denmark	0.025	0.027	0.019	0.037	0.014	0.022
Finland	0.000	0.009	-0.053	-0.016	-0.021	-0.066
Germany	0.017	0.017	0.008	0.011	-0.005	0.012
Hungary	0.036	0.023	0.106	0.057	-0.001	0.090
Italy	-0.012	-0.007	-0.063	-0.004	-0.025	-0.240
Netherlands	0.007	0.002	0.021	0.017	0.001	0.097
Sweden	-0.001	0.012	-0.066	0.002	-0.042	-0.026
United States	-0.014	-0.017	0.116	0.122	-0.056	-0.235
		For domestically produced products				
Austria	0.023	0.102	-0.036	0.207	0.054	-0.115
Belgium	0.058	0.052	0.072	0.222	0.022	-0.040
Denmark	0.043	0.020	0.066	-0.038	0.063	0.077
Finland	0.059	0.055	0.074	0.189	0.047	-0.004
Germany	0.055	0.083	0.041	0.232	0.013	0.114
Hungary	0.088	0.098	-0.025	0.189	0.010	-0.019
Italy	0.013	0.040	0.017	0.040	0.013	0.115
Netherlands	0.014	0.015	0.019	0.148	0.006	0.097
Sweden	-0.005	0.089	-0.047	0.319	0.234	-0.085
United States	0.008	0.020	0.001	0.077	0.003	0.022

Note: The numbers reported here are the estimated values of equations (5) and (6) for each country using data around 1995 (reported in table 5.5) and using data for the year 2000. The computation further assumes an elasticity of demand of 4, and zero elasticities of exchange rate changes to distribution margins in home products, and to the share of imported inputs used in production.

creases in expenditure on distribution services in these industries. In contrast, for the United States the substantial decrease in the distribution expenditures in energy and nonmanufacturing (of almost 25 percent) have resulted in a substantial increase in pass-through for those industries.

The bottom panel of table 5.6 shows the imputed changes in the pass-through of import price changes into the prices of domestic tradable products. Following equation (5), the two forces that would increase this pass through are increases in the share of imported inputs in production, whether for these goods specifically or for the distribution costs of domestically produced goods. This pass-through would also rise if distribution services fall as a share of the total production costs of the respective types of home produced goods. The results in table 5.6 show that the imputed pass-through into home-produced tradable goods has increased in almost all industries and countries. The effect is positive in all cases in manufacturing, food and energy industries. These changes have been larger in absolute value in energy than in the other industries.

This rise in transmission of import price moves into the final prices of domestically-produced goods has been mainly due to changes in the ratio of imported inputs in the production in these industries. The increase in imported inputs in the production of these industries in conjunction with the increase in the use of imported inputs in the production of nontraded goods discussed above have both contributed to a higher sensitivity of final goods prices of domestically produced goods to changes in import prices. The United States has had the smallest overall increase in its pass-through, mainly due to its much lower pass-through rates among the countries in the sample, as reported in table 5.5. However, in percentage terms its pass-through for all industries has increased by 12 percent, among the higher percentage increases of all countries in the sample.

The share of imported inputs in the production of domestic tradables has increased in all countries in the sample over the past decade. This increase has been proportionally larger in energy and manufacturing than in the other three industries. The share of imported inputs in the production of nontradables has also increased in the majority of countries. Only Sweden and Austria show a small decline in this ratio. In contrast, the change in the share of distribution costs has not been so homogeneous across countries. This share increased for Belgium, Finland, Italy, and the United States. The increase in distribution services has been primarily in food (it increased for all countries) and in manufacturing. This pattern results in a higher growth of pass-through into the consumption prices of domestically-produced goods, in most cases, than for imported goods (see table 5.6). This is especially the case for manufactured goods. Given a change in goods prices at the border, the implication is that an induced relative price effect is smaller. This observation may be relevant for discussions of expenditure switching induced by exchange rate changes.

Goldberg and Tille (2006) argue that an adjustment process to current account imbalances is likely to be asymmetric across the United States and its partners in trade, in particular because consumption price sensitivity to exchange rates is expected to be substantially less in the United States. This would lead relative prices of imports for the United States to move to a lesser degree with exchange rate fluctuations than the relative prices of United States' trading partners. The results of table 5.6 provide perspective on how this asymmetry has changed recently. In particularly, focusing only on manufacturing and the all industries columns of table 5.6, we observe that the increased transmission into prices was smaller for the United States than for other countries. This suggests that the asymmetry in adjustment to exchange rate movements may, all else equal, have gotten larger between the United States and some trading partners in the most recent decade.

5.5   Conclusions

This paper has explored the channels for transmission of exchange rates into various types of consumption goods prices and into the aggregate level of prices across eighteen economies. First, we highlight transmission of exchange rates into the border prices of imported goods as the initial step in pass-through into final consumption prices of goods. We find that rates of exchange-rate pass-through into import prices are measured with considerable precision for manufactured goods, but are less precisely measured with respect to nonmanufactured goods, raw materials, and energy. The period since 1995 may have been one of marked changes in pass-through into import prices of manufactured goods, as we observe some countries with higher and others with lower rates of pass-through over the past decade.

Yet, these changes in transmission of exchange rates into the border prices of imports are not analogous to levels or directions of change in the transmission into the consumption prices of the same categories of goods. Thus, the second part of this paper is on the transmission of these border prices into final consumption prices. We take a model-based approach to transmission that highlights the role of sectoral expenditures on imported inputs and on distribution services. Examination of detailed cross-country data leads to the conclusion that changes in transmission into final consumption prices are associated more with the evolution of imported input use in production than to evolution in distribution expenditures at the industry level. In general, use of imported inputs in production grew sharply since the mid-1990s, increasing the sensitivity to exchange rates of the production costs of a broad spectrum of goods. By way of contrast, we observe that expenditures on distribution services have not trended consistently across countries or across industries.

This increase in the sensitivity of consumption prices to the role of imported inputs is particularly important for the East Asian region. The East Asian economies are in general very open to international trade. Not surprisingly, international trade in the region grows at a faster rate than in other parts of the world. This growth is in part driven by the vertical disintegration of production. Hummels, Ishii, and Yi (2001) estimate that vertical specialization accounts for 30 percent of world exports. To the extent that trade in intermediate products continues to increase, the imported input channel for the transmission of changes into consumer prices is likely to play a larger role.

The findings of generalized increases in the calibrated sensitivity of consumption prices of domestically-produced traded goods are important for understanding the potential for expenditure switching and trade adjustment to occur in the aftermath of changes in exchange rates. Goldberg and Tille (2006) argue that an adjustment process to current account imbalances is likely to be asymmetric across the United States and its partners in trade, in particular because price sensitivity to exchange rates is expected to be substantially less in the United States. This would lead to relative prices of imports for the United States to move to a lesser degree with exchange rate fluctuations than the relative prices of United States trading partners. It is useful to explore if this asymmetry is likely growing over time, or declining over time.

Our results imply that the calibrated sensitivity of consumption prices of domestically-produced tradables is rising at a faster rate than the price sensitivity of imported goods. If this is the case, the expenditure switching effects of exchange rate movements are weakened over time, primarily as a result of more integrated production internationally and greater use of imported inputs in production. All else equal, a greater movement in nominal exchange rates would be needed to generate the same elasticity of response of real trade flows. This is an issue that warrants further study.

Another implication of these findings is that increases in the transmission into United States final prices have been smaller than into final prices in other countries. With exchange rate pass-through into border prices already larger outside the United States, the changes over time have magnified the differences in transmission into final consumption prices. With the exchange rate as one instrument of trade balance adjustment, it may be the case that the task of expenditure-switching induced by exchange rates now falls even more heavily on the U.S. trade partners than on the United States. This too warrants further study.

Appendix

Data Sources

OECD Import Price Series

Source: OECD Statistical Compendium. Quarterly time series of aggregate import price indices in local currency for 1975:Q1 to approximately 2004:Q4. We work with the maximum amount of data available by country in our analysis.

Effective Exchange Rate Indices

The nominal exchange rate index is the trade weighted exchange rate index provided by the IMF. Code in IFS database: *neu.* The real effective exchange rate used is code *reu.* Regression analysis uses the inverse of the reported series, so that an increase in the exchange rate is a currency depreciation.

Foreign Price Index

We construct a consolidated export partners cost proxy by taking advantage of the IFS reporting of both real (reu) and nominal (neu) exchange rate series and computing $W_t^{x,j} = neu_t^j \cdot P_t^j / reu_t^j$ by each country in our sample. This gives us a measure of trading partner costs (over all partners x of importing country j), with each partner weighted by its importance in the importing country's trade. The real effective exchange rate is calculated from Unit Labour Costs for developed countries by the IMF. Code in IFS database: reu. The consumer price indices from the *International Financial Statistics.* Code in IFS database. *64.*

Input-Output (I/O) Databases

The Input-Output data for the different countries come from different sources:

- Data for Belgium, Finland, France, Germany, Greece, Italy, Netherlands, Spain, Sweden, and the United Kingdom come from the Eurostat National Accounts database. This database computes the input-output tables for these countries and reports a supply and a use table disaggregated to a total of fifty-nine industries. These fifty-nine industries include twenty-two manufacturing industries, five mining and extraction industries, three agriculture industries, five construction and energy industries, eight trade and transport industries, and seventeen service industries. We report distribution margin data for twenty-nine manufacturing, mining, and agriculture industries (we merge two mining industries into one, given their small production values in most countries).
- Data for Australia on input-output tables comes from the Australian Bureau of Statistics. The data reports supply and final use tables for a total of 237 industries. We convert these industries into the CPA classification of twenty-nine manufacturing, mining, and agriculture industries.
- Data for the United States on input-output tables come from the "Benchmark Input Output Accounts for the U.S. economy" (years 1992 and 1997). The U.S. input-output accounts use a specific IO industry classification, which can then be transformed into the NIPA classification (Nacional Income and Product Account Tables) and then aggregated into the CPA classification of twenty-nine manufacturing, mining, and agriculture industries used in the paper.
- Data for New Zealand on input-output tables come from Statistics New Zealand. The data reports supply, use, and import tables for a total of 210 industries. We aggregate these industries into the CPA classification of twenty-nine manufacturing, mining, and agriculture industries.

Calculation of Distribution Margins

We compute the distribution margins for total supply in the industry as the ratio of the value of trade and transport margins to the value of total supply in the industry at purchasers' prices. Purchaser prices include the cost of supply at basic prices plus the distribution (retail, wholesale, and transportation) costs plus net taxes on products. To the extent that taxation differs significantly across countries for the same industry and across industries within a country, distribution margins may not be perfectly comparable in all cases. See Campa and Goldberg (2006).

Calculation of Imported Input Ratios

The Input-Output tables report the value of the use matrix broken down to the use of inputs by origin: domestic and imported. We calculate imported inputs into the production of each industry as the ratio between the total value of imported intermediate inputs by an industry to the value of total intermediate inputs.

Techniques to construct the imported intermediate flows matrix in the input-output tables vary by country. Most countries used, to some extent, the import proportionality assumption. This technique assumes that an industry uses an import of a particular product in proportion to its total use of that product. This assumption is limiting since some industries may be using inputs from domestic and import sources in different proportions than the average of the economy. Countries made use of this assumption at very different levels of aggregation. For instance, the OECD reports that Germany and Denmark made used of over 2,000 different commodities, while the U.S. and Japan used slightly over 500 and the United Kingdom less than 200.

Table 5A.1   Long-run import price pass-through

	All Imports	Manufactured Goods	Non-manufactured Goods	Energy	Food	Materials Raw
			Pre-1995			
Australia	0.62*+	0.89*	0.16+	-0.51	0.38*+	0.32+
Austria	1.01	0.55	2.27*	2.85	0.49	2.86*
Belgium	1.03	0.6	0.56	-3.13	1.36*	3.18*+
Denmark	0.95*	0.77*	1.10	1.37	0.74	1.95*
Finland	0.72	0.6	1.43	2.01	1.06	0.27
France	0.87*	0.86*	1.12	1.57	1.43*	
Germany	1.00*	0.54*+	1.69*	2.64*	0.55*+	1.45*
Hungary						
Italy	0.32+	0.48+	-0.09	-1.53	0.80*	1.07
Netherlands	0.93*	0.25+	1.77*	2.36	0.73*	2.42*+
New Zealand	0.36+	0.29+	0.99	1.91	0.04+	-0.43+
Norway	0.97*	0.77*	0.31	-0.21	-0.41+	0.83
Portugal	1.18*	1.06*	1.03*	1.06	1.14*	1.48*+
Spain	0.66*	1.00*	0.58	0.06	0.95	1.16*
Sweden	0.32+	0.56*+	-0.30+	-0.88+	0.79*	0.28
United Kingdom	0.45*+	0.46*+	0.36+	0.18	0.50*+	0.55*+
United States	0.44*+	0.47*+	0.15+	-0.22+	0.24+	0.36*+
Average	0.74	0.63	0.82	0.60	0.67	1.18
Standard Deviation	0.29	0.24	0.73	1.66	0.48	1.05

Post-1995

Australia	0.82*	0.93*	0.44	0.45	0.10+	0.43
Austria	-1.40	-1.30	-2.55	-7.60	-1.11	3.02
Belgium	0.25+	0.14+	0.47	2.08	-0.30+	0.73
Denmark	0.83*	0.45*+	1.80*	3.67	1.30*	0.82
Finland	-0.16	-0.24	-1.58	-3.37	2.50	-1.70
France	0.28	0.28+	1.00	0.12	1.31	
Germany	0.68	0.68*	0.63	0.54	0.44	0.93
Hungary	0.78*+	0.79*+	0.67	0.89	0.63*	0.00
Italy	0.85*	0.81*	1.82	4.11*	0.57	0.23
Netherlands						
New Zealand	0.12+	0.19+	-0.26+	-0.62	0.27+	0.18+
Norway	0.09+	0.06+	-0.23	1.90	1.02	-1.27
Portugal	1.96	1.66	-0.64	-16.58	6.47	7.55
Spain	1.18*	1.70	0.84	-3.18	2.23	3.18*+
Sweden	0.21+	0.61*	-1.74*+	-3.22*+	0.67*	-0.19+
United Kingdom	0.32*+	0.26+	0.43	1.30	0.62*	0.08+
United States	0.30*+	0.27*+	0.54	0.97	0.03+	0.34
Average	0.44	0.46	0.10	-1.16	1.05	0.96
Standard Deviation	0.71	0.71	1.22	5.07	1.70	2.23

Notes: * indicates different from 0 with 10% significance; + indicates different from 1 with 10% significance.

Table 5A.2   **Overview of data on imported inputs and distribution margins, by country and industry**

Country	Imported Input Data Availability		Distribution Margin Data Availability	
	Years	Number of Industries	Years	Number of Industries
Austria	1995, 2000	1995: 54, 2000: 56	1995, 2001	1995: 27, 2001: 29, in both: 27
Belgium	1995, 2000	1995: 54, 2000: 55	1995, 2001	1995: 29, 2001: 29, in both: 29
Denmark	1995, 2000	1995: 55, 2000: 55	1995, 2000	1995: 27, 2000: 28, in both: 27
Finland	1995, 2000	1995: 56, 2000: 56	1995, 2002	1995: 29, 2002: 30, in both 29
France	2000	2000: 57	1995, 2001	1995: 30, 2001: 29, in both: 29
Germany	1995, 2001	1995: 57, 2001: 56	1995, 2001	1995: 30, 2001: 30, in both: 30
Greece			1995, 1999	1995: 30, 1999: 30, in both: 30
Hungary	1998, 2000	1998: 57, 2000: 57	1998, 2000	1998: 30, 2000: 30, in both: 30
Ireland	1998	1998: 55	1998	1998: 26
Italy	1995, 2000	1995: 57, 2000: 57	1995, 2001	1995: 29, 2001: 29, in both: 29
Netherlands	1995, 2000	1995: 55, 2000: 55	1995, 2001	1995: 30, 2001: 30, in both: 30
Norway	2001	2001: 57	2002	2002: 29
Portugal	1999	1999: 56	1995, 1999	1995: 28, 1999: 28, in both: 28
Spain	1995	1995: 57	1995, 2000	1995: 29, 2000: 29, in both: 29
Sweden	1995, 2000	1995: 48, 2000: 55	1995, 2001	1995: 29, 2001: 29, in both: 29
United Kingdom	1995	1995: 57	1995, 2001	1995: 29, 2001: 29, in both: 29
United States	1997, 2002	1997: 30, 2002: 30	1992, 1997	1992: 29, 1997: 29, in both: 27

Table 5A.3   **Industry names for disaggregated imported input and distribution margin data**

Number	Industry Name	Mapping
a01	Agriculture, hunting and related service activities	nonmanufacturing
a02	Forestry, logging and related service activities	nonmanufacturing, raw materials
b05	Fishing, operation of fish hatcheries and fish farms; service activities incidental to fishing	nonmanufacturing
ca10	Mining of coal and lignite; extraction of peat	nonmanufacturing, raw materials
ca11	Extraction of crude petroleum and natural gas; service activities incidental to oil and gas extraction excluding surveying	nonmanufacturing, raw materials
ca12+	Mining of uranium and thorium ores	nonmanufacturing, raw materials
cb13	Mining of metal ores	nonmanufacturing, raw materials
cb14	Other mining and quarrying	nonmanufacturing, raw materials
da15	Manufacture of food products and beverages	manufacturing, food
da16	Manufacture of tobacco products	manufacturing, food
db17	Manufacture of textiles	manufacturing
db18	Manufacture of wearing apparel; dressing; dyeing of fur	manufacturing
dc19	Tanning, dressing of leather; manufacture of luggage	manufacturing
de21	Manufacture of pulp, paper and paper products	manufacturing
de22	Publishing, printing, reproduction of recorded media	manufacturing
df23	Manufacturing of Coke, refined petroleum products and nuclear fuel	manufacturing, energy
dg24	Manufacture of chemicals and chemical products	manufacturing

Number	Industry Name	Mapping
dh25	Manufacture of rubber and plastic products	manufacturing
di26	Manufacture of other nonmetallic mineral products	manufacturing
dj27	Manufacture of basic metals	manufacturing
dj28	Manufacture of fabricated metal products, except machinery and equipment	manufacturing
dk29	Manufacture of machinery and equipment n.e.c.	manufacturing
dl30	Manufacture of office machinery and computers	manufacturing
dl31	Manufacture of electrical machinery and apparatus n.e.c.	manufacturing
dl33	Manufacture of medical, precision and optical instruments, watches and clocks	manufacturing
dm34	Manufacture of motor vehicles, trailers and semi-trailers	manufacturing
dm35	Manufacture of other transport equipment	manufacturing
dn36	Manufacture of furniture; manufacturing n.e.c.	manufacturing
dn37	Recycling	nonmanufacturing
e40*	Electricity, gas, steam and hot water supply	nonmanufacturing, energy
e41*	Collection, purification and distribution of water	nonmanufacturing
f45*	Construction	nonmanufacturing
g50*	Sale, maintenance and repair of motor vehicles	nonmanufacturing
g51*	Wholesale trade and commission trade, except of motor and motorcycles	nonmanufacturing
g52*	Retail trade, except of motor vehicles, motorcycles; repair of personal and household goods	nonmanufacturing
h55*	Hotels and restaurants	nonmanufacturing
i60*	Land transport; transport via pipelines	nonmanufacturing
i61*	Water transport	nonmanufacturing
i62*	Air transport	nonmanufacturing
i63*	Supporting and auxiliary transport activities; activities of travel agencies	nonmanufacturing
i64*	Post and telecommunications	nonmanufacturing
j65*	Financial intermediation, except insurance and pension funding	nonmanufacturing
j66*	Insurance and pension funding, except compulsory social security	nonmanufacturing
j67*	Activities auxiliary to financial intermediation	nonmanufacturing
k70*	Real estate activities	nonmanufacturing
k71*	Renting of machinery and equipment without operator and of personal and household goods	nonmanufacturing
k72*	Computer and related activities	nonmanufacturing
k73*	Research and development	nonmanufacturing
l75*	Public administration and defense; compulsory social security	nonmanufacturing
m80*	Education	nonmanufacturing
n85*	Health and social work	nonmanufacturing
o90*	Sewage and refuse disposal, sanitation and similar activities	nonmanufacturing
o91*	Activities of membership organization n.e.c.	nonmanufacturing
o92*	Recreational, cultural and sporting activities	nonmanufacturing
o93*	Other service activities	nonmanufacturing
p95+*	Private households with employed persons	nonmanufacturing

Notes: + Excluded from imported input time trend regressions because of insufficient observations.

Table 5A.4 Distribution margin share

	Year	All Industries	Manufactured Goods	Nonmanufactured Goods	Energy	Food	Raw Materials
Austria	2001	0.14	0.14	0.14	0.19	0.21	0.10
Belgium	2001	0.14	0.13	0.16	0.11	0.16	0.14
Denmark	2000	0.16	0.16	0.14	0.08	0.17	0.22
Finland	2002	0.12	0.12	0.15	0.12	0.28	0.13
France	2001	0.12	0.12	0.12	0.10	0.17	0.04
Germany	2001	0.14	0.13	0.21	0.12	0.25	0.22
Greece	1999	0.20	0.20	0.15	0.18	0.20	0.07
Hungary	2000	0.07	0.08	0.00	0.10	0.18	−0.11
Ireland	1998	0.09	0.10	0.02		0.09	0.04
Italy	2001	0.16	0.15	0.31	0.14	0.28	0.31
Netherlands	2001	0.13	0.14	0.09	0.06	0.17	0.03
Norway	2002	0.17	0.19	0.12	0.17	0.20	0.06
Portugal	1999	0.14	0.14	0.15	0.18	0.19	0.10
Spain	2000	0.13	0.13	0.18	0.07	0.20	0.10
Sweden	2001	0.11	0.11	0.13	0.11	0.20	0.07
United Kingdom	2001	0.21	0.22	0.10	0.05	0.28	0.07
United States	1997	0.29	0.29	0.33	0.34	0.39	0.32
Average		0.15	0.15	0.15	0.13	0.21	0.11
Standard Deviation		0.05	0.05	0.08	0.07	0.07	0.11

References

Antzoulatos, A. A., and Jiawen Yang. 1996. Exchange rate pass-through in U.S. manufacturing industries: A demand side story. *The International Trade Journal* 10 (3): 325–52.

Bacchetta, P., and E. Wincoop. 2003. Why do consumer's prices react less than import prices to exchange rates. *Journal of the European Economics Association* 1 (2–3): 662–70.

Basu, S., and J. Fernald. 1997. Returns to scale in U.S. manufacturing: Estimates and implications. *Journal of Political Economy* 105:123–136.

Bernhofen, D. M., and P. Xu. 2000. Exchange rates and market power: Evidence from the petrochemical industry. *Journal of International Economics* 52 (2): 283–97.

Blonigen, B. A., and S. E. Haynes. 2002. Antidumping investigations and the pass-through of antidumping duties and exchange rates. *American Economic Review* 92 (4): 1044–61.

Burstein, A., J. Neves, and S. Rebelo. 2003. Distribution costs and real exchange rate dynamics during exchange rate based stabilizations. *Journal of Monetary Economics* 50:1189–1214.

Campa, J., and L. Goldberg. 2005. Exchange rate pass-through into import prices. *Review of Economics and Statistics* 87 (4): 679–90.

Campa, J., and L. Goldberg. 2006. Distribution margins, imported inputs, and the sensitivity of the CPI to exchange rates. NBER Working Paper no. 12121. Cambridge, MA: National Bureau of Economic Research, March.

Campa, J., L. Goldberg, and Jose González-Minguez. 2007. Exchange rate pass-through into Euro-area import prices. In *The External Dimension of the Euro Area*, eds. R. Anderton and F. de Mauro. Cambridge, England: Cambridge University Press.

Corsetti, G., and L. Dedola. 2003. The macroeconomics of international price discrimination. Economics Working Papers no. ECO2003/20. Florence, Italy: European University Institute.

Daly, D., R. Hellerstein, and C. Marsh. 2006. Have U.S. import prices become less responsive to changes in the dollar? *Current Issues in Economics and Finance* 12 (6): New York: Federal Reserve Bank of New York.

Engel, C. 1999. Accounting for U.S. real exchange rate changes. *Journal of Political Economy* 107 (3): 507–537.

Feenstra, R. 1989. Symmetric pass-through of tariffs and exchange rates under imperfect competition: An empirical test. *Journal of International Economics* 27 (1/2): 25–45.

Feenstra, R. 1998. Integration of trade and disintegration of production in the global economy. *The Journal of Economic Perspectives* 12:31–50.

Feinberg, R. M. 1989. The effects of foreign exchange movements on U.S. domestic prices. The Review of Economics and Statistics 71 (3): 505–11.

Frankel, J., D. Parsley, and S. Wei. 2005. Slow pass-through around the world: A new import for developing countries? NBER Working Paper no. 11199. Cambridge, MA: National Bureau of Economic Research.

Gagnon, J., and J. Ihrig. 2004. Monetary policy and exchange rate pass-through. *International Journal of Finance and Economics* 9:315–38.

Gil-Pareja, S. 2003. Pricing to market behavior in European car markets. *European Economic Review* 47(6): 945–62.

Goldberg, L., and C. Tille. 2006. The international role of the dollar and trade balance adjustment. NBER Working Paper no. 12495. Cambridge, MA: National Bureau of Economic Research.

Goldberg, P., and F. Verboven. 2001. The evolution of price dispersion in the European car market. *Review of Economic Studies* 68:811–48.

Goldberg, P., and M. Knetter. 1997. Goods prices and exchange rates: What have we learned? *Journal of Economic Literature* 35:1243–92.

Gron, A., and D. L. Swenson. 1996. Incomplete exchange-rate pass-through and imperfect competition: The effect of local production. *American Economic Review Papers and Proceedings* 86 (2): 71–76.

Gust, C., and N. Sheets. 2006. The adjustment of global external imbalances: Does partial pass-through to trade prices matter? International Finance Discussion Papers no. 850. Washington, DC: Board of Governors of the Federal Reserve System, January.

Hellerstein, R. 2004. Who bears the cost of a change in the exchange rate? The case of imported beer. Staff Reports no. 179 (February). New York: Federal Reserve Bank of New York.

Hummels, D., J. Ishii, and K-M. Yi. 2001. The nature and growth of vertical specialization in world trade. *Journal of International Economics* 54:75–96.

Ihrig, J., M. Marazzi, and A. Rothenberg. 2006. Exchange-rate pass-through in the G-7 countries. International Finance Discussion Papers, No. 851. Washington, DC: Board of Governors of the Federal Reserve System, January.

Marazzi, M., N. Sheets, R. Vigfusson, J. Faust, J. Gagnon, J. Marquez, R. Martin, T. Reeve, and S. Rogers. 2005. Exchange rate pass-through to U.S. import prices: Some new evidence. International Finance Discussion Paper No. 833. Washington, DC: Board of Governors of the Federal Reserve System, April.

Marazzi, M., and N. Sheets. 2006. Declining exchange rate pass-through to U.S. import prices: The potential of global factors. Manuscript. Washington, DC: Board of Governors of the Federal Reserve System.

Olivei, G. P. 2002. Exchange rates and the prices of manufacturing products imported into the United States. *New England Economic Review,* First Quarter, 3–18.

Osbat, C. 2005. Sectoral exchange rate pass-through in the Euro area. European Central Bank. Manuscript, December.

Osbat, C., and M. Wagner. 2006. Sectoral exchange rate pass-through in the euro area. European Central Bank. Mimeograph.

Otani, A., S. Shiratsuka, and T. Shirota. 2005. Revisiting the decline in the exchange-rate pass-through: Further evidence from Japan's import prices. IMES Discussion Paper Series no. 2005-E-6, July.

Pollard, P., and C. Coughlin. 2005. Pass-through estimates and the choice of exchange rate. Federal Reserve Bank of St. Louis, Working Paper, 2003–004C.

Rauch, J. 1999. Networks versus markets in international trade. *Journal of International Economics* 48:7–35.

Thomas, C., and J. Marquez. 2006. Measurement matters for modeling U.S. import prices. Federal Reserve Board of Governors, manuscript.

Yang, J. 1997. Exchange rate pass-through into U.S. manufacturing industries. *Review of Economics and Statistics* 79:95–104.

Comment   M. Chatib Basri

Linda Goldberg and Jose Manual Campa have produced a chapter that is both solid and stimulating. This chapter has a strong theoretical base and its empirical findings are important. Using a very rich database that covers sixteen countries in Europe and the United States in the pre- and post-1995 time periods and fifty-nine homogenous manufacturing, primary-industry, and service industry groupings, this chapter explores the role of distribution margins and imported inputs in exchange rate transmission into the consumption prices in five sectors across those countries. This chapter shows that retail price sensitivity to exchange rates may have increased over the past decade. In particular the argument is as follows. First, pass-through may have declined at the level of import prices, but the result is inconclusive over types of goods and countries. Second, there is evidence that imported input used across sectors has expanded largely, making the costs of imported goods as well as home tradable goods more sensitive to import prices and exchange rate. Third, in contrast to the impact of the increase of imported input used in production process, the pass-through effect of exchange rate to consumption prices has been insulated by the distribution margins. Overall, this chapter argues that the balance effect weighs in favor of increased sensitivity of consumption prices to exchange rates.

Following Campa and Goldberg's (2006) approach, which used a two country-model with wage stickiness and monopolistically competitive producers, this paper argues that distribution, services, and so on, provide some insulation. The larger the distribution share, the lower the pass-through impact is on consumer prices. On the contrary, the larger the imported input component of domestically produced goods, the higher the pass-through effect is.

Conceptually, the exchange rate pass-through depends on several variables including market structure, pricing policies, product substitutability, stickiness of wage and nontradable prices, prevailing exchange rate policy, and inflationary environment (Hyder and Shah 2004; Taylor 2000; Otani, Shiratsuka, and Shirota 2003).

There is a vast literature on the exchange rate pass-through, but this chapter specifically and thoroughly goes into the issue of the role of distribution margins and imported input in exchange rate pass-through. This approach seems convincing and is supported by strong methodology. Here Campa and Goldberg specifically show that distribution margins is not a key contributor to changing pass-through into consumption prices of the imported goods over the past decade. Instead, they argue that imported

M. Chatib Basri is Director of the Institute for Economic and Social Research in the Faculty of Economics at the University of Indonesia.

inputs, in the production of both traded and nontraded goods, including distribution services steadily increase, thus increase the predicted sensitivity of retail price to exchange rate. This argument is remarkably interesting because some studies argue that pass-through into import prices of industrialized countries has declined in the past decade (Otani, Shigenori, and Shiratsuka 2003; Marazzi, Sheets, and Vigfusson 2005). These findings are particularly important in enriching the discussion on the impact of exchange rate pass-through to consumption prices.

Now I will go into specific comments:

First, in section 5.2 the authors argue that the exchange rate pass-through into manufacturing industry import prices is relatively low compared to energy and raw materials. This result leads to a question of why the pass-through elasticity of manufacture import prices is rather low, even though it has high imported input shares? On the contrary, the pass-through effect in the raw materials is relatively high, although its imported input is relatively low. Unfortunately, the authors say little on this issue.

Second, this chapter shows that there has been an increase in the pass-through of movement in border prices of imports into the final prices of imported and domestically-produced goods for most countries except for the U.S. and Italy. This finding leads to a question of how we explain this phenomenon in the context of increasing globalization through production net-work and vertical trade/intra-industry trade? Otani, Shigenori, and Shiratsuka (2003), for instance, argue that the pass-through into import prices of industrialized countries has declined due to globalization. As for Japan, they argue that in response to the sharp appreciation of the yen in the mid 1980s, the proportion of the overseas production of Japanese firms increased, as did Japan's re-imports in the 1990s. This phenomenon leads into a decline of exchange rate pass-through in Japanese import prices. I think it will be useful if the authors try to reconcile this contrasting argument.

Third, this chapter shows that pass-through may have declined at the level of import prices, but the results are mixed over the type of goods and countries. I think these mixed findings can be attributed to the increasing globalization through production net-work and vertical trade/intra-industry trade. Thus, it would be useful if the authors try to look at the pass-through effect on countries that are involved in production net-work or vertical trade. By doing this, the authors can reconcile the contrasting argument from Otani, Shigenori, and Shiratsuka.

Fourth, this chapter argues that there has been large expansion of imported input used across sectors, which in turn increased the sensitivity to import price and exchange rates. I think it is very important to observe carefully the impact of increasing imported input to exchange rate pass-through. As pointed out by the authors, it is also of interest to note that the impact of increasing imported input used in the production process can be different if there is vertical or intra-industry trade. Increases in vertical trade also raise the possibility that imported products have value-added that originates in the home market. For example, as shown in the chapter, the U.S. imports of cars from Canada can contain engines that were produced in the United States and eventually re-exported to the United States. Thus, the more important the role of vertical trade, the lower the exchange rate pass-through effect becomes on the consumption prices. As a result, the increase of imported input does not necessarily heighten sensitivity to import prices and exchange rate. On this matter, again the selection of country samples is very important. Looking at the trend of increasing globalization through production-net work, an in-depth study on some particular manufacturing industries—for example electronics or automotive in some East Asian countries like Japan and Korea—is very useful and will give more flavor on the impact of vertical trade into exchange rate pass-through.

Fifth, Taylor (2000) argues the low inflation in the United States during early 2000 has also meant lower persistence of inflation. Conceptually, changes in expectation will reduce the persistence of cost and prices changes. As a result, the volatility in exchange rate is not transmitted into prices. This argument leads into a question of whether the decline in the exchange rate pass-through in the U.S. was due to an inflation (the role of monetary policy) or distribution services? How do we decompose those two effects?

Sixth, what is the role of market shares in the pass-through effect? To maintain the market shares, when there are substitutes available, firms will do some pricing-to-market which will reduce pass-through. I think some comparisons between some competitive and less competitive sectors may be useful to answer this question.

In sum, this chapter is worth reading and offers an important contribution for the study of the role of distribution margins and imported inputs in exchange rate transmission into the consumption prices. This excellent paper also draws some important implications for expenditure switching and trade adjustment from changes in exchange rates over time. In addition, various lessons can be drawn from this paper, particularly in relation to the role of distribution margins and imported input in exchange rate pass-through.

References

Campa, Jose and L. Goldberg. 2006. Distribution margins, imported inputs and the sensitivity of the CPI to exchange rates. NBER Working Paper no. 12121. Cambridge, MA: National Bureau of Economic Research.

Hyder, Z., and S. Sardar. 2005. 2005. Exchange rates pass-through to domestic prices in Pakistan. *Macroeconomics,* no. 0510021, October.

Marazzi, M., N. Sheets, R. Vigfusson, J. Faust, J. Gagnon, J. Marquez, R. Martin,

T. Reeve, and J. Rogers. 2005. Exchange rate pass-through to U.S. import prices: Some evidence. Manuscript. Washington, DC: Board of Governors of the Federal Reserve System.

Otani, A., S. Shiratsuka, and T. Shirota. 2003. The decline in the exchange rate pass-through: Evidence from Japanese import prices. *Monetary and Economic Studies* 21 (3): 51–81.

Taylor, J. 2000. Low inflation, pass-through and pricing power of firms. European Economic Review 44:1389–1408.

Comment   Kiyotaka Sato

This chapter analyzes an important issue of exchange rate pass-through into domestic prices, that is, what causes differences in the degree of exchange rate pass-through between import prices at the border and domestic consumption goods prices. It is well recognized that the extent of exchange rate pass-through into domestic consumption prices is far lower than the corresponding pass-through rate into import prices at the border. Campa and Goldberg attempt to explain such relative insensitivity of consumer prices to exchange rates by using the model-based approach where (a) the share of imported inputs and (b) distribution costs in importing countries play a key role in import-price transmission to domestic consumption prices.

A straightforward solution to this issue is that consumer prices include nontradable goods as well as tradable goods. If the price of nontradable goods were determined entirely by domestic conditions, domestic consumer prices, including nontradable goods, would become less sensitive to exchange rate changes. Indeed, Campa and Goldberg take this aspect into account by incorporating three types of goods in their model: home nontradable goods, home tradable goods, and imported consumption goods. However, they go further into a discussion of cost components for each type of goods. Specifically, home nontradable and tradable goods are assumed to be produced by using imported inputs. As long as pass-through into the border prices of imports is high, a larger share of imported inputs for production leads to a higher exposure of domestically produced products to exchange rate changes.

More importantly, Campa and Goldberg introduce strategic markup adjustments by domestic distributors as another important factor in the relative insensitivity of consumer prices to exchange rate changes. The retail prices of domestic tradable goods and imported consumption goods include nontradable goods and services as cost components, such as trans-

Kiyotaka Sato is associate professor of economics at Yokohama National University.

portation, local storage, marketing costs, and so on. These distribution costs are assumed to be strategically adjusted by local distributors in response to exchange rate changes if their products are being distributed to compete with other products. Thus, strategic adjustments of distribution margins in the distribution sector are likely to dilute sensitivity of imported consumption goods as well as domestic tradable goods to exchange rate changes.

Another important contribution of this study is to empirically investigate the changing pattern of import inputs share and distribution costs across countries and industries by using input-output tables. It is found that imported input use has grown substantially in the sample countries, while distribution expenditures do not show any clear pattern of changes. Moreover, Campa and Goldberg made a connection between these findings and calibrated pass-through elasticities of domestic consumption goods, and concluded that recent changes in import-price transmission to domestic prices are associated more with the increase in the share of imported inputs than that of distribution expenditures.

Thus, Campa and Goldberg have taken some important steps in an analysis of relative insensitivity of domestic consumption prices to exchange rate changes. In particular, they related calibrated pass-through elasticities with actual changes in both imported input shares and distribution costs, which is a significant advance from the existing studies. While they undoubtedly make an important contribution to the literature, there appears to be room for further improvements in their analysis.

First, although table 5.1 shows the extent of exchange rate pass-through into import prices at the border, it will be more informative if the paper presents the estimates of exchange rate pass-through into consumer prices as well. Since the objective of this study is to investigate what plays a key role in making the degree of pass-through lower in domestically produced goods than in imported goods, we first want to know the pass-through rate into domestic consumer goods and then check the difference in the degree of pass-through between import prices and domestic goods prices.

Second, and more importantly, in their calibration exercise, distribution margins are assumed *inelastic* with respect to exchange rate changes, whereas the strategic adjustments of markup by local distributors play a key role in the model of this paper. Owing to this assumption, the degree of pass-through is affected just by the distribution margins per se (i.e., the *share* of distribution costs in the final price of the products). Indeed, Campa and Goldberg calculated the distribution margin by using the input-output data and found that the distribution margin did not show any clear pattern of changes from 1995 to 2000. However, this does not necessarily mean that the distribution margin does not play a major role. It is more important to consider how distribution margins change in response to exchange rate changes during that period. We also need to check to what extent the effective exchange rates changed in each country during the period. In addition, possible differences in elasticities of distribution margins to exchange rates between imported consumption goods and domestic tradable goods are not fully considered in this study. These aspects are worth considering in further analysis of the relative insensitivity of consumer prices to the exchange rate changes.

6

Price Impacts of Deals and Predictability of the Exchange Rate Movements

Takatoshi Ito and Yuko Hashimoto

6.1 Introduction

The overwhelming majority of the spot foreign exchanges are now transacted through the global electronic broking systems—EBS and Reuters D3000.[1] This contrasts to the situation fifteen years ago, when brokers in the interbank market were mostly human and direct dealings between dealers also had a substantial share in the spot market. The euro/dollar and dollar/yen are the key currency pairs that traded on EBS, whereas Reuters has strengths in transactions of sterling/dollar, CAD/dollar, AUD/dollar, and NZD/dollar.

The EBS system works as follows.[2] A bank dealer places a "firm" limit order, either ask or bid, with specified price and units that the dealer is ready to trade if hit. A member bank sets credit limits to each of the possible trading partners in the EBS system when it joins the system. The

Takatoshi Ito is a professor in the Graduate School of Economics at the University of Tokyo, a member of the Japanese Council on Economic and Fiscal Policy, and a research associate of the National Bureau of Economic Research. Yuko Hashimoto is an associate professor of economics at Toyo University.

The authors are grateful to EBS for providing a proprietary data set for academic purpose. The earlier version of the paper was presented at the NBER 17th Annual East Asian Seminar on Economics in Hawaii June 22–24, 2006. We thank Peter Garber, Eli Remolona and Andy Rose for their comments. Helpful comments by Alain Chaboud and seminar participants at the Federal Reserve Board are gratefully acknowledged. The authors receive financial supports from the Japan Society for the Promotion of Science, Grants-in-aid, Basic Research, A-2-15203008 (Ito) and the Japan Society for the Promotion of Science, Grants-in-aid for Young Scientists, B17730211 (Hashimoto).

1. For papers that use electronic broking systems, see Goodhard, Ito, and Payne (1996), Goodhart and Payne (1996), Berger et al. (2005) and Chaboud et al. (2004).

2. Details of the EBS system and characteristics of the data are explained in Ito and Hashimoto (2004).

credit/counterparty risk is controlled by the EBS computer automatically. The computer collects these orders and displays on the screen of each member the following information, "best ask," "best bid," "best ask for the member," and "best bid for the member." The former two do not necessarily agree with the latter two, respectively, because the EBS system controls for the bilateral credit lines and shows the best available for each institution. Hence, if the member does not have a credit line with the market maker(s) that is (are) posting the "best" ask/bid in the market, then the individually available best quotes deviate from the market best quotes. The computer continuously clears the order whenever the sell and buy order matches at the same price—this could happen either when a buyer hits the ask quote posted in the system, or a seller hits the bid quotes posted in the system. The electronic broking system is a centralized network of traders. In a sense, the electronic broking system can be regarded either as a collection of large numbers of market makers or as a continuous (Walrasian) auctioneer. We will use the dollar/yen and euro/dollar data sets provided by EBS.[3]

Retail customers place their buy or sell orders via banks, based on their private information. Then, banks transmit those customers' orders to the electronic broking system. Banks may add their own proprietary trading positions onto the customer orders. As the trading system is highly computerized, trading strategies of banks have evolved too. Until several years ago, bank dealers who received customers' orders were allowed by bank policy to hold their own proprietary positions for profit-taking. They tended to add their own positions when they executed the customers' orders if they felt that customer' orders contained some valuable information. Receiving customers' orders meant a special information advantage in forecasting the direction of the foreign exchange rate. See Lyons (1995, 1996, 1997, 1998, 2001) for modeling of this line of reasoning. In line with the information and pricing in market, Lyons and Moore (2005) applied the information model to the transactions in a triangle of markets, USD/JPY, EUR/USD, and EUR/JPY and found the transaction affected prices.

Dealers in banks now have only very small amounts of their own proprietary positions. Responsibility of proprietary trading has been shifted to an independent department, sometimes characterized as an in-house hedge fund. A proprietary trading section uses more computer modeling than private information extracted from customers' trading. Speeding millions of dollars on programmers (often physics PhDs) and high-speed computers is necessary for high-frequency trading strategy. Clearly they see profit opportunities by betting on directions of the exchange rate in the very short-run, that is, a few minutes to several hours.

In contrast, many economists still believe that the exchange rate is basi-

---

3. The data set was provided for a fee by the EBS Co., for the use at the University of Tokyo, Graduate School of Economics. The authors are grateful to EBS for such an arrangement.

cally a random walk, and it would be a profitless effort to conceive a model that can predict an exchange rate movement. The gap between the academic random walk and millions of dollars invested for a bet on predictable movements in the real world is remarkable, as pointed out by Ito (2005a, b). Evans and Lyons (2005a), for example, examine daily Euro/USD exchange rate returns based on the trades by the end-user and find a persistent (days) effect in currency market induced by news announcement. Still, it is our view that foreign exchange rate modeling in the academic literature is lagging behind the reality.

Conventional wisdom in the academic literature is that the exchange rate follows a random walk for frequencies less than annual, that is, daily, weekly, or even monthly, whereas it shows some time trends, cyclicality or in general history dependence at lower frequencies. For example, Evans and Lyons (2005b) show forecasting performance of a microbased model against a macro and a random walk model using end-user exchange rate. Some studies in the microstructure focuses on very high frequency movements of the exchange rate and show that the exchange rate may respond to pressures of customers' orders. Evans and Lyons (2002), for example, reported a positive relation between daily exchange rate returns and order flows for deutsche mark/dollar. Berger and colleagues (2005) also showed a positive contemporaneous relationship between order flows and the exchange rate, while they reported no evidence of the predicting power of order flows for future exchange rate. In Evans and Lyons (2005c), heterogeneity of order flow was considered in estimating the price impact. Based on the end-user order flow data, they show order flow provides information to market makers.

In this paper, we will examine the relationship between pressures of seller-initiated orders or buyer-initiated orders and the resulting price movements in the following few minutes to half an hour. Although direct observations of customer order flows to banks are not available, deals initiated by sellers and those by buyers in the EBS system are observable. Order flows and executed prices give the information on customers and bank proprietary desks.

Given the organizational change in creating proprietary trading departments in banks, customer orders have to contain both retail customers and bank proprietary positions. Retail customer orders contain information, but orders from computer-generated programs in an in-house proprietary trading department are equally important. It is best to exact information of order flows from seller-initiated and buyer-initiated deals in the system. Therefore we take actual deals done in the market as the buying or selling pressures in the market.

The EBS data record the ask-side deals or bid-side deals for every second. (Lowest given or highest paid are recorded for each second, when at least one deal on either side was executed during the second.) An ask-side deal means that the ready-to-sell quote was hit by a buyer, thus it represents a buyer-initiated deal, that is, a piece of buying pressure. A bid-side deal means that the ready-to-buy quote was hit by a seller, thus it represents a seller-initiated deal, that is, a piece of selling pressure. Therefore, by taking the difference between the number of ask-side deals and the number of bid-side deals in the time frame of x minutes, we can quantify the buy pressure or sell pressure during the x minutes. Then we will measure an impact of buy (sell) pressure to drive up (down) the price contemporaneously or with lags.

The EBS data were exploited in two papers written by Federal Reserve Board economists. Chaboud and colleagues (2004) analyzed the relationship between a macro news announcement and trade volume, and found news releases tend to raise trade volume. Berger and colleagues (2005) showed the correlations between order flows and exchange rate movement. The trading volumes of the buyer-initiated trades (ask-side deals) in excess of the seller-initiated deals (bid-side deals) are considered to be order flows. They examined whether the exchange rate appreciates if there are more buyer initiated trades in several time aggregations, one minutes, five minutes, ten minutes, one hour, and one day. They find strong association of order flows and exchange rate changes, namely, an excess of buyer-initiated trades is associated with a rising price. The contemporary association is strongest in the shortest horizon. Although Berger and colleagues (2005) find a positive contemporaneous price impact of order flow, they argue that there is little evidence for predictability, namely lagged trades impacting on the price change in the next minute.

The objective of our paper is to analyze the forecasting power of order flows (actual deals in the preceding thirty minutes) on future exchange rate movements at various frequencies: one-, five-, fifteen- and thirty-minute windows. The data used in the analysis is extracted from the EBS spanning from January 1999 to October 2003. Our measure of order flows is the "net ask deals" that is defined as the difference between the number of ask deals and bid deals. In our paper, "deal" in one minute is the number of seconds in which at least one deal was done. Although this is not precisely the trading volumes, it is a close substitute.[4]

The prices used to calculate exchange rate returns are based on actual transaction prices, not quoted prices (bid or ask) which may not represent market clearing prices—this is the same as Berger and colleagues (2005) and Chaboud and colleagues (2004). We then estimate price impact of deals in the following time periods up to thirty minutes.

We find strong evidence that order flows (deals) have prediction power for the price movement of one minute to five minutes, while thirty minutes is found to be too long for prediction. The degree of price impact is found

---

4. Berger et al. (2005) and Chaboud et al. (2004) use the actual volume data, but the use of the data is restricted in the central bank community.

to diminish over time, although intervention may induce lagged price impact, and there may be an adjustment process in exchange rate movements. The rest of this paper is organized as follows: In section 6.2 we describe the data. Section 6.3 shows the estimation model and reports the results. Section 6.4 concludes the paper.

6.2   Data[5]

The data set includes information of quote prices and deal prices of the dollar/yen and the euro/dollar currency pairs. The sample period is from January 4, 1998 to October 31, 2003 for USD/JPY, and from January 3, 1999 to October 31, 2003 for EUR/USD.[6] It contains information for, among others, best bid, best ask, deal prices done on the bid side (lowest given), and deal prices done on the ask side (highest paid).[7] It does not contain any information on the volume associated with bid, offer, or deal, or any information on the identity of bid, ask, or deal. The EBS global system consists of three regional computer sites, based in Tokyo, London, and New York, and each region covers Europe, North America, and Asia, respectively. The system matches orders either within the site or across different sites.

We exclude all data from Friday 22:00 (GMT, winter, 21:00 in summer) to Sunday 21:59 (GMT, winter, 20:59 in summer, respectively). If at least one of the three major markets has a national (banking) holiday, then that day is dropped from the sample. In addition, if there is no trade recorded in the time window of the frequency, that particular time is dropped.

To analyze returns at various frequencies, we use the last deal price of the time interval. For the x-minute frequency, we use the last deal price within the x-minute window ($x = 1, 5, 15, 30$). The number of bid and ask deals are separately counted within each frequency. For example, the number of bid deals in 5-minutes equals the total number of seconds in which one or more deals took place.

---

5. The authors are grateful to EBS for providing a proprietary data set for this academic purpose and to EBS analysts in New York for guidance on the nature of the data.

6. Data are of the 1-second time slice. The system records, at every second, bid, offer, deals that are posted and carried out in the world-wide EBS system. Bid and offer rates are recorded at the end of time slice. For example, bid and offer rate at xx hour, yy minute, zz second. Fluctuations of the bid and offer rates within the second (in the time slice) are not recorded and cannot be inferred. It is theoretically possible that bid and offer rates move up and down within the second, but not shown in the data set. Deal rates are recorded on the basis of Highest Paid and Lowest Given at the 1-second time slice. See Ito and Hashimoto (2004, 2006) for details.

7. The deal (on either side) recorded at zz second includes those that took place between zz – 1 second to zz second. When there are multiple trades within one second, "lowest given price" and "highest paid price" will be shown. A highest paid deal means the highest price hit (done) on the ask side within one second and the lowest given deal means the lowest price hit (done) on the bid side within one second.

The *ask quote* means that the institution with the quote is ready to sell (the dollar in exchange for the quoted yen) and the *bid quote* means that the institution with the quote is ready to buy (the dollar in exchange for the quoted yen). When the deal is done at the ask side—we call it *ask deal*—it means that the ask quote is *hit* by a buyer. When the deal is done at the bid side—we call it *bid deal*—it means that the bid quote is hit by a seller. Therefore the ask deal is a buyer-initiated deal, and the bid deal is a seller-initiated deal, according to the description in Berger and colleagues (2005).[8]

By counting the number of ask (bid) deals within a fixed time period (x-minutes), we measure the order flows to buy (or sell, respectively). If the number of the ask deals is larger (smaller) than the number of the bid deals in the time period, it is interpreted that pressure to buy (or sell, respectively) is stronger. When pressure to buy (sell) is stronger, the prices—here the price of the dollar in terms of the yen—tend to rise (or drop, respectively). There are two ways that pressure is materialized into quote and price changes. First, when buy orders hit all volumes at the best ask quotes, then the second best ask quotes becomes the best, and the best ask moves up. Second, by watching that deals are done on the ask side, dealers may withdraw the best ask quote and requote at a higher price. Either way, the ask quote tends to move up when buyers start to hit the best ask quote. If the process continues, then the ask deal prices continue to move up in the subsequent time period. The reverse is true; if selling pressure is strong, then bid deal prices may decline. When the ask quote is rising, the bid quote is likely to rise with it as dealers revise the equilibrium value of the currency.

The above inference leads to a hypothesis that the return of (or changes in) the ask deal price, as well as ask quote price, will be influenced by the buy pressure, while the return of the bid deal price, as well as bid quote price, will be influenced by the sell pressure.

As we differentiate ask-side deals (buy pressure) and bid-side deals (sell pressure), we can identify the direction of order flows from deal data. So, our variables, the difference between the ask-side and bid-side deals, are regarded to represent order flows.

---

8. The buyer-initiated trades (the seller-initiated trades) used in Berger et al. (2005) corresponds to the number of deals on ask side (the number of deals on bid side) in our chapter, respectively. The order flow, the net excess of buyer-initiated trades in Berger et al. corresponds to the *netdeal* in our chapter. Berger et al. had access to the data of actual transaction volumes—proprietary data of EBS—while we use the number of seconds in which at least one deals was done. The number of deals, rather than the signed (actual) volume, is good enough proxy for the volume of transaction. In fact, the actual transaction volume is not revealed to participants other than parties involved, so that they would not be able to be used in prediction of price movement in real time.

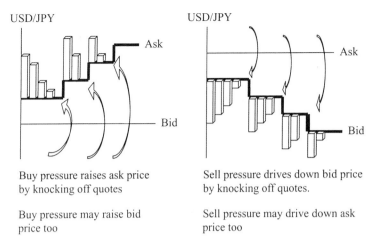

Fig. 6.1   **Stylized process of one-sided deals knocking off best quotes**

6.3   Prediction Window Estimation

In this section, we examine whether order flows in period t will have a predictive power of price movement from period t to $t + 1$. More precisely, we examine whether a relative number of deals on the bid and ask side will drive the price lower or higher x-minute(s) later. For the proxy of order flows in the EBS data, we use *net deals,* defined as the difference between the number of ask deals and that of bid deals during a specified frequency. For testing the predictability of this framework, we use three frequencies: 1-minute, 5-minute, 15-minute and 30-minute windows. The sample period covers from January 4, 1998 to October 31, 2003 for USD/JPY, and from January 3, 1999 to October 31, 2003 for EUR/USD pair.

We will examine *netdeals* at period t to help predict the price movements in period $t + 1$. A similar attempt was made by Berger and colleagues (2005). They regarded a net excess of buyer-initiated trades as order flow. The *net excess of buyer-initiated trades* is the difference between the volume of the buyer-initiated trades, or deals done on the ask side, and the seller-initiated trades, or deals done on the bid side. They note that a dealer tends to break up a large customer's order into small lots and execute them in a staggered manner, in order to avoid large impacts on prices.

One difference of our approach from Berger and colleagues (2005) and Evans and Lyons (2002) is that we do not include contemporaneous effect in this inference, in order to avoid an endogeneity problem, and to test predictability directly.

A variable *netdeal* corresponds to net excess buyer-initiated trade, as a proxy for order flow. We also use a *netdeal ratio (ndr),* or the *netdeal* over the total number of deals (both bid and ask sides) during the period, instead of *netdeal*. Since the overall market activity varies from time to time, the share is able to scale *netdeal* by the degree of market activeness. For example, if # *deal ask* = 700 and # *deal bid* = 690 when the market is active and # *deal ask* = 80 and # *deal bid* = 70 when the market is calm, then *netdeal* is 10 for both cases but *ndr* is 0.0072 and 0.067, respectively.

Therefore, the two definitions of order flows are written as follows:

$$netdeal = \# \, askdeal - \# \, biddeal$$

$$ndr = \frac{\# \, askdeal - \# \, biddeal}{\#askdeal + \# \, biddeal}$$

To reiterate, a conjecture of deal and price movements is as follows: When *ndr* is positive it represents buying pressure, and when *ndr* is negative it represents selling pressure. We expect that buying pressure will raise the ask quote, as explained earlier, and selling pressure will lower the bid quote. Therefore, we construct a variable that would represent buying pressure and selling pressure separately in order to associate with ask- and bid-quote movements separately.

Let us define the buying pressure and the selling pressure as follows, respectively:[9]

$$nd_t^{plus} = \max(netdeal_t, 0), \text{ and}$$

$$nd_t^{minus} = \min(netdeal_t, 0)$$

The regression model is specified as follows. We examine whether deals done at period $t - 1$ at either side help predict the price movement for the next period, t, using information that is contained in the data up to period t:

(1) $$\Delta s_t = \beta_0 + \beta_1 nd_{t-1}^{plus} + \beta_2 nd_{t-1}^{minus} + \sum_j \delta \Delta s_{t-j} + \varepsilon_t,$$

where Δs denotes the exchange rate return from period $t - 1$ to t. Here, nd^{plus} means that the number of deals done at the ask side is larger than the number of deals done on the bid side during period t, and nd^{minus} vice versa.

The estimation methodology is similar to that of Berger and colleagues (2005), in which they estimated the contemporaneous regression with time horizons of 1-minute, 5-minutes, 10-minutes, 1-hour, 1-day, and 1-month. They went on to estimate another regression with lagged Δs and order flows up to five periods. In this paper, we estimate equation (1) with various definitions of returns and explanatory variables.

In the estimation, six different definitions of returns are used for this variable. For deal-price returns we consider the following three patterns:

9. Summary statistics of nd^{plus} and nd^{minus} are summarized in Appendix tables, A-1 and A-2.

the midpoint of the deal-ask and deal-bid prices, the ask-side deal price, and the bid-side deal price. For quote returns, we again consider the three types of returns: the midpoint of the quote prices, the ask price, and the bid price. Berger and colleagues (2005) use the midpoint of the ask- and bid-deal prices, which is a standard practice in the literature. However, the midpoint may not represent a true state of the market, if the last ask side deal was done several minutes prior to the last bid deal. In other words, when the market is thin or one-sided (strong buy pressure or sell pressure) then the midpoint may not be representative. Therefore, we also use the bid-bid return and ask-ask returns, in addition to the midpoint price returns.

Therefore, the regression models to be estimated are the following:

(2) $\quad \Delta s(askdeal)_t = \alpha_0 + \alpha_1 nd_{t-1}^{plus} + \alpha_2 nd_{t-1}^{minus} + \sum_j \delta \Delta s_{t-j} + \varepsilon_t$

(3) $\quad \Delta s(biddeal)_t = \beta_0 + \beta_1 nd_{t-1}^{plus} + \beta_1 nd_{t-1}^{minus} + \sum_j \delta \Delta s_{t-j} + \varepsilon_t$

(4) $\quad \Delta s(midpoint)_t = \gamma_0 + \gamma_1 nd_{t-1}^{plus} + \gamma_2 nd_{t-1}^{minus} + \sum_j \delta \Delta s_{t-j} + \varepsilon_t$

In equation (2), the parameters α_1 captures the direct price impact of ask-side transactions (buy pressures) on the ask-deal price (sell quote) movement. The continuum of ask deals will drive up the price in the following period (dollar appreciation) after eating up orders at the best-ask price and requoting of ask-side dealers. The expected sign is unambiguously positive. The parameter α_2 shows the effect of bid-side deal on the ask quotes in the following period. The expected sign is positive since the negative movement (selling pressure) will drive down the prices. But the effect may not be as significant as α_1 since the causal effect of deals on quotes is not as direct as the ask side deals. If the value of α_1 equals that of α_2 then the effect is symmetric and there is no reason we differentiate nd^{plus} and nd^{minus} but, to use *netdeal* suffices.

In equation (3), the parameter β_2 shows the price impact of bid-side transaction (sell pressures) on bid-price (buy price) returns. Enough bid deals will drive down bid quotes in the following period, knocking-off orders at the best bid price and causing quote revisions on the bid side. The β_2 is expected to be unambiguously positive. The parameter β_1 captures the effect of ask-side transaction (buy pressures) on bid-deal returns (buy quote prices) and the expected sign is positive.

We will call the estimated parameters α_1 and β_2 to represent knocking-off effects, and α_2 and β_1 to represent catch-up effects. (Recall figure 6.1.) Comparing equations (2) and (3), the parameter relationship $\alpha_1 \geq \beta_1$ should hold since it is rather inconceivable that the ask price rises faster than the bid price when the ask-side quotes are transacted by buying pressures. Similarly, $\beta_2 \geq \alpha_2$ is expected since it is more likely that the decline in bid quotes is faster than the ask quotes when the bid quotes are been hit by selling pressure. If both relationships are held constant, $\alpha_1 = \beta_1$ and/or $\alpha_2 = \beta_2$, then the bid-ask spread is interpreted to remain constant:

(5) $\quad \Delta s(bestoffer)_t = \alpha_0 + \alpha_1 nd_{t-1}^{plus} + \alpha_2 nd_{t-1}^{minus} + \sum_j \delta \Delta s_{t-j} + \varepsilon_t$

(6) $\quad \Delta s(bestbid)_t = \beta_0 + \beta_1 nd_{t-1}^{plus} + \beta_2 nd_{t-1}^{minus} + \sum_j \delta \Delta s_{t-j} + \varepsilon_t$

(7) $\quad \Delta s(quotemidpoint)_t = \gamma_0 + \gamma_1 nd_{t-1}^{plus} + \gamma_2 nd_{t-1}^{minus} + \sum_j \delta \Delta s_{t-j} + \varepsilon_t$

We apply the same regression methodology to estimate the price impact of quote-price returns. Interpretations are similar to the previous equations. Equations (5)–(7) show the best offer returns, best bid returns, and the midpoint of quote prices, respectively.

Again, the parameter relationship $\alpha_1 \geq \beta_1$ should hold if the bid prices lagged behind the ask prices in the process of buying pressure moving the prices up. Similarly, $\beta_2 \geq \alpha_2$ is expected if the best ask price lags behind the bid price in declines when selling pressures drives down the prices. If the bid and ask prices move together, the spread remains constant if a relationship $\alpha_1 = \beta_1$ and/or $\alpha_2 = \beta_2$ is found.

For the explanatory variables of nd, we attempt two versions: one with the difference in numbers (*netdeal*) and another with the ratio (*ndr*). Other explanatory variables included in the regression are 1–10 lags of dependent variable. We also control for the time of the day (hour) effect for the regressions.[10]

6.3.1 Results

The regression results are summarized in tables 6.1–6.4 (USD/JPY, deal returns), tables 6.5–6.8 (USD/JPY, quote returns), and tables 6.9–6.12 (EUR/USD, deal returns), and tables 6.13–6.15 (EUR/USD, quote returns).

Overall, the *t*-statistics of variables become insignificant as the chosen frequency becomes lower, regardless of currency pairs and the choice of return definition. For example, the estimated coefficients of explanatory variables (*nd*) are positive and statistically significant in most cases at the 1-minute window, but they become insignificant at the 30-minute window.

The regression results of USD/JPY deal price returns are shown in tables 6.1–6.15. In each table, left-side panels report the results estimated with *netdeal,* and the right-side panels report the results with *ndr.* Tables 6.1 and 6.2 show that price impacts are highly significant at 1- and 5-minute frequencies. The results for 1- and 5-minute periodicity are quite clean and robust. The result is robust with respect to the choice of the ask-deal price,

---

10. It is well known that foreign exchange markets have intra-day seasonality, see Ito and Hashimoto (2004, 2006) and Ito, Lyons, and Melvin (1998) for such a phenomenon for the yen market, and more generally, Andersen and Bollerslev (1997, 1998) and Baillie and Bollerslev (1990).

Table 6.1 Prediction: USD/JPY 1-minute deal return

	netdeal					ndr					
	ndplus	s.e.	ndminus	s.e.	NOB	ndplus	s.e.	NOB	ndminus	s.e.	NOB
Log middle price											
1998	9.34E-04	7.23E-05***	1.09E-03	7.74E-05***	63391	1.25E-02	9.80E-04***	63391	1.21E-02	1.06E-03***	63391
1999	7.66E-04	5.83E-05***	4.95E-04	6.36E-05***	60186	8.69E-03	7.83E-04***	60186	8.40E-03	8.43E-04***	60186
2000	5.90E-04	6.56E-05***	7.81E-04	6.82E-05***	37212	7.88E-03	8.13E-04***	37212	8.32E-03	8.52E-04***	37212
2001	6.17E-04	5.58E-05***	6.69E-04	5.93E-05***	44285	7.73E-03	6.89E-04***	44285	8.38E-03	7.25E-04***	44285
2002	5.89E-04	4.93E-05***	4.85E-04	5.15E-05***	49712	7.69E-03	6.31E-04***	49712	6.29E-03	6.55E-04***	49712
2003	5.51E-04	5.23E-05***	4.76E-04	5.43E-05***	42400	5.56E-03	6.55E-04***	42400	7.49E-03	6.83E-04***	42400
Ask deal return											
1998	1.48E-03	5.97E-05***	9.91E-04	6.23E-05***	90950	8.20E-03	4.84E-04***	90950	1.60E-02	7.16E-04***	108425
1999	1.20E-03	4.89E-05***	5.23E-04	5.18E-05***	88435	5.87E-03	4.07E-04***	88435	1.34E-02	6.05E-04***	99849
2000	1.06E-03	5.09E-05***	7.20E-04	5.13E-05***	62049	4.73E-03	3.74E-04***	62049	1.15E-02	5.75E-04***	69572
2001	9.42E-04	4.53E-05***	6.11E-04	4.68E-05***	70365	5.10E-03	3.34E-04***	70365	1.15E-02	5.08E-04***	79179
2002	9.24E-04	4.02E-05***	5.14E-04	4.12E-05***	76168	5.11E-03	3.09E-04***	76168	1.05E-02	4.59E-04***	85919
2003	9.38E-04	4.27E-05***	4.91E-04	4.32E-05***	64972	3.72E-03	3.28E-04***	64972	1.06E-02	4.86E-04***	71439
Bid deal return											
1998	7.75E-04	5.17E-05***	1.59E-03	5.72E-05***	108425	1.81E-02	7.65E-04***	108425	7.54E-03	6.18E-04***	90950
1999	7.56E-04	4.44E-05***	1.08E-03	4.95E-05***	99849	1.29E-02	6.16E-04***	99849	5.85E-03	4.83E-04***	88435
2000	5.40E-04	4.72E-05***	1.23E-03	5.06E-05***	69572	1.20E-02	5.86E-04***	69572	4.91E-03	4.24E-04***	62049
2001	6.03E-04	4.13E-05***	1.08E-03	4.49E-05***	79179	1.11E-02	5.24E-04***	79179	4.53E-03	3.87E-04***	70365
2002	5.51E-04	3.65E-05***	9.64E-04	3.91E-05***	85919	1.08E-02	4.82E-04***	85919	4.28E-03	3.58E-04***	76168
2003	5.16E-04	3.96E-05***	8.93E-04	4.20E-05***	71439	9.12E-03	4.98E-04***	71439	4.80E-03	3.75E-04***	64972

Note: ***, **, and * indicate the significance at 1, 5, 10%, respectively.

Table 6.2 Prediction: USD/JPY 5-minute deal return

	netdeal					ndr				
	ndplus	s.e.	ndminus	s.e.	NOB	ndplus	s.e.	ndminus	s.e.	NOB
Log middle price										
1998	2.53E-04	6.15E-05***	3.08E-04	7.23E-05***	52922	1.18E-02	2.08E-03***	1.35E-02	2.35E-03***	52922
1999	2.11E-04	5.19E-05***	2.79E-04	6.10E-05***	52425	7.72E-03	1.68E-03***	9.97E-03	1.88E-03***	52425
2000	2.50E-04	4.96E-05***	3.67E-04	5.41E-05***	47782	8.96E-03	1.37E-03***	1.02E-02	1.48E-03***	47782
2001	1.53E-04	4.59E-05***	2.50E-04	5.22E-05***	48571	5.07E-03	1.32E-03***	7.01E-03	1.47E-03***	48571
2002	2.16E-04	4.26E-05***	2.49E-04	4.73E-05***	49883	7.06E-03	1.27E-03***	7.13E-03	1.38E-03***	49883
2003	3.93E-04	4.29E-05***	1.73E-04	4.70E-05***	42979	8.56E-03	1.24E-03***	6.47E-03	1.35E-03***	42979
Ask deal return										
1998	2.82E-04	5.85E-05***	4.75E-04	6.87E-05***	59034	1.67E-02	1.93E-03***	1.13E-02	1.88E-03***	59034
1999	2.42E-04	4.94E-05***	4.17E-04	5.80E-05***	58570	7.39E-03	1.31E-03***	1.27E-02	1.67E-03***	58570
2000	2.43E-04	4.71E-05***	5.02E-04	5.13E-05***	54148	6.50E-03	1.105E-03***	1.27E-02	1.32E-03***	54148
2001	1.86E-04	4.34E-05***	4.03E-04	4.93E-05***	55211	4.64E-03	1.00E-03***	1.02E-02	1.30E-03***	55211
2002	2.32E-04	4.03E-05***	3.58E-04	4.47E-05***	56313	6.53E-03	9.58E-04***	9.18E-03	1.22E-03***	56313
2003	4.01E-04	4.07E-05***	2.74E-04	4.45E-05***	48562	6.42E-03	9.53E-04***	8.40E-03	1.20E-03***	48562
Bid deal return										
1998	4.25E-04	5.93E-05***	3.78E-04	7.01E-05***	57305	1.04E-02	1.64E-03***	1.68E-02	2.11E-03***	57305
1999	3.58E-04	5.01E-05***	3.40E-04	5.91E-05***	56617	1.20E-03	1.56E-03***	8.50E-03	1.52E-03***	56617
2000	4.04E-04	4.73E-05***	4.14E-04	5.20E-05***	52806	1.22E-02	1.25E-03***	7.39E-03	1.15E-03***	52806
2001	2.93E-04	4.42E-05***	2.99E-04	5.04E-05***	53251	8.30E-03	1.22E-03***	6.57E-03	1.14E-03***	53251
2002	3.20E-04	4.09E-05***	2.84E-04	4.57E-05***	54555	9.52E-03	1.16E-03***	6.77E-03	1.08E-03***	54555
2003	4.77E-04	4.15E-05***	1.95E-04	4.56E-05***	46880	1.10E-02	1.15E-03***	5.05E-03	1.07E-03***	46880

Note: ***, ** and * indicate the significance at 1, 5, 10%, respectively.

bid-deal price, or midpoint. The net buy (sell) pressure represented by the order flows has predictive power on the price movements in the following one to five minutes. The result is confirmed in each year in the sample. Tables 6.3 and 6.4 show that these impacts become statistically insignificant in the 15-minute and 30-minute windows.

As for the parameter relationships, we only find significant parameter relationships of $\alpha_1 \geq \beta_1$ and $\beta_2 \geq \alpha_2$ in the 1-minute deal return regression using *netdeal*. In this case, the catch up effects lag behind the knock-off effects. In other cases, it is more common that the bid-ask spread becomes temporarily more narrow in the course of transaction at a very high-frequency (1 minute at the longest) interval.

We can make a rough calculation about the magnitude of predictable movement, provided that data on order flows are available. For example, an increase in ask-deal price when one unit of order flow to buy (nd^{plus}) is observed in the left-panel, the yen/dollar rate, in terms of ask-side deal prices, is supposed to move 0.00148 (the coefficient) in 1998 and around 0.0009 in 2001–2003. The appendix shows that the maximum order flow counts are in the order of 20 to 25. So that the impact of very large order flows on the deal price change is in the order of 0.02 to 0.03. The unit of the left-side variable is the percentage change of the yen/dollar rate, so that 0.02 to 0.03 translates into 0.02 yen or 0.03 yen, when the yen/dollar rate is 100 (and one-percent change means 0.01 yen). This exceeds the average bid-ask spread during the active trading hours.[11]

Similarly, the right-side panel indicates that the ask-side deal prices would respond by 0.018 in 1998, and by a slightly smaller margin by 2003, to a one-sided (100 percent) order-flow direction. The magnitude of 0.018 translates into a change by 0.018 yen/dollar when the yen/dollar level is 100. Similarly, the magnitude exceeds the busiest-hour bid-ask spread.

Tables 6.5–6.8 reports the price impact of USD/JPY quote returns. Results are quite similar to deal-price returns. Price impact is significant at 1-minute and 5-minute frequencies. Predictability of changes in bid and ask quotes in response to order flows, that is, buy or sell pressure, of the preceding time window is clearly established for the 1-minute and 5-minute windows. The number of significant coefficients decreases in the 15-minute window and represents almost no significance in the 30-minute frequency. The transaction at $t - 1$ significantly moves quote prices from $t - 1$ to t up to the 5-minute window, but the price impact disappears at 30-minute frequency.

The parameter relationships of $\alpha_1 \geq \beta_1$ or $\beta_2 \geq \alpha_2$ do not necessarily hold in many cases for 1-minute quote returns and 5-minute quote returns. So, we cannot generalize whether the knocking-off effects are larger than the

11. For descriptions of bid-ask spreads depending on GMT hours (intra-day seasonality), see Ito and Hashimoto (2004).

Table 6.3 Prediction: USD/JPY 15-minute deal return

	netdeal					ndr				
	ndplus	s.e.	ndminus	s.e.	NOB	ndplus	s.e.	ndminus	s.e.	NOB
					Log middle price					
1998	3.16E-05	8.61E-05	8.07E-05	1.14E-04	23149	5.84E-03	6.53E-03	6.74E-03	7.35E-03	23149
1999	-1.81E-04	7.13E-05***	-1.47E-04	9.58E-05*	22821	2.42E-03	5.09E-03	3.76E-03	5.92E-03	22821
2000	6.53E-05	6.79E-05	-1.93E-05	7.93E-05	22292	5.76E-03	3.97E-03*	2.41E-03	4.15E-03	22292
2001	1.15E-04	6.32E-05**	3.49E-05	7.94E-05	22354	4.77E-03	3.73E-03	4.79E-03	4.25E-03	22354
2002	-3.46E-05	5.79E-05	1.73E-04	7.00E-05***	22569	5.97E-03	3.55E-03**	3.58E-03	4.05E-03	22569
2003	2.79E-05	5.92E-05	-7.10E-06	6.98E-05	19113	7.87E-03	3.60E-03**	-4.45E-03	4.04E-03	19113
					Ask deal return					
1998	4.25E-05	8.52E-05	1.14E-04	1.12E-04	23654	5.17E-03	5.98E-03	8.87E-03	7.11E-03	23654
1999	-1.84E-04	7.07E-05***	-1.08E-04	9.49E-05	23272	4.33E-03	4.73E-03	5.56E-03	5.79E-03	23272
2000	9.12E-05	6.70E-05*	1.81E-05	7.82E-05	23057	8.10E-03	3.55E-03**	2.57E-03	4.01E-03	23057
2001	1.15E-04	6.22E-05**	8.00E-05	7.83E-05	23260	4.76E-03	3.30E-03*	7.02E-03	4.07E-03**	23260
2002	-1.96E-05	5.71E-05	2.26E-04	6.91E-05***	23445	5.57E-03	3.11E-03**	5.80E-03	3.90E-03*	23445
2003	5.39E-05	5.86E-05	1.24E-05	6.93E-05	19680	8.30E-03	3.25E-03***	1.29E-03	3.90E-03	19680
					Bid deal return					
1998	9.71E-05	8.66E-05	1.26E-03	1.15E-04	23370	1.02E-02	6.52E-03	9.71E-03	7.17E-03	23370
1999	-1.23E-04	7.09E-05*	-1.12E-04	9.55E-05	23266	7.01E-03	5.00E-03*	1.90E-03	5.33E-03	23266
2000	1.14E-04	6.71E-05**	2.91E-07	7.87E-05	23009	8.82E-03	3.84E-03**	2.28E-03	3.66E-03	23009
2001	1.52E-04	6.27E-05***	6.69E-05	7.89E-05	22926	9.46E-03	3.63E-03***	4.41E-03	3.83E-03	22926
2002	4.93E-06	5.74E-05	1.81E-04	6.97E-05***	23058	8.61E-03	3.47E-03***	2.01E-03	3.67E-03	23058
2003	5.84E-05	5.90E-05	2.62E-05	6.97E-05	19421	1.03E-02	3.54E-03***	-1.35E-03	3.78E-03	19421

Note: ***, ** and * indicate the significance at 1, 5, 10%, respectively.

Table 6.4   **Prediction: USD/JPY 30-minute deal return**

	netdeal					ndr				
	ndplus	s.e.	ndminus	s.e.	NOB	ndplus	s.e.	ndminus	s.e.	NOB
	Log middle price									
1998	-1.88E-04	1.10E-04*	-5.97E-05	1.66E-04	11805	-2.31E-02	1.58E-02	7.52E-04	1.87E-02	11805
1999	-1.86E-04	9.21E-05**	-2.87E-05	1.38E-04	11720	-6.08E-03	1.26E-02	6.20E-03	1.53E-02	11720
2000	2.28E-04	8.94E-05**	-2.65E-05	1.12E-04	11824	3.39E-03	9.50E-03	9.21E-03	1.02E-02	11824
2001	1.09E-04	8.28E-05	-5.41E-05	1.14E-04	11777	4.02E-03	8.75E-03	-8.36E-04	1.03E-02	11777
2002	-3.43E-05	7.68E-05	1.34E-04	9.98E-05	11823	-3.12E-04	8.45E-03	7.33E-03	9.93E-03	11823
2003	-7.96E-05	7.97E-05	5.56E-06	9.98E-05	9890	-4.03E-03	8.99E-03	-6.58E-03	1.03E-02	9890
	Ask deal return									
1998	-2.07E-04	1.10E-04*	-6.34E-05	1.65E-04	11870	-1.92E-02	1.52E-02	-2.23E-03	1.85E-02	11870
1999	-1.70E-04	9.19E-05*	-1.69E-05	1.38E-04	11828	-5.13E-03	1.21E-02	7.00E-03	1.51E-02	11828
2000	2.17E-04	8.88E-05**	6.35E-07	1.11E-04	11946	1.40E-03	8.87E-03	1.13E-02	1.01E-02	11946
2001	1.08E-04	8.27E-05	-3.50E-05	1.14E-04	11894	3.95E-03	8.28E-03	-6.01E-04	1.02E-02	11894
2002	-3.39E-05	7.67E-05	1.63E-04	9.96E-05	11955	-2.26E-03	7.95E-03	1.03E-02	9.75E-03	11955
2003	-5.62E-05	7.95E-05	1.70E-05	9.97E-05	9980	-1.36E-03	8.43E-03	-6.56E-03	1.02E-02	9980
	Bid deal return									
1998	-1.48E-04	1.11E-04	-1.88E-05	1.67E-04	11839	-2.15E-02	1.59E-02	1.76E-02	1.82E-02	11839
1999	-1.73E-04	9.21E-05*	-1.02E-05	1.38E-04	11763	-2.04E-03	1.25E-02	4.11E-03	1.48E-02	11763
2000	2.67E-04	8.96E-05***	-2.63E-05	1.12E-04	11904	5.20E-03	9.43E-03	1.05E-02	9.70E-03	11904
2001	1.36E-04	8.27E-05	-2.95E-05	1.14E-04	11852	7.94E-03	8.69E-03	-1.80E-03	9.92E-03	11852
2002	-9.49E-06	7.67E-05	1.39E-04	9.97E-05	11905	4.70E-03	8.36E-03	4.99E-03	9.50E-03	11905
2003	-7.84E-05	7.98E-05	1.32E-05	1.00E-04	9925	-3.76E-03	8.96E-03	-5.26E-03	1.01E-02	9925

Note: ***, ** and * indicate the significance at 1, 5, 10%, respectively.

Table 6.5 Prediction: USD/JPY 1-minute quote return

	netdeal					ndr				
	ndplus	s.e.	ndminus	s.e.	NOB	ndplus	s.e.	ndminus	s.e.	NOB
Log middle price										
1998	7.03E-04	3.20E-05***	8.80E-04	3.45E-05***	262271	0.0045455	2.29E-04***	3.83E-03	2.42E-04***	251500
1999	3.98E-04	2.76E-05***	3.86E-04	2.99E-05***	233065	2.76E-03	1.93E-04***	2.31E-03	2.03E-04***	225065
2000	3.22E-04	2.71E-05***	4.16E-04	2.82E-05***	191789	2.25E-03	1.67E-04***	1.81E-03	1.73E-04***	184434
2001	3.70E-04	2.47E-05***	3.93E-04	2.62E-05***	208058	2.37E-03	1.55E-04***	2.05E-03	1.62E-04***	200423
2002	3.04E-04	2.22E-05***	3.18E-04	2.34E-05***	214595	1.96E-03	1.44E-04***	1.63E-03	1.50E-04***	206908
2003	3.20E-04	2.44E-05***	3.11E-04	2.55E-05***	170934	1.60E-03	1.56E-04***	1.78E-03	1.63E-04***	165535
Ask deal return										
1998	1.13E-03	3.34E-05***	1.10E-03	3.63E-05***	262271	0.0057625	2.41E-04***	5.29E-03	2.55E-04***	251500
1999	6.95E-04	2.84E-05***	5.17E-04	3.11E-05***	233065	3.50E-03	2.01E-04***	3.29E-03	2.11E-04***	225065
2000	5.82E-04	2.80E-05***	5.59E-04	2.93E-05***	191789	2.93E-03	1.74E-04***	2.59E-03	1.80E-04***	184434
2001	6.31E-04	2.56E-05***	5.41E-04	2.74E-05***	208058	3.03E-03	1.62E-04***	2.91E-03	1.69E-04***	200423
2002	5.30E-04	2.30E-05***	4.67E-04	2.43E-05***	214595	2.61E-03	1.50E-04***	2.39E-03	1.56E-04***	206908
2003	4.32E-04	2.54E-05***	5.06E-04	2.64E-05***	170934	2.16E-03	1.62E-04***	2.32E-03	1.69E-04***	165535
Bid deal return										
1998	1.08E-03	3.54E-05***	1.51E-03	3.79E-05***	262271	0.0069327	2.54E-04***	5.46E-03	2.69E-04***	251500
1999	5.20E-04	2.87E-05***	6.93E-04	3.09E-05***	233065	0.0036533	2.01E-04***	2.82E-03	2.12E-04***	225065
2000	4.91E-04	2.85E-05***	7.18E-04	2.94E-05***	191789	0.0030469	1.75E-04***	2.43E-03	1.82E-04***	184434
2001	5.37E-04	2.60E-05***	7.01E-04	2.74E-05***	208058	3.27E-03	1.64E-04***	2.67E-03	1.71E-04***	200423
2002	4.52E-04	2.33E-05***	5.65E-04	2.43E-05***	214595	2.72E-03	1.51E-04***	2.19E-03	1.58E-04***	206908
2003	5.33E-04	2.52E-05***	4.53E-04	2.66E-05***	170934	0.0022423	1.63E-04***	2.46E-03	1.69E-04***	165535

Note: ***, **, and * indicate the significance at 1, 5, 10%, respectively.

Table 6.6   Prediction: USD/JPY 5-minute quote return

	netdeal					ndr				
	ndplus	s.e.	ndminus	s.e.	NOB	ndplus	s.e.	ndminus	s.e.	NOB
Log middle price										
1998	2.57E-04	5.24E-05***	3.07E-04	6.21E-05***	71787	6.57E-03	1.23E-03***	5.60E-03	1.33E-03***	71359
1999	5.20E-05	4.36E-05	1.04E-04	5.16E-05**	70948	2.99E-03	9.65E-04***	1.99E-03	1.04E-03*	70507
2000	7.97E-05	4.03E-05**	1.78E-04	4.42E-05***	69997	2.38E-03	7.26E-04***	3.46E-03	7.54E-04***	69374
2001	7.16E-05	3.73E-05*	1.41E-04	4.27E-05***	70438	2.23E-03	6.90E-04***	2.74E-03	7.43E-04***	69818
2002	1.06E-04	3.49E-05***	1.29E-04	3.89E-05***	70840	3.42E-03	6.67E-04***	1.95E-03	7.12E-04***	70322
2003	2.67E-04	3.61E-05***	8.46E-05	3.99E-05**	58768	3.56E-03	7.00E-04***	1.73E-03	7.48E-04**	58421
Ask deal return										
1998	6.65E-04	5.51E-05***	7.92E-04	6.54E-05***	71787	0.012117	1.31E-03***	9.71E-03	1.42E-03***	71359
1999	1.08E-04	4.40E-05**	1.85E-04	5.20E-05***	70948	3.60E-03	9.75E-04***	2.45E-03	1.06E-03**	70507
2000	1.62E-04	4.08E-05***	2.73E-04	4.46E-05***	69997	2.95E-03	7.37E-04***	3.99E-03	7.66E-04***	69374
2001	1.59E-04	3.79E-04***	2.31E-04	4.33E-05***	70438	3.02E-03	7.03E-04***	3.27E-03	7.57E-03	69818
2002	1.88E-04	3.53E-05***	2.10E-04	3.94E-05***	70840	4.22E-03	6.77E-04***	2.61E-03	7.24E-04***	70322
2003	3.17E-04	3.65E-05***	1.42E-04	4.03E-05***	58768	3.99E-03	7.10E-04***	1.98E-03	7.59E-04	58421
Bid deal return										
1998	2.75E-04	5.25E-05***	3.11E-04	6.22E-05***	71787	6.75E-03	1.23E-03***	6.21E-03	1.33E-03***	71359
1999	1.57E-04	4.42E-05***	2.04E-04	5.23E-05***	70948	4.22E-03	9.80E-04***	3.12E-03	1.06E-03***	70507
2000	1.53E-04	4.07E-05***	2.50E-04	4.47E-05***	69997	3.20E-03	7.35E-04***	4.29E-03	7.65E-04***	69374
2001	1.64E-04	3.78E-05***	2.57E-04	4.33E-05***	70438	3.17E-03	7.02E-04***	3.79E-03	7.56E-04***	69818
2002	1.57E-04	3.51E-05***	1.96E-04	3.93E-05***	70840	3.93E-03	6.74E-04***	2.50E-03	7.20E-04***	70322
2003	3.26E-04	3.65E-05***	1.41E-04	4.05E-05***	58768	4.24E-03	7.10E-04***	2.54E-03	7.58E-04***	58421

Note: ***, ** and * indicate the significance at 1, 5, 10%, respectively.

Table 6.7 Prediction: USD/JPY 15-minute quote return

	netdeal					ndr				
	ndplus	s.e.	ndminus	s.e.	NOB	ndplus	s.e.	ndminus	s.e.	NOB
Log middle price										
1998	1.05E-04	8.48E-05	1.32E-04	1.12E-04	24118	5.62E-03	5.78E-03	8.13E-03	6.68E-03	24108
1999	-1.96E-04	6.91E-05***	-2.17E-04	9.29E-05**	24141	1.89E-03	4.37E-03	-2.10E-03	4.91E-03	24124
2000	1.57E-05	6.42E-05	-8.59E-05	7.52E-05	24337	2.43E-03	3.18E-03	-1.22E-03	3.30E-03	24314
2001	5.95E-05	5.98E-05	-2.35E-05	7.56E-05	24386	1.38E-03	2.97E-03	2.13E-04	3.39E-03	24355
2002	-7.39E-05	5.51E-05	1.58E-04	6.68E-05**	24477	3.56E-03	2.79E-03	-9.54E-04	3.25E-03	24454
2003	-1.32E-05	5.72E-05	-1.44E-05	6.76E-05	20306	4.10E-03	3.02E-03	-2.39E-03	2.44E-03	20293
Ask deal return										
1998	3.93E-04	8.72E-05***	4.21E-04	1.16E-04***	24118	1.69E-02	5.99E-03***	1.53E-02	6.95E-03**	24108
1999	-1.66E-04	6.93E-05**	-1.97E-04	9.31E-05**	24141	2.55E-03	4.39E-03	-1.75E-03	4.93E-03	24124
2000	4.52E-05	6.44E-05	-6.02E-05	7.54E-05	24337	2.18E-03	3.19E-03	-1.34E-04	3.32E-03	24314
2001	9.45E-05	6.01E-05	5.84E-07	7.59E-05	24386	1.91E-03	2.99E-03	6.04E-04	3.41E-03	24355
2002	-2.80E-05	5.54E-05	1.95E-04	6.71E-05***	24477	4.62E-03	2.81E-03	6.99E-04	3.27E-03	24454
2003	1.04E-05	5.74E-05	-4.06E-07	6.78E-05	20306	3.81E-03	3.03E-03	-1.26E-03	3.46E-03	20293
Bid deal return										
1998	4.38E-05	8.49E-05	1.22E-04	1.12E-04	24118	4.09E-03	5.78E-03	8.99E-03	6.67E-03	24108
1999	-1.80E-04	6.94E-05***	-1.81E-04	9.34E-05*	24141	2.86E-03	4.40E-03	-1.17E-03	4.94E-03	24124
2000	4.10E-05	6.46E-05	-4.99E-05	7.56E-05	24337	4.15E-03	3.20E-03	-1.05E-03	3.32E-03	24314
2001	8.25E-05	6.01E-05	2.03E-05	7.61E-05	24386	2.50E-03	3.00E-03	1.29E-03	3.41E-03	24355
2002	-7.44E-05	5.53E-05	1.71E-04	6.70E-05**	24477	3.78E-03	2.80E-03	-1.37E-03	3.26E-03	24454
2003	4.79E-06	5.76E-05	1.10E-05	6.81E-05	20306	0.0056029	3.05E-03*	-2.38E-03	3.47E-03	20293

Note: ***, ** and * indicate the significance at 1, 5, 10%, respectively.

Table 6.8   Prediction: USD/JPY 30-minute quote return

	netdeal					ndr				
	ndplus	s.e.	ndminus	s.e.	NOB	ndplus	s.e.	ndminus	s.e.	NOB
					Log middle price					
1998	-1.27E-04	1.10E-04	-9.05E-06	1.67E-04	11919	-1.43E-02	1.52E-02	9.74E-03	1.80E-02	11918
1999	-2.06E-04	9.07E-05**	-7.29E-05	1.36E-04	11952	-7.84E-03	1.13E-02	-3.08E-03	1.38E-02	11946
2000	2.03E-04	8.77E-05**	-7.16E-05	1.10E-04	12066	-7.72E-04	8.55E-03	5.78E-03	9.22E-03	12064
2001	8.23E-05	8.14E-05	-4.34E-05	1.12E-04	12075	2.72E-03	7.93E-03	-6.13E-03	9.34E-03	12066
2002	-6.70E-05	7.54E-05	1.18E-04	9.78E-05	12103	-2.37E-03	7.56E-03	7.05E-04	9.00E-03	12097
2003	-9.75E-05	7.88E-05	-4.16E-05	9.88E-05	10033	-5.81E-03	8.29E-03	-1.27E-02	9.69E-03	10032
					Ask deal return					
1998	3.62E-05	1.13E-04	1.93E-04	1.71E-04	11919	-9.26E-04	1.57E-02	2.11E-02	1.86E-02	11918
1999	-1.92E-04	9.08E-05**	-7.11E-05	1.36E-04	11952	-7.92E-03	1.14E-02	3.66E-04	1.38E-02	11946
2000	2.36E-04	8.78E-05***	-6.09E-05	1.10E-04	12066	6.00E-05	8.57E-03	6.84E-03	9.25E-03	12064
2001	8.56E-05	8.16E-05	-6.78E-05	1.13E-04	12075	9.45E-04	7.94E-03	-6.21E-03	9.36E-03	12066
2002	-5.43E-05	7.56E-05	1.39E-04	9.80E-05	12103	-3.15E-03	7.58E-03	2.53E-03	9.02E-03	12097
2003	-8.16E-05	7.89E-05	-4.23E-05	9.89E-05	10033	-6.17E-03	8.30E-03	-1.09E-02	9.70E-03	10032
					Bid deal return					
1998	-1.52E-04	1.11E-04	5.03E-06	1.67E-04	11919	-1.32E-02	1.53E-02	9.54E-03	1.81E-02	11918
1999	-2.00E-04	9.09E-05**	-4.88E-05	1.37E-04	11952	-6.04E-03	1.14E-02	-5.22E-03	1.38E-02	11946
2000	1.93E-04	8.81E-05**	-5.72E-05	1.10E-04	12066	-2.00E-04	8.59E-03	5.86E-03	9.26E-03	12064
2001	1.06E-04	8.18E-05	1.28E-05	1.13E-04	12075	6.32E-03	7.98E-03	-4.59E-03	9.39E-03	12066
2002	-5.60E-05	7.57E-05	1.22E-04	9.82E-05	12103	-1.02E-04	7.59E-03	2.04E-04	9.04E-03	12097
2003	-8.85E-05	7.92E-05	-1.96E-05	9.95E-05	10033	-3.91E-03	8.34E-03	-1.31E-02	9.76E-03	10032

Note: ***, ** and * indicate the significance at 1, 5, 10%, respectively.

catch-up effects. The magnitude of coefficients is not as large as in the case of deal returns.

As for the magnitude of the euro price impacts, rough calculations show that the price impacts (coefficient, like 0.000335 under 1999 in table 6.5 ask-side deals, multiplied by 20 *netdeals* in one minute) when very large order flows occur during busy hours (low bid-ask spread) exceed the size of the lowest bid-ask spread (0.01 EUR/USD). Similarly, the when the net-deal ratio is 1, then the impact was estimated to exceed the bid-ask spread.

Regression results of EUR/USD deal price returns are summarized in tables 6.9–6.12. As clearly seen in these tables, price impact is significant at the 1-minute frequency. Looking at the price impact at 5-minute frequency, some of the price impacts in 1999 and 2000 are not significantly estimated. For example, estimated parameter nd^{minus} for midpoint return and bid-side deal return in 1999 and 2000, parameter nd^{plus} for midpoint return in 1999, and parameters nd^{plus} and nd^{minus} for ask-side deal return in 1999 (all estimated with *netdeal*) are not significant at 10 percent. However, since 2001 deal price returns, both in ask and bid, have been significant at 1 percent in the 5 minute window (table 6.14), just like in the case of USD/JPY (table 6.6). At 15-minute and 30-minute frequencies, most of the coefficients are not statistically significant.

Impacts of order flows on bid and ask prices did not show definite signs of relative magnitude, hence no conclusive statement is possible as for the impacts on the bid-ask spread.

Tables 6.13–6.16 reports the price impact of EUR/USD quote returns. Again, significant price impacts at the 1-minute frequency are found, but some of the parameters in early years are not significant at 5-minute frequency.[12] However, significance disappears at the 15-minute and 30-minute frequencies.

The relative magnitudes of α_1 and β_1 in case of nd^{plus} and of β_2 and α_2 of nd^{minus} show some definite relationships to indicate that the knocking-off effects are faster than the catch-up effects in 1-minute and 5-minute returns.

In sum, our tests turned out to be successful in finding some predictive power of exchange rate changes based on order flows for both USD/JPY and EUR/USD, at least up to 5 minutes. The results are consistent with a wide-spread notion among dealers and market participants that private information on order flows in real time—that is, aggregated every minute—does help predicting the exchange rate movements in the following several minutes. However, the predictability (and information) is short-lived. We fail to detect any predictability even at the 30-minute frequency. In that

12. Parameter nd^{plus} for midpoint return in 1999, 2000 (*netdeal*), 1999 (*ndr*), bid-side deal return in 1999 (*netdeal, ndr*), ask-side deal return in 1999 (*netdeal*), and parameter nd^{plus} for mid point return from 1999–2001, bid-side deal return in 1999 and 2000 (*netdeal* and *ndr*) and ask-side deal return 1999 to 2000 (*netdeal* and *ndr*) are not significant at 10%.

Table 6.9   Prediction: EUR/USD 1-minute deal return

	netdeal					ndr				
	ndplus	s.e.	ndminus	s.e.	NOB	ndplus	s.e.	ndminus	s.e.	NOB
Log middle price										
1999	3.12E-04	2.88E-05***	3.09E-04	3.01E-05***	94682	5.20E-03	4.50E-04***	5.54E-03	4.73E-04***	94682
2000	4.12E-04	3.43E-05***	3.94E-04	3.56E-05***	115301	6.60E-03	5.59E-04***	7.29E-03	5.84E-04***	115301
2001	2.95E-04	3.33E-05***	3.85E-04	3.41E-05***	106335	5.32E-03	5.20E-04***	6.43E-03	5.44E-04***	106335
2002	2.22E-04	2.93E-05***	2.38E-04	3.05E-05***	90761	4.07E-03	4.53E-04***	4.59E-03	4.78E-04***	90761
2003	3.09E-04	2.79E-05***	2.48E-04	2.87E-05***	107231	4.46E-03	4.55E-04***	4.98E-03	4.74E-04***	107231
Ask deal return										
1999	3.35E-04	2.52E-05***	5.59E-04	2.65E-05***	124575	4.22E-03	2.91E-04***	8.09E-03	3.89E-04***	124575
2000	3.99E-04	3.07E-05***	6.59E-04	3.21E-05***	143585	4.69E-03	3.79E-04***	1.05E-02	4.92E-04***	143585
2001	2.86E-04	2.97E-05***	6.31E-04	3.06E-05***	134865	3.84E-03	3.43E-04***	9.07E-03	4.56E-04***	134865
2002	2.28E-04	2.52E-05***	4.26E-04	2.65E-05***	121033	2.72E-03	2.79E-04***	6.70E-03	3.82E-04***	121033
2003	3.02E-04	2.51E-05***	4.15E-04	2.61E-05***	132283	3.53E-03	3.02E-04***	6.80E-03	4.01E-04***	132283
Bid deal return										
1999	5.33E-04	2.61E-05***	3.23E-04	2.69E-05***	118122	7.77E-03	3.86E-04***	4.34E-03	3.24E-04***	118122
2000	6.68E-04	3.15E-05***	4.20E-04	3.24E-05***	138445	9.97E-03	4.87E-04***	5.45E-03	4.12E-04***	138445
2001	4.99E-04	3.05E-05***	3.88E-04	3.10E-05***	128689	8.20E-03	4.49E-04***	4.29E-03	3.78E-04***	128689
2002	3.99E-04	2.63E-05***	2.46E-04	2.70E-05***	114936	6.38E-03	3.82E-04***	3.16E-03	3.09E-04***	114936
2003	4.74E-04	2.56E-05***	2.46E-04	2.63E-05***	128043	6.53E-03	3.94E-04***	3.72E-03	3.28E-04***	128043

Note: ***, ** and * indicate the significance at 1, 5, 10%, respectively.

Table 6.10   Prediction: EUR/USD 5-minute deal return

	netdeal					ndr				
	ndplus	s.e.	ndminus	s.e.	NOB	ndplus	s.e.	ndminus	s.e.	NOB
Log middle price										
1999	5.71E-05	3.63E-05	-4.29E-05	3.95E-05	49697	4.07E-03	1.41E-03**	2.77E-03	1.52E-03*	49697
2000	1.40E-04	4.67E-05**	6.12E-05	5.07E-05	51451	8.26E-03	1.96E-03***	4.22E-03	2.13E-03**	51451
2001	1.43E-04	4.39E.05**	1.53E-04	4.69E-05***	51035	1.01E-02	1.66E-03***	4.25E-03	1.84E-03**	51035
2002	1.22E-04	3.46E-05***	1.45E-04	3.80E-05***	51551	6.11E-03	1.28E-03***	4.52E-03	1.38E-03***	51551
2003	1.21E-04	3.80E-05**	1.43E-04	4.12E-05***	48206	5.78E-03	1.48E-03***	7.86E-03	1.63E-03***	48206
Ask deal return										
1999	5.58E-05	3.47E-05	5.14E-05	3.76E-05	54902	4.27E-03	1.05E-03***	4.35E-03	1.35E-03***	54902
2000	1.49E-04	4.46E-05**	1.59E-04	4.84E-05***	56457	6.00E-03	1.44E-03***	7.47E-03	1.88E-03***	56457
2001	1.53E-04	4.19E-05***	2.19E-04	4.47E-05***	56446	7.68E-03	1.22E-03***	6.59E-03	1.62E-03***	56446
2002	1.32E-04	3.31E-05***	1.98E-04	3.63E-05***	56928	3.77E-03	9.48E-04***	5.98E-03	1.22E-03***	56928
2003	1.28E-04	3.63E-05***	1.87E-04	3.94E-05***	52520	4.72E-03	1.12E-03***	9.21E-03	1.44E-03***	52520
Bid deal return										
1999	1.42E-04	3.51E-05***	-8.16E-06	3.84E-05	53563	6.77E-03	1.30E-03***	2.67E-03	1.20E-03**	53563
2000	2.03E-04	4.51E-05***	7.58E-05	4.92E-05	55121	1.04E-02	1.79E-03***	3.63E-03	1.65E-03**	55121
2001	2.09E-04	4.24E-05***	1.65E-04	4.54E-05***	55093	1.18E-02	1.52E-03***	3.58E-03	1.40E-03**	55093
2002	1.73E-04	3.34E-05***	1.50E-04	3.68E-05***	55772	7.49E-03	1.16E-03***	3.78E-03	1.05E-03***	55772
2003	1.65E-04	3.70E-05***	1.55E-04	4.02E-05***	51031	7.54E-03	1.38E-03***	6.90E-03	1.33E-03***	51031

Note: ***, ** and * indicate the significance at 1, 5, 10%, respectively.

Table 6.11   Prediction: EUR/USD 15-minute deal return

	netdeal					ndr				
	ndplus	s.e.	ndminus	s.e.	NOB	ndplus	s.e.	ndminus	s.e.	NOB
Log middle price										
1999	-9.27E-05	5.24E-05*	-3.54E-05	6.25E-05	21290	1.42E-03	4.05E-03	6.72E-04	4.53E-03	21290
2000	1.27E-05	6.53E-05	-1.67E-04	7.75E-05**	22128	2.88E-03	5.26E-03	-1.64E-03	5.95E-03	22128
2001	-6.66E-05	6.18E-05	1.77E-04	7.04E-05***	22439	5.52E-03	4.43E-03	2.26E-03	4.99E-03	22439
2002	6.21E-05	4.80E-05	-1.29E-04	5.76E-05***	22724	-1.38E-03	3.57E-03	2.31E-03	3.90E-03	22724
2003	7.73E-05	5.58E-05	-1.99E-05	6.38E-05	19881	2.99E-03	4.63E-03	1.36E-02	5.25E-03**	19881
Ask deal return										
1999	-8.45E-05	5.11E-05*	-1.78E-05	6.07E-05	22545	1.04E-03	3.26E-03	6.75E-04	4.19E-03	22545
2000	1.72E-05	6.39E-05	-1.45E-04	7.59E-05*	23110	2.80E-03	4.45E-03	8.25E-04	5.56E-03	23110
2001	-5.06E-05	6.06E-05	1.89E-04	6.92E-05***	23347	4.35E-03	3.82E-03	3.53E-03	4.71E-03	23347
2002	6.41E-05	4.74E-05	-1.15E-04	5.70E-05***	23388	-1.86E-03	3.18E-03	4.43E-03	3.74E-03	23388
2003	7.58E-05	5.54E-05	-1.78E-05	6.35E-05	20132	2.73E-03	4.40E-03	1.43E-02	5.14E-03***	20132
Bid deal return										
1999	-6.71E-05	5.15E-05	-3.07E-05	6.15E-05	22090	4.30E-03	3.86E-03	1.13E-03	3.80E-03	22090
2000	4.08E-05	6.44E-05	-1.53E-04	7.64E-05**	22874	5.53E-03	5.01E-03	-1.27E-03	5.09E-03	22874
2001	-4.50E-05	6.12E-05	1.86E-04	6.98E-05***	23002	7.40E-03	4.28E-03*	3.12E-03	4.46E-03	23002
2002	8.42E-05	4.75E-05*	-1.18E-04	5.70E-05***	23337	9.49E-04	3.45E-03	2.20E-03	3.44E-03	23337
2003	9.56E-05	5.57E-05*	-8.44E-06	6.38E-05	20054	5.09E-03	4.59E-03	1.26E-02	5.02E-03**	20054

Note: ***, ** and * indicate the significance at 1, 5, 10%, respectively.   *Note:* ***, ** and * indicate the significance at 1, 5, 10%, respectively.

Table 6.12   Prediction: EUR/USD 30-minute deal return

	netdeal					ndr				
	ndplus	s.e.	ndminus	s.e.	NOB	ndplus	s.e.	ndminus	s.e.	NOB
Log middle price										
1999	−6.76E-05	6.90E-05	−9.24E-05	8.72E-05	11473	4.24E-03	9.01E-03	−1.23E-02	1.05E-02	11473
2000	−1.80E-04	8.50E-05**	−3.64E-04	1.08E-04***	11840	−1.22E-03	1.19E-02	−2.44E-02	1.37E-02*	11840
2001	−7.01E-05	8.04E-05	1.13E-04	9.66E-05	11865	−4.70E-03	1.05E-02	−5.23E-03	1.22E-02	11865
2002	−9.72E-05	6.31E-05	−3.08E-05	8.19E-05	11914	−1.10E-02	8.59E-03	3.96E-04	9.38E-03	11914
2003	9.64E-06	7.52E-05	−4.65E-05	9.30E-05	10025	−1.84E-02	1.22E-02	1.64E-02	1.42E-02	10025
Ask deal return										
1999	−6.60E-05	6.83E-05	−7.14E-05	8.59E-05	11706	3.69E-03	8.10E-03	−1.04E-02	1.02E-02	11706
2000	−1.80E-04	8.47E-05**	−3.63E-04	1.08E-04***	11948	5.82E-04	1.12E-02	−2.25E-02	1.35E-02*	11948
2001	−6.36E-05	8.02E-05	1.22E-04	9.64E-05	11957	−2.48E-03	9.91E-03	−4.07E-03	1.20E-02	11957
2002	−9.18E-05	6.30E-05	−3.43E-05	8.18E-05	11995	−9.95E-03	8.24E-03	1.14E-03	9.28E-03	11995
2003	1.01E-05	7.52E-05	−3.39E-05	9.29E-05	10044	−1.73E-02	1.19E-02	1.72E-02	1.40E-02	10044
Bid deal return										
1999	−5.19E-05	6.85E-05	−9.24E-05	8.68E-05	11615	5.16E-03	8.90E-03	−7.83E-03	9.67E-03	11615
2000	−1.63E-04	8.50E-05*	−3.48E-04	1.08E-04***	11906	−1.55E-03	1.18E-02	−1.88E-02	1.33E-02	11906
2001	−6.09E-05	8.04E-05	1.14E-04	9.67E-05	11946	−3.28E-03	1.04E-02	−2.11E-03	1.17E-02	11946
2002	−8.87E-05	6.31E-05	−2.73E-05	8.19E-05	11974	−9.24E-03	8.54E-03	1.27E-03	9.03E-03	11974
2003	1.35E-05	7.54E-05	−5.17E-05	9.32E-05	10030	−1.64E-02	1.22E-02	1.58E-02	1.42E-02	10030

Note: ***, **, and * indicate the significance at 1, 5, 10%, respectively.

Table 6.13   Prediction: EUR/USD 1-minute quote return

	netdeal					ndr				
	ndplus	s.e.	ndminus	s.e.	NOB	ndplus	s.e.	ndminus	s.e.	NOB
Log middle price										
1999	1.59E-04	1.97E-05***	1.66E-04	2.05E-05***	195862	1.25E-03	1.73E-04***	1.25E-03	1.80E-04***	191535
2000	2.01E-04	2.47E-05***	2.68E-04	2.57E-05***	208196	1.81E-03	2.33E-04***	1.71E-03	2.43E-04***	204498
2001	1.52E-04	2.46E-05***	2.54E-04	2.53E-05***	188917	1.79E-03	2.20E-04***	1.50E-03	2.30E-04***	185282
2002	1.17E-04	2.20E-05***	1.51E-04	2.31E-05***	156517	1.45E-03	1.98E-04***	1.39E-03	2.07E-04***	153833
2003	1.69E-04	2.09E-05***	1.31E-04	2.16E-05***	180919	1.20E-03	1.96E-04***	1.48E-03	2.03E-04***	178101
Ask deal return										
1999	2.66E-04	2.04E-05***	3.20E-04	2.12E-05***	195862	2.03E-03	1.79E-04***	1.66E-03	1.86E-04***	191535
2000	2.82E-04	2.54E-05***	4.06E-04	2.64E-05***	208196	2.57E-03	2.40E-04***	2.11E-03	2.50E-04***	204498
2001	2.26E-04	2.53E-05***	3.70E-04	2.60E-05***	188917	2.42E-03	2.27E-04***	1.74E-03	2.37E-04***	185282
2002	1.75E-04	2.27E-05***	2.39E-04	2.36E-04***	156517	1.96E-03	2.03E-04***	1.60E-03	2.13E-04***	153833
2003	2.27E-04	2.14E-05***	2.05E-04	2.21E-05***	180919	1.68E-03	2.00E-04***	1.78E-03	2.08E-04***	178101
Bid deal return										
1999	2.68E-04	2.01E-05***	2.37E-04	2.11E-05***	195862	1.61E-03	1.78E-04***	1.91E-03	1.84E-04***	191535
2000	3.55E-04	2.53E-05***	3.74E-04	2.61E-05***	208196	2.36E-03	2.40E-04***	2.59E-03	2.49E-04***	204498
2001	2.70E-04	2.51E-05***	3.45E-04	2.59E-05***	188917	2.24E-03	2.26E-04***	2.31E-03	2.35E-04***	185282
2002	2.02E-04	2.25E-05***	2.09E-04	2.36E-05***	156517	1.78E-03	2.02E-04***	1.97E-03	2.11E-04***	153833
2003	2.44E-04	2.12E-05***	1.92E-04	2.20E-05***	180919	1.50E-03	2.00E-04***	1.96E-03	2.07E-04***	178101

Note: ***, ** and * indicate the significance at 1, 5, 10%, respectively.   *Note:* ***, ** and * indicate the significance at 1, 5, 10%, respectively.

Table 6.14   Prediction: EUR/USD 5-minute quote return

	netdeal					ndr				
	ndplus	s.e.	ndminus	s.e.	NOB	ndplus	s.e.	ndminus	s.e.	NOB
Log middle price										
1999	-1.97E-05	3.02E-05	-8.48E-05	3.31E-05**	67676	9.63E-04	7.16E-04	-3.63E-04	7.66E-04	67050
2000	5.43E-05	3.93E-05	2.84E-05	4.29E-05	68196	3.17E-03	1.00E-03**	5.70E-04	1.08E-03	67641
2001	9.74E-05	3.71E-05***	8.46E-05	3.98E-05**	68079	3.33E-03	8.68E-04***	1.38E-03	9.30E-04	67585
2002	9.04E-05	2.98E-05***	9.70E-05	3.29E-05***	67116	1.28E-03	6.98E-04*	1.94E-03	7.43E-04***	66771
2003	1.04E-04	3.34E-05***	9.89E-05	3.63E-05***	59787	2.12E-03	8.80E-04*	4.55E-03	9.62E-04***	59587
Ask deal return										
1999	3.45E-05	3.06E-05	-1.96E-05	3.35E-05	67676	1.70E-03	7.25E-04*	2.54E-05	7.77E-04	67050
2000	8.48E-05	3.96E-05*	6.74E-05	4.32E-05	68196	3.43E-03	1.01E-03**	7.84E-04	1.09E-03	67641
2001	1.24E-04	3.74E-05**	1.27E-04	4.01E-05***	68079	3.64E-03	8.76E-04***	1.63E-03	9.40E-04*	67585
2002	1.13E-04	3.01E-05***	1.22E-04	3.32E-05***	67116	1.55E-03	7.05E-04*	1.99E-03	7.50E-04***	66771
2003	1.30E-04	3.37E-05***	1.19E-04	3.66E-05***	50787	2.27E-03	8.87E-04*	4.86E-03	9.70E-04***	59587
Bid deal return										
1999	1.23E-05	3.04E-05	-5.49E-05	3.34E-05	67676	1.14E-03	7.22E-04	1.19E-04	7.72E-04	67050
2000	9.25E-05	3.95E-05*	6.49E-05	4.31E-05	68196	3.71E-03	1.01E-03***	1.14E-03	1.09E-03	67641
2001	1.39E-04	3.74E-05***	1.15E-04	4.02E-05***	68079	3.83E-03	8.75E-04***	1.87E-03	9.38E-04**	67585
2002	1.13E-04	3.00E-05***	1.19E-04	3.31E-05***	67116	1.60E-03	7.04E-04*	2.44E-03	7.49E-04***	66771
2003	1.15E-04	3.36E-05***	1.17E-04	3.65E-05***	59787	2.50E-03	8.84E-04**	4.80E-03	9.67E-04***	59587

Note: ***, ** and * indicate the significance at 1, 5, 10%, respectively.   *Note:* ***, ** and * indicate the significance at 1, 5, 10%, respectively.

Table 6.15 Prediction: EUR/USD 15-minute quote return

	netdeal					ndr				
	ndplus	s.e.	ndminus	s.e.	NOB	ndplus	s.e.	ndminus	s.e.	NOB
Log middle price										
1999	−9.99E-05	4.87E-05**	−8.02E-05	5.80E-05	24089	−1.41E-04	2.85E-03	−2.48E-03	3.24E-03	24058
2000	−3.20E-05	6.18E-05	−1.73E-04	7.34E-05**	24325	8.77E-04	4.01E-03	−1.12E-03	4.48E-03	24305
2001	−7.52E-05	5.86E-05	1.60E-04	6.70E-05**	24338	1.85E-03	3.45E-03	7.08E-04	3.93E-03	24317
2002	6.25E-05	4.59E-05	−1.32E-04	5.52E-05**	24372	−1.20E-03	2.89E-03	1.08E-03	3.08E-03	24352
2003	5.70E-05	5.47E-05	−2.21E-05	6.27E-05	20389	5.92E-04	4.24E-03	9.12E-03	4.75E-03*	20385
Ask deal return										
1999	−8.51E-05	4.89E-05*	−6.27E-05	5.82E-05	24089	−3.26E-04	2.86E-03	−2.22E-03	3.26E-03	24058
2000	1.08E-05	6.19E-05	−1.61E-04	7.35E-05**	24325	1.07E-03	4.02E-03	−2.71E-04	4.49E-03	24305
2001	−6.51E-05	5.88E-05	1.58E-04	6.72E-05**	24338	2.03E-03	3.47E-03	6.07E-04	3.94E-03	24317
2002	7.25E-05	4.61E-05	−1.24E-04	5.53E-05**	24372	−1.05E-03	2.90E-03	1.22E-03	3.09E-03	24352
2003	6.57E-05	5.48E-05	−2.25E-05	6.29E-05	20389	4.68E-04	4.25E-03	9.55E-03	4.76E-03**	20385
Bid deal return										
1999	−9.12E-05	4.89E-05*	−7.06E-05	5.82E-05	24089	6.97E-04	2.86E-03	−2.11E-03	3.25E-03	24058
2000	2.12E-06	6.20E-05	−1.63E-04	7.36E-05**	24325	1.35E-03	4.02E-03	−1.35E-03	4.49E-03	24305
2001	−6.47E-05	5.88E-05	1.83E-04	6.72E-05***	24338	2.14E-03	3.48E-03	1.49E-03	3.95E-03	24317
2002	6.53E-05	4.60E-05	−1.27E-04	5.53E-05**	24372	−8.30E-04	2.90E-03	1.39E-03	3.09E-03	24352
2003	5.70E-05	5.48E-05	−1.31E-05	6.28E-05	20389	1.17E-03	4.25E-03	9.16E-03	4.76E-03*	20385

Note: ***, **, and * indicate the significance at 1, 5, 10%, respectively.

Note: ***, **, and * indicate the significance at 1, 5, 10%, respectively.

Table 6.16   Prediction: EUR/USD 30-minute quote return

	netdeal					ndr				
	ndplus	s.e.	ndminus	s.e.	NOB	ndplus	s.e.	ndminus	s.e.	NOB
					Log middle price					
1999	-8.87E-05	6.69E-05	-1.09E-04	8.44E-05	11938	-6.29E-04	7.69E-03	-1.22E-02	9.04E-03	11934
2000	-1.89E-04	8.39E-05**	-3.66E-04	1.07E-04***	12063	-1.23E-03	1.08E-02	-2.20E-02	1.28E-02*	12061
2001	-7.34E-05	7.94E-05	1.03E-04	9.56E-05	12077	-5.29E-03	9.62E-03	-2.48E-03	1.12E-02	12076
2002	-1.09E-04	6.22E-05*	-4.30E-05	8.07E-05	12123	-1.32E-02	7.95E-03*	-3.92E-03	8.67E-03	12118
2003	3.71E-05	7.49E-05	-5.32E-05	9.26E-05	10058	-1.95E-02	1.18E-02	1.42E-02	1.38E-02	10058
					Ask deal return					
1999	-7.93E-05	6.70E-05	-1.00E-04	8.44E-05	11938	-5.23E-04	7.70E-03	-1.01E-02	9.05E-03	11934
2000	-1.74E-04	8.40E-05**	-3.52E-04	1.07E-04***	12063	-7.42E-04	1.08E-02	-2.11E-02	1.28E-02	12061
2001	-6.56E-05	7.97E-05	9.71E-05	9.59E-05	12077	-3.44E-03	9.64E-03	-3.44E-03	1.13E-02	12076
2002	-1.03E-04	6.24E-05*	-3.87E-05	8.09E-05	12123	-1.27E-02	7.96E-03	-3.59E-03	8.69E-03	12118
2003	6.55E-06	7.49E-05	-5.59E-05	9.27E-05	10058	-2.03E-02	1.18E-02*	1.38E-02	1.38E-02	10058
					Bid deal return					
1999	-8.69E-05	6.71E-05	-1.05E-04	8.46E-05	11938	-5.25E-05	7.71E-03	-1.38E-02	9.07E-03	11934
2000	-1.94E-04	8.41E-05**	-3.67E-04	1.07E-04***	12063	-1.00E-03	1.08E-02	-2.23E-02	1.28E-02*	12061
2001	-7.22E-05	7.96E-05	1.18E-04	9.59E-05	12077	-6.30E-03	9.65E-03	-7.85E-04	1.13E-02	12076
2002	-1.09E-04	6.23E-05*	-4.23E-05	8.08E-05	12123	-1.32E-02	7.96E-03*	-3.82E-03	8.68E-03	12118
2003	5.51E-06	7.50E-05	-4.61E-05	9.28E-05	10058	-1.81E-02	1.19E-02	1.52E-02	1.39E-02	10058

Note: ***, ** and * indicate the significance at 1, 5, 10%, respectively.

sense, in time aggregation more coarse than 30 minutes, it would be very difficult to refute a hypothesis that the exchange rate movement is a random walk. What is new here is that there exists a time window, albeit a short period, that the movement is predictable if the right information, which some market participants are able to gather, is available in real time.

6.4 Measuring the Lag Structure of Price Impacts

The preceding section did not test exactly how long the predictable power may persist. In this section, the lagged effects are measured cumulatively so that how long effects may persist can be estimated more precisely. In other words, the estimation will answer a question: How long order flow information will remain valuable. In order to examine the cumulative effect of order flows on the exchange rate changes, the following specification with the 1-minute frequency is adopted:

$$(8) \qquad \Delta s_t = \alpha + \sum_{i=0}^{30} \beta_i ndr_{t-i} + \gamma_i \Delta s_{t-i} + v_t$$

In this specification, the contemporaneous effect β_0 is also included, based on the presumption that order flows Granger-cause the price movement. The past 1-minute effect of the transaction on the current price movement is captured by $\beta_0 + \beta_1$, and the past 14-minute effect is expressed as $\beta_0 + \beta_1 + \beta_2 + \beta_3 + \ldots + \beta_{14}$. We calculate the price impact up to 30 minutes.

In estimating equation (8), again, we use three deal returns (midpoint of the deal-ask and the deal-bid price, deal-ask price, and deal-bid price) for Δs, where ndr denotes the *netdeal ratio*.[13] Lagged independent variables (up to thirty lags) are also included in the estimation. The calculated price impact defined as $\sum_{i=0}^{p} \beta_i$ (p equals up to 30) and associated standard errors are estimated for each of the three candidate return variables and a currency pair. The estimated cumulative price impact with one standard deviation will be examined below.

The price impact, the sum of β_i, is expected to be positive if order flows have predictable power up to the ith minute. For example, if the number of deals done on the ask-side exceeds the number of deals done on the bid-side for USD/JPY, the USD will appreciate *vis-à-vis* the Japanese yen due to more buyer initiated trades occurred. Therefore, ndr is positively associated with the returns.

3.4.1 Results

Results are summarized in figures 6.2–6.7. Figures 6.2–6.4 show the price impact of USD/JPY and figures 6.5–6.7 show the result of EUR/USD.

---

13. Since we do not see a large difference in estimation results of equations through (2) to (7), the estimation in this section was conducted with explanatory variable of *netdeal ratio* only.

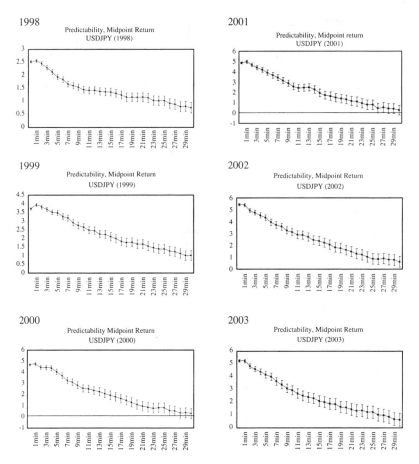

Fig. 6.2   USDJPY: Midpoint deal return

In each figure, the horizontal axis shows the duration from 0 minutes to 30 minutes, and the vertical axis shows the price impact with bars of one standard error. The price impact is not significantly different from zero when vertical bars of s.e. cross the horizontal axis of zero. Overall, the contemporaneous effects are significantly positive regardless of currencies, definition of returns (midpoint returns, bid-side deal returns, or ask-side deal returns), or sample years.

Figures 6.2–6.4 summarize the price impact of order flows on various measures of returns of USD/JPY. Figure 6.2 shows the price impact on midpoint returns. Overall, the contemporaneous price impact (0 minutes) is very large. In some years, the 1-minute period has the peak, and then the cumulative price impact gradually decreases, although it remains significantly positive even after 30 minutes. There is no significant difference in

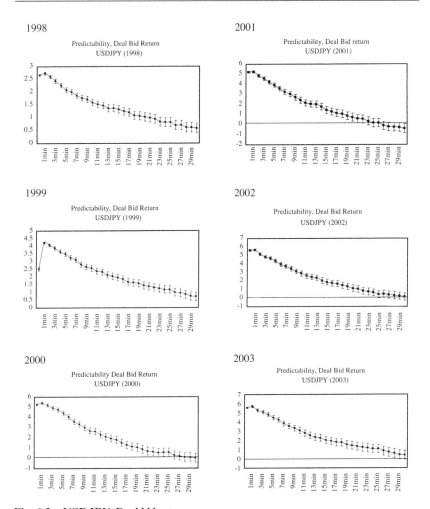

Fig. 6.3   USDJPY: Deal bid return

the price impact patterns over the years. Estimation with bid-side deal returns and ask-side deal returns are shown in figures 6.3 and 6.4, respectively. The size of the contemporaneous price impact (0 minutes) varies
across years, but they are all positive and significant. The cumulative price
impact at 1 minute later is the highest, and then the price impact gradually
decreases. In some years, price impact remains significantly positive after
30 minutes, and in other years, it becomes insignificant at around 25–30
minutes. For bid-side deal returns, price impact becomes insignificant
around 25–30 minutes in 2000, 2001, 2002 and 2003, as shown in figure 6.3.
For ask-side deal returns, price impact becomes insignificant around
28–30 minutes only in 2003, as shown in figure 6.4. For USD/JPY deals, es-

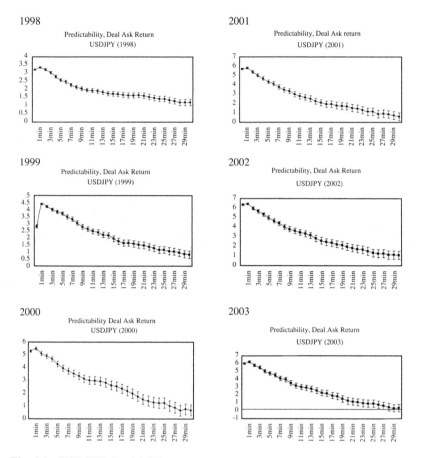

Fig. 6.4   USDJPY: Deal ASK return

timation results show that most of the price impact remains significantly positive after 30 minutes.

Figures 6.5–6.7 show the price impact of order flows on various measures of returns on EUR/USD. Results are mostly the same as the USD/JPY with slight differences. In some years, price impact appears significantly negative at higher lags at around 26–30 minutes. For the midpoint returns, in figure 6.5, the contemporaneous impact is small but positive, and the past-one-minute impact is the largest. Then price impact gradually decreases—but remains significant even at 30 minutes in 1999 and in 2000. Price impact becomes insignificant at 26 minutes in 2001, and significantly negative at around 28 minutes in 2002 and 2003.

Figures 6.6 and 6.7 show the price impact for bid-side deal returns and ask-side deal returns. For bid-side deal returns, price impact remains sig-

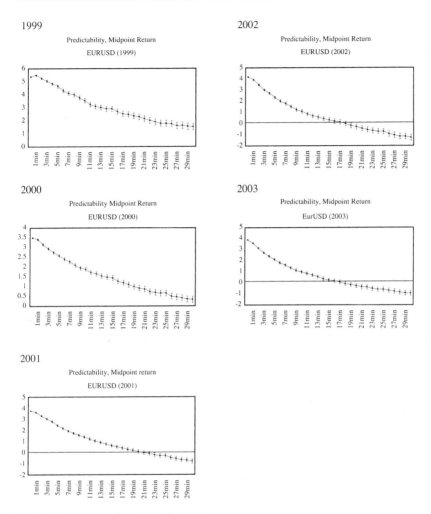

Fig. 6.5   EURUSD: Midpoint deal return

nificant at 30 minutes in 1999 and 2000, whereas it becomes significantly negative around 26 minutes in 2001 and after. For ask-side deal returns, price impact is significant for 30 minutes in 1999, becomes insignificant at 28 minutes in 2000, and becomes significantly negative after 2001.

In summary, the duration of positively significant returns following order flows has become shorter recently. This may be due to advances in technical trading and computer programming, which results in ever short-lived profit opportunities. For USD/JPY, the impact remains significant around 25 minutes (bid-side deal) and 28 minutes (ask-side deal). For EUR/USD, the price impact becomes significantly negative in recent years.

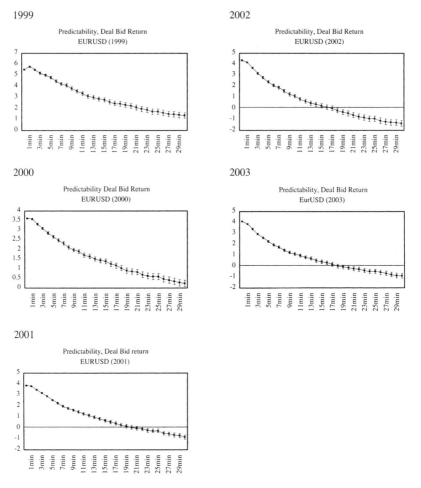

Fig. 6.6   EURUSD: Deal bid return

6.5   Conclusion

We examine the price impact of order flows using the transaction data recorded in the electronic broking system of the both USD/JPY and EUR/USD spot foreign exchange markets. At the 1-minute and 5-minute frequencies, our results show a strong predictive power of order flows for future exchange rate movement, whereas we fail to find any predictability at the half-hour window. In some circumstances, private information in terms of order flows are valuable in real time, but such information is very short-lived.

These findings suggest some profit opportunities if one has detailed information of the second-to-second deal counts/deal volumes in real time. This may explain why the private institutions spend millions of dollars to

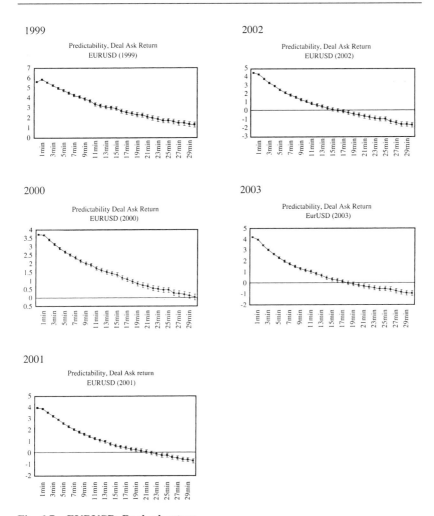

Fig. 6.7   EURUSD: Deal ask return

gather real time information and develop a model to extract buy and sell signals.

Although we found some evidence that price movements are predictable given trades information a minute earlier, this does not necessarily mean that there was a profitable opportunity. The estimation was done for a whole sample, and predictability is tested as an in-sample exercise. To show that profitable opportunity did exist, the exercise has to be done as out-of-sample simulations, taking into account the bid-ask spread, price movements in the preceding minutes, and other information, as well as order flows. A task of more sophisticated out-of-sample simulations is left for future research.

Appendix

Table 6A.1   Summary statistics of nd^{plus} and nd^{minus} of USD/JPY

			1 min				5 min			
			Mean	s.d.	Min	Max	Mean	s.d.	Min	Max
1998	ndplus	(netab)	1.230	2.113	0	24	3.633	5.629	0	57
	ndminus	(netab)	-1.079	1.983	-23	0	-2.644	4.714	-49	0
	ndplus	(ndr)	0.276	0.372	0	1	0.162	0.238	0	1
	ndminus	(ndr)	-0.234	0.354	-1	0	-0.125	0.217	-1	0
1999	ndplus	(netab)	1.140	2.000	0	23	3.361	5.292	0	57
	ndminus	(netab)	-1.025	1.877	-24	0	-2.467	4.433	-49	0
	ndplus	(ndr)	0.272	0.372	0	1	0.160	0.239	0	1
	ndminus	(ndr)	-0.234	0.355	-1	0	-0.125	0.220	-1	0
2000	ndplus	(netab)	0.934	1.705	0	21	2.693	4.370	0	49
	ndminus	(netab)	-0.931	1.693	-23	0	-2.260	3.978	-63	0
	ndplus	(ndr)	0.280	0.385	0	1	0.161	0.248	0	1
	ndminus	(ndr)	-0.255	0.374	-1	0	-0.140	0.237	-1	0
2001	ndplus	(netab)	0.980	1.763	0	21	2.891	4.585	0	43
	ndminus	(netab)	-0.934	1.708	-20	0	-2.243	4.005	-44	0
	ndplus	(ndr)	0.279	0.381	0	1	0.165	0.251	0	1
	ndminus	(ndr)	-0.244	0.366	-1	0	-0.133	0.233	-1	0
2002	ndplus	(netab)	1.011	1.823	0	21	2.926	4.690	0	55
	ndminus	(netab)	-0.980	1.786	-23	0	-2.353	4.183	-51	0
	ndplus	(ndr)	0.274	0.378	0	1	0.160	0.247	0	1
	ndminus	(ndr)	-0.243	0.364	-1	0	-0.132	0.230	-1	0
2003	ndplus	(netab)	0.986	1.764	0	23	2.812	4.487	0	45
	ndminus	(netab)	-0.954	1.733	-27	0	-2.255	4.029	-59	0
	ndplus	(ndr)	0.270	0.375	0	1	0.153	0.236	0	1
	ndminus	(ndr)	-0.242	0.363	-1	0	-0.126	0.221	-1	0

Table 6A.2 Summary statistics of nd^{plus} and nd^{minus} of EUR/USD

		1 min				5 min			
		Mean	s.d.	Min	Max	Mean	s.d.	Min	Max
1999	*ndplus* (netab)	1.159	2.159	0	25	3.146	5.433	0	62
	ndminus (netab)	-1.161	2.150	-27	0	-2.656	4.977	-55	0
	ndplus (ndr)	0.249	0.359	0	1	0.150	0.246	0	1
	ndminus (ndr)	-0.226	0.348	-1	0	-0.127	0.229	-1	0
2000	*ndplus* (netab)	1.216	2.237	0	30	3.276	5.600	0	55
	ndminus (netab)	-1.217	2.223	-27	0	-2.768	5.138	-51	0
	ndplus (ndr)	0.234	0.346	0	1	0.141	0.236	0	1
	ndminus (ndr)	-0.212	0.335	-1	0	-0.118	0.219	-1	0
2001	*ndplus* (netab)	1.131	2.081	0	24	2.980	5.056	0	52
	ndminus (netab)	-1.144	2.096	-24	0	-2.526	4.709	-52	0
	ndplus (ndr)	0.239	0.352	0	1	0.140	0.234	0	1
	ndminus (ndr)	-0.215	0.340	-1	0	-0.118	0.220	-1	0
2002	*ndplus* (netab)	1.116	2.046	0	21	2.948	4.952	0	47
	ndminus (netab)	-1.122	2.033	-25	0	-2.428	4.477	-52	0
	ndplus (ndr)	0.244	0.357	0	1	0.140	0.232	0	1
	ndminus (ndr)	-0.222	0.347	-1	0	-0.119	0.221	-1	0
2003	*ndplus* (netab)	1.260	2.205	0	23	3.274	5.331	0	48
	ndminus (netab)	-1.232	2.175	-27	0	-2.760	4.899	-51	0
	ndplus (ndr)	0.219	0.334	0	1	0.121	0.205	0	1
	ndminus (ndr)	-0.199	0.322	-1	0	-0.101	0.189	-1	0

References

Andersen, T. G., and T. Bollerslev. 1997. Intraday periodicity and volatility persistence in financial markets. *Journal of Empirical Finance* 4:115–58.
Andersen, T. G., and T. Bollerslev. 1998. Deutsche mark-dollar volatility: Intraday activity patterns, macroeconomic announcements, and longer run dependencies. *Journal of Finance* 53 (1): 219–65.
Baillie, R. T., and T. Bollerslev. 1990. Intra-day and inter-market volatility in foreign exchange rates. *Review of Economic Studies* 58:565–85.
Berger, D., A. Chaboud, S. V. Chernenko, E. Howorka, R. S. Knshnasami Iyer, D. Liu, and J. Wright. 2005. Order flow and exchange rate dynamics in electronic brokerage system data. International Finance Discussion Papers No. 830. Washington, DC: Board of Governors of the Federal Reserve System, April.
Chaboud, A. P., S. V. Chernenko, E. Howorka, R. Krishnasami Iyer, D. Liu, and J. H. Wright. 2004. The high-frequency effects of U.S. macroeconomic data releases on prices and trading activity in the global interdealer foreign exchange market. International Finance Discussion Papers, No. 823. Washington, DC: Board of Governors of the Federal Reserve System, November.
Evans, M., and R. K. Lyons. 2002. Order flow and exchange rate dynamics. *Journal of Political Economy,* February: 170–80.
———. 2005a. Do currency markets absorb news quickly? NBER Working Paper no. 11041. Cambridge, MA: National Bureau of Economic Research, January.
———. 2005b. Meese-Rogoff redux: Micro-based exchange rate forecasting. NBER Working Paper no. 11042. Cambridge, MA: National Bureau of Economic Research, January.
———. 2005c. Understanding Order Flow. NBER Working Paper no. 11748. Cambridge, MA: National Bureau of Economic Research, November.
Goodhart, C., T. Ito, and R. Payne. 1996. One day in June 1993: A study of the working of the Reuters 2000–2 electronic foreign exchange trading system. In *The microstructure of foreign exchange markets,* eds. J. A. Frankel, G. Galli, and A. Giovanni, 107–179. Chicago: University of Chicago Press.
Goodhart, C., and M. O'Hara. 1997. High frequency data in financial markets: Issues and applications. *Journal of Empirical Finance* 4:73–114.
Goodhart, C., and R. Payne. 1996. Microstructural dynamics in a foreign exchange electronic broking system. *Journal of International Money and Finance* 15 (6): 829–852.
Ito, T. 2003. Is foreign exchange intervention effective?: The Japanese experiences in the 1990s. In *Monetary history, exchange rates and financial markets: Essays in honor of Charles Goodhart,* vol. 2, ed. Paul Mizen, 126–53. Cheltenham, England: Edward Elgar Publishing.
———. 2004. The yen and the Japanese economy, 2004. In *Dollar adjustment: How far? Against what?* eds. C. F. Bergsten and J. Williamson, 171–96. Washington, DC: Institute for International Economics.
———. 2005a. The exchange rate in the Japanese economy: The past, puzzles, and prospects. *Japanese Economic Review* 56 (1): 1–38.
———. 2005b. Interventions and Japanese Economic recovery. *International Economics and Economics Policy* (IEEP), 2 (2-3): 219–39.
Ito, T., and Y. Hashimoto. 2004. Microstructure of the dollar/yen foreign exchange market: Patterns of intra-day activity in the electronic broking system. NBER Working Paper no. 10856. Cambridge, MA: National Bureau of Economic Research, October.

————. 2006. Intra-day seasonality in activities of the foreign exchange markets: Evidence from the electronic broking system. *Journal of the Japanese and International Economies* 20 (4): 637–64.

Ito, T., R. K. Lyons, and M. T. Melvin. 1998. Is there private information in the FX market? The Tokyo experiment. *The Journal of Finance* LIII (3): 1111–30.

Lyons, R. 1995. Tests of microstructural hypotheses in the foreign exchange market. *Journal of Financial Economics* 39:321–51.

Lyons, R. K. 1996. Foreign exchange volume: Sound and fury signifying nothing? In *The microstructure of foreign exchange markets,* ed. J. A. Frankel, G. Galli, and A. Giovanni, 183–205. Chicago: The University of Chicago Press.

Lyons, R. 1997. A simultaneous trade model of the foreign exchange hot potato. *Journal of International Economics* 42:275–98.

Lyons, R. 1998. Profits and position control: A week of FX dealing. *Journal of International Money and Finance* 17:97–115.

Lyons, R. 2001. *The microstructure approach to exchange rates.* Cambridge, MA: MIT Press.

Lyons, R. K., and M. J. Moore. 2005. An information approach to international currencies. NBER Working Paper no. 11220. Cambridge, MA: National Bureau of Economic Research, March.

Comment   Eli Remolona

This is a very nice empirical microstructure chapter. It is the latest in a series of excellent papers by Taka Ito and various coauthors. The chapter is especially interesting because the market it looks at is one in which the microstructure has changed quite significantly. The market in question is the interdealer market for the world's three major currencies, namely the U.S. dollar, the Japanese yen, and the euro. For this study, Ito and Hashimoto have been able to collect a large amount of high-frequency data, even more than what your typical market microstructure paper would have. Given the number of observations they bring to bear on the analysis, almost any phenomenon the authors wish to find should be evident in the data.

At root, the chapter is about the information content of trades. Here the authors ask two basic questions. First, do trades predict prices? Second, does intervention in the currency market by the Bank of Japan affect the results?

The data are from EBS, which is the electronic broker system that is now used for the bulk of interdealer trades in the U.S. dollar, Japanese yen, and euro. For trades between the dollar and the yen, the authors look at the period from January 1998 to October 2003, and for trades between the euro

Eli Remolona is Head of Economics for Asia and the Pacific, Bank for International Settlements and the dollar, they look at the period from January 1999 to October 2003. The euro, of course, did not exist before January 1999.

For purposes of analysis, rather than analyzing every single trade, the authors aggregate the trades into four very short windows: one minute, five minutes, fifteen minutes and thirty minutes. For each of these windows, they create a proxy for order flows, which is the number of bid deals minus the number of ask deals. This proxy is not controversial; it is the way order flows tend to be constructed in the market microstructure literature.

The basic methodology is to regress currency returns on net-order flows for different windows and for up to ten lags. Days during which the Bank of Japan intervened are distinguished from other days. For robustness, the authors compute currency returns in three ways: based on midpoints between bid and ask quotes, based on just-bid prices, and based on just-ask prices. The different definitions of return seem to produce the same results.

The results are interesting. Order flow predicts returns at one-minute and five-minute horizons but not at thirty-minute horizons. On intervention days, that predictability shortens to one minute. The effect of intervention seems to be to induce lagged price adjustment.

An important question that the authors leave unanswered is whether the change in market microstructure induced by EBS matters. Prior to the advent of EBS, currency dealers traded largely bilaterally through voice brokers. They could therefore not easily observe trades that did not involve themselves. With EBS, dealers see what is going on in almost the entire interdealer market, although they may not know the identities of the counterparties to a given trade.

Lyons (1997) has described the trading activity in the inter-dealer currency market as *hot-potato* trading, in which dealers quickly follow a customer trade with trades with other dealers so as to square their position as soon as possible. When Evans and Lyons (2005) looked at the market with electronic trading already in place, they found that order flow helps predict prices at the one-month horizon, a result that seems to be different from that of Ito and Hashimoto. More recently, Berger and colleagues (2005) use EBS data and find no evidence that trades predict prices at any horizon, again a result that seems to be at odds with those of Ito and Hashimoto. Hence, a question the authors should try to answer is how does one reconcile these seemingly disparate results?

It would also be helpful for the authors to try to shed light on the question of what sorts of information are supposed to be conveyed by order flows that allow them to predict price changes up to the five-minute horizon? In equity markets, the empirical literature suggests that there are trades that convey private information, and this information is what allows trades to move prices. By contrast, Fleming and Remolona (1999) show that the sharpest price movements in U.S. Treasury markets are caused by releases of public macroeconomic information, and these price movements need not be accompanied by trading activity. Berger and colleagues (2005) found something that is still different in currency markets. Here order flow seems to be associated with macroeconomic announcements. Hence, the big unasked question arising from the results of Ito and Hashimoto is what information do currency dealers obtain that seems to remain relevant for five minutes?

References

Evans, M. D. D., and R. K. Lyons. 2005. Do currency markets absorb news quickly? *Journal of International Money and Finance* 24: 197–217.
Fleming, M., and E. Remolona. 1999. Price formation and liquidity in the U.S. treasury market: The response to public information. *Journal of Finance* LIV(5): 1901–15.

7

Adopting a Common Currency Basket Arrangement into the ASEAN Plus Three

Eiji Ogawa and Kentaro Kawasaki

7.1 Introduction

Since the Asian currency crisis, it has been recognized in East Asia that regional monetary and financial cooperation is necessary for preventing and managing future currency crises. The monetary authorities of ASEAN plus three countries (Japan, China, and Korea) established a network of swap arrangements under the Chiang Mai Initiative. They decided to develop the Chiang Mai Initiative at the ASEAN plus three financial ministers' meeting in Istanbul in May of 2005. It is clear that surveillance over the economic situation of the ASEAN plus three countries is necessary for the prevention of currency crises. In fact, monetary authorities have been maintaining surveillance over domestic economic variables such as GDP and inflation rates under the Chiang Mai Initiative.

There still exists a variety of exchange rate regimes in East Asia, although the monetary authorities have been discussing monetary and financial cooperation. For example, Japan and Korea have adopted a free-floating exchange rate system, while China and Malaysia adopted a dollar-peg system prior to mid-2005. Although the monetary authorities of China and Malaysia have announced that they changed their exchange rate regime into a managed floating exchange rate system, they have kept a high weight on the U.S. dollar when conducting exchange rate policy (Ogawa and Sakane 2006; Ito 2005). The variety of exchange rate systems in East Asia shows a possibility of coordination failure in choosing exchange rate regimes (Ogawa and Ito 2002). One of the measures to solve

Eiji Ogawa is a professor at the Graduate School of Commerce and Management at Hitotsubashi University. Kentaro Kawasaki is a professor on the Faculty of Business Administration at Toyo University.

the coordination failure is for the monetary authorities of the ASEAN plus three countries to adopt a common exchange rate policy. The exchange rate policy coordination of the ASEAN plus three countries should contribute to the stability of intraregional exchange rates between the ASEAN plus three currencies.

It is pointed out that the ASEAN plus three countries should be an Optimum Currency Area (OCA) in order to succeed in adopting a common exchange rate policy. At the same time, some impute difficulties in adopting a common exchange rate policy, because the countries are at different stages of economic development. In this chapter we investigate whether the ASEAN plus three countries are an OCA while we take into account the fact that a currency basket system should be desirable for those economies that have strong economic relationships with more than one specific country. It is noted in the fact that both the Chinese and Malaysian monetary authorities have adopted a currency basket system.

A structural vector autoregression model is used to investigate whether economic shocks, especially aggregate supply shocks, are symmetrical between East Asian countries, given that symmetry of shocks is one of the conditions for OCA.[1] The symmetry of shocks that are investigated by the structural VAR are no more than a sufficient condition for OCA. A region is regarded as an OCA if one of the other conditions is satisfied while the shocks are asymmetrical among countries. Therefore, asymmetry of shocks should not always show that the relevant region is not an OCA.

A generalized-purchasing power parity (G-PPP) model is used to investigate whether a region is an OCA. The G-PPP is based on a PPP to extend to a multilateral exchange-rate version. In the case of bilateral exchange rates, the PPP holds in the long-run when a bilateral real exchange rate has stationarity, which means that the real exchange rate converges to a level in the long run. If a region has the convergence of the real exchange rates, it is regarded that the region can be an OCA where the nominal exchange rates can stay fixed with each other, although it is not clear which factors among symmetry of shocks, factor mobility, openness of economy, and fiscal transfers make the region an OCA. According to the G-PPP model, multilateral real exchange rates have a cointegration relationship, which means there is a long-run stable relationship between the relevant currencies. The long-run stable relationship among the regional currencies identified by the G-PPP model can be regarded as an OCA in the region.

In addition, the G-PPP model is used to specify a common currency basket as an anchor currency that the monetary authorities are targeting through their exchange rate policies. The common currency basket system can contribute to reducing fluctuations and misalignments of each regional currency against other regional and outside currencies. Fixing each

---

1. Bayoumi, Eichengreen, and Mauro (2000).

regional currency to common outsider currencies means that not only the regional currencies, but also the anchor currencies should form an OCA. It is important to investigate whether regional currencies can form an OCA with outside currencies as an anchor currency.

This paper addresses the following. We explain a theoretical background of the G-PPP model and the relationship between the G-PPP model and the OCA model. Next, we use the G-PPP model to define a common currency area for the ASEAN plus three countries. We explain the adoption of a common currency basket arrangement into the ASEAN plus three countries. In the fourth section, we conduct an empirical analysis of the possibilities of adopting a common currency basket arrangement into the ASEAN plus three countries. In our conclusion we summarize analytical results.

7.2   OCA Theory and G-PPP Model

7.2.1   Real Effective Exchange Rates and Generalized PPP

Ogawa and Kawasaki (2003), Kawasaki (2005), and Kawasaki and Ogawa (2006) modified the Enders and Hurn's (1994) G-PPP model using a concept of stochastic trends among the real effective exchange rates of countries in the common currency area. We use the extended G-PPP model as well.

The G-PPP model is extended from a simple PPP model by taking into account difficulties in holding PPP, because frequently occurring nominal and real shocks have continuous effects on macrofundamentals. Even in the long run, changes in a bilateral exchange rate depend not only on changes in the relative prices between the related two countries, but also on those in relative prices between the two other countries. Price levels in other countries may effect domestic price levels in the two countries, because prices of intermediate goods imported from abroad may have effects on the prices of domestic products. Therefore it is assumed in the G-PPP model that there are common factors among some bilateral real exchange rates of the home currency vis-à-vis currencies of foreign countries that the home country has strong economic relationships with. Thus, the real exchange rates have a stable equilibrium in the long run if they have strong economic relationships with each other. The G-PPP model explains that a PPP holds if a linear combination of some bilateral real exchange rate series has equilibrium in the long run, even though each of the bilateral rate series is nonstationary. We assume that this linear combination defines the optimum currency area (Mundell 1961).

Suppose that n number of countries are assumed to exist in the world. While country j has n trade partners, it shares strong trade relationships with $m - 1$ countries nearby. We also assume that m number of countries, which includes country j, are expected to form a common currency area because they possess strong economic relationships and share similarities. We could suppose the common currency area as a region where monetary authorities have a common objective to stabilize their trade accounts. Therefore, they conduct a common exchange rate policy and stabilize real effective exchange rates.

Here we define the real effective exchange rates of country j as ree_j, which is composed of its all trade partners. While countries $1, 2, \ldots, j, \ldots, m$ are expected to adopt a common currency policy, countries $m + 1, \ldots, n$ do not share the common currency policy with country j. So, ree_j can be denoted with currency of country j:

$$(1) \qquad ree_j = \xi_j \cdot (\rho_{j,1} re_{j,1} + \rho_{j,2} re_{j,2} + \ldots + \rho_{j,m} re_{j,m})$$
$$+ (1 - \xi_j) \cdot (\rho_{j,m+1} re_{j,m+1} + \ldots + \rho_{j,n} re_{j,n}),$$

where $re_{j,i}$ is the logarithm of the real exchange rate between country i and country j. The coefficients: $\rho_{j,i} (\Sigma_{i=1,i\neq j}^{m} \rho_{j,i} = 1, \Sigma_{i=m+1}^{n} \rho_{j,i} = 1)$ denote that country j's trade weights on country i and ξ are the trade weights of a group of countries that share the common currency.

Here we add one more assumption that the shocks from the outside of the common currency area do not affect the real effective rate of country j permanently, but temporarily. Because of that, in the case where only country j is permanently affected by the countries that do not adopt the common currency basket as an anchor currency, it is difficult to maintain a common currency in the region.

We focus on the part of real effective exchange rates, which is defined by $m - 1$ trade partners who only share the common currency with country j and country $m + 1$, or those who do not share the common currency with country j. While using the currency of country $m + 1$ as a numéraire to define the exchange rate between the regional currencies, equation (1) is rewritten as a currency basket as follows:

$$(2) \qquad cb_j = \omega_{j,1} re_{j,1} + \omega_{j,2} re_{j,2} + \ldots + \omega_{j,m} re_{j,m} + \omega_{j,m+1} re_{j,m+1},$$

where the coefficients $\omega_{j,i}$ $(\Sigma_{i=1,i\neq j}^{m+1} \omega_{j,i} = 1)$ denote country j's trade weights on country i and country $m + 1$.

Furthermore, equation (2) can be rewritten in terms of a currency of country $m + 1$ as follows:

$$cb_{j,t} = \omega_{j,1}(re_{j,1,t} - re_{j,m+1,t}) + \ldots + \omega_{j,m-1}(re_{j,m-1,t} - re_{j,m+1,t}) + re_{j,m+1,t}$$
$$= \omega_{j,1} re_{m+1,1,t} + \ldots + \omega_{j,1} re_{m+1,m,t} - re_{m+1,j,t},$$

where $re_{j,k} = re_{j,n} - re_{k,n} = -re_{n,j} + re_{n,k}$.

Since there exists m number of countries that form a currency area, we focus on m number of real effective exchange rates as a currency basket in the region in terms of the currency of country $m + 1$ and country $m + 1$'s real effective exchange rate defined as a currency basket in the same ways. So, $m + 1$ number of real effective exchange rates can be defined as follows:

$$cb_{1,t} = -re_{m+1,j,t} + \omega_{1,2}re_{m+1,2,t} + \ldots + \omega_{1,m}re_{m+1,m,t}$$
$$cb_{2,t} = \omega_{2,1}re_{m+1,1,t} - re_{m+1,2,t} \ldots + \omega_{2,m}re_{m+1,m,t}$$
$$\vdots$$
$$cb_{m,t} = \omega_{m,1}re_{m+1,1,t} + \ldots + \omega_{m,m-1}re_{m+1,m-1,t} - re_{m+1,m,t}$$
$$cb_{m+1,t} = \omega_{m+1,1}re_{m+1,1,t} + \ldots + \omega_{m+1,m-1}re_{m+1,m-1,t} + \omega_{m+1,m}re_{m+1,m,t}$$

These $m + 1$ currency baskets can also be shown in a vector form. Matrix Ω defines the trade weights, and vector **re**, which includes m elements of the real exchange rate, $re_{m+1,i}$, the vector form of $m + 1$ currency baskets can be written as follows:

(1) $$\mathbf{cb}_t = \Omega \cdot \mathbf{re}_t,$$

where

$$\Omega_{(m+1)\times m} = \begin{bmatrix} -1 & \omega_{1,2} & \ldots & \omega_{1,m-1} & \omega_{1,m} \\ \omega_{2,1} & -1 & \ldots & \omega_{2,m-1} & \omega_{2,m} \\ \vdots & \vdots & \ldots & \vdots & \vdots \\ \omega_{m,1} & \omega_{m,2} & \ldots & \omega_{m,m-1} & -1 \\ \omega_{m+1,1} & \omega_{m+1,2} & \ldots & \omega_{m+1,m-1} & \omega_{m+1,m} \end{bmatrix}$$

and vector **cb** includes $m + 1$ number of currency baskets.

Each of the currency baskets is expected to include a common stochastic trend because the countries have strong trade relationships with each other and seem to share common technologies.[2] We assume that $m + 1$ number of the currency baskets share a common stochastic trend. Using Stock and Watson's (1988) common trend representation for any cointegration system, we can show that vector **cb**, which is characterized by m cointegration relationships, can be described as the sum of a stationary component and a nonstationary component.

(4) $$\mathbf{cb}_t = \overline{\mathbf{cb}}_t + \widetilde{\mathbf{cb}}_t$$

The stationary component, $\overline{\mathbf{cb}}$, is $E(\overline{\mathbf{cb}}_t) = 0$ in this model since the logarithm of the currency baskets can be expected to converge toward the zero-mean in the long run.[3] Therefore, Vector **cb** can be only described as the nonstationary component, $\widetilde{\mathbf{cb}}$. By the definition of common trend in Stock and Watson (1988), the following equation is obtained:

2. Enders and Hurn (1994) developed the G-PPP model based on the real fundamental macroeconomic variables. They assumed these variables shared common trends within a currency area.
3. We focus on the long-run properties of the OCA; however, macroeconomic policy coordination is needed for a short-term sufficient condition for the OCA.

(5) $\mathbf{cb}_t = \Phi \cdot \mathbf{w}_t$,

where Φ is a $(m + 1) \times (m + 1)$ matrix. Vector $\mathbf{w}_t$ is the nonstationary stochastic trend that is characterized by a random walk. Substituting equation (5) into equation (3), then,

(6) $\Phi \cdot \mathbf{w}_t = \Omega \cdot \mathbf{re}_t$.

Here, the non-null matrix Ψ is composed of $(m + 1) \times (m + 1)$ and defined to obtain the following equation from equation (6):

(7) $\Psi \cdot \Phi \cdot \mathbf{w}_t = \Psi \cdot \Omega \cdot \mathbf{re}_t$

If there exists a nonzero $\mathbf{w}$ for which $\Psi \cdot \Phi \cdot \mathbf{w}_t = 0$, $\Psi \cdot \Phi$ does not have a full rank, the rank condition will be expected as follows:

$$\mathrm{rank}(\Psi \cdot \Phi) = \mathrm{rank}(\Phi) < m.$$

As long as the rank condition holds, there exists a non-null matrix Ψ that satisfies the following equation:

(8) $\Psi \cdot \Phi = 0$

When defining $Z = \Psi \cdot \Omega$ and substituting it into equation (7), the following equation is obtained:

(9) $Z \cdot \mathbf{re} = 0$

If we could find a matrix Z, which satisfies rank $(Z) < m$ and equation (9), it means that there exists nonzero $\mathbf{re}$ for $Z \cdot \mathbf{re} = 0$ and that the matrix Ψ is not a null matrix. Accordingly, the number of rank Ω must be smaller than m. Here, it is assumed that rank $(Z) = 1$. Equation (9) can be shown as the following linear combination:

(10) $\zeta_1 \cdot re_{m+1,1} + \zeta_2 \cdot re_{m+1,2} + \ldots + \zeta_m \cdot re_{m+1,m} = 0$

where ζ_i is an element of cointegrating vector.

In our extended G-PPP approach, this linear combination defines that m countries form a common currency area in terms of the currency of country $m + 1$. It means that this area exhibits optimal currency area in the sense of Mundell (1961).[4]

---

4. This linear combination is the same formation as that of Enders and Hurn (1994); however, in our extended G-PPP model, country $m + 1$ does not belong in the common currency area. As Mundell (1961) pointed out, the idea of the optimum currency area works best if each currency shares internal factor mobility and external factor immobility, but may not exhibit enough internal factor mobility because of trade protections or labor policy between these countries. Domestic policies would be changed and obstacles would be omitted after launching their economic union. Therefore, to investigate the candidates of the future monetary union, we should consider not only the internal mobility but also external common immobility and investigate how external shocks affect each economy in the region. Again, to capture the effect from external economies, the common currency area should be evaluated in terms of macrofundamental variables of external countries.

7.3   G-PPP and a Common Currency Basket

7.3.1   Adopting the Common Currency Basket Arrangement into the ASEAN Plus Three

After the Asian currency crisis in 1997, some East Asian countries temporarily changed their exchange rate policy from the *de facto* dollar peg system to a currency basket system. Each country makes reference to a currency basket that includes not only the three major currencies (the U.S. dollar, the euro, and the yen), but also other East Asian currencies.

In the event that an East Asian country adopts six neighboring countries' currencies and the three major trading partners' currencies into its basket currency as their target policy, country i's reference rate can be rewritten as follows:

$$re_{CB,i} = \varphi_{1,i} \cdot re_{1,i} + \ldots + \varphi_{7,i} \cdot re_{7,i} + \varphi_{JP,i} \cdot re_{JP,i} + \varphi_{EU,i} \cdot re_{EU,i} + \varphi_{US,i} \cdot re_{US,i},$$

(11)
$$\sum_{i=1,j\neq i}^{7,JP,EU,US} \varphi_{j,i} = 1$$

Equation (11) can be written in terms of U.S. dollar as follows:

(12)
$$re_{CB,i} = \varphi_{1,i} re_{1,US} + \varphi_{2,i} re_{2,US} + \ldots + \varphi_{m,i} re_{m,US} \\ + \varphi_{JP,i} re_{JP,US} + \varphi_{EU,i} re_{EU,US} + re_{US,i}$$

Here, we suppose that monetary authorities in the seven East Asian countries adopt the currency basket system as their exchange rate policy and refer the same composition of the basket currency. The real exchange rates between each of the East Asian countries and the basket currency can be rewritten as a vector form:

(13)
$$\mathbf{re}_{CB,i} = \mathbf{F} \cdot \mathbf{re}_{(i,JP,EU),US},$$
$$\begin{matrix} (7\times1) & (7\times9) & (9\times1) \end{matrix}$$

where $\mathbf{re}_{CB,i} = (re_{CB,1}, \ldots, re_{CB,7})'$, $\mathbf{re}_{(i,JP,EU),US} = (re_{1,US}, \ldots, re_{7,US}, re_{JP,US}, re_{EU,US})'$, and

$$\mathbf{F} = \begin{pmatrix} -1 & \varphi_{1,2} & \cdots & \varphi_{1,7} & \varphi_{1,JP} & \varphi_{1,EU} \\ \varphi_{2,1} & -1 & \cdots & \varphi_{2,7} & \varphi_{2,JP} & \varphi_{2,EU} \\ \vdots & \vdots & \ddots & \vdots & \vdots & \vdots \\ \varphi_{7,1} & \varphi_{7,2} & \cdots & -1 & \varphi_{7,JP} & \varphi_{7,EU} \end{pmatrix}.$$

By partitioning vector $re_{(i,JP,EU),US}$ into two groups—insider currencies and outsider currencies—and both trade weights, and partitioning matrix

F into the two matrixes for insider and outsider currency, respectively, equation (13) can be rewritten as follows:

$$
(14) \qquad \underset{(7\times1)}{\mathbf{re}_{CB,i}} = \underset{(7\times7)}{\mathbf{F}_1} \cdot \underset{(7\times1)}{\mathbf{re}_1} + \underset{(7\times2)}{\mathbf{F}_2} \cdot \underset{(2\times1)}{\mathbf{re}_2},
$$

where $\mathbf{F} = (\mathbf{F}_1 \ \mathbf{F}_2)$ and $\mathbf{re}_{(i,JP,EU),US} = (\mathbf{re}_1 \ \mathbf{re}_2)'$.

Next, if the Japanese yen is included in the region, as well as seven other East Asian countries, the Japanese yen exchange rates against the U.S. dollar should be included in the first part of partitioning vectors, as well as other East Asian exchange rates against the U.S. dollar. Equation (13) should be rewritten as follows:

$$
(15) \qquad \underset{(8\times1)}{\mathbf{re}_{CB,i}} = \underset{(8\times9)}{\mathbf{F}} \cdot \underset{(9\times1)}{\mathbf{re}_{(i,JP,EU),US}} = \underset{(8\times8)}{\mathbf{F}_1} \cdot \underset{(8\times1)}{\mathbf{re}_1} + \underset{(8\times1)}{\mathbf{F}_2} \cdot \underset{(1\times1)}{\mathbf{re}_2}.
$$

Equations (13) and (15) could be rewritten in a general form as follows:

$$
(16) \qquad \underset{(m\times1)}{\mathbf{re}_{CB,i}} = \underset{(m\times m)}{\mathbf{F}_1} \cdot \underset{(m\times1)}{\mathbf{re}_1} + \underset{[m\times(h-m)]}{\mathbf{F}_2} \cdot \underset{[(h-m)\times1]}{\mathbf{re}_2},
$$

where h is the number of exchange rates that are included in the currency basket and m is the number of countries in the possible region of currency union.

Since matrix $\mathbf{F}_1$ has an inverse matrix, vector $\mathbf{re}_1$ is solved by matrix $\mathbf{F}$ as follows:

$$
(17) \qquad \mathbf{re}_1 = \mathbf{F}_1^{-1} \cdot \mathbf{re}_{CB,i} - \mathbf{F}_1^{-1}\mathbf{F}_2 \cdot \mathbf{re}_2
$$

In equation (17), $\mathbf{re}_1$ is defined by $\mathbf{re}_2$. It means that real exchange rates among East Asian countries in the region would be defined by the currencies outside the region.

If the monetary authorities in the region agree to peg their home currencies to the regional currency basket and intervene in foreign exchange markets to maintain their exchange rate stability, a long-run property of those real exchange rates should be zero: $\mathbf{re}_{CB,i} = 0$. Here, we define the nonnull matrix, $\mathbf{Z}$, which is composed of $m \times m$, equation (16) is written to obtain the following:

$$
(18) \qquad \underset{(m\times m)}{\mathbf{Z}} \cdot \underset{(m\times h)}{\mathbf{F}} \cdot \underset{(h\times1)}{\mathbf{re}_h} = \underset{(m\times m)}{\mathbf{Z}} \cdot \underset{(m\times m)}{\mathbf{F}_1} \cdot \underset{(m\times1)}{\mathbf{re}_1} + \underset{(m\times m)}{\mathbf{Z}} \cdot \underset{[m\times(h-m)]}{\mathbf{F}_2} \cdot \underset{[(h-m)\times1]}{\mathbf{re}_2} = 0,
$$

where vector $\mathbf{re}_h$ includes h number of exchange rates between each of all related currencies and the U.S. dollar.

If there exists a nonzero matrix, $\mathbf{Z}$, for which $\mathbf{Z} \cdot \mathbf{re}_{CB,i} = 0$, $\mathbf{Z}$ does not have a full rank. If we could find a matrix, $\mathbf{Z}$, that satisfies rank $(\mathbf{Z}) < m$, it means that there exists a nonzero re for $\mathbf{Z} \cdot \mathbf{re} = 0$ and that the matrix $\mathbf{Z}$ is not a null matrix. Accordingly, the number of rank $\mathbf{Z}$ must be smaller than

m, using the same logic of the rank condition in equation (9). It means that if the exchange rate between the Japanese yen and the U.S. dollar is included in vector re_2, the number of rank $\mathbf{Z}$ for which $\mathbf{Z} \cdot \mathbf{re}_{CB,i} = 0$ would be $h - m = 2$; if it is included in vector $\mathbf{re}_1$, the number of rank would be $h - m = 1$. There must be a cointegration relationship among real exchange rates, re_h.

7.4 Empirical Analysis

7.4.1 Methodology

In our earlier works we found several linear combinations that had cointegration relationships when we set the basket weight on three major currencies in advance. In this paper, basket weights on the anchor currencies, the U.S. dollar and the euro, will be set by the estimation. The more countries that adopt the common currency basket exchange rate policy, the less robust result we have with a small sample by using the Johansen approach.

In this paper we use the dynamic OLS (DOLS) to estimate the cointegrating vector. We rewrite equation (10) as follows:

(19) $re_{US,EU} = \beta_1 \cdot re_{US,1} + \beta_2 \cdot re_{US,2} + \ldots + \beta_m \cdot re_{US,m} + \beta_{JP} \cdot re_{US,JP}$

Equation (19) represents the long-run relationship, whose coefficients can be estimated by the OLS.[5] To estimate it, we add the leads and lags, deterministic trend, and constant term into equation (19) as follows:

(20) $re_{US,EU} = \beta_0 + \beta_1 \cdot re_{US,1,t} + \beta_2 \cdot re_{US,2,t} + \ldots + \beta_m \cdot re_{US,m,t}$

$$+ \beta_{JP} \cdot re_{US,JP,t} + \sum_{i=1}^{m} \sum_{j=-k}^{k} \gamma_{i,j} \Delta re_{US,i,t \neq j} + \beta \cdot t + u_t$$

Then, the property of the residuals by the DOLS estimates is shown as follows:

(21) $\hat{u}_t = \phi_1 \cdot \hat{u}_{t-1} + \phi_2 \cdot \hat{u}_{t-2} + \phi_3 \cdot \hat{u}_{t-3} + \ldots + \phi_p \cdot \hat{u}_{t-p} + e_t$,

where the sample distribution will be adjusted as:

(22) $$\hat{\sigma}'_u = \frac{\hat{\sigma}_u}{1 - \phi_1 - \phi_2 - \phi_3 - \ldots - \phi_p}.$$

We attempt to estimate the cointegrating vector with endogenous weights in the common currency basket. In this paper, we test combinations: ASEAN 5, ASEAN 5 plus Korea, ASEAN 5 plus China, and ASEAN 5 plus Korea plus China for $r = 2$; and ASEAN 5 plus Japan, ASEAN 5 plus Korea plus Japan, ASEAN 5 plus China plus Japan, and

---

5. See details in the appendix.

ASEAN 5 plus Korea plus China plus Japan for $r = 1$.[6] We assumed serial correlation of residuals was captured by an $AR(4)$, and leads and lags was $k = 2$ in equation (20).

7.4.2   Data

The sample for our empirical tests covers a period between January 1987 and November 2005. Our sample includes data in the period of the Asian currency crisis. We divide the sample periods into a precrisis period from January 1987 to June 1997 and a postcrisis period from January 1999 to November 2005. The eight East Asian countries included are Korea, Singapore, Malaysia, Thailand, the Philippines, Indonesia, China, and Japan. The real exchange rates were based on the monthly data of nominal exchange rates and consumer price indices of the related countries.[7] We calculated the prior euro to estimate before 1997 crisis.[8] These data are from the IMF's *International Financial Statistics* (CD-ROM).[9]

7.4.3   Analytical Results

Table 7.1 shows the result of the DOLS for the precrisis period (from January 1987 to June 1997). In the precrisis period, we could not find any combinations where all the coefficients indicated the significant result among the variables for both of rank conditions. While we could find the combinations where three or four countries could conduct a common exchange rate policy with reference to a common currency basket composed of three major currencies, we could not assure the existence of cointegrating vectors in the combinations in our earlier works that included more than five countries. In most cases, the yen was excluded from the possible currency area, as the rank condition was $r = 1$. The euro may be excluded from the basket if we look at the cases where the rank condition was $r = 2$.

---

6. As using the OLS approach to estimate the coefficients of variables, the researchers assume that related variables are cointegrated and have only one cointegration relationship. To assure this assumption, we should examine whether the related variables are cointegrated or not before we estimate the coefficients by the dynamic OLS. Here, we have a finite sample to conduct the Johansen's ML approach, and critical values should be adjusted by the method shown in Cheung and Lai (1993), or calculated from Monte Carlo simulation. However, we focus on whether the yen is an insider or outsider, if a currency area exists. Therefore, we assume that there exists at least one cointegration relationship among the countries. Thus, we skip the Johansen test here.

7. For the prior euro real exchange rates, we calculated a GDP-weighted average of CPI.

8. The method of calculation of the prior euro is provided by the PACIFIC Exchange rate service of the University of British Colombia (http://fx.sauder.ubc.ca/).

9. The Chinese consumer price index is provided by Yu Yongding, the Chinese Academy of Social Sciences (CASS). Before the 1994 exchange rate unification, there existed a dual foreign exchange rate market in China. As pointed out in Fernald, Edison, and Loungani (1999), 80% of transactions related to the Chinese export were referred to the nonofficial, floating exchange rates, therefore, effective nominal depreciation against the U.S. dollar was estimated smaller than 7%, while official rate depreciated 35% at the 1994 reform. However, the swap date used in their paper was not available to us. We use the official RMB exchange rate in IFS.

Table 7.1 DOLS estimation (pre crisis: 1987:1–1997:6)

Dependent variables	Japan (Yen)	Indonesia (Rupiah)	Malaysia (Ringgit)	The Philippines (Peso)	Singapore ($SG)	Thailand (Baht)	Korea (Won)	China (Yuan)
EU/US	0.0162	-0.9948	0.7092	-0.3870	0.0467	1.1397		
(rank = 1)	(0.32122)	(2.02308)	(0.62715)	(0.42195)	(1.45216)	(3.63366)		
EU/US	—	-0.9583	0.6652	-0.3676	0.0227	1.2014		
(rank = 2)		(1.15805)	(0.50424)	(0.35774)	(0.80176)	(2.23868)		
JP/US	—	5.0534****	0.1892	-0.3717	3.3679****	-7.8083****		
(rank = 2)		(0.98000)	(0.42671)	(0.30274)	(0.67849)	(1.89449)		
EU/US	-0.3104	-1.2086	2.2608***	-0.8616	0.0862	1.2311	1.0006**	
(rank = 1)	(0.20239)	(1.14389)	(0.78621)	(0.35177)	(0.78188)	(1.98842)	(0.44839)	
EU/US		-2.2605**	1.7601**	-0.6484*	-0.7436	3.0897	0.7342	
(rank = 2)		(1.13705)	(0.86317)	(0.39031)	(0.70763)	(2.00540)	(0.44838)	
JP/US		3.2282****	1.6373**	-0.7135**	2.4474**	-5.4477**	0.9098*	
(rank = 2)		(1.19814)	(0.90955)	(0.41129)	(0.74565)	(2.11316)	(0.47248)	
EU/US	-0.0825	-0.6479	0.4326	-0.3605	1.0343	0.6338		0.1931
(rank = 1)	(0.30153)	(1.84107)	(0.62267)	(0.37673)	(1.59292)	(3.35042)		(0.22566)
EU/US		-1.0497	0.3748	-0.3139	0.5836	1.4740		0.1710
(rank = 2)		(1.17591)	(0.55881)	(0.34406)	(0.92062)	(2.33383)		(0.19899)
JP/US		4.4661****	-0.1835	-0.3040	4.0813****	-6.4481****		0.3130*
(rank = 2)		(0.97102)	(0.46144)	(0.28411)	(0.76021)	(1.92718)		(0.16432)
EU/US	-0.3919**	-1.2604	1.7446*	-0.7352	0.8780	1.4663	0.8249*	0.1989
(rank = 1)	(0.19390)	(1.08749)	(0.91614)	(0.37657)	(0.91154)	(1.92056)	(0.48731)	(0.13505)
EU/US		-2.2878*	1.4196	-0.5665	-0.3763	3.2852	0.6266	0.1074
(rank = 2)		(1.22817)	(1.06306)	(0.43579)	(0.90096)	(2.23441)	(0.50100)	(0.16949)
JP/US		2.6400**	1.2918	-0.6293	2.7869***	-4.0726*	0.8312*	0.2112
(rank = 2)		(1.14911)	(0.99463)	(0.40774)	(0.84296)	(2.09059)	(0.46876)	(0.15858)

Note: Significance level: *10%, **5%, ***2.5%, ****1%.

While we could find significant results for the combination, Indonesia, Malaysia, the Philippines, Singapore, Thailand, and Korea, the U.S. dollar and the Japanese yen worked as an outsider currency in the basket, and in addition to other combinations, the euro may be excluded from the currency basket. The de facto dollar peg exchange rate system before the crisis may draw a sharp contrast to much of the fluctuation against the Japanese yen or the euro.

Table 7.2 shows the result of the DOLS for the postcrisis period. All test statistics for the rank condition $r = 1$ indicate significance for the combination ASEAN 5 plus Japan, ASEAN 5 plus Korea plus Japan, and ASEAN 5 plus China plus Japan. However, test statistics for $r = 2$ indicate insignificance in most cases. This means that the yen should be included in the region as the currency that leads the other East Asian currency stability in the long run. East Asian countries, including Japan, seem to satisfy the conditions of optimum currency area in recent years. While test statistics reported here were dramatically changed from that of the postcrisis period, these results are consistent with the recent developments of integration in the region, because East Asian countries have been deepening the interrelationship in terms of international trade, foreign direct investments, and international finance for 1999–2005.[10]

7.5   Conclusion

In this paper we investigate the possibilities of adopting a common currency basket peg arrangement into the ASEAN plus three from a viewpoint of the OCA. A structural VAR model may be used to analyze symmetry of shocks for the OCA, but we point out that the symmetry of shocks is no more than a sufficient condition for the OCA. Instead, we used the DOLS to estimate the cointegrating vector for ASEAN plus three currencies with the currency basket of the U.S. dollar and the euro as the anchor currency according to the modified G-PPP model. In addition, the G-PPP model is useful in specifying a common currency basket as an anchor currency that the monetary authorities are targeting when conducting their exchange rate policies.

We obtained the analytical results that there were only combinations in which three or four countries could conduct a common exchange rate policy with reference to a common currency basket composed of three major currencies in the precrisis period. In the postcrisis period, combinations such as ASEAN 5 plus Japan, ASEAN 5 plus Korea plus Japan, and ASEAN 5 plus China plus Japan are in an area where monetary authorities can conduct a common exchange rate policy with reference to the common

10. Ogawa (2004) found that the linkages of the East Asian currencies with the U.S. dollar have decreased since the Asian currency crisis.

Table 7.2   DOLS Estimation (post crisis: 1998:1–2005:1)

Dependent variables	Japan (Yen)	Indonesia (Rupiah)	Malaysia (Ringgit)	The Philippines (Peso)	Singapore ($SG)	Thailand (Baht)	Korea (Won)	China (Yuan)
EU/US	-0.7691****	0.6302****	-4.7695****	-0.4464**	2.7001****	6.6401**		
(rank = 1)	(0.14485)	(0.08529)	(0.75476)	(0.18897)	(0.43576)	(0.29745)		
EU/US		0.5395****	-5.5718****	-0.3996	2.0716**	0.4252		
(rank = 2)		(0.18520)	(0.59216)	(0.41760)	(0.93066)	(0.63908)		
JP/US		0.1467	1.4802	-0.1484	0.9202	0.3034		
(rank = 2)		(0.21186)	(1.82136)	(0.47772)	(1.06464)	(0.73107)		
EU/US	-0.8305****	0.5539****	-3.1482****	-0.6802****	3.0316****	0.4374**	0.3436****	
(rank = 1)	(0.09914)	(0.06438)	(0.80190)	(0.15433)	(0.30341)	(0.20593)	(0.11760)	
EU/US		0.5784****	-6.0095***	-0.3315	2.1075**	0.4323	-0.0637	
(rank = 2)		(0.21913)	(2.41719)	(0.50826)	(0.97978)	(0.67306)	(0.33892)	
JP/US		0.0080	3.7160	-0.4835	1.1360	0.1182	0.4190	
(rank = 2)		(0.24933)	(2.75032)	(0.57831)	(1.11482)	(0.76582)	(0.38563)	
EU/US	-0.7994****	0.3811****	-3.6697****	-0.3838***	3.5278****	0.9368****		-2.35701****
(rank = 1)	(0.11328)	(0.12513)	(0.77322)	(0.15093)	(0.48399)	(0.27155)		(0.99384)
EU/US		0.39405	-4.9078***	-0.3771	2.4352**	0.6283		-1.2763
(rank = 2)		(0.34461)	(1.91169)	(0.42660)	(1.23349)	(0.73022)		(2.58917)
JP/US		-0.0762	2.1985	-0.0406	1.5688	0.5425		-2.0129
(rank = 2)		(0.42815)	(2.37510)	(0.53001)	(1.53249)	(0.90723)	(3.21681)	
EU/US	-0.8299****	0.4574****	-3.0462****	-0.5830****	3.3451****	0.6392*	0.2442	-1.4172
(rank = 1)	(0.11102)	(0.12950)	(0.95485)	(0.20947)	(0.49622)	(0.34440)	(0.19039)	(1.34229)
EU/US		0.3025	-5.8279	-0.0949	2.9225	1.0064	-0.2994	-3.1035
(rank = 2)		(0.35394)	(2.35729)	(0.56030)	(1.30130)	(0.84758)	(0.42163)	(3.31939)
JP/US	0.0558	3.8811**	-.5069	0.9068**	-0.0168	0.4830	0.6394	
(rank = 2)		(0.44345)	(2.95346)	(0.70200)	(1.63040)	(1.06194)	(0.52827)	(4.15888)

Note: Significance level: *10%, **5%, ***2.5%, ****1%.

currency basket. Thus, we obtained the analytical results that the yen should be included as an endogenous variable in the long-run relationship, as well as other East Asian currencies, while it worked exogenously as well as the U.S. dollar and the euro in the system composed of the East Asian currencies in the precrisis period. It implies that the possible common currency basket arrangement should be adopted into the region of the ASEAN plus three countries that include Japan.

Thus, the ASEAN plus three countries are forming an OCA in terms of the G-PPP model under the developments of economic integration, such as production networks in East Asia gradually converging economic development stages in recent years. It is more likely for the ASEAN plus three countries to succeed in adopting a common exchange rate policy in the postcrisis period than in the precrisis period.

Appendix

If the monetary authorities in the region agree to peg their home currencies to the regional currency basket and intervene in foreign exchange markets to maintain their exchange rate stability, the long-run property of their real exchange rates should be $\mathbf{re}_{CB,i} = 0$ in the long-run. It means the non-null matrix $\mathbf{Z}$ should exist for which $\mathbf{Z} \cdot \mathbf{F} \cdot \mathbf{re}_{(i,JP,EU),US} = 0$ if each of series in vector: $\mathbf{re}_{(i,JP,EU),US}$ has unit root.

Here, we assume the exchange rate between the yen and the U.S. Dollar is included in vector $\mathbf{re}_1$, the number of rank condition for the product of non-null matrix $\mathbf{Z}$ and $\mathbf{F}$ would be $h - m = 1$, we can define non-null matrix $\mathbf{C}$ as follows:

$$
\underset{(m\times m)(m\times h)}{\mathbf{Z} \cdot \mathbf{F}} \cdot \underset{(h\times 1)}{\mathbf{re}_{(i,JP,EU),US}} = \underset{(m\times h)}{\mathbf{C}} \cdot \underset{(h\times 1)}{\mathbf{re}_{(i,JP,EU),US}}
$$

$$
= \begin{bmatrix}
\chi_{1,1} & \chi_{1,1} & \chi_{1,3} & \chi_{1,4} & \chi_{1,5} & \chi_{1,6} & \chi_{1,7} & \chi_{1,8} & \chi_{1,9} \\
a\chi_{1,1} & a\chi_{1,2} & a\chi_{1,3} & a\chi_{1,4} & a\chi_{1,5} & a\chi_{1,6} & a\chi_{1,7} & a\chi_{1,8} & a\chi_{1,9} \\
b\chi_{1,1} & b\chi_{1,2} & b\chi_{1,3} & b\chi_{1,4} & b\chi_{1,5} & b\chi_{1,6} & b\chi_{1,7} & b\chi_{1,8} & b\chi_{1,9} \\
c\chi_{1,1} & c\chi_{1,2} & c\chi_{1,3} & c\chi_{1,4} & c\chi_{1,5} & c\chi_{1,6} & c\chi_{1,7} & c\chi_{1,8} & c\chi_{1,9} \\
d\chi_{1,1} & d\chi_{1,2} & d\chi_{1,3} & d\chi_{1,4} & d\chi_{1,5} & d\chi_{1,6} & d\chi_{1,7} & d\chi_{1,8} & d\chi_{1,9} \\
e\chi_{1,1} & e\chi_{1,2} & e\chi_{1,3} & e\chi_{1,4} & e\chi_{1,5} & e\chi_{1,6} & e\chi_{1,7} & e\chi_{1,8} & e\chi_{1,9} \\
f\chi_{1,1} & f\chi_{1,2} & f\chi_{1,3} & f\chi_{1,4} & f\chi_{1,5} & f\chi_{1,6} & f\chi_{1,7} & f\chi_{1,8} & f\chi_{1,9} \\
g\chi_{1,1} & g\chi_{1,2} & g\chi_{1,3} & g\chi_{1,4} & g\chi_{1,5} & g\chi_{1,6} & g\chi_{1,7} & g\chi_{1,8} & g\chi_{1,9}
\end{bmatrix}
\begin{bmatrix}
re_{1,US} \\
re_{2,US} \\
re_{3,US} \\
re_{4,US} \\
re_{5,US} \\
re_{6,US} \\
re_{7,US} \\
re_{JP,US} \\
re_{EU,US}
\end{bmatrix}
$$

where, $a, b, c, d, e, f,$ and g exhibit the weights of the common currency basket composed of insider currencies, which is normalized at country 1. These can define possible weights of the "regional monetary unit." Therefore:

$$\underset{(m\times h)}{\mathbf{C}} \cdot \underset{(h\times 1)}{\mathbf{re}_{(i,EU,JP),US}}$$

$$= \begin{pmatrix} 1 \\ a \\ b \\ c \\ d \\ e \\ f \\ g \end{pmatrix} (\chi_{1,1} \cdot re_{1,US} + \chi_{1,2} \cdot re_{2,US} + \ldots + \chi_{1,7} \cdot re_{7,US} + \chi_{1,8} \cdot re_{JP,US} + \chi_{1,9} \cdot re_{EU,US})$$

$$= 0$$

We estimate the coefficients $\chi_{1,i}$ of linear combination above by the dynamic OLS. These would satisfy $\chi_{1,i} \neq 0$ for $a, b, c, d, e, f, g > 0$. These are necessary conditions for ensuring that there would be non-null matrix for $re_{CB,i} = 0$.[11]

References

Bayoumi, T., B. Eichengreen, and P. Mauro. 2000. On regional monetary arrangements for ASEAN. CEPR Discussion Paper no. 2411. London: Centre for Economic Policy Research.

Cheung, Y., and K. Lai. 1993. Finite-sample sizes of Johansen's likelihood ratio tests for cointegration. *Oxford Bulletin of Economic and Statistics* 55 (3): 313–28.

Enders, W., and S. Hurn. 1994. Theory and tests of generalized purchasing-power parity: Common trends and real exchange rates in the Pacific Rim. *Review of International Economics* 2 (2): 179–90.

Fernald, J., H. Edison, and P. Loungani. 1999. Was China the first domino? Assessing links between China and other Asian economies. *Journal of International Money and Finance* 18 (4): 515–35.

Frankel, J. A., and S. Wei. 1994. Yen bloc or dollar bloc? Exchange rate policies of the East Asian economies. In *Macroeconomic linkage: Savings, exchange rates*

11. The magnitudes of the coefficients estimated by DOLS in equation (20) exhibit nothing more than the existence of non-null matrix for $re_{CB,i} = 0$. To analyze welfare effects in integrating these economies, we should estimate a, b, c, d, e, f, g, and h by other approaches.

and capital flows, ed. T. Ito and A. O. Krueger, 295–355. Chicago: University of Chicago Press.

Ito, T. 2005. Chinese RMB Reform. RIETI. Mimeograph.

Ito, T., E. Ogawa, and N. Y. Sasaki. 1998. How did the dollar peg fail in Asia? *Journal of the Japanese and International Economies* 12:256–304.

Johansen, S., and K. Juselius. 1990. Maximum likelihood estimation and inference on cointegration; with application to the demand for money. *Oxford Bulletin of Economics and Statistics* 52 (2): 159–210.

Kawai, M., and S. Akiyama. 1998. The role of nominal anchor currencies in exchange arrangements. *Journal of the Japanese and International Economies* 12:334–87.

Kawasaki, K. 2000. A test of OCA in Asian currency area: Empirical analysis based on G-PPP theory (in Japanese). *The Hitotsubashi Review* 124 (6): 127–46.

Kawasaki, K. 2005. Giving a new life to the PPP theory: The modified generalized PPP model (in Japanese). *Keieironshu* 66:111–26.

Kawasaki, K., and E. Ogawa. 2006. What should the weights of the three major currencies be in a common currency basket in East Asia? *Asian Economic Journal* 20 (1): 75–94.

Mundell, R. 1961. A theory of optimum currency areas. *Papers and Proceedings of the American Economic Association* 51:657–64.

Ogawa, E. 2004. Regional monetary cooperation in East Asia against asymmetric responses to the U.S. dollar depreciation. *Journal of Korean Economy* 5 (2): 43–72.

Ogawa, E., and T. Ito. 2002. On the desirability of a regional basket currency arrangement. *Journal of the Japanese and International Economies* 16:317–34.

Ogawa, E., and K. Kawasaki. 2003. Possibility of creating a common currency basket for East Asia. JBICI Discussion Paper no. 5. Tokyo: Japan Bank for International Cooperation.

Ogawa, E., and M. Sakane. 2006. The Chinese yuan after the Chinese exchange rate system reform. *China & World Economy* 14 (6): 39–57.

Stock, J., and M. Watson. 1988. Testing for common trends. *Journal of the American Statistical Association* 83:1097–1107.

Comment   Michael P. Dooley

This chapter addresses an important and difficult issue. For individual Asian countries, managing the nominal exchange rates of a basket of foreign currencies seems a sensible choice. The presumption is that changes in the relative value of major currencies—for example, the dollar, the euro, and the yen, are unlikely to be related to desirable changes in the average real value of the home currency against its trading partners. But we would not assume that any two countries would naturally choose the same basket, or in what amounts to the same thing, would choose to stabilize the value of their currencies within Asia. Clearly, if the Asian countries want greater

Michael P. Dooley is a professor of economics at the University of California, Santa Cruz, and a research associate of the National Bureau of Economic Research.

stability among themselves they have to at the same time adopt the same policy toward the rest of the world.

The authors attack this problem by looking at the history of bilateral real exchange rates and seeing if relative price movements between inside and outside countries have been temporary or permanent. This is equivalent to testing the *feasibility*, not the optimality, of a common basket peg. Clearly, if there have been different and persistent relative price changes in the past, we might conclude that such changes are needed to maintain equilibrium in the balance of payments. Adherence to a common basket peg would have to eventually break down. All this assumes that the inside countries are determined to have the same rate of domestic price inflation.

The logic of the euro currency area was that it would float against the rest of the world. A zone of exchange rate stability within Asia would presumably involve managed nominal exchange rates with the rest of the world. In an important sense this is already occurring, informally, since China's apparent heavy weight for the dollar generates relative price changes with other Asian currencies with less weight on the dollar. This limited independence within Asia would have to be eliminated. Either others would have to adopt the weight preferred by China or that weight would have to be modified.

The real problem for such a system will be the mechanism for financing and adjustment within the currency area. Even if relative price changes are not permanent they can last for a long time. Some rules for fiscal adjustment and financing imbalance within the region will have to be established.

Comment   Kiyotaka Sato

The feasibility of forming a regional monetary union and/or establishing a common currency unit in East Asia has gained a great deal of attention and has been lively debated in recent years. Ogawa and Kawasaki attempt to make an important contribution to the literature by introducing a new approach, a Generalized Purchasing Power Parity (G-PPP) model, to analyze whether a common currency basket can be adopted in ASEAN plus three countries.

To investigate a possible regional monetary arrangement, the existing literature typically relies on the theory of optimum currency area (OCA), which proposes several preconditions for forming a currency area. Specifically, recent studies tend to focus on the similarity of the economic structure and/or the symmetry in (real) shocks as a major precondition. The

Kiyotaka Sato is associate professor of economics at Yokohama National University.

Blanchard and Quah (1989) structural vector autoregression (VAR) technique is generally used in these studies to identify the fundamental shocks and to make a correlation analysis of shocks.

In contrast to these studies, Ogawa and Kawasaki employ the G-PPP model, an extended version of a simple PPP model. Indeed, PPP is less likely to hold because the bilateral real exchange rate tends to reflect nominal and real shocks that continuously affect macroeconomic fundamentals of respective countries. However, the G-PPP model assumes that a linear combination of some bilateral real exchange rates may have a stable long-run equilibrium which reflects the commonality in shocks and a strong economic relationship among the countries.

One drawback of the structural VAR approach is that this approach is based on a correlation analysis in identified shocks and, hence, a country-to-country based analysis. In contrast, the G-PPP model relies on a multi-country framework, which is more appropriate than the structural VAR approach to specify a possible group of countries that forms an OCA. Ogawa and Kawasaki attempt to conduct a multivariate cointegration test and to analyze an important question, that is, whether the Japanese yen can be regarded as an *insider currency* or an *outsider currency* in the regional currency arrangement. Ogawa and Kawasaki found significant cointegrating vectors in the combination of more than five countries only if including Japan as a member country: ASEAN5 plus Japan, ASEAN5 plus Korea plus Japan, and ASEAN 5 plus China plus Japan. It is concluded that the Japanese yen should be included in the region as they appear to satisfy the OCA conditions.

Ogawa and Kawasaki undoubtedly make an important contribution to the literature on monetary arrangement in East Asia by introducing the G-PPP model. Their conclusion is quite interesting and appears to be reasonable because Japan has increased its presence in East Asia as a major trading partner and a major investment source country for the past few decades. However, there seems to be room for further improvements in their study.

First, the G-PPP model is inherently a long-run model, while the precondition for forming an OCA is more pertinent to the short-term aspect of business cycle synchronization. More specifically, the G-PPP model enables us to find a long-run cointegrating relationship of some bilateral real exchange rate series. Even though real exchange rates are cointegrated, however, the countries in question may face very different patterns of short-term economic fluctuations or disturbances. If the countries encounter such idiosyncratic shocks in the short-run, it may be costly for them to renounce their own monetary policy autonomy and, hence, to establish a common currency. Thus, the authors need to further discuss whether it is enough to consider the long-run aspects of real exchange rate comovements as a major precondition for establishing a common currency basket.

Second, Ogawa and Kawasaki use the dynamic OLS (DOLS) method to find a cointegrating relationship for two subperiods: one from January 1987 to June 1997 and the other from January 1999 to November 2005. Whereas the time span is relatively short and the number of observations is small for the cointegration analysis, it is important to focus on the postcrisis monetary arrangement and also to make a comparison between the pre- and postcrisis periods. However, the DOLS method assumes that there is just one cointegrating relationship, although it is not necessarily correct. It seems better to try the Johansen cointegration test to check the number of cointegrating vectors so that they can support the results of the DOLS estimation, even though the relatively small number of observations may cause less robust results of the Johansen test.

Third, Ogawa and Kawasaki report a very interesting result that Japanese yen should be included in a common currency basket arrangement since they found three combinations that show all coefficients are statistically significant: ASEAN5 plus Japan, ASEAN5 plus Korea plus Japan, ASEAN5 plus China plus Japan. This finding is quite suggestive, but the remaining question is whether there are any criteria to assess which combination is the best for establishing a common currency basket. Another important question is how to interpret the sign and the value of coefficients reported in tables 7.1 and 7.2, which may help us to choose the best combination of countries for establishing a common currency basket arrangement. These aspects will be helpful for further improvement of this study.

References

Blanchard, O. J., and D. Quah. 1989. The dynamic effects of aggregate demand and supply disturbances. *American Economic Review* 79:655–673.

III

Liberalization, Market Access, and the Cost of Capital

8

Growth and Returns in Emerging Markets

Peter Blair Henry and Prakash Kannan

8.1 Introduction

Conventional wisdom gives two rationales for investing in the stock markets of developing countries. The first states that the low correlation of developing-country stock returns with those of developed markets provides diversification opportunities that enable investors in developed countries to increase the expected return on their portfolio while reducing their risk. The second states that high rates of economic growth in emerging markets provide great absolute investment opportunities. Because the rate of economic growth in most developing countries is expected to exceed the rate of growth in the developed world for many years to come, the typical discussion presumes that long-run stock returns in emerging markets will also exceed those of developed markets (Malkiel and Mei, 1998; Mobius, 1994).

This chapter focuses on the empirical validity of the second rationale. To what extent do stock returns in developing countries track the real economy—GDP growth in particular—and is it true that stock returns in emerging markets are, on average, higher than in developed countries? The notion that stock returns in fast-growing countries will be higher than stock returns in slow-growing countries sounds almost too obvious to question, but the scatter diagram in figure 8.1 shows that there is no systematic long-run relationship between stock returns and economic growth

Peter Blair Henry is professor of economics and Gunn Faculty Scholar at the Stanford University Graduate School of Business, a faculty research associate of the National Bureau of Economic Research, and a nonresident senior fellow at the Brookings Institution. Prakash Kannan was a doctoral candidate at Stanford University when this paper was written.

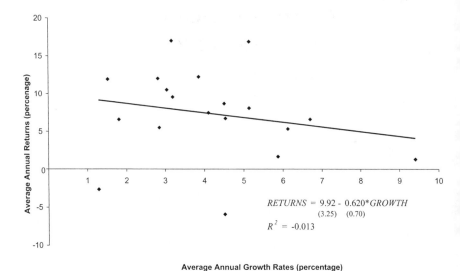

Fig. 8.1   **Stock returns and real GDP growth in emerging market economies are uncorrelated**

in emerging economies over the past 30 years.[1] Not only is the relationship between stock returns and economic growth statistically insignificant, the sign of the relationship actually goes the wrong way—it is negative instead of positive.

A simple example, using the Solow growth model, helps illustrate why higher economic growth does not always imply higher stock returns. Consider two emerging market economies (A and B) that are identical and therefore are growing at the same rate. A standard result of the Solow model is that an increase in the savings rate of country A will temporarily raise its rate of growth. It is also a standard result that an increase in the savings rate will reduce the rate of return to capital. The rate of return falls because the increase in the savings rate of country A drives up its rate of investment. Consequently capital becomes less scarce, and the marginal benefit from an additional unit falls. When diminishing returns has run its course, country A settles down to a new steady state, in which it has the same growth rate as country B, a higher level of GDP per capita, and a lower rate of return to capital.

This specific example illustrates a more general lesson. In order to understand whether a fast-growing emerging market economy will have higher stock returns than a slow-growing one, we must ask what accounts

---

1. Countries included in the scatter plot are Argentina, Brazil, Chile, China, Colombia, India, Indonesia, Jordan, Korea, Malaysia, Mexico, Nigeria, Pakistan, Philippines, South Africa, Thailand, Turkey, Venezuela, and Zimbabwe.

for the difference in the two countries' growth rates of GDP. The stock market is the aggregate collection of financial claims on the real assets of an economy. Therefore, aggregate stock market returns should be tied to the rate of return to real assets in the long run. In turn, the rate of return to real assets depends on their productivity as determined by the interaction of capital, labor, technology, and institutions. For instance, in contrast to the previous savings rate example, the Solow Model predicts that high rates of growth caused by improvements in total factor productivity will raise the rate of return to capital.

These are not merely academic distinctions. Many scholars attribute the exceptionally high growth rates of Asian economies over the past three decades to the rapid rate of capital accumulation, made possible by the thriftiness of their populations rather than increases in the growth rate of total factor productivity (Krugman 1994; Young 1995). In the face of diminishing returns to capital, and an absence of increases in total factor productivity, growth rates of GDP per capita will slow to more pedestrian levels, and the rate of return to capital will fall.

However, a falling rate of return to capital in a given country tells you nothing about the level of its return to capital relative to rates of return elsewhere. This distinction is especially relevant when comparing emerging markets to more developed economies, such as the United States. For this comparison the convergence story within the neoclassical framework is more relevant. Emerging markets, which have lower capital-labor ratios than the United States, will tend to grow faster and have a higher rate of return to capital. Although East Asian economies have experienced significant capital deepening over the past few decades, as mentioned earlier, to the extent that they started from lower capital-labor ratios than the United States, their rates of return may still be higher.

A similar caveat about levels versus changes in rates of return applies to Latin America, a region where country after country in the past two decades have struggled with, and to varying degrees embraced, economic reforms. Reforms such as inflation stabilization, trade liberalization, and privatization all have potential to raise total factor productivity. If these reforms increase total factor productivity in the region, then they probably also drive up rates of return. But even if the rate of return to capital in Latin America is higher today than it was two decades ago, returns there could still be lower than in the United States.

While neoclassical theory provides the framework for the question of whether faster rates of economic growth in emerging markets translate into higher stock returns, our principal goal is to let the data speak for itself. In section 8.2 of this chapter we document that average realized stock returns in emerging markets over the last 30 years have not been significantly higher than realized stock returns in the United States. This finding is particularly striking in the case of fast-growing regions like Asia, which have average realized returns that are actually lower than returns in the United States.

There are legitimate objections to using realized stock returns to test the validity of the view that high growth and high stock returns go together. For instance, high rates of growth may be associated with high expected returns (as opposed to realized returns). To address this concern, section 8.3 constructs measures of expected returns using dividend-price ratios and earnings yields. Unlike the case of average realized rates of return, we find some evidence that average expected returns in emerging markets have been significantly higher than expected returns in the United States. We also document that average realized returns in emerging markets have generally been higher than average expected returns over the past 20 years.

To gain a better understanding of the forces that account for the higher-than-expected returns in emerging markets over the past two decades, section 8.4 presents short vignettes that focus on inflation stabilization and capital account liberalization episodes in Latin America and Asia. The central, if unsurprising, message that emerges from these vignettes is that stock markets respond positively to news about major economic reforms. Insofar as these reforms result in growth that was higher than expected, we find that markets respond positively and yield higher-than-expected returns as well. This significant positive correlation between unexpected growth and unexpected returns is shown to exist in both Latin America and in Asia.

Building on the discussion in section 8.4, section 8.5 discusses a simple and consistent explanation for high growth with low returns in Asia and low growth with high returns in Latin America. High growth implies high returns only if the stock market has not already capitalized the growth into current prices. Entering the 1980s, the Asian Tigers had already experienced two decades of rapid output growth, and expectations for the future were great. In contrast, Latin America entered the 1980s well on its way to a debt crisis. Starting in 1986, and stretching over the next two decades, Latin American countries attempted to stabilize inflation, liberalize trade, and privatize state-owned enterprises. While these efforts were not entirely successful (and similar efforts also occurred in Asia), the very attempt at reform in Latin America was unexpected and thus probably not priced in. Hence, relative to the low expectations for the region at the start of the 1980s, Latin America achieved better outcomes than Asia over the next 20 years. This hypothesis is consistent with the results of the regressions carried out in section 8.4, where unexpected returns were shown to be positively correlated with unexpected growth.

8.2   Data

In order to compare rates of return in emerging economies with those in mature markets, we compute dollar-denominated, inflation-adjusted stock returns for a number of countries. All of the stock market data come from Standard and Poor's (S&P) Emerging Markets Data Base (EMDB). We use the dividend-inclusive, total return index, denominated in U.S. dollars. We compute a real, inflation-adjusted index by deflating the total return index with the U.S. consumer price index. The consumer price index data come from the Bureau of Economic Analysis.

The EMDB provides the most complete and consistent source of stock returns across a wide range of developing countries. Nevertheless, the EMDB data are less than ideal. For some of the larger emerging markets in Latin America and Asia, we have thirty years of stock returns (1976 to 2005). For other countries, most notably those of Eastern Europe, data are only available from the early 1990s. For valuation ratios, the data limitations are even greater. Even in the countries with thirty years of stock price data, price earnings ratios are only available since 1986. By comparison, long-term studies of the U.S. stock market typically employ time series that span close to 100 years (Blanchard 1993; Fama and French 2002).

Stock returns over long periods of time provide a reasonable proxy for the rate of return to capital in an economy, but returns viewed over shorter horizons may not be as easy to interpret. Because of movement in the business cycle and the volatility of returns, our time series may not be long enough to distinguish meaningful information from noise in the data. Nevertheless, a dataset with limitations is better than no dataset at all, so we proceed to calculate long-run returns with the data we have.

Table 8.1 summarizes the average annual realized real return and standard deviation for a selection of twenty emerging market economies during the period 1976 to 2005. For each country in the sample we calculate annual real returns, using continuously compounded growth rates—the natural log of the inflation-adjusted, dividend-inclusive value of the index at the end of the year minus the natural log of the same variable at the beginning of the year. The average annual real return for a country is the simple average of its continuously compounded annual return. In turn, the average annual return for a particular region is the simple average of the average annual real return of all countries in that region.[2]

Panel A of table 8.1 shows that average annual stock returns in emerging markets over the past thirty years have been 7.78 percent per year, while the average return on the U.S. market over the same period was 7.69 percent. The two sets of returns are statistically indistinguishable. Hence, at least from an ex-post point of view, stock returns in emerging markets are no higher than stock returns in the United States. Individual country data in table 8.2 show that the averages are representative of the group as a whole.

The use of country weights to compute regional averages, as opposed to

2. Note that these numbers differ slightly from the regional averages computed by EMDB due to the range of countries included and the use of a simple average here as opposed to a weighted average used in the EMDB computations.

Table 8.1   Realized returns in emerging markets are not significantly higher than realized returns in the United States[a]

	Average Return	Standard Deviation	Sharpe Ratio	Correlation with U.S.
A: Continuously Compounded Returns				
Composite[b]	7.78	23.98	0.22	0.21
Latin America[c]	10.86	35.24	0.24	0.31
Asia[d]	6.62	30.05	0.14	0.09
U.S.	7.69	14.57	0.36	1.00
B: Arithmetic Returns				
Emerging Market Composite[b]	23.57	30.45	0.70	0.22
Latin America[c]	31.01	49.40	0.58	0.25
Asia[d]	16.35	33.83	0.41	0.12
U.S.	9.54	15.81	0.45	1.00

[a] Annual rates from 1976–2005, in %.
[b] Composite returns are the average returns of the following economies: Argentina, Brazil, Chile, China, Colombia, India, Indonesia, Jordan, Korea, Malaysia, Mexico, Nigeria, Pakistan, Philippines, South Africa, Taiwan, Thailand, Turkey, Venezuela, and Zimbabwe.
[c] Latin America returns are the average returns of Argentina, Brazil, Chile, Colombia, Mexico and Venezuela.
[d] Asia returns are the average returns of China, India, Indonesia, Korea, Malaysia, Philippines, Taiwan and Thailand.

simple averages (as used in table 8.1) does not alter our findings. The EMDB dataset contains weighted averages of regional returns where the weighting is done by market capitalization. The average annual return for the EMDB composite during the period 1985–2005 (data for this series are only available from 1985 onward) is 8.30 percent compared to an average return of 9.05 percent in the United States over the same period. Thus, even when weighted, we find that average annual stock returns for emerging market economies are not higher than returns in the United States. The EMDB regional averages, which are weighted, also support our findings from table 8.1. The average annual return for the Latin American aggregate is 14.0 for the period 1985–2005, while the comparable figure for the Asian aggregate is 5.06 percent.

In contrast to the numbers in Panel A, studies that compute stock returns arithmetically find that emerging markets have higher annual returns than the United States. For instance, Harvey (1995) reports a 20.36 percent dollar return on the emerging market composite index as compared to a 13.63 percent return on the United States market.[3] Arithmetic returns overstate the financial performance of emerging markets. Figure 8.2 shows why. It plots the evolution of the inflation-adjusted value of a dollar invested in various stock markets starting in 1975 (with full reinvestment of

3. Panel B of table 8.1 shows that this result obtains in an updated sample.

Table 8.2   **Real annual returns (USD terms, continuously compounded)**

Year	ARG	BRA	CHI	COL	MEX	VEN	CHN	IND	IDN	KOR	MAL	PHI	TAI	THA	JOR	NIG	PAK	SOU	TUR	ZIM	US
1976	166.4	-5.6	67.3		-32.1			20.8		45.3				2.5						-27.3	15.9
1977	-80.3	-19.2	79.4		16.4			4.3		50.1				80.5						-9.9	-13.7
1978	91.3	-27.6	33.5		65.3			24.7		23.1				-16.9						26.4	-1.0
1979	115.4	-46.0	72.8		42.9			5.1		-37.6				-49.6	18.9					75.6	6.3
1980	-23.7	-15.9	46.9		-10.6			19.0		-60.5				-19.7	5.7					18.2	15.5
1981	-86.3	19.9	-64.5		-71.8			16.1		23.2				-27.5	32.2					-109.3	-14.9
1982	-100.5	-20.9	-85.0		-144.4			-8.4		-3.4				21.2	-7.3					-61.7	13.5
1983	36.1	40.2	-41.1		67.2			-1.7		-7.7				16.5	-10.5					-14.9	17.2
1984	-24.5	38.6	-31.3		1.6			-7.1		13.7				-5.7	-17.3					-10.9	1.9
1985	52.4	62.9	36.6	-15.4	13.3	-34.4		68.3		28.8	-18.9	34.7	6.4	-3.4	36.0	1.4	13.3			89.7	24.1
1986	-32.6	-30.1	91.7	89.8	66.1	43.5		-4.8		60.1	9.4	155.6	38.3	54.0	-5.4	-85.6	17.0			15.0	15.3
1987	5.8	-103.2	22.8	54.4	-8.5	-31.7		-20.5		27.5	-2.7	38.5	55.6	28.2	-8.3	-17.8	2.9	125.1		63.0	1.5
1988	28.7	77.3	27.5	-17.2	69.3	-33.7		27.7		71.5	20.4	28.2	61.8	30.1	-14.7	2.8	8.9	-98.4		18.3	11.3
1989	96.8	28.9	36.7	6.8	50.3	-44.9		-0.5		2.1	31.8	42.0	64.6	65.0	-5.8	14.5	1.5	174.9		29.5	22.8
1990	-50.8	-112.2	28.7	26.6	20.7	189.6		11.9	-5.8	-34.5	-17.1	-82.6	-76.4	-28.5	-1.1	28.8	5.3	-8.1		61.5	-8.4
1991	156.2	95.3	64.2	102.8	68.5	32.8		12.8	-59.1	-21.4	7.3	42.2	-4.7	13.4	10.0	28.0	96.0	-58.2	-8.1	-78.2	22.5
1992	-33.7	-2.7	12.0	30.0	16.2	-57.9		17.6	-0.1	0.5	21.7	13.8	-33.9	30.9	19.1	-45.9	-23.3		-78.0	-94.0	4.4
1993	51.7	66.1	26.8	26.8	37.5	-10.1	-10.5	14.2	72.9	16.1	67.8	82.5	60.7	67.9	18.7	-15.2	41.6	57.1	117.7	86.2	6.7
1994	-29.0	50.4	34.6	22.9	-54.7	-32.2	-42.6	4.6	-24.0	14.9	-26.7	-3.1	17.7	-14.5	-12.8	104.3	-11.4	24.7	-54.9	22.4	-1.2
1995	9.1	-25.4	-2.2	-29.9	-32.9	-37.7	-16.0	-44.6	8.5	-9.9	0.7	-18.0	-39.4	-4.2	9.1	-26.2	-40.1	13.6	-14.0	12.6	29.1
1996	17.2	26.7	-18.4	4.8	13.5	84.0	62.0	-5.1	15.2	-51.0	19.0	15.6	28.8	-48.5	-4.2	46.0	-24.6	-21.6	36.9	48.1	17.8
1997	15.9	20.0	4.2	22.5	38.6	19.9	26.2	4.6	-135.9	-118.5	-128.4	-98.8	-10.3	-159.6	11.3	-0.9	20.9	-14.5	75.2	-78.4	26.5
1998	-31.6	-50.9	-33.7	-53.8	-48.2	-69.5	-27.2	-16.1	-35.4	78.2	-0.2	8.8	-23.1	26.7	8.7	-30.4	-83.4	-34.9	-74.3	-87.9	23.6
1999	29.7	54.4	31.4	-18.0	57.5	-9.0	31.0	59.1	67.3	73.6	35.5	7.0	40.1	36.9	-5.3	-3.2	37.6	45.5	127.7	93.6	16.9
2000	-29.6	-8.6	-16.1	-58.1	-24.9	24.6	18.0	-35.9	-89.8	-86.5	-27.3	-58.8	-66.8	-83.6	-23.9	51.5	-12.3	-18.4	-75.2	-25.4	-12.9
2001	-36.3	-22.7	-2.2	24.5	10.8	-15.1	-27.9	-25.2	-18.4	38.5	4.6	-31.0	10.5	4.9	28.0	23.5	-30.7	-23.3	-37.8	85.8	-15.5
2002	-69.3	-37.3	-14.5	14.0	-18.1	-32.3	-19.4	6.5	27.8	5.0	-0.6	-13.6	-33.8	23.9	-0.9	3.9	86.0	39.5	-41.4	70.9	-26.5
2003	81.9	75.0	60.1	27.2	28.0	28.3	31.6	66.5	54.6	27.8	23.4	27.9	33.6	89.9	51.2	48.2	46.5	34.6	74.6	-136.6	23.0
2004	18.9	31.4	21.0	79.0	38.8	45.1	-9.7	20.1	33.6	22.1	13.0	19.0	9.1	-10.5	43.0	21.8	21.8	41.8	28.1	-107.0	7.7
2005	34.7	42.8	13.7	72.5	35.7	-20.2	4.3	27.1	8.9	44.2	-1.5	22.3	4.9	2.2	75.5	18.9	47.3	22.7	41.0	28.7	1.5
Average	12.67	6.73	16.76	19.63	10.41	5.29	1.52	8.70	-4.99	7.84	1.49	11.05	7.80	5.21	9.25	8.00	10.51	12.83	13.74	-1.63	7.69
S.D.	0.68	0.51	0.42	0.44	0.49	0.58	0.30	0.26	0.56	0.46	0.37	0.54	0.43	0.50	0.23	0.40	0.41	0.31	0.83	0.68	0.15

Notes: Selected definition of abbreviations: CHI = Chile, CHN = China, IND = India, IDN = Indonesia, TAI = Taiwan, SOU = South Africa. Latin American returns are the average returns of Argentina, Brazil, Chile, Colombia, Mexico and Venezuela. Asia returns are the average returns of China, India, Indonesia, Korea, Malaysia, Philippines, Taiwan and Thailand

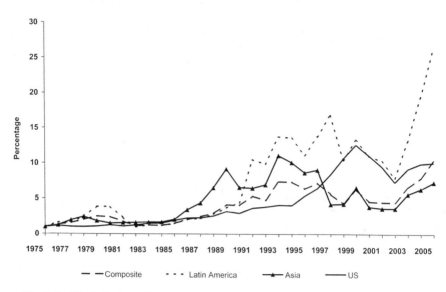

Fig. 8.2   The inflation-adjusted value of a dollar invested in 1975

dividends). The arithmetic average of year-by-year arithmetic returns in the period from 1975 to 1987 is 13.9 percent for Latin America versus 7.8 percent for the United States. This gives the misleading impression that the value of the Latin American investment at the end of the twelve-year period is greater than the value of the U.S. investment when, in fact, the opposite is true. A dollar invested in Latin America in 1975 was worth $2.15 in 1987. A dollar invested in the United States over the same period grew to a value of $2.26.

While continuously compounded mean returns are about the same in emerging markets as in the United States, the emerging market composite index displays substantially higher volatility. Column 2 of table 8.1 shows that the standard deviation of emerging market returns is roughly one and a half times that of the United States. Accordingly, the Sharpe Ratios in column 3 indicate that the higher risk associated with emerging markets has not resulted in higher returns. In spite of the poor absolute performance indicated by their Sharpe ratios, it is well known that emerging markets have the potential to improve the risk-return profile of a balanced portfolio because of their low correlation with developed countries (Harvey 1995). Column 4 of table 8.1 shows that emerging market returns continue to exhibit relatively low correlation with U.S. returns.

Focusing on returns at the broad level of emerging markets masks significant heterogeneity across regions. Compared to returns in the United States, Latin American stocks produced higher average returns over the same period. The average-annual return on Latin American stocks was

10.86 percent, compared to the 7.69 percent return on U.S. stocks (although this difference is not statistically significant). The higher volatility of Latin American stocks, however, means that they also have low Sharpe ratios relative to the United States. Meanwhile, stocks in Asia have performed worse on both counts—they have had lower than average returns than stocks in the United States and higher volatility. Within the group, stocks in Indonesia, for example, produced an average annual real rate of return of negative 5 percent over this 30-year period. Even with the exclusion of Indonesia, average stock returns in Asia are only 6.9 percent over the period.

The relatively low real rate of return on Asian stocks weighs heavily against the view that high growth generates high returns. While Asian countries such as China, India, and Korea experienced high rates of growth relative to the United States and Latin America, the average annual realized return for Asia is the lowest among all three regions. A natural question to ask is whether this observation would still hold if we eliminated the influence of the 1997 Asian Crisis in our calculations. Three points are in order here.

First, even excluding the Asian Crisis, average real returns in Asia remain lower than in Latin America. Real continuously compounded returns in Asia from 1975 to 1996 were 10 percent; in Latin America they were 12.48. If instead of eliminating all of the data after 1996, we calculate returns for Asia using all years except 1997, average returns for Asia are 9.53 percent; returns calculated in the same way for Latin America are 10.54 percent.

Second, given the timing of the 1997 Asian Crisis, there is no theoretical justification for excluding data during that time period from our calculations. The returns series includes an ample number of years following the crisis to balance any undue influence that would occur if the series ended on a down year in the business cycle.

Third, and related to the second point, we are skeptical of throwing away data. The same instinct that suggests you should calculate Asian returns without including the 1997 data would also suggest that you throw away data on stock returns in Latin America during the debt crisis (1982 to 1989). For that matter, why not exclude data from the Mexican and Argentine crisis periods? Indeed, given the volatility of returns in emerging markets, we would soon be left with little of an already-limited sample of data.

The possibility of *survivorship bias* should be mentioned. A sample that disproportionately represents firms or markets that have survived over time will produce average rates of return that are higher than a sample that includes failed firms or markets (see Goetzmann and Jorion 1999). For our comparison of emerging market returns relative to those of the United States, the possibility of survivorship bias actually *strengthens* our conclusion that emerging market returns are not significantly higher than returns in the United States, if we believe that the failure rate of firms in emerging markets is higher than in the United States. The effect of survivorship bias on the comparison between returns in Asia and Latin America, however, is less clear. It could be argued that the higher degree of turbulence in Latin American countries accounts for the higher rate of return relative to Asian economies. However, without more detailed firm-level data in these economies, we cannot know the extent of the bias, if it exists.

On the whole, the data in table 8.1 demonstrate that historical stock returns provide little support to the view that higher growth rates and higher risk in emerging markets produce commensurately higher rates of return. The evidence in table 8.1, however, requires a cautious interpretation. The data on realized returns span a thirty-year period during which a number of crises and reforms occurred in the developing world. As such, it may be the case that the average realized rates of return computed in table 8.1 differ significantly from the average expected returns in these economies over the period. We turn our attention to this distinction in the next section.

8.3   Expected Returns Versus Realized Returns

In order to compute expected rates of return we begin by using the constant dividend-growth model, or as it is more popularly known, the Gordon Model (Gordon 1962). The Gordon model states that the price of a stock should be equal to the dividend payment divided by the difference between the required rate of return for the stock and the expected long-term growth rate of dividends:

$$(1) \qquad P = \frac{D}{\rho - g^e},$$

where D is the dividend, P is the stock price, ρ is the required rate of return, and g^e is the expected growth rate of the dividend stream. Rearranging equation (1) with ρ on the left-hand-side gives an expression that states that the required rate of return on a stock is the sum of its current dividend-price ratio and the expected growth rate of future dividends:

$$(2) \qquad \rho = \frac{D}{P} + g^e$$

In order to use equation (2) to compute expected returns, we need a measure of expected future growth rates that we can add to the dividend-price ratio data we obtain from the EMDB. Because capital's share in national output within a given country does not fluctuate much over time (although it may vary significantly across countries), it is reasonable to assume that in the long-run, earnings grow at the same rate as gross domestic product (GDP). The issue then becomes how to construct a measure of the expected future growth rate of GDP. Here we turn to the International Monetary Fund (IMF) publication, the *World Economic Outlook* (*WEO*).

The *WEO* provides annual analysis and forecasts for the world economy. Every year, the *WEO* produces three sets of numbers for a variety of countries and regions: (a) A forecast of GDP growth for the current year (year [0]); (b) a forecast of growth for the following year (year [+1]); and (c) a forecast of the average expected growth rate for the next four years (years [+2 to +5]).[4] Since the Gordon model assumes a constant expected future growth rate, the proper empirical analogue for g^e is a long-term forecast, not the growth forecast for any single year. In order to capture the spirit of the model, we calculate g^e as the geometric average of the three numbers provided in the *WEO* forecast—in essence, the average expected growth rate over the next five years.

A simple example may help. Suppose that we want to calculate the expected return for Latin America in 1995. The first step is to produce, from the perspective of a market investor in 1995, a forecast of the expected future dividend growth rate. To do so, we open the 1995 issue of the *WEO* and find that the forecast for Latin American growth (as approximated by the Western Hemisphere region) in 1995 was 2.1 percent, the forecast for 1996 was 4.0 percent, and the forecast for 1997 through 2000 was an annual growth rate of 5.3 percent. Given these three numbers, our estimate of the expected future dividend growth rate for Latin America in 1995 is 4.5 percent.

Table 8.3 presents our calculations of average expected returns from 1985 to 2005. The time period in table 8.3 is shorter than that for table 8.1, because data on the dividend price ratio for the individual economies is only available since 1985. Table 8.3 also presents data on the values of the underlying variables that comprise our calculation of expected returns. Column 1 gives the dividend-price ratio, column 2 the expected future growth rate of dividends. Column 3, which presents the sum of the first two columns, shows that over the period 1985–2005, average expected returns for the Composite Emerging Market Index, Latin America, and Asia were all higher than average expected returns in the United States.

To test whether these differences are statistically significant we pooled the expected-returns data and then ran a regression of annual expected returns on a constant and regional dummies (with the United States as a base). The coefficients on all of the regional dummies were significant. In other words, from 1985 to 2005, expected returns in Asia, Latin America, and emerging markets as a whole were significantly higher than expected

---

4. Strictly speaking, the IMF only began to consistently publish forecasts for developing economies along the lines mentioned in the main text from their 1995 issue of the WEO. For the earlier years, we used the regional growth forecasts for "net debtor developing countries." The composition of countries between the two groups is not significantly different. Where possible, we use the September/October issue of the WEO for that year.

Table 8.3   Expected returns in emerging markets versus the United States 1985–2005

	D/P	g^e	Expected return: $DP + g^e$	Expected return: E/P^a	Realized return	Realized Growth
Emerging market composite	3.17	5.24	8.41	6.27	10.32	5.48
Latin America	3.85	3.89	7.74	9.69	14.68	2.94
Asia	1.86	6.47	8.33	4.17	7.01	7.41
U.S.	2.48	2.83	5.31	4.96	9.05	2.98

[a]Earnings-price data only begin from 1986.

returns in the United States. In contrast, the average realized returns for Asia, Latin America, and the composite emerging market index in table 8.1 were not significantly different from the realized returns for the United States.

It is also instructive to compare expected returns with realized returns for a given region. Column 5 in table 8.3 shows the average realized annual return for each region over the same time period. For every emerging market region except Asia, we find that average realized returns exceeded average expected returns over the past two decades. Average realized returns for the United States also exceeded average expected returns over the period. This result is consistent with Fama and French (2002). Using an equation analogous to equation (2), they find that average realized returns for the United States over the period 1951–2000 were much higher than the average expected return.

8.3.1   Expected Returns Using the Earnings Yield

Using the dividend-price ratio to calculate expected returns has its disadvantages. As we can see from equation (2), the expected rate of return depends on dividend policy. For instance, suppose that earnings rise, but firms decide not to increase their cash payouts to shareholders. Because earnings rise, so will the firm's stock price. But without any change in dividend policy, the dividend price ratio will fall, thereby reducing the level of expected returns implied by equation (2). If the increase in earnings were permanent, one would eventually expect an increase in payouts. But given the persistence of dividend policy, the shortness of our earnings-yield series, and the increasing tendency of firms to distribute payouts in forms other than dividends, the change in earnings could have a nontrivial impact on our calculation of expected returns. This is an unattractive feature, because dividend policy is independent of real operations, like investment decisions, that ultimately drive fundamental firm value (Modigliani and Miller 1958).

Since earnings, not dividends, drive long-run value, the earnings yield

E/P provides a more robust measure of aggregate expected returns.[5] It is true that for a given firm, the earnings yield may not accurately measure its expected return. The firm's earnings yield accurately measures the firm's expected returns only when the marginal product of capital equals the cost of capital. When the firm's marginal product of capital exceeds its cost of capital, then the earnings yield will understate the firm's expected rate of return, and vice versa. While it is reasonable to expect that any firm may earn positive or negative economic profits for some period of time, there is no reason to think the same is true for the economy as a whole.

Column 4 of table 8.3 presents average earnings yields for the Composite Emerging Market Index, for Asia, Latin America, and the United States. The basic message about expected returns in emerging markets versus the United States does not change when we use earnings yields. With the exception of Asia, the average earnings yield for all emerging market regions between 1986 and 2005 was higher than in the United States. The average level of expected returns was 9.69 for Latin America, 6.27 for all emerging markets, and 4.17 for Asia. The average level of earnings yields for the United States during this period was 4.96. It is also worth noting that for any given region, average realized returns always exceed average earnings yields. However, given the shortness of the time series and the volatility of realized returns, this result is not statistically significant.

Two main points emerge from table 8.3. First, unlike the realized rates of return computed in table 8.1, expected rates of return in emerging markets are significantly different from expected returns in the United States. Using either the earnings yield or the dividend-price-ratio-based measure, average expected returns over the period 1985–2005 were higher in Latin America and Asia than in the United States. Second, almost without exception, average realized returns in emerging economies over the past two decades have been higher than expected. The question, then, is: what forces drive average realized returns in emerging market economies away from average expected returns? This is the topic to which we now turn.

8.4 Regional Vignettes

There are many potential explanations for the difference between realized and expected returns in emerging markets, but the economic reforms of the past two decades surely play a very prominent role. The most important issue in Latin America is the vanquishing of high inflation. Figure 8.3 shows that inflation began a precipitous decline in 1991 and continued

---

5. Mankiw (2005) also argues for the use of the earnings-price ratio over the dividend price ratio.

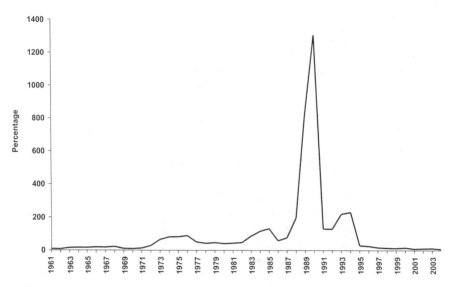

Fig. 8.3   Latin America, average inflation rate (annual percentage change in CPI)

falling through the 1990s. Latin America's disinflation is even more impressive when viewed in event time (figure 8.4).

Year 0 on the *x*-axis of figure 8.4 corresponds to the year in which each of the four successful disinflation episodes in the sample took place: the Mexican *Pacto* in 1987, Argentina's Convertibility Plan in 1991, the Real Plan in Brazil in 1994, and Chile's more garden-variety stabilization in 1989 under its last IMF program to date. Of course, the reduction in inflation is only part of the story. Immediately preceding the drop in inflation in 1991, Mexico became the first country to receive debt relief under the Brady Plan (1989), Brazil substantially liberalized trade (1990), and Venezuela opened its stock market to foreign investment (1990).

To examine whether the good news of economic reforms in Latin America drove up realized returns relative to expected returns, define the variable, *UNEXPECTED RETURNS,* as the realized return on the stock market in a given year, minus the expected return on the stock market (as measured in table 8.3) in the same year. For example, in 1991 the unexpected return is 77.8 percent using the earnings-based measure of expected returns and 81.9 percent using the dividend-based measure. The unexpected returns variable captures the extent to which new information drives a wedge between expected returns and realized returns. For instance, news about changes in policy may lead to unexpected capital gains because changes in policy lead to unexpected changes in growth. Indeed, in 1991 realized growth in Latin America exceeded expected growth by almost a full percentage point (3.9 versus 3.16).

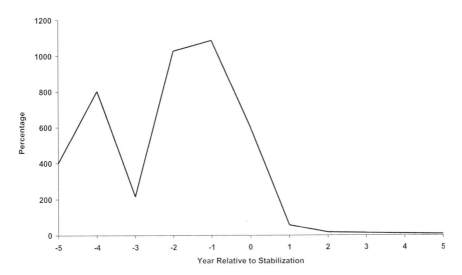

Fig. 8.4   Inflation rates in Latin American countries around stabilization episodes

The relation between unexpected returns and unexpected growth also works in the other direction. In 1994, the *WEO* forecasted that GDP in Latin America would grow by 3.3 percent in 1995. In December of 1994, Mexico devalued the peso, plunging the country into a full-fledged financial crisis. The peso crisis sent shock waves throughout Latin America. In order to maintain its fixed exchange rate, Argentina raised interest rates, financial tightening ensued throughout the region, and economic activity slowed accordingly. As a consequence, Latin America grew by only 1.8 percent in 1995. With realized growth falling 1.5 percentage points (1.8 minus 3.3) short of expectations for that year, Latin American stock returns also came in lower than expected. The unexpected return variable in 1995 was negative 28.7 percent using the earnings measure of expected returns and negative 27.3 percent using the dividend measure.

More generally, a significant correlation exists between unexpected returns and unexpected growth in Latin America:

(3) $UNEXPECTED\ RETURN = 15.2 + 8.7 \cdot UNEXPECTED\ GROWTH$
          (7.0) (3.7)

Adjusted R-Squared $= 0.184$, $N = 21$ (standard errors in parentheses).

8.4.1 East Asia

The emerging economies of East Asia did not have the serious inflation problems of Latin America. But like Latin America, the East Asian economies also began opening their stock markets to foreign investment in the

1980s. Significant liberalizations of restrictions of foreign ownership of domestic stocks took place in the Philippines in 1986, Taiwan in 1986, India in 1986, Malaysia in 1987, South Korea in 1987, and Thailand in 1988. Because emerging economies are capital-scarce relative to the developed world, opening the stock market to foreign investment has the potential to reduce a country's cost of capital.[6] Figure 8.5 suggests that the cost of capital may indeed fall when countries liberalize. The graph displays the profile of the average dividend yield across each of the five Asian economies that liberalized between 1986 and 1988. The average dividend yield falls by 231 basis points as a result of liberalization. The average growth forecast rises by fifty-one basis points. From equation (2), the approximate fall in the cost of capital is equal to the difference—180 basis points.

When a country experiences an unexpected fall in its cost of capital, stock prices should increase, thereby generating a positive unexpected return. Consistent with the notion that liberalization generates positive unexpected returns, during the three-year period from 1986 to 1988, the average wedge between realized returns and expected returns in the five Asian economies was 28.1 percent, according to the earnings-based measure of expected returns, and 25.9 percent according to the dividend-based measure.

A lower cost of capital also has real implications—namely, more investment, and faster economic growth in the short term (Bekaert, Harvey, and Lundblad 2005; Henry 2000b; Henry 2003). Accordingly, over the three-year liberalization period from 1986 to 1988, actual GDP growth in emerging Asia exceeds expected growth by an average of 1.9 percentage points per year (7.8 versus 5.9 percent). Again, as in Latin America, a more general correlation holds between unexpected returns and unexpected growth:

(4) $UNEXPECTED\ RETURN = -13.9 + 13.4 \cdot UNEXPECTED\ GROWTH$
            (8.3)   (5.3)

Adjusted R-Squared $= 0.21$, $N = 21$ (standard errors in parentheses)

The negative intercept term in equation (4) reflects the extreme influence of the Asian crisis on estimates of unexpected returns in a regression with only 21 data points. Nevertheless, we learn a lot from the outlier, which is the Asian crisis of 1997. In 1997, the actual growth rate of GDP in Indonesia, Korea, Malaysia, and Thailand was four percentage points below expected growth, and realized returns were 90.1 percentage points less than expected returns.

Pooling all of the available data, we also estimate the average relationship between unexpected returns and unexpected growth across Latin America, Asia, and developed markets:

---

6. See Stulz (1999), Bekaert and Harvey (2000), and Henry (2000a) for detailed discussions about the impact of liberalization on the cost of capital.

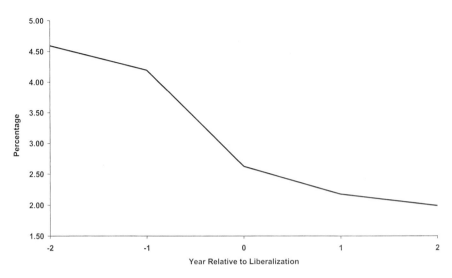

Fig. 8.5   Dividend-yields in Asian economies around capital account liberalization episodes

(5) *UNEXPECTED RETURN* = 2.9 + 5.9 · *UNEXPECTED GROWTH*
                              (3.3) (2.2)

Adjusted *R*-Squared = 0.09, *N* = 63 (standard errors in parentheses)

The general message here is that unexpected growth significantly predicts unexpected returns. Not surprisingly, from 2002 to 2005, GDP growth in emerging markets has been stronger than expected and realized returns have exceeded expected returns.

8.5   Discussion

From 1985 to 2005, the average realized return on Latin American stocks was 14.68 percent per year (table 8.3). Realized returns consist of dividend yields plus capital gains. Since the average dividend yield for Latin America over the period was 3.85 percent per year, average annual capital gains come to 10.83 percent per year. The corresponding figures for Asia are realized returns of 7.01 percent per year, a dividend yield of 1.86 per year, and a capital gain of 5.15 percent per year. In other words, over the past twenty years, capital gains in Latin America exceeded those in Asia by a factor of two. Yet over the same period of time, average annual inflation in Asia was much lower than in Latin America—6.4 percent versus 167 percent—and growth was much higher—7.41 percent per year as compared to 2.91 percent per year. What can explain these facts?

Unexpected changes in the economic environment cause unexpected capital gains (or losses). Relative to initial expectations, Latin America has had better outcomes than Asia over the past two decades. Taken at face value, this assertion sounds a bit far-fetched, but it becomes less so upon deeper reflection. In the 1980s the Asian Tigers were well on their way to achieving the status of newly industrializing countries. They had already experienced two decades of rapid output growth and their expectations for the future were great. Accordingly, price-earnings ratios in Asia were high in 1986—18.29, to be exact. In contrast, the early 1980s saw Latin America fall headlong into a debt crisis. Inflation was high, growth was low, and perhaps most importantly, growth rates in Latin America had begun to diverge substantially from those in Asia (see figure 8.6). The price-earnings ratio of 3.53 for Latin American stocks in 1986 reflected a dismal outlook for the region.

In short, a simple and consistent explanation for high growth with low returns in Asia and low growth with high returns in Latin America goes as follows: High growth implies high returns only if the stock market has not already capitalized the growth into current prices. To the extent that corporate earnings grow, so will stock prices. When there is good news about the future that is not captured in current earnings, prices will increase relative to earnings, and shareholders will experience unexpected capital gains.

In 1986, price-earnings ratios in Latin America and Asia were substantially different. Stock markets in Asia had already priced-in high expected

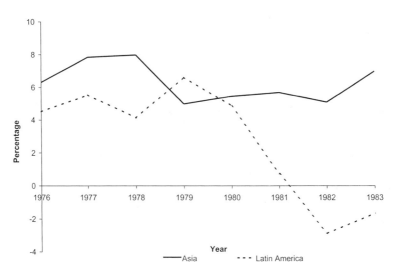

Fig. 8.6   GDP growth in Asia and Latin America, 1976–1983 (converted at market exchange rate)
Source: World Development Indicators, The World Bank

future growth, but by reducing the cost of capital, opening the stock market to foreign investors generated some unexpected capital gains in the mid- to late-1980s (figure 8.5). However, in addition to opening to foreign capital flows, Latin American countries also attempted to stabilize inflation, liberalize trade, and privatize state-owned enterprises. While these efforts were not uniformly successful (and some also occurred in Asia), the very attempt to move the region in this direction was a shock, given low expectations at the time. Hence, the scope of reforms and the magnitude of unexpected capital gains in Asia were modest in comparison with what was yet to occur in Latin America.

References

Bekaert, G., and C. Harvey. 2000. Foreign speculators and emerging equity markets. *Journal of Finance* 55:565–613.
Bekaert, G., C. Harvey, and C. Lundblad. 2005. Does financial liberalization spur growth? *Journal of Financial Economics* 77:3–56.
Blanchard, O. 1993. Movements in the equity premium. *Brookings Papers on Economic Activity* 2:75–138.
Fama, E., and K. French. 2002. The equity premium. *Journal of Finance* 57 (1): 637–59.
Gordon, M. 1962. *The investment, financing, and valuation of the corporation.* Ontario, Canada: Irwin.
Goetzmann, W. N., and P. Jorion. 1999. Re-emerging markets. *Journal of Financial and Quantitative Analysis* 34 (1): 1–32.
Harvey, C. 1995. Predictable risk and return in emerging markets. *Review of Financial Studies* 8 (3): 773–816.
Henry, P. 2000a. Do stock market liberalizations cause investment booms? *Journal of Financial Economics* 58 (1–2): 301–34.
———. 2000b. Stock market liberalization, economic reform and emerging market equity prices. *Journal of Finance* 55 (2): 529–64.
———. 2003. Capital account liberalization, the cost of capital and economic growth. *American Economic Review* 93 (2): 91–96.
International Monetary Fund. 1984–2005. *World Economic Outlook.* (Sept.) Washington, DC: International Monetary Fund.
Krugman, P. 1994. The myth of Asia's miracle. *Foreign Affairs* 73:62–78.
Malkiel, B., and J. P. Mei. 1998. *Global Bargain Hunting: The Investor's Guide to Profits in Emerging Markets.* New York: Simon Schuster.
Mankiw, N. G. 2005. Comment on asset prices and economic growth. *Brookings Papers on Economic Activity* 1:316–21.
Mobius, M. 1994. *The Investor's Guide to Emerging Markets.* Columbus, OH: McGraw-Hill.
Modigliani, F., and M. Miller. 1958. The cost of capital, corporation finance, and the theory of investment. *American Economic Review* 48 (3): 261–97.
Stulz, R. 1999. Globalization, corporate finance and the cost of capital. *Journal of Applied Corporate Finance* 12 (3): 8–25.
Young, A. 1995. The tyranny of numbers: Confronting the statistical realities of the East Asian growth experience. *Quarterly Journal of Economics* 110:641–80.

Comment   Takatoshi Ito

There are good reasons to believe that stock prices will rise in emerging economies with high economic growth rates. High economic growth is usually supported by high corporate earning growth. High corporate earning growth should make stock prices soar.

But, after examining the data of stock returns from emerging market countries, Peter Henry reports that the positive relationship between high economic growth and high stock returns is not confirmed among emerging markets or in a comparison between the emerging market and the United States or even in the comparison of East Asia and Latin America. Then, Henry tries to investigate why the educated guess of the positive association of economic growth and stock returns is not observed in the data.

Is it true that growth theory predicts the positive association? Henry points out that according to a standard Solow model, the positive association may not be obtained. Suppose two economies grow at the same steady state. One economy increases the saving rate, then experiences a temporal increase in growth rate on the way to a new steady state with a higher capital/labor ratio. But when the new steady state is obtained, the growth rate comes back to the original rate (since the growth rate is independent of the saving rate at any steady state), while the return to capital is decreased. However, this comparison, explained by Henry, is not fair. The comparison of the emerging market economies and the United States, or the comparison of low-middle income emerging market and middle-income emerging market economies, should be cast in the convergence story of growth rate. The country with a lower level of income should have higher growth and higher return to capital, while the country with high level of income, near the global steady state, should have a lower growth rate and lower return to capital. The positive association is predicted.

Henry then points out the possibility that the Asian growth may have been expected (at the beginning of the sample period of his study). The stock prices back then may have already discounted the high growth and high returns in the future. Therefore, ex-post returns may not be as high as economic growth. The expected returns were constructed using the IMF World Economic Outlook (WEO) forecasts as expected growth of corporate yields. The table (table 8.2), using data of 1985–2000, shows the following: (a) the expected returns were highest in Asia, followed by Latin America, and last the United States; (b) realized returns were higher than expected returns, especially so in Latin America; (c) realized returns were highest in Latin America, followed by the United States, and last Asia; (d) realized growth was highest in Asia followed by the United States and,

Takatoshi Ito is a professor at the Graduate School of Economics, Tokyo University, and a research associate of the National Bureau of Economic Research.

equally, Latin America. These facts seem to be quite surprising. Henry interpreted the set of results as the already high expectation of Asian growth in 1985, while Latin American countries experienced high unexpected growth and stock returns. Causality may run from stock prices to growth.

However, WEO projections may be too remote to expected growth of earning yields, although the WEO projections may be good proxies for expected economic growth rate. It can be tested in a long-time series of advanced countries whether stock returns really predict future economic growth.

A grouping of Asia and Latin America may be too crude, in that individual countries have very different results, as shown in table 8.2. The returns also widely fluctuate from year to year; for example, in Argentina, from –100.5% in 1982 to +156.2% in 1991. It is important to examine the performance of individual countries as well as the region.

Possible explanations that are not examined in Henry's chapter included the following factors. First, the stock price index of an emerging market economy may not have a representative group of firms. In an emerging market economy, it may be the case that the stock market, that is sometimes heavily regulated with some policy intentions, is represented with unfairly large weights by (former) state-owned companies or traditional resource-related companies, while economic growth is mostly realized by activities of (joint venture) companies with foreign direct investment (FDI), and FDI companies may not be listed in the stock market. Second, the emerging market stock returns, especially those of Asian countries, may be actually high for the U.S. based investors, if the returns are measured in the U.S. dollars, since the exchange rates of high economic growth countries tend to appreciate (i.e., the Balassa-Samuelson effect). Third, several emerging market economies started to grow when they implemented various economic reforms and opened their economies to foreign investment. The opening of the economy had impacts on economic growth, through promoting more investment and introducing modern corporate governance. Stock returns will also rise soon after, if not at the same time, as economic reforms, as the stock prices start to reflect future earning growth. Since timing of economic reform is different for different countries, the event study is called for. A study of lining up the timing of economic reform, a jump in economic growth, and a jump in stock prices may reveal an interesting time-series causality of economic growth and stock returns, and provide richer data to Henry's work.

Comment   Etsuro Shioji

This chapter starts from the observation that, despite higher growth rates, emerging markets are not necessarily characterized by higher stock returns compared to more developed economies. This finding may be at odds with prior expectations of some economists, especially if their intuition comes from the neoclassical growth model (whose main feature is diminishing returns to capital) with no cross country differences in technology. To investigate the source of this contradiction, the authors decompose those realized stock returns into expected and unexpected returns. They find the following two: (a) the average expected returns are no higher in emerging markets than among developed countries, and (b) there is a great deal of heterogeneity among emerging markets. Hence, the objective of the chapter is twofold: to study why the average expected returns are not higher in emerging markets, and to find sources of the differences among those markets. In my view, the latter is the more important (and interesting!) as, given the large diversity within the emerging market group, the group average is not likely to have much economic significance. Results from the regional comparisons are sensitive to the way expected returns are computed, but when they are calculated by the earnings yield (the method that seems to be slightly favored by the authors), Latin America has much higher expected returns than the United States, which in turn has higher expected returns than Asia. The authors propose the following interpretation. At the beginning of the sample period of their analysis (1985), subsequent strong growth of Asia had already been largely anticipated. As a consequence, it was already reflected in its stock prices, not expected returns. By contrast, Latin America's high growth was a consequence of reform efforts by the governments, which were unexpected as of 1985.

This chapter raises important questions. Perhaps some researchers had sensed a need to explore them in the past, but none (to my knowledge) faced them with the same degree of seriousness as do the authors of the chapter. It is my hope that much work will follow to answer the questions put forth by the authors. My comments are as follows:

Survivorship Bias

The authors have at least partially responded to my comments regarding this point in the revised version of the chapter, but let me discuss it one more time here, as it can potentially be important. Presumably, the stock returns data are constructed by taking averages of firms existing in the

Etsuro Shioji is a professor in the Graduate School of Economics at Hitotsubashi University.

market at each point in time (though the authors do not discuss the data construction in much detail). Those firms that disappear in the middle will not be considered in the calculation of the stock indices in subsequent periods. This means that, toward the end of the sample period, "survivors" will be over-represented in the sample. This could introduce an upward bias in the computed average returns: the fact that the average over the sample period was, say, 10 percent does not necessarily mean that one could have earned 10 percent by investing in an average firm at the beginning of the sample. This problem could be particularly serious in crisis-ridden emerging markets. As the authors point out in the revised version, this problem may not be so consequential to the discussion on the comparison between the United States and emerging markets as a whole, but could be important in the comparison between different emerging markets (which, as I said above, is more interesting in my view). As the authors say, it is not clear in which market the bias is stronger. It may be that, as Latin America has had more crises, the bias is larger there than in Asia. But the depth of the crises should also matter. I hope future work will shed more light on this issue.

Was Asia's High Growth Anticipated in 1985?

Note that *Asia* in this chapter includes not only the "tigers," but late-comers such as China and India. To test whether we could have predicted Asia's strong growth based on what we knew as of 1985, I run the following Barro-style cross country regression. The left-hand side variable is each country's growth rate of per capita GDP (PPP based) between 1985 and 2000. The explanatory variables are GDP per capita (denoted by y), ratio of investment to GDP (denoted as I/Y), ratio of government spending to GDP (denoted as G/Y), a measure of openness (exports plus imports as ratio to GDP, denoted as *Open*), all measured as of 1985. I also included dummies for Asia and Latin America (as defined in the same way as in the chapter), denoted *Asia* and *LA,* respectively. Data source is the Penn World Table, and the sample size was 103. Here is the result:

$$\text{(Growth rate, 1985–2000)} = 0.04^*y + 0.045\,(I/Y) - 0.009\,(G/Y)$$
$$+ 0.011^{**}\,Open + 0.033^{**}\,Asia - 0.001\,LA - 0.043 \quad (R^2 = 0.272)$$

In the above, "*," "**," and "***" indicate significance at the 10 percent, 5 percent, and 1 percent levels, respectively. Note that the Asia dummy is highly significantly positive, even after controlling for the effects of other variables that might affect the growth rate. Judging from this, it seems difficult to conclude that Asia's high growth was already anticipated in 1985. I also tried including the growth rate between 1965 and 1985 as an additional explanatory variable, but the results were unchanged. Other modifications did not overturn the results, either.

Degree of Integration into the World Financial Market

Throughout the chapter, the underlying assumption is that the emerging markets are not fully integrated into the world financial market. If they were, expected returns would be identical everywhere, and different prospects for earnings would be reflected entirely in stock price differentials, not in returns differentials. (Of course, realistically, one would also have to worry about risk premia.) This argument suggests that there is a potentially important determinant of expected returns in each market, not fully discussed in the chapter—degree of integration into the world financial market. Suppose, for the sake of argument, that Asia and Latin America would have the same value of expected returns under autarky, and that this rate would be higher than those in developed countries. Suppose, further, that the Asian market is actually more integrated into the world market. Then the actual expected returns would be lower in Asia. A similar argument could be applied along the time series dimension: a country that experiences a reform that enhances the integration would have lower expected returns in the post reform period (though the reform itself is likely to produce windfall gains in the short run, as discussed by the authors). Hence, historical averages may not be very useful indicators for the current expected returns in such a country. I hope future work will deal with this issue properly.

Expected Returns vs. Stock Prices

As stated earlier, the authors' explanation for the low expected returns in Asia (despite its fast growth) was that the growth was largely expected from the beginning, and thus was reflected in the levels of stock prices, not returns. If we push this argument further, and assume that *any* prospect for growth would be reflected in stock prices, we would reach a rather uncomfortable conclusion that there should be no correlation whatsoever between expected growth and expected returns in the world. But this is against our intuition. The relationship between growth and prices/returns is probably a more intricate one, and we need more guidance from growth theory (not the Solow-Swan model, in which expectation plays no role, but the Ramsey-Cass-Koopmans model) to understand what kinds of growth prospects are reflected solely in stock prices, and what kinds affect returns as well. For example, the theory predicts that, if growth is high because of a higher current TFP, the current marginal product of capital would also be higher and that should affect expected returns on financial assets. On the other hand, a higher *future* TFP leaves the current marginal product unchanged but increases current stock prices.

Technology Differentials

As I stated in the beginning, the fact that emerging markets do not necessarily exhibit higher returns may be surprising for students of growth theory, if they assume that the levels of technology are the same across countries. However, recent literature on growth has paid much attention on the differences in the levels of technology "broadly defined." They include the level of financial development (King and Levine 1993), human capital (Lucas 1988, 1990), governmental institutions, public capital, and social capital (Knack and Keefer 1997), among others. By borrowing those ideas from this old literature, I believe this literature on stock market returns will be much more enriched.

Some More Discussions on Institutional Details Would Be Useful

Many emerging markets have experienced fundamental changes in economic institutions in the past few decades. One might worry if a market today can be reasonably considered the same as the beginning of the sample period. Some discussion on the stability (or instability) of institutional features of each market would be quite useful to the reader.

Other Comments

Table 8.2 of the chapter, which shows fluctuations in realized returns in each market, is quite informative. The returns show large year-to-year fluctuations. This makes me wonder if the estimation results in the chapter are sensitive to the sample period, especially in which year the sample ends. In the discussion on the effects of reforms in Latin America, it would be interesting if the authors could separately estimate the effects of reforms per se and those of the foreign assistance that was given to the country conditional on implementation of the reforms.

References

King, R. G., and R. Levine. 1993. Finance and growth: Schumpeter might be right. *Quarterly Journal of Economics* 108:717–37.
Knack, S., and P. Keefer. 1997. Does social capital have an economic payoff? A cross-country investigation. *Quarterly Journal of Economics* 112 (4): 1251–88.
Lucas, R. E. 1988. On the mechanics of economic development. *Journal of Monetary Economics* 22:3–42.
Lucas, R. E. 1990. Why doesn't capital flow from rich to poor countries? *American Economic Review, Papers and Proceedings,* 92–96.

Bond Markets as Conduits
for Capital Flows
How Does Asia Compare?

Barry Eichengreen and Pipat Luengnaruemitchai

9.1 Introduction

Bond market development is high on the policy agenda in East Asia, as demonstrated by the Asian Bond Fund, the Asian Bond Markets Initiative, and a range of related policy initiatives.[1] Building bond markets is designed to free Asian economies from excessive dependence on bank intermediation and foster the development of a more diversified and efficient financial sector. One can think of the desired results as having both domestic and international dimensions. Domestically, banks have the weakness of being closely connected to business and political leaders, but also the strength of long-standing relationships with borrowers, enabling them to bridge information gaps that might otherwise impede lending and bor-

Barry Eichengreen is George C. Pardee and Helen N. Pardee Professor of Economics and Political Science at the University of California, Berkeley, and a research associate of the National Bureau of Economic Research. Pipat Luengnaruemitchai is an economist at the International Monetary Fund.

1. The Asian Bond Fund (ABF) launched by the Executives' Meeting of East Asia-Pacific Central Banks (EMEAP) in June 2003 is designed to catalyze the growth of Asian bond markets by allocating a portion of the reserves of regional central banks to purchases of government and quasi-government securities. The initial $1 billion of investments, known as ABF-1, was devoted exclusively to Asian sovereign and quasi-sovereign issues of dollar-denominated bonds. ABF-2 is twice as large and includes bonds denominated in regional currencies. It has two components: a $1 billion central bank reserve pool to be overseen by professional managers for local bond allocation, and a $1 billion index unit designed to list on eight stock exchanges beginning with Hong Kong in 2005. The latter is designed to facilitate one-stop entry for retail and institutional buyers as well as provide a benchmark structure for tracking pan-Asian performance. The Asian Bond Markets Initiative (AMBI), endorsed by ASEAN+3 finance ministers at their meeting in Manila in August 2003, is designed to foster an active and liquid secondary market in local-currency bonds and to develop the infrastructure needed for the growth of local bond markets, mainly through the activity of six working groups and a focal group intended to coordinate their activities.

rowing. Bond markets have the opposite strengths and weaknesses: transactions are at arm's length, often between anonymous buyers and sellers, but access to the bond market as a source of finance is available only to the largest, longest-established firms about whom the best information is available. Given the existence of long-standing relationships between banks and their clients, the banking system is ideally placed to provide patient financing for investments subject to limited uncertainty but long gestation periods. Bond markets, in contrast, are the channel through which creditors lend to enterprises investing in rival technologies, not all of which will pay off, even with sufficient time. Such are the arguments that a financially mature economy should have diversified sources of finance, including both an efficient banking system and a well-developed bond market.

The international dimension emphasizes that bond markets may have advantages over banks as channels for capital flows. Banks value liquidity, given that some of their funds are raised by offering demand deposits; it follows that bank loans are generally of shorter maturity than bond issues, and the short maturity of foreign liabilities is a notorious problem for countries borrowing abroad (Goldstein and Turner 2004). Banks being too big to fail, market discipline may be weak when such institutions are on the borrowing and/or lending side of the capital flow. These qualms about bank intermediation of capital flows provided an important part of the impetus for the Asian Bond Fund and the Asian Bond Markets Initiative.

In a previous study (Eichengreen and Luengnaruemitchai 2004), we asked how Asia was doing along the domestic dimension—how Asia compared to other regions and how individual Asian countries compared to economies with broadly similar characteristics elsewhere in the world in terms of the depth of domestic markets. Here we provide a complementary analysis of the international aspect. We assess bond markets as a conduit for capital flows (more precisely, as a conduit for cumulated capital flows, that is, stocks). Using bilateral data we analyze the importance of a range of factors determining nonresident holdings of a country's bonds. By permitting us to compare cross-country holdings in Asia with cross-country holdings in other regions, as well as analyze the determinants of holdings across regions, we can gauge the extent of bond market integration and how it compares across regions and over time.[2]

---

2. In principle, one could analyze the integration of bond markets on a number of other dimensions, for example the convergence of interest rates and spreads. Similarly, one would measure bond market development not just in terms of market capital capitalization but also liquidity (turnover), bid-ask spreads, and a number of other measures. Unfortunately, data on these other dimensions are more limited and fragmentary and thus do not permit as extensive an analysis as we undertake here (although data on stock market capitalization, utilized below, can be thought of as providing at least an indirect indication of financial market liquidity). For further discussion, see our 2004 study, and for an analysis of liquidity and spreads that expressly compares Asia with Latin America, see Eichengreen, Borensztein, and Panizza (2006).

The vehicle for this analysis (as some readers will have guessed given use of the word "bilateral" in the preceding sentence) is the gravity model, which provides a natural framework for analyzing trade in financial assets (as well as trade in goods). An advantage of this framework is that it is straightforward to compare the results with previous gravity-model-based studies of the determinants of cross-border capital flows mediated by international banks.[3]

The basic framework explains cross-country bond holdings well. The results point to the significant regionalization of bond markets in the sense that investors are most inclined to hold the bonds of other countries in their same region. Not surprisingly, this phenomenon is most extensive in Europe. Compared to the base case where the investors and the issuing country are in different regions, Europeans hold significantly larger bond-market claims on one another. We would be alarmed and begin to question our methodology if we did not find this, since the single market, the euro, and subsequent efforts at regulatory harmonization provide powerful explanations for this pattern. More striking is that cross holdings are also greater within Asia than across regions when we control for the basic arguments of the gravity model. Bond market integration in Asia may have significantly further to go before it reaches European levels or meets the expectations of regional officials, but our results suggest that there has already been some progress.[4]

A number of our results also caution that bond markets are not a panacea for countries seeking to tame volatile capital flows. They indicate that bond-market transactions are heavily influenced by financial conditions in the investing country, in turn suggesting that emerging economies utilizing bond markets to access foreign finance can suffer disruptions for reasons largely beyond their control. This was a conclusion of the literature analyzing early post-Brady Plan bond flows to emerging markets (see Calvo, Liederman, and Reinhart 1993); it is timely again today, when questions are being raised about whether flows into local bond markets reflect better fundamentals in emerging-market economies or simply the fact that the advanced economies are awash with liquidity.[5] Our results also indicate that bondholders are attracted to the securities of countries whose returns

---

3. This literature is surveyed in section 9.2.

4. A contrasting case is Latin America, where we find that bond market integration, so measured, is even less than is typical of pairs of countries located in different parts of the world. This result is fully explained, it turns out, by the weakness of institutions in Latin American countries, which continues to discourage foreign investors in the region (as well as foreign investors outside) from holding their bonds—and is associated with financial underdevelopment generally. Thus, Eichengreen, Borenstein, and Panizza (2006) compare bond market development in Asia and Latin America to show that Asian countries rank significantly higher in terms of cost and reliability of contract enforcement, compliance with international account standards, etc.

5. Empirical evidence that both sets of factors are at work is in Buchanan (2005) and Borensztein, Eichengreen, and Panizza (2006).

co-vary positively with their own; this result would seem to support return-chasing rather than diversification motives for holding foreign bonds. This evidence of limited diversification again raises questions about the prospective stability of the market.

Section 9.2 starts with a review of previous studies, after which we introduce the data in section 9.3. Section 9.4 reports the basic results, while section 9.5 examines their robustness. In section 9.6 we turn to the key issue of how cross-holdings of bonds within Asia and globally are related to the development of national financial systems. This leads us in section 9.7 to the role of institutional investors (banks, insurance companies, and mutual funds). Section 9.8 reiterates the main findings and draws out their policy implications.

9.2   Review of Previous Studies

There are now a substantial number of theoretical and empirical studies using the gravity model to analyze bilateral commodity trade. Why the size and distance between importing and exporting countries should successfully explain patterns of merchandise trade is intuitive: country size is a proxy for both the supply and demand for tradeable goods, while distance between the trading partners is correlated with transport costs. More recently there has developed a rapidly growing, if still largely unpublished, literature using the gravity model to explain trade in assets.[6] In that context the meaning of the distance variable is less straightforward.[7] Physical transport costs are negligible in this case; more likely is that distance to a country is correlated with availability of information about its financial instruments and the determinants of their performance (investors are likely to know more about these things in neighboring countries, to which travel is relatively cheap). This perspective suggests augmenting the traditional distance measure with more direct proxies for ease of information flows, such as bilateral telephone traffic and imports and exports of newspapers and periodicals.

There is some theoretical basis for these relationships. Martin and Rey (2004) show that if markets for financial assets are segmented, cross-border asset trade entails transaction or information costs, and the supply of assets is endogenous, then bilateral asset holdings are positively related to the size of the markets, negatively related to the transaction or information costs, and positively related to expected returns of the assets.[8] Using a similar theoretical model, Faraqee, Li and Yan (2004) also show that the grav-

6. In contrast to the substantial literature on bank-intermediated flows and the growing literature on equity flows, studies of the bond market—our particular concern in this chapter—utilizing this framework are relatively few and far between.

7. We return to this in the following.

8. This assumption is consistent with the views that financial assets are imperfect substitutes as they insure against different risks.

ity equation emerges naturally. While these models are developed for equity investment, one can show that the results can be applied for risky bond investments.

9.2.1   Studies Using Data on Bank Claims

From the early 1980s the Bank for International Settlements (BIS) has provided information on the international claims of BIS-reporting banks. Banks reporting to the BIS tend to be larger and more internationally-active than the typical commercial bank, a form of selectivity that should be taken into account when interpreting the findings of studies utilizing this source.[9] This measure of international bank lending is organized by the country of origin of the bank extending the claims (specifically, the country in which the head office of the reporting bank is located).[10] The underlying information is drawn from supervisory and statistical returns of the countries in which the banks are headquartered. Data are broken down by the national destination of the loans.

To our knowledge the first studies to use these data are by Claudia Buch. Buch (2000a) uses BIS consolidated data for one year, 1999, and limits her source countries to France, Italy, Japan, Spain, the United Kingdom, and the United States (while distinguishing 75 destination countries). The most important determinant of the extent of cross-border lending is financial development in the destination country (as measured by the ratio of bank credit to GDP). Curiously, the presence or absence of capital controls does not appear to have a significant impact on the extent of lending. In a follow-up study, Buch (2000b) then uses BIS consolidated claims data for the longer period 1983–99. In addition to the standard gravity variables, she includes in her specification the volume of bilateral trade (which enters positively and significantly, where lagged trade is used as an instrument for current trade).[11] She also considers a dummy for OECD membership as a

9. A not unrelated fact is that country coverage has expanded over time. At most recent report banks and other lending institutions in some 30 jurisdictions contribute to the construction of the BIS data.

10. This is in contrast to the BIS's locational data (not published on the institution's web site), which distinguishes banks by location rather than nationality. Arguably, the consolidated data are more relevant for studies of financial integration insofar as they focus on both the cross-border and within-destination-country lending activities of foreign-headquartered banks.

11. Rose and Spiegel (2004) focus on the connection between trade and lending as well. Their strongest finding is that an increase in trade is associated with an increase in bilateral bank lending. They instrument trade with distance and therefore do not include distance as an explanatory variable for lending. They also use a common language dummy and a regional trade agreement dummy. An alternative approach is that of Aviat and Coeurdacier (2005), who use 2001 BIS data. They estimate two simultaneous equations for trade in goods and trade in assets (using transport costs—UPS shipping rates—as an instrument for trade in goods and hence omitting it from the trade in assets equation). In addition, they compute the correlation of the average gross return on equity in the two countries. Interestingly, they find the same thing we do when we consider bonds below: a higher correlation leads to more claims (they refer to this as the "correlation puzzle"). Another study that reaches the same result is Coeurdacier and Guibaud (2005).

measure of the differential effects of the Basle Accord (which enters positively), the Grilli-Milesi-Ferretti capital controls measure (which has a negative but quantitatively small impact on cross-border bank claims), the share of the banking system that is government owned (which affects cross border lending negatively), and a measure of exchange rate volatility (which has no discernible effect on the volume of cross-border lending).

Kawai and Liu (2001) use BIS data for the period 1985–2000. They consider ten OECD source countries and a sample of developing country destinations. Unlike other studies, they do not pool the annual data for successive years but consider a series of sixteen cross sections. Like Buch, they find that trade flows encourage cross-border banking lending. In addition, the volume of bank-related inflows declines with measures of consumption and rises with the credit rating of the recipient country (especially after 1996, suggesting a growing sensitivity to credit-quality-related considerations). Countries receiving more bilateral foreign aid also receive more bank loans from the same source. In contrast to Buch's earlier conclusion, the authors find that a more volatile exchange rate discourages bank lending (this coefficient is consistently negative, though not always significant). The interest differential between the source and destination country has no consistent effect.

Jeanneau and Micu (2002) study lending flows from OECD countries to ten emerging markets. Their principal findings include that aggregate flows are procyclical with respect to growth in the lending countries. They find a positive correlation between fixed exchange rates and bank lending (reinforcing the earlier finding of Kawai and Liu). Ferrucci (2004) studies BIS-reporting banks' lending to nineteen emerging markets, and distinguishes six advanced lending countries. The results support the significance of business cycles in the borrowing country (but not in the lending country, which is contrary to Jeanneau and Micu), bilateral exchange rate variability (which reduces lending), the overall level of indebtedness of the borrower (which again reduces lending), bilateral trade (which enters positively), global equity returns (which enter negatively), and the yield spread between low- and high-rated U.S. corporate bonds as a measure of risk tolerance (which enters negatively).

The most recent wave of studies (Eichengreen and Park 2005; Kim, Lee, and Shin 2005) focuses on comparisons between Asia and Europe. To shed more light on intra-Asian flows, Eichengreen and Park (2005) supplement the BIS data with unpublished data for Taiwan, Hong Kong, Singapore, and Korea.[12] Banks are distinguished by nationality rather than location. They find that cross-border bank claims are smaller in Asia than in Europe. The standard gravity variables explain some, but by no means all, of this difference. The remainder is explained by policy variables: more intrare-

12. Obtained from the national authorities in each country.

gional trade in Europe makes for more financial flows, past capital controls influence current claims, and less developed financial markets (as measured by bank credit as a share of GDP) make for fewer flows. Kim, Lee, and Shin (2005) augment the BIS data base with data for Korea. Unlike Eichengreen and Park, they report results suggesting there is no remaining significant difference between the volume of intra-European and intra-East Asian flows once one controls for the standard gravity models. This may however reflect their limited geographical coverage for Asia.

The most comprehensive study in this vein is Papaioannou (2005), who uses BIS locational banking data from the mid-1980s through 2002. Standard gravity variables perform as expected, but there is also a role for political risk ratings, in that recent declines in country risk in developing countries have led to a significant increase in cross-border bank claims, other things equal. Papaioannou then tries to unbundle this variable by substituting bureaucratic quality (which discourages foreign bank investment), time required to complete a legal case (which has a significant negative effect on cross-border bank claims), and government ownership of the banking system (which has a significant negative effect). When political risk is reintroduced, it matters as well; "politics and institutions are both key determinants of international capital transactions" (p. 5). Papaioannou also considers the Reinhart-Rogoff de facto classification of exchange rate regimes and finds that foreign banks prefer investing in countries with more stable exchange rates.

Finally, Liu (2005) uses BIS data to test for the significance of General Agreement on Trade and Services (GATS) commitments—which are highly significant in his specification. In contrast to other studies, he finds no effect of exchange rate volatility or the presence of capital controls.

9.2.2 Studies Using Data on Equity Markets

An early contribution to the literature on international equity transactions is Ghosh and Wolf (2000), who consider flows from Germany, Italy, the United Kingdom, and the United States to nine recipient countries. They include only the basic gravity variables, finding that most of these perform reasonably well. Portes and Rey (2005), in a more comprehensive effort, consider bilateral equity purchases and sales between fourteen source and destination countries in the period 1989–1996.[13] They compare the performance of two measures of information costs: distance and telephone traffic. The number of bank branches in country i of banks headquartered in country j consistently matters, as if banks and equity-market flows are complements rather than substitutes. They use market capitalization in the source and destination countries as a measure of market size.

---

13. The data are from Cross-Border Capital. Their Asian countries include Japan, Hong Kong, and Singapore.

Interestingly (and in contrast to our results for bonds below), destination country returns do not appear to matter.

Izquierdo, Morriset, and Olarreaga (2003) use the same data as Portes and Rey (2005) for a similar period (1990–1996). They again use bilateral telephone traffic as a measure of information flows but also consider bilateral trade in newspapers and periodicals; by distinguishing imports and exports of newspapers they can say something about the direction of the information flow. Their most important finding, which is somewhat counterintuitive, is that information flowing from the source to the destination country matters most for bilateral equity flows (newspaper exports from the United States to Argentina matter more than newspaper exports from Brazil to the United States in explaining U.S. purchases of Brazilian equities). They interpret this as an indication of the importance of information about the liquidity of the U.S. market.[14]

9.2.3   Studies Using Data on Bonds

Studies concerned with bond markets, our focus in this chapter, are few and far between. Ghosh and Wolf (2000), in the same study noted in section 9.2.2, estimate the impact of the basic gravity variables on debt outflows from Germany, the United States, and Italy to a number of different destinations. Interestingly, these estimates do not appear to fit the data particularly well, except in the case of the United States. Buch (2000b) uses IMF data on debt securities for 1997 only. In her study the basic gravity variables are well behaved and look similar to those in regressions for bank claims.[15] The impact of having a larger domestic banking system is ambiguous, with the sign of the effect varying by source country. Finally, coefficients on the ratio of bank loans to total debt finance suggest the relative importance of bond finance rises with the financial development of the host country, while country (population) size is otherwise insignificant, suggesting minimal economies of scale.[16]

Thus, the few previous studies that have utilized the gravity model to study the bond market raise as many questions as they answer. In what follows we therefore see whether we can push this literature forward another step.

---

14. In addition they attempt to identify the relationship between trade flows and financial flows, using import and export taxes as instruments in the commodity trade equation and stock market capitalization as an instrument in the equities trade equation; the two relationships are estimated simultaneously.

15. Suggesting in turn that the relatively poor results in the study by Ghosh and Wolf reflect the very limited nature of their sample.

16. In the study otherwise closest to our own, Kim, Lee, and Shin (2005) use IMF data on total portfolio claims (portfolio equity, debt securities, and bank claims) rather than just bonds for 1997 and 2001 through 2004. They find trade is positively associated with financial integration. When trade is added, the dummy variable indicating that both the source and recipient country are in East Asia goes to zero. They also include a variable for whether one of the pair is a global financial center and find that this matters strongly for Asia, as if countries in the region are more heavily linked with global financial centers than with one another.

9.3   Data and Specification

The dependent variable in our analysis is the log of bilateral international portfolio holdings of long-term debt securities from the Coordinated Portfolio Investment Survey (CPIS) compiled by the IMF for the years 2001–2003.[17] The purpose of the survey is to collect information on the stock of cross-border holdings of equities, long-term debt securities, and short-term debt securities, all valued at market prices and broken down by the economy of residence of the issuer. Central bank reserve holdings are excluded.[18]

To date, the IMF has released five waves of CPIS data.[19] The first wave was for end-1997; twenty-nine economies participated. The second through fourth waves were released annually from end-2001 through end-2003. The number of countries participating tended to rise over time; sixty-nine economies participated in 2003. For each participating economy, the survey reports holdings in all destination economies. The list of reporting economies appears in Appendix A. For this study we create an unbalanced panel using data for 2001–2003.[20]

In designing this survey the IMF has attempted to ensure comprehensiveness and consistency across countries. All national surveys are conducted simultaneously, use consistent definitions, and are structured to encourage the use of best practices in data collection. Specific procedures are recommended to minimize the danger of misclassification and double counting. For example, the issuance of depository receipts creates the potential for double counting since there will then exist two securities that can be reported as held, but only one underlying liability.[21] Depository receipts are therefore recorded by looking through the financial institution that issues the receipts; instead the holder of the receipts is taken to have a claim on the underlying asset. In this case American Depository Receipts (ADRs) are recorded as liabilities of the non-U.S. enterprise whose securi-

17. To avoid the problem of log of zero, we use natural logs of (1 + the variable). The data set and data description are available on the internet at http://www.imf.org/external/np/sta/pi/cpis.htm.
18. Thus, our results concerning the determinants of such positions should be understood as reflecting the investment decisions of private agents and, where appropriate, government agencies with foreign holdings. Although central bank reserves are excluded from the CPIS data, it still could be that large reserves are a signal that exchange rates will be relatively stable, capital markets will remain open, and liquidity will be ensured through backstopping operations. In the section on sensitivity analysis below, we therefore add reserves in both the sending and receiving countries to our baseline specification.
19. Since the first draft of this paper was written, the fifth wave of CPIS data has been released, but the amount of information made publicly available, especially at the disaggregated level, is still limited. We prefer to wait for the complete data set before extending our analysis.
20. We drop the 1997 data since the smaller and less representative sample would likely aggravate problems of selectivity (addressed in the following).
21. Depository receipts are securities that represent ownership of securities held by a depository.

ties underlie the ADR issue, and not of the U.S. financial institution that issues the ADRs.

Despite all this, there are problems with the CPIS (see also Lane and Milesi-Ferretti 2004). These include (a) incomplete country coverage, as some large holders of portfolio assets, such as China, Saudi Arabia, and the United Arab Emirates, have not participated in the survey; (b) under-reporting of assets by CPIS participants due to incomplete institutional coverage; (c) third party holding, as the survey responses in some countries may be based on custodians instead of end-investors; and (d) problems with collection methods, especially for those participating in the survey for the first time. The exclusion of China may be consequential for comparisons of Asia with other regions, although we would note that flows *from* other Asian countries responding to the survey *to* China are included in our analysis.[22] Note that we are unable to analyze separately the determinants of cross-border holdings of corporate bonds and government bonds, since the CPIS reports only data on the sum of the two.[23] Nor do we have information on the currency composition of bilateral holdings.

The years 2001 to 2003, spanned by our survey data, were special ones in international financial markets. The beginning of this period was disturbed by default in Argentina and financial difficulties in Turkey, while its end was dominated by low global interest rates and surging cross-border investment.[24] It is not clear in what direction these particular conditions might influence our estimates of the coefficients of interest. Still, it will clearly be important to include year fixed effects or to apply equivalent treatments to prevent our results from being contaminated by temporal effects.

Tables 9.1 and 9.2 provide summary statistics of the CPIS data by region of source and destination countries. Table 9.3 provides analogous information broken down by the sector of the holder. Table 9.1 shows the average amount of cross-border bond holdings. It is not surprising that the cross-

---

22. Also, since central bank holdings of foreign bonds are not included in the aggregates analyzed here, as noted previously, the fact that China is not included is somewhat less troubling. In addition to China, some readers may also be concerned about the results because of the exclusion of India from the sample. According to the IMF's International Investment Position Statistics, India invested $300–400 million in foreign portfolio debt securities during the sample period. The exclusion of bond investment from India should affect the results only marginally.

23. Doing otherwise would violate the IMF's commitment to keep confidential the information it obtains on the composition of individual central banks' foreign reserves. Other evidence (such as that reported in Eichengreen, Borensztein, and Panizza 2006) suggests that the cross-border holdings analyzed here predominantly take the form of government bonds. We are, however, able to analyze the determinants of domestic market capitalization (as opposed to regional and global bond market integration, our focus here) separately for corporate and government bonds in our companion paper.

24. Note, however, that 2005 and the first quarter of 2006, when emerging market spreads fell to unprecedentedly low levels and enormous volumes of capital flowed into emerging markets as a corollary of the so-called carry trade, are not included in our sample period.

Table 9.1   Average cross-border portfolio holdings of long-term debt, 2001–2003

Investments From/To	U.S. & Canada	Asia	EU15	Eastern Europe	Latin America	Others	Total
U.S. & Canada	12,299	51,524	326,252	6,313	65,230	250,916	712,535
Asia	444,215	41,920	527,525	3,124	10,771	254,125	1,281,679
EU15	624,247	86,538	2,914,030	46,689	51,621	404,261	4,127,386
Eastern Europe	2,140	9	6,669	1,033	46	1,028	10,926
Latin America	15,193	78	2,225	22	6,999	1,161	25,678
Others	260,587	19,503	324,228	3,090	14,189	76,259	697,856
Total	1,358,682	199,573	4,100,929	60,271	148,856	987,749	6,856,060

Sources: IMF; Authors' calculation.
Note: Figures are in millions of U.S. dollars.

Table 9.2   Average cross-border portfolio holdings of long-term debt as percentages of destination countries' total outstanding debt securities

Investment From/To	U.S. & Canada	Asia	EU15	Eastern Europe	Latin America	Others
U.S. & Canada	0.06	0.64	2.60	2.05	7.97	9.65
Asia	2.34	0.52	4.20	1.02	1.32	9.77
EU15	3.29	1.07	23.18	15.20	6.31	15.54
Eastern Europe	0.01	0.00	0.05	0.34	0.01	0.04
Latin America	0.08	0.00	0.02	0.01	0.86	0.04
Others	1.38	0.24	2.58	1.01	1.73	2.93
Total	7.17	2.48	32.62	19.62	18.20	37.98

Sources: IMF; BIS; Authors' calculation.

border holdings of long-term debt securities are the highest within the European Union, as the region's financial integration and financial development are well advanced. While Asian countries hold a large sum of foreign bonds issued by countries outside the region, their holdings of bonds issued by countries within the region are relatively small. Latin America, on the other hand, holds small positions in foreign debt securities, and the intraregional holdings are smaller than those of Asia. Table 9.2 shows cross-border bond investment in percent of the total bonds outstanding of the destination region.[25] In other words, the table shows the share of each region's outstanding debt securities held by foreign investors, as reported by the CPIS.[26]

Our empirical strategy is to estimate the gravity model, augmented by various control variables. Specifically, we estimate the following equation:

25. The total bonds outstanding are the sum of domestic and international debt securities from BIS securities debt statistics.
26. The share of intraregional bond holdings in Asia appears to be smaller than in Latin America because of the larger amount of bonds outstanding.

Table 9.3   **Average cross-border portfolio holdings of long-term debt, by sector of holders, 2001–2003**

Investment from	Investment to						
	U.S. & Canada	Asia	EU15	Eastern Europe	Latin America	Others	Total
Asia							
Banks	129,438.7	5,689.3	122,740.3	174.7	632.3	88,296.3	346,971.7
Insurance companies	79,301.7	1,228.7	62,933.7	12.3	629.3	35,074.7	179,180.3
Mutual funds	20,187.7	297.7	20,691.7	178.3	1,110.0	6,402.7	48,868.0
Nonfinancial corporations	29,971.7	2,384.0	72,740.3	1,259.3	4,122.0	34,666.3	145,143.7
EU15							
Banks	160,959.0	51,952.7	792,584.7	19,756.3	17,033.7	168,458.7	1,210,745.0
Insurance companies	105,456.3	6,570.7	373,012.0	1,476.7	902.3	43,001.3	530,419.3
Mutual funds	40,387.3	4,105.7	211,480.0	1,538.0	4,121.7	21,861.0	283,493.7
Nonfinancial corporations	29,592.0	981.3	103,420.7	2,243.3	13,031.0	31,213.7	180,482.0
Eastern Europe							
Banks	293.3	5.7	750.3	50.7	25.7	58.3	1,184.0
Insurance companies	0.7	—	4.7	—	—	2.7	8.0
Mutual funds	3.3	—	5.7	1.3	—	1.7	12.0
Nonfinancial corporations	64.3	1.3	86.0	—	15.3	18.7	185.7
Latin America							
Banks	4,596.3	53.0	996.7	5.0	4,659.0	812.3	11,122.3
Insurance companies	689.7	18.3	277.7	8.7	131.0	51.7	1,177.0
Mutual funds	131.3	0.7	17.7	3.0	218.0	8.0	378.7
Nonfinancial corporations.	3,568.7	0.3	114.0	—	739.3	67.0	4,489.3
Others							
Banks	19,519.0	851.0	29,469.7	592.0	550.0	6,583.0	57,564.7
Insurance companies	37,889.7	679.0	22,482.7	33.7	196.3	2,512.0	63,793.3
Mutual funds	15,836.7	1,439.0	13,357.3	142.3	886.0	3,216.0	34,877.3
Nonfinancial corporations	820.0	11.3	1,634.3	15.0	24.0	230.3	2,735.0

Source: IMF; Authors' calculation.
Note: Figures in millions of U.S. dollars.

$$\ln(bond_{ijt}) = \alpha + \beta_1 \ln(Size_{it}) + \beta_2 \ln(Size_{jt}) + \beta_3 \ln(distance_{ij})$$
$$+ \boldsymbol{\beta}_w' \mathbf{w}_{it} + \boldsymbol{\beta}_x' \mathbf{x}_{jt} + \boldsymbol{\beta}_z' \mathbf{z}_{ijt} + \varepsilon_{ijt}$$

where i denotes the source; j denotes the destination country of bond investments; and t denotes time, which spans from 2001–2003 in the sample. The variable $bond_{ijt}$ is the cross-border holdings of long term debt securities from country i to country j at time t. The variable $\mathbf{w}_{it}$ is a vector of source country-specific explanatory variables, $\mathbf{x}_{jt}$ is a vector of destination country-specific explanatory variables, and $\mathbf{z}_{it}$ is a vector of bilateral explanatory variables. The descriptions and sources of these explanatory variables are listed in Appendix B. Finally, ε_{ijt} is an error term, which can be specified differently depending on the estimation method. For example, in an OLS model ε_{ijt} would be independently and identically distributed $IID(0, \sigma_\varepsilon^2)^0$. If we assume a destination-country fixed-effects model, then $\varepsilon_{ijt} = u_j + v_{ijt}$, where u_j is constant for each destination country and v_{ijt} is independently and identically distributed $IID(0, \sigma_v^2)$. In a random effects model, u_j would be drawn from $IID(0, \sigma_u^2)$ where u_j and all explanatory variables are uncorrelated with v_{ijt}.

9.4   Basic Results

To implement the gravity model, we will start with ordinary least squares, then add destination-country random effects and fixed effects (where the latter forces us to eliminate time-invariant recipient country variables), and finally use country-pair fixed effects (forcing us to drop country pair variables that do not vary over time).

As shown in table 9.4, the basic gravity variables (country size, log of distance, land border dummy, common language dummy) behave well in our pooled OLS specifications. In table 9.5 we add recipient country fixed and random effects. The Breusch-Pagan Lagrange Multiplier (LM) test suggests that random effects are preferred to pooled OLS, and Hausman's specification test prefers fixed effects to random effects. Table 9.6 reports the baseline results using country-pair random effects model.[27]

We find, similar to results in the literature, that country size matters: larger countries invest more in other countries' bonds. At the same time, larger countries attract more bond investment from other countries. The results are similar whether we measure country size by GDP, land area, or population. Distance between countries enters negatively, consistent with the information-cost hypothesis. The coefficients on the land-border dummy are positive but not robust. This implies that contiguity is a less important determinant of information and transaction costs for finance than

---

27. Again, the LM test rejects the null hypothesis of pooled OLS. The results with fixed effects are not reported, as we are forced to drop all country-pair, time-invariant variables (e.g., distance, intraregional dummy variables), many of which are of particular interest.

Table 9.4   Baseline results: Pooled OLS

	(1)	(2)	(3)	(4)	(5)
log of GDP—source country	0.405	0.419			0.307
	(38.71)**	(36.48)**			(27.43)**
log of GDP—destination country	0.636	0.654			0.524
	(85.38)**	(80.27)**			(58.72)**
log of GDP, PPP—source country			0.384		
			(28.15)**		
log of GDP, PPP—destination country			0.666		
			(67.91)**		
log of GDP per capita—source country				0.900	0.764
				(34.36)**	(32.18)**
log of GDP per capita—destination country				0.902	0.445
				(60.27)**	(29.22)**
log of distance	−0.579	−0.545	−0.470	−0.244	−0.456
	(24.47)**	(21.24)**	(16.90)**	(8.99)**	(19.16)**
Land border dummy	0.133	0.198	0.266	1.277	0.535
	(1.22)	(1.74)	(2.18)*	(10.45)**	(5.07)**
Common Language Dummy	0.415	0.335	0.445	0.151	0.259
	(8.46)**	(6.36)**	(7.74)**	(2.65)**	(5.32)**
Control on bond transactions (inflow)	−0.359	−0.411	−0.654	−0.009	0.012
	(9.99)**	(10.41)**	(15.21)**	(0.21)	(8.92)**
Control on bond transactions (outflow)	−0.806	−0.816	−1.079	−0.080	0.002
	(20.15)**	(18.56)**	(22.42)**	(1.48)	(1.51)
LIBOR—Source country interest rate	0.020	0.021	0.012	−0.122	
	(14.38)**	(13.77)**	(7.93)**	(3.19)**	
Destination country interest rate—LIBOR	−0.010	−0.018	−0.000	−0.149	
	(6.85)**	(11.09)**	(0.04)	(3.21)**	
Asia	0.860	0.643	0.803	2.305	1.112
	(5.72)**	(4.24)**	(4.95)**	(14.19)**	(7.92)**
EU15	3.808	3.516	3.940	3.683	3.056
	(43.57)**	(39.34)**	(41.43)**	(38.20)**	(36.69)**
Latin America	−0.279	0.199	0.306	0.187	0.407
	(2.83)**	(1.80)	(2.55)*	(1.57)	(3.98)**
Constant	−19.034	−19.694	−20.157	−11.876	−25.709
	(50.56)**	(48.57)**	(41.38)**	(31.79)**	(63.07)**
Observations	12,481	10,654	10,180	10,654	10,654
R-squared	0.58	0.61	0.57	0.55	0.67

Note: Absolute value of t statistics in parentheses.
*Significant at 5%
**Significant at 1%

trade (which makes sense in that physical transportation costs, which are often minimized by contiguity, matter more for the latter).

The interest rate variables highlight the importance of push factors: investments do not always go to the countries with higher interest rates, but they clearly come from countries with lower interest rates. We find the same when we instead use the average monthly return on home country bonds

Table 9.5   Baseline results: Destination country fixed and random effects

	(1) RE	(2) FE	(3) RE	(4) FE	(5) RE	(6) FE	(7) RE	(8) FE	(9) RE	(10) FE
log of GDP—source country	0.428	0.430	0.439	0.440					0.317	0.318
	(45.63)**	(45.91)**	(42.10)**	(42.25)**					(30.49)**	(30.65)**
log of GDP—destination country	0.585	0.814	0.620	0.809					0.489	-0.068
	(23.45)**	(2.04)*	(22.44)**	(1.75)					(18.72)**	(0.05)
log of GDP, PPP—source country					0.425	0.429				
					(35.36)**	(35.80)**				
log of GDP, PPP—destination country					0.633	0.459				
					(20.56)**	(0.97)				
log of GDP per capita—source country							1.006	1.014	0.794	0.797
							(46.06)**	(46.87)**	(36.17)**	(36.36)**
log of GDP per capita—destination country							0.838	1.328	0.423	1.068
							(19.81)**	(2.53)*	(9.89)**	(0.65)
log of distance	-0.714	-0.730	-0.657	-0.669	-0.575	-0.586	-0.373	-0.377	-0.566	-0.584
	(27.65)**	(27.84)**	(22.87)**	(22.87)**	(19.09)**	(19.15)**	(13.47)**	(13.45)**	(20.98)**	(21.09)**
Land border dummy	-0.098	-0.121	0.011	-0.006	0.078	0.060	0.764	0.733	0.349	0.323
	(0.98)	(1.22)	(0.11)	(0.06)	(0.71)	(0.55)	(7.34)**	(7.10)**	(3.50)**	(3.23)**
Common Language Dummy	0.353	0.348	0.323	0.322	0.403	0.396	0.301	0.323	0.278	0.284
	(7.50)**	(7.38)**	(6.33)**	(6.27)**	(7.43)**	(7.31)**	(5.94)**	(6.39)**	(5.78)**	(5.87)**
Control on bond transactions (inflow)	-0.178	-0.105	-0.259	-0.183	-0.351	-0.132	-0.129	-0.143	-0.144	-0.167
	(2.20)*	(1.01)	(2.83)**	(1.55)	(3.59)**	(0.98)	(1.43)	(1.22)	(1.78)	(1.48)
Control on bond transactions (outflow)	-0.874	-0.877	-0.870	-0.872	-1.219	-1.230	-0.143	-0.149	-0.147	-0.147
	(24.17)**	(24.25)**	(21.71)**	(21.75)**	(28.51)**	(28.84)**	(3.17)**	(3.34)**	(3.44)**	(3.45)**
LIBOR—Source country interest rate			0.018	0.018	0.019	0.019	0.012	0.012	0.009	0.009
			(14.28)**	(14.17)**	(14.49)**	(14.51)**	(9.03)**	(9.14)**	(7.59)**	(7.33)**
Destination country interest rate—LIBOR			-0.005	-0.001	-0.010	-0.002	-0.001	0.000	0.000	-0.000
			(1.59)	(0.11)	(2.91)**	(0.37)	(0.20)	(0.05)	(0.06)	(0.08)

(continued)

Table 9.5   (continued)

	(1) RE	(2) FE	(3) RE	(4) FE	(5) RE	(6) FE	(7) RE	(8) FE	(9) RE	(10) FE
Asia	0.932	0.911	0.897	0.893	1.049	1.048	1.910	1.864	1.358	1.351
	(6.32)**	(6.16)**	(5.95)**	(5.89)**	(6.69)**	(6.66)**	(12.82)**	(12.54)**	(9.54)**	(9.42)**
EU15	3.183	3.121	3.058	3.010	3.259	3.181	3.115	3.061	2.790	2.746
	(36.04)**	(35.16)**	(33.49)**	(32.76)**	(34.35)**	(33.41)**	(34.52)**	(33.99)**	(32.37)**	(31.59)**
Latin America	-0.576	-0.611	-0.103	-0.132	-0.025	-0.055	0.162	0.159	0.251	0.221
	(5.85)**	(6.16)**	(0.93)	(1.18)	(0.22)	(0.47)	(1.47)	(1.44)	(2.39)*	(2.08)*
Constant	-17.393	-22.747	-18.636	-23.137	-19.825	-15.512	-11.431	-15.261	-24.345	-16.008
	(25.91)**	(2.37)*	(24.84)**	(2.07)*	(23.02)**	(1.31)	(23.55)**	(3.54)**	(38.15)**	(0.72)
Observations	12,481	12,481	10,654	10,654	10,180	10,180	10,654	10,654	10,654	10,654
Number of group (destination countries)	156	156	133	133	129	129	133	133	133	133
R2-overall	0.58	0.57	0.61	0.60	0.56	0.53	0.54	0.53	0.67	0.53
R2-within	0.40	0.40	0.43	0.43	0.41	0.41	0.44	0.44	0.49	0.49
R2-between	0.74	0.74	0.79	0.78	0.70	0.69	0.62	0.62	0.86	0.53
Breusch-Pagan LM Test for Random Effects	25,192.19		17,716.94		25,205.25		57,638.89		13,214.07	
Prob > Chi2	0.00		0.00		0.00		0.00		0.00	
Hausman Specification Test		49.36		22.97		123.60		48.81		69.50
Prob > Chi2		0.00		0.03		0.00		0.00		0.00

Note: Absolute value of *t* statistics in parentheses.

*Significant at 5%

**Significant at 1%

Table 9.6   Baseline results: Country pair random effects

	(1)	(2)	(3)	(4)	(5)
log of GDP—source country	0.407 (26.44)**	0.438 (26.18)**			0.301 (18.10)**
log of GDP—destination country	0.605 (55.29)**	0.622 (52.30)**			0.493 (37.61)**
log of GDP, PPP—source country			0.378 (19.44)**		
log of GDP, PPP—destination country			0.623 (43.64)**		
log of GDP per capita—source country				0.878 (25.92)**	0.745 (23.31)**
log of GDP per capita—destination country				0.826 (41.21)**	0.419 (19.99)**
log of distance	−0.579 (16.58)**	−0.604 (16.09)**	−0.558 (13.84)**	−0.292 (7.38)**	−0.479 (13.79)**
Land border dummy	0.007 (0.04)	−0.037 (0.21)	−0.021 (0.11)	1.152 (6.17)**	0.408 (2.51)*
Common Language Dummy	0.467 (6.44)**	0.434 (5.60)**	0.561 (6.64)**	0.180 (2.17)*	0.288 (4.03)**
Control on bond transactions (inflow)	−0.190 (5.66)**	−0.264 (7.00)**	−0.336 (8.14)**	−0.106 (2.71)**	−0.141 (3.80)**
Control on bond transactions (outflow)	−0.488 (12.43)**	−0.518 (12.12)**	−0.574 (12.94)**	−0.197 (4.26)**	−0.225 (5.18)**
LIBOR—Source country interest rate		0.005 (5.32)**	0.005 (5.33)**	0.002 (1.76)	0.002 (2.41)*
Destination country interest rate—LIBOR		−0.006 (3.86)**	−0.009 (5.87)**	−0.001 (0.68)	0.000 (0.09)
Asia	0.769 (3.27)**	0.581 (2.45)*	0.655 (2.57)*	2.442 (9.66)**	1.213 (5.52)**
EU15	4.131 (29.60)**	3.846 (26.88)**	4.362 (28.68)**	3.895 (25.39)**	3.254 (24.47)**
Latin America	−0.159 (1.10)	−0.046 (0.30)	−0.077 (0.46)	0.043 (0.26)	0.313 (2.21)*
Constant	−18.611 (33.15)**	−19.376 (31.99)**	−18.803 (26.58)**	−10.790 (20.89)**	−24.340 (41.30)**
Observations	12,481	10,654	10,180	10,654	10,654
Number of group (country pair)	5,166	4,436	4,342	4,436	4,436
R2-overall	0.58	0.61	0.55	0.55	0.67
R2-within	0.02	0.02	0.02	0.03	0.03
R2-between	0.57	0.60	0.54	0.54	0.66
Breusch-Pagan LM Test for Random Effects	8,971.53	7,422.27	7,226.88	8,132.88	7,092.55
Prob > Chi2	0.00	0.00	0.00	0.00	0.00

Note: Absolute value of t statistics in parentheses.
*Significant at 5%
**Significant at 1%

and the average monthly return on foreign country bonds in home country currency (table 9.7).[28] (We interpret the average monthly return as the historical or backward-looking return and the interest differential as the contemporaneous or forward-looking return.) These results are consistent with accounts emphasizing the importance of global factors and conditions in the financial centers as determinants of conditions in emerging markets (see Calvo 1999). They are suggestive for a paper presented in the summer of 2006, since the first half of the year was marked by substantial flows into emerging market bonds and, in turn, prompted a debate over whether this reflected mainly improved fundamentals in the emerging markets or the low level of interest rates and abundant liquidity in the advanced economies. Our results provide some support for the second interpretation.

The correlation of bond returns enters positively in our equations, which is easier to interpret in terms of return chasing than diversification.[29] This is the correlation puzzle identified by McCauley and Jiang (2004) in their analysis of bank-intermediated flows. McCauley and Jiang (2004) observe that arbitrage has done little to equalize returns between Asian local currency bonds and their industrial-country counterparts, consistent with this finding, but they also suggest that this pattern should make diversification attractive; our results suggest that there has been little such diversification to date. This result is also consistent with interpretations of recent trends emphasizing the high level of liquidity in the financial centers in driving flows to emerging markets, as well as trend-chasing behavior as opposed to diversification motives.[30]

In contrast to the mixed results in studies of bank loans, for bond markets

28. We measure past bond returns using total return indices, taking into account changes in bilateral exchange rates by using own-currency returns for source countries and source-country-currency returns for destination countries. For emerging market countries, we use J. P. Morgan's Emerging Market Bond Indices (EMBI) total returns, which compute capital gains and interest returns on U.S. dollar-denominated debt instruments issued by sovereign and quasi-sovereign entities. For mature market countries, we use J. P. Morgan's Government Bond Indices (GBI), which track total returns on local currency government debt instruments. For source countries we calculate returns from its bond index and, if applicable, convert the returns into its own currency. For destination countries we use unhedged bond returns in source country currency to take into account changes in bilateral exchange rates. In principle, it would be desirable to measure the extent of hedging behavior directly, perhaps using data on the level of activity on hedging markets. However, information on the activity of such markets, and even on their existence, is available in systematic form only for a relatively small subset of countries.

29. We compute the correlation of bond returns using the three-year rolling correlation of the past total bond returns (as described earlier). Given expected returns and portfolio weights, the lower the correlation of returns on two assets, the lower the variance of the portfolio they comprise. Hence one would expect a risk adverse investor to choose foreign assets with a lower return correlation with their local portfolio in order to diversify and minimize portfolio risks. The positive coefficient on the return correlation implies that investors choose foreign bonds with returns more correlated with their local bond portfolio.

30. We should note that this result is also consistent with reverse causality, in the sense that larger cross-border investments between two countries could result in higher correlations of domestic and foreign returns.

	(1) Destination FE	(2) Pair RE	(3) Destination FE	(4) Pair RE
Table 9.7 Historical total bond returns vs. interest rates				
log of GDP—source country	0.961 (50.33)**	1.013 (31.05)**	0.976 (45.90)**	1.038 (29.56)**
log of GDP—destination country	2.520 (2.98)**	0.864 (28.28)**	1.996 (2.17)*	0.887 (26.15)**
log of distance	−0.580 (12.30)**	−0.560 (8.75)**	−0.593 (11.53)**	−0.611 (8.90)**
Land border dummy	−0.146 (1.00)	−0.114 (0.47)	−0.188 (1.22)	−0.237 (0.93)
Common Language Dummy	0.804 (9.60)**	0.864 (6.69)**	0.805 (9.12)**	0.927 (6.83)**
Control on bond transactions (inflow)	−0.184 (0.79)	−0.262 (3.62)**	−0.060 (0.20)	−0.297 (3.58)**
Control on bond transactions (outflow)	−1.624 (25.88)**	−1.129 (15.06)**	−1.589 (23.97)**	−1.107 (14.04)**
Historical Bond Returns—source country	−0.094 (4.56)**	−0.013 (1.18)		
Historical Bond Returns—destination country	0.043 (2.25)*	0.016 (1.77)		
LIBOR—Source country interest rate			0.006 (2.69)**	−0.002 (0.98)
Destination country interest rate—LIBOR			0.007 (1.07)	0.003 (1.17)
Correlation of Bond Returns	1.598 (11.70)**	0.979 (7.73)**	1.804 (12.19)**	1.154 (8.38)**
Volatility of Bilateral Exchange Rates	−0.101 (5.74)**	−0.027 (2.90)**	−0.054 (3.17)**	−0.020 (2.09)*
Asia	1.416 (7.88)**	0.817 (2.93)**	1.391 (7.58)**	0.710 (2.51)*
EU15	1.736 (11.88)**	2.645 (13.19)**	1.642 (10.63)**	2.450 (11.71)**
Latin America	−0.930 (4.90)**	−0.661 (2.46)**	−0.964 (4.48)**	−0.897 (3.04)**
Constant	−82.063 (3.74)**	−41.079 (32.67)**	−69.033 (2.88)**	−41.933 (30.95)**
Observations	4,072	4,072	3,682	3,682
Number of groups	52	1,615	47	1,461
R2-overall	0.52	0.57	0.58	0.67
R2-within	0.65	0.04	0.65	0.04
R2-between	0.67	0.69	0.68	0.69
Hausman Specification Test	41.36		29.79	
Prob > Chi2	0.00		0.00	
Breusch-Pagan LM Test for Random Effects		2,592.41		2,309.43
Prob > Chi2		0.00		0.00

Note: Absolute value of t statistics in parentheses.

*Significant at 5%

**Significant at 1%

we consistently find that capital controls are important.[31] The regressions suggest that controls in both source and destination countries matter in an anticipated fashion. Controls on outflows from the investing country always enter with the larger coefficient (in absolute value terms), as if these measures are especially binding. All this is consistent with findings in our earlier paper on the domestic dimension of bond market development— that capital controls are negatively associated with domestic bond-market capitalization.

The volatility of the bilateral exchange rate enters with a strong negative coefficient.[32] Again, this is consistent with our earlier analysis of domestic bond-market capitalization, where we found that more volatile exchange rates had a negative effect (which we interpreted as evidence that exchange rate volatility discourages foreign participation).

Interestingly, when we add the Asia dummy to the preceding specifications, it enters with a positive coefficient, as if Asian bond markets are more integrated, so measured, than a randomly selected pair of bond markets.[33] But this coefficient goes to zero in table 9.8, where we include financial sector variables (domestic credit provided by the banking sector as a percent of GDP and stock market capitalization as a percent of GDP). When we add an analogous dummy for members of the European Union (as of 2001–2003), it is also positive and significant, and the point estimate is even larger. In contrast to Asia, the EU dummy is not wiped out by adding financial sector measures. Thus, cross border participation in Europe appears to reflect more than simply the advanced nature of the region's financial sector and the absence of capital controls; it presumably also reflects the extent of, inter alia, regulatory harmonization.[34]

In table 9.9, we add several proxies for the quality of institutions of the destination country.[35] Not surprisingly, measures of the quality of institutions in the destination country are consistently important in explaining cross-border holdings. Indices measuring law and order, corruption, bureaucratic quality, and the investment risks (higher values mean better

31. We use the lines for restrictions on capital transactions in bonds and other debt instruments from the IMF's *Annual Report on Exchange Arrangements and Exchange Restrictions.* The data are entered as a dummy variable where "1" means there is a restriction on capital transactions in bonds and other debt instruments, and "0" means there is not.

32. The volatility of the bilateral exchange rate is measured as the annual standard deviation of monthly changes of logs of bilateral exchange rates.

33. The Asia dummy is equal to 1 for Hong Kong SAR, Indonesia, Japan, Korea, Macao SAR, Malaysia, the Philippines, Singapore, Taiwan Province of China, and Thailand. Note that it leaves out Laos, Myanmar, Cambodia, Brunei, and Vietnam, for which data are spotty and that do not participate fully in the region's entire range of financial-market initiatives.

34. The Latin America dummy is opposite in sign. It also tends to lose some of its statistical significance when we add financial sector variables, but not across the board.

35. While these recipient-country-specific control variables are not time-invariant, the variations over time are small compared to cross-country variations. Thus, results using a destination country fixed effects model may not be very meaningful. As a result, we will report the results from the random effects model only.

Table 9.8   Development of financial sector

	(1) Destination RE	(2) Pair RE	(3) Destination RE	(4) Pair RE
log of GDP—source country	0.303	0.366	0.387	0.454
	(29.59)**	(23.36)**	(28.32)**	(22.00)**
log of GDP—destination country	0.530	0.547	0.676	0.653
	(20.32)**	(45.33)**	(15.24)**	(33.87)**
log of distance	-0.705	-0.590	-0.857	-0.740
	(28.00)**	(17.49)**	(27.92)**	(18.24)**
Land border dummy	0.107	0.115	0.027	0.048
	(1.10)	(0.71)	(0.25)	(0.27)
Common Language Dummy	0.286	0.364	0.331	0.369
	(6.24)**	(5.19)**	(5.17)**	(3.86)**
Control on bond transactions (inflow)	-0.166	-0.174	-0.189	-0.231
	(2.16)*	(5.18)**	(1.80)	(4.85)**
Control on bond transactions (outflow)	-0.657	-0.474	-0.938	-0.705
	(18.10)**	(12.01)**	(19.98)**	(13.36)**
Size of banking sector—source country	0.009	0.003	0.011	0.005
	(29.14)**	(11.13)**	(24.99)**	(11.29)**
Size of banking sector—destination country	0.006	0.005	0.003	0.003
	(5.87)**	(11.03)**	(2.60)**	(5.44)**
Size of stock market—source country			0.008	0.005
			(20.75)**	(11.87)**
Size of stock market—destination country			0.001	0.001
			(1.23)	(3.23)**
Asia	0.716	0.541	0.160	0.036
	(4.99)**	(2.39)*	(1.02)	(0.15)
EU15	3.110	3.917	2.606	3.357
	(36.17)**	(29.0)**	(27.65)**	(22.8)**
Latin America	-0.269	0.036	-0.479	-0.080
	(2.80)**	(0.26)	(3.35)**	(0.42)
Constant	-14.351	-16.744	-19.318	-20.752
	(21.35)**	(29.96)**	(17.23)**	(27.75)**
Observations	12,214	12,214	7,961	7,961
Number of Groups	153	5,088	96	3,499
R2-overall	0.62	0.61	0.063	0.62
R2-within	0.44	0.01	0.56	0.01
R2-between	0.80	0.60	0.78	0.63
Breusch-Pagan LM Test for Random Effects	20,862.50	8,336.51	13,797.59	4,952.58
Prob > Chi2	0.00	0.00	0.00	0.00

Notes: Number of group(pair); absolute value of t statistics in parentheses.
*Significant at 5%
**Significant at 1%

Table 9.9   **Quality of institutions: Destination country random effects (usual gravity model variables not reported)**

	(1)	(2)	(3)	(4)	(5)
log of GDP per capita—source country		0.872			
		(27.37)**			
log of GDP per capita—destination country		0.447			
		(11.37)**			
Law and order risk	0.224	0.163			0.195
	(11.21)**	(8.37)**			(6.59)**
Corruption risk	−0.045	−0.214			0.021
	(2.13)*	(9.92)**			(0.68)
Bureaucratic quality	0.237	−0.133			0.319
	(7.71)**	(4.05)**			(7.09)**
Investment profile	0.148	0.095			0.307
	(10.36)**	(6.85)**			(15.47)**
LIBOR–Source country interest rate			0.025	0.007	
			(15.50)**	(4.25)**	
Destination country interest rate–LIBOR			0.011	0.009	
			(2.34)*	(1.97)*	
Sovereign Credit Ratings (S&P)			0.093	0.109	
			(5.49)**	(6.56)**	
English legal origin					−0.418
					(1.17)
French legal origin					−0.155
					(0.44)
German legal origin					−0.208
					(0.55)
Socialist legal origin					−0.516
					(1.28)
Creditor rights					−0.020
					(0.33)
Contract enforcement days					−0.001
					(2.09)*
Asia	1.405	1.532	0.811	1.533	0.920
	(9.82)**	(11.06)**	(4.78)**	(9.52)**	(5.96)**
EU15	3.069	2.917	2.598	2.386	3.164
	(35.97)**	(35.28)**	(24.31)**	(23.72)**	(33.14)**
Latin America	0.403	0.299	0.180	1.159	−0.697
	(3.95)**	(3.02)**	(1.31)	(8.59)**	(6.04)**
Constant	−22.425	−24.410	−22.685	−30.615	−21.381
	(33.81)**	(39.90)**	(21.77)**	(28.89)**	(23.13)**
Observations	12,343	12,343	7,159	7,048	10,420
Number of destination countries	156	156	75	75	121
R2-overall	0.60	0.65	0.60	0.64	0.60
R2-within	0.44	0.47	0.49	0.56	0.42
R2-between	0.75	0.83	0.82	0.81	0.81
Breusch-Pagan LM Test for Random Effects	30,081.25	19,210.76	5,777.85	8,106.69	13,159.93
Prob > Chi2	0.00	0.00	0.00	0.00	0.00

Note: Robust *t* statistics in parentheses.
*Significant at 5%
**Significant at 1%

institutions) all tend to enter with positive coefficients.[36] We similarly obtain a negative coefficient on the number of days required to enforce a contract (from Djankov et al. 2005).[37]

Even when we control for institutional quality and interest rates, credit ratings continue to matter. The direction of the effect is plausible: higher ratings mean higher foreign holdings. It may be that the rating agencies are capturing something in addition to the standard measures of institutional quality, or it could be that restrictive covenants preventing institutional investors from holding bonds of issuers with sub-investment-grade ratings are driving this result.

Interestingly, the intraregional dummy variable for Latin America turns positive and significant when we control for the quality of institutions. The importance of institutional weaknesses for various aspects of bond market development in Latin America has been widely remarked upon. Thus, de la Torre and Schmuker (2004) observe that the high cost of judicial proceedings is a factor discouraging foreign investors from holding the bonds of a number of Latin American countries. Inter-American Development Bank (2005) observes that Latin America fares poorly when rated on both investor and creditor rights. In both cases the highest ranked Latin American country—Chile—has values according to the standard indices that are lower than the Asian average. Eichengreen, Borensztein, and Panizza (2006) show that Latin American countries comply less fully with international accounting standards than do their Asian counterparts. What is interesting here is that the low level of financial integration in Latin America is fully (indeed, more than fully) explained by the low quality of institutions.

9.5   Sensitivity Checks

We now provide a series of robustness checks of the results reported above.

1. We adjust the standard errors for the fact that a number of our institutional variables do not vary over time by clustering on destination countries.[38] Clustering increases the standard errors on the institutional vari-

---

36. An exception is the corruption measure. However, there appears to be strong colinearity between per capita income and the institutional variables (not surprisingly): the sign and significance of the latter are sensitive to whether per capita income is included (since this is associated with other hard-to-observe dimensions of the strength of institutions).

37. The measures of legal origin, which are negative for both English and French law (where Nordic law is the omitted alternative), are hard to reconcile with the standard La Porta et al. (1999) view. Recall that these same variables similarly entered with counterintuitive signs in our earlier study using domestic-capitalization data and that Djankov et al. (2005) also find that these variables do not always have the anticipated effects. The mystery deepens.

38. In other words, we assume that observations are independent across destination countries, but not necessarily within them.

ables, as expected, but few of the latter lose their statistical significance.[39] Overall, the results are very similar to before.

2. We check for selectivity, which may be important given that only some seventy source countries (of some 180-plus IMF members) participated in the CPIS surveys. We reestimated the basic equations using a Heckman selectivity correction. From the first-stage selection equations, we find, plausibly, that countries participating in the survey are larger, richer, and have larger banking systems and stock markets. But even after controlling for these selection criteria, the results remain similar to those obtained before. The results are reported in table 9.10.

3. We experiment with alternative measures of the de facto exchange rate regime. When we replace exchange rate variability, the measure used above, with dummy variables constructed on the basis of Reinhart and Rogoff's exchange rate regime classification, the results remain basically the same.[40] We find that pegged exchange rates have positive effects on cross-border bond holdings (compared to floating and managed floating regimes), while regimes of limited flexibility enter with significantly negative signs.[41] See table 9.11.

4. We experiment with alternative measures of policies toward the capital account. For example, we substitute the alternative measures of the absence of restrictions on all inflows and outflows as well as the financial openness index kindly made available by Nancy Brune.[42] Again, the results are largely the same. We then substitute Chinn and Ito's (2005) measure of financial openness.[43] Once again, the results are consistent with before: as

---

39. The results, while not reported, are available on request.

40. We use the update through 2003 of the Reinhart and Rogoff de facto classification of Eichengreen and Razo-Garcia (2006). For tractability we reclassify their more detailed classifications into three main categories: peg, limited flexibility, and floating/managed floating, and assign a dummy variable for each category. Floating/managed floating is the alternative omitted from the regressions.

41. These results, however, are not robust to the measures of the rate of return. The coefficients lose their significance when we use historical returns instead of the interest rate differential.

42. The measure of capital openness of all inflows is the sum of five dummy variables, measuring controls on inflows of invisible transactions, controls on inflows of export transactions, controls on inflows pertaining to capital and money market securities, controls on inflows pertaining to credit operations, and controls on inward direct investment. For each component, a value of one means open (no restriction) while zero means closed (restriction in place). The resulting measure ranges from zero to five, where higher values imply more open capital account on inflow transactions. Similarly, the measure of capital openness of all outflows is the sum of four variables: controls on outflows of all transactions mentioned previously, except export transactions. The resulting measure ranges from zero to four, where higher values imply a more open capital account on outflow transactions. The financial openness index is the sum of the measures of capital openness of inflows and outflows as well as dummy variables indicating controls on inward direct investment, controls on outward direct investment, controls on real estate transactions, provisions specific to commercial banks, and exchange rate structure (where this last variable takes on a value of zero if a country has dual or multiple exchange rates). The resulting index ranges from zero to twelve.

43. A note on calculation of this measure is available at http://www.pdx.edu/~ito/Readme_kaopen163.pdf.

Table 9.10   **Heckman selectivity bias correction**

	(1)	(2)	(3)
log of GDP—source country	0.152	0.232	0.704
	(10.39)**	(18.48)**	(21.65)**
log of GDP—destination country	0.637	0.637	0.906
	(87.98)**	(87.81)**	(41.79)**
log of distance	−0.540	−0.546	−0.659
	(23.57)**	(23.72)**	(14.59)**
Land border dummy	0.275	0.381	−0.046
	(2.61)**	(3.63)**	(0.29)
Common Language Dummy	0.401	0.326	0.615
	(8.33)**	(6.67)**	(7.10)**
Control on bond transactions (inflow)	−0.380	−0.385	−0.526
	(10.80)**	(10.95)**	(7.68)**
Control on bond transactions (outflow)	−0.430	−0.458	−0.825
	(10.46)**	(11.17)**	(10.79)**
LIBOR—Source country interest rate			0.026
			(7.61)**
Destination country interest rate—LIBOR			0.011
			(4.15)**
Correlation of Bond Returns			1.547
			(10.47)**
Volatility of Bilateral Exchange Rates			−0.069
			(4.13)**
Asia	0.968	0.874	0.354
	(6.68)**	(6.04)**	(2.07)*
EU15	3.607	3.551	1.448
	(41.34)**	(40.87)**	(9.53)**
Latin America	−0.035	−0.155	−0.275
	(0.38)	(1.53)	(1.33)
Constant	−12.308	−14.431	−32.144
	(26.44)**	(34.39)**	(28.66)**
Selection Equation			
log of GDP—source country	0.404	0.267	0.367
	(80.29)**	(39.67)**	(34.14)**
log of GDP per capita—source country	0.764	0.718	0.673
	(94.78)**	(66.70)**	(46.07)**
Market Capitalization		0.003	0.007
		(9.97)**	(13.63)**
Domestic Bank Credit		0.008	0.005
		(29.70)**	(11.58)**
Constant	−16.967	−13.715	−16.363
	(124.07)**	(72.32)**	(55.30)**
Observations	93,791	35,435	26,902

Note: Absolute value of z statistics in parentheses.
*Significant at 5%
**Significant at 1%

Table 9.11   Sensitivity checks: Destination country random effects (usual gravity model variables not reported)

	(1)	(2)	(3)	(4)	(5)
Historical bond returns—source country	-0.091 (4.42)**	-0.095 (4.57)**	0.062 (3.03)**	-0.189 (8.26)**	-0.152 (7.43)**
Historical bond returns—destination country	0.035 (1.90)	-0.034 (2.46)*	-0.005 (0.37)	-0.096 (6.30)**	-0.041 (2.94)**
Correlation of bond returns	1.588 (11.62)**	1.713 (12.64)**	1.511 (11.81)**	1.348 (9.01)**	1.782 (13.15)**
Volatility of Bilateral Exchange Rates	-0.100 (5.82)**				
Pegged exchange rate regime (Reinhart-Rogoff)		0.197 (1.06)	0.206 (1.13)	0.033 (0.17)	0.210 (1.12)
Limited flexibility (Reinhart-Rogoff)		-0.259 (1.66)	-0.195 (1.31)	-0.385 (2.27)*	-0.235 (1.49)
Control on bond transactions (inflow)	-0.340 (2.14)*	-0.159 (0.97)			
Control on bond transactions (outflow)	-1.618 (25.72)**	-1.639 (25.98)**			
NB capital openness—inflow			0.092 (2.26)*		
NB capital openness—outflow			-0.085 (2.14)*		
NB financial openness index—destination country			0.340 (20.71)**		
Chinn-Ito capital control—destination country				0.158 (2.74)**	

Share of last 5 years with capital controls on bond inflow					-0.320
					(1.53)
Share of last 5 years with capital controls on bond outflow					-1.999
					(26.42)**
Dummy for IMF program—destination country	0.105	0.064	0.111	0.187	0.055
	(0.60)	(0.36)	(0.65)	(0.91)	(0.31)
Asia	1.380	1.434	1.800	0.853	1.594
	(7.74)**	(8.03)**	(10.55)**	(4.40)**	(8.90)**
EU15	1.769	1.817	1.557	2.348	1.479
	(12.15)**	(12.46)**	(11.19)**	(14.55)**	(10.01)**
Latin America	-0.845	-0.956	-0.927	-1.271	-0.743
	(4.50)**	(5.09)**	(5.17)**	(6.21)**	(3.94)**
Constant	-39.256	-38.902	-42.633	-38.632	-35.946
	(20.43)**	(19.23)**	(21.54)**	(18.43)**	(17.33)**
Observations	4,072	4,072	4,072	3,876	4,072
Number of destination countries	52	52	52	49	52
R2-overall	0.67	0.68	0.70	0.64	0.68
R2-within	0.65	0.65	0.69	0.59	0.65
R2-between	0.71	0.73	0.73	0.77	0.73
Breusch-Pagan LM Test for Random Effects	4,886.47	4,275.74	5,183.11	2,315.52	4,485.49
Prob > Chi2	0.00	0.00	0.00	0.00	0.00

Note: Absolute value of z statistics in parentheses.

*Significant at 5%

**Significant at 1%

expected, financial openness has a positive effect on foreign holdings of portfolio debt securities. Again, see table 9.11.

5. We add a lagged dependent variable to see whether the patterns we detect are robust to a model that explicitly allows for hysteresis or habit formation. Previous work on the determinants of bilateral trade flows using purely cross section data (e.g., Eichengreen and Irwin 1996) showed that such habit formation can be important in practice. To see whether this holds in the present context, we add the lagged dependent variable to a cross section regression estimated on 2003 data.[44] To correct for the bias resulting from adding a lagged dependent variable, we also instrument for the lagged dependent variable using the lagged independent variables and two-stage least squares. The results are shown in table 9.12. In all specifications, we find that there is strong evidence of habit formation. While most other coefficients remain unchanged, the Asia dummy becomes insignificant when we control for bond holdings in the previous year. This suggests that whatever is distinctive about cross-border bond holdings within Asia is persistent over time.

6. Although central bank reserves are excluded from the CPIS data, it still could be, as noted above, that large reserves are a signal that exchange rates will be relatively stable, capital markets will remain open, and liquidity will be ensured through backstopping operations. Countries with ample reserves will be more sanguine, intuition suggests, about policies of benign neglect toward outward investment. On the inward investment side, some authors (e.g., Dooley and Garber 2005) have argued that reserves should be thought of as collateral, so that high reserve levels make it easier for emerging markets to access foreign financial markets. We therefore add reserves scaled by GDP in the sending and receiving countries to our baseline specification. As shown in the first column of table 9.13, the coefficient on the reserves of the sending country is positive and significant; as expected, countries with ample reserves can invest abroad with fewer worries. However, reserves in the receiving country enter negatively, which is inconsistent with the collateral hypothesis.

7. We explored further possible interpretations of the coefficient on distance. In table 9.13, we also added to the basic framework measures of incoming and outgoing telephone traffic and the cost of telephone calls on the grounds that these tell us something about the information flows that are important in portfolio investment decisions, and that this may be what the distance variable is picking up. These additional variables also enter with the expected signs (positive and negative, respectively) and are strongly significant. But the distance variable is still negative and significant as well. This suggests

---

44. We also add a lagged dependent variable to the panel estimates. However, this may create problems for the consistency of the estimates; hence, we prefer to rely on the simple cross section for 2003.

Table 9.12   Sensitivity checks: Lagged dependent variable

	(1) OLS	(2) RE	(3) IV	(4) OLS	(5) IV
Lagged Dependent Variable	0.942 (130.96)**	0.931 (126.05)**	1.061 (24.06)**	0.899 (71.26)**	0.975 (24.04)**
log of GDP—source country	-0.005 (0.49)	0.001 (0.07)	-0.056 (2.63)**	0.066 (3.22)**	0.001 (0.03)
log of GDP—destination country	0.078 (9.95)**	0.086 (9.57)**	-0.003 (0.09)	0.119 (6.01)**	0.053 (1.33)
Log of distance	-0.121 (6.12)**	-0.126 (5.98)**	-0.063 (2.12)**	-0.218 (5.99)**	-0.194 (5.01)**
Land border dummy	-0.171 (2.07)*	-0.168 (2.05)*	-0.222 (2.51)*	-0.380 (3.00)**	-0.407 (3.15)**
1 for Common Language	-0.044 (1.12)	-0.027 (0.69)	-0.082 (1.90)	-0.017 (0.25)	-0.064 (0.88)
LIBOR—Source country interest rate	0.011 (4.90)**	0.012 (5.21)**	0.005 (1.52)		
Destination country interest rate—LIBOR	-0.001 (0.97)	-0.002 (1.11)	0.001 (0.64)		
control on bond or other debt instruments (inflow)	-0.036 (1.19)	-0.042 (1.14)	0.022 (0.58)	0.006 (0.10)	0.032 (0.55)
control on bond or other debt instruments (outflow)	-0.122 (3.13)**	-0.129 (3.37)**	-0.038 (0.76)	-0.270 (4.35)**	-0.150 (1.71)
Historical Bond Returns—source country				-0.083 (2.78)**	-0.055 (1.64)

(continued)

Table 9.12 (continued)

	(1) OLS	(2) RE	(3) IV	(4) OLS	(5) IV
Historical Bond Returns—destination country				0.066	0.054
				(3.55)**	(2.71)**
Correlation of Bond Returns				0.236	0.170
				(2.01)*	(1.37)
Volatility of Bilateral Exchange Rates				-0.019	-0.008
				(1.02)	(0.40)
Asia	-0.133	-0.099	-0.198	-0.206	-0.261
	(1.24)	(0.90)	(1.73)	(1.50)	(1.83)
EU15	0.149	0.158	-0.249	-0.012	-0.188
	(2.22)*	(2.27)*	(1.54)	(0.09)	(1.21)
Latin America	0.158	0.106	0.173	0.002	-0.021
	(1.72)	(1.13)	(1.80)	(0.01)	(0.13)
Constant	-0.313	-0.578	2.152	-2.296	0.642
	(0.92)	(1.61)	(2.21)*	(2.76)**	(0.38)
Observations	3,014	3,014	3,014	1,241	1,241
R-squared	0.95		0.94	0.94	0.94
Number of Destination countries		129			

Note: Absolute value of t statistics in parentheses.

*Significant at 5%

**Significant at 1%

Table 9.13   Sensitivity check: Reserves, distance, time zone, and information costs

	(1) Full Sample	(2) Full Sample	(3) Full Sample	(4) Exclude U.S. and Japan	(5) Full Sample
log of GDP—source country	0.473	0.385	0.416	0.336	0.669
	(21.41)**	(33.25)**	(36.39)**	(27.80)**	(36.15)**
log of GDP—destination country	0.663	0.653	0.647	0.624	0.577
	(44.35)**	(78.30)**	(79.24)**	(76.00)**	(15.92)**
Log of distance	−0.629		−0.778	−0.779	−0.537
	(13.50)**		(21.55)**	(21.88)**	(12.41)**
Time Zone Difference		−0.050	0.075	0.082	
		(8.40)**	(9.13)**	(9.89)**	
Phone traffic					0.000
					(9.75)**
Phone cost					−0.548
					(11.24)**
Land border dummy	0.123	0.955	0.019	−0.010	−0.004
	(0.62)	(8.76)**	(0.17)	(0.09)	(0.02)
1 for Common Language	0.259	0.241	0.343	0.274	0.647
	(2.73)**	(4.52)**	(6.54)**	(5.19)**	(7.04)**
LIBOR—Source country interest rate	0.047	0.024	0.020	0.019	0.034
	(10.80)**	(16.82)**	(13.97)**	(13.99)**	(15.73)**
Destination country interest rate—LIBOR	−0.017	−0.014	−0.008	−0.007	0.014
	(5.65)**	(9.60)**	(5.28)**	(4.90)**	(4.48)**
Control on bond or other debt instruments (inflow)	−0.433	−0.453	−0.406	−0.417	−0.121
	(6.11)*	(11.28)**	(10.31)**	(10.71)**	(1.37)

(continued)

Table 9.13   (continued)

	(1) Full Sample	(2) Full Sample	(3) Full Sample	(4) Exclude U.S. and Japan	(5) Full Sample
Control on bond or other debt instruments (outflow)	-0.946 (10.09)**	-0.914 (20.55)**	-0.807 (18.41)**	-0.760 (17.70)**	-1.505 (21.38)**
Reserves/GDP—source country	2.186 (8.36)**				
Reserves/GDP—destination country	-0.785 (3.56)**				
Asia	-0.044 (0.16)	0.937 (6.07)**	0.745 (4.92)**	1.137 (7.31)**	0.845 (4.27)**
EU15	3.555 (22.29)**	4.047 (46.47)**	3.492 (39.21)**	3.653 (41.94)**	2.867 (25.18)**
Latin America	0.101 (0.51)	0.463 (4.13)**	0.257 (2.34)*	0.225 (2.09)*	0.472 (2.21)*
Constant	-20.389 (27.10)**	-22.934 (58.51)**	-17.898 (39.84)**	-15.358 (33.35)**	-23.678 (22.57)**
Observations	3,387	10,654	10,654	10,220	4,501
R-squared	0.64	0.60	0.62	0.62	0.61

Note: Absolute value of *t* statistics in parentheses.

*Significant at 5%

**Significant at 1%

that distance is picking up something besides information communicated through these channels.

8. One possibility is that distance is simply a stand-in for the additional difficulty of investing across time zones. Insofar as claims on countries are traded primarily in their own time zones, portfolio managers and others may find it inconvenient to get up in the middle of the night to check market conditions and transact. Those impressed by the ease of obtaining information on far distant markets in the internet age may be inclined toward this alternative interpretation. We therefore experimented with a measure of the number of time zones separating the source and destination markets (see table 9.13). When this is substituted for distance in our basic specifications, it is again negative and significant (not surprisingly, as distance and time zone differences are positively correlated). But when we include both distance and time zone differences, the former is still significantly negative, as before, while the latter is not positive and significant. It would appear, in other words, that distance is not simply a proxy for time zone differences. The positive coefficient on the latter appears to be capturing a tendency for investors to prefer transactions with countries to their east and west rather than to their north or south, although why this should be the case remains an open question.[45]

9.6 Connections with Other Aspects of Financial Development

In this section we consider further variables and specifications designed to shed light on the impact of other aspects of financial development on bond market integration.

We first ask whether stock and bond markets are substitutes or complements. We start by adding the value of listed companies in the source and destination countries as a way of capturing the depth of their financial markets. Both variables enter positively (table 9.14), but it is the size of stock markets in the source (investing) country that seems to matter. This may indicate that these countries have an active institutional investor community inclined to take positions in the securities issued by foreign countries. We attempt to provide more direct evidence on this in the following.

We also ask, again following up on our previous work, whether having a large and well-developing banking system encourages or discourages efforts to place bonds with foreign investors. For both the source and destination countries, domestic credit provided by the banking sector as a share of GDP is positive, suggesting that a large and active banking system encourages foreign participation in domestic bond markets. This is the

---

45. In particular, this result is not being driven by the inclusion of the major financial centers (the United States, United Kingdom, and Japan) in the sample. The results are largely the same when we exclude them from the sample (see table 9.13).

Table 9.14   Financial development: Recipient country random effects

	(1)	(2)	(3)	(4)
log of GDP—source country	0.317	0.336	0.326	0.418
	(28.42)**	(19.75)**	(28.13)**	(28.51)**
log of GDP—destination country	0.560	0.648	0.605	0.726
	(20.24)**	(17.96)**	(21.28)**	(16.13)**
log of distance	−0.673	−0.664	−0.664	−0.834
	(24.14)**	(20.25)**	(23.36)**	(24.91)**
Land border dummy	0.175	0.228	0.178	0.074
	(1.71)	(2.04)*	(1.72)	(0.64)
Common Language Dummy	0.271	0.431	0.288	0.273
	(5.46)**	(6.39)**	(5.62)**	(4.09)**
Control on bond transactions (inflow)	−0.239	−0.241	−0.249	−0.306
	(2.77)**	(2.28)*	(2.90)**	(2.67)**
Control on bond transactions (outflow)	−0.683	−0.840	−0.724	−0.876
	(17.20)**	(15.66)**	(17.75)**	(16.89)**
LIBOR—Source country interest rate	0.012	0.015	0.008	0.019
	(9.48)**	(9.94)**	(6.10)**	(7.53)**
Destination country interest rate—LIBOR	−0.005	−0.004	−0.005	−0.003
	(1.53)	(0.96)	(1.51)	(0.43)
Size of Banking Sector—source country	0.009	0.012	0.009	0.010
	(26.04)**	(24.73)**	(23.40)**	(21.17)**
Size of Banking Sector—destination country	0.005	0.005	0.005	0.003
	(4.78)**	(4.32)**	(4.69)**	(2.07)*
Bank Concentration Index—source country		−0.325		
		(2.31)*		
Bank Concentration Index—destination country		−0.224		
		(0.80)		
Share of public bank assets—source country			−0.013	
			(9.28)**	
Share of public bank assets—destination country			−0.007	
			(3.65)**	
Size of Stock Market—source country				0.008
				(19.41)**
				0.001
				(0.59)
Asia	0.692	0.539	0.736	0.121
	(4.73)**	(3.37)**	(4.98)**	(0.77)
EU15	3.015	2.752	2.932	2.513
	(33.99)**	(28.35)**	(32.70)**	(26.20)**
Latin America	0.042	0.275	0.160	−0.201
	(0.39)	(2.29)*	(1.46)	(1.25)
Constant	−15.371	−18.222	−16.542	−21.137
	(21.24)**	(17.70)**	(22.11)**	(18.21)**
Observations	10,557	7,553	10,102	7,038
Number of Destination Country	132	89	124	85
R2-overall	0.64	0.65	0.65	0.65
R2-within	0.46	0.51	0.47	0.57
R2-between	0.82	0.84	0.85	0.82
Breusch-Pagan LM Test for Random Effects	16,397.08	9,351.59	11,799.28	10,667.40
Prob > Chi2	0.00	0.00	0.00	0.00

Note: Absolute value of z statistics in parentheses.

*Significant at 5%

**Significant at 1%

same thing found in our previous study on the size of domestic bond markets. There we suggested a number of reasons why this might be so. Banks are producers of information about conditions in financial markets and about the characteristics of financial instruments that may be particularly valuable to foreign investors. They provide underwriting services for domestic issuers, advising the issuer on the terms and timing of the offer. They provide bridge finance in the period when the marketing of bonds is still underway. They provide distribution channels for government bonds and form an important part of the primary dealer network. Their institutional support may also be conducive to secondary-market liquidity. Finally and most directly, banks owing to their relatively large size can be major issuers of bonds themselves.

Conversely, there is the fear that an inefficient banking system may hinder bond market development and participation, and that an imperfectly competitive system, in which banks have significant market power, may allow them to use their incumbency advantage to hinder the advance of securitization and disintermediation.[46] We therefore constructed measures of the concentration of the banking system in both the source and destination countries (as a Herfindahl-Hirschman index of commercial bank assets, using data from Bankscope—thus, a higher value indicates greater concentration). Here, measures for both the source and destination countries enter negatively as expected, although the signs and levels of statistical significance are sensitive to what control variables are included. We similarly added the share of bank assets accounted for by public-sector banks as an additional measure of banking sector efficiency.[47] Again, this enters in the expected fashion (negatively). It suggests interpreting this set of results in terms of the negative impact of a relatively inefficient banking system on various aspects of bond market development, more than in terms of strategic behavior by banks with market power.

While our other results remain unchanged, the negative coefficient on cross-holdings within Latin America now goes to zero even without the addition of measures of the quality of institutions.[48] Borensztein, Eichengreen, and Panizza (2006a) show that Latin America generally looks better in terms of other dimensions of bond market development when one controls for the underdevelopment of the region's financial system.[49] We

---

46. They may do so by limiting access to the payment system and by supporting the maintenance of regulations that increase the cost of underwriting and issuance (Schinasi and Smith 1998; Rajan and Zingales 2003; Eichengreen and Luengnaruemitchai 2004).

47. We compute country-level public bank assets by summing assets of commercial banks with a share of public ownership of more than 50 percent, using the data from Micco, Panizza, and Yañez (2004).

48. Sometimes we even get a significantly positive, albeit small, coefficient.

49. Another way of putting the point is that the region's bond markets are underdeveloped for the same reasons that the rest of the region's financial system is underdeveloped (those reasons having to do with the institutional variables that also caused the coefficients for intra-Latin American cross holdings to go to zero in section 9.4 above).

find the same thing here. Note that institutional (and other) factors stunting the development of the banking system do not appear to be what is holding back bond market integration in Asia (the coefficients on the dummy variable for intra-Asian cross holdings is little different than before).

9.7   The Composition of the Investor Base

Another approach to analyzing the importance of institutional factors is to make use of the fact that the CPIS reports data by type of institutional investor (banks, insurance companies, and mutual funds). East Asia and other regions are making considerable efforts to cultivate the participation of institutional investors in their bond markets. We can use the CPIS data to analyze the importance of these agents for cross-border investment both within the region and globally.

In table 9.15 we run three parallel regressions for the three categories of holders—banks, insurance companies, and mutual funds—estimating them by seemingly unrelated regression to capitalize on the correlation of disturbance terms across types of holders for given country pairs. These results should be interpreted cautiously, since the sample size is now considerably smaller than before. (There turn out to be a non-negligible number of empty cells when we disaggregate by type of investor.)

The results show that the basic gravity variables are well behaved (virtually without exception the signs remain the same as before). When we turn to the dummy variables for intraregional cross holdings, the comparison of Asia and Europe is particularly interesting. For banks, insurance companies, and mutual funds alike, we get large positive coefficients for intraregional positions in bond markets in Europe. In Asia, however, we get a positive coefficient for insurance companies but a strongly negative coefficient for mutual funds. This points to the development and behavior of the mutual fund industry as a potential constraint on bond market development in the region. We want to be careful here and to reiterate the provisional nature of these findings, since we have information on the foreign asset positions of mutual funds for only a limited number of Asian countries. Still, the results appear to make sense; in a number of Asian countries assets under management by insurance companies remain significant larger than those under management by mutual funds. Total assets under management by mutual funds are of roughly the same size relative to GDP in East Asia and Latin America (IMF 2005). Despite the fact that Latin American financial markets are relatively underdeveloped along a number of other dimensions, regulators there have taken aggressive steps to encourage the participation of institutional investors, mutual funds, and pension funds in particular.[50] But, in both regions, cross-border investment by mutual funds

50. Again, see Borensztein, Eichengreen, and Panizza (2006a).

Table 9.15 Investor Base Equations

	Destination RE			Destination FE			SUR		
	(1) Banks	(2) Insurance	(3) Mutual Funds	(4) Banks	(5) Insurance	(6) Mutual Funds	(7) Banks	(8) Insurance	(9) Mutual Funds
log of GDP—source country	0.927	0.692	0.857	0.927	0.703	0.847	0.927	0.681	0.881
	(36.38)**	(25.08)**	(28.04)**	(36.26)**	(25.40)**	(27.50)**	(26.30)**	(21.68)**	(26.70)**
log of GDP—destination country	0.666	0.648	0.530	0.077	0.332	-1.825	0.739	0.734	0.564
	(10.82)**	(11.62)**	(10.10)**	(0.07)	(0.29)	(1.33)	(21.80)**	(24.28)**	(17.79)**
log of distance	-0.391	0.094	-0.308	-0.382	0.139	-0.346	-0.246	-0.072	-0.266
	(6.35)**	(1.37)	(4.06)**	(5.87)**	(1.91)	(4.14)**	(3.17)**	(1.04)	(3.66)**
Land border dummy	0.441	0.346	0.110	0.442	0.416	0.076	0.349	0.114	0.168
	(2.47)*	(1.77)	(0.47)	(2.46)*	(2.12)*	(0.32)	(1.28)	(0.47)	(0.65)
Common Language Dummy	0.644	0.503	0.061	0.662	0.502	0.030	0.538	0.375	0.075
	(5.50)**	(4.35)**	(0.44)	(5.60)**	(4.29)**	(0.22)	(3.45)**	(2.69)**	(0.51)
Control on bond transactions (inflow)	-0.241	-0.403	-0.192	-0.182	0.044	0.152	-0.359	-0.570	-0.258
	(1.46)	(2.60)**	(1.25)	(0.62)	(0.14)	(0.43)	(3.29)**	(5.86)**	(2.53)*
Control on bond transactions (outflow)	-1.380	-1.409	-1.073	-1.389	-1.457	-1.073	-1.198	-1.257	-1.140
	(16.75)**	(17.32)**	(10.11)**	(16.72)**	(17.75)**	(9.90)**	(9.50)**	(11.17)**	(9.65)**
Bond Returns—source country	0.044	0.041	0.048	0.046	0.045	0.049	0.061	0.047	0.056
	(2.03)*	(2.16)*	(2.03)*	(2.07)*	(2.33)*	(2.08)*	(2.28)*	(1.97)*	(2.24)*
Bond Returns—destination country	0.043	0.047	0.054	0.047	0.034	0.056	0.075	0.097	0.055
	(1.95)	(2.20)*	(2.15)*	(2.01)*	(1.47)	(1.99)*	(2.88)**	(4.17)**	(2.23)*
Correlation of Bond Returns	1.067	2.302	0.659	1.063	2.410	0.688	0.323	1.918	0.562
	(5.49)**	(10.98)**	(2.70)**	(5.41)**	(11.33)**	(2.74)**	(1.15)	(7.66)**	(2.14)*

(continued)

Table 9.15   (continued)

	Destination RE			Destination FE			SUR		
	(1) Banks	(2) Insurance	(3) Mutual Funds	(4) Banks	(5) Insurance	(6) Mutual Funds	(7) Banks	(8) Insurance	(9) Mutual Funds
Volatility of Bilateral Exchange Rates	-0.039	-0.016	-0.067	-0.043	-0.002	-0.067	-0.080	-0.077	-0.070
	(1.99)*	(0.83)	(2.73)**	(2.08)*	(0.12)	(2.49)*	(3.20)**	(3.47)**	(2.99)**
Asia	0.330	0.652	-1.075	0.396	0.841	-1.014	0.064	0.265	-1.334
	(1.32)	(2.36)*	(3.24)**	(1.55)	(2.99)**	(2.96)**	(0.18)	(0.84)	(4.01)**
EU15	2.244	2.676	1.739	2.272	2.578	1.771	2.802	2.697	1.705
	(10.76)**	(11.61)**	(7.08)**	(10.54)**	(10.74)**	(6.67)**	(10.59)**	(11.42)**	(6.88)**
Latin America	-0.588	0.390	-0.207	-0.614	0.540	-0.428	0.131	0.162	0.062
	(2.56)*	(1.74)	(0.84)	(2.59)**	(2.30)*	(1.62)	(0.49)	(0.67)	(0.24)
Constant	-35.908	-33.980	-31.487	-20.726	-26.616	29.997	-39.148	-34.300	-33.245
	(19.81)**	(19.26)**	(18.12)**	(0.74)	(0.91)	(0.84)	(26.21)**	(25.74)**	(23.78)**
Observations	2,517	1,749	1,509	2,517	1,749	1,509	1,351	1,351	1,351
Number of Destination Country	52	52	52	52	52	52			
R-squared	0.81	0.83	0.73	0.62	0.65	0.58	0.68	0.72	0.63

Note: Absolute value of t statistics in parentheses.

*Significant at 5%

**Significant at 1%

continues to be hindered by a dearth of appropriate assets.[51] Note that the Asian Bond Fund, by creating a set of passively managed index funds of regional bonds, is designed to address precisely this problem.[52]

9.8   Conclusions and Policy Implications

The development of bond markets can be gauged in a number of ways. In this chapter we have concentrated on the international dimension. We used data on the extent to which residents of one country hold the bonds of issuers resident in another as a measure of financial integration or interrelatedness, asking how Asia compares with Europe and Latin America, and with the base case in which the purchaser and issuer of the bonds reside in different regions. It is no surprise that Europe is head and shoulders above other regions in terms of financial integration. More interesting is that Asia already seems to have made some progress on this front compared to Latin America and the world as a whole. The contrast with Latin America is largely explained by stronger creditor and investor rights, more expeditious and less costly contract enforcement, and greater transparency that lead to larger and better developed financial systems in Asia, something that is conducive to foreign participation in local markets and to intraregional cross holdings of Asian bonds generally. Further results based on a limited sample suggest that one factor holding back investment in foreign bonds in East Asia may be limited geographical diversification by mutual funds, in turn reflecting a dearth of appropriate assets. Asian Bond Fund 2, by creating a passively managed portfolio of local currency bonds potentially attractive to mutual fund managers and investors, may help to relax this constraint.

We also find evidence that cross-holdings are heavily driven by financial conditions in the investing country, which suggests that bond market conditions could adjust abruptly for reasons having nothing to do with policies in the borrowing economy. Our results also indicate that bondholders are attracted to the securities of countries whose returns co-vary with their own, suggesting return chasing rather than diversification behavior. These are reasons for skepticism that the development of bond markets is a panacea for stabilizing capital flows.

51. A problem that is compounded by the existence of restrictive covenants that limit the classes of assets in which funds can invest.
52. As noted above, Asian Bond Fund 2 has two components: a $1 billion central bank reserve pool to be overseen by professional managers for local bond allocation, and a $1 billion index unit designed to list on eight stock exchanges beginning with Hong Kong. The regional index is designed to provide a benchmark structure for tracking pan-Asian performance as well as facilitating one-stop entry for retail and institutional buyers in particular.

Appendix A

Table 9A.1 **List of Participants in CPIS**

	2001	2002	2003		2001	2002	2003
Argentina	1	1	1	Kazakhstan	1	1	1
Aruba	1	1	1	Korea, Republic of	1	1	1
Australia	1	1	1	Lebanon	1	1	1
Austria	1	1	1	Luxembourg	1	1	1
Bahamas, The	1	1	1	Macao SAR of China	1	1	1
Bahrain	1	0	0	Malaysia	1	1	1
Barbados	0	0	1	Malta	1	1	1
Belgium	1	1	1	Mauritius	1	1	1
Bermuda	1	1	1	Mexico	0	0	1
Brazil	1	1	1	Netherlands	1	1	1
Bulgaria	1	1	1	Netherlands Antilles	1	1	1
Canada	1	1	1	New Zealand	1	1	1
Cayman Islands	1	1	1	Norway	1	1	1
Chile	1	1	1	Pakistan	0	1	1
Colombia	1	1	1	Panama	1	1	1
Costa Rica	1	1	1	Philippines	1	1	1
Cyprus	1	1	1	Poland	1	1	1
Czech Republic	1	1	1	Portugal	1	1	1
Denmark	1	1	1	Romania	1	1	1
Egypt	1	1	1	Russian Federation	1	1	1
Estonia	1	1	1	Singapore	1	1	1
Finland	1	1	1	Slovak Republic	1	1	1
France	1	1	1	South Africa	1	1	1
Germany	1	1	1	Spain	1	1	1
Greece	1	1	1	Sweden	1	1	1
Guernsey	1	1	1	Switzerland	1	1	1
Hong Kong SAR of China	1	1	1	Thailand	1	1	1
Hungary	1	1	1	Turkey	1	1	1
Iceland	1	1	1	Ukraine	1	1	1
Indonesia	1	1	1	United Kingdom	1	1	1
Ireland	1	1	1	United States	1	1	1
Isle of Man	1	1	1	Uruguay	1	1	1
Israel	1	1	1	Vanuatu	1	1	1
Italy	1	1	1	Venezuela	1	1	1
Japan	1	1	1	Total	67	67	69
Jersey	1	1	1				

Appendix B

Table 9B.1   Data Description

Variable	Description	Source
GDP	GDP at current US$	World Bank's WDI
GDP per capita	GDP per capita at current US$	World Bank's WDI
GDP, PPP	GDP adjusted for purchasing power parity	World Bank's WDI
Distance	Distance between countries (in logs)	Andrew Rose's web site
Land border dummy	Dummy variable = 1 if the two countries share a land border	Andrew Rose's web site
Common Language Dummy	Dummy variable = 1 if the two countries have a common language	Andrew Rose's web site
Time zone difference	Time difference between financial centers of the countries in hours (in June). The variable ranges from 0 to 12.	www.worldtimezone.com
Control on bond transactions (inflow)	Dummy variable = 1 if there is a restriction on inflow transaction of bonds or other debt securities	IMF's Annual Report on Exchange Arrangements and Exchange Restrictions
Control on bond transactions (outflow)	Dummy variable = 1 if there is a restriction on outflow transaction of bonds or other debt securities	IMF's Annual Report on Exchange Arrangements and Exchange Restrictions
LIBOR	London Interbank Offer Rate	IMF's International Financial Statistics
Interest rate	Treasury bill rate	IMF's International Financial Statistics
Exchange Rate	Bilateral (crossed) exchange rate	IMF's International Financial Statistics
Historical Bond Returns	Total bond return index—see text	Bloomberg
Size of Banking Sector	Bank credit to private sector	IMF's International Financial

(*continued*)

Table 9B.1 (continued)

Variable	Description	Source
Size of Stock Market	Stock market capitalization	IMF's International Financial Statistics
Law and Order Risk	Political risk rating component on law and order (higher values means lower risks)	International Country Risk Guide
Corruption Risk	Political risk rating component on corruption (higher values means lower risks)	International Country Risk Guide
Bureaucratic Quality	Political risk rating component on quality of bureaucracy (higher values means lower risks)	International Country Risk Guide
Investment Profile	Political risk rating component on assessment of investment risks (higher values means lower risks)	International Country Risk Guide
Sovereign Credit Ratings	Numerical variable ranging from 0–20; 0 is equivalent to the rating "default" and 20 is AAA	Standard & Poor's
Legal origin	Dummy variables identifying the legal origin of the company law or commercial code of each country. The five origins are English, French, German, Nordic, and Socialist.	Djankov, McLiesh, and Shleifer (2005)
Creditor's rights	Index of creditor rights, ranging from 0 (weak) to 4 (strong creditor rights)	Djankov, McLiesh, and Shleifer
Contract enforcement	The number of days to resolve a payment dispute through courts	Djankov, McLiesh, and Shleifer
Share of public bank assets	Ratio of public commercial banks' assets to total banking assets	Micco, Panizza, and Yañez (2004) and Bankscope
Bank concentration	HHI index of commercial bank assets	Bankscope
de facto exchange rate regime	Reinhart-Rogoff de facto exchange rate regime classification	Eichengreen and Razo-Garcia (2006)
Phone traffics	Minutes of incoming and outgoing telephone traffics	International Telecommunication Union
Phone costs	Cost of international call (US$ per 3 minutes in peak hours to the U.S.A.; for the U.S.A. to Europe)	World Competitiveness Yearbook

References

Aviat, A., and N. Coeurdacier. 2005. The geography of trade in goods and asset holdings. CNRS-EHESS-PNPC-ENS. Unpublished Manuscript.

Borensztein, E., B. Eichengreen, and U. Panizza. 2006a. Building bond markets in Latin America. Inter-American Development Bank. Unpublished Manuscript, March.

———. 2006b. Debt instruments and policies for the new millennium: New markets and new opportunities. Inter-American Development Bank. Unpublished Manuscript, March.

Buch, C. 2000a. Are banks different? Evidence from international data. Kiel Working Paper no. 1012. Kiel, Germany: Kiel Institute of World Economics.

———. 2000b. Information or regulation: What is driving the international activities of commercial banks? Kiel Working Paper no. 1011. Kiel, Germany: Kiel Institute of World Economics.

Buchanan, M. 2005. Emerging markets and the global economy—Hysteresis not hysteria. *Global Economics Weekly,* 30 November.

Calvo, G. 1999. Contagion in emerging markets: When Wall Street is a carrier. University of Maryland, Department of Economics. Unpublished Manuscript, May.

Calvo, G., L. Liederman, and C. Reinhart. 1994. Capital inflows and real exchange rate appreciation in Latin America. *IMF Staff Papers* 40:108–51. Washington, DC: International Monetary Fund.

Chinn, M., and H. Ito. 2005. What matters for financial development? Capital controls, institutions, and interactions. NBER Working Paper no. 11370. Cambridge, MA: National Bureau of Economic Research.

Coeurdacier, N., and S. Guibaud. 2005. International equity holdings and stock return correlations: Does diversification matter at all for portfolio choice? PSE-ENS-EHESS. Unpublished Manuscript, July.

De la Torre, A., and S. Schmukler. 2004. *Whither Latin American Capital Markets?* Washington, DC: The World Bank.

Djankov, S., C. McLiesh, and A. Shleifer. 2005. Private credit in 129 countries. NBER Working Paper no. 11078. Cambridge, MA: National Bureau of Economic Research, January.

Dooley, M., and P. Garber. 2005. Is it 1958 or 1968? Three notes on the longevity of the revived Bretton Woods system. *Brookings Papers on Economic Activity* 1:147–87.

Eichengreen, B., E. Borensztein, and U. Panizza. 2006. A tale of two markets: Bond market development in Latin America and East Asia. Hong Kong Institute for Monetary Research. Occasional Paper no. 3, October.

Eichengreen, B., and D. Irwin. The role of history in bilateral trade flows. NBER Working Paper no. 5565. Cambridge, MA: National Bureau of Economic Research, May.

Eichengreen, B., and P. Luengnaruemitchai. 2004. Why doesn't Asia have bigger bond markets? NBER Working Paper no. 10576. Cambridge, MA: National Bureau of Economic Research.

Eichengreen, B., and Y. C. Park. 2005. Why has there been less financial integration in East Asia than in Europe? In *A new financial market structure for East Asia,* eds. Y. C. Park, T. Ito, and Y. Wang, 84–103. Cheltenham, England: Edward Elgar.

Eichengreen, B., and R. Razo-Garcia. 2006. The International Monetary System in the last and next 20 years. *Economic Policy* 47 (July): 393–442.

Faruqee, H., S. Li, and I. K. Yan. 2004. The determinants of international portfolio holdings and home bias. IMF Working Paper no. WP/04/34. Washington, DC: International Monetary Fund., February.

Ferrucci, G. 2004. Understanding capital flows to emerging market economies. *Financial Stability Review* (June): 89–97.

Ghosh, S., and H. Wolf. 2000. Is there a curse of location? Spatial determinants of capital flows to emerging markets. In *Capital flows and the emerging economies,* ed. Sebastian Edwards, 137–58. Chicago: University of Chicago Press.

Goldstein, M., and P. Turner. 2004. *Controlling currency mismatches in emerging market economies: An alternative to the original sin hypothesis.* Washington, DC: Institute for International Economics.

Inter-American Development Bank. 2005. *Unlocking credit: The quest for deep and stable bank lending.* Washington, DC: Inter-American Development Bank.

International Monetary Fund. 2005. Development of corporate bond markets in emerging market economies. *Global financial stability report,* 103–41. Washington, DC: International Monetary Fund.

Izquierdo, A., J. Morriset, and M. Olarreaga. 2003. Information diffusion in international markets. Working Paper no. 488, Research Department. Washington, DC: Inter-American Development Bank.

Jeanneau, S., and M. Micu. 2002. Determinants of international bank lending to emerging market countries. BIS Working Paper no. 112, June.

Kawai, M., and L.-G. Liu. 2001. Determinants of international commercial bank loans to developing countries. University of Tokyo and Asian Development Bank Institute. Unpublished Manuscript, June.

Kim, S., J.-W. Lee, and K. Shin. 2005. Regional and global financial integration in East Asia. Korea University, Department of Economics. Unpublished Manuscript.

La Porta, R., F. Lopez-de-Silanes, A. Shleifer, and R. Vishny. 1999. Investor protection: Origins, consequences and reform. NBER Working Paper no. 7429. Washington, DC: National Bureau of Economic Research, December.

Lane, P. R., and G. M. Milesi-Ferretti. 2004. International investment patterns. CEPR Discussion Paper no. 4499. London: Centre for Economic Policy Research.

Lui, L.-G. (2005). Impact of financial services trade liberalization on capital flows: The case of China's banking sector. Hong Kong Monetary Authority. Unpublished Manuscript.

Papaioannou, E. 2005. What drives international bank flows? Politics, institutions and other determinants. Working Paper no. 437. Frankfurt: ECB.

Martin, P., and H. Rey. 2004. Financial super-markets: Size matters for asset trade. *Journal of International Economics* 64:335–61.

McCauley, R., and G. Jiang. 2004. Diversifying with Asian local currency bonds. *BIS Quarterly Review,* September: 51–66.

Micco, A., U. Panizza, and M. Yañez. 2004. Bank ownership and performance. IADB Working Paper no. 518. Washington, DC: Inter-American Development Bank.

Portes, R., and H. Rey. 2005. The determinants of cross-border equity flows. *Journal of International Economics* 65:269–95.

Rajan, R., and L. Zingales. 2003. Banks and markets: The changing character of European finance. NBER Working Paper no. 9595. Washington, DC: National Bureau of Economic Research.

Reinhart, C. M., and K. S. Rogoff, (2002) . The modern history of exchange rate arrangements: A reinterpretation. NBER Working Paper no. 8963. Washington, DC: National Bureau of Economic Research.

Rose, A., and M. Spiegel. 2004. A gravity model of sovereign lending: Trade, default and credit. *IMF Staff Papers* 51 (special issue): 50–63. Washington, DC: International Monetary Fund.

Schinasi, G., and T. Smith. 1998. Fixed income markets in the United States, Europe and Japan: Some lessons for emerging markets. IMF Working Paper no. 98–173. Washington, DC: International Monetary Fund.

Comment   Eiji Ogawa

This chapter focuses on an international aspect of the Asian bond markets to investigate how capital flows for Asia in comparison with other regions such as Europe and Latin America. In this chapter, the authors assessed bond markets as a conduit for capital flows. They have already written a paper that focused on a domestic aspect of the Asian bond markets. This chapter is complementary to that previous study.

The monetary authorities of East Asian countries have recognized the underlying problems caused by a double overdependence on the banking sector in their financial systems and on the U.S. dollar in their currency systems since East Asian economies experienced the Asian Currency Crisis in 1997. We have the problem of how efficiently we should match savings with investments within East Asia through regional financial markets, although there are both an abundance of savings in East Asia and profitable investment opportunities in East Asian emerging market countries. One solution should be to establish and activate regional bond markets in East Asia.

The monetary authorities of East Asian countries are actually promoting the Asian Bond Market Initiative, that is, a regional financial cooperation to establish Asian bond markets in East Asia. Recent discussions of the Asian Bond Market Initiative have focused on the choice of denomination currency and the credit guarantee and rating agency. Ito (2003) proposed an Asian bond designed to be a fund of the local currency denominated bonds issued by governments of East Asian countries. However, as an initiative of the EMEAP, the Asian Bond Fund (ABF) was launched in its first version (ABF1) in June 2003 as a basket of U.S. dollar denominated bonds issued by Asian sovereign and quasi-sovereign entities in EMEAP economies (excluding Australia, Japan and New Zealand). The EMEAP has worked to extend the ABF concept to bonds denominated in local currencies and has announced the launch of the second stage of ABF (ABF2) in December 2004.

In this chapter, the authors used bilateral data to analyze the importance of a range of factors determining nonresident holdings of a country's

Eiji Ogawa is a professor in the Graduate School of Commerce and Management, Hitotsubashi University.

bonds as well as analyzing the determinants of holdings across regions. They used the gravity model to analyze determinants of cross-border capital flows. They used the log of bilateral international portfolio holdings of long-term debt securities as the dependent variable. The data came from the Coordinated Portfolio Investment Survey (CPIS) compiled by the IMF for the years 2001–2003. The gravity model, augmented by various control variables used in the literature, were estimated.

The authors obtained interesting analytical results from the estimation of the gravity model. Country size matters in determining capital flows. Distance between countries has negative effects on capital flows. The interest rate variables in source countries have stronger effects on capital flows. Capital controls on bond transactions have negative effect on capital flows. The volatility of the bilateral exchange rates has negative effects on capital flows. As for the Asia dummy, it enters with a positive coefficient. However, this coefficient goes to zero when control variables of "size of stock market" are included. Measures of the quality of institutions in the destination country are important in explaining capital flows. Insurance companies and mutual funds have asymmetric effects on capital flows in Asia. The former has a positive effect while the latter has a negative effect.

I have five comments for the authors.

The first comment is related to using the gravity model to analyze determinants of capital flows. The gravity model is used to analyze determinants of bilateral capital flows in a framework where both sizes of the two economies and a distance between the two economies basically determine trade volumes between them. It is supposed that investors have only options of investing into their home and one foreign country. Rather, investors make international portfolio investments to diversify foreign assets for risk management. I question whether the gravity model is consistent with the international portfolio investments into several foreign countries. For example, assuming a very simple case where a portfolio share of the international portfolio investments to one country is a constant, total size of investments from one country to the rest of the world should have effects on capital flows from one country to another.

The second comment is related to calculation of bond returns. Capital flows are in theory affected by expected return differentials that are the interest rate differentials plus the expected rate of change in exchange rates. It seems to be inconsistent with the chapter's investigation of whether interest rate variables work as push factors or pull factors when determining capital flows. In addition, the expected rate of change in exchange rates should be considered when analyzing the effect of bond returns on capital flows. The authors should take into account the expected rate of change in exchange rates when calculating the bond returns.

The third comment is related to the Asia dummy. The Asia dummy refers to capital flows from one Asian country to the other Asian countries. The authors used the Asia dummy to investigate characteristics of the intraregional capital flows in Asia. The dummy is an intercept dummy. They can use coefficient dummies by set cross-terms that are products of the Asia dummy and explanatory variables. They should use cross terms such as the Asia dummy times the size of stock market—source country and stock market—destination country to analyze sensitivity of Asian countries to the size of the stock market. Thus, they can use coefficient dummies to obtain more fruitful characterization of the Asian intraregional bond transactions, which is related to Asian bond market issues.

The fourth comment is related to the analytical result of negative factors on the Asian mutual funds' investments into the Asian region. Given that the Asia dummy refers to capital flows from one Asian country to the other Asian countries, the result does not always imply both that the Asian mutual funds' investments are significantly smaller and that their investments into the Asia are significantly smaller. This is why Asian mutual funds are significantly smaller, because household's savings tend to go into less risky financial instruments of banks and insurance companies. If this is true, the ABF 2 might not improve the situation, contrary to what the authors suggest. However, the ABF 2 is expected to stimulate investments into the Asia, especially local-currency denominated Asian bonds.

Lastly, I suggest the authors investigate effects on liquidity in bond markets on capital flows. Ogawa and Shimizu (2004) and Shimizu and Ogawa (2005) investigated advantages and disadvantages of choosing a common regional currency basket unit over an international currency as a denomination currency for bond issuers and foreign investors in terms of both foreign exchange risks and liquidity in the case of Asian bond market. Although the basket currency denominated bonds would contribute to decreasing the foreign exchange risks, bond issuers and investors may prefer the U.S. dollar denominated bonds to the currency basket denominated bonds as long as they care about liquidity rather than foreign exchange risks. The liquidity problem is key in fostering the regional bond market in Asia.

References

Ito, T. 2003. Construction of infrastructures for the development of regional bonds market. In *Financial Development and Integration in East Asia*, eds. C. Y. Ahn, T. Ito, M. Kawai, and Y. C. Park, 206–21. Korea Institute for International Economic Policy.

Ogawa, E., and J. Shimizu. 2004. Bonds issuers' trade-off for common currency basket denominated bonds in East Asia. *Journal of Asian Economics* 15:719–38.

Shimizu, J., and E. Ogawa. 2005. Risk properties of AMU denominated Asian bonds. *Journal of Asian Economics* 16:590–611.

10

Financial Liberalization under the WTO and Its Relationship with the Macro Economy

Lee-Rong Wang, Chung-Hua Shen, and
Ching-Yang Liang

10.1 Introduction

The effect of financial liberalization on growth has recently attracted a significant amount of attention. Financial liberalization, through giving banks and other financial intermediaries more freedom of action, results in resources being governed by the market mechanism and hence being more efficiently allocated. Three broad types of financial liberalization are discussed. One is concerned with lifting the restrictions on the domestic financial sector, which includes the deregulation of the interest rate, the exchange rate, allowing new financial instruments to be introduced, and encouraging mergers among financial institutions, to name but a few. Demirgüç-Kunt and Detragiache (2001) have chosen the deregulation of bank interest rates as the centerpiece of financial liberalization. Montes-Negret and Landa (2001) study the Mexican financial process.

The second broad liberalization concerns the opening up of the domestic market to international participants, that is, allowing the domestic market to be parallel to the international one. Claessens and Glaessner (1998) point out that internationalization has helped build more robust and efficient financial systems by introducing international practices and standards, by allowing more stable sources of funds, and by improving the quality, efficiency, and breadth of financial services. Claessens, Demirgüç-

Lee-Rong Wang is a research fellow in the Taiwan WTO Center at the Chung-Hua Institution for Economic Research. Chung-Hua Shen is a professor in the Department of Finance at National Taiwan University. Ching-Yang Liang is a Ph.D. student in the Department of Public Finance at National Chengchi University.

This paper was prepared for the NBER 17th Annual East Asian Seminar on Economics held at the Mauna Lani Bay Hotel, 68-1400 Mauna Lani Drive, Kohala, Hawaii on June 22–24, 2006.

Kunt, and Huizinga (2001) study the effects of foreign bank entry on the efficiency of domestic banks. The experiences of various countries seem to suggest that a foreign bank presence can facilitate increased competition, improve the allocation of credit, and help increase access to international capital markets. Henry (2000) and Beakers and Harvey (2000) show that the liberalization of equity markets, through a reduction in the cost of capital, leads to an increase in real economic growth on an annual basis.

The third approach is to construct a financial liberalization index on the basis of the World Trade Organization (WTO) commitments. The members of the *General Agreement on Tariffs and Trade* (GATT), the predecessor of the WTO,[1] commenced bilateral negotiations on services in 1994 and have started to submit liberalization commitments and schedules since then. Each member, in considering its own domestic situation, has progressively liberalized its trade in services according to these schedules.

There are twelve sectors covered in the services negotiation under the WTO; we focus particularly on the largest one, the financial services sector. For each subsector of financial services, each country promises three types of commitment: *unbound* (no commitment), *bound* (partial commitment), and *none* (full commitment). By employing the commitments data as of mid-1994, Hoekman (1995, 1996) uses values of 0, 0.5, and 1 to enumerate the above three kinds of commitments, with a higher number denoting a higher degree of liberalization. They use this frequency measures method to quantify the impediments to trade and investment in services, which are less transparent and more difficult to quantify.

The first purpose of this chapter is to extend and improve the method suggested by Hoekman (1995, 1996) in calculating the financial liberalization indices. However, we make several revisions. The first revision is concerned with covering the services supply mode[2] that deals with the movement/presence of natural persons and all sub-sectors listed in the Annex on Financial Services. The second revision is to employ weighting on four modes of services supply. The last revision, instead of unanimously giving a 0.5 score to the partial commitments as Hoekman (1995, 1996) and Hoekman and Primo Braga (1997) did, is intended to analyze in more detail the information involved within different degrees of liberalization and thus score further on the partial commitments.

---

1. The WTO began life on January 1, 1995, but its trading system is half a century older. Since 1948, the GATT has provided the rules for the system. The last and largest GATT round was the Uruguay Round, which lasted from 1986 to 1994 and led to the WTO's creation. Whereas the GATT dealt mainly with trade in goods, the WTO and its agreements now cover trade in services, in the context of the General Agreement on Trade in Services (GATS), and other areas.

2. The GATS distinguishes the ways in which services are supplied into four possible modes, which are listed as cross-border supply (Mode 1), consumption abroad (Mode 2), commercial presence (Mode 3), and the presence of natural persons (Mode 4). Section 10.2 of this chapter will further explain these modes.

The second purpose of this chapter is to study the effect of liberalization on economic growth. By employing our newly-constructed financial index, we investigate the effects of liberalization on economic growth. In the literature, the different spheres of liberalization are threefold, namely, trade, financial, and equity liberalization. For studies using the trade liberalization as the proxy for liberalization, Francois and Schuknecht (1999), who employ the openness in trade, find a strong positive relationship between growth and competition within the financial sector. Eschenbach, Francois, and Schuknecht (2000) also place emphasis on the procompetitive effects of trade in financial services. Since financial services are the nexus of the savings and accumulation mechanism that drives economic growth, they consider it appropriate to emphasize trade in services and growth. By working with a cross-country sample of ninety-three countries, Tornell, Westerman, and Martinez (2004) have recently found that trade liberalization enhances growth but that financial liberalization does not necessarily lead to more rapid growth, in large part because it is associated with risky capital flows, lending booms, and crises. With regard to financial liberalization, Demirgüç-Kunt and Detragiache (1998) find that financial liberalization has a very large and statistically significant effect on the probability of a banking crisis. Shen and Lee (2006), in using the liberalization dates suggested by Kaminsky and Reinhert (2002), find that the liberalization has little effect on the relationship between financial development and economic growth. Finally, for studies using equity liberalization, Henry (2000) reports that equity liberalization has preceded private investment booms in nine of eleven developed countries. Although they discuss a slightly different issue, Kawakatsu and Morey (1999) reject the hypothesis that market liberalization affects the economy. There is no research that uses the WTO liberalization index to study the same issue.

The remainder of this chapter is organized as follows. Section 10.2 introduces the history of WTO commitments and describes how we construct the financial liberalization index. Section 10.3 discusses some interesting patterns of the financial liberalization under the WTO. Section 10.4 describes the empirical models and data, while section 10.5 presents the empirical findings. Finally, section 10.6 summarizes the conclusions that are drawn.

10.2   WTO Commitments and the Liberalization Index for Financial Services

10.2.1   Introduction to WTO Commitments for Financial Services

The construction of a financial liberalization index in our chapter is based on the negotiation results within the WTO. The WTO requests that member countries negotiate with each other on the liberalization of trade in goods, trade in services, and trade-related intellectual property rights.[3] This chapter deals only with the second category, that is, trade in services. There are twelve sectors that are included in these services and we particularly focus on the financial services sector, which is the largest service sector in the context of the *General Agreement on Trade in Services* (GATS). Furthermore, this service sector can be categorized into two major subsectors, one being the *banking and other financial services* subsector and the other the *insurance and insurance-related services* subsector. In our chapter, the negotiation results within the WTO for both subsectors are taken into account when the financial liberalization index is constructed.

The GATS negotiations on trade in services have so far gone through two stages. The first stage started in 1994 and continued until 2000, whereas the second started in 2001 and extended through 2006. During the first period, the critical part of the GATS negotiations that was referred to as "specific commitments" in regard to the liberalization schedules, was submitted by the WTO members beginning in 1994.

After that, the first round of negotiations on financial services in the context of the GATS was concluded in December 1997 and became fully subject to multilateral trade rules. Some members, nevertheless, did not provide their liberalization schedules until 2000 for the sake of their domestic situation. Not only did the agreement consolidate the relatively open policies of industrial countries that account for much of the world trade in financial services, but it also evoked wide participation from both developing countries and countries in transition. The wide coverage of the WTO members is the reason why, in this chapter, we build the financial liberalization index based on the GATS commitments.

The next round of negotiations to further liberalize trade in services started March 28, 2001, when the WTO Council for Trade in Services adopted the *Guidelines and Procedures for the Negotiations* as the basis for continuing the negotiations. Participants were to submit requests and offers for specific commitments by certain deadlines. However, as the request and offer negotiations continued among WTO members, the contents of the specific commitments also continued to be updated until 2006. As a result, our data for financial liberalization and the coordinating macroeconomic data are classified into the two periods, as previously shown.

The GATS also distinguishes ways of categorizing supply into four possible modes, which are listed as cross-border supply (mode 1),[4] consump-

3. These three parts are stipulated under the General Agreement on Tariffs and Trade (GATT), the General Agreement on Trade in Services (GATS), and Trade Related Intellectual Property Rights (TRIPS), respectively.
4. Under the mode for cross-border supply, the services suppliers and consumers remain in their own domestic territories, while tackling the trading business between them via the Internet or through the use of other electronic tools, such as facsimiles.

tion abroad (mode 2),[5] commercial presence (mode 3),[6] and the movement of natural persons (mode 4). One example of financial services in mode 1 is buying overseas mutual funds via the Internet. Buying insurance in a foreign country when a person travels abroad is an example of mode 2. As for mode 3, the worldwide Citi-Group branch establishments would be a typical case. Sending intracorporate transferees to one specific branch is a mode 4. Basically, modes 1, 2, and 4 are all different forms of cross-border trade, whereas mode 3 generally involves investment (foreign direct investment) in the service-importing economy.

It is interesting to explore, at least to some degree, how the GATS commitments relate to actual liberalization measures in the real world. The extent of the new liberalization effected by GATS commitments on financial services is somewhat limited, with many members binding either at the level of their existing practices or at a level lower than their existing practices (PECC International Secretariat 2003). In the latter cases, GATS commitments (the de jure indication) were a misleading indicator of the extent to which liberalization had actually taken place (the de facto indicators). There are reasons for WTO members choosing to have this kind of situation. The WTO commitment schedule is legally binding for all members. Strict dispute settlement procedures will be initiated by members whenever their benefits are impeded once the commitment schedule is not followed by a certain member or members. To avoid the legal constraints mentioned above, some members would end up having their GATS commitments no more favorable than the real regulation.

Besides, recognizing the benefits of liberalizing trade in services has encouraged a number of economies, including some in the APEC region such as Korea, Singapore, and Taiwan, to undertake unilateral liberalization in this sector. Subsequent unilateral liberalization by some members has widened the gap between GATS commitments and actual measures. The credit for such autonomous liberalization is currently an important negotiating issue for those economies that have engaged in it (PECC International Secretariat 2003).

10.2.2   Construction of the Financial Liberalization Index

Our liberalization index is constructed by using the commitments of the four modes within various subsectors of financial services. As mentioned in the Introduction, three types of commitments, *unbound* (no commitment), *bound* (partial commitment), and *none* (full commitment), are promised by each country. Because the impediments to trade and invest-

5. Consumption abroad keeps services suppliers in their own domestic territory, while consumers move into the territory of the services suppliers and proceed to trade there.

6. Commercial presence keeps services consumers in their own domestic territory, while suppliers move into the territory of the consumers and proceed to trade there.

ment in services tend to be in the form of nontariff barriers (NTBs), which are less transparent and difficult to quantify, researchers often adopt the frequency measures method.[7] PECC (1995), Hoekman (1995, 1996), and Hoekman and Primo Braga (1997) are among the seminal studies to employ the frequency measures methodology to compile indices of services to measure the degree of restrictiveness or liberalization of trade in services. McGuire and Schuele (2000) also propose a restrictiveness index[8] for banking services and compile a list of nonprudential regulations on entry and operations for banking services from various sources. These sources include the GATS commitments, the information from APEC Individual Action Plans, WTO Trade Policy Reviews, and information provided by several countries to the IMF as a requirement for receiving standby credit facilities. Mattoo (1998, 2000) constructs commitment indices for the Second Protocol using a specific weighting scheme, considering the importance of modes (based on U.S. data) for 105 countries' market access commitments in banking (deposits and lending) and direct insurance (life and nonlife). Mattoo, Rathindran, and Subramanian (2006) present a financial index of openness to quantify the nature and extent of restrictions on international trade in financial services.

The estimates of the measures for the liberalization of services trade in the previous literature, however, contain several shortcomings. Our chapter revises the previously produced financial liberalization index in three respects. First, we cover mode 4 and all subsectors listed in the "Annex on Financial Services" of the GATS. Then we assign weights for the four modes. Finally, and most importantly, we score partial commitments, which are ignored in earlier works. These three major types of revisions are accounted for below.

First, our liberalization index covers mode 4, which is the movement of natural persons. Except for Hoekman (1995, 1996), McGuire and Schuele (2000), and Claessens and Glaessner (1998), who cover only some parts of mode 4, past studies typically do not take this mode into account.[9] The criteria for scoring the liberalization index and the categories for mode 4 are listed in table 10.1, where higher scores denote higher degrees of liberalization. The two extreme cases, "unbound" (no commitment) and "none" (full commitment), are assigned scores of 0 and 1, respectively. Partial commitments are here assigned scores from 0.25 to 0.75, depending on the respective degrees of openness as described in table 10.1.

---

7. This is also referred to as index methodology.
8. McGuire and Schuele (2000) use higher scores to denote higher degrees of restriction, whereas we use higher scores to denote higher degrees of liberalization. In other words, the restrictiveness index produced in McGuire and Schuele (2000) is similar to our liberalization index in terms of the concept, yet opposite in terms of the content's meaning.
9. For example, Barth, Caprio, and Levine (2001), Mattoo (1998, 2000), and Mattoo, Rathindran, and Subramanian (2006) do not take mode 4 into account.

Table 10.1   **Scoring liberalization index for M4**

The Criteria	Score
Unbound	0
(1) Only referring to general requirements for entry, including the economic need test (ENT) or making reference to laws and regulations	0.25
(2) Conditionally allowing the entry of 1~2 kinds of the above-mentioned natural persons	
(1) Unconditionally allowing the entry of 2 kinds of the above-mentioned natural persons	0.5
(2) Conditionally allowing the entry of 3~4 kinds of the above-mentioned natural persons	
Unconditionally allowing the entry of 4 kinds of the above-mentioned natural persons	0.75
None	1

Note: This paper computes these scores based on the classification summarized in the WTO document (JOB[03]/195), which describes frequently-used categories of natural persons included under mode 4 in the horizontal section of members' schedules of specific commitments. The four main categories are intracorporate transferees (ICT), business visitors (BV) and service salespersons (SS), contractual service suppliers (CSS) and other categories. CSS includes employees of juridical persons and independent professionals. Other categories contain graduate trainees and spouses and partners of ICT.

This chapter also takes into account all of the subsectors covered in the context of the GATS.[10] By contrast, Claessens and Glaessner (1998), Mattoo (1998, 2000), and McGuire and Schuele (2000)[11] do not cover the subsectors as completely as we do here.

The second revision concerns the weighting of the four modes. Most countries do not provide a precise identification of the patterns of trade based on different modes,[12] except the United States. Therefore, previous studies often use a simple-weighted average. By considering that commitments with heavier amounts trade should be assigned more weight, we therefore follow Mattoo's (1998, 2000) method to adopt the data from the *United States Financial Services Trade by Mode of Supply, 1994*. Mattoo (1998, 2000), however, does not include mode 4 and covers only parts of the subsectors.[13] We therefore make some revisions to his approach and present the final weight in table 10.2. After our revisions, the trade that takes place as a result of the commercial presence in the insurance subsector is about four times that generated through across-border trade. In banking

10. These subsectors are listed in the Annex on Financial Services of the GATS.
11. For instance, McGuire and Schuele (2000) cover only the banking subsector.
12. Maurer (2005) reported the weights for the four modes as 0.35, 0.12–0.15, 0.5, and 0.01–0.02, respectively. However, these figures are derived on an aggregated level and cover all of the service sectors.
13. Mattoo (1998, 2000) covers only life and nonlife insurance in the insurance subsector, and deposits and lending in the banking subsector, as shown in table 10.2.

Table 10.2   Comparison of weights among four modes in the financial sector

Mode	All Insurance and Insurance-Related Services			Banking and Other Financial Services		
	Mattoo (1998, 2000)			Mattoo (1998, 2000)		
	Life Services	Non-life Services	Weights adopted by the authors	Deposits Services	Lending Services	Weights adopted by the authors
Mode 1	0.12	0.20	0.18	0.12	0.20	0.24
Mode 2	0.03	0.05	0.045	0.03	0.05	0.06
Mode 3	0.85	0.75	0.75	0.85	0.75	0.6
Mode 4	—	—	0.025	—	—	0.1

Note: According to Article I of the GATS, the four modes of the supply of a service are defined as: Mode 1 (cross-border supply)—the supply of a service from the territory of one member into the territory of any other member; Mode 2 (consumption abroad)—the supply of a service in the territory of one member to the service consumer of any other member; Mode 3 (commercial presence)—the supply of a service by a service supplier of one member, through commercial presence in the territory of any other member; Mode 4 (the movement/presence of natural persons)—the supply of a service by a service supplier of one member, through the presence of natural persons of a member in the territory of any other member.

and securities services, the trade arising through the commercial presence is two and a half times that achieved through the cross-border trade.

Finally, partial commitments are scored. Due to the difficulty in judging how the presence of specific restrictions is to be evaluated, Hoekman (1995, 1996) assigned a score of 0.5 for each partial commitment. Although this method has its merits in that it is simple and straightforward, the information resulting from different degrees of liberalization has been lost. Mattoo (1998, 2000) adopts a slightly more sophisticated approach, but only handles the commitments in relation to mode 3. Qian (2000) and Valckx (2002) also adopt the same method. Furthermore, Valckx (2002) believes that the unbound feature is slightly better than a blank entry, and hence the score 0.05 is given instead of 0. Valckx (2002) also gives licensing subject to requirements a slightly higher score than discretionary licensing, in order to make a distinction between the two limitations. This chapter employs the formula proposed by Switzerland (TN/S/W/51, September 2005) to deal with this issue more delicately.

Our methodology of scoring partial commitments deserves description. As suggested by Switzerland, each member's specific commitments are entered according to an arithmetic formula (continuous function) referred to as the formula C^n, where C denotes any coefficient between 0 and 1, and superscript n denotes the number of scheduled restrictions in one entry. For practical purposes, the coefficient C is set at 0.5, although it could be any number given that it equally applies to all schedules.[14] The formula is

14. The value of the coefficient is not of particular relevance since comparability across commitments and members lies at the heart of the exercise.

based on two considerations. First, each limitation to market access and/or national treatment is an additional burden for the service supplier (or consumer). Therefore, an accurate and reliable methodology has to allow barriers to trade for every scheduled limitation to be tracked. Second, it is assumed that the marginal burden that falls on the service supplier due to an additional limitation is decreasing.

For simplicity, this chapter counts the number of scheduled restrictions affecting market access and national treatment according to the classification specified in Bosworth et al. (2000). Besides the classification specified in Article XVI of the GATS,[15] Bosworth et al. (2000) add one more measure affecting market access, "other" to avoid missing any other kinds of restrictions.

10.3   Interesting Patterns of the Financial Liberalization under the WTO

After the construction of the financial liberalization index based on GATS commitments, we highlight seven important patterns.

First, as can be seen in table 10.3, the degree of liberalization of financial services over the 2001–2006 period is overall higher than that during the 1994–2000 period. The low income countries and high income non-OECD countries have improved the most among the five income level groups. High income non-OECD countries are observed to have improved a great deal, especially in the subsector for insurance and insurance-related services.

Second, a member with a high degree of liberalization in one of these two subsectors in financial services tends to have a high degree of liberalization in the other subsector. This is because the correlation of the liberalization indices between the insurance industry and the banking-and-others industry is 70.04 percent during the period 1994–2000, and is also 71.03 percent during 2001–2006.

Third, under modes 1, 2 and 3, the degree of liberalization in relation to market access is positively correlated with the income level; however, there is no such link under mode 4. This is probably because mode 4 is related to the natural persons and because developing countries have abundant labor resources; thus, developing countries promote liberalization under mode 4 the most. By contrast, developed countries are modest in terms of liberal-

---

15. The classification of the scheduled restrictions specified in Bosworth, Findlay, Trewin, and Warren (2000) is as follows: (a) measures affecting market access include limitations on the number of service suppliers, limitations on the total value of service transactions or assets, limitations on the total number of service operations or on the total quantity of service outputs, limitations on the total number of natural persons that may be employed in a sector, measures which restrict or require specific types of legal entity or joint venture, limitations on the participation of foreign capital, and other measures affecting market access; (b) measures affecting national treatment include discriminatory taxes, discriminatory incentives/subsidies, government procurement policies, local content requirements, nationality, citizenship or residence requirements, and other measures affecting national treatment.

Table 10.3   Comparison of the liberalization index of financial services in the two periods of 1994–2000 and 2001–2006 classified by income level

Income Level	No. of Countries	Time Period/% of Change	All Insurance and Insurance-related Services	Banking and Other Financial Services	All Financial Services
High income OECD countries	24	1994–2000	0.6904	0.7173	0.7038
		2001–2006	0.7584	0.7763	0.7674
		% of change	9.85	8.23	9.04
High income Non-OECD countries	13	1994–2000	0.4821	0.432	0.4571
		2001–2006	0.6364	0.4708	0.5536
		% of change	32.01	8.98	21.11
Upper-middle income countries	25	1994–2000	0.4947	0.4569	0.4758
		2001–2006	0.5625	0.4577	0.5101
		% of change	13.71	0.18	7.21
Low-middle income countries	27	1994–2000	0.4428	0.3625	0.4027
		2001–2006	0.4708	0.3761	0.4235
		% of change	6.32	3.75	5.17
Low income countries	4	1994–2000	0.2658	0.233	0.2494
		2001–2006	0.3319	0.2852	0.3086
		% of change	24.87	22.40	23.74

Notes: High income OECD countries include Australia, Austria, Belgium, Canada, Denmark, Finland, France, Germany, Greece, Iceland, Ireland, Italy, Japan, Korea, Luxembourg, the Netherlands, New Zealand, Norway, Portugal, Spain, Sweden, Switzerland, the United Kingdom, and the United States. High income non-OECD countries include Bahrain, Brunei, Cyprus, Hong Kong, Israel, Liechtenstein, Macao, Malta, Qatar, Singapore, Slovenia, Taiwan, and United Arab Emirates. Upper-middle income countries include Argentina, Barbados, Chile, Costa Rica, Croatia, the Czech Republic, Dominica, Estonia, Gabon, Grenada, Hungary, Latvia, Lithuania, Malaysia, Mauritius, Mexico, Panama, Poland, the Slovak Republic, Saint Kitts and Nevis, Saint Lucia, Saint Vincent and the Grenadines, Trinidad and Tobago, Uruguay, and Oman. Low-middle income countries include Albania, Bolivia, Brazil, Bulgaria, China, Colombia, Cuba, Dominican Republic, Egypt, El Salvador, Fiji, Guatemala, Guyana, Honduras, Indonesia, Jamaica, Jordan, Macedonia, Morocco, Paraguay, Peru, the Philippines, Sri Lanka, Suriname, Thailand, Tunisia, and Turkey. Low income countries include India, Kenya, Nicaragua, and Pakistan. Weights among the four modes are the same as those adopted by the authors in 10.2.

izing under mode 4 and focus more on the issues of improving transparency and procedures related to the movement of natural persons.

Fourth, we compare the performance of liberalization across the four modes. Higher income members[16] have, on average, the highest level of market access liberalization under mode 2. Considering the difficulty involved in regulating consumption abroad, many WTO members therefore choose to liberalize the market access under mode 2. However, with regard to the national treatment part, mode 3 appears to have the highest degree of liberalization regardless of the income level.

Furthermore, it is found in table 10.4, in which countries are classified by

16. These include high income OECD countries, high income non-OECD countries, and upper-middle income countries.

Table 10.4 The liberalization index of all insurance and insurance-related services classified by geographic region in the 2001–2006 period

Geographic Region	No. of Countries	Market Access					National Treatment					Total
		M1	M2	M3	M4	Weighted Average	M1	M2	M3	M4	Weighted Average	
East Asia and Pacific	14	0.4152	0.5402	0.5452	0.3973	0.5179	0.4911	0.5714	0.7254	0.3571	0.6671	0.5925
South Asia	4	0.3125	0.2656	0.1797	0.4063	0.2131	0.1875	0.1875	0.2188	0.2656	0.2129	0.2130
Europe and Central Asia	33	0.7391	0.8409	0.6813	0.4867	0.6941	0.8845	0.9242	0.8958	0.4905	0.8849	0.7895
North America	2	0.4688	0.9375	0.3594	0.5313	0.4094	0.8125	0.9375	0.7188	0.0000	0.7275	0.5684
Latin America and Caribbean	27	0.2348	0.2404	0.3501	0.2043	0.3207	0.2564	0.2452	0.4663	0.2103	0.4122	0.3665
Middle East and North Africa	10	0.5116	0.6366	0.5347	0.3854	0.5314	0.5394	0.5914	0.7361	0.3715	0.6851	0.6082
Sub-Saharan Africa	3	0.6875	0.7083	0.6667	0.4167	0.6660	0.8750	0.8750	0.9167	0.4167	0.8948	0.7804

Notes: East Asia and Pacific includes Australia, Japan, Korea, New Zealand, Brunei, Taiwan, Hong Kong, Macao, Singapore, Malaysia, China, Fiji, the Philippines, and Thailand. South Asia includes Indonesia, India, Sri Lanka, and Pakistan. Europe and Central Asia includes Austria, Belgium, Denmark, Finland, France, Germany, Greece, Iceland, Ireland, Italy, Luxembourg, the Netherlands, Norway, Portugal, Spain, Sweden, Switzerland, the United Kingdom, Cyprus, Liechtenstein, Slovenia, Croatia, the Czech Republic, Estonia, Hungary, Latvia, Lithuania, Poland, the Slovak Republic, Albania, Bulgaria, Macedonia, and Turkey. North America incudes Canada and the United States. Latin America and Caribbean includes Argentina, Barbados, Chile, Costa Rica, Grenada, Mexico, Nicaragua, Panama, St. Kitts and Nevis, St. Lucia, St. Vincent and the Grenadines, Trinidad and Tobago, Uruguay, Bolivia, Brazil, Colombia, Cuba, Dominican Republic, El Salvador, Guatemala, Guyana, Honduras, Jamaica, Paraguay, Peru, and Suriname. Middle East and North Africa includes Bahrain, Israel, Malta, Qatar, United Arab Emirates, Egypt, Jordan, Morocco, Oman and Tunisia. Sub-Saharan Africa includes Gabon, Mauritius, and Kenya. Weights among the four modes are the same as those adopted by the authors in table 10.2. The index for each mode in each region is the simple average among the same geographic region.

geographic region, that East Asia and the Pacific, and Latin America and the Caribbean liberalize mode 3 the most in the insurance and insurance-related services subsector. On the other hand, Europe and Central Asia, the Middle East and North Africa, and North American countries choose to liberalize less under mode 3 compared to modes 1 and 2. The degree of liberalization in the banking and other financial services subsector under mode 3 for East Asia and the Pacific region, though not the highest, still remains high among the four modes, as shown in table 10.5. East Asia and the Pacific, and Latin American and the Caribbean regions comprise many developing countries, which attract experienced foreign financial institutions through foreign direct investment (i.e., mode 3) that in a great way help develop their own domestic financial industries. Due to the liberalization in relation to mode 3, and by attracting much incoming foreign direct investment, these countries not only enhance industrial development and technology transfer, but also raise their domestic employment in these areas. Mode 3, as a result, is traditionally the most popular liberalization mode for the governments in these regions.

Under the WTO, commitments to liberalize mode 1 of a service oblige a member to allow the necessary capital movements. To reduce the chances of the occurrence of a financial crisis facilitated by capital movements, many WTO members therefore choose to liberalize mode 1 as little as possible. Compared with other regions, European and Central Asian and North American (except for the insurance subsector) countries have a higher degree of liberalization in regard to mode 1, as shown in table 10.4 and table 10.5. Does this have anything to do with their performance in the trade in financial services or with the occurrence of financial crises? The next two patterns would be a good, yet preliminary, kickoff for examining this issue. From table 10.4 and table 10.5, we find that some regions have similar liberalization performances across different subsectors, but that some regions do not. In the former cases, East Asia and the Pacific region ranks fourth and Europe and the Central Asia region ranks first in both subsectors. By contrast, the financial liberalization in North America and the Sub-Saharan African regions is very different in the different subsectors. For instance, North America is the second most liberal region in regards to the banking and other financial services subsector, whereas it only ranks as the fifth most liberal region in relation to the insurance and insurance-related services subsector. The degree of liberalization in North America in the latter subsector surprisingly lags behind many other less developed regions, such as East Asia and Pacific and the Sub-Saharan Africa regions.

Finally, we examine the correlation between the financial liberalization index and the trade balance (i.e., the current account) of financial services for ninety-three WTO members. It is found in table 10.6 that, regardless of the subsectors, the liberalization index has a higher degree of correlation with the total trade balance (i.e., exports plus imports) than the net trade

Table 10.5 The liberalization index of banking and other financial services classified by geographic region in the 2001–2006 period

Geographic Region	No. of Countries	Market Access					National Treatment					Total
		M1	M2	M3	M4	Weighted Average	M1	M2	M3	M4	Weighted Average	
East Asia and Pacific	14	0.2979	0.5146	0.4359	0.3589	0.3998	0.4727	0.5412	0.6362	0.3063	0.5582	0.4790
South Asia	4	0.2205	0.2431	0.4933	0.5486	0.4183	0.1667	0.2188	0.5855	0.4045	0.4449	0.4316
Europe and Central Asia	33	0.8007	0.8181	0.7168	0.4883	0.7201	0.9007	0.9171	0.8228	0.5254	0.8174	0.7688
North America	2	0.8932	0.9384	0.4141	0.6250	0.5816	1.0000	1.0000	0.6389	0.3750	0.7208	0.6512
Latin America and the Caribbean	27	0.1122	0.1469	0.2587	0.1651	0.2075	0.1082	0.1405	0.3691	0.1629	0.2722	0.2398
Middle East and North Africa	10	0.4290	0.5193	0.4390	0.3484	0.4324	0.4491	0.5556	0.5787	0.4120	0.5295	0.4810
Sub-Saharan Africa	3	0.4537	0.5231	0.3495	0.2095	0.3709	0.4120	0.5231	0.3287	0.2095	0.3484	0.3597

Notes: The classification of countries is the same as that in table 10.4. Weights among the four modes are the same as those adopted by the authors in table 10.2. The index for each of M1–M4 is the simple average for the respective geographic region.

Table 10.6   The relationship (correlation coefficient) between the financial liberalization index and the trade balance (current account) of financial services for WTO members

Sub-sectors	Trade Balance	Weights adopted by the authors	$0.8 * M1 + 0.2 * M2$
Insurance services	Net Trade Balance	0.102965	0.276626
	Total Trade Balance	0.137906	0.150024
Banking and other services	Net Trade Balance	0.094380	0.179390
	Total Trade Balance	0.306151	0.377653
Financial services	Net Trade Balance	0.154236	0.294957
	Total Trade Balance	0.270827	0.328254

balance (i.e., exports minus imports). The net trade balance, theoretically speaking, should be more closely connected with each member's exchange rate and competitiveness in their respective areas. The existing current account statistics for services from the IMF, however, do not cover the trading volume defined by mode 3 and mode 4. It is therefore more reasonable to consider only the degree of liberalization for mode 1 and mode 2 when examining this issue. The liberalization index that is composed of only mode 1 and mode 2 (with 0.8 and 0.2 weights, respectively) is further established to explore the above relationship. As shown in the last column of table 10.6, the correlation between the liberalization index and both trade balances, respectively, is raised when only mode 1 and mode 2 are covered. Again, the liberalization index for overall financial services has a higher degree of correlation with the total trade balance than with the net trade balance.

10.4   Econometric Model

This section specifies the relationship between financial liberalization and macroeconomic performance, which is measured in terms of the average growth rate for per capita GDP for the periods 1994–2000 and 2001–2006, respectively. By employing a similar model to that in Eschenbach, Francois, and Schuknecht (2000), our model is,

Model (A):

$$(1) \quad PCGDPGR_I = a_0 + a_1 COMMITTOBANK_i \\ + a_2 CONCENTRATION_i + a_3 CREDIT_i + a_4 TRADE_i \\ + a_5 STDINFLA_i + a_6 PCGDP90_i \\ + a_7 SECOND90_i + a_8 INSTITUTION_i \\ + a_9 POPGR + \varepsilon_i$$

$$(2) \quad CONCENTRATION_j = b_0 + b_1 COMMITTOBANK_j + b_2 SIZE_j + \varepsilon_j$$

Model (B):

(1) $PCGDPGR_i = a_0 + a_1 CONCENTRATION_i + a_2 CREDIT_i$
$+ a_3 TRADE_i + a_4 STDINFLA_i + a_5 PCGDP90_i$
$+ a_6 SECOND90_i + a_7 INSTITUTION_i$
$+ a_8 POPGR_i + \varepsilon_i$

(2) $CONCENTRATION_j = b_0 + b_1 COMMITTOBANK_j + b_2 SIZE_j + \varepsilon_j$

Model (C):

(1) $PCGDPGR_i = a_0 + a_1 COMMITTOALL_i + a_2 COMMITTOALL_i^2$
$+ a_3 CONCENTRATION_i + a_4 CREDIT_i$
$+ a_5 TRADE_i + a_6 STDINFLA_i + a_7 PCGDP90_i$
$+ a_8 SECOND90_i + a_9 INSTITUTION_i + \varepsilon_i$

Model (D):

(1) $PCGDPGR_i = a_0 + a_1 COMMITTOBANK_j$
$+ a_2 CONCENTRATION_i + a_3 CREDIT_i$
$+ a_4 TRADE_i + a_2 STDINFLA_i + a_6 PCGDP90_i$
$+ a_7 SECOND90_i + a_8 INSTITUTION_i + a_9 POPGR_i$
$+ a_{10} INVESTMENT_i + \varepsilon_i$

(2) $CONCENTRATION_j = b_0 + b_1 COMMITTOBANK_j + b_2 SIZE_i + \varepsilon_j$

(3) $a_1 = c_0 + c_1 \mathbf{GOVERNANCE} + c_2 \mathbf{REGION};$

where *COMMITTOBANK* is the constructed liberalization index described in the previous section; *CONCENTRATION* is the concentration ratio of the banking sector, which is the sum of the market shares (measured in total assets) of the three largest banks in a country; *CREDIT* is the private credit to total credit; *TRADE* depicts the trade openness, which is the sum of exports and imports divided by GDP; *STDINFLA* is the standard deviation of the inflation rate; *PCGDP90* is the per capita GDP in 1990, which is the proxy for the initial endowment; *SECOND90* denotes the primary school enrollment and secondary school enrollment ratio in 1990; *SIZE* is included because, as discussed in Francois and Schuknecht (1999), larger markets can imply more scope for competition, particularly if scale economies are present.

There are two vectors of conditional variables in Model (D). The first vector of variables is **GOVERNANCE,** which contains five government governance variables. The first one is *GOVEFFECT,* which denotes government effectiveness and regulatory quality taken from Kaufmann, Kraay, and Mastruzzi (2005, hereafter KKZ). Next, *SUPERVISION,* which denotes the official supervisory power, examines whether the supervisory authorities possess the power to take corrective action when confronted with violations of regulations or other imprudent behavior on the part of banks. The larger the number, the more the authority has the power to supervise the banks. The variable is taken from Barth, Caprio, and Levine (2006). Third, *PRIVATEMONITOR* denotes the private monitoring index, which is also taken from Barth, Caprio, and Levine (2006). It means that bank behavior is affected by private market forces and the greater the figure, the more the public has access to information regarding the overall condition of the banking industry. Fourth, *CAPITALREGU,* which is the capital regulatory index and is taken from Barth, Caprio, and Levine (2006), examines whether there are explicit regulatory requirements regarding the amount of capital. Last, *INSTITUTION* denotes the corruption, law and order, and bureaucracy quality, which is taken from the *International Country Risk Guide* (ICRG).

The second set **REGION** includes three regional dummies, which are *EASIA,* denoting the dummy variable for the East Asian and Pacific countries; *LATIN,* denoting the dummy variable for the Latin American and Caribbean countries; and *SAHARAN,* denoting the dummy variable for the Sub-Saharan African countries. Detailed definitions and sources of these and other variables are reported in table 10.7.

The four models can be accounted for as follows. Model (A) investigates the direct and indirect links between banking liberalization and economic growth. If there is a direct impact, *COMMITTOBANK* in equation (1) will have a positive effect on growth and a_1 is significant. If there is an indirect impact, *COMMITTOBANK* should have a negative effect on *CONCENTRATION*, which also has a negative effect on growth. This suggests that a_2 and b_1 are negative.

Model (B) is similar to Model (A) but does not consider the direct effect by taking *COMMITTOBANK* out of equation (1). Thus, only the indirect link between banking liberalization and economic growth is examined, whereas the effects related to trade in financial services are then subsumed into the *CONCENTRATION* term.

Model (C) is opposite to Model (B) in that it only explores the direct relationship between the total financial liberalization and economic growth. Thus, the variable *COMMITTOALL* appears in equation (1), and equation (2) is removed. The concept can also be found in Mattoo, Rathindran, and Subramanian (2006), where the term *COMMITTOBANK* is replaced by the term *COMMITTOALL* to take into account the impact of liberalization of the financial subsectors overall.

In contrast to the above three models, where the impact of *COMMITTOBANK* is constant, Model (D) permits the direct impacts to be influenced by the two sets of variables, **GOVERNANCE** and **REGION**. As suggested by Shen and Lee (2006), good governance should strengthen the impact of liberalization. We do not have priors regarding the impacts of the regional effects.

The control variables in the four models are similar to those reported in

Table 10.7   **Mnemonics and description and sources of variables**

Variable Name	Description	Source
PCGDPGR	The average of the per capita growth rate over the respective 1994–2000 and 2001–2006 periods	WDI and IFS
COMMITTOBANK	Score on the index of financial liberalization calculated from each WTO member's GATS commitments in financial services (excluding insurance).	Constructed by authors
COMMITTOALL	Score on the index of financial liberalization calculated from each WTO member's GATS commitments in financial services (including insurance).	Constructed by authors
CONCENTRATION	Concentration in the financial sector: the assets of the 3 largest banks as a share of total assets expressed as a percentage, averaged over 1994–2000 and 2001–2006, respectively.	BDL
CREDIT	Credit to the private sector as a percentage of total credit, averaged over the periods 1994–2000 and 2001–2006, respectively.	WDI and IFS
TRADE	Trade openness, exports plus imports over GDP, averaged over the periods 1994–2000 and 2001–2006, respectively.	WDI and IFS
STDINFLA	The standard deviation of the inflation rate over the respective 1994–2000 and 2001–2006 periods.	WDI and IFS
PCGDP90	Per capita GDP in 1990.	WDI and IFS
SECOND90	The primary school enrollment and secondary school enrollment ratio in 1990.	WDI
INSTITUTION	General conditions of corruption, law and order, and bureaucratic quality (from Political Risk Services), ranging from 0 to 6, where 6 is the best, averaged over the periods 1994–2000 and 2001–2006, respectively.	ICRG
POPGR	Average rate of population growth over the periods 1994–2000 and 2001–2006.	WDI and IFS
INVESTMENT	Gross capital formation as a percentage of GDP, averaged over the periods 1994–2000 and 2001–2006, respectively.	WDI
SIZE	Total value of GDP as a percentage of world GDP, averaged over the periods 1994–2000 and 2001–2006, respectively.	WDI and IFS
SUPERVISION	Official supervisory power, which examines whether the supervisory authorities possess the power to take corrective action when confronted with violations of regulations or other imprudent behavior on the part of banks. This variable ranges from 0 to 14, with a higher value indicating greater power.	BCL
PRIVATEMONITOR	The private monitor index, which tries to capture market or private monitoring existing in different countries. The greater the number, the more the public has access to information about the overall condition of the banking industry. This variable ranges from 0 to 9 with a higher value indicating more supervision.	BCL

(continued)

Table 10.7   (continued)

Variable Name	Description	Source
CAPITALREGU	The conditions of overall capital stringency and initial capital stringency. It captures both the amount of capital and verifiable sources of capital that a bank is required to possess. This variable ranges from 0 to 9 with a higher value indicating greater stringency.	BCL
GOVEFFECT	The conditions of government effectiveness and regulatory quality. Government effectiveness combines responses on the quality of public service provisions, the quality of the bureaucracy, the competence of civil servants, the independence of the civil service from political pressures, and the credibility of the government's commitment to policies. Regulatory quality instead focuses more on the policies themselves, including measures of the incidence of market-unfriendly policies such as price controls or inadequate bank supervision, as well as perceptions of the burdens imposed by excessive regulation in areas such as foreign trade and business development.	KKZ
EASIA	East Asian and Pacific countries = 1, otherwise = 0.	WDI
LATIN	Latin American and Caribbean countries = 1, otherwise = 0.	WDI
SAHARAN	Sub-Saharan African countries = 1, otherwise = 0.	WDI

Notes: WDI: *World Development Indicators,* published by the World Bank. IFS: *International Financial Statistics,* published by the IMF. BDL: Beck, Demirgüç-Kunt and Levine (2000). ICRG: *International Country Risk Guide,* published by the PRS Group. BCL: Barth, Caprio, and Levine (2006). KKZ: Kaufmann, Kraay, and Mastruzzi (2005).

Eschenbach et al. (2000), Levine and Zervos (1998), and Shen and Lee (2006). For example, *CREDIT* describes the role of financial development in the growth equation, *TRADE* controls the effect of trade openness, *STDINFLA* reflects the uncertainty of inflation on the growth, *PCGDP90* serves as the initial endowment effect, *SECOND90* is schooling levels, and *INSTITUTION* is institutional factors (measures of corruption, law and order, and bureaucratic quality), as well as population growth over the two periods.

Country size is measured by GDP, and scaled by world GDP. We employ the share of domestic banking assets held by the three largest banks to measure the degree of competition in banking.[17]

17. The concentration ratio is an outcome-based variable, and, moreover, a misleading indicator of the level of competition in the banking system because a concentrated market for banking services can still be contestable. A large number of developed countries such as Canada and many European countries have banking systems characterized by a small number of banks, but still produce competitive outcomes.

10.5   Empirical Results

Table 10.8 reports the estimated results of equation (1) for our four models by using two-stage least squares (TSLS), where the second stage adopts weighted least squares (WLS).[18] Table 10.9 reports the estimated results of equation (2). The TSLS procedure is applied to remove the endogenous effects so as to yield consistent estimates. The WLS is employed to take into account the heteroskedasticity problem. The weights of the WLS are the *institution* and residual squared, but only the former is reported.

In table 10.8, the estimated coefficient of our liberalization variable *COMMITTOBANK* in Model (A) is insignificantly positive, suggesting that a country which commits to bank opening does not increase the growth of GDP per capita. The controlled variables emerge with the expected sign, though not always with significant coefficients. The most robust variables in this regard are *PCGDP90* (the initial per capita GDP), which is overwhelmingly significantly negative, indicating that the higher the initial income, the lower the growth. This is consistent with the income convergence theory (Barro and Sala-i-Martin 2004). The term *INSTITUTION*, which is the indicator of the general conditions regarding corruption, law and order, and bureaucratic quality, appears to be significantly positive in all specifications, suggesting that good governance enhances economic growth. Our measures of financial sector competition, *CONCENTRATION*, consistently emerge with a significantly negative sign. This should not be surprising because Demirgüç-Kunt and Levine (2001) also find that the correlation coefficient between the concentration ratio and growth is almost zero. The term *CREDIT* is overwhelmingly insignificant, which is partly similar to the findings in Shen and Lee (2006).[19]

Model (B) does not consider the liberalization and mainly examines the indirect effect of *COMMITTOBANK* through the *CONCENTRATION*. Thus, the focus is on the coefficient of *CONCENTRATION* reported in table 10.8 and the coefficient of *COMMITTOBANK* in equation (2) reported in table 10.9. The coefficient of *CONCENTRATION* in table 10.8 is equal to −0. 0447 and is significant, suggesting that the higher the ratio, the lower the growth. Because the coefficient of *COMMITTOBANK* in table 10.9 is −15.1629 and is significant, we do find an indirect effect that the liberalization of the banking industry decreases the concentration ratio, which then increases the growth.

When the square of *COMMITTOALL* is added, as shown in Model (C), the estimated coefficients of *COMMITTOALL* and $COMMITTOALL^2$

---

18. Our TSLS approach uses all exogenous variables to first predict the *CONCENTRATION.* The resulting predicted variables secondly replace the actual variables. The WLS simply uses the variable *INSTITUTION* as the weight to minimize the effect of the heteroskedasticity.

19. The coefficients of *CREDIT* in their regression are either insignificant or negative.

Table 10.8　　　　The GDP per capita growth equation: Equation (1) of four models

Independent Variables	Model A	Model B	Model C	Model D	Model D
CONSTANT	1.6559	1.7604***	0.4187	-2.8994**	-2.0923
	(1.589)	(1.651)	(0.287)	(-2.245)	(-1.518)
COMMITTOBANK	0.3051			8.4426*	8.1972**
	(0.336)			(2.620)	(2.556)
COMMITTOALL			-5.3429***		
			(-1.939)		
COMMITTOALL^2			5.5680**		
			(2.285)		
COMMITTOBANK× SUPERVISION				0.0535	0.0437
				(0.594)	(0.467)
COMMITTOBANK× PRIVATE MONITOR				-0.1337	0.0142
				(-0.517)	(0.057)
COMMITTOBANK× CAPITALREGU				-0.2442**	-0.2275**
				(-2.406)	(-2.349)
COMMITTOBANK× GOVEFFECT				0.5968***	0.6125***
				(1.699)	(1.820)
COMMITTOBANK× INSTITUTION				-0.7341*	-0.7754*
				(-3.252)	(-3.372)
COMMITTOBANK× EASIA					-0.5974
					(-1.257)
COMMITTOBANK× LATIN					-2.2099*
					(-3.806)
COMMITTOBANK× SAHARAN					-2.7684***
					(-1.913)
CONCENTRATION	-0.0458*	-0.0447**	-0.0514*	-0.0116	-0.0087
	(-2.605)	(-2.459)	(-2.755)	(-0.778)	(-0.598)
CREDIT	0.0014	0.0012	-0.00003	0.0011	0.0007
	(1.206)	(0.914)	(-0.022)	(1.056)	(0.659)
TRADE	0.0055**	0.0054**	0.0053**	-0.0005	-0.0012
	(2.096)	(1.971)	(2.154)	(-0.176)	(-0.426)
STDINFLA	-0.0022	-0.0022	-0.0011	-0.0017	-0.0013
	(-1.105)	(-1.065)	(-0.953)	(-1.231)	(-0.935)
PCGDP90	-0.0002*	-0.0002*	-0.0002*	-0.0001*	-0.0001*
	(-5.282)	(-4.671)	(-4.765)	(-3.487)	(-3.211)
SECOND90	0.0090	0.0093	0.0176**	0.0011	-0.00001
	(1.424)	(1.537)	(2.105)	(0.204)	(-0.003)
INSTITUTION	0.3771*	0.3729*	0.4170*	0.5397*	0.4644*
	(3.579)	(3.508)	(3.909)	(3.557)	(3.124)
POPGR	-0.9839*	-1.0006*		-0.9169*	-0.8209*
	(-5.476)	(-5.624)		(-5.312)	(-4.866)
INVESTMENT				0.1043*	0.1049*
				(2.595)	(2.583)
R^2	0.349	0.338	0.208	0.472	0.500
Number of observations	138	138	141	130	130

Notes: Heteroskedasticity-robust *t*-values are in parentheses; *, **, and *** denote significance at the 1%, 5%, and 10% levels, respectively. The model is estimated by Two-Stage Least Squares (TSLS), while the second stage uses Weighted Least Squares (WLS) with the weight being equal to *institution*.

Table 10.9   The bank concentration equation: *concentration*

Independent Variables	Model A	Model B	Model D
CONSTANT	76.5271*	76.5271*	78.3417*
	(17.530)	(17.530)	(17.898)
COMMITTOBANK	–15.1629**	–15.1629**	–17.4480**
	(–2.109)	(–2.109)	(–2.496)
SIZE	–1.5466*	–1.5466*	–1.5735*
	(–7.479)	(–7.479)	(–7.476)
R^2	0.764	0.764	0.779
Number of observations	138	138	130

Notes: Heteroskedasticity-robust *t*-values are in parentheses; *, **, and *** denote significance at the 1%, 5%, and 10% levels, respectively. The model is estimated by Weighted Least Squares (WLS) with the weight being equal to COMMITTOBANK.

are –5.3429 and 5.5680, respectively. Thus, the influence of overall financial liberalization that includes the insurance, banking, and other sectors on the growth of income takes the form of a U-shaped curve; it first decreases the growth of income and then increases it. As the commitments start to increase, the burden and costs raised by short-run adjustments from the industries decrease the growth rate. As more and more liberalization measures are introduced, however, competition will bring about long-run benefits and will raise the growth of income.

The fourth column of table 10.8 reports the estimated results using Model (D), which incorporates the interaction variables. The estimated coefficient of the liberalization variable COMMITTOBANK is significantly positive, implying that the liberalization of the banking sector can increase the growth. Furthermore, the coefficient of the interaction variable COMMITTOBANK × GOVEFFECT is significantly positive, suggesting that good government effectiveness and regulatory quality can enhance the liberalization effect. The coefficients of the interaction variables COMMITTOBANK × SUPERVISION and COMMITTOBANK × PRIVATEMONITOR are insignificant. To our surprise, though, the coefficients of COMMITTOBANK × CAPITALREGU and COMMITTO-BANK × INSTITUTION are small, and are significantly negative. Accordingly, the stringency of the requirements of capital regulations and a decrease in the corruption may lessen the effect of liberalization. Because the coefficient of COMMITTOBANK is much larger (8.4426) than those of the two interaction variables (–0.2442 and –0.7341), the reduced effect is small, except for large CAPITALREGU and INSTITUTION.[20]

The last column of table 10.8 reports the estimated results when the re-

20. This negative effect may be due to the short-run pain and long-run gain as suggested by Kaminsky and Schmukler (2003).

gional dummies are included. The coefficients of the *COMMITTOBANK* remain significantly positive, with the coefficient being equal to 8.1972. The coefficients of the interaction variables between *COMMITTOBANK* and the three regional dummies, *EASIA, LATIN* and *SAHARAN* are overwhelmingly negative (−0.5974, −2.2099, and −2.768, respectively). However, only the latter two are significant. Thus, liberalization indeed increases the growth, but this positive effect is lessened only when it is implemented in Latin America and the Sub-Saharan area.

Table 10.9 reports the estimated results of equation (2) for models (A), (B) and (D). The coefficients of *COMMITTOBANK* are significantly negative regardless of the models, suggesting that the country that commits to bank opening decreases the concentration ratio of the banking sector. This may be because once the restrictions and regulations of the banking market are lessened, the establishment of new banks becomes more common, which decreases the concentration ratio.

To sum up, these results with regard to financial sector competition and growth, which are taken together with the apparent link between competition and liberalization, point to the following pattern in the data. Open financial sectors are more competitive, and more competitive financial sectors are strongly correlated with higher growth rates. Hence, through procompetitive effects, trade in financial services may enhance growth rates.

10.6   Discussion and Concluding Remarks

This chapter constructs a new financial liberalization index and then examines the impact of liberalization on economic growth. Although our chapter focuses on the liberalization of the trade in services (finance) sector, it is interesting to discuss the link between trade in services liberalization and trade in the goods sector first. Mattoo, Rathindran, and Subramanian (2006), for example, conclude that services liberalization differs from trade in goods because the former involves factor mobility and leads to scale effects that are distinctive, though not unique. Goods liberalization in the absence of services liberalization could well result in negative effective protection of goods, thus highlighting the need for the latter to keep pace with the former. Deardorff (2001) even stresses that the service liberalization can improve the trade liberalization. He examines the role played by services liberalization and finds that it can stimulate the trade not only in services, but also in goods. In particular, international trade in goods requires inputs from trade in services, too. Restrictions on movements in services across borders add costs and barriers to international trade in goods. Liberalizing trade in services could thus facilitate trade in goods.

Our new financial liberalization index is constructed based on the WTO commitment schedules of ninety-three countries in relation to financial services, and covers the 1994–2006 period. In the analysis we introduce several revisions, based on the method adopted by Hoekman (1995, 1996), to calculate the financial liberalization indices. These revisions include the covering mode 4 and all subsectors listed in the *Annex on Financial Services,* the weighting assigned to each of the four modes, and further scoring for partial commitments.

Our results show that the degree of liberalization is positively correlated with income level under modes 1, 2, and 3, but not mode 4. The liberalization index has a higher degree of correlation with the total trade balance than with the net trade balance, regardless of the subsectors. The correlation between the liberalization index and both trade balances, respectively, is raised when only mode 1 and mode 2 are covered in the liberalization index, probably because the existing statistics for the trade in services from the IMF only cover the trading volume under mode 1 and mode 2. In addition, the liberalization in relation to market access and to national treatment is highly correlated. Also, a member country with a high degree of liberalization in one of these two subsectors tends to also have a high degree of liberalization in the other subsector.

We also find that East Asia and the Pacific and Latin America and the Caribbean are liberalized under mode 3 the most, whereas European and Central Asian and North American countries have chosen to liberalize less under mode 3 as compared with mode 1 and mode 2. East Asia and Pacific, and Latin America and Caribbean regions comprise many developing countries, which traditionally attract experienced foreign financial institutions through foreign direct investment (i.e., mode 3) in order to help develop their own domestic financial industries. By liberalizing under mode 3, which enables countries to attract incoming foreign direct investment, these countries not only enhance their industrial development and technology transfer, but they also increase their domestic employment in these areas.

Once the index is constructed, regression analyses are employed to investigate the direct and indirect effects of the liberalization on growth, where the indirect effect is examined through the concentration ratio of banks in each country. Furthermore, we examine whether the direct effect is affected by the governance variable in a broad sense and based on the regional variables. Our results show that the liberalization of the banking sector does directly enhance growth when all variables are included; however, it is only slightly sensitive to the model's specifications. The indirect effect also exists since the liberalization is found to negatively affect concentration, which will then negatively affect the growth.

Turning to the case of governance, the results also show that good government effectiveness and regulatory quality can enhance the liberalization effect. In addition, the stringency of the requirements of capital regulations and a decrease in corruption may lessen the effect of liberalization, although the effect is small. With respect to the regional effect, liberalization indeed increases the growth in East Asia, but this positive effect is lessened only when it is implemented in Latin America and the Sub-Saharan area.

Appendix

Table 10A.1   **The GDP per capita growth equation: Equation (1) of four models**

Independent Variables	Model A (TSLS)	Model B (TSLS)	Model C (TSLS)	Model D (TSLS)	Model D (TSLS)
CONSTANT	1.8685***	1.8699***	0.7873	−2.4521***	−1.6581
	(1.739)	(1.780)	(0.578)	(−1.674)	(−1.075)
COMMITTOBANK	0.0035			7.0865**	6.7332**
	(0.004)			(2.109)	(2.000)
COMMITTOALL			−4.4379***		
			(−1.677)		
COMMITTOALL^2			4.2766***		
			(1.920)		
COMMITTOBANK× SUPERVISION				0.0266	0.0178
				(0.297)	(0.192)
COMMITTOBANK× PRIVATEMONITOR				−0.0614	0.0704
				(−0.251)	(0.293)
COMMITTOBANK× CAPITALREGU				−0.2485*	−0.2458*
				(−2.580)	(−2.580)
COMMITTOBANK× GOVEFFECT				0.5088	0.4923
				(1.442)	(1.434)
COMMITTOBANK× INSTITUTION				−0.6025**	−0.6177**
				(−2.413)	(−2.447)
COMMITTOBANK× EASIA					−0.7996***
					(−1.769)
COMMITTOBANK× LATIN					−2.1054*
					(−3.498)
COMMITTOBANK× SAHARAN					−3.0113**
					(−1.964)
CONCENTRATION	−0.0356**	−0.0356**	−0.0389*	−0.0124	−0.0108
	(−2.548)	(−2.484)	(−2.697)	(−0.854)	(−0.766)
CREDIT	0.0009	0.0009	−0.0006	0.0011	0.0008
	(0.775)	(0.741)	(−0.399)	(1.021)	(0.658)
TRADE	0.0054**	0.0054**	0.0047***	0.0006	0.0001
	(2.068)	(2.020)	(1.955)	(0.218)	(0.019)
STDINFLA	−0.0024	−0.0024	−0.0014	−0.0017	−0.0015
	(−1.120)	(−1.079)	(−1.093)	(−1.190)	(−0.949)
PCGDP90	−0.0002*	−0.0002*	−0.0002*	−0.0001*	−0.0001*
	(−5.307)	(−4.870)	(−4.997)	(−3.356)	(−3.068)
SECOND90	0.0060	0.0060	0.0131***	0.0002	−0.0010
	(1.028)	(1.073)	(1.763)	(0.042)	(−0.209)
INSTITUTION	0.3372*	0.3372*	0.3641*	0.4761*	0.4087**
	(3.647)	(3.692)	(3.935)	(2.891)	(2.564)
POPGR	−0.8936*	−0.8938*		−0.8556*	−0.7660*
	(−5.090)	(−5.291)		(−5.061)	(−4.555)
INVESTMENT				0.1109*	0.1147*
				(2.803)	(2.811)
R^2	0.301	0.298	0.174	0.424	0.447
Number of observations	138	138	141	130	130

Notes: Heteroskedasticity-robust t-values are in parentheses; *, **, and *** denote significance at the 1%, 5%, and 10% levels, respectively. The model is estimated by Two-Stage Least Squares (TSLS).

Table 10A.2   The bank concentration equation: *CONCENTRATION*

Independent Variables	Model A	Model B	Model D
CONSTANT	68.1093*	68.1093*	69.6667*
	(17.544)	(17.544)	(17.798)
COMMITTOBANK	–0.5034	–0.5034	–2.6828
	(–0.081)	(–0.081)	(–0.437)
SIZE	–1.5759*	–1.5759*	–1.5833*
	(–7.225)	(–7.225)	(–7.332)
R^2	0.112	0.112	0.120
Number of observations	138	138	130

Notes: Heteroskedasticity-robust t-values are in parentheses; *, **, and *** denote significance at the 1%, 5%, and 10% levels, respectively. The model is estimated by OLS.

References

Barro, R., and X. Sala-i-Martin. 2004. *Economic Growth,* 2nd ed. Cambridge, MA: MIT Press.

Barth, J., G. Caprio, Jr., and R. Levine. 2001. The regulation and supervision of banks around the world: A new database. Policy Research Working Paper no. 2588. Washington, DC: World Bank.

Barth, J., G. Caprio, Jr., and R. Levine. 2006. *Rethinking bank regulation: Till angels govern.* Cambridge, England: Cambridge University Press.

Beck, T., A. Demirgüç-Kunt, and R. Levine. 2000. A new database on financial development and structure. *World Bank Economic Review* 14:597–605.

Bekaer, G., and C. R. Harvey. 2000. Foreign speculators and emerging equity markets. *Journal of Finance* 55 (2): 565–613.

Bosworth, M., C. Findlay, R. Trewin, and T. Warren. 2000. Price-impact measures of impediments to services trade. In *Impediments to trade in services: Measurement and policy implications,* ed. C. Findlay and T. Warren, 42–51. London: Routledge.

Claessens, S., A. Demirgüç-Kunt, and H. Huizinga. 2001. How does foreign entry affect domestic banking markets? *Journal of Banking and Finance* 25:891–911.

Claessens, S., and T. Glaessner. 1998. The internationalization of financial services in Asia. Policy Research Working Paper no. 1911. Washington, DC: World Bank.

Deardorff, A. V. 2001. International provision of trade services, trade, and fragmentation. *Review of International Economics* 9 (2): 233–48.

Demirgüç-Kunt, A., and E. Detragiache. 1998. The determinants of banking crises in developing and developed countries. *IMF Staff Papers* 45 (1): 81–109.

Demirgüç-Kunt, A., and E. Detragiache. 2001. Financial liberalization and financial fragility. In *Financial liberalization: How far, how fast?,* eds. G. Caprio, P. Honahan, and J. E. Stiglitz, 96–124. Cambridge, England: Cambridge University Press.

Demirgüç-Kunt, A., and R. Levine. 2001. Bank-based and market-based financial systems: Cross-country comparisons. In *Financial structure and economic growth: A cross-country comparison of banks, markets, and development,* eds. A. Demirgüç-Kunt and R. Levine, 81–140. Cambridge, MA: MIT Press.

Eschenbach, F., J. F. Francois, and L. Schuknecht. 2000. Financial sector openness and economic growth. In *The internationalization of financial services: Issues and lessons for developing countries,* eds. S. Claessens and J. Jansen, 103–15. London: Kluwer Law International.

Francois, J. F., and L. Schuknecht. 1999. Trade in financial services: Procompetitive effects and growth performance. CEPR Discussion Paper no. 2144. London: Centre for Economic Policy Research.

Henry, P. 2000. Do stock market liberalizations cause investment booms? *Journal of Financial Economics* 58:301–34.

Hoekman, B. 1995. Tentative first step: An assessment of the Uruguay round agreement on services. Policy Research Working Paper no. 1455. World Bank.

Hoekman, B. 1996. Assessing the general agreement on trade in services. In *The Uruguay Round and the Developing Countries,* eds. W. Martin and L. A. Winters, 88–124. Cambridge, England: Cambridge University Press.

Hoekman, B., and C. A. Primo Braga. 1997. Protection and trade in services: A survey. *Open Economies Review* 8:285–308.

Kaminsky, G. L., and C. M. Reinhart. 2002. Financial markets in times of stress. *Journal of Development Economics* 69 (2): 451–70.

Kaminsky, G. L., and S. L. Schmukler. 2003. Short-run pain, long-run gain: The effects of financial liberalization. IMF Working Paper no. 03/34. World Trade Organization.

Kaufmann, D., A. Kraay, and M. Mastruzzi. 2005. Governance matters IV: Governance indicators for 1996–2004. Draft. World Bank.

Kawakatsu, H., and M. R. Morey. 1999. An empirical examination of financial liberalization and the efficiency of emerging market stock prices. *Journal of Financial Research* 4:385–411.

Levine, R., and S. Zervos. 1998. Stock market, banks and economic growth. *American Economic Review* 88 (3): 537–58.

Mattoo, A. 1998. Financial services and the WTO: Liberalization in the developing and transition economies. Staff Working Paper no. TISD9803. World Trade Organization.

Mattoo, A. 2000. Financial services and the WTO: Liberalization commitments of the developing and transition economies. *World Economy* 23 (3): 351–86.

Mattoo, A., R. Rathindran, and A. Subramanian. 2006. Measuring services trade liberalization and its impact on economic growth: An illustration. *Journal of Economic Integration* 21:64–98.

Maurer, A. 2005. Economic importance of cross-border trade in services—Recent developments. Symposium on the Cross-border Supply of Services, 28–29 April 2005, Geneva: World Trade Organization.

McGuire, G., and M. Schuele. 2000. Restrictiveness of international trade in banking services. In *Impediments to trade in services: Measurement and policy implications,* eds. C. Findlay and T. Warren, 172–88. London: Routledge.

Montes-Negret, F., and L. Landa. 2001. Interest rate spreads in Mexico during liberalization. In *Financial liberalization: How far, how fast?* eds. G. Caprio, P. Honohan, and J. E. Stiglitz, 188–207. Cambridge, England: Cambridge University Press.

PECC. 1995. *Survey of impediments to trade and investment in the APEC region.* Pacific Economic Cooperation Council.

PECC International Secretariat. 2003. *Financial services liberalization and its sequencing in the APEC region: WTO and RTAS.* Pacific Economic Cooperation Council.

Qian, Y. 2000. Financial services liberalization and GATS. In *The internationalization of financial services: Issues and lessons for developing countries,* eds. S. Claessens and M. Jansen, 63–101. London: Kluwer Law International.

Shen, C. H., and C. C. Lee. 2006. Same financial development yet different economic growth—Why? *Journal of Money, Credit, and Banking* 38 (7): 1907–44.

Tornell, A., F. Westermann, and L. Martinez. 2004. The positive link between financial liberalization growth and crises. NBER Working Paper no. 10293. Cambridge, MA: National Bureau of Economic Research.

Valckx, N. 2002. WTO financial services liberalization: Measurement, choice and impact on financial stability. Research Memorandum *Wo* no. 705. De Nederlandsche Bank.

Comment   Shin-ichi Fukuda

The motivation of this chapter is to explore the relationship between liberalization of financial services and economic growth by cross-country regression. There are several previous studies that have explored the same issue. But how to measure the depth and growth of financial markets is very controversial in these studies. There are some measures of the depth and growth of financial markets in literature: liquid liabilities and gross claims on the private sector in King and Levine (1993), private sector credit in De Gregorio and Guidotti (1995), real interest rate distortions and lending-deposit spread in Roubini and Sala-i-Martin (1992), and stock market activities in Levine and Zervos (1998). Problems with these measures are that they are endogenous variables. Causality was not necessarily clear in these studies. Some common factor may derive both financial development and growth. Financial development—typically measured by the level of credit and the size of the stock market—may predict economic growth simply because financial markets anticipate future growth.

What is new in this chapter is the use of measures on liberalization on international trade in financial services based on the GATS commitments in overall financial sectors. The measures may not be purely exogenous, but less endogenous than those in previous studies. By using the measures, the authors constructed an index to measure nontariff barriers and found a more clear and less biased link from financial liberalization to economic growth. The main result is a positive link between the liberalization of the financial sector and economic growth. But the link is indirect. The liberalization of the financial sector leads to more competition within the financial sector and this leads to higher economic growth. An implication of this chapter is that the liberalization of the financial sector is important because it makes the financial sector more competitive. The result seems plausible.

However, there are alternative views in the literature for the impacts of financial market liberalization: a positive view, a negative view, and a positive view with some reservations. A positive view, which is this chapter's

Shin-ichi Fukuda is a professor of economics at the University of Tokyo.

view, includes Goldsmith (1969), McKinnon (1973), and King and Levine (1993). They assert that financial market liberalization will channel investment funds to their most productive uses so that it will enhance capital accumulation and promote economic growth. In contrast, a negative view, such as Stiglitz (2004), insists that the positive views are based on the neoclassical model with perfect information, perfect capital market, and perfect competition. Capital-market liberalization was systematically associated with instability in developing countries. Crises in East Asia and Latin America in recent decades are good examples for the instability. A positive view with some reservations asserts that the liberalization of foreign direct investment (FDI) has a positive effect on economic growth. But the liberalization of short-term capital flows does not. The economic crises of the late 1990s were attributable to worldwide capital-market liberalization of short-term capital flows in the 1980s and 1990s. Another positive view with some reservations proposes that we need some preconditions for successful capital-market liberalization, such as good corporate governance, transparent accounting rules, legal protections of investors, prudential regulation by government, some possible extensions, and so on. This chapter attempts to identify some of the channels through which capital-market liberalization leads to faster economic growth, but it does not seem to attempt to test the alternative hypothesis, including the positive views with some reservations. We need to include alternative measures in the regressions to test the alternative hypothesis. The use of some measures on capital-market liberalization of short-term capital flows may be desirable.

To check the robustness of the interesting findings, we call for further investigations in the chapter. In the growth regression, the index of financial liberalization becomes insignificant when concentration in the financial sector is included in the explanatory variables. The liberalization of the financial sector may not enhance economic growth unless it makes the financial sector more competitive. This is somewhat consistent with the positive view with some reservations. Model (C) finds that there is a nonlinear relationship between the index of financial liberalization and economic growth. The overall financial liberalization first has a negative impact on economic growth, and then the impact becomes positive. This finding may also be consistent with the alternative views. We probably need to add further deliberate interpretations, as well as further regressions, to the robustness.

The sample periods may be too short to discuss long-run economic growth. The chapter used the average growth rate for the periods 1994–2000 and 2001–2005. The average growth rate in the short sample periods may reflect short-run business cycles. In particular, a series of crises occurred during the sample periods. Ideally, we need longer sample periods.

We may also need to use alternative economic indicators in the regressions. Economic indicators that are included in standard growth regressions are initial income level, investment rates (or saving rates), population growth, and human capital. These variables are consistent with Solow's growth model (Mankiw, Romer, and Weil 1992). The chapter included most of them. But investment rates (or saving rates) are missing in this chapter. Investment rates are usually the most significant variable. In this chapter, the level of human capital is controlled by the secondary school enrollment ratio. But this is a flow data. Theoretically, it is more desirable to use some stock data of human capital such as accumulation of previous school enrollments (see Barro and Lee 1993).

References

Barro, R. J., and J. W. Lee. 1993. International comparisons of educational attainment. *Journal of Monetary Economics* 32 (3): 363–94.

De Gregorio, J., and P. E. Guidotti. 1995. Financial development and economic growth. *World Development* 23 (3): 433–48.

Goldsmith, R. W. 1969. *Financial structure and development.* New Haven, CT: Yale University Press.

King, R. G., and R. Levine. 1993. Finance and growth: Schumpeter might be right. *Quarterly Journal of Economics* 108 (3): 717–37.

Levine, R., and S. Zervos. 1998. Stock markets, banks, and economic growth. *American Economic Review* 88 (3): 537–58.

McKinnon, R. I. 1973. Money and capital in economic development. Washington, DC: Brookings Institution.

Mankiw, N. G., D. Romer, D. N. Weil. 1992. A contribution to the empirics of economic growth. *Quarterly Journal of Economics* 107 (2): 407–37.

Roubini, N., and S. Xavier. 1992. Financial repression and economic growth. *Journal of Development Economics* 39 (1): 5–30.

Stiglitz, J. E. 2004. Globalization and growth in emerging markets. *Journal of Policy Modeling* 25:465–84.

Comment   Roberto S. Mariano

This chapter utilizes panel cross-country regressions, of the partial reduced-form type, to analyze the overall contribution of the financial sector to economic growth and the role of liberalization in the financial sector (as well as the competition within the sector) in this process. One main contribution of the chapter lies in the way in which financial liberalization is measured—namely, through the financial liberalization commitments of countries under the *General Agreement on Trade in Services* (GATS).

The financial sector liberalization index in the chapter is based on esti-

Roberto S. Mariano is a professor of economics and statistics, dean of the School of Economics, and Vice Provost for Research at Singapore Management University, and Professor Emeritus of Economics and Statistics at the University of Pennsylvania.

mates of tariff-equivalents for trade in financial services utilizing GATS commitments within the WTO—as submitted by each member country within the periods 1994–2000 and 2001–2005. Two liberalization indices are constructed: one for all financial services (banking, insurance, and others) and one for banking alone. These indices are constructed through a disaggregate treatment of subsectors of financial services and the four possible modes of supply identified by GATS, with appropriate weighting of the four modes and with scoring for partial commitments, and in the context of market access and national treatment. The four modes of supply identified by GATS are cross-border supply, consumption abroad, commercial presence, and movement of natural persons.

Patterns of correlation of these liberalization indices with the trade balance for WTO members, and differences among these indices across geographical regions as well as income levels are described in the chapter. The empirical analysis in the chapter points to a "positive pattern linking the financial sector competition indicators with . . . financial sector liberalization, and economic growth with the financial sector competition." The positive effect is increased further when a government is effective and has good regulation. However, when a country has stringent requirements on capital regulation and decreased corruption, the positive effects of an open banking sector are lessened.

The authors go through a painstaking process of constructing their indices and they are to be commended for the detailed work and discussion of this process as well as their literature review and discussion of patterns of financial liberalization under the WTO. These are covered in the first three sections of the chapter. In their discussion, the authors allude to one possible major deficiency of their liberalization index—that is, being based on GATS commitments rather than on extent of liberalization that actually took place. It could very well be that these commitments are the best observable proxy for actual liberalization. But, the authors themselves point out that "subsequent unilateral liberalization undertaken by some members has widened the gap between GATS commitments and actual measures."

The fourth and fifth sections of the chapter deal with the empirics of financial liberalization and growth. In footnote 19, the authors comment that the variable *CONCENTRATION* is a misleading indicator of the level of competition in the banking system. If this is the case, why use this variable in the empirical exercise at all? The estimation results reported in tables 10.8 and 10.9 apparently are based on panel data for ninety-three countries for the two periods 1994–2000 and 2001–2005. I wonder how this number of ninety-three countries fits with the reported numbers of observations in tables 10.8 and 10.9 (between 130 and 141). It is good to see that the authors have included Model (D) in tables 10.8 and 10.9, which shows statistically significant interaction terms—such as the interaction of financial liberalization in banks (*COMMITTOBANK*) with capital regulation (*CAPITALREGU*), government effectiveness (*GOVEFFECT*), and corruption (*INSTITUTION*). Regarding estimating procedure, as remarked by the authors in footnote 20, the estimated equations in table 10.8 are obtained by a two-stage least squares procedure which uses all the exogenous variables to correct for the endogeneity of *CONCENTRATION*. In the second stage, weighted least squares is implemented by using *INSTITUTION* as the weight in the correction for heteroskedasticity. The authors need to re-examine this approach on various counts. Concerning the correction for heteroskedasticity, if *INSTITUTION* is categorical, (and this is not clear in the chapter), why not use estimated standard deviations in each *INSTITUTION* category as the weights?

As to the correction for endogeneity, some of the other regressors in the equation for growth in per capita GDP in Model (D) also may be endogenous, such as trade openness (*TRADE*), percent of credit to the private sector (*CREDIT*), standard deviation of inflation (*STDINFLA*), and financial liberalization itself (*COMMITTOBANK*). If so, these variables cannot be used as instruments in the first stage and, indeed, corrections for their endogeneity also should be made.

11

Cross-Border Acquisitions and Target Firms' Performance
Evidence from Japanese Firm-Level Data

Kyoji Fukao, Keiko Ito, Hyeog Ug Kwon,
and Miho Takizawa

11.1 Introduction

The flow of inward foreign direct investments (FDI) to Japan has increased dramatically since the latter half of the 1990s. According to Japan's international-investment-position statistics, the stock of inward FDI in Japan rose 3.4 fold to 10.1 trillion yen during the six years from 1998 to 2004. Although Japan's inward FDI stock/GDP ratio (2.0 percent in 2004) is only about one seventh of the corresponding value of the United States (14.1 percent in 2003), employment in foreign affiliates as a share of total employment is 2.75 percent, which is equivalent to about half of the corresponding value, 5.61 percent for the United States (table 11.1).

FDI is a form of international capital flows that are accompanied by intangible assets, such as technology, management skills, and marketing know-how. Because of such intangible assets, foreign-owned firms will have higher productivity and higher profit rates. International economics theory suggests that the inflow of such intangible assets should benefit Japan. Being aware of this benefit, the Japanese government set the goal to double the inward FDI stock relative to GDP, first in 2003 and again in 2006, as part of its policies to restructure the Japanese economy and boost economic growth. To promote inward FDI, the Japanese government in May 2007

Kyoji Fukao is a Professor in the Institute of Economic Research at Hitotsubashi University. Keiko Ito is an associate professor of economics at Senshu University. Hyeog Ug Kwon is an assistant professor of economics at Nihon University. Miho Takizawa is a research fellow of the Japan Society for the Promotion of Science (JSPS).

The authors would like to thank the editors of this volume, the discussants, M. Chatib Basri and Robert Mariano, and participants of the seventeenth annual NBER-East Asia Seminar on Economics. Financial support from the Japan Securities Scholarship Foundation and the Japan Society for the Promotion of Science (JSPS) is gratefully acknowledged.

Table 11.1   Employment in foreign affiliates as a share of total employment (in %)

Industry	JAFF (33.4%) 1996	JAFF (33.4%) 2001	JAFF (20%, single owner) 2001	USAFF (10%, single owner) 1997
Food products	0.29	0.34	1.32	8.38
Textiles & apparel	0.15	0.17	0.93	5.83
Wood and paper products	0.06	0.16	0.83	4.95
Publishing & printing	0.13	0.22	0.38	7.83
Chemical products	3.61	3.27	13.5	21.8
Drugs & medicine	7.21	15.49	15.27	31.9
Petroleum and coal products	7.24	2.91	2.31	22.2
Plastic products	0.41	0.45	3.22	10.03
Rubber products	1.08	1.15	2.81	40.18
Ceramic, stone and clay	0.28	0.35	1.55	21.45
Iron & steel	0.01	0.13	0.27	19.35
Non-ferrous metals	1.61	0.44	7.72	15.73
Metal products	0.31	0.2	0.72	7.52
General machinery	1.68	1.78	6.82	12.75
Electrical machinery	2.46	2.48	12.51	13.78
Motor vehicles & parts	4.72	10.79	18.32	15.6
Miscellaneous transport equipment	0.7	0.62	12.71	4.23
Precision instruments	0.41	0.9	5.04	11.16
Miscellaneous manufacturing	0.47	0.72	1.71	6.62
Manufacturing total	**1.36**	**1.94**	**5.91**	**10.78**
Construction & civil engineering	0.05	0.05	0.03	1.72
Electricity, gas, steam and water supply, etc.	0	0	0.04	1.96
Wholesale trade	2.31	2.57	4.24	7.89
Retail trade	0.29	0.49	0.77	4.5
Financial intermediary services	1.47	1.75	10	6.1
Insurance	1.67	6.69	12.57	6.4
Real estate	0.02	0.08	0.28	1.64
Transportation & postal service	0.5	0.27	3.52	4.82
Telecommunications & broadcasting	0.22	2.31	6.55	7.66
Education & research institutes	0.34	0.97	1.76	6.39
Medical services, health and hygiene	0.02	0.04	0.16	1.99
Computer programming & Information services	1.83	2.55	4.33	3.88
Goods & equipment rental & leasing	0.88	1.2	0.49	3.66
Other business services	0.52	1.71	2.1	4.77
Eating & drinking places	1.58	2.36	3.89	2.48
Other personal services	0.12	0.39	0.38	4.23
Other services	0.01	0	0	n.a.
Services total	**0.65**	**0.97**	**2.04**	**4.31**
Total: all sectors	**n.a.**	**1.15**	**2.75**	**5.61**

Source: Paprzycki and Fukao (2005). Original data is compiled from the microdata of the Ministry of Internal Affairs and Communications' *Establishment and Enterprise Census for 1996 and 2001* and the Bureau of Economic Analysis' *Foreign Direct Investment in the United States: Establishment Data for 1997*, online: http://www.bea.gov/bea/ai/iidguide.htm#FDIUS.

Notes: JAFF (33.4%): Japanese Affiliates of Foreign Firms (33.4% or more foreign-owned by one or more foreign companies); JAFF (20%): Japanese Affiliates of Foreign Firms (20% or more foreign-owned by a single foreign company); USAFF: U.S. Affiliates of Foreign Firms (10% or more foreign-owned by a single foreign company).

lifted the ban on triangular mergers involving foreign firms. In addition, the Japan External Trade Organization (JETRO), a government-related institution, provides a one-stop window and other services to facilitate foreign investment.

Despite the importance of the subject, there are few meaningful empirical studies on the implications of the increase in inward FDI for the Japanese economy. In fact, some observers have argued that Japan does not need more FDI. Like FDI in other developed economies, the largest part of recent inflows to Japan took the form of mergers and acquisitions (M&As). The critics fear that inward M&As are dominated by "vulture" funds seeking to reap quick profits by taking advantage of troubled firms (*Nihon Keizai Shimbun* 2003). Another argument is that some inward M&As are in fact aimed at acquiring advanced technologies (Werner 2003) rather than at transferring and employing intangible assets in Japan.

According to quantitative studies on corporate performance in Japan, such as Kimura and Kiyota (2004) and Fukao and Murakami (2005), foreign-owned firms tend to show higher productivity than domestically-owned firms. However, the positive correlation between foreign ownership and productivity does not necessarily mean Japanese firms that were acquired by foreign firms receive new technologies and management skills from their foreign owners, or that this transfer of intangible assets is responsible for their higher TFP (the technology-transfer effect). There is another possible theoretical explanation for the positive correlation: foreign-owned firms enjoy greater productivity because foreign firms choose firms with higher TFP as their M&A targets (the selection effect).

In a previous study (Fukao, Ito and Kwon 2005), we conducted two empirical tests using firm-level data for Japan's manufacturing industry in order to determine which one of the two effects is responsible for the positive correlation between foreign ownership and productivity. In that study, we first estimated a Probit model explaining whether a firm is chosen as an M&A target based on its TFP level and other characteristics. Second, we tested whether the TFP of Japanese firms that were acquired by foreign firms improved after the investments.[1] Estimating a Probit model, we found that foreign firms who acquired Japanese firms enjoyed higher TFP levels and higher profit rates. In contrast, in-in M&As seemed to have the characteristics of rescue missions, as they tended to target small firms with

---

1. Although the majority of FDI in developed economies has taken the form of cross-border acquisitions, studies on cross-border M&As are rather scarce. Conyon et al. (2002) conducted an empirical analysis on the impact of foreign ownership on productivity in the United Kingdom for the period 1989–1994. By observing firms' productivity before and after acquisition, they showed that firms that were acquired by foreign firms exhibited an increase in labor productivity of 13%. Arnold and Javorcik (2005) and Bertrand and Zitouna (2005) found that foreign acquisitions improved the productivity of target firms in Indonesia and France. On the other hand, Gugler et al. (2003) did not find any significant differences in the effect on profits of cross-border and domestic M&As.

a higher total liability/total asset ratio. Estimating the dynamic effects of M&As on target firms, we found that out-in M&As improved target firms' TFP level and current profit/sales ratio. Compared with in-in M&As, out-in M&As brought a larger and quicker improvement in TFP and profit rates but no increase in target firms' employment two years after the acquisition. Based on these results, we concluded that both the selection effect and the technology-transfer effect play a role in explaining the positive correlation between foreign ownership and productivity.

Our previous study has several limitations, which this chapter seeks to overcome. First, although our study found that in-in M&As had the characteristics of rescue missions, this result may have been influenced by the fact that some in-in M&As are conducted within groups of related firms. In the case of M&As within firm groups, acquisitions are conducted as part of a restructuring of the firm group and will indeed have the characteristics of rescue missions. On the other hand, in-in M&As involving outsiders of firm groups may have similar effects as out-in M&As. In this chapter, using data on Japanese firm groups compiled by Toyo Keizai Shinposha, we distinguish in-in M&As within firm groups and in-in M&As involving outsiders.

Second, although 72 percent of FDI during the 1997–2002 period went into nonmanufacturing sectors, such as the finance and insurance, telecommunications, service, and retail/wholesale sectors (which experienced deregulation), Fukao, Ito, and Kwon (2005) only examined M&As in Japan's manufacturing industry. In this chapter, we look at M&As not only in the manufacturing sector, but also in the wholesale and retail industry.

Third, estimation results on the dynamic effects of M&As on target firms may suffer from a selection bias problem. Suppose foreign investors somehow acquire more promising Japanese firms than Japanese investors do. Then the ex post facto improvement of out-in M&A target firms' performance should not be regarded as evidence of technology-transfer from foreign investors to acquired firms. In order to solve this selection bias problem, following Arnold and Javorcik (2005), we combine a difference-in-differences approach with propensity score matching. We employ the propensity score matching technique proposed by Rosenbaum and Rubin (1983). The basic idea is that we first look for firms that were not acquired by foreign firms, but had similar characteristics to firms that were acquired by foreigners. Using these firms as control subjects while comparing treated (out-in M&A targets) and control subjects, we examine whether firms acquired by foreigners show a greater improvement in performance than firms not acquired by foreigners.

Fourth, using data for the period from 1994 to 2001, Fukao, Ito, and Kwon (2005) investigated the performance of target firms for only two years after each M&A. By adding data of one more year, 2002, we now study dynamic effects of M&A with a longer time span.

The remainder of this chapter is organized as follows: In section 11.2, we provide an overview of out-in M&As in Japan. Section 11.3 then presents an outline of our data and reports our empirical results. Section 11.4 summarizes our results.

11.2   An Overview of M&As in Japan

Probably the most comprehensive data on M&As in Japan are published by the private information service company RECOF. In this section, we provide an overview of M&A activity in Japan using these data. Figure 11.1 shows the number of out-in and in-in M&A cases in Japan by year. Both M&A cases have dramatically increased since the end of the 1990s.

Several factors seem to have contributed to the increase in M&A cases during this period. First, in order to speed up the restructuring of Japanese firms, Japan's corporate law was amended at the end of the 1990s to facilitate M&As. Second, advances in information and communication technology, as well as deregulation during the 1990s, mean the optimal size and optimal scope of firms in many sectors, such as electronics, pharmaceuticals, telecommunications, finance, insurance, and commerce may have changed. Third, deregulation in Japan has removed barriers to inward FDI in some industries, such as broadcasting, telecommunications, finance, and insurance. Fourth, there was a worldwide boom in M&As during this period and foreign investors, including private equity funds, and foreign agents of M&A, including investment banks, brought their M&A techniques and the M&A boom to Japan. Fifth, as a result of the prolonged

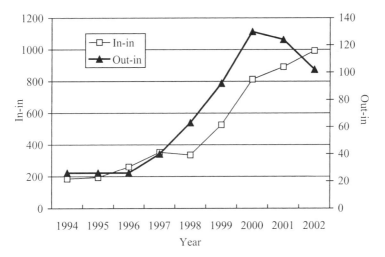

Fig. 11.1   Number of in-in and out-in M&A transactions in Japan by year: 1994–2002

Source: RECOF (2003).

Note: M&A transactions include mergers, purchases of substantial minority interests, and purchases of additional shares and acquisitions.

recession and the financial crisis in 1998, Japanese stock prices plunged and financially distressed firms and banks were forced to unwind their cross-shareholdings, creating a fire sale situation that allowed foreign firms to acquire Japanese companies.

Probably as a result of the last three of these factors, the rapid increase in out-in M&As preceded the boom for in-in M&As (figure 11.1). Figure 11.2 shows the number of out-in M&A cases by source region and by year. United States and European firms were the major investors. One interesting new trend is that since 2000 investments from Asian countries have also been increasing. Among the total ninety-seven out-in M&As involving firms from Asia in the period between 1994–2002, thirty-six involved firms from China, twenty-four from Korea, nineteen from Taiwan, and eight from Singapore.

An interesting question is whether there are any differences in the industry distribution of target firms between M&A investments from Western countries and from Asia. Table 11.2 shows the industry distribution of out-in M&A target firms by source region. Compared with investments from Western countries, M&A investments from Asia tend to be concentrated in electrical machinery, communication and broadcasting, and software. One possible explanation regarding these differences is that Asian firms conduct M&A investments in Japan in order to gain access to the technology of Japanese high-tech firms.

Another issue concerns the extent to which the out-in M&A boom in Japan was dominated by private equity funds (vulture funds). Table 11.3,

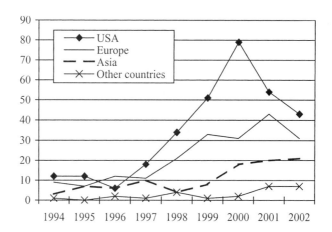

Fig. 11.2   Number of out-in M&A transactions in Japan by year and by regions
Source: RECOF (2003).
Note: M&A transactions include mergers, purchases of substantial minority interests, and purchases of additional shares and acquisitions.

Table 11.2   **Industry distribution of target firms in out-in M&A transactions: By source region, 1994–2002**

Target firms' industry	Source region			
	USA	Europe	Asia	Other countries
Mining	0.0	0.0	0.0	4.0
Construction	1.6	1.0	0.0	8.0
Food	1.9	1.0	2.1	0.0
Textiles	0.0	0.5	2.1	0.0
Paper and pulp	0.3	0.0	1.0	0.0
Chemicals	2.6	13.6	3.1	0.0
Medical supplies	2.3	7.1	1.0	0.0
Petroleum and coal	1.0	0.5	0.0	0.0
Rubber	0.6	0.0	1.0	0.0
Publishing and printing	1.0	1.0	0.0	4.0
Stone, clay and glass	0.3	2.0	1.0	0.0
Steel	1.0	0.0	2.1	0.0
Nonferrous metals	1.3	2.0	3.1	4.0
General machinery	4.5	5.1	3.1	4.0
Transportation	5.5	10.1	3.1	0.0
Precision machinery	1.0	1.0	2.1	4.0
Other manufacturing	0.6	0.0	0.0	4.0
General trading company	0.6	1.0	1.0	0.0
Food wholesale	0.6	2.0	0.0	4.0
Medical-supplies wholesale	0.0	0.5	0.0	4.0
Other wholesale	9.1	8.1	8.2	12.0
Department stores	0.3	0.0	0.0	0.0
Supermarkets, convenience stores	1.0	0.0	0.0	0.0
Other retail	0.6	2.5	0.0	0.0
Food services	0.0	0.5	0.0	0.0
Banks	1.3	1.5	0.0	0.0
Life insurance, damage insurance	1.6	3.0	0.0	0.0
Security	2.9	1.0	8.2	0.0
Other finance	7.1	5.6	0.0	4.0
Transportation, warehouses	1.0	1.0	1.0	4.0
Communication, broadcasting	7.8	5.1	12.4	8.0
Real estate, hotels	1.3	1.5	2.1	0.0
Amusement	1.6	1.5	2.1	0.0
Software	16.8	6.1	12.4	12.0
Services	11.3	5.6	6.2	8.0
Total # of out-in M&As	309	198	97	25

Source: RECOF (2003).

Notes: All figures are in %. M&A transactions include mergers, purchases of substantial minority interests, and purchases of additional shares and acquisitions.

Table 11.3   Number of out-in acquisition cases by purchasers' industry and by target firms' industry: 1994–2002

Purchasers' industry	Target firms' industry					
	Manufacturing	Commerce	Finance	Other services	Primary industry and construction	Total
Manufacturing	118(98)	31	0	13	0	162
Commerce	2	8(7)	0	1	0	11
Finance	7	4	32(23)	16	0	59
Other services	8	4	5	54(47)	2	73
Primary industry and construction	2	0	0	0	4(4)	6
Total	137	47	37	84	6	311

Source: RECOF (2003).
Notes: Figures in parentheses denote the number of acquisition cases between the same industries at a 2-digit industry classification. (See table 11.2 for the 2-digit industry classification.)

which shows the number of out-in acquisitions by purchasers' industry and by target firms' industry, provides a clue. The table shows that out-in M&As in the same industry are much more common than cross-industry out-in M&As. There were only seven acquisitions of Japanese manufacturing firms by foreign investors from the financial sector, which includes M&As by private equity funds. It is also interesting to note that in the case of out-in M&As in the commerce sector, the majority of purchasers were manufacturing firms (see table 11.3). This is probably because manufacturers of differentiated products, such as automobiles and electronic machinery, usually try to integrate the overseas sales of their products in order to control and promote their exports.

11.3 Research Approach, Empirical Model, and Results

Attempts to provide a theoretical explanation for changes in ownership and the causes and consequences of acquisitions have produced two different hypotheses: the synergy hypothesis and the managerial-discipline hypothesis.[2] The synergy hypothesis claims acquisitions take place when the value of the combined new hierarchical firm group to be created by the acquisition is expected to be greater than the sum of the values of the inde-

2. Lichtenberg and Siegel (1987) and McGuckin and Nguyen (1995) tested these hypotheses using U.S. plant level data. Lichtenberg and Siegel (1987) found that firms with low productivity were chosen and productivity increased after the acquisition. McGuckin and Nguyen (1995) found a positive relationship between changes in ownership and both initial productivity and productivity growth after the acquisition.

pendent firms. As Nguyen and Ollinger (2002) have pointed out, if an acquisition is motivated by this synergy effect, acquiring firms tend to target only productive and efficient firms. After a merger, synergies between the firms are expected to improve the performance of the acquired firm. In contrast, the managerial-discipline hypothesis claims acquisitions are driven by the intention to strengthen managerial control over entrenched managers, who try to maximize their own benefits rather than owners' wealth. Therefore, takeover targets are likely to be inefficient firms and their performance, especially the rate of return on capital, is expected to improve after the acquisition (Jensen 1988).

In our previous study, Fukao, Ito, and Kwon (2005), we examined the characteristics of firms acquired by in-in and out-in M&As by estimating Probit models. We also estimated the dynamic effects of M&As on target firms by regressing changes in performance on a set of control variables and dummy variables which represent firms acquired by in-in or out-in M&As. Through these estimations, we found foreign firms acquired better performing Japanese firms with higher TFP levels and higher profit rates. Moreover, out-in M&As improved target firms' TFP level and current profit-sales ratio, and compared with in-in M&As, out-in M&As brought a larger and quicker improvement in the performance of acquired firms. Therefore, we concluded that the motivation for out-in M&As tended to be to achieve synergy effects, while the motivation for in-in M&As tended to be to improve managerial efficiency. The analysis in Fukao, Ito, and Kwon (2005) was based on the firm-level data for the period from 1994 to 2001 underlying the *Basic Survey of Japanese Business Structure and Activities* and the analysis focused on the manufacturing sector. In this chapter, we extend the sample period until 2002 and include the data on nonmanufacturing industries. The survey covers many nonmanufacturing industries: wholesale and retail trade, electricity and gas, information and communication services, credit and finance business, restaurants, private education services, and other services such as amusement and recreation, business services, and personal services. In the 2003 survey, 27,545 firms answered the survey. Of these, 12,946 firms are classified in the manufacturing sector (47 percent of the total number of responding firms). In this chapter, using a new dataset, we analyze the effect of out-in M&As on target firms' performance for both the manufacturing sector and the nonmanufacturing sector, following the methodology employed by Fukao, Ito, and Kwon (2005). We examine whether the effects of M&As are temporary or long-lasting by analyzing the dynamic effects over a longer time span. Moreover, we investigate whether there are differences between the effects of in-in M&As within a corporate group and those of in-in M&As by outsiders.

However, one possible concern is firms acquired by foreign firms show better performance simply because foreign firms acquired better performing firms or firms that would potentially perform well, even under local ownership.[3] As Arnold and Javorcik (2005, p. 6) point out, "plants acquired by foreign investors are unlikely to be a random sample from the populations. To the extent that the acquisition targets differ systematically from other plants, a problem of simultaneity between ownership status and other performance-relevant variables will arise and bias the estimate of the productivity advantage." In order to control for this selection bias, we apply a matching technique in this chapter. Using this technique, we identify for each foreign-acquired firm a suitable domestically-owned firm for comparison.[4] In other words, we find firms that were not acquired by foreign firms but had similar characteristics as firms that were acquired by foreigners. Comparing the treated group (out-in M&A targets) and the control group, we examine whether firms acquired by foreigners show a greater or faster improvement in performance than firms not acquired by foreigners.

In order to examine this issue, we compare the growth rates of performance measures of acquired firms with those of firms remaining under domestic ownership using a difference-in-differences (DID) technique. The difference-in-differences technique compares the difference in average outcome before and after the treatment for the treated group with the difference in average outcome during the same period for the control group.[5] However, before applying the difference-in-differences technique, we need to overcome, or at least reduce, the problem of sample selection bias. Following Arnold and Javorcik (2005), we combine the difference-in-differences approach with propensity score matching.[6] We employ the propensity score matching technique proposed by Rosenbaum and Rubin (1983). In studies evaluating the effects of economic policy interventions, and so on, data often come from (nonrandomized) observational studies, and the estimation of the effect of treatment may be biased by the existence of confounding factors. The propensity score matching method provides a

3. Many FDI-related studies show that compared with domestically-owned firms, foreign-owned firms tend to be larger in size, more capital- and skill-intensive, and show better business performance in terms of, for instance, productivity and profitability. See, for example, Doms and Jensen (1998) for the United States, Griffith and Simpson (2001) for the United Kingdom, Ramstetter (1999), Takii (2004), and Ito (2004) for Asian countries. Fukao, Ito, and Kwon (2005) also compared differences in performance and other characteristics of local and foreign-owned firms in Japanese manufacturing and found that foreign-owned firms showed a better performance.
4. Arnold and Javorcik (2005), using plant-level data on the Indonesian manufacturing sector, apply the matching technique and compare TFP levels and other performance measures of domestic plants and plants acquired by foreign firms.
5. The DID estimator assumes that unobserved macroeconomic shocks affect the treatment and the control group in the same way (common trends assumption).
6. This type of strategy is often employed in studies in the field of labor economics such as Heckman, Ichimura, and Todd (1997) and Heckman, Ichimura, Smith, and Todd (1998). Moreover, the matching estimator has become increasingly popular in international economics and other areas of economics. See, for example, Girma, Greenaway, and Kneller (2004), Barba Navaretti, Castellani, and Disdier (2006) and Hijzen, Jean, and Mayer (2006).

way to reduce the bias of the estimation of treatment effects and control for the existence of the confounding effect by comparing treated and control subjects that are as similar as possible. Since matching subjects on an n-dimensional vector of characteristics is typically unfeasible for large n, the propensity score matching method summarizes the pretreatment characteristics of each subject into a single-index variable (i.e., the propensity score) which makes the matching feasible.[7]

11.3.1 The Propensity Score Matching and the Difference-in-Differences Estimator

The propensity score is defined by Rosenbaum and Rubin (1983) as the conditional probability of assignment to a particular treatment given the pretreatment characteristics:

$$(1) \qquad p(x) \equiv \Pr\{z = 1 | x\} = E\{z | x\}$$

where $z = \{0, 1\}$ is the indicator of receiving the treatment and x is a vector of observed pretreatment characteristics. Rosenbaum and Rubin (1983) show that if the recipient of the treatment is randomly chosen within cells defined by x, it is also random within cells defined by the values of the single-index variable $p(x)$. Therefore, for each treatment case i, if the propensity score $p(x_i)$ is known, the average effect of treatment on the treated (ATT) can be estimated as follows:

$$(2) \quad \hat{\alpha}_{ATT} = E\{y_{1i} - y_{0i} | z_i = 1\}$$
$$= E\{E\{y_{1i} - y_{0i} | z_i = 1, p(x_i)\}\}$$
$$= E\{E\{y_{1i} | z_i = 1, p(x_i)\} - E\{y_{0i} | z_i = 0, p(x_i)\} | z_i = 1\}$$

where y_1 and y_0 denote the potential outcomes in the two counterfactual situations of treatment and no treatment, respectively. Therefore, according to the last line of equation (2), the ATT can be estimated as the average difference between the outcome of recipients and nonrecipients of the treatment whose propensity scores $p(x_i)$ are identical.

In the case of this study, we consider two types of treatment: acquisition by foreign investors and acquisition by domestic investors. Therefore, we focus on the difference in ex post facto performance between firms acquired by foreigners and firms that remain independent (nonacquired firms), as well as between firms acquired by domestic investors and independent firms (acquired by neither foreigners nor domestic investors). Therefore, in our case, z denotes one of three possible outcomes: remaining independent (nonacquired), acquired by foreigners, or acquired by do-

---

7. For details on the method and an explanation of the Stata program for the method, see Becker and Ichino (2002).

mestic investors. Variable x is a vector of various characteristics of a firm such as firm size, length of business experience, ex ante performance, and so on. Therefore, by estimating a multinomial logit model at the first stage, we investigate important determinants of acquisition by foreigners and by domestic firms and compute the two propensity scores (i.e., the probabilities of a firm being acquired by a foreign firm or by a domestic firm) for each firm. Making use of this result, we conduct propensity score matching and compare the performance of firms within the pairs of observations matched on the propensity score. In our matching process, firms are matched separately for each year and industry using one-to-one nearest matching with replacement.[8]

In the second stage, we estimate a difference-in-differences (DID) estimator to evaluate the causal effect of acquisition on a set of performance variables of interest. Once matched, the only difference between acquired and nonacquired firms is their acquisition status. Therefore, we focus on the ATT. The ATT can be estimated as equation (2) above, which in the case of this study is equivalent to the following equation:

$$(3) \qquad \hat{\alpha}_{ATT} = \frac{1}{n} \sum_{1}^{n} (y^{treated}_{acquisition\ year+s} - y^{control}_{acquisition\ year+s})$$

$$- \frac{1}{n} \sum_{1}^{n} (y^{treated}_{pre-acquisition\ year} - y^{control}_{pre-acquisition\ year})$$

$$s = \{0, 1, 2, 3, 4\}$$

where n denotes the number of observations and y denotes outcome variables.

In the following subsections, we (a) provide details on our dataset (section 11.3.2); (b) show the result of the multinomial logit estimation on the determinants of acquisition (section 11.3.3); (c) examine, by OLS regression analysis, whether the acquired firms saw an improvement in performance after the acquisition using unmatched samples (section 11.3.4); and finally (d) examine the ex post facto performance differences between firms acquired by foreigners and nonacquired firms, as well as between firms acquired by domestic investors and nonacquired firms, using matched samples (section 11.3.5).

11.3.2   Data Source

Our analysis on the effects of acquisitions is based on the firm-level data of the *Kigyo Katsudo Kihon Chosa* (*Basic Survey of Japanese Business*

---

8. Our matching procedure is implemented in Stata 9 using a modified version of the procedure provided by Leuven and Sianesi (2001). As we match firms separately for each year and industry (thirteen manufacturing industries and nine nonmanufacturing industries), we had to modify the program.

Structure and Activities) compiled by the Ministry of Economy, Trade, and Industry (METI).[9] Our data cover the period from 1994 to 2002.[10] We define out-in M&As as cases where a firm did not have a foreign parent firm with majority ownership at time $t - 1$ comes to have a foreign parent firm with majority ownership at time t. Similarly, we define in-in M&As as cases where a firm did not have a parent firm with majority ownership at time $t - 1$ comes to have a domestic parent firm with majority ownership at time t. Therefore, if a firm is sold from a domestic parent firm to another domestic parent firm, such cases are not counted as in-in M&As in our above definition.

Tables 11.4 and 11.5 show the number of out-in and in-in M&A cases in our dataset. We have 156 cases of out-in M&As and 3,132 cases of in-in M&As for the period from 1994 to 2002. As shown in table 11.5, our unbalanced panel consists of 186,080 observations, of which 53 percent fall into the manufacturing sector. More than 80 percent of the nonmanufacturing observations fall into the wholesale and retail trade sector. Table 11.5 also shows that out-in M&As are heavily concentrated in a relatively small number of industries, which include chemicals, machinery, and wholesale and retail trade.[11] Although in-in M&As also tend to be concentrated in these industries, they are more widely dispersed, covering all industries except agriculture, forestry, and fishing.

Data on sales, purchases, total assets, profits, total liabilities, firm age, the number of employees, the number of nonproduction workers, exports, R&D expenditure, and advertising expenditure are taken from the *Basic Survey of Japanese Business Structure and Activities.* We mainly use newly constructed industry-level deflators, which were taken from the JIP (Japan Industry Productivity) Database 2006.[12] We use the industry-level output and input deflators to deflate firms' sales and intermediate inputs, respectively. Exports and R&D expenditure are deflated by the export price index compiled by Bank of Japan and the R&D price index compiled by the Science and Technology Agency and reported in *Kagaku Gijutsu Yoran 2003,* respectively. Advertising expenditure is deflated by the corporate services

---

9. The survey covers all firms with at least fifty employees or thirty million yen of paid-in capital in the Japanese manufacturing, mining, commerce, and several other service sectors.

10. The compilation of the micro data of the METI survey was conducted as part of the project *Study Group on the Internationalization of Japanese Business* at the Research Institute of Economy, Trade and Industry (RIETI).

11. These industries have a higher share of foreign-owned firms than other industries. For detailed statistics on foreign-owned firms in Japan, see Fukao, Ito, and Kwon (2005) and Ito and Fukao (2005).

12. The JIP Database 2006 was compiled as part of the RIETI (Research Institute of Economy, Trade and Industry) research project *Development of a RIETI Manufacturing Database and Study of Productivity by Industry* for fiscal 2004–05. The JIP 2006 contains sector-level information on 108 sectors from 1970 to 2002 that can be used for total factor productivity analyses. These sectors cover the whole Japanese economy. A preliminary version of the JIP database is available from the RIETI website http://www.rieti.go.jp/jp/database/d04.html.

Table 11.4   Number of out-in and in-in acquisitions, by year

Year	Out-in	In-in
1994–1995	20	410
1995–1996	17	417
1996–1997	32	516
1997–1998	16	352
1998–1999	14	406
1999–2000	20	314
2000–2001	26	473
2001–2002	11	244
Total	156	3,132

Source: Authors' calculation.

Table 11.5   Number of out-in and in-in acquisitions, by industry: 1994–2002

Industry	Out-in	In-in	Number of observations
Agriculture, forestry and fishing	0	0	80
Mining	0	5	395
Food products and beverages	2	203	11,799
Textiles	1	44	2,733
Pulp, paper and paper products	2	65	3,264
Chemicals	20	105	7,010
Petroleum and coal products	2	7	430
Non-metallic mineral products	1	64	4,271
Basic metals	1	88	5,451
Fabricated metal products	0	102	7,144
General machinery	10	147	11,349
Electrical machinery, equipment and supplies	15	234	14,919
Transport equipment	7	166	8,616
Precision instruments	5	35	2,624
Manufacturing not elsewhere classified	9	262	19,812
Construction	0	42	3,206
Electricity, gas and water supply	0	3	392
Wholesale and retail trade	77	1,351	71,175
Finance and insurance	0	8	297
Real estate	0	3	230
Transport and communications	0	13	678
Service activities	4	185	10,205
Total	156	3,132	186,080

Source: Authors' calculation.

Table 11.6   **Definition of variables**

Variable name	Definition
TFP	Multilateral TFP index (see Appendix)
ROA	Return on assets measured as: (after-tax profits + interest payments)/total assets
log(size)	Firm size measured as the log of the number of workers
Age	Number of years since the foundation of the firm
Number of nonproduction workers/number of workers	Quality of firms' human capital measured as the share of nonproduction workers
R&D intensity	R&D expenditure divided by total sales
Advertising intensity	Advertising expenditure divided by total sales
Export intensity	Export ratio measured as exports divided by total sales
Debt/total assets	Debt-asset ratio measured as total liabilities divided by total assets

price index provided by the Bank of Japan. ROA is defined as the ratio of after-tax profits inclusive of interest payments to total assets. Table 11.6 provides a description of the variables used in our econometric analysis. The summary statistics for the variables are shown in Appendix table 11A.1, and a detailed description of our TFP measure is provided in the Appendix.

11.3.3   Are Acquisition Targets Better Than the Rest? A Multinomial Logit Estimation

Using our panel data for the period 1994–2002, we estimate multinomial logit models designed to test whether a firm is chosen as an M&A target based on its productivity or profitability level, or whether other characteristics are more important. The multinomial logit estimation allows us to compute the probability of remaining independent and the probability of being acquired by foreign investors or domestic investors.

We consider three outcomes: outcome 1 (not-acquired), outcome 2 (acquired by foreigners, *Out-in*), and outcome 3 (acquired by domestic investors, *In-in*).[13] As explanatory variables, we use the logarithm of TFP, ROA (return on assets), the logarithm of employment to represent firm size, firm age, the share of the number of non-production workers in the total number of workers as an indicator of human capital, R&D intensity, ad-

13. We were also interested in the difference between determinants of out-in M&As by Asian firms and by Western firms and the difference between the outcomes for these two types of out-in M&As. However, the number of observations for M&A cases by Asian firms is very small and almost no observations were left after we screened the data. Therefore, we gave up investigating the characteristics or outcomes of out-in M&As by Asian firms in this study. Nonetheless, as mentioned in section 11.2, the number of out-in M&A cases by Asian firms has been increasing in recent years and M&As by Asian firms are an issue that deserves further investigation in future studies.

vertising intensity, export intensity, and the debt-asset ratio.[14] All the explanatory variables are values in year $t - 1$, for example, the year preceding the year of acquisition, t. The model also includes a full set of industry and year dummies.

The results from the multinomial logit estimation are presented in table 11.7. The determinants of acquisition are quite different for out-in acquisitions and in-in acquisitions. In the case of out-in acquisitions, consistent with the preceding results of Fukao, Ito, and Kwon (2005) and Conyon et al. (2002), we find that firms with higher TFP, a higher profit rate, a higher share of nonproduction workers, a higher export intensity, and of larger size are chosen as targets in the manufacturing sector (equation (1) of table 11.7). As for the nonmanufacturing sector, firms with a higher profit rate and higher advertising tend to be chosen as out-in M&A targets (equation (3) of table 11.7). This result implies that foreign firms acquire well-performing Japanese firms. In contrast, in the case of in-in acquisitions, many of these performance measures are not significant determinants of acquisitions (equation (2) of table 11.7). Moreover, in the case of in-in acquisitions in the nonmanufacturing sector, firms with a higher profit rate are less likely to be acquired, which is conspicuously different from the case of out-in acquisitions (equation (4) of table 11.7). Another important difference between out-in and in-in acquisitions is that firms with a higher debt-asset ratio are chosen as targets in the case of in-in acquisitions, while firms with a lower debt-asset ratio are chosen as targets in the case of out-in acquisitions.[15] This result implies that in-in acquisitions may have the characteristics of rescue missions. As discussed in Fukao, Ito, and Kwon (2005), in-in acquisitions in Japan may be mainly conducted within vertical and horizontal *keiretsu* networks or within a corporate group, and financially distressed firms are salvaged by other member firms or parent firms through M&As. We will return to this issue in the next subsection.

---

14. In the case of the nonmanufacturing sector, the share of the number of nonproduction workers in the total number of workers, R&D intensity, and export intensity are excluded from the explanatory variables. We define "production workers" as the workers who are working in manufacturing plants and consequently, our definition of the share of nonproduction is not appropriate as a proxy for human capital or skilled labor in the case of the nonmanufacturing sector. The data on R&D expenditure are not very reliable for many firms in the nonmanufacturing sector in our dataset. As for exports, most of exporting firms are trading companies and there are very few firms who export their products or services in other nonmanufacturing industries. Therefore, we think these variables are not appropriate explanatory variables in the case of the nonmanufacturing sector.

15. In the latter half of the 1990s, it was argued that Japanese banks were reluctant to advance loans because of the severe nonperforming loan problem. In order to check whether foreign capital helped to remove credit constraints, we included the short-term debt to assets ratio instead of the total debt to assets ratio as an explanatory variable. Short-term debt was defined as total debt minus fixed debt. The estimated coefficient on the short-term debt-asset ratio was not statistically significant in the case of out-in acquisitions, while it was positive and significant in the case of in-in acquisitions. Therefore, at least based on our dataset, we cannot conclude that foreign capital rescued Japanese firms suffering from credit constraints.

Table 11.7   What firms are chosen as acquisition targets? Multinomial logit analysis

	Manufacturing				Nonmanufacturing			
	(1) Out-in Acquisitions		(2) In-in Acquisitions		(3) Out-in Acquisitions		(4) In-in Acquisitions	
Dependent variable	Coefficient.	z-value	Coefficient	z-value	Coefficient	z-value	Coefficient	z-value
$TFP(t-1)$	1.213	2.55**	0.236	1.14	-0.179	-0.43	-0.038	-0.34
$ROA(t-1)$	0.417	3.40***	-0.018	-0.07	2.541	4.74***	-0.522	-1.73*
$\log(size)(t-1)$	0.376	4.30***	-0.065	-1.93*	0.181	1.10	0.023	0.78
$Age(t-1)$	-0.053	-5.84***	-0.015	-7.27***	-0.060	-5.79***	-0.017	-8.74***
(Number of non-production workers/ number of workers) $(t-1)$	2.011	4.42***	-0.121	-0.92				
R&D intensity$(t-1)$	3.091	1.02	-2.036	-1.16				
Advertising intensity$(t-1)$	-8.441	-0.79	-9.284	-1.91*	9.308	4.49***	-0.180	-0.10
Export intensity$(t-1)$	2.785	4.65***	-0.429	-1.18				
(Debt/total assets) $(t-1)$	-0.286	-0.45	0.487	7.44***	-1.152	-2.05**	0.386	6.05***
Constant	-33.582	-24.01***	-3.686	-13.93***	-27.668	-23.80***	-26.425	-25.50***
Observations	89,168				74,644			
Pseudo R^2	0.0402				0.046			

Notes: Estimated coefficients of year dummies and 3-digit industry dummies are not shown in the table. Z-values are White-corrected for heteroskedasticity.
*Significant at the 10% level (two-tailed test).
**Significant at the 5% level.
***Significant at the 1% level.

The results from the multinomial logit estimation generally indicate foreign firms tend to target firms that are more productive and have a higher ROA, while Japanese firms target firms with low profitability. There are two potential explanations for these revealed preferences of foreign firms. One is the synergy hypothesis. Foreign firms seek synergy effects when they purchase Japanese firms. In order to make sure they reap synergy effects, foreign firms prefer excellent Japanese firms. The other explanation, which is not necessarily inconsistent with the first, is an asymmetric information problem. Foreign firms are disadvantaged in gathering information on small Japanese firms. It is a very difficult task for foreign firms to correctly evaluate whether they can restructure a small Japanese firm teetering on the brink of bankruptcy and negotiate from their home country debt rescheduling with the Japanese main bank of such a firm. Because of this problem, foreign firms may prefer better Japanese firms as their target.

In the case of cross-border portfolio investment, it is well known that investors tend to prefer stocks of excellent and large manufacturing firms with high export intensity. Probably in the case of out-in M&As, the problem of asymmetric information causes a similar phenomenon. After establishing a beachhead by purchasing an excellent Japanese firm, foreign firms probably can gather more information on smaller and inferior Japanese firms and then start purchasing such firms. But if this new purchase is conducted by the beachhead Japanese affiliate, our data on out-in M&As do not cover such cases.

In the case of in-in M&As, we found that Japanese firms tend to target inefficient firms with low profits or with a high debt-asset ratio. This finding is consistent with the managerial-discipline hypothesis.

11.3.4 Do Acquisitions Improve the Performance of Target Firms? An Analysis of the Dynamic Effects Based on the Unmatched Sample

In this subsection, we examine how the performance of targeted firms changes after the acquisition. First, following Fukao, Ito, and Kwon (2005), we estimate the following model of the dynamic effects of an acquisition in order to see whether the improvement in performance is significantly faster for acquired firms than for nonacquired firms:

$$(4) \qquad y_{f,t+s} - y_{f,t-1} = \alpha + \beta_1 Out\text{-}in_{f,t} + \beta_2 In\text{-}in_{f,t} + x_{f,t-1}\phi$$
$$+ \sum_t \lambda_\tau YearDummy(t, \tau) + \sum_i \delta_j IndustryDummy(i, j) + \varepsilon_{f,t}$$
$$s = \{1, 2, 3, 4\}$$

where $y_{f,t}$ denotes the performance of firm f in year t and $x_{f,t-1}$ is a vector of various firm characteristics that are expected to affect the performance of firm f in year $t-1$. As variables to measure targeted firms' performance we use the logarithm of TFP, the return on assets (ROA) ratio, the logarithm of sales, and the logarithm of employment. It likely takes several years for the performance improving effects of an acquisition to materialize. In order to take this time lag into account, we examine whether the performance of acquired firms has improved s ($= 1, 2, 3, 4$) years after the acquisition compared with the performance in the year prior to the acquisition. As explanatory variables, we use out-in and in-in acquisition dummies (*Out-in* and *In-in*) that take 1 for an acquired firm in year t when the acquisition occurs, the lagged values of the two performance variables (the *TFP* level and the *ROA*), the lagged logarithm of the number of employees in year $t - 1$, and several additional firm characteristics, such as the length of business experience (*Age*), the ratio of the number of nonproduction workers to the number of total workers, R&D intensity, advertising intensity, export intensity, and the debt-asset ratio.[16] A full set of industry and year dummies is also included, λ_τ and δ_j denote the coefficients of the year and industry dummies, respectively By looking at the coefficients on the *Out-in* and *In-in* dummy variables, β_1 and β_2, we will evaluate whether the performance of acquired firms improved faster than that of nonacquired firms once other characteristics are controlled for.

The estimation results for the manufacturing sector on the effects of the acquisition are reported in tables 11.8 and 11.9. Table 11.8 presents the effect of the acquisition on the TFP growth rate. Panels (a), (b), and (c) of table 11.9 show the effect of the acquisition on the ROA ratio, sales growth, and employment growth, respectively. Although the explanatory variables in all the equations are exactly same as those in the TFP growth equations, the estimated coefficients of the variables representing all other firm characteristics except out-in and in-in dummy variables are not reported in table 11.9. The results in table 11.8 suggest that compared to nonacquired firms, both firms acquired by foreigners and firms acquired by another domestic firm show a significantly higher TFP growth rate during the four-year period from the year prior to the acquisition to three years after the acquisition. The coefficient on the out-in dummy variable is much larger than that on the in-in dummy in the cases of the three-year window (equation [2] of table 11.8) and the 4-year window (equation [3] of table 11.8), which implies that out-in acquisitions may have a larger positive effect on TFP growth. In the case of the five-year window (equation [4] of table 11.8), the coefficient on the out-in dummy becomes insignificant while the coefficient on the in-in dummy remains positive and significant. Therefore, regarding the effects of acquisitions on the TFP growth rate, the results in table 11.8 suggest out-in acquisitions tend to bring a larger productivity

16. In the case of the nonmanufacturing sector, we exclude the share of nonproduction workers, R&D intensity, and export intensity for the same reasons as in the multinomial logit estimation in the previous subsection.

Table 11.8   **Dynamic effects of acquisition on TFP growth: Manufacturing sector**

Manufacturing Sector
Dependent variable: Growth rate of total factor productivity

Variable	(1) 2 windows ([t+1]−[t−1])		(2) 3 windows ([t+2]−[t−1])		(3) 4 windows ([t+3]−[t−1])		(4) 5 windows ([t+4]−[t−1])	
	Coefficient	t-value	Coefficient	t-value	Coefficient	t-value	Coefficient	t-value
Out-in	−0.006	−0.33	0.011	0.68	0.042	2.25**	0.012	0.81
In-in	0.001	0.34	0.003	0.74	0.006	1.75*	0.012	3.18***
TFP	−0.391	−16.02***	−0.450	−17.83***	−0.496	−18.82***	−0.491	−13.90***
ROA	−0.046	−1.15	−0.040	−1.10	−0.009	−0.30	−0.005	−0.17
log(size)	0.011	19.13***	0.012	20.61***	0.014	21.80***	0.015	20.32***
Age	0.000	−8.93***	0.000	−8.93***	0.000	−9.88***	0.000	−10.74***
Number of non-production workers/number of workers	0.012	6.91***	0.017	8.52***	0.018	8.34***	0.018	6.78***
R&D intensity	0.318	7.74***	0.284	6.02***	0.337	6.56***	0.343	4.97***
Advertising intensity	0.094	1.46	0.101	1.44	0.089	1.22	0.113	1.27
Export intensity	0.009	1.64	0.014	2.18**	0.014	1.94*	0.016	2.10**
Debt/total assets	−0.008	−2.71***	−0.008	−2.63***	−0.007	−2.17**	−0.003	−0.64
Constant	−0.018	−0.19	0.115	10.89***	0.098	9.81***	0.042	3.51***
Observations	72,585		59,306		47,467		36,390	
R^2	0.2833		0.3170		0.3433		0.3919	

Notes: Estimated coefficients of year dummies and 3-digit industry dummies are not shown in the table. White-corrected *t*-values are reported in the table.

*Significant at the 10% level (two-tailed test).

**Significant at the 5% level.

***Significant at the 1% level.

Table 11.9 Dynamic effects of acquisition: Manufacturing sector

	Manufacturing Sector							
	(1) 2 windows ($[t+1]-[t-1]$)		(2) 3 windows ($[t+2]-[t-1]$)		(3) 4 windows ($[t+3]-[t-1]$)		(4) 5 windows ($[t+4]-[t-1]$)	
Variable	Coefficient	t-value	Coefficient	t-value	Coefficient	t-value	Coefficient	t-value
(a) Dependent variable: Difference in ROA								
Out-in	−0.008	−0.57	0.011	1.06	0.022	1.71*	0.021	2.18**
In-in	−0.004	−1.28	−0.002	−0.92	−0.002	−1.03	0.001	0.29
(b) Dependent variable: Growth rate of sales								
Out-in	−0.038	−0.76	0.044	0.43	0.041	0.48	0.073	0.77
In-in	0.001	0.15	0.012	1.03	0.024	1.84*	0.043	2.87***
(c) Dependent variable: Growth rate of employment								
Out-in	0.025	0.69	−0.044	−0.92	−0.044	−0.77	0.017	0.22
In-in	−0.006	−0.92	0.005	0.61	0.003	0.29	0.007	0.56
(d) Dependent variable: Growth rate of TFP								
In-in (within group)	0.007	1.38	0.007	1.13	0.020	3.1***	0.021	2.85***
In-in (by outsider)	−0.001	−0.26	0.001	0.31	0.003	0.66	0.010	2.31**
(e) Dependent variable: Difference in ROA								
In-in (within group)	−0.006	−1.83*	−0.008	−1.91**	−0.004	−1.04	−0.007	−1.50
In-in (by outsider)	−0.003	−0.80	0.000	−0.06	−0.002	−0.74	0.003	0.87
(f) Dependent variable: Growth rate of sales								
In-in (within group)	−0.011	−0.61	−0.012	−0.46	0.018	0.68	0.014	0.45
In-in (by outsider)	0.005	0.52	0.020	1.56	0.027	1.79*	0.052	3.06***
(g) Dependent variable: Growth rate of employment								
In-in (within group)	−0.001	−0.09	0.015	0.88	0.009	0.51	0.003	0.15
In-in (by outsider)	−0.007	−0.99	0.002	0.22	0.001	0.10	0.007	0.55
Observations	72,585		59,306		47,467		36,390	

Notes: Estimated coefficients of variables representing other firm characteristics, year dummies, and 3-digit industry dummies are not shown in the table. White-corrected t-values are reported in the table.

*Significant at the 10% level (two-tailed test).

**Significant at the 5% level.

***Significant at the 1% level.

improvement than in-in acquisitions three years after the acquisition, but the productivity improvements from out-in acquisitions do not last long. On the other hand, the results in panel (a) of table 11.9 indicate out-in acquisitions lead to a significant improvement in target firms' profitability (measured as ROA) three and four years after the acquisition. Although no immediate improvement in profitability can be observed after out-in acquisitions, the results clearly indicate out-in acquisitions contribute to higher profitability while in-in acquisitions do not have any impact on target firms' profitability. In contrast, in-in acquisitions contribute to significantly higher sales growth three and four years after the acquisition as shown in panel (b) of table 11.9. Both out-in and in-in acquisitions do not have any significant impact on target firms' employment growth (panel [c] of table 11.9).

In the case of the nonmanufacturing sector, the impact of out-in acquisitions on target firms' performance differs more sharply from that of in-in acquisitions (tables 11.10 and 11.11).[17] Out-in acquisitions result in higher TFP growth for target firms three years after the acquisition, while the TFP improvement effect of in-in acquisitions is very small or even negative and not statistically significant (table 11.10). As for ROA, out-in acquisitions have a significant positive effect beginning immediately after the acquisition, while the effects of in-in acquisitions are negative but insignificant in all equations except one in panel (a) of table 11.11. As for sales growth and employment growth, both out-in and in-in acquisitions do not have any significant impact on target firms (panels [b] and [c] of table 11.11).

Overall, we find some evidence that out-in acquisitions lead to an improvement in target firms' ROA both in the manufacturing and the nonmanufacturing sector. Moreover, out-in acquisitions also lead to a TFP improvement three years after the acquisition both in the manufacturing and the non-manufacturing sector. These results regarding out-in acquisitions are consistent with the synergy hypotheses. On the other hand, in the case of in-in acquisitions, the result that there is no significant improvement in ROA does not provide much support for the managerial-discipline hypotheses. However, we find some positive impact of in-in acquisitions on target firms' sales growth in the case of the manufacturing sector.[18]

17. As in table 11.9, the estimated coefficients of variables representing all other firm characteristics except out-in and in-in dummy variables are not reported in table 11.11.

18. As argued by Froot and Stein (1991) and others, a depreciation of the domestic currency can lead to foreign acquisitions of certain domestic assets. Given the important role played by the exchange rate in cross-border M&A decisions, we tried to test whether the outcome of M&As differs during periods of strong yen and a weak yen. We defined as strong yen periods years in which the average rate for the U.S. dollar was less than 115 yen and identified 1994, 1995, 1996, 1999 and 2000 as periods of a strong yen. All other years were defined as weak yen periods. We divided our data sample into two periods and the results were mostly consistent with those in tables 11.8 to 11.11. However, out-in acquisitions in strong yen periods tended to lead to significantly higher TFP growth in the manufacturing sector and significantly higher sales growth in the nonmanufacturing sector. These findings suggest that the

Although our results do not seem to support the managerial-discipline hypotheses, in the case of in-in acquisitions, firms with a lower profit rate (for the nonmanufacturing sector) and a higher debt-asset ratio (for both the manufacturing and the nonmanufacturing sectors) are, as discussed in section 11.3.3, more likely to be acquired. This result implies that in-in acquisitions may have the characteristics of rescue missions, which may be one reason why there is no conspicuous improvement in profitability but some improvement in sales after an in-in acquisition. As mentioned above, many cases of in-in acquisitions in Japan are conducted within vertical and horizontal *keiretsu* networks or within a corporate group. In the case of within-group acquisitions, since workers and managers of acquired firms expect further support by group firms, it may be difficult to accomplish drastic restructuring. On the other hand, in-in acquisitions involving outsiders may have a positive effect on performance after the acquisition in a way that is similar to out-in acquisitions. In order to test this hypothesis, we examine the dynamic effects of in-in acquisitions within firm groups and of in-in acquisitions involving outsiders.

For information on firm groups, we use the *Kankei Kaisha* database (subsidiary firms database) compiled by Toyo Keizai Shinposha. We define acquisitions as conducted within a group if, prior to the acquisition, between 20 and 50 percent of the paid-in capital of the acquired firm was held by a related company. It is important to note, however, that if firm A was partly owned by related firm B, but the majority of firm A's equity is newly acquired by another firm C, which did not have a close relationship with firm A before the acquisition, such a case is incorrectly included in our sample as a *within-group acquisitions*. Using the Toyo Keizai information, we find 518 within-group in-in acquisition cases in our dataset for the period from 1994 to 2002, which is approximately one sixth of the total of in-in acquisition cases (refer to table 11.4). The estimation results, including the within-group in-in acquisition dummy variable and the dummy for in-in acquisitions by outsiders, are reported in panels (d)–(g) in tables 11.9 and 11.11. The explanatory variables are the out-in acquisition dummy, the within-group in-in acquisition dummy, the dummy for in-in acquisitions, and the same other firm characteristics as in tables 11.8 and 11.10. In panels (d)–(g) in tables 11.9 and 11.11, the estimated coefficients on the within-group in-in acquisition dummy and the dummy for in-in acquisitions by outsiders are reported.

---

role of the exchange rate in the outcome of cross-border M&As deserves more detailed investigation in the future. Calculated TFP levels tend to be affected by demand shocks. We adjusted capital utilization and hours worked by using the industry-level capital utilization ratio provided by the Ministry of Economy, Trade and Industry, and the sectoral working hours taken from the JIP database 2006. Moreover, we control for economy-wide demand shocks by including year dummies. We tried to eliminate the influence of demand fluctuation as much as possible in the calculation of our TFP measure.

Table 11.10   Dynamic effects of acquisition on TFP growth: Nonmanufacturing sector

		Nonmanufacturing Sector						
		Dependent variable: Growth rate of total factor productivity						
Variable	(1) 2 windows $([t+1]-[t-1])$		(2) 3 windows $([t+2]-[t-1])$		(3) 4 windows $([t+3]-[t-1])$		(4) 5 windows $([t+4]-[t-1])$	
	Coefficient	t-value	Coefficient	t-value	Coefficient	t-value	Coefficient	t-value
Out-in	−0.016	−0.51	0.013	0.38	0.090	2.45**	0.053	1.02
In-in	−0.004	−0.63	−0.003	−0.43	−0.008	−1.00	0.004	0.46
TFP	−0.604	−65.67***	−0.647	−66.97***	−0.678	−66.97***	−0.701	−63.17***
ROA	−0.057	−2.42**	−0.057	−2.68***	−0.053	−2.35**	−0.051	−2.57***
log(size)	−0.010	−11.12***	−0.011	−10.34***	−0.010	−8.45***	−0.011	−8.27***
Age	0.000	7.53***	0.000	6.55***	0.000	4.08**	0.000	3.44***
Advertising intensity	−0.669	−11.31***	−0.772	−13.51***	−0.754	−12.18***	−0.769	−10.58***
Debt/total assets	−0.035	−8.87***	−0.042	−9.25***	−0.037	−7.19***	−0.07	−4.33***
Constant	0.169	6.82***	0.138	4.43***	0.140	3.94***	0.188	11.44***
Observations	55,425		43,155		33,991		25,650	
R^2	0.4287		0.4395		0.4503		0.4755	

Notes: Estimated coefficients of year dummies and 3-digit industry dummies are not shown in the table. White-corrected *t*-values are reported in the table.

*Significant at the 10% level (two-tailed test).

**Significant at the 5% level.

***Significant at the 1% level.

Table 11.11   Dynamic effects of acquisition: Nonmanufacturing sector

Variable	(1) 2 windows $([t+1]-[t-1])$ Coefficient	t-value	(2) 3 windows $([t+2]-[t-1])$ Coefficient	t-value	(3) 4 windows $([t+3]-[t-1])$ Coefficient	t-value	(4) 5 windows $([t+4]-[t-1])$ Coefficient	t-value
(a) Dependent variable: Difference in ROA								
Out-in	0.035	2.98***	0.058	4.75***	0.093	4.21***	0.087	2.50**
In-in	−0.003	−1.74*	−0.002	−0.98	−0.001	−0.56	−0.001	−0.58
(b) Dependent variable: Growth rate of sales								
Out-in	0.033	0.59	0.098	1.61	0.114	1.33	0.090	0.77
In-in	0.009	1.12	0.002	0.19	−0.001	−0.04	−0.012	−0.64
(c) Dependent variable: Growth rate of employment								
Out-in	0.020	0.51	−0.026	−0.64	−0.020	−0.31	−0.076	−0.9
In-in	0.015	1.79*	0.006	0.6	0.013	0.96	−0.002	−0.12
(d) Dependent variable: Growth rate of TFP								
In-in (within group)	−0.006	−0.29	−0.027	−1.38	0.015	0.71	0.050	1.72*
In-in (by outsider)	−0.003	−0.56	0.000	−0.03	−0.011	−1.29	−0.001	−0.06
(e) Dependent variable: Difference in ROA								
In-in (within group)	−0.004	−1.29	−0.005	−1.13	0.002	0.31	−0.003	−0.43
In-in (by outsider)	−0.002	−1.50	−0.001	−0.70	−0.001	−0.70	−0.001	−0.48
(f) Dependent variable: Growth rate of sales								
In-in (within group)	−0.022	−0.85	−0.056	−1.33	−0.033	−0.87	−0.038	−0.77
In-in (by outsider)	0.013	1.54	0.010	0.87	0.004	0.27	−0.009	−0.45
(g) Dependent variable: Growth rate of employment								
In-in (within group)	−0.009	−0.37	−0.041	−1.08	−0.004	−0.10	−0.070	−1.47
In-in (by outsider)	0.017	1.99**	0.012	1.07	0.014	1.03	0.005	0.26
Observations	55,425		43,155		33,991		25,640	

Notes: Estimated coefficients of variables representing other firm characteristics, year dummies, and 3-digit industry dummies are not shown in the table. White-corrected t-values are reported in the table.

*Significant at the 10% level (two-tailed test).

**Significant at the 5% level.

***Significant at the 1% level.

Panels (d)–(g) in table 11.9 show the results for the manufacturing sector. Contrary to our expectation, target firms of within-group in-in acquisitions tend to show a higher TFP growth rate than target firms of in-in acquisitions by outsiders. The TFP growth rate during the period from a year prior to the acquisition to three years after the acquisition is significantly higher for firms acquired by a group firm than for firms acquired by a domestic outsider firm. As for ROA performance, however, within-group in-in acquisitions tend to have a significant negative impact, while acquisitions by domestic outsiders did not have any significant effects. These results imply that again, the managerial-discipline hypothesis does not seem to apply in the case of in-in acquisitions in Japan. Rather, the results may be interpreted as follows: in the case of within-group in-in acquisitions, parent firms may try to quickly restructure acquired firms, which temporarily worsens their profitability. However, after the business restructuring is completed, the acquired firms may be able to enjoy higher productivity by effectively utilizing managerial and technological resources within the corporate group. Although acquisitions by domestic outsiders lead to higher sales growth, both within-group in-in acquisitions and acquisitions by domestic outsiders do not have any significant impact on target firms' employment growth.

According to the results for the nonmanufacturing sector shown in panels (d)–(g) in table 11.11, there is a significant positive impact of within-group in-in acquisitions on the TFP growth rate only in the case of the five-year window (equation [4] of panel [d] in table 11.11). There is also a significant positive impact of acquisitions by domestic outsiders on employment growth only in the case of the two-year window (equation [1] of panel [g] in table 11.11). In all the other cases, the coefficients for within-group in-in acquisitions and in-in acquisitions by outsiders are not statistically significant. Although out-in acquisitions positively affect the return on assets in the case of the nonmanufacturing sector, neither type of in-in acquisitions has a positive impact on ROA. In the case of the nonmanufacturing sector, our results suggest that there is no conspicuous difference between the effects of within-group in-in acquisitions and in-in acquisitions by outsiders. That is, in the nonmanufacturing sector, even acquisitions by domestic outsiders do not lead to an improvement in the acquired firms' performance.

11.3.5   Do M&As Improve the Performance of Target Firms? Analysis Based on Difference-in-Differences Estimates from the Matched Sample

Our estimation results on the dynamic effects of out-in and in-in acquisitions in the previous subsection indicate that both in the manufacturing and the nonmanufacturing sectors out-in acquisitions lead to improvements in target firms' TFP and ROA. These results are consistent with those in Fukao, Ito, and Kwon (2005), although the results of that study indicated out-in acquisitions improve target firms' performance more quickly.[19] However, as described at the beginning of section 11.3, the Fukao, Ito, and Kwon (2005) study does not address the selection bias problem and therefore suffers from the problem of simultaneity between ownership status and other performance variables, because out-in acquisition targets differ systematically from other firms as indicated by the results of the multinomial logit analysis.

Also, the analysis in this study so far has not addressed the simultaneity problem. Therefore, we now employ the propensity score matching and the difference-in-differences (DID) techniques described in section 11.3.1 and examine whether we still find that out-in acquisitions lead to an improvement in acquired firms' performance even after the simultaneity problem has been overcome or at least reduced. What we are interested in is the causal effect of acquisition on target firms' performance. However, changes in performance following an acquisition are not exclusively the result of the acquisition, but also depend on other factors. Applying the DID technique, the change in performance before and after the acquisition therefore is further differenced with respect to changes in performance of the control group of non-acquired firms. Therefore, the DID estimator removes the effects of common shocks and more accurately measures the causal effect of the acquisition.

Using the multinomial logit estimation results shown in table 11.7, we first identify the probability of acquisition (or "propensity score") for all firms in our dataset.[20] Our multinomial logit estimation model in table 11.7 assumes that the propensity of firms to be acquired by other firms is a function of the TFP level, firm size, the number of years since establishment, the share of the number of nonproduction workers, R&D intensity, advertisement intensity, export intensity, and the debt-asset ratio.[21] A nonacquired firm which is closest in terms of its propensity score to an acquired firm is

19. The difference between the results of that study and the present one is probably due to the fact that (a) the data for this study cover the period 1994–2002, which is one year longer than the observation period in Fukao, Ito, and Kwon (2005); (b) this study uses newly compiled and detailed industry-level deflators taken from the JIP database 2006; and (c) the explanatory variables employed in the regression analyses are not exactly the same as those in Fukao, Ito, and Kwon (2005).

20. In order to verify whether the balancing condition is satisfied in our matched sample, we conduct two tests, following Hijzen, Jean, and Mayer (2006). First, we examine the standardized bias for variables included in the propensity score estimation before and after matching (see Smith and Todd 2005). Rosenbaum and Rubin (1983) assume that a standardized bias in excess of 20 percent is large, although there is no formal criterion to assess the bias. Second, for each variable in the propensity score estimation, we perform standard t-tests for equality of means of each variable between the treated group and the control group before and after matching. The results of these two tests are presented in appendix tables 11A.2 and 11A.3. The standardized bias and t-test for equality of means before and after matching indicate that the balancing property is satisfied for all of our variables except one (advertising intensity in the case of non-manufacturing).

21. In the case of the non-manufacturing sector, we exclude the share of nonproduction workers, R&D intensity, and export intensity.

selected as a match for an actually acquired firm using the one-to-one nearest neighbor matching method. One-to-one nearest neighbor matching means that we can use data only from a subset of the sample. Using nonacquired firms as the control group, we conduct one-to-one nearest neighbor matching on firms acquired by foreigners and then match firms acquired by domestic investors using, again, the sample of nonacquired firms as the control group. In the case of out-in acquisitions, our matched sample contains 132 firms not acquired by foreigners as a match for the 132 firms acquired by foreigners (sixty-four firms in manufacturing and sixty-eight firms in nonmanufacturing). In the case of in-in acquisitions, our matched sample contains 2,827 firms not acquired by domestic firms as a match for the 2,827 firms acquired by domestic firms (1,369 firms in manufacturing and 1,458 firms in nonmanufacturing).

Using the subsets of the sample, we estimate a difference-in-differences (DID) estimator, which in our case is equivalent to calculating the ATT based on equation (3) in section 11.3.1. The calculated effects of out-in and in-in acquisitions are presented in table 11.12. In the case of the manufacturing sector (upper panel), a foreign acquisition leads to an additional 4 percentage point TFP growth in the firms acquired by foreigners two years after the acquisition. The result also shows that firms acquired by foreign firms enjoy higher TFP growth than the control group equivalent to 2.4 percentage-points at the end of the third year of foreign ownership, although the difference is not statistically significant (probably partly due to the small sample size). The lower panel of table 11.12 shows that foreign ownership improved the ROA of acquired firms in the nonmanufacturing sector at the end of the third year of foreign acquisition. On the other hand, in-in acquisitions had a significant negative impact on the TFP and ROA growth of acquired firms. Moreover, as for TFP and ROA, the sign of the DID tends to be positive for out-in acquisitions in both the manufacturing and the nonmanufacturing sector, while for in-in acquisitions it tends to be negative (although in many cases the DID is not statistically significant).

However, out-in acquisitions tend to have a negative impact on employment, while in-in acquisitions lead to an additional 4–6 percentage-point increase in the sales growth rate for the acquired firm three or four years after the acquisition, in the case of the manufacturing sector. Although many of the DID estimators are not statistically significant, foreign acquisitions tend to be associated with cost cutting and profit or productivity improvements, while domestic acquisitions tend to be associated with increases in output.

The results from the matched sample indicate foreign acquisitions improve target firms' productivity and profitability, while acquisitions by domestic firms hardly have any positive impact on productivity and profitability. The significant positive effect of foreign acquisitions shows up only two years after acquisition, implying that the realization of synergy

Table 11.12   The effect of acquisition: Matching results

	Effect of foreign acquisition					Effect of domestic acquisition				
	TFP	ROA	Emp	Sales	Obs.	TFP	ROA	Emp	Sales	Obs.
	(a) Manufacturing sector									
Acquisition year	0.022	0.000	−0.020	−0.052	64	0.001	−0.004	−0.013**	−0.012	1,369
	(0.02)	(0.01)	(0.05)	(0.04)		(0.00)	(0.00)	(0.01)	(0.01)	
One year later	−0.008	0.000	0.022	−0.058	47	−0.004	−0.004	−0.005	−0.002	1,003
	(0.03)	(0.01)	(0.08)	(0.06)		(0.00)	(0.00)	(0.01)	(0.01)	
Two years later	0.039*	0.001	−0.067	0.022	31	0.004	−0.001	0.007	0.022	717
	(0.02)	(0.01)	(0.08)	(0.08)		(0.00)	(0.00)	(0.01)	(0.02)	
Three years later	0.024	−0.011	−0.152**	−0.055	26	0.011	−0.002	0.014	0.042*	550
	(0.04)	(0.02)	(0.06)	(0.12)		(0.01)	(0.00)	(0.02)	(0.02)	
Four years later	−0.010	−0.016	−0.015	−0.018	23	−0.003	−0.007	0.025	0.058*	387
	(0.05)	(0.02)	(0.12)	(0.013)		(0.01)	(0.01)	(0.02)	(0.03)	
	(b) Nonmanufacturing sector									
Acquisition year	0.004	−0.001	0.036	0.061	68	−0.008	−0.003	0.008	−0.006	1,458
	(0.04)	(0.01)	(0.03)	(0.04)		(0.01)	(0.00)	(0.01)	(0.01)	
One year later	0.036	−0.009	0.061	0.025	44	−0.012	−0.005	0.020*	0.013	975
	(0.07)	(0.02)	(0.05)	(0.07)		(0.01)	(0.00)	(0.01)	(0.01)	
Two years later	0.052	0.025	−0.015	0.013	33	−0.025*	−0.005	0.002	−0.015	633
	(0.08)	(0.03)	(0.07)	(0.14)		(0.01)	(0.00)	(0.02)	(0.02)	
Three years later	0.058	0.075*	−0.056	0.124	23	−0.026	−0.004	0.011	−0.034	468
	(0.07)	(0.04)	(0.10)	(0.16)		(0.02)	(0.00)	(0.02)	(0.02)	
Four years later	0.026	0.071	−0.188**	0.014	15	−0.026	−0.007*	−0.036	−0.036	299
	(0.09)	(0.06)	(0.09)	(0.23)		(0.02)	(0.00)	(0.03)	(0.03)	

Note: Standard errors in parentheses. *, ** statistically significant at 10% and 5%.

effects from acquisitions or the restructuring of acquired firms take at least two years. Moreover, according to the results, improvements experienced by firms acquired by foreigners are likely to be a temporary phenomenon. Although the matching results provide only weak evidence that acquisition by a foreign firm improves the performance of acquired firms, they do confirm that such a positive effect exists, even when the sample selection bias is removed.[22]

11.4 Conclusion

In recent years, the Japanese government has been actively promoting inward foreign direct investment with the aim of accelerating structural adjustment and achieving a full-scale economic recovery. In order to examine whether the entry of foreign firms does indeed provide a stimulus to the Japanese economy and contribute to a better performance of Japanese firms, we investigated the effects of out-in M&As on target firms' performance in a previous study (Fukao, Ito, and Kwon 2005). Although the study found some evidence that out-in M&As brought larger and quicker improvements in TFP and the profit-to-sales ratio than in-in M&As, the study had several limitations. This chapter sought to overcome these limitations by conducting (a) a much more careful investigation of the effect of in-in acquisitions by distinguishing within-group in-in acquisitions and in-in acquisitions by outsiders; (b) an analysis of firms in the nonmanufacturing sector; (c) a more rigorous analysis by employing propensity score matching and the difference-in-differences technique; and (d) an analysis using a new dataset that contains the most recent data available.

The results of this chapter were generally consistent with those in Fukao, Ito, and Kwon (2005). However, the present study also produced several new findings. First, we found that there was no positive impact on target firms' ROA in the case of both within-group in-in acquisitions and in-in acquisitions by domestic outsiders. In fact, in the manufacturing sector the return on assets even deteriorated one year and two years after within-group in-in acquisitions. The results thus did not support the managerial-discipline hypothesis, which suggests that acquisitions are intended to strengthen managerial control over entrenched managers who are more interested in their own benefit than the wealth of the firm's owners, and

22. Instead of calculating propensity scores using multinomial logit estimation, we also tried to calculate propensity scores using probit estimation. In the latter case, we estimated the probability of being acquired by a foreign firm and the probability of being acquired by a domestic firm separately. Next we estimated the probit model, and then compared the difference in performance with the matched sample. We found both TFP growth and ROA improvement to be significantly higher three years after the acquisition in firms acquired by foreigners both in the manufacturing and the nonmanufacturing sector. In the case of in-in acquisitions, the DID was not statistically significant in all cases except one.

which therefore predicts the profitability of acquired firms improves after the acquisition. Rather, our results imply that in the case of within-group in-in acquisitions, parent firms may be trying to quickly restructure acquired firms even at the cost of deteriorating profitability. Our results also showed that within-group in-in acquisitions brought a larger and quicker improvement in TFP compared with in-in acquisitions by domestic outsiders both in the manufacturing and nonmanufacturing sectors.

Second, we found that foreign acquisitions improved target firms' productivity and profitability significantly more and quicker than acquisitions by domestic firms. We confirmed these results by employing a methodology that combines propensity score matching and difference-in-differences techniques. The methodology enabled us to ensure that the characteristics of acquired firms and nonaquired firms are as close as possible and to isolate causal effects that can be reliably attributed to acquisitions. However, we also found that foreign acquisitions lead to a lower employment growth rate in acquired firms while domestic acquisitions in the manufacturing sector lead to a higher sales growth rate in acquired firms. According to these results, it seems the outcome of M&As is quite different between foreign acquisitions and domestic acquisitions: the former is productivity- and profitability-improving but employment-reducing, while the latter is not. Although domestic acquisitions improve sales growth, this positive effect can be seen only in the manufacturing sector. One potential concern is that our results from the matched sample may not be very strong. A possible reason for our somewhat weak results may be the accuracy of the matching. As mentioned in Girma, Greenaway, and Kneller (2004), the importance of appropriate matching cannot be overemphasized. If acquired firms experience a surge in productivity just before the acquisition, their productivity is likely to grow more slowly in subsequent periods. In such a case, a difference-in-differences estimator based on randomly matched firms is likely to underestimate the performance impact of acquisitions. There may be room for further improvement of the matching methodology in future studies.

Another possible concern is that the reliability of the difference-in-differences methodology is dependent on the assumption that acquired and nonacquired firms are similarly affected by macroeconomic factors. However, the bias arising from this assumption is mitigated as much as possible in this study because firms are matched in the same industry and year in our matching process.

Our major finding that acquisitions by foreign firms have a positive effect on target firms' productivity are in line with several preceding studies on this issue in other countries, including Conyon et al. (2002), Arnold and Javorcik (2005), and Bertrand and Zitouna (2005). Comparing our results with those of Arnold and Javorcik's (2005) study on Indonesia, however, the magnitude of the positive effect is much smaller in our study than in theirs.[23] This is not surprising, because the difference in technological and managerial capabilities between domestic and foreign firms is much larger in Indonesia than in Japan, and technology transfer effects from foreign firms to domestic firms should be less relevant in Japan. However, our results in this study imply that even in Japan, where many domestic firms are closer to the technology frontier, performance improvement effects from foreign acquisitions are present. Moreover, taking into account that inward FDI tends to generate productivity spillovers, as suggested by Blomström and Kokko (1998) and Blomström, Kokko, and Globerman (2001), our results support the idea that promoting inward FDI and facilitating cross-border M&As could help to improve productivity in Japan.[24] Since the inward FDI penetration in Japan remains low (Ito and Fukao 2005), there appears to be ample room for improvements in productivity through inward FDI.

In addition, we find that the positive effects of foreign acquisitions tend to be much larger in the case of the nonmanufacturing sector than in the case of the manufacturing sector. It is often argued anecdotally that the productivity of Japanese nonmanufacturing firms is relatively low compared with firms in other developed countries. If this is true, the positive effect of foreign acquisitions in the nonmanufacturing sector may have very important policy implications: foreign acquisitions possibly contribute to a better performance of target firms in the nonmanufacturing sector by transferring advanced technology or managerial know-how. However, in our dataset most out-in acquisitions in the nonmanufacturing sector occur in the wholesale and retail trade industries. The majority of out-in acquisitions in these industries consist of acquisitions by manufacturing firms, suggesting foreign manufacturing firms often acquire Japanese wholesalers or retailers in order to obtain their own distribution channels. Although technology and managerial know-how transfer effects may not be relevant, such cases possibly contribute to the streamlining of dis-

23. Our results cannot be directly compared with those obtained by Conyon et al. (2002) for the United Kingdom who used labor productivity as their measure of productivity. Bertrand and Zitouna's (2005) study on France, although employing a slightly different analytical model than the one used by Arnold and Javorcik (2005) and in our study, shows that firms acquired by foreigners have nearly 40 percent higher TFP than nonacquired firms. Why the impact of cross-border M&As on TFP is so much greater in France than in Japan certainly is an issue that it would be worth investigating. Moreover, Bertrand and Zitouna (2005) suggest that non-European M&As are more efficiency-improving than domestic or intra-EU M&As. This result highlights the fact that the country origin of the buyer firm matters, providing a further interesting line for enquiry for future studies.

24. A detailed survey of the literature on the various economic effects of FDI and a discussion of the mixed evidence on productivity and knowledge spillovers to domestic firms in previous studies is provided by Lipsey (2004). Although no universal relationships are evident, Lipsey (2004) concludes that "there is substantial evidence from several countries that inward FDI has been most beneficial to the productivity of local firms where the local firms are not extremely far behind the multinationals' affiliates (p. 365)."

tribution networks in the Japanese commerce sector. A more detailed investigation of technology transfer effects, particularly in the nonmanufacturing sector, is an issue warranting further investigation.

Appendix
Construction of the Multilateral Index

The dataset employed in this chapter was obtained from *Kigyo Katsudo Kihon Chosa* (*Basic Survey of Japanese Business Structure and Activities*), which is conducted annually by the Ministry of Economy, Trade and Industry (METI).

We define the productivity level of firm i in year t in a certain industry in comparison with the productivity level of a hypothetical representative firm in base year 0 in that industry.

The TFP level is defined as follows:

$$(A1) \quad \ln TFP_{i,t} = (\ln Q_{i,t} - \overline{\ln Q_t}) - \sum_{f=1}^{n} \frac{1}{2}(S_{f,i,t} + \overline{S_{f,t}})(\ln X_{f,i,t} - \overline{\ln X_{f,t}})$$

$$+ \sum_{s=1}^{t}(\overline{\ln Q_s} - \overline{\ln Q_{s-1}})$$

$$- \sum_{s=1}^{t}\sum_{f=1}^{n} \frac{1}{2}(\overline{S_{f,s}} + \overline{S_{f,s-1}})(\overline{\ln X_{f,s}} - \overline{\ln X_{f,s-1}})$$

where $Q_{i,t}$, $S_{f,i,t}$, and $X_{f,i,t}$ denote the output of firm i in year t, the cost share of factor f for firm i in year t, and firm i's input of factor f in year t, respectively. Variables with an upper bar denote the industry average of that variable.

Output: Except for the commerce sector, gross output is defined as firms' total sales. For the commerce sector, gross output is measured as sales minus expenses for purchased materials. Gross output is deflated by the output deflator derived from the JIP 2006.

Intermediate inputs: For the commerce sector, intermediate inputs are calculated as (Cost of sales + Operating costs) – (Wages + Depreciation costs + Expenses for purchased materials). The intermediate inputs of other sectors are defined as (Cost of sales + Operating costs) – (Wages + Depreciation costs). Intermediate inputs are deflated by the intermediate input deflator provided in the JIP 2006.

Labor input: As labor input, we used each firm's total number of workers multiplied by the sectoral working hours from the JIP 2006.

Capital stock: For capital stock, the only data available are the nominal book values of tangible fixed assets. Using these data, we calculated the net capital stock of firm i in industry j in constant 1995 prices as follows:

$$K_{it} = BV_{it} * (INK_{jt}/IBV_{jt})$$

where BV_{it} represents the book value of firm i's tangible fixed capital in year t, INK_{jt} stands for the net capital stock of industry j in constant 1995 prices, and IBV_{jt} denotes the book value of industry j's capital. INK_{jt} was calculated as follows. First, as a benchmark, we took the data on the book value of tangible fixed assets in 1975 from the *Financial Statements Statistics of Corporations* published by the Ministry of Finance. We then converted the book value of year 1975 into the real value in constant 1995 prices using the investment deflator provided in the JIP 2006. Second, the net capital stock of industry j, INK_{jt}, for succeeding years was calculated using the perpetual inventory method. We used the investment deflator in the JIP 2006. The sectoral depreciation rate used is taken from the JIP 2006.

Cost Shares: Total cost of labor is measured as total wages. We used nominal intermediate input as the intermediate input cost. Capital cost was calculated by multiplying the real net capital stock with the user cost of capital. The latter was estimated as follows:

$$c_k = \frac{1-z}{1-u} p_k \left[\lambda r + (1-u)(1-\lambda)i + \delta_i - \left(\frac{\dot{p}_k}{p_k} \right) \right],$$

where p_k, i, δ, u, λ, and z are the price of investment goods, the interest rate, the depreciation rate, the corporate tax rate, the equity ratio, and the present value of depreciation deduction on a unit of nominal investment, respectively. Data on investment goods prices, interest rates, and corporate tax rates were taken from the JIP 2006, the Bank of Japan's web site, and the *Ministry of Finance Statistics Monthly,* respectively. The depreciation rate for each sector was taken from the JIP 2006. We calculated the cost shares of each factor by dividing the cost of each factor by total costs, which consist of the sum of labor costs, intermediate inputs costs, and capital costs.

Table 11A.1   **Summary statistics**

Lagged variables	Obs	Mean	Std. Dev.	Min.	Max.
	Whole sample				
TFP	163,812	−0.004	0.204	−5.554	4.024
ROA	163,812	0.048	0.094	−13.249	15.504
log(size)	163,812	5.237	0.998	3.912	11.563
Age	163,812	36.101	15.502	0.000	125.000
Number of non-production workers/number of workers	163,812	0.606	0.368	0.000	1.000
R&D expenditure/sales	163,812	0.006	0.030	0.000	7.339
Advertising expenditure/sales	163,812	0.006	0.019	0.000	3.009
Export/sales	163,812	0.022	0.082	0.000	1.090
Debt/total assets	163,812	0.739	0.277	0.000	12.383
	Manufacturing sector				
TFP	90,075	−0.010	0.127	−4.468	1.297
ROA	90,075	0.049	0.098	−13.249	15.504
log(size)	90,075	5.259	1.007	3.912	11.254
Age	90,075	37.471	15.315	0.000	111.000
Number of non-production workers/number of workers	90,075	0.339	0.250	0.000	1.000
R&D expenditure/sales	90,075	0.009	0.021	0.000	0.734
Advertising expenditure/sales	90,075	0.005	0.019	0.000	3.009
Export/sales	90,075	0.031	0.097	0.000	1.090
Debt/total assets	90,075	0.704	0.274	0.000	8.101
	Nonmanufacturing sector				
TFP	73,737	0.002	0.270	−5.554	4.024
ROA	73,737	0.046	0.089	−3.928	12.229
log(size)	73,737	5.211	0.987	3.912	11.563
Age	73,737	34.427	15.565	0.000	125.000
Advertising expenditure/sales	73,737	0.008	0.018	0.000	0.528
Debt/total assets	73,737	0.781	0.274	0.000	12.383

Table 11A.2   Balancing tests for matching: Manufacturing sector

Variable	Sample	Foreign acquisition Mean Treated	Mean Control	% bias	% reduct bias	t-test t	p > t	Domestic acquisition Mean Treated	Mean Control	% bias	% reduct bias	t-test t	p > t
TFP(t − 1)	Unmatched	0.058	−0.011	43.9		4.16	0.000	−0.016	−0.011	−3.9		−1.4	0.153
	Matched	0.042	0.046	−2.4	94.5	−0.13	0.896	−0.015	−0.013	−1.5	60.3	−0.4	0.670
ROA(t − 1)	Unmatched	0.088	0.049	43		3.33	0.001	0.049	0.049	0.2		0.01	0.943
	Matched	0.078	0.077	1	97.6	0.08	0.938	0.050	0.049	0.9	−318.7	0.3	0.772
log(size) (t − 1)	Unmatched	5.741	5.256	45		4.01	0.000	5.140	5.258	−12.1		−4.3	0.000
	Matched	5.696	5.836	−13	71.2	−0.65	0.514	5.138	5.138	0.0	99.9	0.0	0.997
Age(t − 1)	Unmatched	28.449	37.493	−57.4		−4.9	0.000	32.917	37.557	−29.6		−11.2	0.000
	Matched	30.078	32.031	−12.4	78.4	−0.68	0.500	32.907	32.934	−0.2	99.4	−0.1	0.964
(Number of nonproduction workers/ number of R&D intensity(t − 1)	Unmatched	0.506	0.334	65.5		5.83	0.000	0.307	0.335	−10.9		−4.1	0.000
	Matched	0.496	0.521	−9.7	85.2	−0.53	0.599	0.308	0.305	0.8	92.4	0.2	0.825
R&D intensity(t − 1)	Unmatched	0.028	0.010	56.1		7.16	0.000	0.008	0.010	−9.8		−3.4	0.001
	Matched	0.029	0.028	3.8	93.2	0.17	0.867	0.008	0.008	−1.4	85.9	−0.4	0.693
Advertising intensity(t − 1)	Unmatched	0.007	0.005	11.5		0.92	0.356	0.003	0.005	−10.6		−3.4	0.001
	Matched	0.007	0.007	−3.6	68.9	−0.24	0.810	0.003	0.003	−0.8	92.7	−0.3	0.784
Export intensity(t − 1)	Unmatched	0.117	0.031	55.5		7.34	0.000	0.023	0.032	−8.9		−3.1	0.002
	Matched	0.093	0.106	−8.3	85.1	−0.41	0.685	0.023	0.022	1.1	87.6	0.3	0.745
(Debt/total assets) (t − 1)	Unmatched	0.658	0.705	−16.6		−1.4	0.162	0.782	0.704	26.8		10.5	0.000
	Matched	0.666	0.681	−5.6	66.2	−0.32	0.747	0.777	0.759	6.3	76.5	1.8	0.071

Table 11.A3   Balancing tests for matching: Nonmanufacturing sector

Variable	Sample	Foreign acquisition Mean Treated	Control	% bias	% reduct bias	t-test t	p > t	Domestic acquisition Mean Treated	Control	% bias	% reduct bias	t-test t	p > t
TFP(t − 1)	Unmatched	0.017	0.003	5.4		0.44	0.659	−0.002	0.003	−1.9		−0.7	0.457
	Matched	0.017	0.029	−4.6	14.1	−0.24	0.810	−0.002	0.000	−0.6	68.6	−0.2	0.871
ROA(t − 1)	Unmatched	0.109	0.046	62.5		5.87	0.000	0.042	0.046	−5.5		−1.9	0.052
	Matched	0.109	0.087	22	64.8	1.25	0.212	0.042	0.044	−2.4	56.6	−0.8	0.445
log(size) (t − 1)	Unmatched	5.225	5.215	0.9		0.8	0.934	5.251	5.214	3.7		1.4	0.158
	Matched	5.225	5.192	3.1	−22.79	0.18	0.856	5.250	5.200	5.0	−34.0	1.4	0.172
Age(t − 1)	Unmatched	21.382	34.459	−83.2		−6.93	0.000	29.339	34.549	−33.9		−12.7	0.000
	Matched	21.382	20.334	6.7	91.9	0.41	0.679	29.314	28.719	3.9	88.6	1.1	0.287
Advertising intensity(t − 1)	Unmatched	0.027	0.008	55.7		8.91	0.000	0.009	0.008	5.8		2.5	0.012
	Matched	0.027	0.014	38.7	30.4	2.08	0.040	0.009	0.008	3.7	35.3	1.0	0.306
(Debt/total assets) (t − 1)	Unmatched	0.726	0.779	−19.8		−1.6	0.109	0.859	0.777	27.6		11.3	0.000
	Matched	0.726	0.708	6.7	66	0.43	0.670	0.859	0.823	12.0	56.5	3.3	0.001

References

Arnold, J., and B. Smarzynska Javorcik. 2005. Gifted kids or pushy parents? Foreign acquisitions and plant performance in Indonesia. CEPR Discussion Paper Series no. 5065. London: Centre for Economic Policy Research, May.

Barba Navaretti, G., D. Castellani, and A.-C. Disdier. 2006. How does investing in cheap labour countries affect performance at home? France and Italy. CEPR Discussion Paper no. 5765. London: Center for Economic Policy Research, July.

Becker, S. O., and A. Ichino. 2002. Estimation of average treatment effects based on propensity scores. *Stata Journal* 2 (4): 358–77.

Bertrand, O., and H. Zitouna. 2005. Domestic versus cross-border acquisitions: Which impact on the target firms' performance? IUI Working Paper no. 647. Stockholm, Sweden: The Research Institute of Industrial Economics.

Blomström, M., and A. Kokko. 1998. Multinational corporations and spillovers. *Journal of Economic Surveys* 12 (2): 247–77.

Blomström, M., A. Kokko, and S. Globerman. 2001. The determinants of host country spillovers from foreign direct investment: A review and synthesis of the literature. In *Inward Investment, Technological Change, and Growth: The Impact of Multinational Corporations on the UK Economy,* ed. N. Pain, 34–65. Basingstoke, England: Palgrave.

Conyon, M. J., S. Girma, S. Thompson, P. W. Wright. 2002. The productivity and wage effects of foreign acquisitions in the United Kingdom. *Journal of Industrial Economics* 50:85–102.

Doms, M. E., and J. Bradford Jensen. 1998. Comparing wages, skills, and productivity between domestically and foreign-owned manufacturing establishments in the United States. In *Geography and ownership as bases for economic accounting,* eds. R. E. Baldwin, R. E. Lipsey, and J. D. Richardson, 235–55. NBER Studies in Income and Wealth, vol. 59. Chicago and London: University of Chicago Press.

Froot, K. A., and J. C. Stein. 1991. Exchange rates and foreign direct investment: An imperfect capital markets approach. *Quarterly Journal of Economics* 106 (4): 1191–1217.

Fukao, K., K. Ito, and H. Ug Kwon. 2005. Do out-in M&As bring higher TFP to Japan? An empirical analysis based on micro-data on Japanese manufacturing firms. *Journal of the Japanese and International Economies* 19:272–301.

Fukao, K., and Y. Murakami. 2005. Do foreign firms bring greater total factor productivity to Japan? *Journal of the Asia Pacific Economy* 10 (2): 237–54.

Girma, S., D. Greenaway, and R. Kneller. 2004. Does exporting increase productivity? A microeconometric analysis of matched firms. *Review of International Economics* 12 (5): 855–66.

Griffith, R., and H. Simpson. 2001. Characteristics for foreign-owned firms in British manufacturing. Working Paper No. 01/10. London: The Institute for Fiscal Studies.

Gugler, K., D. C. Mueller, B. Burcin Yurtouglu, and C. Zulehmer. 2003. The effects of mergers: An international comparison. *International Journal of Industrial Organization* 21 (5): 625–53.

Heckman, J. J., H. Ichimura, and P. E. Todd. 1997. Matching as an econometric evaluation estimator: Evidence from evaluating a job training programme. *Review of Economic Studies* 64:605–54.

Heckman, J. J., H. Ichimura, J. Smith, and P. Todd. 1998. Characterizing selection bias using experimental data. *Econometrica* 66 (5): 1017–98.

Hijzen, A., S. Jean, and T. Mayer. 2006. The effects at home of initiating production abroad: Evidence from matched French firms: What happens to the biological kids of foster parents? Mimeograph. Paris: CEPII, November.

Ito, K. 2004. Foreign ownership and productivity in the Indonesian automobile industry: Evidence from establishment data for 1990–99. In *Growth and Productivity in East Asia,* vol. 13, eds. T. Ito and A. K. Rose, 229–70. Chicago and London: University of Chicago Press.

Ito, K., and K. Fukao. 2005. Foreign direct investment and trade in Japan: An empirical analysis based on the establishment and enterprise census for 1996. *Journal of the Japanese and International Economies* 19:414–55.

Jensen, M. 1988. Takeovers: Their causes and consequences. *Journal of Economic Perspectives* 2:21–48.

Kimura, F., and K. Kiyota. 2004. Foreign-owned versus domestically-owned firms: Economic performance in Japan. *Review of Development Economics* 11 (1): 31–48.

Leuven, E., and B. Sianesi. 2001. PSMATCH2: Stata module to perform full mehalanobis and propensity score matching, common support graphing, and covariate imbalance testing. Retrieved from http://ideas.repec.org/c/boc/bocode/s432001.html. Version 1.2.3. 7 June, 2006.

Lichtenberg, F. R., and D. Siegel. 1987. Productivity changes in ownership of manufacturing plants. *Brookings Papers on Economic Activity* 3:643–73.

Lipsey, R. E. 2004. Home- and host-country effects of foreign direct investment. In *Challenges to Globalization: Analyzing the Economics,* eds. R. E. Baldwin and L. A. Winters, 333–79. Chicago and London: University of Chicago Press.

McGuckin, R. H., and S. V. Nguyen. 1995. On productivity and plant ownership change: New evidence from the longitudinal research database. *RAND Journal of Economics* 26:257–76.

Nguyen, S. V., and M. Ollinger. 2002. Mergers and acquisitions and productivity in the U.S. meat products industries: Evidence from the micro data. CES-WP-02-07, Center for Economic Studies. Washington, DC: U.S. Bureau of the Census.

Nihon Keizai Shimbun. 2003. Haiena kara hiro e: Gaikoku-jin butai no funsen [From "Hyenas" to heroes: Brave fights of a foreign legion]. Evening edition, March 26.

Paprzycki, R., and K. Fukao. 2005. The extent and history of foreign direct investment in Japan. Hi-stat discussion paper series, no. 84. Tokyo: Hitotsubashi University.

Ramstetter, E. D. 1999. Comparisons of foreign multinationals and local firms in Asian manufacturing over time. *Asian Economic Journal* 13 (2): 163–203.

RECOF. 2003. *M & A databook of Japanese companies 1988 to 2002.* Tokyo: RECOF Corporation.

Rosenbaum, P. R., and D. B. Rubin. 1983. The central role of the propensity score in observational studies for causal effects. *Biometrika* 70 (1): 41–55.

Smith, J., and P. Todd. 2005. Rejoinder. *Journal of Econometrics* 125:365–75.

Swenson, D. L. 1993. Foreign mergers and acquisitions in the United States. In *Foreign Direct Investment,* ed. K. A. Froot, 255–81. Chicago: University of Chicago Press.

Takii, S. 2004. Productivity differentials between foreign and local plants in Indonesian manufacturing, 1995. *World Development* 32 (11): 1957–69.

Werner, R. A. 2003. Foreign money won't help Japan's economy. *The Daily Yomiuri,* 20 June.

Comment   M. Chatib Basri

This is a commendable chapter and a valuable reading. It addresses the issue of the relationship between merger and acquisition (M&A) and productivity and company performance. This topic is particularly valuable because, as stated by the authors, there is a growing concern today that M&A are dominated by "vulture" funds seeking to reap profits from troubled companies. As a result, understanding the relationship between M&A and productivity is particularly important.

Consistent with the previous study, this chapter shows that M&A improved the productivity of the target firms. However, there is a question of causality direction here: whether the M&A increase the productivity of the target firms or if the high productivity of the target firms attracts some companies to pursue mergers and acquisitions. In particular this chapter tries to elucidate two questions: first, whether a firm is chosen as M&A target based on its productivity or whether it is determined by other characteristics. Second, does the M&A improve the target firms' performance.

This study pointed out that the previous study done by Fukao, Ito, and Kwon (2005) has a limitation due to the selection bias problem. This study aims to fill the gap by employing the combination of Difference-in-Difference (DID) and propensity score matching approach. I think this is a major contribution made by this chapter, which carefully takes care the issues of methodology by handling problems of selection bias. In addition, this chapter extends the coverage of the study, which is not limited to the manufacturing sector, but also includes the nonmanufacturing sector. The other contribution made by this chapter is the distinction between M&A within the group and outside the group.

The results show that in the case of out-in acquisitions, foreign firms acquire well performing Japanese firms. This was indicated by the results that the selection of the target firms was based on higher TFP, profit rate, share of nonproduction workers, export intensity, and larger size in manufacturing industries. As for nonmanufacturing industries, firm with higher advertising and low debt/sales ratio are chosen as targets. In the case of in-in acquisitions this study finds no positive impact on profit rates, in either the case of within group in-in acquisitions or in-in acquisitions by domestic outsiders. On the second question, this study also finds that foreign acquisitions improve target firms productivity and profitability, whereas domestic firms hardly have any impact on performance. The results seem compelling and supported by strong methodology. Nevertheless, to make these results more robust it is worth to address some specific issues:

M. Chatib Basri is Director of the Institute for Economic and Social Research in the Faculty of Economics at the University of Indonesia.

1. Is the increase of productivity merely due to acquisition by the new company or it is caused by scale effects? It is true that the matching results on TFP show a productivity increase after three years. However, the econometrics results also shows that the impacts on productivity vanish in the fourth year. Could this finding be attributed to the increase of capacity utilization or scale effect and not to the improvement of the technology that was brought by the new company? It is therefore important to check the constant return to scale assumption on this matter.[1]

2. Some studies, including Ishikawa and Tsutsui (2005) show that a credit crunch occurred in Japan during the period 1996–2001. Thus, it is important to ask whether the improvement of productivity was due to foreign acquisitions' lessening credit constraint?

3. As argued by Arnold and Javorcik (2005), improvement in productivity could also be attributed to preparation for entering the export market. Thus, it is important to investigate whether the improvement in productivity occurred due to exporter effect rather than M&A. This argument is particularly important bearing in mind that the result of this study shows that export intensity significantly determined the M&A.

4. It is particularly important to pay attention to the interpretation of the increase of TFP. It is true that TFP is proximity for productivity, but one needs to carefully interpret the change of TFP growth for the short-run, because it can also be attributed to the demand side rather than increase of productivity. This is also true for the short-run case where capital is fixed. The change of TFP growth for the short-run can be caused by rigidity rather than by productivity.

5. This chapter argues that M&A significantly increased after the Japanese government amended the corporate law on M&A, deregulated some sectors and foreign direct investment, and also because of a "fire sale" due to the economic crisis. It is also of interest to note that these patterns are similar in many countries. In addition, Hausman and Fernandes-Arias (2000) show that M&A occurs when an institution is weaker. Thus the increase of M&A could also reflect a signal of weakening institution. For these reasons it is worth it to complete some comparative studies.

6. It is useful to delve into a more disaggregated level, particularly in relation to acquisitions in some manufacturing industries, including electronics and machinery, and to look at the impact of M&A on productivity with regard to an increasing pattern of production net-work.

This chapter offers a lot of potential to draw out policy implications, including the positive effect of M&A in nonmanufacturing for production net-work. It comes to my surprise that Japan, as almost the most frontier in technology, has yet to improve its own technological productivity. It

---

1. For detail on this issue see Arnold and Javorcik (2005).

raises a concern that in the future Japanese companies will face strong competition pressures from their competitors.

In sum, this chapter is commendable and offers an important contribution for the study on the relationship between M&A and productivity.

References

Arnold, J., and B. Smarzynska Javorcik. 2005. Gifted kids or pushy parents? Foreign acquisitions and plants performance in Indonesia. CEPR Discussion Paper No. 5065. London: Centre for Economic Policy Research.
Fukao, K., K. Ito, and H. Ug Kwon. 2005. Do foreign firms bring greater total factor productivity to Japan? An empirical analysis based on micro-data on Japanese manufacturing firms. *Journal of the Japanese and International Economics* 19:272–301.
Hausman, R., and E. Fernande-Arias. 2000. foreign direct investment: Good cholesterol? Working Paper #417, Inter American Development Bank, Research Department.
Ishikawa, D., and Y. Tsutsui. 2005. Has credit crunch occurred in Japan in 1990s. RIETI Discussion Paper No. 06-E-012. Tokyo: Research Institute of Economy, Trade, and Industry, Japan.

Comment   Roberto S. Mariano

This chapter extends an earlier work (2005) to further examine the basis for acquisition and the impact on firms' performance when firms are acquired by foreign and domestic investors in Japan. In this chapter, the authors use Japanese firm-level data covering an extra year relative to their previous study and extend the scope to include nonmanufacturing industries.

The authors use a multinomial logit analysis (instead of their binomial probit analysis in 2005) to investigate the basis for firm acquisition as the analysis distinguishes three categories: nonacquired firms, foreign-acquired (out-in M&As), and domestic-acquired (in-in M&As). They further employ propensity score matching and difference-in-differences (DID) techniques to account for selection bias in foreign investors' choice of firms for acquisition. This is for purposes of assessing the impact of foreign versus domestic acquisition on a firm's productivity, profitability, sales, and employment growth.

The authors calculate the propensity scores through a multinomial logit model of firm acquisition—the appropriate approach since the categorical acquisition variable is trinomial. Probit estimation, as applied by the au-

Roberto S. Mariano is a professor of economics and statistics and dean of the School of Economics, as well as the Vice Provost for Research, at Singapore Management University, and professor emeritus of economics and statistics at the University of Pennsylvania.

thors in their earlier study to foreign-acquired firms versus others and domestic-acquired firms versus others, may result in biased estimates of propensity scores except in special cases and, consequently, lead to mismatches in the implementation of the DID technique.

As the authors point out, the findings in the chapter are generally consistent with their earlier results. In particular, the authors find that "foreign acquisitions improved target firms' productivity and profitability significantly more and quicker than acquisitions by domestic firms."

In applying the DID, the authors keep in mind that there are three categories. They use the nonacquired firms as the control group and "conduct one-to-one nearest neighbor matching on firms acquired by foreigners and then match firms acquired by domestic investors using again the sample of nonacquired firms as the control." The differences in measured effects for foreign-acquired and for domestic-acquired firms are partly due to the fact that the matching control sets are different for the two categories. The nearest neighbor choices (from the control group) for foreign-acquired firms are based on estimated propensity scores that would be quite different from those used to get matches for domestic-acquired firms. This could account for what the authors call somewhat weak results regarding the impact of foreign acquisition relative to that of domestic acquisition.

The authors appropriately caution that matching must be done carefully when implementing the DID technique. Indeed, further research on appropriate matching methodology is needed, especially when dealing with multinomial situations.

Stock Market Opening
and the Cost of Capital
The Case of Korea

Inseok Shin and Chang-Gyun Park

12.1 Introduction

Literature on emerging capital markets is growing rapidly. While the literature covers diverse topics (see Bekaert and Harvey 2002 for a recent review), one of the key issues that constantly draws researchers' attention is effect of stock market openings on the cost of capital. The prediction of theories is well known. In a standard international asset pricing model, a stock market opening reduces the opening economy's cost of capital by allowing risk sharing between domestic and foreign agents (Bekaert and Harvey 1995; Eun and Janakiramanan 1986; Errunza and Losq 1989; Errunza, Senbet, and Hogan 1998). Several studies have tested the theoretical prediction using cross-country data from emerging markets, and report the cross-country data indeed confirms the prediction (Bekaert and Harvey 2000; Henry 2000; Kim and Singal 2000). It is important to note that empirical studies find desirable effects of market openings on the cost of capital, while empirical evidence for impacts on market volatility of opening produces ambiguous results (Bekaert and Harvey 2000; Aggarwal, Inclan, and Leal 1999).

In this chapter, we follow previous research and study changes in the cost of capital after a stock market opening. The difference between this chapter and existing works is that we focus on the Korean experience. By restricting the scope of research to a single country, this chapter takes the risk of lower empirical power than previous works, which utilize cross-country data sets. Despite the potential caveat, we seek to complement existing studies in the following manner. First, we take a longer-term perspective in

Inseok Shin and Chang-Gyun Park are Professors of Finance at Chung-Ang University, College of Business Administration.

examining effects of Korean stock market opening on the cost of capital. A stock market opening is a gradual process. When we measure the progress of openings by regulatory liberalization, emerging economies' experiences show liberalization processes usually take several years to be completed. In Korea, for example, the first deregulation that allowed foreign investment in the Korean stock market occurred in 1992. But, final elimination of regulatory restrictions on foreign investment did not take place until 1998. Partly because completion of market opening is a relatively recent event in most emerging economies, existing studies focus on initial opening dates when examining the effect of market openings on the cost of capital. Also their windows of examination are limited to two or three years around initial opening dates. As for Korea, Henry's (2000) sample covers only up to the end of 1994, and Bekaert and Harvey (2000) stop at the end of 1995. As a result, existing works are vulnerable to the *hot money* problem. They may find a decrease in the cost of capital not because the stock market is opened to foreign investors, but because horizons of their analysis are confined to when markets are doing well. In this chapter, we examine changes in the cost of capital of the Korea stock market for the past thirteen years, from 1992 to 2004. We compare the cost of capital during the liberalization era with the post-liberalization era, with each era including about six years. Following Bekaert and Harvey's (2000) argument, we employ the dividend yield as a measure of the cost of capital. We find that the dividend yield is larger in the post-liberalization era when the Korean stock market is fully opened. In fact, the dividend yield appears to have decreased only around 1992, the initial opening year, and then continued to rise as liberalization of the Korean stock market advanced.

Using firm level panel data we analyze, in detail, what effects greater foreign presence in the Korean stock market has brought on the dividend yield. We examine what trends emerge when controlling other factors and regressing the dividend yield on degrees of foreign ownership. We obtain an interesting result. The higher the degree of foreign ownership in a firm, the lower the dividend yield is. Notably, the negative relationship between foreign ownership and the dividend yield is only significant during recent years when the Korea stock market has been fully opened.

The results of this chapter are in contrast to the existing studies based on cross-country data sets that find most of the effects of market opening on the cost of capital tend to appear around the initial liberalization dates (Bekaert and Harvey 2000; Henry 2000; Kim and Singal 2000). According to the existing studies, the cost of capital goes down, responding to the initial market opening as further risk sharing becomes feasible. If this risk sharing story is correct, revaluation of stocks triggered by the market opening is likely to be concentrated in those stocks that attract foreign investment. This likely because foreign ownership of a stock indicates the stock now belongs to the global portfolio.[1] The conclusion of this chapter—that higher foreign ownership produces lower dividend yield—is consistent with the hypothesis that market opening decreases the cost of capital. However, our finding that the negative relationship between foreign ownership and dividend yield is only visible after the liberalization process is completed suggests that the mere beginning of a liberalization process may not be enough to produce the negative effect of market opening on the cost of capital.

The rest of the chapter is structured as follows. In section 12.2, we briefly describe the stock market opening process in Korea and examine the trend in the cost of capital. In section 12.3, we present the analysis based on the panel data set. Section 12.4 contains concluding remarks.

12.2 Descriptive Findings

12.2.1 Regulatory Changes

Foreign investor's direct access to the Korean stock market[2] was prohibited until January 1992. At that time, the Korean government began allowing foreign participation in the Korean stock market, but with ceiling regulations. Foreign ownership was limited to 10 percent in, so-called, ordinary companies and 8 percent in public interest companies that were deemed of national interest, such as defense and communications. The 10 percent ceiling was subsequently raised to 12 percent in December 1994 and to 15 percent in July 1995 (see table 12.1). The pace of deregulation was accelerated during 1996 and 1997 when the Korean economy was under foreign liquidity problems. The foreign investment restriction was relaxed six times over the two years, raising the ceiling to 55 percent for ordinary companies. Toward the end of 1997 the Korean economy fell victim to a currency crisis. To deal with the currency crisis, the ceiling regulation for ordinary companies finally was eliminated in May 1998.

Another notable deregulation measure taken during the currency crisis period was the relaxation of the limit on foreign individual ownership. Initially the individual ownership ceiling was set at 3 percent in 1992. Although there were subsequent moderations, it still stood at 7 percent as of November 1997, rendering foreign controlling ownership in Korean companies impossible. In December 1997 when the Korean currency crisis erupted, the individual ceiling was raised to 50 percent. The individual ceil-

---

1. For a detailed explanation on stock revaluation due to risk sharing, see Chari and Henry (2005).

2. There are two stock exchanges in Korea: the Korea Stock Exchange and the Kosdaq Market. The former is a main board and traditional market, while the latter is a Korean version of the Nasdaq. In the paper, we focus on the Korea Stock Exchange.

Table 12.1   Stock market opening in Korea: Changes in foreign investment ceilings

	1992	1994	1995	1996		1997				1998	2000
	1	12	7	4	10	5	11	12.11	12.30	5	11
Company-level ceiling											
Ordinary companies	10	12	15	18	20	23	26	50	55	—	—
Public interest companies	8	8	10	12	15	18	21	25	25	30	40
Individual-level ceiling											
Ordinary companies	3	3	3	4	5	6	7	50	50	—	—
Public interest companies	1	1	1	1	1	1	1	1	1	3	3

Source: Financial Supervisory Service.

ing regulation was finally abolished in May 1998, together with the company level ceiling regulation.

Though the ceiling regulation for public interest companies still remains, the Korean stock market has been practically fully opened since May 1998. The ceiling on public interest companies was raised to 30 percent in May 1998 and to 40 percent in November 2000. As of 2005, the ratio of noninvestible stocks for foreigners is 5.3 percent (see table 12.2).

Foreign Investment Flows into the Korean Stock Market

Since the implementation of the initial opening measure in January 1992, there has been a steady flow of foreign capital into the Korean stock market (see figures 12.1, 12.2). When the market was fully opened in May 1998, the pace of capital inflow accelerated significantly. As a result, the foreign participation ratio has continued to be on an upward trend since 1992. The pace of the trend stayed mild until 1997, as the ratio rose to 12.9 percent over the six years from 1992 to 1997 (see figure 12.3). After the full opening in 1998, the slope of the upward trend became steep. The foreign participation rate jumped to 21.9 percent in 1999, and then continued to increase, reaching 30 percent in 2000. The rate remained on an upward trend, except for a slight setback in 2002. At the end of 2005 foreign investors claim around 40 percent of the Korean stock market capitalization.

12.2.2   Change in the Dividend Yield

Bekaert and Harvey (2000) argue that the dividend yield is a better measure of the capital of cost than expected returns. Following their argument, we examine the trend in the dividend yield during the stock market opening and the post-opening years in Korea.

Figure 12.4 shows the trend in the dividend yield of listed companies in the Korean stock market for the past sixteen years starting from 1990. Each year's dividend yield is computed as a ratio of the total value of dividends paid by listed companies during the year to the market capitalization

Table 12.2	Stock market opening in Korea: Trend in share of noninvestible stocks by foreigners					
	2000	2001	2002	2003	2004	2005
Number of companies under restriction	10	8	7	7	8	8
Value of stocks under restriction[a]	23.5	12.6	10.5	7.2	7.4	5.3

[a]Ratio to Market Capitalization.

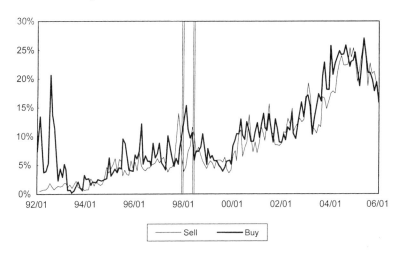

Fig. 12.1 Trend in foreign investors' trading in the Korea stock exchange: Ratio to the total

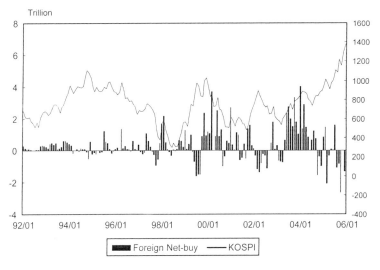

Fig. 12.2 Trend in net-buy by foreign investors in the Korea stock exchange: Trend

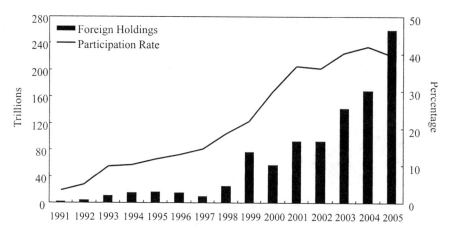

Fig. 12.3   Trend in foreign investors' participation rate in the Korea stock exchange

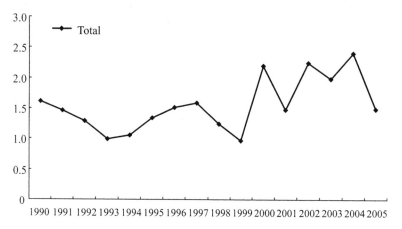

Fig. 12.4   Trend in the cost of capital: Dividend yield (1990–2005)

measured at the end of the year. The presented figure illustrates that the dividend yield was on a downward trend before the initial market opening in 1992. After the implementation of the partial opening measure in 1992, the decreasing trend lasted one more year, but was overturned in 1994. For the following years until the eruption of the currency crisis of 1997, it appears that the dividend yield remained on an upward trend.

Descriptive statistics of the dividend yield are reported in table 12.3. Dividing the sixteen years into the precrisis and the postcrisis period, means and standard deviations of the dividend yield for each period are computed. A simple test comparing mean-differences between the precrisis and postcrisis period is conducted. The result shows that the mean of the dividend yield for the postcrisis period is significantly larger.

Table 12.3   **Difference in the dividend yield: During and after the market opening**

	1992–1998(A)	1999–2005(B)	B – A
Mean	1.29	1.82	0.48
Standard deviation	0.22	0.52	(4.07)

Note: ( ) is a *t*-statistic for the hypothesis 'B – A = 0.'

12.3   Regression Strategy and Data

12.3.1   Question and Potential Explanations

The inspection of the trend in the dividend yield gives rise to a natural question: why have dividend yields increased after the economic crisis of 1997 when the Korean stock market is fully opened and foreign investor participation in the market is rising?

In measuring the effect of market opening on the cost of capital through the dividend yield, some factors may blur the relationships between the two need to be considered. The dividend yield is a function of not only the cost of capital but also future dividend flows. Hence, negative relationship of the market opening on the dividend yield holds when the future dividend flows remain constant. Any factor that changes future dividend flows may hinder one from observing the negative effect of the market opening on the dividend yield. Indeed, Henry (2000) reports that macroeconomic reform measures, other than capital market openings, also make significant impacts on the cost of capital in emerging economies, presumably by changing their growth prospects.

Even if one can hold future dividend flows constant, it still may not be easy to identify the impact of market opening on the dividend yield process. A standard theory predicts the effect of market opening on the cost of capital and the dividend yield to be negative because market opening changes marginal investor groups from domestic investors to foreign. But, it is not clear at which level of foreign ownership the change in the marginal investor group occurs.

Taking these factors into account, four possible explanations arise regarding the effect of the market opening and interpretation of the observed trend in the dividend yield of the Korean stock market. Based on his cross-country examination, Henry (2000) argues that the impact of market opening on the cost of capital is visible only around the first opening years. Though the market opening-process is always gradual in emerging economies, later opening measures in economies of his sample do not produce statistically significant effects on the cost of capital. The Korean experience may be interpreted along this line. One may argue the decreasing effect of the market opening on the cost of capital and the dividend yield had already been realized around 1992, namely the initial period of the market opening. One can then claim the movement of the dividend yield during the postcrisis period should not be connected to the market opening. Instead, the increase in the dividend yield may be attributed to other changes, such as the lowered growth prospect of the Korean economy after the economic crisis of 1997.

A second and opposing explanation would be that the decreasing effect of the market opening has actually been materializing during the postcrisis years, but disguised by other developments; the decrease in the dividend yield during the precrisis period is then an effect of other factors instead of the initial market opening measures. This hypothesis may be justified on the ground that foreign participation in the Korean stock market had not reached a critical level before the crisis, which would have been necessary for the change in the marginal investor group. Only after the crisis, when foreign ownership in Korean companies rose further, did foreign investors replace domestic investors as the marginal investor group and begin affecting the cost of capital.

The third hypothesis is that the cost of capital has been declining all along the liberalization process since the first opening in 1992. The reason why its effect on the cost of capital is not shown clearly in the movement of the dividend yield in recent years can be attributed to other factors that affect dividend flows.

The final possibility is an outright rejection of the prediction that market opening should lower the cost of capital. For example, in contrast to what the theory predicts, foreign investors may be myopic, so that they seek to maximize short-term returns from their investment in Korean companies. If foreign investors' myopic behavior leads them to demand exploiting dividends from Korean companies that cannot be sustained, one may observe a temporary increase in the dividend yield, as occurred during the post-crisis period.

12.3.2   Regression Strategy

Strategy

To identify the impact of market opening on the cost of capital, existing studies such as Bekaert and Harvey (2000) and Henry (2000) employ cross-country regressions. Their strategy is to control the effects of other factors on the cost of capital by considering differences among emerging economies. As long as macroeconomic profiles and histories of economic reforms are different among emerging economies, it may be argued that cross-country regressions will correctly identify impacts of stock market openings.[3]

---

3. Henry (2000) includes some dummy variables for macroeconomic reforms in his regression as an additional attempt to control their effects on measures of the cost of capital. But,

Our approach is different. We employ a one-country, firm level panel regression approach instead of a cross-country panel regression. While the dependent variable in the existing studies is dividend yields of emerging economies, the dependent variable in our regression is firm level dividend yields of the Korean stock market. In our regression, macroeconomic events, including economic reforms that may affect the dividend yield, will be controlled by time effects. We seek to identify the effect of market opening on the cost of capital and the dividend yield through foreign participation rates in each company. Our identifying assumption is that if market opening decreases the cost of capital as foreign investors become marginal investors, the impact of market opening will be more visible in firms with higher foreign participation rates. The following is the basic form of the regression equation we run:

(1) $$DY_{it} = \alpha + \beta' X_{it} + \gamma FS_{it-1} + \delta T_t + \mu_i + \varepsilon_{it}$$

In the equation, X_{it} stands for firm level characteristics that may affect each firm's dividend yield. Changes in economic environment such as reforms and global market conditions will be controlled by a time-dummy variable T_t. The variable μ_i is to allow individual fixed effect. The parameter of key interest is γ that is the coefficient to the foreign participation rate denoted by FS_{it}.

Control Variables

It has been suggested by many studies in the field of corporate finance that irrelevance of dividend policy à la Modigliani-Miller does not hold, and so a firm's dividend policy is influenced by a variety of variables. Following the literature, we include five variables to control possible variation in dividend yields due to corporate financial policy: change in investment, return on asset, change in fixed debt, cash flow, and size of the firm.[4]

Change in investment (Investment) is defined as the ratio of the change in investment in fixed assets to the total asset. Inclusion of the variable as an explanatory variable is primarily based on the theory that regards dividends as a signaling device for a firm's future profitability. One may presume that if the prospect of future profitability improves, managers would increase investment and concurrently increase dividend payout as an attempt to signal their private information to the outside investors.

On the contrary, one can deduce the opposite implication from the signaling motivation on the relationship between investment activities and dividend policy. Since it is possible for investors to observe the investment activities of a firm, increase in investment itself may contain rich enough

---

identifying economic reforms that may have taken effects on measures of the cost of capital is hard. It seems that his main strategy to control other variables' effects on measures of the cost of capital may exploit cross-country differences.

4. For a standard reference, see Frankfurter, Wood, and Wansley (2003).

information on a firm's future growth prospect for the outside investors. In that case, it is unnecessary for managers to employ dividend policy as an additional signaling device. This is so because dividends are a relatively costly signal device due to tax treatment on dividend income. Hence, any sign of the coefficient to the change in investment would be consistent with the signaling theory of dividends.

Return on asset (ROA) is the ratio of earnings net of dividend distribution to preferred stocks to total asset. Earning is the most frequently used variable in empirical study to explain dividend decisions ever since Lintner's seminal work (1956). Earnings net of dividend distributed to preferred stocks constitute the source of funds for either retained earnings or dividends to common stocks. Therefore, the presumption is that better earning performance in general leads to higher dividends if liquidity constraint is present for some reason.

Both change in fixed debt (Fixed debt) and "cash flow" are variables included to take into account cash flow hypothesis (Eckbo and Verma 1994). Change in fixed debt is normalized by total assets to neutralize scale effect, and cash flow is defined as operating profit less corporate income tax and total dividends, which are also normalized by total assets. Cash flow hypothesis argues that investors use dividends as a discipline device for managers by minimizing free cash flow that can be arbitrarily disposed of by managers. Less dependence on internal sources of funding, in general, bring in lower monitoring cost through wider exposure to capital markets.

Finally, "size" is measured as the log of real assets and is included to capture the empirical regularity that larger firms tend to pay out more dividends. It is also possible to justify the inclusion of size variables in terms of the agency cost argument. Larger firms are more likely to be subject to negative effects of asymmetric information and have stronger incentive to use dividends as a signaling device for future profitability.

12.3.3   Data

Sample Selection

In principle, we want to construct a sample consisting of all nonfinancial firms that have been continuously listed at the Korea Stock Market during the period 1992–2004. One potential problem with this sampling approach is survival bias. The dividend yield process of the sample of surviving firms may be different from the total sample. To see whether there are any tangible differences in the dividend yield, we present two dividend yield processes in figure 12.5. As shown, the two processes have moved closely together since 1994. But, there appears a visible gap between the two in 1992 and 1993. We take two remedies. First, we restrict our sample period to 1994–2004 when the sample of surviving firms closely represent the total sample, as far as movement in the dividend yield is concerned. Second, we repeat the same regression analysis with the total sample, which includes delisted firms.

We exclude those firms for which crucial information such as foreign participation rate or dividends is unavailable. By excluding those firms, we end up with 411 nonfinancial firms in the surviving firm sample. Table 12.4 describes the basic features of the panel sample.

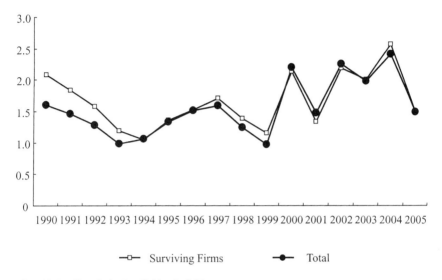

Fig. 12.5   Trends in the dividend yield

Table 12.4   **Industry composition and relative size of the panel sample to the market**

	Machinery & chemistry	Services	Electronics	Steel & metal	Others	Total
Sample	140	62	49	29	131	411
1996	204	76	85	43	241	649(760)
1997	213	79	90	43	238	663(776)
1998	211	74	91	43	230	649(748)
1999	211	73	89	43	213	629(725)
2000	209	74	88	42	207	620(704)
2001	208	76	88	41	201	614(689)
2002	212	76	81	39	197	605(683)
2003	212	76	79	41	190	598(684)
2004	214	84	73	40	175	586(683)

Note: ( ) denotes the number of all listed companies including finance industry each year.

Data Source

Stock prices and the share of foreign investors for each listed firm are extracted from a database maintained by the Korea Security Computing Corporation (Koscom). Information on all other variables are obtained from financial statements for listed firms provided by the Korea Information Service (KIS).

12.4   Result

12.4.1   Basic Model

Main results of the regression analysis are contained in table 12.5 and 12.6. For simplicity, we do not report the coefficients of individual fixed effects and time effects. Table 12.5 reports the result when the dividend yield is regressed on foreign participation rates or the share of foreign investors' holding in a firm. The regression is implemented three times for the changing sample periods: first for the whole sample period, second for the precrisis sample period, and finally for the postcrisis period. This is to

Table 12.5   Dividend yields and shares of foreign investors: Regression (1)

	Basic Model		
Variable	1994–2004	1994–1998	1999–2004
FS(t - 1)	–0.0114**	0.0020	–0.0187**
	(0.0052)	(0.0086)	(0.0082)
Investment	0.0030	0.0023	0.0040
	(0.0032)	(0.0030)	(0.0073)
ROA	0.0027**	0.0087***	0.0022
	(0.0013)	(0.0034)	(0.0015)
Fixed debt	0.0028**	–0.0043	0.0024
	(0.0014)	(0.0027)	(0.0016)
Cash flow	0.0008	–0.0025	–0.0044
	(0.0045)	(0.0098)	(0.0056)
Size	0.5533***	0.1387	0.4911**
	(0.0956)	(0.1795)	(0.1943)
Number of observations	4,521	2,055	2,466
R^2	0.0437	0.0505	0.0274
Wald test	352.48***(16)	111.4***(10)	69.63***(11)

Notes: Dependent variable = dividend yield. Standard errors are in parentheses. Wald is the test statistic for the null hypothesis that all coefficients except for constant term are jointly zero and degrees of freedom are in the parentheses.

**Statistically significant at 5%

***Statistically significant at 1%

see if the trend in the dividend yield observed in figure 12.4 can be confirmed by the regression analysis.

For the whole sample period of 1994–2004, the estimate of the coefficient to the foreign participation rate is negative and significant, which is encouraging since it implies that the stock market opening and the increase in foreign participation in the domestic stock market indeed reduces the cost of capital.

When the whole sample is divided into the two subperiods, an interesting finding emerges. The estimate of the coefficient to the foreign participation rate remains negative and significant for the postcrisis sample. However, for the precrisis sample it is estimated positive and insignificant. The result is a contrast to Henry (2000) and Bekaert and Harvey (2000), as they report the decreasing effect of market opening on the cost of capital appears in the early stages of market opening.

12.4.2 Alternative Model

We repeat the regression analysis now allowing for serial correlation in the dividend yield. Studies exist on dividend policy that emphasize the presence of inertia in the dividend process (Lintner 1956; Waud 1966). These studies suggest various empirical specifications based on partial adjustment model for dividend change. Allowing for the possibility of inertia in dividend adjustment, we estimate the following dynamic panel model:

$$(2) \qquad DY_{it} = \alpha + \beta' x_{it} + \gamma FS_{it-1} + \delta DY_{it-1} + \mu_i + \varepsilon_{it}$$

It is well-known that a typical estimation strategy for a static panel like equation (1) leads to an inconsistent estimator. Therefore, we resort to an Arellano and Bond (1988) style GMM estimation procedure in estimating the dynamic panel model.

The result is presented in table 12.6. The coefficient to the lagged dividend yield is estimated to be positive and significant, indicating the existence of persistence in the each year process. But, focusing on the coefficient to the foreign participation rate, we report that the result is qualitatively unchanged from the basic regression model. Before ending this section, we redo the regression analyses with the unbalanced panel including delisted companies sometime during the sample period. Results are contained in table 12.7 and 12.8. Significance of the coefficient to the foreign participation rate becomes marginal in the basic model regression. The result for the dynamic model remains qualitatively same.

12.4.3 Causality Check

In this section, we conduct a supplementary analysis on the effect of foreign investors on dividend yield. We test the existence of a causal relationship in the Granger sense between share of foreign investors and dividend

Table 12.6   **Dividend yields and shares of foreign investors: Regression (2)**

	Dynamic Model		
Variable	1995–2004	1995–1998	1999–2004
FS($t-1$)	-0.0246***	-0.0141	-0.0381**
	(0.0090)	(0.0224)	(0.0130)
Investment	0.0015	0.0055	-0.0041
	(0.0032)	(0.0053)	(0.0083)
ROA	0.0015	0.0026	0.0025
	(0.0014)	(0.0071)	(0.0019)
Fixed debt	0.0012	-0.0155***	0.0026
	(0.0014)	(0.0059)	(0.0021)
Cash flow	-0.0083	-0.0299	-0.0102
	(0.0055)	(0.0210)	(0.0075)
Size	0.3004*	-0.0080	0.2273
	(0.1798)	(0.4435)	(0.3339)
DY($t-1$)	0.1383***	0.6823***	0.2706***
	(0.0260)	(0.2429)	(0.0486)
Number of observations	3,699	1,233	1,644
Sargan test	256.76***(44)	9.66**(5)	96.33**(9)

Notes: Dependent variable = dividend yield. Standard errors are in parentheses. Sargan is the test statistic for overidentifying restrictions and degrees of freedom are in the parentheses.
*Statistically significant at 10%
***Statistically significant at 1%
**Statistically significant at 5%

yield by taking advantage of the panel vector autoregression (VAR) technique suggested by Holtz-Eakin, Newey, and Rosen (1988), which has been recently developed and applied by Grinstein and Michaely (2005) for investigating firms' payout policy.

Suppose the following bivariate panel VAR, allowing for time varying coefficients and individual fixed effect, such that:

$$(3) \qquad DY_{it} = \alpha_{0t} + \sum_{l=1}^{m} \alpha_{lt}DY_{it-l} + \sum_{l=1}^{m} \beta_{lt}FS_{it-l} + \varphi_t f_i + \varepsilon_{it}$$

$$FS_{it} = \gamma_{0t} + \sum_{l=1}^{m} \gamma_{lt}DY_{it-l} + \sum_{l=1}^{m} \delta_{lt}FS_{it-l} + \omega_t g_i + \eta_{it},$$

where $i = 1, 2, \ldots, N$ is the number of firms and $t = 1, 2, \ldots,$ and T is the number of years in the sample. The variable l is the number of time lags included for estimation and f_i and g_i are individual fixed effects allowed for dividend yield and share of foreign investors, respectively. The variables (α, β, φ, γ, δ, ω) are the vector of parameters to be estimated and (ε_{it}, η_{it}) is a sequence of serially independent stochastic error terms with a well-defined joint distribution.

Table 12.7   **Dividend yields and shares of foreign investors: Regression (3)**

	Basic model: Total listed companies		
Variable	1992–2004	1992–1998	1999–2004
FS($t-1$)	−0.0015	0.0021	−0.0093
	(0.0057)	(0.0106)	(0.0064)
			(p-value 14.5%)
Investment	0.0002	-0.0004	-0.0002
	(0.0011)	(0.0023)	(0.0011)
ROA	0.0009	0.0152***	0.0003
	(0.0009)	(0.0049)	(0.0006)
Fixed debt	0.0018	−0.0012	−0.0028
	(0.0236)	(0.0321)	(0.0417)
Cash flow	0.0035	−0.0183*	0.0001
	(0.0043)	(0.0107)	(0.0040)
Size	0.5141***	-0.2668	0.5382***
	(0.1093)	(0.2504)	(0.1488)
number of observations.	7,873	4,156	3,717
R^2	0.0143	0.0037	0.0171
Wald test	173.12***(16)	34.56***(9)	92.5***(10)

Notes: Dependent variable = dividend yield. Standard errors are in parentheses. Wald is the test statistic for the null hypothesis that all coefficients except for constant term are jointly zero and degrees of freedom are in the parentheses. The sample includes all firms both listed and delisted for each period.
*Statistically significant at 10%
**Statistically significant at 5%
***Statistically significant at 1%

Following Holtz-Eakin, Newey, and Rosen (1988), one can transform equation (3) into a set of two estimating functions without individual fixed effect:

(4)
$$DY_{it} = \alpha_{0t} + \sum_{l=1}^{m+1} \alpha_{lt} DY_{it-l} + \sum_{l=1}^{m+1} b_{lt} FS_{it-l} + u_{it}$$

$$FS_{it} = c_{0t} + \sum_{l=1}^{m+1} c_{lt} DY_{it-l} + \sum_{l=1}^{m+1} d_{lt} FS_{it-l} + v_{it}$$

GMM with the following orthogonality conditions bring us a consistent estimator:

$$E[DY_{is} u_{it}] = E[FS_{is} u_{it}] = 0 \text{ for } s < (t-1)$$

$$E[DY_{is} v_{it}] = E[FS_{is} v_{it}] = 0 \text{ for } s < (t-1)$$

The null hypotheses of the traditional Granger causality test are given as:

(5)
$$H_0 : \beta_{1t} = \beta_{2t} = \ldots = \beta_{mt} = 0 \ \forall t$$

$$H_0 : \gamma_{1t} = \gamma_{2t} = \ldots = \gamma_{mt} = 0 \ \forall t$$

Table 12.8   **Dividend yields and shares of foreign investors: Regression (4)**

	Dynamic Model		
Variable	1994–2004	1994–1998	1999–2004
FS($t - 1$)	–0.0044	0.0049	–0.0331***
	(0.0083)	(0.0135)	(0.0105)
Investment	–0.0015	–0.0006	–0.0043
	(0.0040)	(0.0053)	(0.0067)
ROA	0.0006	0.0163	0.0005
	(0.0010)	(0.0058)	(0.0011)
Fixed debt	0.0004	0.0005	0.0005
	(0.0011)	(0.0034)	(0.0013)
Cash flow	–0.0117***	–0.0331***	–0.0006
	(0.0048)	(0.0120)	(0.0051)
Size	0.1889	–0.7420**	0.0740
	(0.1781)	(0.3448)	(0.2438)
DY($t - 1$)	0.5262***	-0.0081	0.2838***
	(0.0130)	(0.0323)	(0.0410)
Number of observations	6,387	2,832	2,339
Sargan test	4,227.5***(65)	2,467.06***(14)	111.89***(9)

Notes: Dependent variable = dividend yield. Standard errors are in parentheses. Sargan is the test statistic for overidentifying restrictions and degrees of freedom are in the parentheses. The sample includes all firms both listed and de-listed for each period.
*Statistically significant at 10%
**Statistically significant at 5%
***Statistically significant at 1%

Holtz-Eakin, Newey, and Rosen (1988) show that testing equation (5) in (3) is equivalent to testing the following null hypotheses in (4):

$$(6) \qquad H_0 : b_{1t} = b_{2t} = \ldots = b_{mt} = b_{(m+1),t} = 0 \; \forall t$$
$$H_0 : c_{1t} = c_{2t} = \ldots = c_{mt} = c_{(m+1),t} = 0 \; \forall t$$

Holtz-Eakin, Newey, and Rosen (1988) also suggest a Wald-type test statistic based on the difference between the residuals of a restricted and unrestricted model.

The test statistics are reported in table 12.9. We reject the null hypothesis that share of foreign investors does not Granger-cause dividend yield for the period from 1994 to 2004. However, we cannot reject the null hypothesis that dividend yield does not Granger-cause share of foreign investors for the same period. Second, for the precrisis period, we do not obtain a consistent conclusion on the interaction between share of foreign investors and dividend yield. Third, for the postcrisis period, share of foreign investors help explain dividend yield, but not vice versa.

In sum, Granger causality tests in this section confirm that the effect of foreign investors on the cost of capital (dividend yield) unfolded its poten-

Table 12.9   **Granger causality test**

	FS → DY			DY → FS		
# of lags	χ^2-statistics	d.f.	p-value	χ^2-statistics	d.f.	p-value
1994–2004						
1	43.2231	16	0.0003	22.1696	16	0.1378
2	47.3938	21	0.0008	28.5234	21	0.1259
1994–1998						
1	8.0402	4	0.0901	15.5057	4	0.0038
2	3.5896	3	0.3093	5.1844	3	0.1578
1999–2004						
1	15.3385	6	0.0178	9.6124	6	0.1646
2	20.4021	6	0.0023	10.085	6	0.1211

tial in full scale after 1999, when capital market liberalization was completed and the foreign participation rate rose.

12.5 Conclusion

We have examined the effect of market opening on the dividend yield based on the Korean data. We employed firm level panel regression approaches, focusing on relationships between foreign participation rates and dividend yields. We found that the larger the foreign participation rate is, the lower the dividend yield is. But, the relationship is only significant in the postcrisis period when the Korean stock market was fully opened and foreign participation rate was relatively higher. The results are different from the existing studies based on cross-country data that find the effect of market opening realizes in the early stage of opening.

The purpose of this chapter is focused on testing the prediction of a standard asset-pricing model that market opening allows further risk sharing and so reduces the cost of capital. Hence, we intentionally interpreted results of the chapter in view of the risk-sharing story. However, a number of alternative interpretations are possible. Specifically, the negative relationship between foreign participation rates and dividend yields may be due to some other factors. Shleifer's (1986) price pressure is one candidate. Foreign investors' trading advantage as argued by Froot, O'Connell, and Seasholes (2001) is another. In addition, if foreign shareholders can induce better management of firms by improving corporate governance, the governance channel can make a third factor.

Given these alternative interpretations, we have no intention to conclude that an increase in foreign participation indicates expanded risk-sharing opportunities. Rather, by showing that the negative relationship between foreign participation and the cost of capital exists in the postliberalization period, in contrast to the existing works on the effect of market opening on the cost of capital, this chapter cautions that market opening may not automatically induce foreign investors to exploit expanded risk-sharing opportunities. At the minimum, this chapter suggests we need more work to understand why market opening leads to revaluation of stocks.

References

Aggarwal, R., C. Inclan, and R. Leal. 1999. Volatility in emerging stock markets. *Journal of Financial Quantitative Analysis* 34:33–55.
Arellano, M. S., and R. Bond. 1988. Dynamic panel estimation using DPD—A guide for users. Working Paper 88/15. London: Institute for Fiscal Studies.
Bekaert, G., and C. Harvey. 1995. Time-varying world market integration. *Journal of Finance* 50:403–44.
———. 2000. Foreign speculators and emerging equity markets. *Journal of Finance* 55:565–613.
———. 2002. Research in emerging market finance: Looking to the future. *Emerging Markets Review* 3:429–48.
Chari, A., and P. Henry. 2005. Risk sharing and asset prices: Evidence from a natural experiment. *Journal of Finance* 59:1295–1324.
Eckbo, B., and S. Verma. 1994. Managerial share-ownership, voting power, and cash dividend policy. *Journal of Corporate Finance* 1:33–62.
Errunza, V., and E. Losq. 1989. Capital flow controls, international asset pricing, and investors welfare: A multi-country framework. *Journal of Finance* 44:1025–37.
Errunza, V., L. W. Senbet, and K. Hogan. 1998. The pricing of country funds from emerging markets: Theory and evidence. *International Journal of Theoretical and Applied Finance* 1:111–43.
Eun, C. S., and S. Janakiramanan. 1986. A model of international asset pricing with a constraint on the foreign equity ownership. *Journal of Finance* 41:897–914.
Frankfurter, G. M., B. Wood, and J. Wansley. 2003. Dividend policy. Burlington, MA: Academic Press Inc.
Froot, K., P. O'Connell, and M. Seasholes. 2001. The portfolio flows of international investors. *Journal of Financial Economics* 59:151–93.
Grinstein, Y., and R. Michaely. 2005. Institutional holdings and payout policy. *Journal of Finance* 60:1389–1426.
Henry, P. 2000. Stock market liberalization, economic reform, and emerging market equity prices. *Journal of Finance* 55:529–64.
Holtz-Eakin, D. W., W. Newey, and H. Rosen. 1988. Estimating vector autoregression with panel data. *Econometrica* 56:1371–95.
Kim, E. H., and V. Singal. 2000. Stock markets openings: Experiences of emerging economies. *Journal of Business* 73:25–66.
Lintner, J. 1956. Distribution of incomes of corporations among dividends, retained earnings and taxes. *American Economic Review* 46:97–113.
Shleifer, A. 1986. Do demand curves for stocks slope down? *Journal of Finance* 41:579–590.
Waud, R. 1966. Small sample bias due to misspecification in the "Partial Adjustment" and "Adapted Expectations" Models. *Journal of the American Statistical Association* 1966:134–45.

Comment   Yuko Hashimoto

The purpose of this chapter is to investigate the impacts of the liberalization of the Korea stock market on the cost of capital. The research covers a decade, from 1994 to 2005, of the liberalization process of the Korean stock market. The authors estimate the effect of foreign participation rate on dividend yield and consider causality between the two. There is literature that focuses on the Korean stock market from the cost of capital point of view but this research is perhaps the first to expand the sample period to the post-currency crisis period. By dividing the sample period into two, a partially regulated period from 1994 to 1997 and a deregulated period from and after 1998, the authors try to compare the performance of the surviving firms and all (dead + listed) firms.

The authors find that foreign participation significantly reduced the dividend yield for the period 1999–2004, while it significantly increased the dividend yield for the period 1995–98, regardless of the estimation methodology. These results are opposite to the existing literature in that the effect of deregulation appears at the early stage of liberalization. It is also found that during the partial deregulation period, the dividend yield granger-caused foreign participation, while the foreign participation granger-caused the dividend yield during the deregulated period.

These findings are interpreted as the fact that it takes some time before the liberalization effect (reduction of cost of capital) emerges in the process, and the negative relationship between foreign ownership and the dividend yield became significant only recent years.

The chapter is well summarized, the objective is clear, and the findings are interesting. This is a very good chapter. Still, I would like to make three comments.

The first comment is about the story. This chapter confirms previous studies that liberalization does reduce the cost of capital. That is, this chapter shows that the liberalization effect appears in the latter stages of the liberalization process, whereas existing papers say it appears at the early stage. But it seems that results depend on the choice of variables and sample period. As the liberalization progresses and market becomes much more open to the world, the share of foreign participation rises as well. As is clear from figure 12.3, there is a big jump in the change in the share of foreign participation (slope of the participation) from 1992–1993, when the liberalization started, and 1999–2001, the final stages of the process. The results perhaps only reflect this fact, the endogeneity between the liberalization and the share of foreign participation. As for the sample-period problem, the latter subsample period in the estimation exactly overlaps the post-Asian currency crisis. The reduction of cost of capital is partly due to

Yuko Hashimoto is an associate professor of economics at Toyo University.

a strong stock price recovery after 1997. It would be favorable to separate the Asian crisis factors from the dividend yield.

The second comment relates to the interpretation of the results. The chapter tries to study "the cost of capital after a stock market opening" based on the assumption that "the cost of capital (= dividend yield) decreases in response to market opening because . . . foreigners become marginal investors." Another interpretation is applicable to this research. Foreign participants are also attracted to a firm with good balance sheets, ROA, cash flow, and high dividends. In this line, a positive relationship between dividend yield and foreign participation is possible. The authors should also take into account the potential investment opportunity, that is, a firm facing good investment opportunities will invest its earnings rather than pay dividends. Include Tobin's q or sales growth rate as control variables for potential investment opportunity and see whether the results are robust.

The third comment relates to the deregulation in December of 1997. There were twice relaxations in the foreign investment ceilings in the Korean stock market that month, on December 11 and 30. Foreign investment ceilings for ordinary companies were raised from 26 percent to 50 percent on December 11, and the limit on foreign individual ownership was raised from 7 percent to 50 percent on the same day (and then both ceilings were raised up to 55 percent on December 30). Obviously, this was when the Korean currency crisis was erupting. I am just curious why the ceiling was raised twice at that time. Is it something to do with IMF conditionality, or did the Korean authority intend to invite money from abroad in order to create appreciation pressure on the Korean Won? In any case, the authors should try to devote one or two pages for the background of the Korean stock market at this time, which would improve the contribution of this chapter more and help readers to understand the deregulation process in Korea. The regime change in the foreign exchange rate system must have affected the behavior of foreign investors to some extent, and the cost of capital as well. Therefore, exchange rate regime switch should be controlled for in the estimation. The easiest way is to use a dummy.

Comment   Chulsoo Kim

In a standard international asset pricing model, stock market opening reduces an opening economy's cost of capital by allowing for risk sharing between domestic and foreign agents. Using cross-country data, current literature, Bekaert-Harvey (2000), Henry (2000), and Kim-Singal (2000),

Chulsoo Kim is a professor of economics at Sookmyung Women's University.

confirms this implication. This chapter examines the cost of capital after the stock market opening in Korea with two distinctive approaches. First, the chapter uses a longer time horizon (fifteen years). Stock market opening is a gradual process, taking several years to be completed. Yet, the literature examines two or three years around the initial opening. It is interesting to see the effects on the cost of capital around and after the initial opening. Second, the chapter uses a firm-level data set. This chapter examines if firms with higher foreign ownership will see more reduction in the cost of capital.

This chapter finds that the higher the degree of foreign ownership in a firm, the lower the dividend yield is. It has been significant, however, only during the recent years when the Korea stock market has been fully opened, which is a contrast to the literature that finds the effects around the initial liberalization dates.

This chapter makes an important contribution to the literature by examining the effects of a stock market opening on individual stocks instead of aggregate cross-country data. The individual-firm data set contains rich information that we cannot get in the aggregate cross-country data set. Therefore, this chapter can shed new light on the effects of a stock market opening. I have several comments that may help to strengthen this chapter's claim.

First, in this chapter, the cost of capital is equal to dividend yield. Yet, we are ultimately interested in how the stock market opening may benefit or hurt a country. When the volatility increases, however, a country may not be better off even if the cost of capital decreases. For example, short-term capital inflow may lead to a sudden withdrawal from the country, which may in turn cause an economic crisis as in Asia in 1997. Hence, the cost of capital would be better examined in terms of volatility as well as dividend yield.

Second, the chapter needs to examine if the foreign participation rate is a good proxy for the stock market opening. The identification assumption of this chapter is that if market opening decreases the cost of capital with more foreign investors, the impact of the market opening would be more visible in firms with higher foreign participation rates. Yet, the foreign participation rate can increase due to several reasons.

The increase in the foreign participation rate could be due to the stock market opening as the chapter claims. This explanation may be important in the initial opening of 1992, but less important after that. Mean and median foreign participation rates have been under a ceiling constraint. For most firms, the ceiling constraint did not bind. Many foreign investors bought less than they were allowed except for a small number of popular stocks. If the stock market opening is the main driving force behind the increase in the foreign participation rate, the foreign investors should be indifferent among stocks and the participation rate should increase for all stocks. There are, however, some stocks that foreign investors like to buy and other stocks foreign investors do not like to buy, which suggests that the foreign participation rate depends on more than the market opening. Specifically, the foreign participation rate may increase when the foreign investors expect better prospects in the Korean economy or in a particular stock. Hence, foreign participation rate alone may not be a good measure of market opening. This chapter needs a structural model of the foreign participation rate and needs to sort out the market opening effect. Although this paper conducts Granger causality tests between dividend yields and the share of foreign investors, foreign investors may use more information than dividend yields in picking stocks, and hence the foreign participation rate should be explicitly modeled.

Third, this chapter needs to distinguish between the Asian crisis of 1997 and the stock market opening in 1998. Economic reforms after the crisis may have caused higher foreign participation rates. Although economic reforms are controlled by a time-dummy variable in this chapter, some reforms affect individual firms differently. For example, after the fall of Daewoo, the "too big to fail" policy is no longer expected. Foreign banks started to monitor loans more carefully. Some grassroots groups demanded more shareholder rights from certain firms. These changes led to more transparency in certain firms, but the effects were not uniformly distributed across firms. Therefore, a time-dummy would not be able to capture all these effects, and the chapter needs to control for economic reforms after the Asian crisis.

Fourth, do lower dividend yields with higher foreign participations confirm the benefit of the market opening? Maybe, but there exists another possibility. Korean investors often imitate foreign investors, possibly because Koreans may think that foreigners have better skills in picking winning stocks. In this case, Koreans shift their portfolio from the stocks that foreigners do not prefer to the stocks they do. This would lead to lower dividend yields for the stocks that foreigners prefer and higher dividend yields for the stocks which they do not. This can be tested since the chapter has all the individual data. When the foreign participation rates increase, it could be due to the market opening or the higher demand for the stock. When the foreign participation rates decrease, however, it could not be due to the market opening and it must be due to the lower demand for the stock. In other words, when the foreign participation rate decreases, the negative change has nothing to do with the market opening. Therefore, if dividend yields increase when the foreign participation rate has decreased, the dividend yield change is caused by the lower demand for the stock, instead of the market opening.

Fifth, this chapter can try a counterfactual study. Assuming there was no stock market opening in 1992 or 1998, this chapter can examine the dividend yield. Then, the chapter can examine interesting implications, such as how many firms have benefited or lost from the market opening, how much the cost of capital has decreased, and how many changes in volatilities there have been.

Sixth, this chapter discusses why dividend yields have increased after the economic crisis of 1997, when the Korean stock market was fully opened and foreign participation in the market were increasing. This chapter then provides four possible explanations. The first explanation is that the decreasing effect of the market opening was realized around the initial period of market opening. Other changes, such as the lowered growth prospect of the Korean economy after the Asian crisis of 1997, may be responsible. The second explanation is that the decrease in the dividend yield during the precrisis period is an effect of other factors instead of the initial market opening measures. The third explanation is that other factors that affect dividend flows are responsible. The fourth explanation is the rejection of the prediction that the market opening should lower the cost of capital. Foreign investors may be myopic and seek to maximize short-term returns. Yet, these four explanations seem to contradict the findings in the chapter. Therefore, this chapter should attempt to reconcile the increase in dividend yields after 1997 with the results from this chapter.

Seventh, Korea started to open a stock market in 1992 and completed the opening in 1998. Even if the stock market was partially opened in 1992, most of the effect of the opening should have taken place around 1992, since market participants rationally expect the full opening later and incorporate that information in 1992. The expected future increase of the foreign participation rate would be reflected in 1992, while the unexpected increase would be reflected in 1998. This chapter hence needs to discuss when the government announced the market opening, and if the government exactly followed the initial plan for the opening, so that the chapter can test the expected and unexpected effects of the event.

References

Bekaert, G., and C. Harvey. 2000. Foreign speculators and emerging equity markets. *Journal of Finance* 55:565–613.

Henry, P. 2000. Stock market liberalization, economic reform, and emerging market equity prices. *Journal of Finance* 55:529–564.

Kim, E. H., and V. Singal. 2000. Stock markets openings: Experiences of emerging economies. *Journal of Business* 73:25–66.

Contributors

Ashvin Ahuja
Bank of Thailand
273 Samsen Road
Bangkhunphrom
Bangkok, Thailand 10200

M. Chatib Basri
Institute for Economic and Social
    Research
University of Indonesia
Jl. Salemba Raya 4
Jakarta, Indonesia 10430

José Manual Campa
IESE Business School
Camino del Cerro del Aguila 3
Madrid, Spain 28023

Dante B. Canlas
School of Economics
University of the Philippines
Diliman, Quezon City
The Philippines 1101

Michael P. Dooley
Department of Economics
Engineering II
University of California, Santa Cruz
Santa Cruz, CA 95064

Barry Eichengreen
Department of Economics
University of California
549 Evans Hall 3880
Berkeley, CA 94720-3880

David Folkerts-Landau
Deutsche Bank
Great Winchester Street
London EC2N 2DB, England

Kyoji Fukao
Institute of Economic Research
Hitotsubashi University
Naka 2-1, Kunitachi
Tokyo, Japan 186

Shin-ichi Fukuda
Faculty of Economics
The University of Tokyo
7-3-1 Hongo, Bunkyo-ku
Tokyo, Japan 113-0033

Peter Garber
Deutsche Bank
60 Wall Street
New York, NY 10005

Linda S. Goldberg
Research Department
Federal Reserve Bank of New York
33 Liberty Street
New York, NY 10045

Yuko Hashimoto
Faculty of Economics
Toyo University
5-28-20-Hakusan, Bunkyo-ku
Tokyo, Japan 112-8606

Peter Blair Henry
Graduate School of Business
Stanford University
Littlefield 277
Stanford, CA 94305-5015

Keiko Ito
Faculty of Economics
Senshu University
2-1-1 Higashi-mita, Tama-ku
Kawasaki, Kanagawa, Japan 214-8580

Takatoshi Ito
Graduate School of Economics
University of Tokyo
7-3-1 Hongo, Bunkyo-ku
Tokyo, Japan 113-0033

Prakash Kannan
Research Department
International Monetary Fund
700 19th Street NW
Washington, DC 20431

Kentaro Kawasaki
Faculty of Business Administration
Toyo University
5-28-20 Hakusan, Bunkyo-ku
Tokyo, Japan 112-8606

Chulsoo Kim
Department of Economics
Sookmyung Women's University
Seoul, Korea 140-742

Yoshifumi Kon
Department of Economics
University of Tokyo
7-3-1 Hongo, Bunkyo-ku
Tokyo, Japan 113-0033

Hyeog Ug Kwon
College of Economics
Nihon University
1-3-2 Misaki-cho, Chiyoda-ku
Tokyo, Japan 102-8360

Ching-Yang Liang
Department of Public Finance
National Chengchi University
Wenshan District
Taipei City, Taiwan 11605

Jin-Lung Lin
Institute of Economics
Academia Sinica
No. 128, Sec. 2, Academia Rd.
Nankang, Taipei, Taiwan 11529

Pipat Luengnaruemitchai
International Monetary Fund
700 19th Street, NW
Washington, DC 20431

Roberto S. Mariano
School of Economics
Singapore Management University
90 Stamford Road
Singapore 178903

Eiji Ogawa
Graduate School of Commerce and
    Management
Hitotsubashi University
2-1 Naka, Kunitachi
Tokyo, Japan 186-8601

Chang-Gyun Park
College of Business Administration
Chung-Ang University
221 Heukseok-dong, Dongjak-gu
Seoul, Korea 156-756

Eli Remolona
Bank for International Settlements
    (BIS)
Representative Office for Asia and the
    Pacific
78/F Two International Financial
    Centre 8
Finance Street, Central, Hong Kong

Andrew K. Rose
Haas School of Business
 Administration
University of California
Berkeley, CA 94720-1900

Kiyotaka Sato
Faculty of Economics
Yokohama National University
79-3 Tokiwadai, Hodogaya-ku
Yokohama, Japan 240-8501

Chung-Hua Shen
Department of Money and Banking
National Chengchi University
Wenshan District
Taipei, Taiwan

Jianhuai Shi
China Center for Economic Research
 (CCER)
Peking University
Beijing, China 100871

Inseok Shin
College of Business Administration
Chung-Ang University
221, Heukseok-dong, Dongjak-gu
Seoul, Korea 156-756

Etsuro Shioji
Graduate School of Economics
Hitotsubashi University
Naka 2-1, Kunitachi
Tokyo, Japan 186-8601

John Simon
Payments Policy Department
Reserve Bank of Australia
GPO Box 3947
Sydney NSW 2001, Australia

Miho Takizawa
Hi-Stat COE visiting research associate
Institute of Economic Research
Hitotsubashi University
Naka 2-1, Kunitachi
Tokyo, Japan 186

Lee-Rong Wang
Taiwan WTO Center
Chung-Hua Institution for Economic
 Research
75 Chang-Hsing Street
Taipei, Taiwan 106

Chung-Shu Wu
The Institute of Economics
Academia Sinica
115 Nankang, Taipei, Taiwan

Author Index

Aggarwal, R., 391
Aizenman, J., 40
Akinlo, A. E., 74
Andersen, T. G., 186n10
Antzoulatos, A. A., 142
Arellano, M. S., 403
Arnold, J., 349n1, 350, 356, 356n4, 377, 378n23, 387, 387n1
Aviat, A., 271n11

Bacchetta, P., 140
Baillie, R. T., 186n10
Barba Navaretti, G., 356n6
Barro, R. J., 135, 333, 343
Barth, J., 320n9, 330
Basu, S., 153
Bayoumi, T., 126n12, 220n1
Becker, S. O., 357
Bekaert, G., 256, 256n6, 316, 391, 392, 394, 398, 403, 410
Berger, D., 180, 180n4, 183, 184, 185, 216, 217
Bernanke, B. S., 40
Bernhofen, D. M., 142
Bertrand, O., 349n1, 377, 378n23
Berument, H., 74
Blanchard, O., 3, 22n9, 39, 236, 245
Blomström, M., 378
Blonigen, B. A., 142
Bollerslev, T., 186n10
Bond, R., 403
Borensztein, E., 268n2, 269n4, 269n6, 289, 301

Bosworth, M., 323
Branson, W., 29n14
Branson, W. H., 74
Broner, F., 43
Brune, N., 290
Bruno, M., 73, 74
Buch, C., 271, 272, 274
Buchanan, M., 269n5
Burstein, A., 146n6

Caballero, R., 40
Calvo, G., 269, 284
Campa, J. M., 5, 139, 140, 141, 143, 144, 145, 147, 149n8, 171
Caprio, G., 320n9, 330
Castellani, D., 356n6
Caves, R. E., 73n5
Chaboud, A. P., 180, 180n4
Chari, A., 393
Cheung, Y., 228n6
Claessens, S., 315, 320, 321
Cochrane, J. H., 84
Coeurdacier, N., 271n11
Conyon, M. J., 349n1, 362, 377, 378n23
Cooper, R. N., 30n15, 73
Corsetti, G., 40, 140n1
Coughlin, C., 142, 144, 148

Daly, D., 140
Deardorff, A. V., 336
Dedola, L., 140n1
De Gregorio, J., 341

Demirgüç-Kunt, A., 315, 316, 317, 333
Detragiache, E., 315, 317
Diaz-Alejandro, C. F., 73
Disdier, A.-C., 356n6
Djankov, S., 289, 289n37
Doms, M. E., 356n3
Dooley, M. P., 2, 15n4, 15n5, 24n12, 40, 294

Eckbo, B., 400
Edison, H., 228n9
Edwards, S., 74, 85
Eichengreen, B., 8, 14n2, 24n11, 220n1, 268,
    268n2, 269n5, 272, 273, 290n40, 294,
    301, 301n46
Enders, W., 221, 223n2, 224n4
Engle, R. R., 91
Erceg, C. L., 66
Errunza, V., 391
Eschenbach, F., 317, 328, 332
Eun, C. S., 391
Evans, M., 179, 183, 216

Fama, E., 245, 252
Faraqee, H., 270
Farhi, E., 40
Faruqee, H., 66
Feenstra, R., 142, 148n7
Feinberg, R. M., 142
Fernald, J., 153, 228n9
Fernandes-Arias, E., 387
Ferrucci, G., 272
Findlay, C., 323
Folkerts-Landau, David, 2, 15n5, 24n12, 40
Francois, J. F., 317, 328
Frankel, J. A., 71, 73, 73n5, 99, 140
Frankfurter, G. M., 399n4
French, K., 245, 252
Froot, K. A., 368n18
Fukao, K., 348, 349, 350, 355, 356n3,
    359n11, 362, 365, 372, 373, 373n19,
    376, 378, 386
Fukao, Kyoji, 9
Fukuda, S., 2, 3, 43
Fung, B. S. C., 126n12

Gagnon, J., 141, 143
Garber, Peter, 2, 15n4, 15n5, 22n12, 40, 294
Ghosh, S., 273, 274
Giavazzi, F., 3, 22n9, 39
Gil-Pareja, S., 142
Girma, S., 356n6, 377
Glaessner, T., 315, 320, 321
Globerman, S., 378

Goetzmann, W. N., 249
Goldberg, Linda S., 5, 68, 139, 140, 141,
    143, 144, 145, 145n5, 147, 149n8, 159,
    160, 171
Goldberg, P., 142
Goldsmith, R. W., 342
Goldstein, M., 71, 268
González-Mínguez, J., 140, 141, 143, 144,
    145
Goodhard, C., 177n1
Gordon, D. B., 135
Gordon, M., 250
Gourinchas, P.-O., 40
Granger, C. W. J., 91
Greenaway, D., 356n6, 377
Griffith, R., 356n3
Grinstein, Y., 404
Gron, A., 142
Guerrieri, L., 66
Guibaud, S., 271n11
Guidotti, P. E., 341
Gust, C., 66, 141
Gylfason, T., 73, 74

Harvey, C., 246, 256n6, 316, 391, 392, 394,
    411
Hashimoto, Y., 5, 177n2, 181n6, 186n10,
    189
Hausman, R., 387
Hayes, S. E., 142
Heckman, J. J., 356n6
Hellerstein, R., 140, 146
Henderson, D., 22n8, 29n14
Henry, P. B., 7, 256, 316, 317, 391, 392, 393,
    397, 398, 398n3, 403, 410
Hijzen, A., 356n6, 373n20
Hirschman, A. O., 73
Hoekman, B., 316, 320, 322, 336
Hoffmaister, A. W., 74
Holtz-Eakin, D. W., 404, 405, 406
Hsu, J. D., 115n7
Hu, S. C., 126n12
Hudak, G. B., 126n12
Huizinga, H., 316
Hummels, D., 160
Hurn, S., 221, 223n2, 224n4
Hyder, Z., 171

Ichimura, H., 356n6
Ichino, A., 357
Ihrig, J., 140, 141, 143, 145
Inclan, C., 391
Irwin, D., 294

Ishii, J., 160
Ishikawa, D., 387
Ito, K., 9, 349, 350, 355, 356n3, 359n11, 362, 372, 373, 373n19, 376, 378, 386
Ito, T., 5, 177n1, 177n2, 181n6, 186n10, 189, 219, 311, 365
Izquierdo, A., 274

Janakiramanan, S., 391
Javorcik, B. S., 349n1, 350, 356, 356n4, 377, 378n23, 387, 387n1
Jean, S., 356n6, 373n20
Jeanne, O., 43
Jeanneau, S., 272
Jensen, J. B., 356n3
Jensen, M., 355
Jiang, G., 284
Jones, R. W., 73n5
Jorion, P., 249
Juselius, K., 126n12

Kamin, S. B., 73, 74, 79, 81, 81n10, 85, 91, 92, 97
Kaminsky, G. L., 317, 335n20
Kannan, P., 7
Kaufmann, D., 329
Kawai, M., 272
Kawakatsu, H., 317
Kawasaki, K., 6, 221
Keefer, P., 265
Kim, E. H., 391, 392, 410
Kim, S., 272, 273, 274n16
Kimura, F., 349
King, R. G., 265, 341, 342
Kiyota, K., 349
Knack, S., 265
Kneller, R., 356n6, 377
Knetter, M., 142
Kokko, A., 378
Kon, Y., 2, 3
Kraay, A., 329
Krugman, P., 73, 99, 243
Kwon, H. U., 9, 349, 350, 355, 356n3, 359n11, 362, 365, 372, 373, 373n19, 376, 386

Lai, K., 228n6
Landa, 315
Lane, P. R., 28n13, 109, 276
La Porta, R., 289n37
Laxton, D., 66
Leahy, M., 22n8
Leal, R., 391

Lee, C. C., 317, 330, 332
Lee, J., 40
Lee, J-W., 272, 273, 274n16, 343
Leuven, E., 358
Levine, R., 265, 320n9, 330, 332, 333, 341, 342
Li, S., 270
Liang, C-Y., 8–9
Lichtenberg, F. R., 354n2
Liederman, L., 269
Lin, J. L., 126
Lin, Jin-Lung, 4
Lintner, J., 400, 403
Lipsey, R. E., 378n24
Liu, L.-G., 272, 273
Liu, L. M., 126n12
Lizondo, S., 73n5
Lorenzoni, G., 43
Losq, E., 391
Loungani, P., 228n9
Lucas, R. E., 265
Luengnaruemitchai, P., 8, 268, 301n46
Lundblad, C., 256
Lyons, R. K., 178, 179, 183, 186n10, 216

Malkiel, B., 241
Mankiw, N. G., 253n5, 343
Marazzi, M., 140, 143, 145, 148, 172
Marquez, J., 140
Marsh, C., 140
Martin, P., 270
Martinez, L., 317
Marz, 141
Mastruzzi, M., 329
Mattoo, A., 320, 320n9, 321, 321n13, 336
Maurer, A., 321n12
Mauro, P., 220n1
Mayer, T., 356n6, 373n20
McCauley, R., 284
McGuckin, R. H., 354n2
McGuire, G., 320, 320n8, 321, 321n11
McKinnon, R. I., 342
Mei, J. P., 241
Melvin, M. T., 186n10
Micco, A., 301n47
Michaely, R., 404
Micu, M., 272
Milesi-Ferretti, G. M., 28n13, 276
Miller, M., 252
Mobius, M., 241
Modigliani, F., 252
Montes-Negret, F., 315
Montiel, P. J., 73n5

Moore, M. J., 178
Morey, M. R., 317
Morriset, J., 274
Morsink, J., 126n12
Muir, D., 66
Mundell, R., 221, 224, 224n4
Murakama, Y., 349

Neves, J., 146n6
Newey, W., 404, 405, 406
Nguyen, S. V., 354n2, 355

Obstfeld, M., 14n2, 30n16, 39, 78n8
Odusola, A., 74
Ogawa, E., 6, 219, 221, 230n10, 313
Olarreaga, M., 274
Olivei, G. P., 142, 148
Ollinger, M., 355
Osbat, C., 143
Otani, A., 140, 171, 172
Oxley, L., 126n12
Ozeki, Y., 57, 57n2

Panizza, U., 268n2, 269n4, 269n5, 289, 301, 301n47
Papaioannou, E., 273
Paprzycki, R., 348
Park, C-G., 9
Park, Y. C., 272, 273
Parsley, D., 140
Pasaogullari, M., 74
Payne, R., 177n1
Pesaran, H. H., 126
Pesenti, P., 40, 66
Phillips, P. C. B., 126
Pollard, P., 142, 144, 148
Portes, R., 273, 274
Primo Braga, C. A., 316, 320

Qian, Y., 322
Quah, D., 236

Radelet, S., 40
Radetzki, M., 73, 74
Rajan, R., 301n46
Rathindran, R., 320, 320n9, 336
Rauch, J., 148n7
Razo-Garcia, R., 290n40
Rebelo, S., 146n6
Reinhart, C., 269
Reinhert, C. M., 317
Rey, H., 270, 273, 274

Rodrik, D., 40, 43
Rogers, J. H., 73, 74, 79, 81, 81n10, 85, 91, 92, 97
Rogoff, K., 5, 14n2, 30n16, 39, 42, 61, 78n8, 133
Romer, D., 4, 109, 110, 111, 115, 115n6, 118, 118n8, 126, 129, 130, 131, 133, 343
Rose, A., 271n11
Rosen, H., 404, 405, 406
Rosenbaum, P. R., 356, 373n20
Rothenberg, A., 140, 145
Roubini, N., 14n2, 39, 40, 341
Rubin, D. B., 356, 373n20

Sa, F., 22n9, 39
Sachs, J., 40
Sakane, M., 219
Sala-i-Martin, X., 333, 341
Sardar, S., 171
Schinasi, G., 301n46
Schmukler, S., 43, 335n20
Schuele, M., 320, 320n8, 321, 321n11
Schuknecht, L., 317, 328
Setser, B., 14n2, 39
Sheets, N., 140, 141, 143, 145, 172
Shen, C. H., 8–9, 317, 330, 332
Shi, J., 3, 72, 99
Shimizu, J., 313
Shin, I., 9
Shin, K., 272, 273, 274n16
Shiratsuka, S., 140, 171, 172
Shirota, T., 140, 171
Sianesi, B., 358
Siegel, D., 354n2
Simpson, H., 356n3
Sims, C., 81, 83
Sin, Y., 126
Singal, V., 391, 392, 410
Smith, J., 356n6
Smith, T., 301n46
Spiegel, M., 271n11
Stein, J. C., 368n18
Stiglitz, J. E., 342
Stock, J., 83, 223
Stulz, R., 256n6
Subramanian, A., 320, 320n9, 336
Swenson, D. L., 142

Takizawa, M., 9
Tavlas, G. S., 57, 57n2
Taylor, J., 171
Taylor, L., 73, 99

Temple, J., 110, 110n1
Terra, M. C. T., 110
Thomas, C., 140
Tille, C., 68, 145n5, 159, 160
Todd, P. E., 356n6
Tornell, A., 317
Trewin, R., 323
Tsutsui, Y., 387
Turner, P., 268

Valckx, N., 322
Van Wijnberger, S. V., 74
Van Wincoop, E., 140
Vegh, C., 74
Velasco, A., 43
Verboven, F., 142
Verma, S., 400
Vesperoni, E., 43
Vigfusson, R., 140, 143, 145, 172

Wang, L-R., 8–9
Wansley, J., 399n4
Warren, T., 323
Watson, M., 83, 223
Waud, R., 403
Wei, S., 140
Weil, N., 343
Werner, R. A., 349
Westerman, F., 317
Wolf, H., 273, 274
Wood, B., 399n4
Wu, C. S., 4, 115n7, 126n12

Xu, P., 142

Yan, I. K., 270
Yañez, M., 301n47
Yang, J., 142, 144
Yi, K-M., 160
Young, A., 243

Zervos, S., 332, 341
Zingales, L., 301n46
Zitouna, H., 349n1, 377, 378n23

Subject Index

Page numbers followed by t *or* f *refer to tables and figures, respectively.*

ABF (Asian Bond Fund), 267, 267n1
ABMI (Asian Bond Markets Initiative),
    267, 267n1
Acquisitions. *See* Mergers and acquisitions
    (M&As)
ADRs (American Depository Receipts),
    275–76
American Depository Receipts (ADRs),
    275–76
Appreciations, 73
ASEAN plus three countries, 219–20
Asia, 19; effects of savings exports of, 22;
    real interest rates for, 20f; savings and,
    19–20. *See also* East Asian economies
Asia, emerging, financial markets of,
    15, 16
Asian Bond Fund (ABF), 267, 267n1
Asian Bond Markets Initiative (ABMI),
    267, 267n1
Asian real exchange rates, 18, 19
Augmented Dickey-Fuller (ADF) test, 83

Bank for International Settlements (BIS),
    271, 271n9, 271n10
Bond markets: composition of investor base
    and, 302–5; data for, 275–79; in East
    Asia, 267–70; impact of other aspects
    of financial development on, 299–302;
    policy implications of study for, 305;
    review of previous studies of, 270–74;

sensitivity checks for study of, 289–99;
    studies using data on, 274; study re-
    sults of, 279–89
Bretton Woods II system, 13, 15

Capital, changes in cost of, 9
Capital flows, 6–7; bond markets and, 268
Chiang Mai Initiative, 219
China: gross domestic product data for
    VAR model of, 81–84; output of,
    RMB real exchange rate and, 74–79;
    results of VAR model of, 84–98; VAR
    model for studying relationship be-
    tween RMB real exchange rate and
    output of, 79–81. *See also* Renminbi
    (RMB)
Cointegration tests, 83–84, 84t
Common currency basket: data for analysis
    of, 228; G-PPP and, 225–27; methodol-
    ogy for analysis of, 227–28; results for
    analysis of, 228–30
Common exchange rate policy, ASEAN,
    220. *See also* Optimum Currency Area
    (OCA)
Consumption prices: calibrating pass
    through of exchange rates into, 153–59;
    mapping imported inputs and distribu-
    tion margins into, 145–49
Contractional devaluations effect, 73
Contractionary devaluations literature, 73

Coordinated Portfolio Investment Survey (CPIS) database, 8, 275; problems with, 276
CPIS, 8, 275; problems with, 276
Currency reevaluations, 73–74
Current accounts, understanding, 19

Depreciations, 73
Distribution expenditures, patterns in, 149–53
Dividend yield, change in, Korean stock market and, 394–97; analysis of, 397–98
Dollar (U.S), depreciation of, 2, 17, 22–23
Double marginalization, 147
Double mismatches, 8

East Asian capital flows, changes in, United States current account deficits and, 57–60
East Asian economies: as net lenders, 40; trade balances of, 40, 41t
EBS system, 177–78
Economic growth, effect of financial liberalization on, 317
Emerging capital markets: introduction to, 391–93; literature on, 391
Emerging markets: data for, 244–50; discussion of study results, 257–59; expected returns vs. realized returns of, 250–53; introduction, 241–44; in Latin America, 253–57; regional vignettes, 253–57
Emerging Markets Data Base (EMDB), 7, 245, 284n28
Euro, 3, 17
Euroland, 15, 20; financial markets of, 16; real interest rates for, 19; savings and, 19–20
Exchange rate adjustments, global imbalances and, 4
Exchange rate changes: effects of, on macro economy, 5–6; import prices of goods and, 142–45; inflation and, 4–5
Exchange rate collapses, 6
Exchange rate regimes, in East Asia, 219–20
Exchange rates: calibrating pass through of, into consumption prices, 153–59; data for predicting movement of, 181–82; disturbances along adjustment path and, 24–29; forces contributing to less than complete pass-through of, 139–40; import price elasticities and, 142–

45; measuring lag structure of price impacts on movements of, 205–10; predicting movement of, 180–81; prediction window estimation of, 183–86; random walk and, 178–79; reconciling expectations and, 29–30; results for predicting movement of, 186–205. *See also* Pass-through
Expectations, reconciling exchange rates and, 29–30

Financial liberalization: discussion of results of econometric model of, 336–37; econometric model of, 328–32; effect of, on economic growth, 317; empirical results of econometric model of, 333–36; internationalization and, 315–16; macroeconomic performance and, 328–32; patterns of, under WTO, 323–28; types of, 315–16
Financial liberalization index, construction of, 319–23
Foreign direct investment (FDI), into Japan, 9. *See also* Inward foreign direct investment (FDI); Mergers and acquisitions (M&As)
Foreign exchange markets, 21–22
Foreign reserves, liquidity risk and, 47–50

GBI (Government Bond Indices), 284n28
Generalized-purchasing power parity (G-PPP) model: common currency basket and, 225–27; empirical analysis of, 227–30; OCA theory and, 221–24
Global imbalances, 1–2; actors in phenomenon of, 2; exchange rate adjustments and, 4
Gordon Model, 250
Government Bond Indices (GBI), 284n28
Government loss minimization problem, 47–50
G-PPP model. *See* Generalized-purchasing power parity (G-PPP) model
Granger causality tests, 78, 79t
Gravity model, 269
Group of Seven (G7), 109. *See also* Newly Industrialized Economies (NIEs)
Growth, 317
Growth rates, aggregate: stock market returns of emerging markets and, 7–8

Imported inputs, mapping, 145–49
Imported input use, patterns in, 149–53

Import price elasticities, exchange rates and, 142–45
Import prices, exchange rate changes and, 142–45
Impulse response analysis, variable ordering and, 126
Impulse response functions (IRFs), 85–88
Inflation, 4; effect of exchange rate changes and, 4–5; empirical analysis of panel data for, 115–18; historical patterns of openness and, in G7 and NIEs, 111–14; openness and, 109–11; time series approach to, 118–26. *See also* Openness
Interest rates, disturbances along adjustment path and, 24–29
Internationalization, financial liberalization and, 315–16
Inward foreign direct investment (FDI): Japan and, 347–49. *See also* Foreign direct investment (FDI), into Japan

Japan: flow of inward foreign direct investment and, 347–49; foreign direct investment in, 9; overview of M&As in, 351–54; studies of corporate performance in, 349–50. *See also* Mergers and acquisitions (M&As)
Japan External Trade Organization (JETRO), 349
Johansen cointegration tests, 83–84, 84t

Korean stock market: analysis of dividend yield of, 397–98; change in dividend yield and, 394–96; changes in cost of capital after opening of, 97; data for analysis of, 400–402; foreign investment flows into, 394; regression strategy for cost of capital and, 398–400; regulatory changes for, 393–94; results for analysis of, 402–8

Latin America: bond market integration in, 269n4; emerging markets in, 248, 253–57
Liberalization. *See* Financial liberalization
Liquidity risk: East Asian examples of, 53–57; foreign reserves and, 47–50; government loss minimization problem, 47–50; impacts on unanticipated changes in macroeconomic variables, 45–47; numerical examples of, 50–53; small open economy model of, 43–45

Liquidity risk aversion: impact of, on real exchange rates, 60–62; impacts of unanticipated changes in, 47–50; impacts when economy suddenly increases its, 45–47

Macroeconomic performance, financial liberalization and, 328–32
Macroeconomy, effects of exchange rate on, 5–6
Mapping, 145–49
M&As. *See* Mergers and acquisitions (M&As)
Mergers and acquisitions (M&As), 349; data sources for, 358–61; overview of, in Japan, 351–54; performance of target firms after, 365–76; research approach for studying, 354–58; results of study of, 361–64. *See also* Foreign direct investment (FDI), into Japan
Models of international monetary system: analysis of, 17–24; assumptions for, 15–16; departures from conventional approach to, 16; intervention and, 30–31; introduction, 13–15; summarization of results of paper, 16–17
Money supply, real output and, 126–29

National inflation performance, 4
Net deals, 183–86
Newly Industrialized Economies (NIEs), historical patterns of openness and inflation of, 109, 111. *See also* Group of Seven (G7)

OCA. *See* Optimum Currency Area (OCA)
Openness, 4; empirical analysis of panel data for, 115–18; historical patterns of inflation and, in G7 and NIEs, 111–14; inflation and, 109–11; time series approach to, 118–26. *See also* Inflation
Optimum Currency Area (OCA): generalized-purchasing power parity (G-PPP) model for, 220–24; theory, 221–24
Output, real, money supply and, 126–29

Pass-through: calibrating, of exchange rates into consumption prices, 153–59; introduction to, 139–42; micro-oriented studies of, 142. *See also* Exchange rates
People's Republic of China (PRC). *See* China

Phillips-Perron test, 83
Price impacts, measuring lag structure of, 205–10
Proprietary trading, 178

Random walk, 178–79
Real exchange rates: Asian, 18–19; impacts of increased liquidity risk aversion on, 60–62; output and, 74
Real output, money supply and, 126–29
Renminbi (RMB), 17; brief history of exchange rate evaluation of, 75–79; inflexibility of, 3; introduction to, 71–75; real exchange rate, China's output and, 74–79. *See also* China
Reuters D3000, 177
"Revived Bretton Woods," 13, 15
Robustness analysis, 91–98

Sensitivity checks, 289–99
Spot foreign exchanges, 177
Stock market returns of emerging markets, aggregate growth rates and, 7–8
Survivorship bias, 249–50
Swan Diagram, 72

Target firms, performance of, after M&As, 365–76
Total factor productivity (TFP), 9

United States: financial markets of, 15, 16; real interest rates for, 19, 20f; savings and, 19–20
United States current account, 39
United States current account deficits, 3, 18, 19f; changes in East Asian capital flows and, 57–60
Unit root tests, 83

Variable ordering, impulse response analysis and, 126
Variance decompositions, from VAR model, 88–91
VAR model, 79–81

"Wal-Mart effect," 140
World Economic Outlook (WEO), 251
World Trade Organization (WTO) commitments, 316; introduction to, 317–19

Yuan (China), 2. *See also* Renminbi (RMB)